UNPITIED AND UNKNOWN

"Then dropped into the grave, unpitied and unknown."

J. Beattie, "The Minstrel"

By the same author

Katyn – A Crime without Parallel
(Tom Stacey, 1971)
The Katyn Cover-up
(Tom Stacey, 1972)

DEBATE: Publisher's Foreword

The DEBATE series is a collection of personal, political writings. We, as publishers, believe that our responsibility to readers is best served by giving them access to all points of view and all types of literature. We do not wish to act as censors nor to attempt to mould public opinion by refusing to publish cogently-expressed beliefs.

UNPITIED AND UNKNOWN

Katyn ... Bologoye ... Dergachi

LOUIS FITZGIBBON

Foreword by Lord George-Brown, PC

Bachman & Turner
London

Bachman & Turner
45 Calthorpe Street
London
WC1X 0HH

© Louis FitzGibbon 1975
First published 1975

ISBN 0 85974 029 3

Computer typeset by Input Typesetting Limited, 4 Valentine Place,
London SE1
Printed in England by Ferrygrove Ltd, Coggeshall, Essex.

Dedication

This book is dedicated to the concept of Justice.

Every man has a right to justice, including the 14,471 who still lie uneasy beneath the pines of Katyn, at Dergachi and near Bologoye. Justice is also awaited by their relatives and friends for whom the behaviour of erstwhile allies can be only an imitation of Pontius Pilate.

And there are those who have been and continue to be wrongly accused: the German Army and, through it, the German nation.

The author fervently hopes that this book may bring justice nearer.

> Though the mills of God grind slowly,
> yet they grind exceeding small:
> Though with patience He stands waiting,
> with exactness grinds He all.

H. W. Longfellow,
translated from Friedrich von Logau

Acknowledgements

I have received help from so many people since I first began my study of the Katyn case in 1970 that it would be impossible to thank them all. I must therefore confine myself to offering a word of gratitude to those directly concerned with the material in this book and with its production.

First, I thank my wife, Madeleine, who found the verse from which the title is taken, and then my children, Simone, James and Michele each of whom solemnly considered and then rejected other titles I had thought of. I am, of course, much in debt to Lord George-Brown, who generously provided the Foreword. My gratitude is due to my good Polish friends Stefan Soboniewski and Adam Treszka who originally informed me about Katyn and thus helped with Chapters 1 and 2, and to the British Library where the staff found me the material for Chapter 3, as well as to the staff at 43 Eaton Place, London, residence of His Excellency the President of Poland, who volunteered the information in Chapter 4. For much of the contents of Chapter 6 I thank Miss Susan Hodge, the assistant solicitor of the Royal Borough of Kensington and Chelsea, and I am most grateful to His Excellency the German Ambassador and his staff for the vital material in Chapter 7. I am also much indebted to David Floyd of the *Daily Telegraph* for the data which constitute Appendix II. I would like to thank Mr and Mrs Arora for their introduction to Paul Davis, in whose tiny north London flat I found that peace and solitude so essential to my task. Finally I am grateful to my publisher whose faith in me enabled this book to reach the public and, it is fervently hoped, the hands of those who may one day pronounce a judgement at international level.

Contents

Illustrations

The photographs between pages 243 and 393 are reproduced by permission of the United States Information Agency.

Foreword
by Lord George-Brown, PC

Secretary of State for Foreign Affairs 1966-8

From time to time over the years I have felt uneasy about the Katyn case in that it rests *in vacuo* through lack of a judgement, and my disquiet has not diminished with the passage of time. It was with pleasure therefore that I accepted an invitation to add a few words by way of prologue to this book and thus, as it were, make some personal contribution, however small.

Louis FitzGibbon takes us from the startling discovery of April 1943 to the hardly courageous display at Nuremberg and on to the investigation of the US Select Committee in 1952 which, by the following year, must have seemed fruitless to those who made such an effort to arrive at the truth. The recital is sharply updated to the explosion of interest shown in 1971 and brings us right to the present day into the current struggle to erect a memorial to the victims of this unique crime.

Then suddenly, and with a sense of shock, we are confronted with the horrible solution of a problem which seemingly has baffled even the Poles: the fate of "the other 10,000" and the probable whereabouts of their remains. The impact is the greater for the ice-cold simplicity of the 1940 NKVD Report which, in a few lines, disposes of nearly 15,000 innocent men.

In dedicating his book to Justice, Louis FitzGibbon sounds the right note, albeit a sombre and dolorous knell, for perhaps nowhere is justice so totally lacking as in the matter of Katyn. Here is a concise book containing all the evidence needed to reach a simple conclusion. It remains for courageous and determined action to follow so that this unjudged case may close after a proper pronouncement from an international legal forum – for it matters not that the Katyn crime was committed thirty-five years ago. Thus I join the author in hoping that the day of judgement may not now be too far distant. In the meantime, and while Justice waits, I commend this book to all, whether in authority or not, and of whatever nationality, as a testament to the truth and a fragment of history which must not much longer continue to be ignored.

Introduction

This is a book without an end. The story of what is collectively known as the Katyn Massacre is yet without its final chapter.

I have not attempted to describe the massacre of 4,254 of the total 14,471 in detail, hoping that those facts are by now reasonably well known. I have, however, tried to clear up the evidence, presenting it in full, which points to the murderers; evidence which is not surmise, but the painstaking conclusions of legal and quasi-legal bodies and which is capped by the secret NKVD report of 1940 which, for the first time, reveals what befell the "other 10,000".

It is a horrible story, a story which makes most people recoil and which offends the very essence of human reason. It is because people cannot bear to look the facts in the face that the story is so far without its proper conclusion.

This book is dedicated to the concept of Justice. For it tries to disperse doubts where none should exist, to give the answers to convenient facile questions, and certain people will find it an inconvenient book. But no difficulty was ever solved by running away. 14,471 dead men will not vanish as if they had never been; Justice does not allow it. Furthermore, their widows and other relatives survive amongst us.

I invite international authority to examine the case, disregarding expediency and special pleading, and to find room for that compassion which should be followed by anger that this injustice be allowed to continue. I urge all concerned to summon their courage so that Justice may at last be done.

1 Rejection of the International Red Cross 1943

At 2.15 pm London time in April 1943, the following news was broadcast by Radio Berlin:

"A report has reached us from Smolensk to the effect that the local inhabitants have mentioned to the German authorities the existence of a place where mass executions had been carried out by the Bolsheviks and where 10,000 Polish officers had been murdered by the GPU [initials for the previous name of the Soviet secret state police, at that time already the NKVD]. The German authorities accordingly went to the place called Kozy Gory ('Goat's Hill' – a small forested hill inside Katyn), a Soviet health resort situated twelve miles west of Smolensk, where a terrible discovery was made. A ditch was found, 28 metres long and 16 metres wide, in which the bodies of 3,000 Polish officers were piled up in twelve layers. They were fully dressed in military uniforms, some were bound, and all had pistol shot wounds in the back of their heads. There will be no difficulty in identifying the bodies as, owing to the nature of the ground, they are in a state of mumification and the Russians had left on the bodies their personal documents. It has been stated today that General Smorawinski from Lublin has been found amongst other murdered officers. Previously these officers were in a camp at Kozielsk near Orel and, in February and March 1940, were brought in 'cattle' freight-cars to Smolensk. Thence they were taken in lorries (trucks) to Kozy Gory and were

13

murdered there by the Bolsheviks. The search for further pits is in progress. New layers may be found under those already discovered. It is estimated that the total number of officers killed amounts to 10,000, which would correspond to the entire cadre of Polish officers taken prisoner by the Russians. The correspondents of Norwegian newspapers, who were on the spot and were thus able to obtain direct evidence of the crime, immediately sent their despatches to their papers in Oslo."

It was as if a mighty thunderclap had burst upon the world, huge and reverberating, to be followed by silence, a silence complete and endless. For a second in time the world stood still, appalled at this momentous revelation, just as a few years later it again paused before the gigantic horror of Hiroshima. It was as if the pulse of humanity momentarily stopped, shocked by the very enormity of that which so suddenly forced itself upon the mind. It was unbelievable; impossible; but there was no denying that it had been announced.

Berlin Radio went inexorably on:

"In the summer months of 1942 a few Poles, members of labour units attached to the German Army, and some civilians who had been liberated from enslavement by the Bolsheviks had learned from the local population that the Bolsheviks had carried out executions of Poles in the neighbourhood of Smolensk. From these rumours it was further made known that the murdered men were buried most probably in the Katyn wood, to the right of the road leading from the Smolensk-Katyn highway to the summer resthouse of the NKVD (formerly GPU). Apparently, to the railway station of Gniezdovo arrived repeated transports of prisoners, Polish officers, who were next loaded into trucks and driven to the neighbourhood of Katyn wood. The persons mentioned took interest in the fate of their countrymen and started digging up a little hillock which already at first glance seemed artificial and did not fit the natural surroundings. And indeed they soon

14

One of the death pits at Katyn partially emptied.

struck upon the body of a Polish officer, judging by the uniform in which it was clad. But initially nobody supposed that it was a mass grave which had been discovered. As the German unit to which these Poles were attached had to leave the neighbourhood, they had to give up further investigation. Terrorized by the Bolshevik rule, the local population was unwilling to repeat what it had lived through in 1940. It was only in Spring 1943 that the news about the bodies buried in the Katyn wood first reached the German authorities. Upon which the authorities undertook systematic and thorough enquiries, which gradually allowed them to reconstruct with terrifying exactness the event which immediately preceded the mass murder and one by one the horrific details were revealed. Statements given under oath by many witnesses clearly elucidate the whole matter and they conform with the observations derived from the exhumation researches. These statements also testify that the Katyn wood has already for many years been used as a place of execution by the GPU."

Radio Berlin further announced that new mass-graves continued to be discovered up to 16 April, bringing to light an additional 1,500 bodies. The Germans also broadcast the text of the statement given by old Partemon Kisielev from which the world learnt of the visit to his cottage in 1942 by the Poles in the "Todt" organisation. Apparently they had heard about Polish officers being murdered and they were told that Kisielev knew more about it than any of the other local inhabitants, because he lived nearest to the place. And so these ten Poles paid him a visit.

They asked him to show them the exact spot. They took spades with them. After having ascertained the truth, they filled up the holes they had dug and raised two crosses, cut out of birch wood, upon the grave. The silence which attended the first German announcement lasted throughout 14 April; a day, it could be said, when the Allies held their breath, each one wondering what to do and what to say. The British Government well knew that the numbers quoted by the Germans tallied well with the

16

total of missing officers, for which the Polish Government had been searching in Russia since the summer of 1941, and it also knew all about the Diplomatic Notes which had been exchanged on the subject. It knew also the answers given by the Soviet authorities. Here was a dilemma of massive proportions; Britain was allied both to the Poles and to the Russians and yet the common enemy had revealed a fact which, if true, must drive a wedge between these allies.

First to break the silence was Radio Moscow which, on 15 April 1943, made this announcement:

"In the past two or three days Goebbel's slanderers have been spreading vile fabrications alleging that the Soviet authorities carried out a mass shooting of Polish officers in the Spring of 1940 in the Smolensk area. In launching this monstrous invention the German-Fascist scoundrels did not hesitate to spread the most unscrupulous and base lies, in their attempts to cover up crimes which, as has now become evident, they perpetrated themselves. The German-Fascist report on this subject leaves no doubt as to the fate of the former Polish prisoners of war who in 1941 were engaged in construction work in areas west of the Smolensk region and who fell into the hands of German-Fascist hangmen in the summer of 1941, after the withdrawal of the Soviet troops from the Smolensk area. Beyond doubt Goebbel's slanderers are now trying with lies and calumnies to cover up the bloody crimes of the Hitlerite gangsters. In their clumsily concocted fabrication about the numerous graves which the Germans allegedly discovered near Smolensk, the Hitlerite liars mention the village of Gniezdovo. But, like the swindlers they are, they remain silent about the fact that it was near the village of Gniezdovo that the archaeological excavations of the historic 'Gniezdovo burial place' were made."

Here, at least, was a lead, and the British Government was not slow to follow. At 7.15 on 15 April the BBC announced:

"In a statement broadcast today, Moscow Radio officially and categorically denied the news propounded by the Germans about the alleged shooting of Polish officers by the Soviet authorities.

These German lies indicate the fate which met these officers whom the Germans had employed in 1941 for construction works in the neighbourhood. The Moscow transmission was interrupted all along and deafened by Berlin."

From that moment Radio Moscow and the Soviet press consolidated this version, namely that the "Polish prisoners, since 1940 assembled in camps around Smolensk, and employed in the neighbourhood, fell into the German hands in July 1941 and were subsequently shot by the Germans in August-September of the same year." It is a version which the *Soviet Weekly* repeated as recently as October 1971!

On the same day, 15 April 1943, the Poles also reacted violently, and from his HQ in the Middle East, General Anders sent the following telegram to the Polish Minister of Defence in London:

"From the moment of my release from prison I tried to find our soldiers from Starobielsk, Kozielsk and Ostashkow. I always received evasive replies from the Soviet authorities. The Commander-in-Chief of the Polish Army, General W. Sikorski, when in Moscow made a personal appeal to Stalin and received the answer that they had probably escaped. During the whole time I was in the USSR, I for my part, made prodigious efforts to discover something about their fate from the Soviet authorities and from Stalin himself. I sent people in all directions to search for them. In private conversations some of the Soviet officials declared that a *rokovoya oshibka* (fatal mistake) had been made over this. News reached us that some of our officers had been deliberately drowned in the Arctic Ocean. But it is quite possible that those moved from Kozielsk were murdered near Smolensk. A number of the names given by the

18

German radio are in our card index. It is a fact that not one of the 8,300 officers from the camps at Kozielsk and Starobielsk, nor any of the 4,000 NCOs of the military and civil police from Ostashkow camp have joined the army. In spite of tremendous efforts on our part, we have received absolutely no news of any of them. It has long been our conviction that none of them are alive, but that they were deliberately murdered. Nevertheless the announcement of the German discoveries made a tremendous impression and caused deep dismay. I consider it necessary for the Government to intervene in this affair with the object of obtaining official explanations from the Soviets, especially as our soldiers are convinced that the rest of our people in the USSR will also be exterminated."

Thus, whereas the British Government was content to follow behind the Soviets, the Poles were not; obviously General Anders who had spent time in the Lubianka knew more about Stalin than his British allies.

On the 17 April 1943, the Polish Government in London issued the following statement:

"On Saturday a cabinet meeting of the Polish Government was held in London at which all information concerning the discovery of the mass graves near Smolensk and the news received from Poland in connection with this discovery, was examined; after which the following communiqué was issued:

'No Pole can help being deeply shocked by the news to which the Germans are now giving the widest publicity, that is to say the discovery of the bodies in a common grave near Smolensk of the Polish officers missing in the USSR, and of the mass execution which was their lot.

'German propaganda is trying to give the greatest possible publicity to this news. The Polish Government have instructed their representative in Switzerland to request the International Red Cross in Geneva to send a delegation to investigate the true state of affairs on the spot. It is desirable that the results of the investigation of this protective institution, which is entrusted with the task of clarifying the matter and establishing the responsibility, should be made public without delay.' "

On the same day General Kukiel, the Polish Minister of Defence, also issued a communiqué, which concluded with this paragraph:

"We have become accustomed to the lies of German propaganda and we understand the purpose behind its latest revelations. In view however of the abundant and detailed German information concerning the discovery of the bodies of many thousands of Polish officers near Smolensk, and the categorical statement that they were murdered by the Soviet authorities in the Spring of 1940, the necessity has arisen that the mass graves discovered should be investigated and the facts alleged verified by a competent international body, such as the International Red Cross. The Polish Government has therefore approached this institution with a view to their sending a delegation to the place where the massacre of Polish prisoners of war is said to have taken place."

At the same time the Polish Government decided to make a final approach to the Soviet Government asking for an explanation, and a Note was sent to the Soviet Ambassador in London on 20 April 1943. After recalling that the question of the missing officers had been raised many times, the Note continued by saying:

"If, however, as shown by the communiqué of the Soviet Information Bureau of 15 April 1943 (ie the Russian reaction to the German revelations quoted above), the Government of the USSR should be in possession of further information on this matter than was communicated to the representatives of the Polish Government some time ago, I beg you once more, Mr Ambassador, to communicate to the Polish Government detailed and precise information as to the fate of the prisoners of war and civilians previously detained in the camps at Kozielsk, Starobielsk and Ostashkow.

Public opinion in Poland and throughout the world has quite rightly been so deeply shocked, that only irrefutable facts can outweigh the numerous and detailed German statements concerning the discovery of the bodies of many thousands of Polish officers murdered near Smolensk in the Spring of 1940."

To this Note, *no reply was ever received*. Neither were the Germans slow in seeking the assistance of the International Red Cross, and on 16 April 1943 the following message was sent by the German Red Cross to the International Red Cross in Geneva:

"Reference the news published on the discovery of thousands of bodies of Polish officers in Katyn Forest near Smolensk. In view of the international importance of the affair we regard the participation of the International Committee as very desirable, particularly in view of many cases of disappearance of persons in the USSR reported by the German Red Cross, the Polish Red Cross and other bodies. According to information obtained by the German Red Cross all facilities will be given to the representatives of the Committee to enable them to proceed forthwith to the place to take part in the investigations."

The message was signed "Grawitz". A similar message was later sent to Geneva by Prince von Koburg, President of the German Red Cross.

At 4.30 pm on the following day (17 April) Prince S. Radziwill, deputy of the Polish Red Cross delegate in Switzerland, handed a Note to Mr Rueger, a representative of the International Red Cross, also requesting an investigation. Prince Radziwill was informed that the International Red Cross would consider the matter on 20 April 1943. It is most important to note the German attitude in this application to the International Red Cross, as if the German version were untrue, as the Russians said

21

it was, then the Germans would have been inviting certain condemnation throughout the world just at a time when they held in their hands a propaganda weapon of massive importance. In all this Great Britain stood back – as it has continued to do even up to the hearing before the London consistory court on 15 January 1975.

Returning to 1943 and the month of April, the International Committee of the Red Cross found itself under increasing pressure to open investigations at Katyn. It was at this point that the Soviets exerted pressure of their own, sufficient indeed to cause the cancellation of the meeting proposed for 20 April. Instead the Executive Council replied with a short memorandum, the third paragraph of which stated: "3. The context of the Memorandum of 12 September 1939 does not permit us to consider sending experts to take part in the technical procedure of identification except with the agreement of all interested parties."

In fact the International Committee of the Red Cross had intended to send a team of experts composed of Swedish, Portugese and Swiss experts under the leadership of a Swiss, but it was then pointed out that the Soviet Government, as an "interested party" would not agree. Thus there was no alternative but to issue the short memorandum of which the essence is given above.

The moment for handling the matter discreetly had passed, for the world was awaiting the outcome with keen expectancy. In the event the International Committee had no alternative but to publish, on 23 April 1943, the following communiqué:

"The German Red Cross and the Polish Government in London have approached the International Red Cross with a request for its participation in the identification of bodies which, according to German reports, have been discovered near Smolensk. In both instances the International Red Cross replied that in principle it is prepared to afford assistance by selecting experts, on condition that similar appeals are received from all other parties interested in this

22

question. This is in accordance with the memorandum sent by the International Red Cross, on 12 September 1939, to all belligerent nations, defining the principles on the basis of which the International Red Cross may participate in this kind of investigation."

Here was an open invitation to the Soviet Government also to request this impartial investigation and thus prove before the world that its accusations against the Germans were true. But the die had already been cast, for on 21 April 1943 *Pravda* had published an article entitled "Polish collaboration of Hitler".

No reply was ever given by the Russians to the communiqué issued by the International Red Cross on 23 April, but instead Molotov summoned the Polish Ambassador on 25 April and informed him that relations between the Soviet Union and Poland were severed as a result of this so-called collaboration between the Germans and the Poles. Thus the dual call by the Germans and the Poles resulted unexpectedly in a political situation which portended grave possibilities, namely that the USSR might attempt a separate peace with Germany. This came at a time when both Great Britain and the United States were making every endeavour to secure Soviet friendship. Churchill had had a friendly meeting with Stalin in Moscow a few months earlier. Less than a year later King George VI was to send Stalin, in honour of the city named after him, a Sword of Honour with a golden hilt. On the night of 24/25 April pressure was brought to bear on General Sikorski in the hope that he would issue an official statement denying the possibility that the Katyn victims had been murdered by the Russians and proclaiming the whole business as a German propaganda trick.

Now General Sikorski, in most difficult circumstances, was doing his best to prosecute the war against Germany, and he made every possible concession leading to the Polish-Soviet treaty of 30 July 1941. It must have been infinitely painful for him to brush aside the treacherous attack on Poland by the USSR of 17 September 1939 and the subsequent deportation and martyrdom of thousands of Poles in the bad lands of Siberia. Even after the attempt to fight alongside the Russians after July 1941, Sikorski knew only too well of the pitiable condition in which some shattered remnants of his countrymen wandered back to join General Anders' army from the far reaches of Asian Russia. Starved, frostbitten, suffering from scurvy and almost broken by ill-treatment, these Poles nevertheless found it in their hearts to continue the struggle against the all-powerful Wehrmacht. All this Sikorski forced himself to put aside; but to agree to the lie that it was the Germans who had committed the ghastly crime of Katyn was too much. He refused.

It was this refusal which also contributed to the Soviet excuse for severing relations with the Polish Government on 25 April 1943 at 0.15 am.

All of this was viewed with dismay in England, and on 4 May 1943 the British Foreign Secretary, Anthony Eden (now Lord Avon), addressed the House of Commons as follows:

"The House will no doubt wish me to make a brief statement about the unfortunate difficulties between the Soviet and Polish Governments which have arisen since the House rose. There is no need for me to enter into the immediate origins of the dispute. I would only draw attention, as indeed the Soviet and Polish Governments have already done in their published statements, to the cynicism which permits the Nazi murderers of hundreds of thousands of innocent Poles and Russians to make use of a story of mass murder in an attempt to disturb the unity of the Allies.

From the outset His Majesty's Government have used their best efforts to persuade both the Poles and the Russians not to allow these German manoeuvres to have even the semblance of success. It was, therefore, with regret that they learned that, following an appeal by the Polish Government to the International Red Cross to investigate the German story, the Soviet Government felt compelled to

24

General Wladyslaw Sikorski.

interrupt relations with the Polish Government. His Majesty's Government have no wish to attribute blame for these events *to anyone except the common enemy*" (author's italics).

But even this attempt at appeasement made no difference to the Soviets, who still did not reply to the communiqué of the International Red Cross. Meanwhile the press in neutral countries such as Switzerland, Sweden and Turkey quite openly maintained that the gruesome mass murder at Katyn was the work of the Soviets.

Perhaps this is the moment to refer to an event of July 1943. General Sikorski flew to Cairo to visit the Polish Army under General Anders which by then had had a couple of months to digest the fact and aftermath of Katyn. General Sikorski was on his way back to England, perhaps with new data about the missing officers murdered in the forest, when he was killed in an air crash at Gibraltar on 4 July. Only the pilot survived, and although the bodies of the other passengers were retrieved, there is no sign of General Sikorski's briefcase or its contents. But was that crash an accident? Or was it engineered by the Soviets to get rid of an honourable and brave man who refused to help them about Katyn and who still demanded back the eastern part of Poland? The head of British Intelligence in the Iberian Peninsular was none other than Kim Philby, at that time not known to be a spy. It leaves room for considerable thought.

Tempting as it is to continue this theme about Sikorski, it must be abandoned to return to the major question which hung in the air in April 1943 and still remains unanswered. Why, if the Soviets accuse the Germans of the massacre at Katyn, did they refuse agreement for an impartial investigation by the International Committee of the Red Cross?

2 The International Medical Commission 1943 and the Soviet Commission 1944

Frustrated by the Soviet refusal to allow the International Committee of the Red Cross to conduct an impartial investigation in Katyn forest, the Germans decided to do the next best thing, that is to say to obtain the verdict of an "International" body of their own composition. They lost no time, and what they termed the "International Medical Commission" was brought together from experts in Belgium, Bulgaria, Denmark, Finland, Yugoslavia (Croatia), Italy, Switzerland, Holland, Czechoslovakia (Behemia and Moravia), Romania, Switzerland, Slovakia (also Czechoslovakia) and Hungary. It is important to note that whereas all those taking part came from countries under German control and included one from her ally, Italy, it also had the benefit of advice from Professor Francois Naville from neutral Switzerland.

Dated at Smolensk on 30 April 1943, the text of the official communiqué or protocol reads as follows:

"A Commission consisting of the representatives from the Institutes of Forensic Medicine and Criminology of European Universities, as well as of other professors of medicine, conducted a scientific examination of the mass-graves of Polish officers in Katyn Forest near Smolensk, between April 28 and 30, 1943.

The Commission was composed of the following members:

1. Belgium: Speelers, MD, Professor of Ophthalmology,

Ghent University.

2. Bulgaria: Markov, MD, Reader in Forensic Medicine and Criminology, Sofia University.

3. Denmark: Tramsen, MD, Assistant at the Institute of Forensic Medicine in Copenhagen.

4. Finland: Saxén, MD, Professor of Pathological Anatomy, Helsinki University.

5. Croatia (ie Yugoslavia): Miloslavich, MD, Professor of Forensic Medicine and Criminology, Zagreb University.

6. Italy: Palmieri, MD, Professor of Forensic Medicine and Criminology, Naples University.

7. Holland: De Burlet, MD, Professor of Anatomy, Groningen University.

8. Bohemia and Moravia (ie Czechoslovakia): Hájek, MD, Professor of Forensic Medicine and Criminology, Prague University.

9. Rumania: Birkle, MD, Expert in Forensic Medicine at the Rumanian Ministry of Justice.

10. Switzerland: Naville, MD, Professor of Forensic Medicine and Criminology, Geneva University.

11. Slovakia (ie Czechoslovakia): Subik, MD, Professor of Pathological Anatomy, Bratislava University.

12. Hungary: Orsós, MD, Professor of Forensic Medicine and Criminology, Budapest University.

Further, the investigations and meetings of the Commission were attended by:

1. Buhtz, MD, Professor of Forensic Medicine and Criminology at Breslau (Wroclaw) University, entrusted with the exhumation work at Katyn by the German High Command.

· 2. Costedoat, Medical Inspector, attending the work of the Commission on behalf of the Head of the French Government.

The discovery of the mass-graves of Polish officers in Katyn Forest, near Smolensk, recently brought to the attention of the German authorities, induced Doctor Conti, the Head of the Reich Health Department, to ask the above-mentioned specialists from various European countries to investigate the Katyn discovery and thus to

Two victims side by side.

assist in elucidating this unique case.

The Commission personally questioned a number of Russian witnesses from the vicinity who testified that in March and April, 1940, large transports of Polish officers arrived almost daily at the railway station of Gniezdovo, near Katyn, where they were unloaded and sent in lorries (trucks) towards the Katyn forest, never to be heard of again. The Commission also examined the discoveries and the results of previous investigations, as well as such evidence as had been collected. Up to April 30, 1943, 982 bodies had been exhumed. Of these, about 70 per cent were gradually identified; documents found on the remaining victims could not be used for identification until they had

29

been properly cleaned. All bodies exhumed prior to the arrival of the Commission had been examined and in most cases a post mortem had been carried out by Professor Buhtz and his colleagues. Up till now seven mass graves have been excavated. The largest contained the bodies of about 2,500 officers.

The members of the Commission personally conducted a post mortem on nine of the bodies, and proceeded to establish the evidence in specially selected cases.

All bodies so far exhumed show that death was caused by a shot in the head. These shots were without exception fired into the nape of the neck; generally one shot had been fired, in some instances two, and in one instance three. In every case the bullet had entered the lower part of the nape, piercing the occipital bone, close to the opening of the lower part of the skull; the point of exit was in the forehead, generally on the line of the hair-growth, in some rare cases in the lower part of the forehead. The shots were without exception those of a pistol with a calibre of less than eight millimetres.

That the shots had been fired from a barrel touching the nape of the neck or at extremely close range is proved by the cracks in the skull, by traces of gunpowder on the base of the skull close to the entrance of the bullet, and by the similarity of the exit orifices caused by the bullet. This may also be deduced from the fact that, apart from a few isolated cases, the path of the bullet is identical. The striking uniformity of the injuries and the position of the bullet's entry, all within a very small circumference on the lower part of the skull, point to experienced hands having been at work. The wrists of a large number of victims were found to have been tied in exactly the same way and in a few cases light bayonet stabs were noticed in the skin and in the clothes. The way in which the hands of the victims were tied is similar to that observed in the case of corpses of Russian civilians, also exhumed in Katyn Forest, but buried much earlier. Further, it has been established that the shots in the nape of the neck of these civilians had likewise been the work of experienced men.

Corpses in Katyn Forest.

Part of Katyn Forest showing bodies among the pines.

A stray bullet which had penetrated the head of a Polish officer previously killed by the usual shot in the nape of the neck, and which was wedged in the exterior part of the bone, proves that the bullet first killed another officer and then struck this officer who already lay dead in the pit. This fact warrants the assertion that shooting also took place in the pits themselves, in order to avoid transferring the corpses to the burial ground.

The mass-graves are situated in clearings, which had been completely levelled and then planted with pine trees. According to personal examinations carried out by the members of the Commission and the statements of senior forestry inspector Von Herff, who had been summoned as an expert, the pine trees in question were at least five years old, rather stunted owing to their being in the shade of older trees, and had been planted in that area three years ago.

The pits were dug in stepped terraces in a hilly area and in sandy soil. In places they penetrated to underground water.

The bodies were almost without exception laid face downwards, pressed together, fairly tidily around the sides of the pit but more irregularly in the centre. In almost all cases the legs were extended. It is clear that the bodies were arranged systematically. The Commission observed that the uniforms of the exhumed bodies, especially in respect of buttons, badges of rank, decorations, boots, marks on the underwear, etc., were typically Polish. The uniforms in question were winter ones. Fur coats, leather jackets, pullovers, officers' boots and caps customarily worn by Polish officers were frequently found. Only a few bodies of other ranks were discovered; the body of a priest was also found. All the uniforms were well-fitting despite the varying sizes of the wearers. The underclothes were buttoned up in the normal way; the braces of the trousers were properly adjusted. The Commission arrived at the conclusion that the victims were buried in the uniforms worn by them up to the moment of their death.

No watches or rings were found on the bodies although,

Corpse of a Polish major.

judging from the entries in the notebooks in which the exact time had been recorded, the officers must have been in possession of watches until the last moment. Valuable articles of metal were found concealed on a few bodies only. Bank-notes were found in large quantities and quite often some small change. Boxes of matches and Polish cigarettes were also found, and in some cases tobacco pouches, and cigarette cases bearing the inscription 'Kozielsk' (the name of the last Russian POW camp where the majority of the murdered officers had been imprisoned). The documents found on the bodies (notebooks, letters, newspapers) bear the dates covering the period between the Autumn of 1939 and the months of April and March, 1940. So far, the most recent date that has come to light is that on a Russian newspaper dated April 22, 1940.

The stages of decay were found to vary in accordance with the position of the bodies in the pits. Whilst mummification had taken place on the top and at the sides of the mass of bodies, a humid process could be observed caused by the damp nearer the centre. Adjacent bodies were stuck together with a thick putrid liquid. The peculiar deformations due to pressure clearly show that the bodies remained in the position they had assumed when they were first thrown into the pits.

Neither insects nor any traces of them, such as could have dated from the time of the burial, were found on the bodies. This proves that the shooting of the victims and their burial took place in the cold season, when there were no insects.

Several skulls were examined with a view to seeing whether they showed a condition which, if present, constitutes, according to the experiments made by Professor Orsós, clear evidence regarding the date of death. This appears as a crust, formed of layers of necrotic structure, around the surface of the brain which is turned into a uniform clay, like pulp. Bodies that have been in graves less than three years do not show this condition. Amongst others, body No 526, which was discovered on the surface of a big mass grave, bore distinct traces of this

Corpses awaiting examination.

One of the corpses lying in a mass grave.

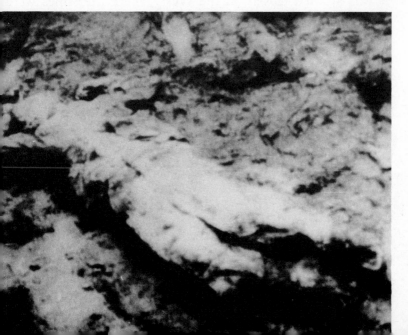

phenomenon."

Then followed a brief summary, which contained the following paragraph.

"The death of all these victims was caused exclusively by a shot in the nape of the neck. From statements made by witnesses, as well as from letters, diaries, newspapers, etc. found on the bodies, it follows that the executions took place in March and April, 1940. There is a complete conformity between the statements concerning the mass-graves and the results of the examination of single bodies of Polish officers."

The whole report was signed by all members of the Commission.

Here was an authoritative statement signed by experts in the field of forensic medicine. Attention is particularly invited to the signatures of 1. Professor Naville of Switzerland, the one neutral participant, who was later to be attacked in his own country for taking part; 2. Dr Markov of Bulgaria who, with Dr Hajek of Czechoslovakia, was later to recant under Soviet threats; 3. Dr Tramsen of Denmark and Dr Palmieri of Italy, both of whom were to reiterate their opinions as recently as 1974.

It was a statement which gave much food for thought and it was studied closely in the West, where the Allies were still searching for a way out of the terrible dilemma into which the German find and subsequent investigation had thrown them.

On 24 May 1943, Mr Owen O'Malley, His Majesty's Ambassador to the Polish Government in London addressed this despatch to the British Foreign Office, attaching to it a translation of a telegram received by the Polish Government from the Polish underground organisation in Warsaw dated 15 May 1943. These documents were marked "Most Secret".

Mr O'Malley to Mr Eden

British Embassy to Poland
45, Lowndes Square, S.W.1.
24th May, 1943.

Sir,

My despatch No 43 of the 30th April dwelt on the probability that no confederation in Eastern Europe could play an effective part in European politics unless it were affiliated to the Soviet Government, and suggested that so long as the policy of this Government was as enigmatic as it now is, it would be inconsistent with British interests that Russia should enjoy a sphere of influence extending from Danzig to the Aegean and Adriatic Seas. The suppression of the Comintern on the 20th May may be considered to have brought to an end what was in the past the most objectionable phase of Soviet foreign policy and to entitle the Soviet Government to be regarded less distrustfully than formerly. It is not, then, without hesitation that I address this further despatch to you, which also gives grounds for misgivings about the character and policy of the present rulers in Russia.

2. We do not know for certain who murdered a lot of Polish officers in the forest of Katyn in April and May 1940, but this at least is already clear, that it was the scene of terrible events which will live long in the memory of the Polish nation. Accordingly, I shall try to describe how this affair looks to my Polish friends and acquaintances, of whom many had brothers and sons and lovers among those known to have been taken off just three years ago from the prison camps at Kozielsk, Starobielsk and Ostashkow to an uncertain destination: how it looks, for instance, to General Sikorski, who there lost Captain Fuhrman, his former ADC and close personal friend; to M. Morawski, who lost a brother-in-law called Zoltowski and a newphew; or to M. Zaleski, who lost a brother and two cousins.

3. The number of Polish prisoners taken by the Russian armies when they invaded Poland, in September 1939, was about 180,000, including police and gendarmerie and a certain number of civilian officials. The total number of

37

army officers was round about 15,000. At the beginning of 1940 there were in the three camps named above round about 9,000 or 10,000 officers and 6,000 other ranks, policemen and civil officials. Less public reference has been made to these 6,000 than to the 10,000 officers, not because the Polish Government are less indignant about the disappearance of other ranks than about the disappearance of officers, or were less insistent in enquiries for them, but because the need of officers to command the Polish troops recruited in Russia was more urgent than the need to increase the total ration strength of the Polish army. There is no reason to suppose that these 6,000 other ranks and the police and the civilians were treated by the Soviet Government differently to the officers, and mystery covers the fate of all. For the sake of simplicity, however, I shall write in this despatch only of the missing officers, without specific reference to other ranks, to police prisoners or to civilians. Of the 10,000 officers, only some 3,000 or 4,000 were regular officers. The remainder were reserve officers who in peace time earned their living, many with distinction, in the professions, in business and so on.

4. In March of 1940 word went round the camps at Kozielsk, Starobielsk and Ostashkow that, under orders from Moscow, the prisoners were to be moved to camps where conditions would be more agreeable, and that they might look forward to eventual release. All were cheered by the prospect of a change from the rigours which prisoners must endure to the hazards and vicissitudes of relative freedom in Soviet or German territory. Even their captors seemed to wish the prisoners well, who were now daily entrained in parties of 50 to 350 for the place at which, so they hoped, the formalities of their discharge would be completed. As each prisoner was listed for transfer, all the usual particulars about him were rechecked and reregistered. Fresh finger-prints were taken. The prisoners were inoculated afresh and certificates of inoculation furnished to them. Sometimes the prisoners' Polish documents were taken away, but in many such cases these were returned before departure. All were furnished with

38

rations for the journey, and, as a mark of special regard, the sandwiches furnished to senior officers were wrapped in clean white paper – a commodity seldom seen anywhere in Russia. Anticipations of a better future were clouded only by the fact that 400 or 500 Poles had been listed for further detention, first at Pavlishchev Bor and eventually at Griazovetz. These were, as it turned out later, to be the only known survivors of the lost legion, and some of them are in England now; but at the time, although no principle could be discovered on which they had been selected, they supposed that they had been condemned to a further period of captivity; and some even feared that they had been chosen out for execution.

5. Our information about these events is derived for the most part from those routed to Griazovetz, all of whom were released in 1941, and some of whom – notably M. Komarnicki, the Polish Minister for Justice – are now in England.

6. Entrainment of the 10,000 officers from the three camps went on all through April and the first half of May, and the lorries, lined with cheerful faces, which took them from camp to station, were, in fact, the last that was even seen of them alive by any witness to whom we have access. Until the revelations made by the German broadcast of the 12th April, 1943, and apart from a few words let drop at the time by the prison guards, only the testimony of scribblings on the railway wagons in which they were transported affords any indication of their destination. The same wagons seem to have done a shuttle service between Kozielsk and the detraining station; and on these some of the first parties to be transported had scratched the words: "Don't believe that we are going home," and the news that their destination had turned out to be a small station near Smolensk. These messages were noticed when the vans returned to Smolensk station, and have been reported to us by prisoners at Kozielsk, who were later sent to Griazovetz.

7. But though of positive indication as to what subsequently happened to the 10,000 officers there was none until the grave at Katyn was opened, there is now

available a good deal of negative evidence, the cumulative effect of which is to throw serious doubt on Russian disclaimers of responsibility for the massacre. (See also my despatch No 52 Secret of today's date.)

8. In the first place there is the evidence to be derived from the prisoners' correspondence, in respect to which information has been furnished by officers' families in Poland, by officers now with the Polish army in the Middle East, and by the Polish Red Cross Society. Up till the end of March 1940 large numbers of letters had been despatched, which were later received by their relatives, from the officers confined at Kozielsk, Starobielsk and Ostashkow; whereas no letters from any of them (excepting from the 400 moved to Grizovetz) have been received by anybody which had been despatched subsequent to that date. The Germans overran Smolensk in July 1941, and there is no easy answer to the question why, if any of the 10,000 had been alive between the end of May 1940 and July 1941, none of them ever succeeded in getting any word through to their families.

9. In the second place there is the evidence of the correspondence between the Soviet Government and the Polish Government. The first request for information about the 10,000 was made by M. Kot of M. Vyshinsky on the 6th October, 1941. On the 3rd December, 1941, General Sikorski backed up his enquiry with a list of 3,845 names of officers included among them. General Anders furnished the Soviet Government with a further list of 800 names on the 18th March, 1942. Enquiries about the fate of the 10,000 were made again and again to Russian Government verbally and in writing by General Sikorski, M. Kot, M. Romer, Count Raczyński and General Anders between October 1941 and April 1943. The Polish Red Cross between August and October 1940 sent no less than 500 *questionnaires* about individual officers to the Russian Government. To none of all these enquiries extending over a period of two and a half years was a single positive answer of any kind ever returned. The enquirers were told either that the officers had been released, or that "perhaps they

General von Gersdorff addressing French and Turkish journalists in Katyn Forest, 1943. Photograph taken by a member of the Wehrmacht.

Corpses being arranged in rows.

are already in Germany," or that "no information" of their whereabouts was available, or (M. Molotov to M. Kot, October 1941) that complete lists of the prisoners were available and that they would all be delivered to the Polish authorities "dead or alive." But it is incredible that if any of the 10,000 were released, not one of them has ever appeared again anywhere, and it is almost equally incredible, if they were not released, that not one of them should have escaped subsequent to May 1940 and reported himself to the Polish authorities in Russia or Persia. That the Russian authorities should have said of any Polish officer in Soviet jurisdiction that they had "no information" also provokes incredulity; for it is notorious that the NKVD collect and record the movements of individuals with the most meticulous care.

10. In the third place there is the evidence of those who have visited the grave: first, a Polish commission including, among others, doctors, journalists and members of the Polish Assistance Committee, a former president of the Polish Academy of Literature and a representative of the Mayor of Warsaw; secondly, another Polish commission which included priests, doctors and representatives of the Polish Red Cross Society; thirdly, an international commission of criminologists and pathologists, of which the personnel is given in Annex I. The report of this commission forms Annex II to this despatch, and the reports of the two Polish commissions add little to it. It is deposed by all that several hundred identifications have been established. All this evidence would normally be highly suspect since the inspections took place under German auspices and the results reached us through German broadcasts. There are fair grounds for presuming that the German broadcasts accurately represented the findings of the commissions, that the commissions' findings were at any rate in some respects well founded, and that the grounds were sound on which at any rate some of the identifications were made.

11. In the fourth place there is the fact that a mass execution of officer prisoners would be inconsistent with

what we know of the German army. The German army has committed innumerable brutalities, but the murder by them of prisoners of war, even of Poles, is rare. Had the German authorities ever had these 10,000 Polish officers in their hands we can be sure that they would have placed some or all of them in the camps in Germany already allotted to Polish prisoners, while the 6,000 other ranks, policemen and civil officials would have been put to forced labour. In such case the Polish authorities would in the course of two years certainly have got into touch with some of the prisoners; but, in fact, none of the men from Kozielsk, Starobielsk or Ostashkow have ever been heard of from Germany.

12. Finally there is the evidence to be derived from the confusion which characterises explanations elicited from or volunteered by the Sovet Government. Between August 1941 and the 12th April, 1943, when the Germans announced the discovery of the grave at Katyn, the Russian Government had, among other excuses, maintained that all Polish officers taken prisoner in 1939 had been released. On the other hand, in conversation with the Polish Ambassador, a Russian official who had drunk more than was good for him, once referred to the disposal of these officers as "a tragic error." On the 16th April, immediately after the German announcement, the Soviet Information Bureau in Moscow suggested that the Germans were misrepresenting as victims of Russian barbarity skeletons dug up by archaeologists at Gniezdowo, which lies next door to Katyn. On the 26th April M. Molotov, in a note to the Polish Ambassador in Moscow, said that the bodies at Katyn were those of Poles who had at one time been prisoners of the Russians but had subsequently been captured by the Germans in their advance at Smolensk in July 1941 and had been murdered then by them. On a later occasion, and when the German broadcasts gave reason to think that some bodies were sufficiently well preserved to be identifiable, the Russian Government put forward a statement that the Polish officers had been captured by the Germans in July 1941, had been employed upon

construction work, and had only been murdered shortly before the German "discovery" was announced. This confusion cannot easily be understood except on the assumption that the Russian Government had something to hide.

13. The cumulative effect of this evidence is, as I said earlier, to throw serious doubt on Russian disclaimers of responsibility for a massacre. Such doubts are not diminished by rumours which have been current during the last two and a half years that some of the inmates of Kozielsk, Starobielsk and Ostashkow had been transported towards Kolyma, Franz Joseph Land or Novaya Zemlya, some or all of these being killed *en route*. It may be that this was so, and it may be that some less number than ten thousand odd were destroyed and buried at Katyn; but whether the massacre occurred (if it did occur) in one place or two places or three places naturally makes no difference to Polish sentiments. These will accordingly be described without reference to the uncertainty which exists as to the exact number of victims buried near Smolensk.

14. With all that precedes in mind it is comprehensible that the relatives and fellow-officers of the men who disappeared should have concluded that these had in fact been murdered by their Russian captors and should picture their last hours – somewhat as follows – with bitter distress. The picture is a composite one to which knowledge of the district, the German broadcasts, experience of Russian methods and the reports of visitors to the grave have all contributed, but it is not so much an evidentially established description of events as a reconstruction in the light of the evidence – sometimes partial and obviously defective – of what may have happened. But it – or something like it – is what most Poles believe to have happened, and what I myself, in the light of all the evidence, such as it is, incline to think happened. Many months or years may elapse before the truth is known, but because in the meantime curiosity is unsatisfied and judgment in suspense, we cannot, even if we would – and much less can Poles – make our thoughts and feelings

unresponsive to the dreadful probabilities of the case.

15. Smolensk lies some 20 km. from the spot where the common graves were discovered. It has two stations and in or near the town the main lines from Moscow to Warsaw and from Riga to Orel cross and recross each other. Some 15 km. to the west of Smolensk stands the unimportant station of Gniezdowo, and it is but a short mile from Gniezdowo to a place known locally as Kozlinaya Gora or "The Hill of Goats." The district of Katyn, in which this little hill stands, is covered with primeval forest which has been allowed to go to rack and ruin. The forest is mostly coniferous, but the pine trees are interspersed here and there with hardwoods and scrub. The month of April normally brings spring to this part of the country, and by early May the trees are green; but the winter of 1939-40 had been the hardest on record, and when the first parties from Kozielsk arrived on the 8th April there would still have been occasional patches of snow in deep shade and, of course, much mud on the rough road from the station to the Hill of Goats. At Gniezdowo the prison vans from Kozielsk, Starobielsk and Ostashkow discharged their passengers into a barbed-wire cage surrounded by a strong force of Russian soldiers, and the preparations made here for their reception must have filled most of the Polish officers with disquiet, and some indeed with dismay who remembered that the forest of Katyn had been used by the Bolsheviks in 1919 as a convenient place for the killing of many Czarist officers. For such was the case, and a Pole now in London, Janusz Laskowski, tells me that when he was eleven years old he had to listen every evening to an account of his day's work from one of the executioners, Afanaziev, who was billeted in his mother's house. From the cage the prisoners were taken in lorries along a country road to the Hill of Goats, and it must have been when they were unloaded from the lorries that their hands were bound and that dismay gave way to despair. If a man struggled, it seems that the executioner threw his coat over his head, tying it round his neck and leading him hooded to the pit's edge, for in many cases a body was found to be thus hooded and

45

the coat to have been pierced by a bullet where it covered the base of the skull. But those who went quietly to their death must have seen a monstrous sight. In the broad deep pit their comrades lay, packed closely round the edge, head to feet, like sardines in a tin, but in the middle of the grave disposed less orderly. Up and down on the bodies the executioners tramped, hauling the dead bodies about and treading in the blood like butchers in a stockyard. When it was all over and the last shot had been fired and the last Polish head been punctured, the butchers – perhaps trained in youth to husbandry – seem to have turned their hands to one of the most innocent of occupations: smoothing the clods and planting little conifers all over what had been a shambles. It was, of course, rather late in the year for transplanting young trees, but not too late; for the sap was beginning to run in the young Scots pines when, three years later, the Polish representatives visited the site.

16. The climate and the conifers are not without significance. The climate of Smolensk accounts for the fact that, though the Germans first got wind of the existence of the mass graves in the autumn of 1942, it was only in April of 1943 that they published to the world an account of what had been unearthed. The explanation is surely this: not that the German propagandists had chosen a politically opportune moment for their revelations, but that during the winter the ground at Smolensk is frozen so hard that it would have been impossible to uncover corpses without dynamite or such other violent means as would have destroyed the possibility of identifying dead bodies. The winter of 1942-43 was exceptionally mild and the German authorities probably got to work as soon as the soil was sufficiently soft. The little conifers also deserve more attention than they have received. In the first place they are presumptive evidence of Russian guilt; for, considering the conditions under which the German army advanced through Smolensk in July 1941 in full expectation of early and complete victory, it is most unlikely, if the Polish officers had been murdered by Germans and not Russians,

Head of a victim showing mouth stuffed with sawdust.

that the Germans would have bothered to cover up their victims' graves with young trees. In the second place, one of these young trees under examination by a competent botanist would reveal beyond any possibility of doubt whether it had last been transplanted in May 1940 or some time subsequent to July 1941. Perhaps this test of Russian veracity will presently be made.

17. The political background against which the events described in paragraph 15 are viewed by Poles is by contrast a matter of undisputed history, including as it does all the long story of partitions, rebellions and repressions, the Russo-Polish war of 1919-20, the mutual suspicions which this left behind it, the unannounced invasion of Poland by Russia in September 1939, the subsequent occupation of half Poland by Russia and the carrying into captivity of some million and a half of its inhabitants. More recently comes the virtual annexation of the occupied eastern parts of Poland, the refusal of the Russian Government to recognise as Polish citizens the inhabitants of the occupied districts, the suppression of relief organisations for Poles in Russia and the persecution of Poles refusing to change their own for Russian nationality. When Poles learned that, in addition to all these misfortunes, round about 10,000 men of the best breeding stock in Poland had (according to Russian accounts) been either dispersed and "lost" somewhere in the Soviet Union or else abandoned to the advancing German armies, or had (according to German accounts) been found to have been murdered by the Russians, many of them naturally concluded (though I do not here give it as my own conclusion) that the Soviet Government's intention had been to destroy the very foundations upon which their own Poland could be rebuilt. This sinister political intention imputed by Poles to Russia poisoned the wound and enhanced the sufferings of a nation already outraged and dismayed by the conduct of the Soviet Government. Some Poles, remembering Lenin's attitude to the holocausts of 1917 and subsequent years, and probing the dark recesses of Stalin's mind when he took (if take he did) the dreadful

decision, compare disciple with master. Lenin would have broken apart the heads of ten thousand Polish officers with the insouciance of a monkey cracking walnuts. Did corpses pitching into a common grave with the precision of machines coming off a production-belt similarly satisfy a nature habituated to manipulate blood and lives with uncompassionate detachment? Some at any rate so interpret Stalin's mind. "These men are no use to us," they imagine him as saying; "in fact they are a nuisance and a danger. Here is an *élite* of talent, here is valour and a hostile purpose. These stallions must not live to sire a whole herd of hostile Christian thoroughbreds. Many of the brood-mares have already been sold to Siberian peasants and the camel-pullers of Kazakstan. Their foals and yearlings can be broken to Communist harness. Rid me of this stud farm altogether and send all this turbulent bloodstock to the knackers."

18. The men who were taken to Katyn are dead, and their death is a very serious loss to Poland. Nevertheless, unless the Russians are cleared of the presumption of guilt, the moral repercussions in Poland, in the other occupied countries and in England of the massacre of Polish officers may well have more enduring results than the massacre itself; and this aspect of things, therefore, deserves attention. As I have as yet seen no reliable reports on public feeling in Poland and German-occupied Europe, my comments will relate only to our own reaction to the uncovering of the graves.

19. This despatch is not primarily concerned with the reaction of the British public, press or Parliament, who are not in such a good position as His Majesty's Government to form an opinion as to what actually happened. We ourselves, on the other hand, who have access to all the available information, though we can draw no final conclusions on vital matters of fact, have a considerable body of circumstantial evidence at our disposal, and I think most of us are more than half convinced that a large number of Polish officers were indeed murdered by the Russian authorities, and that it is indeed their bodies (as

well, maybe, as other bodies) which have now been unearthed. This being so, I am impelled to examine the effect on myself of the facts and allegations, and to adjust my mind to the shocking probabilities of the case. Since the Polish Government is in London and since the affair has been handled directly by yourself and the Prime Minister with General Sikorski and Count Raczyński, it may seem redundant for me to comment on it, as I should naturally do were the Polish Government and I both abroad; but, though all important conversations have been between Ministers and the leaders of the Polish Government, my contacts have doubtless been more numerous than yours during the last few weeks with Poles of all kinds, and they have possibly spoken to me with less reserve than to yourself. I hope therefore I may, without impertinence, submit to you the reflections which follow.

20. In handling the publicity side of the Katyn affair we have been constrained by the urgent need for cordial relations with the Soviet Government to appear to appraise the evidence with more hesitation and lenience than we should do in forming a common-sense judgment on events occurring in normal times or in the ordinary course of our private lives; we have been obliged to appear to distort the normal and healthy operation of our intellectual and moral judgments; we have been obliged to give undue prominence to the tactlessness or impulsiveness of Poles, to restrain the Poles from putting their case clearly before the public, to discourage any attempt by the public and the press to probe the ugly story to the bottom. In general we have been obliged to deflect attention from possibilities which in the ordinary affairs of life would cry to high heaven for elucidation, and to withhold the full measure of solicitude which, in other circumstances would be shown to acquaintances situated as a large number of Poles now are. We have in fact perforce used the good name of England like the murderers used the little conifers to cover up a massacre; and, in view of the immense importance of an appearance of Allied unity and of the heroic resistance of Russia to Germany, few will think that any other course

would have been wise or right.

21. This dislocation between our public attitude and our private feelings we may know to be deliberate and inevitable; but at the same time we may perhaps wonder whether, by representing to others something less than the whole truth so far as we know it, and something less than the probabilities so far as they seem to us probable, we are not incurring a risk of what – not to put a fine point on it – might darken our vision and take the edge off our moral sensibility. If so, how is this risk to be avoided?

22. At first sight it seems that nothing less appropriate to a political despatch than a discourse upon morals can be imagined; but yet, as we look at the changing nature of the international world of today, it seems that morals and international politics are becoming more and more closely involved with each other. This proposition has important consequences; but since it is not universally accepted I hope the following remarks in support of it are not out of place.

23. Nobody doubts that morals now enter into the domestic politics of the United Kingdom, but it was not always so. There was a time when the acts of the Government in London were less often the fruit of consultation and compromise in the general interests of all than of the ascendancy of one class or group of citizens who had been temporarily successful in the domestic arena. It was realisation of the interdependence of all classes and groups of the population of England, Scotland and Wales which discouraged the play of intestine power-politics and set the welfare of all above the advantage of the strong. Similar causes are producing similar results in the relations of States to each other. "During the last four centuries of our modern era," writes Professor Pollard, "the last word in political organisation has been the nation; but now that the world is being unified by science and culture" the conception of the nation state as the largest group in which human beings are organically associated with each other is being superseded by the conception of a larger, it may be of a European, or indeed of a world-wide unity; and "the

nation is taking its place as the bridge, the half-way house, between the individual and the human family." Europe, and indeed the world, are in process of integrating themselves, and "the men and women of Britain," as you said at Maryland, "are alive to the fact that they live in one world with their neighbours." This being so, it would be strange if the same movement towards the coalescence of smaller into larger groups which brought about the infiltration of morals into domestic politics were not also now bringing about the infiltration of morals into international politics. This, in fact, it seems to many of us is exactly what is happening, and is why, as the late Mr Headlam Morley said, "what in the international sphere is morally indefensible generally turns out in the long run to have been politically inept." It is surely the case that many of the politicial troubles of neighbouring countries and some of our own have in the past arisen because they and we were incapable of seeing this or unwilling to admit it.

24. If, then, morals have become involved with international politics, if it be the case that a monstrous crime has been committed by a foreign Government – albeit a friendly one – and that, we, for however valid reasons, have been obliged to behave as if the deed was not theirs, may it not be that we now stand in danger of bemusing not only others but ourselves: of falling, as Mr. Winant said recently at Birmingham, under St. Paul's curse on those who can see cruelty "and burn not"? If so, and since no remedy can be found in an early alteration of our public attitude towards the Katyn affair, we ought, maybe, to ask ourselves how, consistently with the necessities of our relations with the Soviet Government, the voice of our political conscience is to be kept up to concert pitch. It may be that the answer lies, for the moment, only in something to be done inside our own hearts and minds where we are masters. Here at any rate we can make a compensatory contribution – a reaffirmation of our allegiance to truth and justice and compassion. If we do this we shall at least be predisposing ourselves to the exercise of a right judgment on all those half political, half

moral, questions (such as the fate of Polish deportees now in Russia) which will confront us both elsewhere and more particularly in respect to Polish-Russian relations as the war pursues its course and draws to its end; and so, if the facts about the Katyn massacre turn out to be as most of us incline to think, shall we vindicate the spirit of these brave unlucky men and justify the living to the dead.

I have the honour to be, with the highest respect,

Sir,

Your most obedient,

humble Servant,

OWEN O'MALLEY

Enclosure in Mr O. St C. O'Malley's despatch No 52 Most Secret of May 24th, 1943

Translation. Telegram from Poland, dated May 15, 1943.

1. At the foot of a hillock is an "L"-shaped mass-grave, which has been completely opened up. Its dimensions are: 16 x 26 x 6 metres. The bodies of the murdered men have been carefully arranged in from 9 to 12 layers, one on the top of the other, each layer with the heads laid in opposite directions. The uniforms, notes in the pockets, passports and decorations are well preserved. The skin, hair and tendons have remained in such a good state that in order to carry out the trepanning it was necessary to cut under the skin and tendons. The faces were however unrecognizable.

2. Perpendicular to the first grave is a second mass-grave which up to now has only been partially opened up. Its dimensions are 14 x 16 metres. All the bodies in this grave have the hands tied behind them with a plait of string: in some cases the mouths have been gagged with handkerchiefs or rags: in some the head has been wrapped round with the skirt of an overcoat.

3. Up to now 906 bodies have been extracted, 76 per cent of which have been identified on the strength of passports, letters, etc., found on them.

4. It is presumed that in the two graves together there lie the bodies of from 2,500 to 4,000 officers: in only a few cases

53

are they reserve officers in civilian dress.

5. Twelve persons, including one doctor and three non-commissioned officers of an ambulance unit, were present on behalf of the Polish Red Cross when the graves were opened up, the bodies identified and the documents found on them collected.

6. A characteristic feature is that nothing except watches has been removed from the murdered men: note-cases, money and papers are still in their pockets: sometimes even rings are still on the fingers.

7. All the bodies have a bullet wound in the back of the skull. The representatives of the Polish Red Cross who were present at the exhumation took pains to collect the bullets extracted from the heads of the murdered men, the revolver shells and ammunition lying in the mass-graves as well as the cords with which the hands of the murdered men had been tied. The entire material found was sent to the Polish Red Cross in Warsaw for Dr. Gorczycki.

8. In the presence of the author of this report there was taken from the clothing of Major Solski a diary written up to April 21st. The writer of the diary stated that from Kozielsk they were taken in prison vans to their destination, then taken to Smolensk where they spent the night: reveille was sounded at 4 a.m. and they were placed in prison motor cars. At a clearing in the forest they were turned out of the motor cars and at 6.30 taken to some buildings there, where they were told to give up their jewellery and watches. At this point the diary ends.

9. Under the supervision of the German authorities the Delegate of the Polish Red Cross is carrying out the exhumation and autopsies, besides collecting the papers. He has moreover established private contact with the local population. Whenever a body is identified a small tablet with a Red Cross number is attached to the bones. Afterwards all the bodies are put into a freshly dug, common grave. All of the officers identified were from Kozielsk with the exception of one from Starobielsk.

10. The clearing in the forest at Katyn covers several square kilometres: on it there used to be NKVD

rest-houses. The local civilian population state that in March and April 1940 one transport of Polish officers to the number of from 200 to 300 used to arrive every day.

The following comments were made by senior members of the Foreign Office.

"This is a brilliant, unorthodox and disquieting despatch.

In the first thirteen paragraphs Mr O'Malley confines himself to an examination of the evidence as to German or Russian responsibility for the Katyn massacres. This is useful and the material is skilfully assembled. On the evidence available it is, I think, not difficult to share his conclusion that at any rate a strong presumption exists that the Russians were responsible.

In the next five paragraphs Mr O'Malley embarks upon what he admits is a 'sometimes partial and obviously defective' reconstruction of what may have happened at Katyn, leading up to a final ghoulish vision of Stalin condemning the Poles to the knacker's yard. This passage seems to serve no other purpose than to arouse anti-Soviet passions and prejudices in the reader's mind.

Mr O'Malley then applies himself to the question of how passions and prejudices may best be turned to account. By way of a devious argument about the infiltration of morals into international politics he recommends, while recognizing the present necessity of avoiding public accusations of our Russian allies, that we should at least redress the balance in our own minds and in all our future dealings with the Soviet Government refuse to forget the Soviet crime of Katyn. Our future dealings with the Russians should in fact be governed by the moral necessity of 'vindicating the spirit of these brave, unlucky men and justifying the living to the dead'. In effect Mr O'Malley urges that we should follow the example which the Poles themselves are unhappily so prone to offer us and in our diplomacy allow our heads to be governed by our hearts. The minutes on Mr O'Malley's earlier despatch in U 2011/58/72 suggest that this is the one thing above all to be

avoided, at any rate in our dealings with Soviet Russia."
(SIR WILLIAM DENIS ALLEN KCMG, then a member of HM
Diplomatic Service.)

"I agree with Mr Allen's dissection of this despatch into
three very different and unequal parts. I do not think that
many people who have been able to follow this question at
all closely would disagree with Mr O'Malley's conclusion
that the presumption of guilt rests very strongly on the
Soviet Government. It is obviously a very awkward matter
when we are fighting for a moral cause and when we intend
to deal adequately with war criminals, that our Allies
should be open to accusations of this kind and to others
relating to the deportation of hundreds of thousands of
Poles and to their subsequent treatment in Soviet Russia.
However, as Mr O'Malley says himself, there is no point in
our assisting German propaganda on these issues and there
is no reason why we cannot maintain our own moral
standards and values whilst at the same time endeavouring
in every way possible to improve our relations with the
Russians and incidentally perhaps to bring about an
improvement in Soviet conduct.

It is unfortunately the case that the Polish case has rather
tended to go by default owing to the circumstances in
which the Katyn question first became public knowledge.

It would, therefore, I think, be useful for the facts
assembled by Mr O'Malley in paragraphs 1 to 13 to be
circulated at all events to the Cabinet. But I cannot help
feeling that his subsequent imaginative reconstruction of
the scene in paragraphs 14 to 17, and more particularly
paragraph 17, and his moral observation in paragraphs 19
to 24 cast very little light upon this problem and merely
leave the reader with the impression that Mr O'Malley is
working up the maximum prejudice against the Soviet
Union. The last paragraphs of his despatch therefore tend
to discount the impression left by the introductory factual
paragraphs. I know that Mr O'Malley is very anxious that
this despatch should be circulated. I think myself that there
would be advantage in printing and circulating to the War

Cabinet paragraphs 1 to 13 only without the last sentence of paragraph 13 and without the passages I have marked in paragraphs 7 and 10."
(SIR FRANK KENYON ROBERTS, Foreign Office 1937-45.)

"I should be inclined to print this as it stands (except the first enclosure) and circulate to King and War Cabinet only. It is a powerful piece of work and deserves to be read."
(W. STRANG Lord William Strang, then Assistant Under-Secretary (of State in the Foreign Office.)

"I agree."
(O. SARGENT Sir Orme Sargent, then Deputy Under-Secretary of State in the Foreign Office.)

"This is very disturbing. I confess that, in cowardly fashion, I had rather turned my head away from the scene at Katyn – for fear of what I should find there.

There may be evidence, that we do not know of, that may point in another direction. But on the evidence that we have, it is difficult to escape from the presumption of Russian guilt.

This of course raises terrible problems, but I think no one has pointed out that, on the purely moral plane, these are not new. How many thousand of its citizens has the Soviet régime butchered? And I don't know that the blood of a Pole cries louder to Heaven than that of a Russian. But we have perforce welcomed the Russians as Allies and have set ourselves to work with them in war and peace.

The ominous thing about this incident is the ultimate political repercussion. How, if Russian guilt is established, can we expect Poles to live amicably side by side with Russians for generations to come? I fear there is no answer to that question.

And the other disturbing thought is that we may eventually, by agreement and in collaboration with Russians, proceed to the trial and perhaps execution of Axis 'war criminals' while condoning this atrocity. I confess

I shall find that extremely difficult to swallow.

However, quite clearly for the moment there is nothing to be done. As to what circulation we give to this explosive material, I find it difficult to make up my mind. Of course it would be only honest to circulate it. But as we know (all admit) that the knowledge of this evidence cannot affect our course of action, or policy, is there any advantage in exposing more individuals than necessary to the spiritual conflict that a reading of this document excites?''
(A.C. Rt Hon Sir Alexander Cadogan, then Permanent Under-Secretary of State for Foreign Affairs.)

It is interesting to note that Mr. O'Malley's despatch, dated May 1943, had been lying quietly in the archives of the British Foreign Office right up until 1 January 1972, when it, together with his second despatch dated 11 February 1944, were released. In the meantime a debate had been initiated by Lord Barnby in the Upper House on 17 June 1971, when Lord Aberdare for the Government made a statement which, *inter alia*, reads as follows:

"I would emphasise that Her Majesty's Government were in no way associated with any of these investigations (referring to the German investigation of 1943, the Soviet investigation of 1944 and the American Congressional investigation of 1952), nor have Her Majesty's Government accepted any of their various conclusions. The only enquiry in which Britain was involved took place at the Nuremberg War Crimes Tribunal in 1946. The results were inconclusive and the judgments issued by the Nuremberg Tribunal contained no reference to the Katyn massacre."

Later he went on:

"Is it likely, is it even conceivable, that the truth about these events could be established now to universal satisfaction, when it was not established in 1941, in 1944, in 1946 or in 1952? ... I suggest to the House that the only result of a new inquiry would be to re-open old wounds ...

58

The Noble Lord's Question invites Her Majesty's Government to take certain action, and this action we regard as not only beyond our competence, but likely to lead to nothing but pain, disagreement, and ill-will."

The implication of these soothing comments was that Great Britain was unsure in the matter; did not wish to make statements when there was doubt, and generally wished to ignore the whole subject for lack of facts. And yet, within six months, previously Most Secret documents were released which show that ever since 1943 and 1944 it had been well known who had committed this horrible massacre.

Further on in the debate of 17 June 1971, Lord Aberdare had promised the late Marquess of Salisbury that he would "convey that point to my right honourable friend" (referring to the then Foreign Secretary) and in response to a suggestion that "Her Majesty's Government ... do something which we have not done up to now, and that is to express their own view about the Katyn massacre?" Lord St Oswald continued to press the point on 29 June and 21 July 1971, but he did not obtain a satisfactory reply. What a great pity that the O'Malley despatches were not available in the summer of 1971!

So much, then, for the German investigation and its echoes in Great Britain in 1943 and as recently as 1971. We come now to the Russian investigation of 1944, and what that brought forth.

Within a few weeks of the publication of the *Amtliches Material* in mid-1943, the German Army was driven from the Smolensk region. After unusually heavy fighting the attacks launched by General Sokolowski's Army on Jartsevo and by General Jermienko's Army on Duchovshtchizna on 15 September 1943 led to the capture of Smolensk by the Soviet armies on September 25. Soon afterwards they also retook the region of the Katyn graves, with the result that the "resumption" of the exhumations which the Germans had declared would take place in the autumn became impossible.

The publication of the *Amtliches Material* was therefore the "swan song" of German propaganda about the Katyn affair. For some months the Germans had used it to shock public opinion in Europe and the world; but by October 1943 almost nothing was heard of it.

It was, however, taken up by the Russians when their forces re-occupied the area in the autumn of 1943.

By a Decree of the Supreme Council of the USSR dated 2 November 1943 an "Extraordinary State Commission for Ascertaining and Investigating the Crimes committed by the German Fascist Invaders and their Associates" was set up. The Extraordinary Commission set up a "Special Commission for Ascertaining and Investigating the Circumstances of the Shooting of Polish Officer Prisoners by the German Fascist Invaders in the Katyn Wood." The first mention of this "Special Commission" was made in Moscow on 17 January, 1944.

The composition of this Special Commission was as follows: Chairman: M. N. Burdenko – surgeon and Academician.

Members: A. N. Tolstoy – Academician, Author; Nikolai – Metropolitan of Kiev and Halich; Lt. Gen. Gundurov – President of the All-Slav Committee; S. Kolesnikov – Chairman of the Executive Committee of the Union of Red Cross and Red Crescent Societies; W. Potemkin – Peoples' Commissar of Education of the Russian SFSR, Academician; Col. Gen. E. Smirnov – Chief of the Central Medical Administration of the Red Army; B. Mielnikov – Chairman of the Smolensk Regional Executive Committee.

It appears from the Report of the Special Commission that a member of the Extraordinary State Commission, M. N. Burdenko, together with his collaborators and medico-legal experts (none of whom are named in the Report), proceeded to Smolensk on 26 October, 1943, that is on the day following the capture of that city by the Red Army, and for a period of nearly four months "carried out preliminary study and investigation of the circumstances of all the crimes perpetrated by the Germans".

The vast amount of material collected in those four

months defined as "study and investigation" in the Report, was then put at the disposal of the Special Commission, operating under the Chairmanship of the same Burdenko. By 24 January, 1944 the Report of the Special Commission was ready.

The Report opened with the statement that "the Katyn forest had for long been the favourite resort of Smolensk people, where they used to rest on holidays. The population of the neighbourhood grazed cattle and gathered fuel in the Katyn forest. Access to the Katyn Forest was not banned or restricted in any way."

The Special Commission recalled as a proof of this statement the fact that even in the summer of 1941 there was a Young Pioneers Camp of the "Industrial Insurance Board in this forest, and it was not liquidated until July 1941." But the Report said nothing of the site of that Pioneers Camp in the Katyn wood and as it extended over a fairly large area and consisted of different parts, some of them bearing separate names, the mere fact of a Pioneers Camp having existed in one part of the wood and not having been liquidated "until July 1941" did not exclude the possibility of other parts having been used for different purposes. The fact that the various parts of the Katyn wood were called by different names was confirmed in the last paragraph of Chapter 1 of the Report, which said that "the part of the Katyn Forest named Kosy Gory was guarded particularly strictly" by the Germans. The Report of the Special Commission definitely failed to mention how far that Pioneers Camp lay from the "Rest House of the Smolensk Administration of the Peoples' Commissariat of International Affairs" (NKVD).

The Report went on to refer to the Polish prisoners who were alleged to have been in the Smolensk area when it was taken by the Germans in 1941. Except however for a vague reference in the testimony of one of the witnesses (Savatiexev – see below) to the fact that those prisoners were brought to the region of Smolensk in the spring of 1940 and were disembarked at the Gniezdovo station, it confined itself to stating that "Polish war prisoners, officers and men, worked in the Western district of the Region, building and repairing roads" and that they were "quartered in three special camps named: Camp No 1 O.N., Camp No 2 O.N. and Camp No 3 O.N. These camps were located 25-45 kilometres (about 15½-28 miles) West of Smolensk".

Unfortunately the Report made no mention of such important and essential points as: 1. The general number of Polish prisoners who were supposed to have been in that region in 1941; 2. The number of prisoners in each of the three camps; 3. The Polish military ranks of the prisoners, which should have presented no difficulty to the Soviet authorities in view of the detailed records made in the camps; 4. The actual site of each of those camps, which could have been named after the geographical names of the places in which they were supposed to have been situated instead of being referred to only by numbers.

The report also did not explain why those particular POW camps for Polish officers and soldiers near Smolensk were called "special" camps, nor did it give any indication of specialised features that might have distinguished them from other "ordinary" POW camps.

In general there was no answer to be found in the Report to the many questions which naturally arose if, as the Soviets maintained, the Polish POWs from Kozielsk, Starobielsk and Ostashkov had been moved to "special camps" in the Smolensk area:

1. Why, in 1940 and 1941, 97 per cent of Polish officers captured by the Soviets were detained in the special camps Nos 1 O.N., 2 O.N. and 3 O.N., and engaged in "building and repairing roads", while the remaining 3 per cent, at that time in the camp at Pavlishtchev Bor and subsequently at Griazovetz, were exempt from all forced labour?

2. Why – as appears from an article by Warrant Officer Marian Klimczak entitled "I was a prisoner in the Katyn Forest", published in No 7/48 of the Moscow *Wolna Polska* of 24 February, 1944 – were the prisoners in camp No 2 O. N. (in which the author of the article is supposed to have passed "a certain time" in 1941 with "a group of 300

persons") kept on normal rations for Soviet correctional labour camps which depended on the results of their work, while those in the camps of Pavlishtschev Bor and Griazovetz were receiving full rations regardless of the fact that they did no work?

3. Why did families in Poland receive no news for eighteen months from Polish prisoners-of-war in special camps No 1 O.N., 2 O.N. and 3 O.N., while they were able to correspond comparatively freely with prisoners of war at Griazovietz?

4. Why, in camps No 1 O.N., 2 O.N. and 3 O.N., did Generals and staff officers have to work at "building and repairing roads" while in other camps such officers were not only exempt from all work but had batmen and even adjutants assigned to them?

5. Why and for what purpose were even invalids and people with artificial arms and legs transferred from Kozielsk to these "special" camps? And why were prisoners sent to these special camps for building roads without regard to their age or state of health, among them people over 60 years of age, while from the camp for internees at Kozielsk (Kozielsk III) only those pronounced fit for work by the medical commission were sent to labour camps?

6. If in the period from October 1940 in the POW camp of Griazovetz and the camp for internees at Kozielsk the Soviet authorities were taking steps to find people to organise the already planned "Polish Division" of Army, why were similar steps not taken in special camps Nos 1 O.N., 2 O.N. and 3 O.N. which contained 97 per cent of Polish officer prisoners-of-war?

7. Why, finally, were such large numbers (over 10,000) of Polish prisoners of war, particularly officers, concentrated for the work of "building and repairing roads" in the Western district of the Smolensk region, when – as is stated in the *Short Soviet Encyclopaedia*, pub. 1941, vol. IX, p. 810 – the lines of communication in the region of Smolensk were as fully developed as in any place in the whole Soviet Union?

The Report of the Special Commission went on to explain why Polish prisoners-of-war from the three "special" camps in the Western areas of the Smolensk region had not been evacuated before the German advance. It stated that: "Testimony of witnesses and documentary evidence establish that after the outbreak of hostilities, in view of the situation that arose, the camps could not be evacuated in time and all the Polish war prisoners, as well as some members of the guard and staff of the camps fell prisoner to the Germans."

The "documentary evidence" mentioned in the foregoing paragraph was neither quoted in the Report of the Special Commission nor discussed in any detail, so that we know nothing about it. As far as statements of witnesses in this matter are concerned, the Report quoted two of the depositions:

"The former Chief of Camp No 1 O.N. Major of State Security Vetoshnikov interrogated by the Special Commission testified:

'I was waiting for the order on the removal of the camp, but communication with Smolensk section of the Western Railway, Ivanov, asking him to provide the camp with railway cars for evacuation of the Polish war prisoners. But Ivanov answered that I could not count on receiving cars. I also tried to get in touch with Moscow, to obtain permission to set out on foot, but I failed. By this time Smolensk was already cut off from the camp by the Germans, and I did not know what happened to the Polish war prisoners and guards who remained in the camp.'

Engineeer Ivanov, who in July 1941, was acting Chief of Traffic of the Smolensk Section of the Western Railway, testified before the Special Commission:

'The Administration of the Polish War Prisoners' Camps applied to my office for cars for evacuation of the Poles, but we had none to spare. Besides, we could not send cars to the Gussino line, where the majority of the Polish war prisoners were, since that line was already under fire. Therefore, we could not comply with the request of the

Camps Administration. Thus the Polish war prisoners remained in the Smolensk region.' "

The report did not mention if both these witnesses were interrogated during the public session of the Special Commission. Jerzy Borejsza, special correspondent of the *Wolna Polska* mentioned in his report "On the trail of the crime" only Ivanov's depositions and he quoted from it extremely important and essential factual details, which were entirely omitted in the report of the Special Commission.

"The former stationmaster of Gniezdovo" (the Report of the Special Commission referred to Ivanov as the acting Chief of Traffic of the Smolensk Station) Ivanov, a precise, neat old man, recalled the circumstances of the evacuation of Smolensk. On 12 July 1941 he was asked by the Chief of one of the Polish war prisoner camps to extend to him facilities to evacuate the war prisoners. But the German offensive was so rapid that it was impossible even to evacuate certain factories and some of the workers. "How many wagons were you asked to provide for the prisoners – I asked. I was asked for at least 40 wagons – replied Ivanov."

This quotation shows that the Soviet journalist succeeded in recording a very important detail from the testimony of the witness Ivanov – a detail completely ignored in the report of the Special Commission – namely the *date* on which he was supposed to have been approached by the chief of the War Prisoner Camp with the request for wagons.

The brief German communiqué of 7 August 1941 states that "on 11 July we captured Vitebsk. On the next day flying columns attacked on a far-flung front East of the Orsha-Smolensk road."

This attack cannot have been very successful and could not have advanced very rapidly, since it was not until the 15th of July that the German communiqué stated that "the last fort on the Eastern-most point of the Stalin Line in the Vitebsk region has been captured." This is also borne out

65

by Soviet communiqué of 13, 14 and 15 July, which spoke of stubborn fighting "in the direction of" or "in the sector of" Vitebsk and the Soviet communiqué of 16 July stated that "near Vitebsk enemy attempts to penetrate this region have failed completely."

In the light of the communiqués by both combatants the situation on 15 July 1941 appeared to have been as follows: stubborn fighting was going on in the region of Vitebsk on Orsha, while pressure of the German forces to the East was – according to the Soviet communiqué of 16 July – being successfully held or, at least, delayed.

If at the same time we bear in mind the fact that according to the Soviet version the three "special" Polish war prisoner camps were supposed to have been situated at a distance of 15-28 miles West of Smolensk, ie 50-62 miles East of Vitebsk, we cannot but conclude that it would have been possible to evacuate these camps as late as 15 July 1941.

The German communiqué of 17 July speaks of the capture of Smolensk but the Soviet communiqué of July 23 states that "Smolensk continues to be held, German formations which had reached it several days previously, have been ejected." It may be assumed, therefore, that the German communiqué of 17 July was not quite accurate and that on 16 July only some light German units had reached Smolensk and had possibly entered the outskirts of the city – a fact which supplied the Germans with a foundation for the communiqué about the capture of the city. This hypothesis is confirmed by the historians W. E. D. Allen and P. Muratov, who say that German units were in the region of Smolensk as early as 17 July, but remark that "it was not the end but only the beginning of the battle of Smolensk". The battle of Smolensk, during which there were no major moves by either army, continued for two weeks.

As late as 28 July, the German communiqué stated:

"The Battle of Smolensk is nearing a favourable conclusion" but it was not until 6 August that the Germans published a special communiqué announcing the completion of this operation and describing its course.

This short summary of the military operations in the sector of Smolensk suggests without any doubt that, not only on 12 July, but even on 13, 14 and probably also on 15 the "special" camps might have been evacuated on foot, without any difficulty. These camps could easily have been transferred in one day to the city of Smolensk, some $15\frac{1}{2}$-28 miles distant, after which there would have been two weeks in which to evacuate them further, no matter how slowly, under cover of the armies fighting in the battle of Smolensk. During that fortnight they might have easily marched to some railway station which was still functioning, or even gone on foot to Moscow which was only about 187 miles away. In any case such a march would have been much shorter and less exhausting than the long marches, lasting many weeks and covering distances of several hundred miles, done by other Polish prisoners-of-war, such as the march from Brody to Ztotonosz.

The question arises, therefore, why the commandant of the Special Camp No 1 O. N., major of the NKVD Vetoshnikov, who on an unspecified date left "together with several staff members" the camp entrusted to his care and made attempts in Smolensk on 12 July to secure wagons, did not return during the period of three, four or more days between 12 July and the capture of Smolensk by the Germans. The assertions of Vetoshnikov that he had unsuccessfully tried to get in touch with Moscow in order to receive from the Central Authorities "permission to start on foot" are not convincing. In the face of the enemy and in direct danger one would expect a senior officer to show initiative and not to wait passively for orders or "permission" from his superiors, especially in this case since the railway network in the Smolensk region was particularly well developed.

It is extremely odd that such ill luck should have haunted the three "special" camps of the Polish officer prisoners-of-war. Situated on the most important sector from an operational point of view, distant only by 200 miles from the chief dispositional centre, Moscow, and by more

67

than 350 miles from the boundary of "Soviet-German interests" in a region which was captured by the enemy at the earliest on the twenty-fourth day of the war – it was still not possible to evacuate them. The senior authorities, of whom very many were stationed in this important sector, forgot all about them, and their immediate superiors proved criminally negligent. Silently, entirely without publicity, all of them apparently fell into German hands and no trace was ever found of them until the discovery of the bodies in the Katyn graves.

This particular misfortune becomes even more amazing when one recalls the fate of other Polish prisoner-of-war camps. The Sknilow Camp near Lwow, 40 miles from the Soviet-German frontier, situated in a region which the Germans captured a few days after the outbreak of the war, was successfully evacuated on foot to Zolotonosha on the Dnieper and thence by rail; it was not forgotten by the superior authorities in spite of the fact that it was some 800 miles distant from Moscow. The Brody Camp, in a region which the Germans reached on July 2 (and distant by 65 miles from the Soviet-German frontier) also was successfully evacuated to Zolotonosha, although it was situated right off the beaten track, far from any large town or the CHQ of senior authorities.

More such examples could be given but taking these two alone into consideration the fate of the three "special" camps near Smolensk becomes so improbable that the question whether these camps really existed spontaneously arises, especially since, up to the time of the publication of the Soviet communiqué of 15 April 1943, no one was aware of the presence of special Officers' Camps in these regions.

The Special Commission evidently realised that such a doubt must of necessity arise in the minds of critical observers, and, therefore, quoted the statements of the two witnesses, given above, to the effect that it was not possible to evacuate the Polish prisoners-of-war from the Smolensk area before it was captured by the Germans. The "proofs" are limited to the statement made by a certain Sashneva who sheltered one of the prisoners for one night, and to the statement of one Danilenkov who "in August and September 1941 saw groups of Poles of 15-20 men working on the roads", a fact confirmed by a further twelve witnesses who made "similar statements".

It is impossible not to wonder that so very large a group of Polish prisoners-of-war – numbering more than 10,000 officers and men, for the most part, young and healthy – were inefficient and indolent in escaping in such circumstances.

During the second world war, Poles have achieved a certain measure of renown for their skill in slipping across frontiers, for moving about in enemy-occupied territory, and for escaping from prisons and camps. Those abilities of the Poles in this respect have even been confirmed by Stalin, who in his conversation with General Sikorski on December 3, 1941 expressed his supposition that several thousand of the Polish officers searched for in the Northernmost parts of the USSR had probably succeeded, after their release from Soviet camps, in escaping to Manchuria without the knowledge of the local authorities.

Therefore the fact that out of several thousand Polish prisoners-of-war not a single one managed to make his way to Poland, neither during work on road constructions under Soviet or German supervision, nor in the chaos caused by the capture of the camps by the Germans, coupled with the fact that those who escaped did not succeed, in spite of the most favourable conditions, present such an improbable picture as to be wholly unbelievable. Inevitably the critical inquirer is inclined to doubt whether the three "special" camps from which no sign of life was given and about the existence of which the world was wholly unaware until the publication of the Soviet communiqué of 15 April 1943 had ever really existed at all.

In the Report the signatures of the medicolegal experts were placed at the end of their Conclusions and after them the Report listed the documents found by them on the bodies, which it considered were deserving of "special attention".

Of these there were nine in all, found on six bodies which

69

were not identified by the Commission but only numbered. By a strange coincidence although in all 925 bodies had been exhumed, according to the Report, the body bearing the highest number on which such documents had been found was No 101. It may of course have been the case that all the important documents from the Commission's point of view had been found in the hundred or so bodies lying in the upper layers of the graves.

These revealing documents were not listed in the Report in any particular order nor were they given, as one might have expected, in the order of the numbers of the bodies on which they were found. Those body numbers were not listed in numerical order and, where more than one document had been found on the same body, it was listed as a separate item and not grouped with the other documents from the body, so that the same body number appeared several times in the list. This arrangement naturally makes the analysis of the documents unnecessarily difficult.

The analysis however, of the contents of the documents as given in the Report is very interesting. They fall into three groups: 1. Letters; 2. Receipts; 3. An ikon.

1. Three letters were said to have been found:

(a) A postcard stamped at Tarnopol on 12 November 1940, bearing no text or address ("written text and address are discoloured"). Found on body No 4.

(b) A letter from Warsaw dated 12 September 1940, addressed to the Central War Prisoners Bureau of the Red Cross, Moscow, and written by the wife of one Tomasz Zigon, enquiring after his whereabouts. This letter bore the stamp of Central Post Office, Moscow, and an anonymous inscription in Russian: "Ascertain and forward for delivery, November 15 1940." Found on body No 92.

(c) An unmailed postcard addressed to Warsaw by one Stanislaw Kuczinski and dated 20 June 1941. Found on body No 53.

2. Five receipts were found made out to two people and given by the Soviet Authorities.

(a) Three were made out to one Araszkevicz. The first

dated 16 December 1939 for a gold watch had been issued at Starobielsk camp. On the back it bore a note dated 25 March 1941, stating that the watch had been sold to the Jewellery Trading Trust. It was not said whether this note had been signed.

The second was dated 6 April 1941, issued at Camp 1 O. N., for an unknown sum of roubles. (In the Edition of the Report published in Polish the sum is given as 226 roubles.)

The third was dated 5 May 1941, issued at camp 1 O.N. for 102 roubles.

All three documents said to have been found on the same body, No 46, were numbered on the list given in the Report as 4, 6 and 7.

(b) Two receipts said to have been found on body No 101 were made out to one Lewandowski. The first dated 19 December 1939, issued at Kozielsk camp, was for a gold watch and bore a similar inscription on the back about the watch having been sold to the Jewellery Trading Trust dated 14 March 1941.

The second issued at camp 1 O.N. on 15 May 1941, was made out for 175 roubles. On the list these documents were numbered 3 and 8.

3. The paper "ikon".

The paper "ikon" with the image of Christ was said to have been found on body No 71. This body was not identified in the Report, although care was taken to point out that the picture was found "between pages 144 and 145 of a Catholic prayer book". This ikon was said to have borne the inscription "Jadwiga" and the date 4 April 1941.

In considering the list of documents as a whole, the following reflections spring to mind. The Soviet reaction to the Katyn revelations was much concerned from first to last with the documents found on the bodies in the graves. Very early on they asserted that the documents which the Germans declared had been found in the graves had, in reality, been taken from the archieves of the Gestapo and placed on the bodies by the Germans themselves.

The same accusation was brought against the Germans in the report of the Special Commission, namely in the testimony of Moskovskaya when she related how Yegorev had told her that "the Germans made the prisoners put into the pockets of the Polish officers some papers which they took from cases and suitcases (I don't remember exactly) which they had brought along."

By giving so much prominence to the whole question of the documents found with the bodies, and stressing their belief that they had been planted by the Germans, the Russians to some extent laid themselves open to the possibility of similar accusations being brought against themselves. In this connection it might well be pointed out that the documents found in the spring of 1943 and inspected by the Polish professional team, the "International Commission" and many journalists and visitors, were mostly personal papers, photographs of which were published throughout the world. Those described by the Russians' medico-legal experts were in no case personal documents and all but one (the ikon) had either been issued by the Russian authorities themselves or had passed through their hands. They were moreover only made known to the public by the vague description of them found in the Report itself.

Once again Mr Owen O'Malley, Ambassador of the British Government to the Poles, was not slow to act. As has been shown earlier, he was obviously convinced that the Soviets had committed the Katyn massacre, and his reading of the Soviet Report confirmed his belief. In a further Most Secret Report addressed to The Rt Hon. Anthony Eden and dated 11 February 1944 he commented in no uncertain terms.

No 25   *British Embassy to Poland,*
(15/90/44)   *45 Lowndes Square, SW1*
            11th February, 1944

Sir,

On January 24th the Soviet Government issued the report of a special commission appointed for "ascertaining and investigating the circumstances of the shooting of Polish Officer Prisoners by German Fascist invaders in the

Katyn Forest". This report appears in full in the *Soviet War News* of January 27, 28 and 31 and February 1, runs to some 20,000 words, and finishes with the conclusions which are enclosed herein. Having dealt with the German account of this affair at some length in my despatch No 51 of May 24, 1943, I ought perhaps now to deal with the question of what new light, if any, is thrown upon it by our Allies who, having regained possession of Smolensk, have been able to revisit the scene of the massacre and make an enquiry on the spot.

2. There was a difference between the methods employed by the German Government on the one hand and the Soviet Government on the other for convincing the world of the truth of the conclusion which each has levelled against each. The Germans relied primarily upon the findings of an international commission of fourteen pathologists and criminologists of whom two came from Germany, eleven from satellite or occupied states, and one from Switzerland. Basing itself on the findings of this body, the German Government told its story to the world through every available publicity agency, and they reinforced their case by bringing to Katyn a purely Polish delegation composed of well known Poles from many different professions and classes of society, a delegation from the Polish Red Cross Society, and delegations from Lodz and Poznan. The Russian Government on the other hand relied mainly upon the report of a purely Russian commission composed of eight Government officials who had the assistance of a medico-legal sub-commission composed of five Russian scientists. The Russian Government and the German Government, however, acted alike in this, that they both invited foreign journalists to visit the scene of the crime, and both did their best to make the visit a pleasant one. The most up-to-date sleeping-cars were provided by the Russians and aeroplanes by the Germans for their guests; in both cases, after a busy day among the corpses, these were served with smoked salmon, caviare, champagne and other delicacies. In both cases a religious ceremony terminated the proceedings.

3. No definite conclusion can, I think, be drawn from the differences between German and Russian procedure, except perhaps that we shall be slightly more inclined to credit the opinion of the international experts brought to the spot by the Germans than the opinion of a scientific sub-commission composed exclusively of Russians; for since it would clearly have strengthened their case if the Soviet Government had invited British and American scientists to participate in the investigation, one can only suppose that a guilty conscience prevented them from doing so. This inclination is strengthened by the facts, first, that Polish visitors to the graves (including members of the Underground Movement) who hate Germans and Russians equally were in no doubt that the latter had carried out the massacre; and secondly, that the journalists who accompanied the Russian investigators from Moscow were, with the exception of Miss Kate Harriman, not favourably impressed by the Russian evidence or the means by which it was elicited.

4. Both Germans and Russians relied, among other things, upon two classes of testimony; first, verbal testimony given at first or second hand by individuals who might be supposed to have personal knowledge of what occurred at Katyn in April and May 1940 (according to the German story) or in the last four months of 1941 (according to the Russian story); and secondly, the findings of experts who examined the corpses. It would, I think, be futile to try to appraise the trustworthiness of the testimony of witnesses examined by either the German Government or the Russian Government. Both were in a position to intimidate the soldiers, servants, peasants or other local residents who were called upon to give evidence, and both are notoriously prone to use intimidation. Both allege that material witnesses had been murdered by the other side. The Germans, for instance, say that the Soviet Government itself gave orders for the destruction of the executioners employed by them; while the Russians affirm that the Gestapo liquidated no less than 500 Russian prisoners who had been ordereed to open the graves at Katyn and assist

with the examination of the corpses. It was for this reason that my despatch No 51 made no reference to any part of the verbal evidence given to the German investigators; and for the same reason I do not propose to discuss similar evidence given to the Russian investigators although it occupies not less than nine-tenths of their report.

5. Since I enclosed in my despatch No 51 the findings of the German (international) Scientific sub-commission, it is only fair that I should annexe to the present despatch the findings of the Russian Scientific sub-commission. The following are the most important discrepancies between the two, The German Sub-commission claims to have exhumed 982 bodies: the Russian 925.

The Germans say that "a considerable number of bodies were dissected": the Russians say "no external examination of the bodies ... and no medico-legal examination of the bodies ... had been effected previously". The Germans say that "there are varying degrees of decomposition of the bodies; that a large number of skulls were examined" for certain changes which only occur three years after death, and that "this change was observed to a marked degree on skull No 526": the Russians say that "there are absolutely no bodies in a condition of decay or disintegration", that "the bodies had not remained in the earth "for long" and that "the shooting dates back to ... between September and December 1941." The Germans say the latest document found on any corpse was dated April 22, 1940; the Russians say that numerous documents were found with dates between September 12, 1940, and June 20, 1941. It would be rash to draw any conclusions from these discrepancies; but it would be very interesting if His Majesty's Minister in Berne could get an opinion of the whole matter from Dr Naville, Professor of Forensic Medicine at Geneva, who was a member of the German Sub-commission, and is the only neutral and accessible expert from either side.

6. Dismissing as more or less unreliable the verbal accounts of supposed eye witnesses and the findings of the scientific commissions on both sides, let us summarise the Russian story and see whether it affords reason for

doubting the conclusion tentatively reached in my former despatch on the subject, namely that it it was by order of the Soviet Government that the Polish officers were massacred.

7. The Russian report may be summarised as follows: Before the capture of Smolensk by the Germans, Polish prisoners were quartered in three camps 25 to 45 kilometres west of Smolensk. After the outbreak of hostilities the camps could not be evacuated in time, and all the Polish war prisoners as well as some members of the guard were taken prisoner by the Germans. Polish prisoners were seen working on the roads round Smolensk in August and September 1941 but not later. German soldiers frequently combed the neighbouring villages for escaped Polish prisoners. Access to the localities where the executions took place were strictly barred, but lorry-loads of Polish prisoners were often seen being driven thither and many shots were heard. The report then passes on to the Spring of 1943 when the Germans were alleged to have been preparing the ground for the announcements made on their broadcast system on April 12th of that year, and states that witnesses were tortured by the Germans into giving false evidence of Russian culpability; that 500 Russian prisoners, subsequently murdered, had been employed in March 1943 by the Germans to dig up the corpses and to introduce forged documents into their pockets, and that lorry-loads of corpses were brought to Katyn in March 1943. In short, the Russian case amounts to this: that the occupants of the camps at Kozielsk, Starobielsk and Ostashkov were moved in April and May 1940 to three Russian labour camps near Smolensk, captured by the advancing German armies in July 1941, and shot at various dates during the subsequent four months.

8. If the evidence of the Soviet Government's witnesses and experts could be trusted, it would be just possible to believe in the truth of the Russian story; but it would nevertheless be very difficult to do so because it makes at least one essential assumption which is incredible, and because it leaves altogether unexplained at least one

76

indisputable set of facts which urgently require explanation before we can accept the Soviet Government's account of events.

9. The Russian story assumes that about 10,000 Polish officers and men, employed on forced labour, lived in the district of Smolensk from April 1940 till July 1941 and passed into German captivity when the Germans captured it in July 1941 without a single one of them having escaped or fallen again into Russian hands or reported to a Polish consul in Russia or to the Polish Underground Movement in Poland. This is quite incredible; and not only is it incredible to anyone who knows anything about prisoners-of-war labour camps in Russia, or who pictures to himself the disorganisation and confusion which must have attended the Russian exit and German entry into Smolensk, but the assumption which I have described as essential to the Russian case is actually destroyed by the words of the Russian investigating commission itself. The commission asserts that many Polish prisoners did in fact escape after the district of Smolensk had been overrun by the Germans, and describe the frequent "round-ups" of escaped prisoners which the Germans organised. The Russian story gives no explanation of why in these circumstances not a single one of the Poles who were allegedly transferred from Kozielsk, Starobielsk and Ostashkov to the labour camps Nos 1 O.N., 2 O.N., and 3 O.N. has never been seen or heard of alive again.

10. So much for the assumption essential to the credibility of the Russian story. The unexplained set of facts is the same set of facts which has dominated this controversy throughout, namely that from April 1940 onwards no single letter or message was ever received by anybody from the Poles who were until then at Kozielsk, Starobielsk and Ostashkow (excepting the 400 to 500 sent to Griazovetz); that no single enquiry about these men out of some 500 actually addressed by the Polish Red Cross Society to the Soviet authorities was ever answered, and that no enquiries by representatives of the Polish Government elicited any definite or consistent information

about them from the Soviet Government. If they had, as the Soviet Government now allege, been transferred from Kozielsk, Starobielsk and Ostashkow to camps Nos 1, 2 and 3 O.N., why did not the Soviet Government say so long ago?

11. To all this I am afraid I can only reply, as I did in my previous despatch on the same subject, that, while "we do not know for certain who murdered the Polish officers buried at Katyn ... the cumulative effect of the evidence is to throw serious doubts on Russian disclaimers of responsibility". The defective nature of the report now issued by the Russian commission of enquiry makes these doubts even stronger than they were before. Stronger anyhow in the view of well informed persons in the United Kingdom, for having made enquiries through appropriate channels, I am satisfied that the great majority of responsible British journalists have during the last nine months come round to the same opinions as I have held myself throughout. Consistently with this, the Russian report was coldly received by the British press.

12. Let us think of these things always and speak of them never. To speak of them never is the advice which I have been giving to the Polish Government, but it has been unnecessary. They have received the Russian report in silence. Affliction and residence in this country seem to be teaching them how much better it is in political life to leave unsaid those things about which one feels most passionately.

I have the honour to be, with highest respect,
Sir,
Your most obedient,
humble Servant,
(Signed) OWEN O'MALLEY

The Right Honourable
Anthony Eden, MC, MP, etc.

Thus the events of 1943 and 1944: investigations by both the Germans and the Soviets, the counter-accused and the accused, with a secret comment by the then enemies of the first and at that time allied to the second. What does it all add up to? – An obviously sincere attempt by the Germans to fill the gap made by the Soviets in forbidding elucidation by the International Committee of the Red Cross and a conclusive verdict; an obviously insincere attempt by the Soviets to prove their point and thus smudge the truth; an attempt by Great Britain to avoid the issue and even to continue avoiding it up to a debate in the House of Lords in 1971. The facts speak plainly for themselves, as do the discrepancies, as the next chapters will show.

3   Nuremberg 1946

In 1945 the Allies set up an apparatus of justice known as
the International Military Tribunal charged with the trial
of major War Criminals, otherwise known as the German
Major War Criminals. The place chosen for this pageant of
condemnation was Nuremberg, and like an anticipatory
audience before the curtain rises the world waited for what
was to come – some sadly, others with relish, depending
upon their nationality. When a war is over people are
exhausted, but nonetheless they wait for the final act in the
drama. It is a sad moment, a sort of vacuum. All the
bloodshed finished, an unexpected hush settles upon the
ravaged countries which took part and they wait like the
crowds gathered about the guillotine. If there are those who
wished it otherwise, there are others who lick their lips at
the thought of revenge, and yet others again for whom
malice is the prime mover. Whatever may be said for and
against retribution, how will human nature stand up to the
rigours to come? It is not just a question of the accused and
their probable march to the scaffold; it is a matter of how
the judge will conduct himself and what kind of an example
he will set in the broader and timeless plane of honour and
justice.

The verbatim reports of the Nuremberg Trial proceedings alone run to forty-two volumes and additionally there
are tens of thousands of written and printed documents.
Any trial is concerned not only with the essence of crime,
but also with procedure, legal niceties, minutiae of all kinds

and matters of little interest except to the professional lawyer. At Nuremberg there was also the element of *lex talionis*, the law of retribution, and this in the face of slaughter on an immense scale confused and compounded by years of war propaganda. As the judges assembled they must have been oppressed by what lay before them, and perhaps this is best expressed by a passage from the opening speech of Mr Jackson, the Chief Prosecutor, who said:

"Modern civilisation puts limitless weapons of destruction into the hands of mankind ... Every recourse to war, to any kind of war, is recourse to measures which by their very nature are criminal. War is inevitably a web of killing, invasion, loss of freedom and destruction of property ... Human reason demands that the law should not be considered adequate if it punishes only petty crimes of which lesser people are guilty.

The law must also reach the men who seize power and deliberately combine to make use of it to commit an evil which affects every home in the world. The last step in preventing the periodic outbreak of war, which is unavoidable with international lawlessness, is to make statesmen responsible before the law. [Mr Jackson raised his voice] Let me say it quite clearly: this law is here first applied to German aggressors, but it includes, and must do if it is to be of service, the condemnation of aggression by any other nation, not excepting those who now sit here in judgment."

Weighty words and indeed, had Mr Jackson known, only too appropriate. "... *those who now sit here in judgment.*" What feelings, one must wonder, did that phrase arouse in the judges? At that second they had not started their long pilgrimage through the evidence, nor had they realised through what tortuous paths they were to be led. If it is true to say that the actual evidence given at Nuremberg is far from well known, this must apply especially to that concerning the Katyn massacre, for it was a shortly-told story with no end and thus no focus. In all that mass of verbiage, argument, horror and dry legal discussion, Katyn vanished almost as if it had never been mentioned. While other terrible matters were exposed to the public gaze, Katyn was shown to the world unexpectedly and most briefly – like the wolf which scratched at the mound in Katyn wood and which surprised the Germans by its presence. Even during its brief appearance, Katyn was fogged with small arguments to an extent where its true frightfulness was lost except for those with a special interest or unusual perception. The subject occupied perhaps a couple of summer days during all the long months when the world grew impatient for the outcome – the sentence which was either anticipated with glee or with dread. There was so much else. For that reason, if for no other, space must be found to portray what there is in full, unadulterated and as it was, so that it can find a place in the record more fitting to what it constituted – one of the most appalling and ghastly crimes of recent centuries. It was the subject of a counter-accusation, and this must have been in the minds of at least some of the judges as they listened to Mr Jackson. That no mention of Katyn appears in the final judgment is a matter for international shame. It makes a mockery of international justice and should, but apparently does not, torture the international conscience. The disclosures about Katyn at Nuremberg are a part of history, a history in this case not yet resolved.

On 14 February 1946, the Tribunal's attention was drawn to the Katyn massacre by the Soviet prosecution in these words, uttered by Colonel Pokrovsky:

I should now like to turn to the brutalities committed by the Hitlerites towards members of the Czechoslovakian, Polish, and Yugoslavian Armies. We find, in the Indictment, that one of the most important criminal acts for which the major war criminals are responsible was the mass execution of Polish prisoners of war, shot in the Katyn Forest near Smolensk by the German fascist invaders.

I submit to the Tribunal, as a proof of this crime, official documents of the special commission for the establishment and the investigation of the circumstances which attended the executions. The commission acted in accordance with a directive of the Extraordinary State Commission of the Soviet Union. In addition to members of the Extraordinary State Commission—namely Academicians Burdenko, Alexis Tolstoy, and the Metropolitan Nicolas—this commission was composed of the President of the Pan-Slavonia Committee, Lieutenant General Gundorov; the chairman of the Executive Committee of the Union of the Red Cross and Red Crescent, Kolesnikov; of the People's Commissar for Education in the R.S.S.F.R., Academician Potemkin; the Supreme Chief of the Medical Department of the Red Army, General Smirnov; and the Chairman of the District Executive Committee of Smolensk, Melnikov. The commission also included several of the best known medico-legal experts.

It would take too long to read into the record that precise and detailed document which I now submit to you as Exhibit Number USSR-54 (Document Number USSR-54), which is a result of the investigation. I shall read into the record only a few comparatively short excerpts. On Page 2 of the document, which is Page 223 in your document book, we read—this passage is marked in your file:

"According to the estimates of medico-legal experts, the total number of bodies amounts to over 11,000. The medico-legal experts carried out a thorough examination of the bodies exhumed, and of the documents and material evidence found on the bodies and in the graves. During the exhumation and examination of the corpses, the commission questioned many witnesses among the local inhabitants. Their testimony permitted the determination of the exact time and circumstances of the crimes committed by the German invaders."

I believe that I need not quote everything that the Extraordinary Commission ascertained during its investigation about the crimes of the Germans. I only read into the record the general conclusions, which summarize the work of the commission. You will find the lines read into the record on Page 43 of Exhibit Number USSR-54 if you turn to the original document, or on Page 264 of your document book:

"General conclusions:

"On perusal of all the material at the disposal of the special commission, that is, the depositions of over 100 witnesses questioned, the data of the medico-legal experts, the documents and the material evidence and belongings taken from the graves in Katyn Forest, we can arrive at the following definite conclusions:

"1. The Polish prisoners of war imprisoned in the three camps west of Smolensk and engaged in railway construction before the war, remained there after the occupation of Smolensk by the Germans, right up to September 1941.

"2. In the autumn of 1941, in Katyn Forest, the German occupational authorities carried out mass shootings of the Polish prisoners of war from the above-mentioned camps.

"3. Mass shootings of Polish prisoners of war in Katyn Forest were carried out by German military organizations disguised under the specific name, 'Staff 537, Engineer Construction Battalion,' commanded by Oberleutnant Arnes and his colleagues, Oberleutnant Rex and Leutnant Hott.

"4. In connection with the deterioration, for Germany, of the general military and political machinery at the beginning of 1943, the German occupational authorities, with a view to provoking incidents, undertook a whole series of measures to ascribe their own misdeeds to organizations of the Soviet authorities, in order to make mischief between the Russians and the Poles.

"5. For these purposes:

"a. The German fascist invaders, by persuasion, attempts at bribery, threats, and by barbarous tortures, endeavored to find 'witnesses' among the Soviet citizens from whom they obtained false testimony, alleging that the Polish prisoners of war had been shot by organizations of the Soviet authorities in the spring of 1940.

"b. The German occupational authorities, in the spring of 1943, brought from other places the bodies of Polish prisoners of war whom they had shot, and laid them in the turned up graves of Katyn Forest with the dual purpose of covering up the traces of their own atrocities and of increasing the numbers of 'victims of Bolshevist atrocities' in Katyn Forest.

"c. While preparing their provocative measures, the German occupational authorities employed up to 500 Russian prisoners of war for the task of digging up the graves in Katyn Forest. Once the graves had been dug, the Russian prisoners of war were shot by the Germans in order to destroy thus all proof and material evidence on the matter.

"6. The date of the legal and medical examination determined, without any shadow of doubt:

"a. That the time of shooting was autumn 1941.

"b. The application by the German executioners, when shooting Polish prisoners of war, of the identical method—a pistol shot in the nape of the neck—as used by them in the mass murders of the Soviet citizens in other towns, especially in Orel, Voronetz, Krasnodar and in Smolensk itself."

THE PRESIDENT: The Tribunal will now recess.

[The Tribunal recessed until 1400 hours.]

COL. POKROVSKY: Point 7 of the general conclusions of the Extraordinary State Commission of the Soviet Union, on which I reported in the preceding session, states:

"The conclusions reached, after studying the affidavits and medico-legal examinations concerning the shooting of Polish military prisoners of war by Germans in the autumn of 1941, fully confirmed the material evidence and documents discovered in the Katyn graves.

"8. By shooting the Polish prisoners of war in Katyn Forest, the German fascist invaders consistently realized their policy for the physical extermination of the Slav peoples."

Here follow the signatures of all the members of the Commission.

I think we can now pass on at once to the general conclusions and to read into the Record to this end Subparagraph g on Page 39—Page 287 of the document book:

"The above-mentioned treatment of Polish prisoners of war by individuals as well as by the German military authorities, flagrantly violated the articles of the Geneva Convention of 1929, Articles 2, 3, 9, 10, 11, 29, 30, 50, and 54. The convention in question had been ratified by Germany on 21 February 1934."

The Tribunal occupied itself with other matters until 8 March 1946, when it was again brought back to the Katyn case – all subsequent to the inclusion in the indictment of this statement: "In September 1941, 11,000 Polish officers who were prisoners of war were killed in the Katyn Forest near Smolensk."

DR. OTTO STAHMER (Counsel for Defendant Göring): Mr. President and Gentlemen of the Tribunal, before I start with my presentation I beg to make two supplementary applications. I am aware of the fact that supplementary requests as such should be put in writing. But since it is a question of several requests, I should like to have your decision whether I should submit these applications now or whether the Tribunal desires a written request.

THE PRESIDENT: You may put your request now, verbally, but we would prefer to have it in writing afterwards as soon as possible.

DR. STAHMER: I name first Major Bütz, who is in custody here in Nuremberg, as a witness for .the following facts: Reich Marshal Göring repeatedly opposed in the summer of 1944 the measures which Hitler had ordered against aviators taking part in terror attacks. Furthermore, he knows that no order was issued either by the Luftwaffe or by the Wehrmacht corresponding to Hitler's orders regarding terror aviators. Finally, he can give evidence in regard to the following: An officer of the Luftwaffe in May 1944 in Munich protected an airman, who had bailed out, from the lynching which the crowd wanted to carry out. Hitler, who had knowledge of this incident, demanded of Göring the name of this officer, and that he be punished. In spite of repeated inquiries on Hitler's part, Göring did not give the name of this officer, although he knew it, and in this way protected him. This is the application regarding the witness Bütz. Another supplementary request is concerned with the following: In the session of 14 February 1946 the Soviet Prosecution submitted that a German military formation, Staff 537, Pioneer Battalion, carried out mass shootings of Polish prisoners of war in the forests near Katyn. As the responsible leaders of this formation, Colonel Ahrens, First Lieutenant Rex, and Second Lieutenant Hodt were mentioned. As proof the Prosecution referred to Document USSR-64. It is an official report of the Extraordinary State Commission of the Soviet Union which was ordered to investigate the facts of the well-known Katyn case. The document I have not yet received. As a result of the publication of this speech by the Prosecution in the press, members of the staff of the Army Group Center, to which Staff 537 was directly subordinate and which was stationed 4 to 5 kilometers from Staff 537, came forward. These people stated that the evidence upon which the Prosecution have based the statement submitted was not correct.

The following witnesses are mentioned in this connection:

Colonel Ahrens, at that time commander of 537, later chief of army armament and commander of the auxiliary army; First Lieutenant Rex, probably taken as a prisoner of war at Stalingrad; Lieutenant Hodt, probably taken prisoner by the Russians in or near Königsberg; Major General of intelligence troops, Eugen Oberhauser, probably taken prisoner of war by the Americans; First Lieutenant Graf Berg—later ordnance officer with Field Marshal Von Kluge— a prisoner of war in British hands in Canada. Other members of the units which are accused are still to be mentioned. I name these

Lord Justice Lawrence, the President of the Tribunal, at Nuremberg.

witnesses to prove that the conclusion as to the complicity of Göring drawn by the Prosecution in the above-mentioned statement is not justified according to the Indictment.

This morning I received another communication bearing on the same question, which calls for the following request: Professor Naville, professor of forensic medicine at the University of Geneva, carried out, with an international commission at Smolensk, investigations of the bodies at that time. He established from the state of preservation of these corpses, from the notes found in the pockets of their clothes, and other means of evidence, that the deed must have been committed in the year 1940.

Those are my requests.

The final plea of Hermann Goering.

SIR DAVID MAXWELL-FYFE: If Your Lordship pleases.

Then I think that only leaves an application of the Defendant Keitel for the use of a decree of Hitler of 20 July 1944, and the Prosecution has no objection to that.

My Lord, I think I have dealt with every one except the first one, which my friend General Rudenko will deal with—the application of the Defendant Göring.

GENERAL R. A. RUDENKO (Chief Prosecutor for the U.S.S.R.): Members of the Tribunal, the Soviet Prosecution have several times expressed their view respecting the application of Defense Counsel to call witnesses with regard to the mass shooting of Polish officers by the Fascist criminals in Katyn Forest. Our position is that this episode of criminal activity on the part of the Hitlerites has been fully established by the evidence presented by the Soviet Prosecution, which was a communication of the special Extraordinary State Commission investigating the circumstances of the mass shooting of Polish officer prisoners of war by the German Fascist aggressors in Katyn Forest. This document was presented by the Soviet Prosecution under the Document Number USSR-54 on 14 February

1946, and was admitted by the Tribunal; and, as provided by Article 21 of the Charter, it is not subject to argument.

Now the Defense once again are putting in an application for the calling of three supplementary witnesses—a psychiatrist, Stockert; a former adjutant of the Engineer Corps, Böhmert; and a special expert of the staff of the Army Group Center, Eichborn.

We object to the calling of these three witnesses for the following reasons:

The calling of the psychiatrist Stockert as a witness must be considered completely pointless as the Tribunal cannot be interested in the question of how the commission drew its conclusion—a conclusion which was published in a Hitlerite *White Book*. No matter how this conclusion was drawn, the fact of the mass shooting of Poles by Germans in Katyn Forest has been unequivocally established by the Soviet Extraordinary State Commission.

Stockert himself is not a doctor of forensic medicine but a psychiatrist—at that time a member of the Hitlerite commission, not on the basis of his competence in the field of forensic medicine, but as a representative of the German Fascist military command.

The former adjutant, Captain Böhmert, is himself a participant in the crimes of Katyn Forest, having been a member of the Engineer Corps which carried out the executions. As he is an interested party, he cannot give any useful testimony for clarifying the circumstances of this matter.

Third, the expert of the staff of the Army Group Center also cannot be admitted as a witness because he, in general, knew nothing at all about the camp of the Polish prisoners of war, and could not have known all that pertained to the matter. The same reasons apply to his potential testimony to the fact that the Germans never perpetrated any mass shooting of Poles in the district of Katyn. Moreover, Eichborn cannot be considered an unprejudiced witness.

Regardless of these objections which express the opinion of all the prosecutors, the Soviet Prosecution especially emphasize the fact that these bestial crimes of the Germans in Katyn were investigated by the special authoritative State Investigating Committee, which went with great precision into all the details. The result of this investigation has established the fact that the crimes in Katyn were perpetrated by Germans, and are but a link in the chain of many bestial crimes perpetrated by the Hitlerites, a great many proofs of which have previously been submitted to the Tribunal.

For these reasons the Soviet Prosecution categorically insists on the rejection of the application of the Defense Counsel.

I have finished my statement.

DR. KAUFFMANN: Thank you.

DR. OTTO STAHMER (Counsel for Defendant Göring): May I make a brief statement with reference to General Rudenko's motion?

General Rudenko wishes to reject my application for evidence, referring to Article 21, I believe, of the Charter. I do not believe that this regulation opposes my application. It is true of course, that government reports are evidence...

THE PRESIDENT: Dr. Stahmer, I think the Tribunal has already ruled that that article does not prevent the calling of witnesses; but General Rudenko, in addition to an argument based upon Article 21, also gave particular reasons why he said that these particular witnesses were not witnesses who ought to be called. He said that one of them was a psychiatrist, and the other one could not give any evidence of any value. We should like to hear you upon that.

DR. STAHMER: In the report submitted by the Soviet Union, the charge is made that members of the engineer staff which was stationed near Katyn carried out the execution of these Polish officers. They are mentioned by name, and I am bringing counter-evidence—namely members of the same staff—to prove that during the whole time that this staff was stationed there no killings of Polish officers occurred. I consider this is a pertinent assertion and a presentation of relevant evidence. One cannot eliminate a witness by saying that he was involved in the act. With reference to these people, that is not yet settled, and it is not mentioned at all in the record. Neither are these people, whom I have now named, listed in the Russian record as having taken part in the deed. Apart from that, I consider it out of the question to eliminate a witness by saying that he committed the deed. That is what has to be proved by hearing him.

THE PRESIDENT: About the psychiatrist, was he a member of the German commission?

DR. STAHMER: Yes.

THE PRESIDENT: He was a member of it?

DR. STAHMER: Yes. He was present at the unloading, and he ascertained from the condition of the corpses that the executions must have been carried out at some time before the occupation by the German Army.

THE PRESIDENT: But he does not actually say in the application that he was a member. He said he was present during the visit of the military commission; he knows how the resolution of the commission was produced.

DR. STAHMER: I do not think he was an appointed member, but he took part in this inspection and in the duties connected with it.

As far as I know, he was a regimental doctor in some regiment near—he was a regimental doctor of a regimental staff in the vicinity.

THE PRESIDENT: Very well, we will consider your argument.

On 5 June 1946, while dealing with another aspect, Katyn again made a brief appearance.

DR. LATERNSER: What do you know about the case of Katyn?

JODL: Regarding the finding of these mass graves, I received the first report through my propaganda department, which was informed through its propaganda company attached to the army group. I heard that the Reich Police Criminal Department had been given the task of investigating the whole affair, and I then sent an officer from my propaganda department to the exhumation to check the findings of the foreign experts. I received a report which, in general, tallies with the report which is contained in the *White Book* issued, I think, by the Foreign Office. I have never heard anyone raise any doubts as to the facts as they were presented.

It was not until the end of June, on 29 June 1946 to be precise, that the Tribunal really started to give its full attention to this massacre. What follows is a full exposé of what was actually said, on that day when Katyn was fully discussed (1 July 1946) and again on the following day.

The cells at Nuremberg.

The defendants at Nuremberg: left to right, Raeder, Doenitz, Schirach, Sauckel, Goering, Hess, Ribbentrop, Keitel, Kaltenbrunner.

Colonel Pokrovsky, the Tribunal would like to know whether you have arrived at any agreement with Dr. Stahmer on behalf of the Defendant Göring with reference to affidavit evidence or witnesses, with reference to the Katyn matter.

COLONEL Y. V. POKROVSKY (Deputy Chief Prosecutor for the U.S.S.R.): My Lord, we have had three conferences with the Defense Counsel. After the second meeting I told the Tribunal that, in order to shorten the proceedings, the Soviet Prosecution was willing to read into the record only a part of the evidence submitted. About 15 minutes ago I had a meeting with Dr. Exner and Dr. Stahmer, and they told me that their understanding of the Tribunal's ruling was that the old decision for the summoning of two witnesses was still in force and that only additional documents were now under discussion.

In view of this interpretation of the Tribunal's ruling, I do not think that we shall be able to come to an agreement with the Defense. As I see it, the decision in this matter must now rest in the hands of the Tribunal.

THE PRESIDENT: The Tribunal orders that, unless an agreement is arrived at, the evidence shall not be given entirely by affidavits and that the three witnesses on either side shall be called first thing on Monday morning at 10 o'clock, unless you can arrive at an agreement before that, that the evidence is to be offered in affidavits.

DR. SIEMERS: Mr. President, may I say something on this subject?

A number of counsel who are interested in the Katyn case had a conference this morning; among them were Professor Exner and Dr. Stahmer. We agreed to ask the Tribunal to allow two witnesses to be examined here in person by the Defense. These witnesses would be Colonel Ahrens and First Lieutenant Von Eichborn. We also agreed to dispense with the hearing of the third witness but decided to request that an affidavit of this witness, and in addition two other affidavits, be submitted. I believe this to be a suggestion which both satisfies us and saves the most time: Two witnesses would be heard and three affidavits submitted.

THE PRESIDENT: Dr. Siemers, the Tribunal sees no objection to there being two witnesses called and one affidavit. But their order was that three witnesses on either side—that the evidence should be limited to three witnesses on either side; and they, therefore, are not prepared to allow further affidavits to be given. The evidence must be confined to the evidence of three persons on either side. They may give their evidence either by oral evidence or by affidavit.

DR. SIEMERS: Mr. President, as far as I was informed, the original decision stated that three witnesses were allowed but did not mention affidavits. That was the reason why Dr. Stahmer and Professor Exner assumed that, regardless of the witnesses, certain individual points could be proved by means of affidavits. I think that the hearing of two witnesses and three affidavits would be quicker than the examination of three witnesses.

THE PRESIDENT: I am afraid Dr. Stahmer and Dr. Exner drew a wrong inference from the order of the Tribunal. The Tribunal intended and intends that the evidence should be limited to the evidence of three witnesses on either side, and whether they give their evidence orally or by affidavit does not matter. We left it to the Soviet Prosecution and to defendant's counsel to see whether they could agree that it should be given by affidavit in order to save time. But that was not intended to extend the number of witnesses who might give evidence.

DR. SIEMERS: Mr. President, in that case, I should be grateful if Dr. Stahmer and Professor Exner would be heard. I myself have not been in Nuremberg recently; I was therefore not present when these details were discussed and it is difficult for me—I see that Dr. Stahmer is now—perhaps Dr. Stahmer himself could speak about it.

DR. STAHMER: I have just heard Dr. Siemers' report, at least a part of it. I mentioned already during the last discussion, Mr. President, that Professor Exner and I had understood the decision to mean that besides the three witnesses we were also allowed to submit affidavits. Indeed, the original decision granted us five witnesses, though it made the reservation that only three of them could give evidence here in Court. We assumed, therefore, that we could submit affidavits of those witnesses out of the five who had been originally granted us but who would not give evidence in Court. The original decision granted us five witnesses, and then a later decision of the Tribunal . . .

THE PRESIDENT: Listen, that is not the recollection of the Tribunal; and if you say so, you must produce written evidence that that was the decision. The Tribunal's recollection is not that five witnesses were allowed.

DR. STAHMER: Yes, yes, yes. I shall submit written evidence of these decisions to the Tribunal. I cannot remember offhand when they were made, but originally five witnesses were granted; then I named another witness, who was also granted, and it was only afterwards that the decision to allow only three witnesses to give evidence in Court was announced.

THE PRESIDENT: Dr. Stahmer, when the order was made limiting it to three out of five, there was no reference in that order to affidavits, as far as I know.

DR. STAHMER: No, affidavits were not mentioned then.

THE PRESIDENT: What I am telling you is that the Tribunal in making that order of limitation intended to limit the whole of the evidence to three witnesses on either side, because the matter is only a subsidiary allegation of fact; and the Tribunal thinks that at this stage of the proceedings such an allegation of fact ought not to be investigated by a great number of witnesses, and three witnesses are quite sufficient on either side.

Therefore the Tribunal does not desire to hear and did not intend that it should have to hear any evidence except the evidence of three witnesses, either orally or by affidavit.

The Tribunal will now adjourn.

[The Tribunal adjourned until Monday 1 July at 1000 hours.]

Monday, 1 July 1946

Morning Session

THE PRESIDENT: I have an announcement to make.

The Tribunal orders that any of the evidence taken on commission which the Defense Counsel or the Prosecution wish to use shall be offered in evidence by them. This evidence will then become a part of the record, subject to any objections.

Counsel for the organizations should begin to make up their document books as soon as possible and put in their requests for translations.

That is all.

Dr. Stahmer.

DR. STAHMER: With reference to the events at Katyn, the Indictment contains only the remark: "In September 1941 11,000 Polish officers, prisoners of war, were killed in the Katyn woods near Smolensk." The Russian Prosecution only submitted the details at the session of 14 February 1946. Document USSR-54 was then submitted to the Tribunal. This document is an official report by the Extraordinary State Commission, which was officially authorized to investigate the Katyn case. This commission, after questioning the witnesses...

THE PRESIDENT: Dr. Stahmer, the Tribunal are aware of the document and they only want you to call your evidence; that is all.

DR. STAHMER: I wanted only to add, Mr. President, that according to this document, there are two accusations: One, that the period of the shooting of the Polish prisoners of war was the autumn of 1941; and the second assertion is, that the killing was carried out by some German military authority, camouflaged under the name of "Staff of Engineer Battalion 537."

THE PRESIDENT: That is all in the document, is it not? I have just told you we know the document. We only want you to call your evidence.

DR. STAHMER: Then, as my first witness for the Defense, I shall call Colonel Friedrich Ahrens to the witness stand.

DR. SIEMERS: Mr. President, I have a request to make before the evidence is heard in the Katyn case. The Tribunal decided that three witnesses should be heard, and it hinted that in the interests of equality, the Prosecution could also produce only three witnesses, either by means of direct examination or by means of an affidavit. In the interests of that same principle of equality, I should be grateful if the Soviet Delegation, in the same way as the Defense, would state the names of their witnesses before the hearing of the evidence. The Defense submitted the names of their witnesses weeks ago. Unfortunately, up to now, I note that in the interests of equality and with regard to the treatment of the Defense and the Prosecution, the Soviet Delegation has so far not given the names of the witnesses.

THE PRESIDENT: General Rudenko, were you going to give me the names of the witnesses?

GEN. RUDENKO: Yes, Mr. President. Today we notified the General Secretary of the Tribunal that the Soviet Prosecution intends to call three witnesses to the stand: Professor Prosorovsky, who is the Chief of the Medico-Legal Experts Commission; the Bulgarian subject, Professor of Legal Medicine at Sofia University Markov, who at the same time was a member of the so-called International Commission created by the Germans; and Professor Bazilevsky, who was the deputy mayor of Smolensk during the time of the German occupation.

[The witness Ahrens took the stand.]

THE PRESIDENT: Will you state your full name?

FRIEDRICH AHRENS (Witness): Friedrich Ahrens.

THE PRESIDENT: Will you repeat this oath after me: I swear by God—the Almighty and Omniscient—that I will speak the pure truth—and will withhold and add nothing.

[The witness repeated the oath.]

THE PRESIDENT: You may sit down.

DR. STAHMER: Witness, did you, as a professional officer in the German Armed Forces, participate in the second World War?

AHRENS: Yes, of course; as a professional officer I participated in the second World War.

DR. STAHMER: What rank did you hold finally?

AHRENS: At the end as colonel.

DR. STAHMER: Were you stationed in the eastern theater of war?

AHRENS: Yes.

DR. STAHMER: In what capacity?

AHRENS: I was the commanding officer of a signal regiment of an army group.

DR. STAHMER: What were the tasks of your regiment?

AHRENS: The signal regiment of an army group had the task of setting up and maintaining communications between the army group and the neighboring units and subordinate units, as well as preparing the necessary lines of communication for new operations.

DR. STAHMER: Did your regiment have any special tasks apart from that?

AHRENS: No, with the exception of the duty of defending themselves, of taking all measures to hinder a sudden attack and of holding themselves in readiness to defend themselves with the forces at their disposal, so as to prevent the capture of the regimental battle headquarters.

This was particularly important for an army group signal regiment and its battle headquarters because we had to keep a lot of highly secret material in our staff.

DR. STAHMER: Your regiment was the Signal Regiment 537. Was there also an Engineer Battalion 537, the same number?

AHRENS: During the time when I was in the Army Group Center I heard of no unit with the same number, nor do I believe that there was such a unit.

DR. STAHMER: And to whom were you subordinated?

AHRENS: I was directly subordinated to the staff of the Army Group Center, and that was the case during the entire period when I was with the army group. My superior was General Oberhäuser.

With regard to defense, the signal staff of the regiment with its first battalion, which was in close touch with the regimental staff, was at times subordinated to the commander of Smolensk; all orders which I received from that last-named command came via General Oberhäuser, who either approved or refused to allow the regiment to be employed for a particular purpose.

In other words, I received my orders exclusively from General Oberhäuser.

DR. STAHMER: Where was your staff accommodated?

AHRENS: I prepared a sketch of the position of the staff headquarters west of Smolensk.

DR. STAHMER: I am having the sketch shown to you. Please tell us whether that is your sketch.

AHRENS: That sketch was drawn by me from memory.

DR. STAHMER: I am now going to have a second sketch shown to you. Will you please have a look at that one also, and will you tell me whether it presents a correct picture of the situation?

AHRENS: May I briefly explain this sketch to you? At the right-hand margin, that large red spot is the town of Smolensk. West of Smolensk, and on either side of the road to Vitebsk, the staff of the army group was situated together with the Air Force corps, that is south of Krasnibor. On my sketch I have marked the actual area occupied by the Army Group Center.

That part of my sketch which has a dark line around it was very densely occupied by troops who came directly under the army group; there was hardly a house empty in that area.

The regimental staff of my regiment was in the so-called little Katyn wood. That is the white spot which is indicated on the sketch; it measures about 1 square kilometer of the large forest and is a part of the entire forest around Katyn. On the southern edge of· this small wood there lay the so-called Dnieper Castle, which was the regimental staff headquarters.

Two and a half kilometers to the east of the staff headquarters of the regiment there was the first company of the regiment. which was the operating company, which did teleprinting and telephone work for the army group. About 3 kilometers west of the reg-imental staff headquarters there was the wireless company. There were no buildings within the radius of about 1 kilometer of the regimental staff headquarters.

This house was a large two-story building with about 14 ·to 15 rooms, several bath installations, a cinema, a rifle range, garages, Sauna (steam baths) and so on, and was most suitable for accom-modating the regimental staff. Our regiment permanently retained this battle headquarters.

DR. STAHMER: Were there also any other high-ranking staff headquarters nearby?

AHRENS: As higher staff headquarters there was the army group, which I have already mentioned, then a corps staff from the Air Force, and several battalion staffs. Then there was the delegate of the railway for the army group, who was at Gnesdovo in a special train.

DR. STAHMER: It has been stated in this Trial that certain events which have taken place in your neighborhood had been most secret and most suspicious. Will you please, therefore, answer the following questions with particular care?

How many Germans were there in the staff personnel, and what positions did they fill?

AHRENS: I had 3 officers on my staff to begin with, and then 2, and approximately 18 to 20 noncommissioned officers and men; that is to say, as few as I could have in my regimental staff, and every man in the staff was fully occupied.

DR. STAHMER: Did you have Russian personnel in your staff?

AHRENS: Yes, we had four auxiliary volunteers and some female personnel living in the immediate vicinity of the regimental staff quarters. The auxiliary volunteers remained permanently with the regimental staff, whereas the female personnel changed from time to time. Some of these women also came from Smolensk and they lived in a separate building near the regimental staff.

DR. STAHMER: Did this Russian personnel receive special instructions from you about their conduct?

AHRENS: I issued general instructions on conduct for the regimental headquarters, which did not solely apply to the Russian personnel.

I have already mentioned the importance of secrecy with reference to this regimental headquarters, which not only kept the records of the position of the army group, but also that of its neighboring units, and on which the intentions of the army group were clearly recognizable. Therefore, it was my duty to keep this material particularly secret. Consequently, I had the rooms containing this material barred to ordinary access. Only those persons were admitted—generally officers—who had been passed by me, but also a few noncommissioned officers and other ranks who were put under special oath.

DR. STAHMER: To which rooms did this "no admission" order refer?

AHRENS: In the first place, it referred to the telephone expert's room, it also referred to my own room and partly, although to a smaller degree, to the adjutant's room. All remaining rooms in the house and on the site were not off limits.

THE PRESIDENT: Dr. Stahmer, how is this evidence about the actual conditions in these staff headquarters relevant to this question?

DR. STAHMER: Mr. President, in the Russian document the allegation is contained that events of a particularly secret nature had taken place in this staff building and that a ban of silence had been imposed on the Russian personnel by Colonel Ahrens, that the rooms had been locked, and that one was only permitted to enter the rooms when accompanied by guards. I have put the questions in this connection in order to clear up the case and to prove that these events have a perfectly natural explanation on account of the tasks entrusted to the regiment and which necessitated quite obviously, a certain amount of secrecy.

For that reason, I have put these questions. May I be permitted...

THE PRESIDENT: Very well.

DR. STAHMER: I have almost finished with these questions.

[Turning to the witness.] Was the Katyn wood cordoned off, and especially strictly guarded by soldiers?

Mr. President, may I remark with reference to this question that here also it had been alleged that this cordon had only been introduced by the regiment. Previously, there had been free access to the woods, and from this conclusions are drawn which are detrimental to the regiment.

AHRENS: In order to secure antiaircraft cover for the regimental staff headquarters, I stopped any timber from being cut for fuel in the immediate vicinity of the regimental staff headquarters. During this winter the situation was such that the units cut wood wherever they could get it.

On 22 January, there was a fairly heavy air attack on my position during which half a house was torn away. It was quite impossible to find any other accommodation because of the overcrowding of the area, and I therefore took additional precautions to make sure that this already fairly thin wood would be preserved so as to serve as cover. Since, on the other hand, I am against the putting up of prohibition signs, I asked the other troop units by way of verses to leave us our trees as antiaircraft cover. The wood was not closed off at all, particularly as the road had to be kept open for heavy traffic, and I only sent sentries now and then into the wood to see whether our trees were left intact.

DR. STAHMER: The Prosecution...

THE PRESIDENT: Dr. Stahmer, at a time that is convenient to you, you will, of course, draw our attention to the necessary dates, the date at which this unit took over its headquarters and the date at which it left.

DR. STAHMER: Very well.

[Turning to the witness.] When did your unit, your regiment, move into this Dnieper Castle?

AHRENS: As far as I know, this house was taken over immediately after the combat troops had left that area in August 1941, and it was confiscated together with the other army group accommodations, and was occupied by advance parties. It was then permanently occupied by the regimental headquarters as long as I was there up to August 1943.

DR. STAHMER: So, if I understand you correctly, it was first of all in August 1941 that an advance party took it over?

AHRENS: Yes, as far as I know.

DR. STAHMER: When did the staff actually arrive?

AHRENS: A few weeks later.

DR. STAHMER: Who was the regimental commander at that time?

AHRENS: My predecessor was Colonel Bedenck.

DR. STAHMER: When did you take over the regiment?

AHRENS: I joined the army group during the second half of November 1941, and after getting thoroughly acquainted with all details I took over the command of the regiment, at the end of November, if I remember rightly, on 30 November.

DR. STAHMER: Was there a proper handing over from Bedenck to you?

AHRENS: A very careful, detailed, and lengthy transfer took place, on account of the very considerable tasks entrusted to this regiment. Added to that, my superior, General Oberhäuser, was an extraordinarily painstaking superior, and he took great pains to convince himself personally whether, by the transfer negotiations and the instructions which I had received, I was fully capable of taking over the responsibilities of the regiment.

DR. STAHMER: The Prosecution further alleges and claims that it was suspicious that shots were often fired in the forest. Is that true, and to what would you attribute that?

AHRENS: I have already mentioned that it was one of the main tasks of the regiment to take all the necessary measures to defend themselves against sudden attack. Considering the small number of men which I had in my regimental staff, I had to organize and take the necessary steps to enable me to obtain replacements in the shortest time possible. This was arranged through wireless communication with the regimental headquarters. I ordered that defensive maneuvers should be carried out and that defense works should be prepared around the regimental headquarters sector and that there should be maneuvers and exercises in these works together with the members of the regimental headquarters. I personally participated in these maneuvers at times and, of course, shots were fired, particularly since we were preparing ourselves for night fighting.

DR. STAHMER: There is supposed to have been a very lively and rather suspicious traffic to and around your staff building. Will you please tell us quite briefly what this traffic signified?

AHRENS: There was an extraordinary lively traffic around staff headquarters which still increased in the spring of 1941 as I was having the house rebuilt. I think I mentioned that it had been destroyed through air attacks. But, of course, the traffic increased also through the maneuvers which were held nearby. The battalions in the front area operating at 300 and 400 kilometers distance had to, and could perform their job only by maintaining personal contact with the regiment and its staff headquarters.

DR. STAHMER: There is supposed to have been considerable truck traffic which has been described as suspicious.

AHRENS: Besides our supplies, which were relatively small, the Kommandos, as I have just mentioned, were brought in by trucks; but so was, of course, all the building material which I required. Apart from that, the traffic was not unusually heavy.

DR. STAHMER: Do you know that about 25 kilometers west of Smolensk there were three Russian prisoner-of-war camps, which had originally been inhabited by Poles and which had been abandoned by the Russians when the German troops approached in July 1941?

AHRENS: At that time I had not yet arrived. But never during the entire period I served in Russia did I see a single Pole; nor did I hear of Poles.

DR. STAHMER: It has been alleged that an order had been issued from Berlin according to which Polish prisoners of war were to be shot. Did you know of such an order?

AHRENS: No. I have never heard of such an order.

DR. STAHMER: Did you possibly receive such an order from any other office?

AHRENS: I told you already that I never heard of such an order and I therefore did not receive it, either.

DR. STAHMER: Were any Poles shot on your instructions, your direct instructions?

AHRENS: No Poles were shot on my instructions. Nobody at all was ever shot upon my order. I have never given such an order in all my life.

DR. STAHMER: Well, you did not arrive until November 1941. Have you heard anything about your predecessor, Colonel Bedenck, having given any similar orders?

AHRENS: I have not heard anything about it. With my regimental staff, with whom I lived closely together for 21 months, I had such close connections, I knew my people so well, and they also knew me, that I am perfectly convinced that this deed was not perpetrated by my predecessor nor by any member of my former regiment. I would undoubtedly have heard rumors of it at the very least.

THE PRESIDENT: This is argument, you know, Dr. Stahmer. This is not evidence; it is argument. He is telling you what he thinks might have been the case.

DR. STAHMER: I asked whether he had heard of it from members of his regiment.

THE PRESIDENT: The answer to that would be "no," I suppose, that he had not heard—not that he was convinced that he had not done it.

DR. STAHMER: Very well.

[Turning to the witness.] After your arrival at Katyn, did you notice that there was a grave mound in the woods at Katyn?

AHRENS: Shortly after I arrived—the ground was covered by snow—one of my soldiers pointed out to me that at a certain spot there was some sort of a mound, which one could hardly describe as such, on which there was a birch cross. I have seen that birch cross. In the course of 1942 my soldiers kept telling me that here in our woods shootings were supposed to have taken place, but at first I did not pay any attention to it. However, in the summer of 1942 this topic was referred to in an order of the army group later commanded by General Von Harsdorff. He told me that he had also heard about it.

DR. STAHMER: Did these stories prove true later on?

AHRENS: Yes, they did turn out to be true and I was able to confirm, quite by accident, that there was actually a grave here. During the winter of 1943—I think either January or February—quite accidentally I saw a wolf in this wood and at first I did not believe that it was a wolf; when I followed the tracks with an expert, we saw that there were traces of scratchings on the mound with the cross. I had investigations made as to what kind of bones these were. The doctors told me "human bones." Thereupon I informed the officer responsible for war graves in the area of this fact, because I believed that it was a soldier's grave, as there were a number of such graves in our immediate vicinity.

DR. STAHMER: Then, how did the exhumation take place?

AHRENS: I do not know about all the details. Professor Dr. Butz arrived one day on orders from the army group, and informed me that following the rumors in my little wood, he had to make exhumations, and that he had to inform me that these exhumations would take place in my wood.

DR. STAHMER: Did Professor Butz later give you details of the result of his exhumations?

AHRENS: Yes, he did occasionally give me details and I remember that he told me that he had conclusive evidence regarding the date of the shootings. Among other things, he showed me letters, of which I cannot remember much now; but I do remember some sort of a diary which he passed over to me in which there were dates followed by some notes which I could not read because they were written in Polish. In this connection he explained to me that these notes had been made by a Polish officer regarding events of the past months, and that at the end—the diary ended with the spring of 1940—the fear was expressed in these notes that something horrible was going to happen. I am giving only a broad outline of the meaning.

DR. STAHMER: Did he give you any further indication regarding the period, he assumed the shooting had taken place?

AHRENS: Professor Butz, on the basis of the proofs which he had found, was convinced that the shootings had taken place in the spring of 1940 and I often heard him express these convictions in my presence, and also later on, when commissions visited the grave and I had to place my house at the disposal of these commissions to accommodate them. I personally did not have anything to do whatsoever with the exhumations or with the commissions. All I had to do was to place the house at their disposal and act as host.

DR. STAHMER: It was alleged that in March 1943 lorries had transported bodies to Katyn from outside and these bodies were buried in the little wood. Do you know anything about that?

AHRENS: No, I know nothing about that.

DR. STAHMER: Would you have had to take notice of it?

AHRENS: I would have had to take notice of it—at least my officers would have reported it to me. because my officers were constantly at the regimental battle headquarters, whereas I, as a regimental commander, was of course, frequently on the way. The officer who in those days was there constantly was First Lieutenant Hodt, whose address I got to know last night from a letter.

DR. STAHMER: Were Russian prisoners of war used for these exhumations?

AHRENS: As far as I remember, yes.

DR. STAHMER: Can you tell us the number?

AHRENS: I cannot say exactly as I did not concern myself any further with these exhumations on account of the dreadful and revolting stench around our house, but I should estimate the number as being about 40 to 50 men.

DR. STAHMER: It has been alleged that they were shot afterward; have you any knowledge of that?

AHRENS: I have no knowledge of that and I also never heard of it.

DR. STAHMER: I have no further questions, Mr. President.

FLOTTENRICHTER OTTO KRANZBÜHLER (Counsel for Defendant Dönitz): Colonel, did you yourself ever discuss the events of 1940 with any of the local inhabitants?

AHRENS: Yes. At the beginning of 1943 a Russian married couple were living near my regimental headquarters; they lived 800 meters away and they were beekeepers. I, too, kept bees, and I came into close contact with this married couple. When the exhumations had been completed, approximately in May 1943, I told them that, after all, they ought to know when these shootings had taken place, since they were living in close proximity to the graves. Thereupon, these people told me it had occurred in the spring of 1940, and that at the Gnesdovo station more than 200 Poles in uniform had arrived in railway trucks of 50 tons each and were then taken to the woods in lorries. They had heard lots of shots and screams, too.

FLOTTENRICHTER KRANZBÜHLER: Was the wood off limits to the local inhabitants at the time?

AHRENS: We have ...

THE PRESIDENT: That is a leading question. I do not think you should ask leading questions.

FLOTTENRICHTER KRANZBÜHLER: Do you know whether the local inhabitants could enter the woods at the time?

AHRENS: There was a fence around the wood and according to the statements of the local inhabitants, civilians could not enter it during the time the Russians were there. The remains of the fence were still visible when I was there, and this fence is indicated on my sketch and is marked with a black line.

FLOTTENRICHTER KRANZBÜHLER: When you moved into Dnieper Castle did you make inquiries as to who the former owners were?

AHRENS: Yes, I did make inquiries because I was interested. The house was built in a rather peculiar way. It had a cinema installation and its own rifle range and of course that interested me; but I failed to ascertain anything definite during the whole time I was there.

FLOTTENRICHTER KRANZBÜHLER: Apart from mass graves in the neighborhood of the castle, were there any other graves found?

AHRENS: I have indicated by a few dots on my sketch, that in the vicinity of the castle there were found a number of other small graves which contained decayed bodies; that is to say, skeletons which had disintegrated. These graves contained perhaps six, eight, or a few more male and female skeletons. Even I, a layman, could recognize that very clearly, because most of them had rubber shoes on which were in good condition, and there were also remains of handbags.

FLOTTENRICHTER KRANZBÜHLER: How long had these skeletons been in the ground?

AHRENS: That I cannot tell you. I know only that they were decayed and had disintegrated. The bones were preserved, but the skeleton structure was no longer intact.

FLOTTENRICHTER KRANZBÜHLER: Thank you, that is all.

DR. HANS LATERNSER (Counsel for General Staff and High Command of the German Armed Forces): Mr. President...

THE PRESIDENT: Dr. Laternser, you know the Tribunal's ruling.

DR. LATERNSER: Yes, Sir.

THE PRESIDENT: Well, you have no right to ask any questions of the witness here.

DR. LATERNSER: Mr. President, I just wanted to ask you, in this unusual case, to allow me to put questions...

THE PRESIDENT: I said to you that you know the Tribunal's ruling and the Tribunal will not hear you. We have already ruled upon this once or twice in consequence of your objections and the Tribunal will not hear you.

DR. LATERNSER: Mr. President, the Katyn case is one of the most serious accusations raised against the group.

THE PRESIDENT: The Tribunal is perfectly well aware of the nature of the allegations about Katyn and the Tribunal does not propose to make any exceptional rule in that case and it therefore will not hear you and you will kindly sit down.

DR. LATERNSER: Mr. President, I wish to state that on account of this ruling I feel myself unduly handicapped in my defense.

THE PRESIDENT: As Dr. Laternser knows perfectly well, he is entitled to apply to the Commission to call any witness who is called here, if his evidence bears upon the case of the particular organizations for which Dr. Laternser appears. I do not want to hear anything further.

DR. LATERNSER: Mr. President, the channel you point out to me is of no practical importance. I cannot have every witness who appears here called by the Commission.

THE PRESIDENT: Dr. Siemers, you are appearing for the Defendant Dönitz, or is it Raeder?

DR. SIEMERS: Defendant Raeder.

THE PRESIDENT: Well, unless the questions you are going to ask particularly refer to the case of the Defendant Raeder, the Tribunal is not prepared to hear any further examination. The matter has been generally covered by Dr. Stahmer and also by Dr. Kranzbühler. Therefore, unless the questions which you want to ask have some particular reference to the case of Raeder, the Tribunal will not hear you.

DR. SIEMERS: Mr. President, I had merely assumed that there were two reasons on the strength of which I could put a few questions: First, because the Tribunal itself has stated that within the framework of the conspiracy all defendants had been participants; and second, that according to the statements by the Prosecution Grossadmiral Raeder, too, is considered a member of the alleged criminal organizations, the General Staff and the OKW. It was for that reason I wanted to ask one or two supplementary questions.

THE PRESIDENT: Dr. Siemers, if there were any allegations that in any way bore on the case against Defendant Raeder, the Tribunal would of course allow you to ask questions; but there is no allegation which in any way connects the Defendant Raeder with the allegations about the Katyn woods.

DR. SIEMERS: I am grateful to the Tribunal for that statement, Mr. President.

DR. LATERNSER: Mr. President, may I be allowed to ask something else? May I have the question put to the Prosecution, who is to be made responsible for the Katyn case?

THE PRESIDENT: I do not propose to answer questions of that sort.

The Prosecution may now cross-examine if they want to.

CHIEF COUNSELLOR OF JUSTICE L. N. SMIRNOV (Assistant Prosecutor for the U.S.S.R.): Please tell me, Witness, since when, exactly, have you been in the Smolensk district territory?

AHRENS: I have already answered that question: since the second half of November 1941.

MR. COUNSELLOR SMIRNOV: Please answer me further, where were you prior to the second part of 1941? Did you in any way have anything to do with Katyn or Smolensk or this district in general? Were you there personally in September and October 1941?

107

AHRENS: No, I was not there.

MR. COUNSELLOR SMIRNOV: That is to say that you were not there, either in September or in October 1941, and therefore do not know what happened at that time in the Katyn forest?

AHRENS: I was not there at that time, but I mentioned earlier on that...

MR. COUNSELLOR SMIRNOV: No, I am actually only interested in a short question. Were you there personally or not? Were you able to see for yourself what was happening there or not?

THE PRESIDENT: He says he was not there.

AHRENS: No, I was not there.

THE PRESIDENT: He said he was not there in September or October 1941.

MR. COUNSELLOR SMIRNOV: Thank you, Mr. President.

[Turning to the witness.] Maybe you recall the family names of the Russian women workers who were employed at the country house in the woods?

AHRENS: Those female workers were not working in different houses. They merely worked as auxiliary kitchen personnel in our Dnieper Castle. I have not known their names at all.

MR. COUNSELLOR SMIRNOV: That means that the Russian women workers were employed only in the villa situated in Katyn forest where the staff headquarters were located?

AHRENS: I believe that question was not translated well. I did not understand it.

MR. COUNSELLOR SMIRNOV: I asked you whether the Russian women workers were employed exclusively in the villa in Kosig Gory where the staff headquarters were located? Is that right?

AHRENS: The women workers worked for the regimental headquarters as kitchen help, and as kitchen helpers they worked on our premises; and by our premises I mean this particular house with the adjoining houses—for instance, the stables, the garage, the cellars, the boiler room.

MR. COUNSELLOR SMIRNOV: I will mention a few names of German military employees. Will you please tell me whether they belonged to your unit? First Lieutenant Rex?

AHRENS: First Lieutenant Rex was my regimental adjutant.

MR. COUNSELLOR SMIRNOV: Please tell me, was he already assigned to that unit before your arrival at Katyn?

AHRENS: Yes, he was there before I came.

MR. COUNSELLOR SMIRNOV: He was your adjutant, was he not?

AHRENS: Yes, he was my adjutant.

MR. COUNSELLOR SMIRNOV: Lieutenant Hodt? Hodt or Hoth?

AHRENS: Lieutenant Hodt is right; but what question are you putting about Lieutenant Hodt?

MR. COUNSELLOR SMIRNOV: I am only questioning you about whether he belonged to your unit or not.

AHRENS: Lieutenant Hodt was a member of the regiment. Whether ...

MR. COUNSELLOR SMIRNOV: Yes, that is what I was asking. He belonged to the regiment which you commanded, to your army unit?

AHRENS: I did not say by that that he was a member of the regimental staff, but that he belonged to the regiment. The regiment consisted of three units.

MR. COUNSELLOR SMIRNOV: But he lived in the same villa, did he not?

AHRENS: That I do not know. When I arrived he was not there. I ordered him to report to me there for the first time.

MR. COUNSELLOR SMIRNOV: I will enumerate a few other names. Corporal Rose, Private Giesecken, Oberfeldwebel Krimmenski, Feldwebel Lummert, a cook named Gustav. Were these members of the Armed Forces who were billeted in the villa?

AHRENS: May I ask you to mention the names individually once again, and I will answer you individually.

MR. COUNSELLOR SMIRNOV: Feldwebel Lummert?

AHRENS: Yes.

MR. COUNSELLOR SMIRNOV: Corporal Rose?

AHRENS: Yes.

MR. COUNSELLOR SMIRNOV: And I believe, if my memory serves me correctly, Storekeeper Giesecke.

AHRENS: That man's name was Giesecken.

MR. COUNSELLOR SMIRNOV: Yes, that is right. I did not pronounce this name quite correctly. These were all your people or at least they belonged to your unit, did they not?'

AHRENS: Yes.

MR. COUNSELLOR SMIRNOV: And you assert that you did not know what these people were doing in September and October 1941?

AHRENS: As I was not there, I cannot tell you for certain.

THE PRESIDENT: We will adjourn now.

[A recess was taken.]

MR. COUNSELLOR SMIRNOV: May I continue? Mr. President, since the witness has stated that he cannot give any testimony concerning the period of September to October 1941, I will limit myself to very short questions.

[*Turning to the witness.*] Witness, would you please point out the location of the villa and the forest with respect to the Smolensk-Vitebsk highway? Did the estate cover a large area?

AHRENS: My sketch is on a scale of 1 to 100,000 and is drawn from memory. I estimate, therefore, that the graves were situated 200 to 300 meters directly west of the road to our Dnieper Castle, and 200 to 300 meters south of the Smolensk-Vitebsk road so that the Dnieper Castle lay a further 600 meters away.

THE PRESIDENT: Will you repeat that?

AHRENS: South of the Smolensk-Vitebsk highway, approximately 15 kilometers west of Smolensk. According to the scale 1 to 100,000, as far as one is able to draw such a sketch accurately from memory, the site of these graves was 200 to 300 meters to the south, and a further 600 meters to the south, directly on the northern bend of the Dnieper, was situated our regimental staff quarters, the Dnieper Castle.

MR. COUNSELLOR SMIRNOV: Consequently, the villa was approximately 600 meters away from the Smolensk-Vitebsk highway?

AHRENS: No, that is not correct. What I said . . .

MR. COUNSELLOR SMIRNOV: Please give a more or less exact figure. What was the distance between the highway and the villa, please?

AHRENS: I just mentioned it in my testimony, that is to say, the graves were about 200 to 300 meters away, and there were a further 600 meters to the castle, therefore, in all about 900 to 1,000 meters. It might have been 800 meters, but that is the approximate distance as can also be seen by this sketch.

THE PRESIDENT: I am not following this. Your question, Colonel Smirnov, was: How far was it from the road to what you called the country house? Was it not?

MR. COUNSELLOR SMIRNOV: No, Mr. President, I asked how far was the villa from the Smolensk-Vitebsk highway.

THE PRESIDENT: What do you mean by the "Villa"?

MR. COUNSELLOR SMIRNOV: The headquarters of the unit commanded by the witness in 1941 was quartered in a villa, and this villa was situated not far from the Dnieper River, at a distance of about 900 meters from the highroad. The graves were nearer to the highway. I would like to know how far away were the headquarters from the highway, and how far away from the highway were the graves in Katyn forest.

THE PRESIDENT: What you want to know is: How far was the house in which the headquarters was situated from the highway? Is that right?

MR. COUNSELLOR SMIRNOV: Yes, that is exactly what I wanted to know, Mr. President.

AHRENS: You put two questions to me: first of all, how far were the graves from the highway; and secondly, how far was the house from the highway. I will repeat the answer once more, the house was 800 to 1,000 meters south of the Smolensk-Vitebsk highway.

MR. COUNSELLOR SMIRNOV: One minute, please. I asked you primarily only about the house. Your answer concerning the graves was given on your own initiative. Now I will ask you about the graves, how far were these mass graves from the Smolensk-Vitebsk highway?

AHRENS: From 200 to 300 meters. It might also have been 350 meters.

MR. COUNSELLOR SMIRNOV: Consequently, the graves were 200 or 300 meters from the main road which connected two important centers? Is that right?

AHRENS: Yes, indeed. They were at a distance of 200 to 300 meters south of this, and I may say that at my time this was the most frequented road I ever saw in Russia.

MR. COUNSELLOR SMIRNOV: That was just what I was asking you. Now, please tell me: Was the Katyn wood a real forest, or was it, rather, a park or a grove?

AHRENS: Up to now I have only spoken about the wood of Katyn. This wood of Katyn is the fenced-in wooded area of about 1 square kilometer, which I drew in my sketch. This wood is of mixed growth, of older and younger trees. There were many birch trees in this little wood. However, there were clearings in this wood, and I should say that from 30 to 40 percent was cleared. One could see this from the stumps of newly felled trees.

Under no circumstances could you describe this wood as a park; at any rate one could not come to such a conclusion. Fighting had taken place in this wood, as one could still see trenches and fox holes.

MR. COUNSELLOR SMIRNOV: Yes, but anyway, you would not call Katyn wood a real forest since it was relatively a small grove in the immediate vicinity of the Smolensk-Vitebsk highway. Is that right?

AHRENS: No, that is not right. It was a forest. The entire Katyn forest was a regular forest which began near our grove and extended far beyond that. Of this Katyn forest, which was a mixed forest, part of it had been fenced in, and this part, extending over 1 square kilometer, was what we called the little Katyn wood, but it did belong to this entire wooded region south of the highway. The forest began with our little wood and extended to the west.

MR. COUNSELLOR SMIRNOV: I am not interested in the general characteristics of the wood. I would like you to answer the following short question: Were the mass graves located in this grove?

AHRENS: The mass graves were situated directly west of our entrance drive in a clearing in the wood, where there was a growth of young trees.

MR. COUNSELLOR SMIRNOV: Yes, but this clearing, this growth of young trees, was located inside this small grove, near the Smolensk-Vitebsk highway, is that correct?

AHRENS: It was 200 to 300 meters south of the Smolensk-Vitebsk highway, and directly west of the entrance drive leading from this road to the Dnieper Castle. I have marked this spot on my sketch with a fairly large white dot.

MR. COUNSELLOR SMIRNOV: One more question. As far as you know did the Smolensk-Vitebsk highway exist before the German occupation of Smolensk, or was it constructed only after the occupation?

AHRENS: When I arrived in Russia at the end of November 1941, everything was covered with snow. Later I got the impression that this was an old road, whereas the road Minsk-Moscow was newer. That was my impression.

MR. COUNSELLOR SMIRNOV: I understand. Now tell me, under what circumstances, or rather, when did you first discover the cross in the grove?

AHRENS: I cannot tell the exact date. My soldiers told me about it, and on one occasion when I was going past there, about the beginning of January 1942—it could also have been at the end of December 1941—I saw this cross rising above the snow.

MR. COUNSELLOR SMIRNOV: This means you saw it already in 1941 or at the latest the beginning of 1942?

AHRENS: That is what I have just testified.

MR. COUNSELLOR SMIRNOV: Yes, certainly. Now, please be more specific concerning the date when a wolf brought you to this cross. Was it in winter or summer and what year?

AHRENS: It was the beginning of 1943.

MR. COUNSELLOR SMIRNOV: In 1943? And around the cross you saw bones, did you not?

AHRENS: No.

MR. COUNSELLOR SMIRNOV: No?

AHRENS: No, at first I did not see them. In order to find out whether I had not been mistaken about seeing a wolf, for it seemed rather impossible that a wolf should be so near to Smolensk, I examined the tracks together with a gamekeeper and found traces of scratching on the ground. However, the ground was frozen hard, there was snow on the ground and I did not see anything further there. Only later on, after it had been thawing my men found various bones. However, this was months later and then, at a suitable opportunity I showed these bones to a doctor and he said that these were human bones. Thereupon I said, "Then most likely it is a grave, left as a result of the fighting which has taken place here," and that the war graves registration officer would have to take care of the graves in the same way in which we were taking care of other graves of fallen soldiers. That was the reason why I spoke to this gentleman—but only after the snow had melted.

MR. COUNSELLOR SMIRNOV: By the way, did you personally see the Katyn graves?

AHRENS: Open or before they were opened?

MR. COUNSELLOR SMIRNOV: Open, yes.

AHRENS: When they were open I had constantly to drive past these graves, as generally they were approximately 30 meters away from the entrance drive. Therefore, I could hardly go past without taking any notice of them.

MR. COUNSELLOR SMIRNOV: I am interested in the following: Do you remember what the depth of the layer of earth was, which covered the mass of human bodies in these graves?

AHRENS: That I do not know. I have already said that I was so nauseated by the stench which we had to put up with for several weeks, that when I drove past I closed the windows of my car and rushed through as fast as I could.

MR. COUNSELLOR SMIRNOV: However, even if you only casually glanced at those graves, perhaps you noticed whether the layer of earth covering the corpses was deep or shallow? Was it several centimeters or several meters deep? Maybe Professor Butz told you something about it?

AHRENS: As commander of a signal regiment I was concerned with a region which was almost half as large as Greater Germany and I was on the road a great deal. My work was not entirely carried out at the regimental battle headquarters. Therefore, in general, from Monday or Tuesday until Saturday I was with my units. For that reason, when I drove through, I did cast an occasional glance at these graves; but I was not especially interested in the details and I did not speak to Professor Butz about such details. For this reason I have only a faint recollection of this matter.

MR. COUNSELLOR SMIRNOV: According to the material submitted to the High Tribunal by the Soviet Prosecution, it has been established that the bodies were buried at a depth of 1¹/₂ to 2 meters. I wonder where you met a wolf who could scratch the ground up to a depth of 2 meters.

AHRENS: I did not meet this wolf, but I saw it.

MR. COUNSELLOR SMIRNOV: Tell me please, why you started the exhumation on these mass graves in March 1943 only, after having discovered the cross and learned about the mass graves already in 1941?

AHRENS: That was not my concern, but a matter for the army group. I have already told you that in the course of 1942 the stories became more substantial. I frequently heard about them and spoke about it to Colonel Von Gersdorff, Chief of Intelligence, Army Group Center, who intimated to me that he knew all about this matter and with that my obligation ended. I had reported what I had seen and heard. Apart from that, all this matter did not concern me and I did not concern myself with it. I had enough worries of my own.

MR. COUNSELLOR SMIRNOV: And now the last question. Please tell me who were these two persons with whom you had this conversation, and maybe you can recollect the names of the couple who told you about the shootings in the Katyn woods?

AHRENS: This couple lived in a small house about 800 to 1,000 meters north of the entrance to our drive leading to the Vitebsk road. I do not recall their names.

MR. COUNSELLOR SMIRNOV: So you do not remember the names of this couple?

AHRENS: No, I do not recall the names.

MR. COUNSELLOR SMIRNOV: So you heard about the Katyn events from a couple whose names you do not remember, and you did not hear anything about it from other local inhabitants?

AHRENS: Please repeat the question for me.

MR. COUNSELLOR SMIRNOV: Consequently, you heard about these Katyn events only from this couple, whose names you do not remember? From none of the other local inhabitants did you hear anything about the events in Katyn?

AHRENS: I personally heard the facts only from this couple, whereas my soldiers told me the stories current among the other inhabitants.

MR. COUNSELLOR SMIRNOV: Do you know that during the investigation of the Katyn affair, or rather of the Katyn provocation, posters were placarded by the German Police in the streets of Smolensk, promising a reward to anyone giving any information in connection with the Katyn event? It was signed by Lieutenant Voss.

AHRENS: I personally did not see that poster. Lieutenant Voss is known to me by name only.

MR. COUNSELLOR SMIRNOV: And the very last question. Do you know of the report of the Extraordinary State Commission concerning Katyn?

AHRENS: Do you mean the Russian *White Paper* when you mention this report?

MR. COUNSELLOR SMIRNOV: No, I mean the report of the Soviet Extraordinary State Commission, concerning Katyn, the Soviet report.

AHRENS: Yes, I read that report.

MR. COUNSELLOR SMIRNOV: Therefore, you are acquainted with the fact that the Extraordinary State Commission names you as being one of the persons responsible for the crimes committed in Katyn?

AHRENS: It mentions a Lieutenant Colonel Arnes.

MR. COUNSELLOR SMIRNOV: I have no further questions, Mr. President.

THE PRESIDENT: Dr. Stahmer, do you wish to re-examine?

DR. STAHMER: Witness, just a little while ago you said that you did not know when First Lieutenant Hodt joined your staff. Do you know when he joined the regiment?

AHRENS: I know that he belonged to the regiment during the Russian campaign and actually right from the beginning.

DR. STAHMER: That is, he belonged to the regiment from the beginning?

AHRENS: Yes. He belonged to this regiment ever since the beginning of the Russian campaign.

DR. STAHMER: Just one more question dealing with your discussion with Professor Butz. Did Professor Butz mention anything about the last dates on the letters which he found?

AHRENS: He told me about the spring of 1940. He also showed me this diary and I looked at it and I also saw the dates, but I do not recall in detail just which date or dates they were. But they ended with the spring of 1940.

DR. STAHMER: Therefore no documents were found of a later date?

AHRENS: Professor Butz told me that no documents or notes were found which might have given indications of a later date, and he expressed his conviction that these shootings must have taken place in the spring of 1940.

DR. STAHMER: Mr. President, I have no further questions to put to the witness.

THE TRIBUNAL (Gen. Nikitchenko): Witness, can you not remember exactly when Professor Butz discussed with you the date at which the corpses were buried in the mass graves?

AHRENS: May I ask to have the question repeated?

THE TRIBUNAL (Gen. Nikitchenko): When did Professor Butz speak to you about the mass graves and assert that the burial of the corpses must have taken place in the spring of 1940?

AHRENS: I cannot tell you the date exactly, but it was in the spring of 1943, before these exhumations had started—I beg your pardon—he told me that he had been instructed to undertake the exhumation and during the exhumations he was with me from time to time; therefore it may have been in May or the end of April. In the middle of May he gave me details of his exhumations and told me among other things that which I have testified here. I cannot now tell you exactly on which days Professor Butz visited me.

THE TRIBUNAL (Gen. Nikitchenko): So far as I can remember, you stated that Professor Butz arrived in Katyn. When did he actually arrive there?

AHRENS: In the spring of 1940 Professor Butz came to me and told me that on instructions of the army group, he was to undertake exhumations in my woods. The exhumations were started, and in the course of ...

THE TRIBUNAL (Gen. Nikitchenko): You say 1940? Or perhaps the translation is wrong?

AHRENS: 1943, in the spring of 1943. A few weeks after the beginning of the exhumations, Professor Butz visited me, when I happened to be there, and informed me; or, rather, he discussed this matter with me, and he told me that to which I have testified here. It may have been the middle of May 1943.

THE TRIBUNAL (Gen. Nikitchenko): According to your testimony, I understood you to say in answer to a question put by the defense counsel, that Professor Butz asserted that the shootings had taken place in the spring of 1940 before the arrival of the commission for the exhumations. Is that correct?

AHRENS: May I repeat once more that Professor Butz...

THE TRIBUNAL (Gen. Nikitchenko): It is not necessary to repeat what you have already said. I am only asking you, is it correct or not? Maybe the translation was incorrect, or maybe your testimony was incorrect at the beginning.

AHRENS: I did not understand the question just put to me. That is the reason why I wanted to explain this once more. I do not know just what is meant by this last question. May I ask this question be repeated?

THE TRIBUNAL (Gen. Nikitchenko): At the beginning, when you were interrogated by the defense counsel, I understood you to say that Professor Butz told you that the shooting had taken place in the spring of 1940, that is before the arrival of the commission for the exhumations.

AHRENS: No, that has not been understood correctly. I testified that Professor Butz came to me and told me that he was to make exhumations since it concerned my woods. These exhumations then took place, and approximately 6 to 8 weeks later Professor Butz came to me—of course, he visited me on other occasions as well—but approximately 6 to 8 weeks later he came to me and told me that he was convinced that, as a result of his discoveries, he was now able to fix the date of the shootings. This statement which he made to me, refers approximately to the middle of May.

THE TRIBUNAL (Gen. Nikitchenko): Were you present when the diary and the other documents which were shown to you by Professor Butz were found?

AHRENS: No.

THE TRIBUNAL (Gen. Nikitchenko): You do not know where he found the diary and other documents?

AHRENS: No, that I do not know.

THE PRESIDENT: When did you first report to superior authority the fact that you suspected that there was a grave there?

AHRENS: At first, I was not suspicious. I have already mentioned that fighting had taken place there; and at first I did not attach any importance to the stories told to me and did not give this matter any credence. I believed that it was a question of soldiers who had been killed there—of war graves, like several in the vicinity.

117

THE PRESIDENT: You are not answering my question. I am asking you, when did you first report to superior authority that there was a grave there?

AHRENS: In the course of the summer 1942 I spoke to Colonel Von Gersdorff about these stories which had come to my knowledge. Gersdorff told me that he had heard that too, and that ended my conversation with Von Gersdorff. He did not believe it to be true; in any case he was not thoroughly convinced. That I do not know, however.

Then in the spring of 1943, when the snow had melted, the bones which had been found there were brought to me, and I then telephoned to the officer in charge of war graves and told him that apparently there were some soldiers' graves here. That was before Professor Butz had visited me.

THE PRESIDENT: Did you make any report in writing?

AHRENS: No, I did not do that.

THE PRESIDENT: Never?

AHRENS: No, I was not in any way concerned with this matter.

THE PRESIDENT: The witness can retire.

DR. STAHMER: Then, as another witness, I should like to call Lieutenant Reinhard von Eichborn.

THE PRESIDENT: Yes.

[The witness Von Eichborn took the stand.]

Will you state your full name please.

REINHARD VON EICHBORN (Witness): Reinhard von Eichborn.

THE PRESIDENT: Will you repeat this oath after me: I swear by God—the Almighty and Omniscient—that I will speak the pure truth—and will withhold and add nothing.

[The witness repeated the oath.]

THE PRESIDENT: You may sit down.

DR. STAHMER: Witness, what is your occupation?

VON EICHBORN: Assistant judge.

DR. STAHMER: Were you called up for service in the German Armed Forces during this war?

VON EICHBORN: Yes, in August 1939.

DR. STAHMER: And what was your unit?

VON EICHBORN: Army Group Signal Regiment 537.

DR. STAHMER: And what was your rank?

118

VON EICHBORN: At the outbreak of the war, platoon leader and lieutenant.

DR. STAHMER: And at the end?

VON EICHBORN: First lieutenant.

DR. STAHMER: Were you on the Eastern Front during the war?

VON EICHBORN: Yes, from the beginning.

DR. STAHMER: With your regiment?

VON EICHBORN: No, from 1940 onward, on the staff of Army Group Center.

DR. STAHMER: Apart from this Regiment 537, was there an Engineer Battalion 537?

VON EICHBORN: In the sphere of the Army Group Center there was no Engineer Battalion 537.

DR. STAHMER: When did you arrive with your unit in the vicinity of Katyn?

VON EICHBORN: About 20 September the staff of Army Group Center transferred its headquarters to Smolensk, that is to say in the Smolensk region.

DR. STAHMER: Where had you been stationed before?

VON EICHBORN: How am I to understand this question?

DR. STAHMER: Where did you come from?

VON EICHBORN: We came from Borisov.

THE PRESIDENT: One moment. The witness said 20 September. That does not identify the year.

DR. STAHMER: In what year was this 20 September?

VON EICHBORN: 20 September 1941.

DR. STAHMER: Was Regiment 537 already there at that time?

VON EICHBORN: The staff of Regiment 537 was transferred at about the same time together with the staff of the army group to the place where the headquarters of the army group was. Advance units had already been stationed there previously, in order to set up communication facilities.

DR. STAHMER: And where was this staff accommodated?

VON EICHBORN: The staff of Army Group Signal Regiment 537 was accommodated in the so-called Dnieper Castle.

DR. STAHMER: Where was the advance unit?

VON EICHBORN: The advance unit may have occupied this building, too—or at least a part of this advance unit did—to safeguard this building for the regimental staff.

DR. STAHMER: Do you know who was in command of this advance unit?

VON EICHBORN: Lieutenant Hodt was in command of this advance unit.

DR. STAHMER: When did this advance unit come to Katyn?

VON EICHBORN: Smolensk fell on about 17 July 1941. The army group had planned to put up its headquarters in the immediate vicinity of Smolensk, and, after this group had selected its quarters, this region was seized immediately after the fall of the city. The advance unit arrived at the same time as this area was seized, and that was probably in the second half of July of 1941.

DR. STAHMER: Therefore the advance unit was there from July of 1941 until 20 September 1941?

VON EICHBORN: Yes.

DR. STAHMER: And the entire staff was there from 20 September 1941?

VON EICHBORN: Yes. It may be that part of the staff arrived somewhat later, but the majority of the staff arrived on 20 September.

THE PRESIDENT: Are you speaking of the staff of the army group or the staff of the signal regiment?

VON EICHBORN: I am speaking of both staffs, because the moving of large staffs such as that of an army group could not be undertaken in 1 day; usually 2 to 3 days were needed for that. The operations of the signal corps had to be assured, and therefore the regiment had to leave some of the staff behind until the entire staff had been moved.

DR. STAHMER: Where was the advance unit accommodated?

VON EICHBORN: At least part of the advance unit was accommodated in the Dnieper Castle. Some of the others were in the neighborhood of those places where later on the companies were billeted. The reason for that was to keep the billets ready for this regiment until the bulk of it had been moved.

DR. STAHMER: How about the Regimental Staff 537?

VON EICHBORN: That was in the Dnieper Castle.

DR. STAHMER: Can you give us the names of the officers who belonged to the regimental staff?

VON EICHBORN: At that time there was Lieutenant Colonel Bedenck, the commanding officer; Lieutenant Rex, adjutant; Lieutenant Hodt, orderly officer; and a Captain Schäfer, who was a telephone expert. It may be that one or two others were there as well, but I can no longer remember their names.

DR. STAHMER: The preceding witness has already told us about the tasks of the regimental staff. How were the activities of the regimental staff controlled?

VON EICHBORN: The regiment, which consisted of 10 to 12 companies, had to give an exact report each evening as to what work had been allotted to the various companies. This was necessary as we had to know what forces were available in case of emergency, for undertaking any new tasks.

DR. STAHMER: How far away from the Dnieper Castle were you billeted?

VON EICHBORN: Approximately 4 to 5 kilometers. I cannot give you the exact distance as I always made it by car, but it would be about 4 to 5 kilometers.

DR. STAHMER: Did you frequently go to Dnieper Castle?

VON EICHBORN: Very frequently when I was off duty, as I had belonged to this regiment and knew most of the officers, with whom I was on friendly terms.

DR. STAHMER: Can you tell us about the kind and extent of the traffic to the Dnieper Castle?

VON EICHBORN: In order to judge this you have to differentiate between persons and things. So far as people were concerned, the traffic was very lively because the regiment had to be very centrally organized in order to be equal to its tasks. Therefore, many couriers came and commanders of the various companies frequently came to visit the regimental staff.

On the other hand there was a heavy traffic of trucks and passenger cars, because the regiment tried to improve its billets there; and since we remained there for some time all sorts of building alterations were carried out in the house.

DR. STAHMER: Did you hear anything about there being three Russian camps with captured Polish officers, 25 to 45 kilometers west of Smolensk, which had allegedly fallen into German hands?

VON EICHBORN: I never heard anything about any kind of Polish officers' camps or Polish prisoner-of-war camps.

DR. STAHMER: Did your army group receive reports about the capture of such Polish officers?

VON EICHBORN: No. I would have noticed that, since the number of prisoners, and especially the number of officers, was always submitted to me in the evening reports of the armies which took these prisoners. It was our responsibility to receive these signal reports and we therefore saw them every evening.

DR. STAHMER: You did not receive a report to that effect?

VON EICHBORN: I neither saw such a report from an army, which would have issued it, nor did I ever receive a report from an army group which would have had to transmit this report in their evening bulletin to the High Command of the Army (OKH).

DR. STAHMER: Could a report like that have been handed in from another source or been sent to another office?

VON EICHBORN: The official channel in the Army was very stringent, and the staffs saw to it that official channels were strictly adhered to. In any case the armies were always required to make the detailed reports, following the lines stipulated in the form sheets and this applied especially to the figures concerning prisoners. Therefore, it is quite out of the question that if such a number of officers had fallen into the hands of an army, it would not have reported the matter through the appropriate channel.

DR. STAHMER: You said, just a little while ago, that you were in particularly close relationship with the officers of this regiment. Did you ever hear that Polish prisoners of war, officers, were shot at some time or other in the Katyn forest at the instigation of Regiment 537 under Colonel Bedenck or under Colonel Ahrens?

VON EICHBORN: I knew nearly all the officers of the regiment, as I myself had been over a year with the regiment, and I was on such familiar terms with most of the officers that they told me everything that took place, even anything of an unofficial nature. Therefore, it is quite out of the question that such an important matter should not have come to my knowledge. From the nature of the whole character moulding in the regiment, it is quite impossible that there should not have been at least one who would have come to tell me about it immediately.

DR. STAHMER: Were all the operational orders for Regiment 537 officially known to you?

VON EICHBORN: The operational orders for this army group signal regiment were twofold: The orders which concerned only the wireless company and those which applied to the nine telephone companies. Since I was a telephone expert, it was quite natural for me to draft these orders and submit them to my superior, General Oberhäuser. Therefore, each order which was issued had either been drafted by me or I had seen it beforehand.

DR. STAHMER: Was there ever at any time an order given out by your office to shoot Polish prisoners of war?

VON EICHBORN: Such an order was neither given to the regiment by our office nor by any other office. Neither did we receive a report to this effect, nor did we hear about things like that through any other channel.

DR. STAHMER: If an order like that came through official channels, it could come only through you?

VON EICHBORN: This order would have necessitated a great many members of the regiment being taken away from their own duties, which were to safeguard the system of communications. As we were very short of signallers, we had to know what almost every man in the regiment was doing. It would have been quite out of the question for any member of the regiment to have been taken away from such a duty without our knowledge.

DR. STAHMER: I have no further questions, Mr. President.

THE PRESIDENT: Dr. Kranzbühler, whom are you appearing on behalf of?

FLOTTENRICHTER KRANZBÜHLER: For Grossadmiral Dönitz, Mr. President.

THE PRESIDENT: There is no charge made against Grossadmiral Dönitz in connection with this offense at all.

FLOTTENRICHTER KRANZBÜHLER: Mr. President, the exhumations and the propaganda connected with them occurred during the period when Grossadmiral Dönitz was Commander-in-Chief of the Navy. The Prosecution alleges that at that time Grossadmiral Dönitz was a member of the Cabinet and had participated in all acts taken by the Government. Therefore, I must consider him as being implicated in all the problems arising out of the Katyn case.

THE PRESIDENT: That would mean that we should have to hear examination from everybody who was connected with the Government. And the Tribunal has already pointed out, with reference to Admiral Raeder, that his case was not connected with this matter. It is only when a case is directly connected with the matter that counsel for the individual defendants are allowed to cross-examine, in addition to the defendant's counsel who calls the witness. If there is any suggestion that you want to make to the counsel who is calling the witness, you can make it to him, but you are not entitled ...

FLOTTENRICHTER KRANZBÜHLER: But I am asking your permission to put two or three questions to this witness.

THE PRESIDENT: If you have any special questions to put, you may suggest them to Dr. Stahmer, and Dr. Stahmer will put them. Dr. Kranzbühler, if you want to put any questions, you may put them to Dr. Stahmer, and he will put them to the witness.

FLOTTENRICHTER KRANZBÜHLER: Mr. President, I did not quite understand. Shall I propose to Dr. Stahmer to put the questions or...

THE PRESIDENT: If you cannot do it verbally, you may do it in writing, and you may do it later on. But I really do not think there can be any questions which are so difficult to suggest to Dr. Stahmer as all that.

FLOTTENRICHTER KRANZBÜHLER: They can also be put through Dr. Stahmer. I was only thinking that I would save some time by putting the questions myself.

THE PRESIDENT: I told you if you wish to ask any questions, you must ask them through Dr. Stahmer.

FLOTTENRICHTER KRANZBÜHLER: Thank you, Mr. President.

THE PRESIDENT: In the meantime, the Tribunal will go on with the cross-examination, and any questions which you wish to put can be put in re-examination.

Does the Prosecution wish to cross-examine?

MR. COUNSELLOR SMIRNOV: Witness, I am interested to know your exact function in the army. Were you in charge of teleprinter communications at the headquarters of Army Group Center or were you a wireless expert?

VON EICHBORN: No, Mr. Prosecutor, you are wrong. I was the telephone expert of Army Group Center, not the wireless expert.

MR. COUNSELLOR SMIRNOV: That is exactly what I am asking you. The translation was evidently incorrect. So you were in charge of telephone communications, were you not?

VON EICHBORN: Yes; you are right.

MR. COUNSELLOR SMIRNOV: Ordinary telegrams, or ciphered telegrams?

VON EICHBORN: The task of a telephone expert connected with an army group consisted in keeping the telephone lines intact.

MR. COUNSELLOR SMIRNOV: No, I am not interested in the tasks in a general way. I would like to know whether these were secret ciphered telegrams or the ordinary army mail, army communications which were not secret.

VON EICHBORN: There were two kinds of telegrams, open and secret.

MR. COUNSELLOR SMIRNOV: Were secret telegrams transmitted by you, too?

VON EICHBORN: Both came through me.

MR. COUNSELLOR SMIRNOV: Consequently, all communications between the Wehrmacht, between Army units and the highest police authorities also passed through you; is that correct?

VON EICHBORN: The most important telegrams, and especially the secret ones were submitted to the telephone expert.

MR. COUNSELLOR SMIRNOV: Yes. Consequently, the correspondence between the police authorities and the Armed Forces units passed through you; is that correct? I am asking you this question for a second time.

VON EICHBORN: I must answer with the reservation that the messages did not pass through the telephone expert, but only the most important secret teletype matters were submitted to him—not the whole correspondence, because that went also through the mail as well as by courier service.

MR. COUNSELLOR SMIRNOV: That is clear. Do you know in this case that in September and October 1941 there were special detachments in Smolensk whose duty, in close co-operation with the Army, was to carry out the so-called purge of the prisoner-of-war camps and the extermination of prisoners of war?

DR. LATERNSER: Mr. President, I must decisively object to this questioning of the witness. This questioning can have only the purpose of determining the relations between the General Staff and the OKW and any commands of the Security Service. Therefore, they are accusing the General Staff and the OKW; and if I, Mr. President, as defense counsel for the General Staff and the OKW am not permitted to put questions, then on the basis of equal treatment, the same rules must apply to the Prosecution as well.

MR. COUNSELLOR SMIRNOV: May I, Mr. President, make a short statement?

THE PRESIDENT: Colonel Smirnov, the question is competent.

MR. COUNSELLOR SMIRNOV: I beg your pardon.

THE PRESIDENT: I said the question was competent. You may ask the question.

MR. COUNSELLOR SMIRNOV: I would like to ask you the following question, Witness. Since all secret teletypes passed through you, did you ever encounter among these telegrams any from the so-called 1st Einsatzgruppe "B"—that was the so-called first command—or from the Special Command "Moscow" which at that time was located at Smolensk and kept in reserve in anticipation of better times? The latter had the order to perpetrate mass murders in Moscow. Both commands were located at Smolensk at that time.

VON EICHBORN: No such reports came into my hands. I can fully explain this to you, Mr. Prosecutor. When any detachments of this sort had been established in the area of Army Group Center, these detachments had their own wireless stations. It was only later on in the course of the Russian campaign that these posts had teletype facilities as well; then they used the army group network. However, that only happened later.

MR. COUNSELLOR SMIRNOV: Consequently, the telegrams of those special units which, by order of high police authorities, were assigned to carry out special actions in co-operation with military units, did not pass through your hands in September and October of 1941?

VON EICHBORN: That is correct. At that time, there were no teletype facilities and offices for such special units, even if they were in that area at all.

MR. COUNSELLOR SMIRNOV: Mr. President, this document was already presented to the Court together with the Extraordinary State Commission Report, Document Number USSR-3. If the High Tribunal will permit it, I should like to present to the Tribunal and to the Defense photostatic copies of one of the documents which was attached to the report of the Extraordinary State Commission. If the Tribunal will look at Page 2 of this document, it will see that the Special Command "Moscow" and the Einsatzgruppe "B" were both located in Smolensk. It says on the first page that these detachments together with units of the Armed Forces, were assigned to carry out mass killings in the camps. If the Tribunal will permit me, I shall submit this document now . . .

THE PRESIDENT: Colonel Smirnov, that is a matter of argument. We shall take judicial notice of it, of course, of everything which is in the Soviet Government's publication. And I understand you to say that this document is a part of the Soviet Government communication or Soviet Government report.

MR. COUNSELLOR SMIRNOV: Yes, Mr. President; but I would like to ask permission to present an original German document, a secret document, which states that in the Smolensk area there were two large special commands whose duties were to carry out mass murders in the camps, and that these actions had to be carried out together with the Armed Forces units which had to co-operate with them.

THE PRESIDENT: Colonel Smirnov, is this document which you have just handed up to us a part of the report USSR-3?

MR. COUNSELLOR SMIRNOV: Yes, Mr. President, it is a part of the report, Document USSR-3, called "Special Directives of the Hitler Government Concerning the Annihilation of Prisoners of War." I would like to ask the Tribunal to allow me to present one of the original documents even if the report, USSR-3, has been already submitted in full.

It says there that these special units were located in Smolensk and were assigned together with the Armed Forces units to carry out mass killings in the camps.

THE PRESIDENT: Yes, Colonel Smirnov. This document is already in evidence, if the Tribunal understands correctly.

MR. COUNSELLOR SMIRNOV: Thank you, Mr. President.

[Turning to the witness.] Consequently, we may consider it as an established fact that the correspondence, the telegraphic messages of these special detachments did not pass through your hands; is that correct?

THE PRESIDENT: He has said that twice already.

MR. COUNSELLOR SMIRNOV: Excuse me, Mr. President.

[Turning to the witness.] Why did you assert with such certainty that there were no reports about the killing of the Poles? You know that the killing of the Polish prisoners of war was a special action, and any report about this action would have to pass through your hands? Is that correct?

VON EICHBORN: I answered the prosecutor—rather, I answered Dr. Stahmer—that if in the area of Army Group Signal Regiment 537 killings of that sort had taken place, I would undoubtedly have known about them. I did not state what the prosecutor is now trying to ascribe to me.

THE PRESIDENT: Colonel Smirnov, the Tribunal think you had better read this passage from this document, which is in the German language, to the Tribunal so that it will go into the record.

MR. COUNSELLOR SMIRNOV: In this document, Mr. President, it is stated...

THE PRESIDENT: Go on, Colonel Smirnov.

MR. COUNSELLOR SMIRNOV: Thank you, Mr. President.

This document is dated "Berlin, 29 October 1941." It is headed, "The Chief of the Security Police and of the Security Service." It has a classification, "Top Secret; Urgent letter; Operational Order Number-14." Reference is made to decrees of 17 July and 12 September 1941. I shall now read a few short sentences, and I shall begin with the first sentence:

"In the appendix, I am sending directions for the evacuation of Soviet civilian prisoners and prisoners of war out of permanent prisoner-of-war camps and transit camps in the rear of the Army...

"These directives have been worked out in collaboration with the Army High Command. The Army High Command has notified the commanders of the armies in the rear as well as the local commanders of the prisoner-of-war camps and of the transit camps.

"The task force groups, depending on the size of the camp in their territory, are setting up special commands in sufficient strength under the leadership of an SS leader. The commands are instructed immediately to start work in the camps."

I break off here, and will continue reading the last paragraph:

"I emphasize especially that Operational Orders Number 8 and 14 as well as the appendix are to be destroyed immediately in the case of immediate danger."

I shall finish my reading and now I shall only mention the distribution list. On Page 2 I quote the part concerning Smolensk. It says here that in Smolensk the Einsatzgruppe "B" was located, consisting of Special Commands 7a, 7b, 8, and 9; and in addition to this, there was already located in Smolensk a special command, which had been rather prematurely named "Moscow" by its organizers.

These are the contents of the document, Mr. President.

THE PRESIDENT: The Tribunal directs that the whole document shall be translated. We will now recess until 5 minutes past 2 o'clock.

[The Tribunal recessed until 1405 hours.]

Afternoon Session

MR. COUNSELLOR SMIRNOV: Mr. President, I have no more questions to put to this witness.

THE PRESIDENT: Dr. Stahmer.

DR. STAHMER: Witness, do you know who owned that little castle near the Dnieper before the occupation by German troops? Who owned it, who lived there?

VON EICHBORN: I cannot say that for certain. We noticed that the little castle was astonishingly well furnished. It was very well laid out. It had two bathrooms, a rifle range, and a cinema. We drew certain conclusions therefrom, when the facts became known, but I do not know anything about the previous owner.

DR. STAHMER: The Russian Prosecutor submitted to you a document dated 29 October 1941, "Directives to the Chief of the Sipo for the Detachments in the Stalags." With reference to that document, I want to ask you whether you had an opportunity personally to ascertain the attitude of Field Marshal Kluge, your commander of Army Group Center, regarding the shooting of prisoners of war?

VON EICHBORN: By chance I became the ear-witness of a conversation between the Commanders Bock and Kluge. That conversation took place about 3 or 4 weeks before the beginning of the Russian campaign. I cannot tell you the exact time. At the time Field Marshal Von Bock was the commander of Army Group Center, and Field Marshal Von Kluge was commander of the 4th Army. The army group was in Posen and the 4th Army at Warsaw. One day I was called by the aide-de-camp of Field Marshal Von Bock, who was Lieutenant Colonel Count Hardenberg. He gave me the order...

THE PRESIDENT: These details are entirely irrelevant, aren't they. All you want to ask him is: What was the attitude of Von Kluge? That is all.

DR. STAHMER: The answer did not come through. I did not understand what you said, Mr. President.

THE PRESIDENT: What I said was that all these details about the particular place where Von Kluge met some other army group commander are utterly irrelevant. All you are trying to ask him is: What was Von Kluge's attitude toward the murder of war prisoners? Isn't that all?

DR. STAHMER: Yes.

[Turning to the witness.] Will you answer the question briefly, Witness. Please just tell us what Von Kluge said.

VON EICHBORN: Von Kluge told Von Bock, during a telephone conversation, that the order for the shooting of certain prisoners of war was an impossibility and could not be carried out, with regard to the discipline of the troops. Von Bock shared this point of view and both these gentlemen talked for half an hour about the measures which they wanted to adopt against this order.

DR. STAHMER: According to the allegations of the Prosecution, the shooting of these 11,000 Polish officers is supposed to have been carried out sometime in September 1941. The question now is: Do you consider it possible, in view of local conditions, that such mass shootings and burials could have been carried out next door to the regimental headquarters without you yourself having heard about it?

VON EICHBORN: We were very busy in preparation for the move of the army group to Smolensk. We had assigned a great number of signal troops for setting up perfect installations. On the entire site there was a constant going and coming of troops laying cables and telephone lines. It is out of the question that anything of this kind could have occurred in that particular area without the regiment and I getting knowledge of it.

DR. STAHMER: I have no further questions to put to the witness, Mr. President.

THE PRESIDENT: The witness can retire.

DR. STAHMER: Mr. President, before calling my third witness, Lieutenant General Oberhäuser, may I ask your permission to make the following remarks?

The Prosecution has up to now only alleged that Regiment Number 537 was the one which had carried out these shootings and that under Colonel Ahrens' command. Today again, Colonel Ahrens has been named by the Prosecution as being the perpetrator. Apparently this allegation has been dropped and it has been said that if it was not Ahrens then it must have been his predecessor, Colonel Bedenck; and if Colonel Bedenck did not do it, then apparently—and this seems to be the third version—it was done by the SD. The Defense had taken the position solely that Colonel Ahrens was accused as the perpetrator and it has refuted that allegation. Considering the changed situation and the attitude adopted by the Prosecution, I shall have to name a fourth witness in addition. That is First Lieutenant Hodt, who has been mentioned today as the perpetrator and who was with the regimental staff right from the beginning and who was, as we have told, the senior of the advance party which arrived at the Dnieper Castle in July. I got the address of First Lieutenant Hodt by chance yesterday. He is at Glücksburg near Flensburg; and I, therefore, ask to be allowed to name as a witness First Lieutenant Hodt, who will give evidence that during the time between July and September such shootings did not occur

130

THE PRESIDENT: Dr. Stahmer, the Tribunal will consider your application, when they adjourn at half past 3, with reference to this extra witness.

DR. STAHMER: Yes, Sir. Then I shall now call Lieutenant General Oberhäuser as witness.

[The witness Oberhäuser took the stand.]

THE PRESIDENT: Will you state your full name, please?

EUGEN OBERHÄUSER (Witness): Eugen Oberhäuser.

THE PRESIDENT: Will you repeat this oath after me: I swear by God—the Almighty and Omniscient—that I will speak the pure truth—and will withhold and add nothing.

[The witness repeated the oath.]

THE PRESIDENT: You may sit down.

DR. STAHMER: General, what position did you hold during the war?

OBERHÄUSER: I was the signal commander in an army group, first of all during the Polish campaign, in Army Group North; then, in the Western campaign Army Group B; and then in Russia, Army Group Center.

DR. STAHMER: When did you and your staff reach the neighborhood of Katyn?

OBERHÄUSER: Sometime during September 1941.

DR. STAHMER: Where was your staff located?

OBERHÄUSER: My staff was located in the immediate vicinity of the commander of the army group; that is to say, about 12 kilometers west of Smolensk, near the railroad station of Krasnibor.

DR. STAHMER: Was Regiment Number 537 under your command?

OBERHÄUSER: Regiment 537 was directly under my command.

DR. STAHMER: What task did that regiment have?

OBERHÄUSER: That regiment had the task of establishing both telegraph and wireless communications between the command of the army group and the various armies and other units which were directly under its command.

DR. STAHMER: Was the staff of the regiment stationed near you?

OBERHÄUSER: The staff of that regiment was located about 3, perhaps 4 kilometers west from my own position.

DR. STAHMER: Can you give us more detailed information regarding the exact location of the staff headquarters of Number 537?

OBERHÄUSER: The staff headquarters of 537 was in a very nice Russian timber house. Commissars were supposed to have been living there before. It was on the steep bank of the Dnieper River. It was somewhat off the road, perhaps 400 to 500 meters away. It was, from my place, 4 kilometers west of the main highway Smolensk to Vitebsk.

DR. STAHMER: Who was the commanding officer of the regiment after the capture of Smolensk?

OBERHÄUSER: After the capture of Smolensk, Colonel Bedenck was the commander of the regiment.

DR. STAHMER: For how long?

OBERHÄUSER: Until about November 1941.

DR. STAHMER: Who was his successor?

OBERHÄUSER: His successor was Colonel Ahrens.

DR. STAHMER: How long?

OBERHÄUSER: Approximately until September—it may have been August—1943.

DR. STAHMER: Were you near Katyn as long as that, too?

OBERHÄUSER: I was there until the command of the army group transferred its headquarters farther west.

DR. STAHMER: What were your relations with the commanders of this regiment?

OBERHÄUSER: My relations with the regimental commanders were most hearty, both officially and privately, which is due to the fact that I had been the first commander of that regiment. I myself had formed the regiment and I was most attached to it.

DR. STAHMER: Did you personally visit the little Dnieper Castle frequently?

OBERHÄUSER: I went to the Dnieper Castle frequently; I can well say in normal times once or twice a week.

DR. STAHMER: Did the commanders visit you in the meantime?

OBERHÄUSER: The commanders came to see me more frequently than I went to see them.

DR. STAHMER: Did you know anything about the fact that near Smolensk, about 25 to 45 kilometers to the west, there were three Russian camps which contained Polish prisoners of war ...

OBERHÄUSER: I knew nothing of that.

DR. STAHMER: ... who had fallen into the hands of the Germans?

OBERHÄUSER: I never heard anything about it.

DR. STAHMER: Was there an order, which is supposed to have come from Berlin, that Polish officers who were prisoners of war were to be shot?

OBERHÄUSER: No, such an order was never issued.

DR. STAHMER: Did you yourself ever give such an order?

OBERHÄUSER: I have never given such an order.

DR. STAHMER: Do you know whether Colonel Bedenck or Colonel Ahrens ever caused such shootings to be carried out?

OBERHÄUSER: I am not informed, but I consider it absolutely impossible.

DR. STAHMER: Why?

OBERHÄUSER: First, because such a decisive order would necessarily have gone through me, for I was the direct superior of the regiment; and second, because if such an order had been given, for a reason which I could not understand, and transmitted to the regiment through some obscure channel, then the commanders would most certainly have rung me up or they would have come to see me and said, "General, they are asking something here which we cannot understand."

DR. STAHMER: Do you know First Lieutenant Hodt?

OBERHÄUSER: Yes, I know him.

DR. STAHMER: What position did he have in Regiment 537?

OBERHÄUSER: Hodt held various posts in the regiment. Usually, he was sent ahead because he was a particularly qualified officer—especially in regard to technical qualifications—in order to make preparations when headquarters was being changed. He was therefore used as advance party of the so-called technical company in order to establish the new command posts; and then he was the regimental expert for the telephone system, dealing with all matters relating to the telephone and teletype system with the command headquarters of the army group. In my staff he was occasionally detailed to fill the positions of any of my officers when they were on leave.

DR. STAHMER: Was he also in charge of the advance party during the advance on Katyn?

OBERHÄUSER: That I cannot say. I can only say that I personally heard from my staff signal commander that he had sent an officer ahead, after it had been ascertained how the headquarters were to be laid out, that this officer was acting on my behalf, as at the time I still remained in the old quarters, and he was preparing things in the way I wanted them from the point of view of the signal commander. I do not know who was in charge of that advance party at the time, but it is quite possible that it was First Lieutenant Hodt.

DR. STAHMER: Were you in Katyn or the vicinity during the period after the capture of Smolensk, which was, I believe, on or about 20 July 1941, and up to the transfer of your staff to Katyn on 20 September?

OBERHÄUSER: I was in the vicinity. I was where the headquarters of the army. group wanted to settle down; that is, in the woods west of Smolensk, where Katyn is located.

DR. STAHMER: Were you frequently there during that time?

OBERHÄUSER: I should say three or four times.

DR. STAHMER: Did you talk to Hodt on those occasions?

OBERHÄUSER: If he was the officer in charge of the advance party, which I cannot say today, then I must certainly have talked to him. At any rate, I did talk to the officer whom I had sent ahead and also to the one from my regiment.

DR. STAHMER: Did you hear anything about shootings occurring during that time?

OBERHÄUSER: I heard nothing, nor did I hear anything at all except in 1943, when the graves were opened.

DR. STAHMER: Did you or Regiment 537 have the necessary technical means, pistols, ammunition, and so on, at your disposal which would have made it possible to carry out shootings on such a scale?

OBERHÄUSER: The regiment, being a signal regiment in the rear area, was not equipped with weapons and ammunition as well as the actual fighting troops. Such a task, however, would have been something unusual for the regiment; first, because a signal regiment has completely different tasks, and secondly it would not have been in a position technically to carry out such mass executions.

DR. STAHMER: Do you know the place where these graves were discovered later on?

OBERHÄUSER: I know the site because I drove past it a great deal.

DR. STAHMER: Can you describe it more accurately?

OBERHÄUSER: Taking the main road Smolensk-Vitebsk, a path led through wooded undulating ground. There were sandy spaces, which were, however, covered with scrub and heather, and along that narrow path one got to the Dnieper Castle from the main road.

DR. STAHMER: Were the places where these graves were later discovered already overgrown when you got there?

OBERHÄUSER: They were overgrown just like the surrounding ground, and there was no difference between them and the rest of the surroundings.

DR. STAHMER: In view of your knowledge of the place, would you consider it possible that 11,000 Poles could have been buried at that spot, people who may have been shot between June and September 1941?

OBERHÄUSER: I consider that it is out of the question, for the mere reason that if the commander had known it at the time he would certainly never have chosen this spot for his headquarters, next to 11,000 dead.

DR. STAHMER: Can you tell me how the graves were discovered?

OBERHÄUSER: Officially I had nothing to do with that. I only heard that through local inhabitants or somebody else it had become known that large-scale executions had taken place there years ago.

DR. STAHMER: From whom did you hear that?

OBERHÄUSER: Quite probably from the commander himself, who, because he was located on the spot, had heard more about it than I had. But I cannot remember exactly now.

DR. STAHMER: So you did not receive official notice about the discovery of the graves, did you?

OBERHÄUSER: No, I never did.

DR. STAHMER: After the opening of the graves, did you talk to the German or foreign members of the commission?

OBERHÄUSER: I have never talked to any members of that commission.

DR. STAHMER: I have no further questions, Mr. President.

THE PRESIDENT: Colonel Smirnov.

MR. COUNSELLOR SMIRNOV: Witness, you arrived in the region of Katyn in September 1943?

OBERHÄUSER: 1941, not 1943.

MR. COUNSELLOR SMIRNOV: Excuse me, I meant September 1941. Is that correct?

OBERHÄUSER: Yes, September 1941.

MR. COUNSELLOR SMIRNOV: And you contend that you did not know anything either about the camps for Polish prisoners of war or the prisoners in the hands of the German troops, is that so?

OBERHÄUSER: I have never heard anything about Polish prisoners of war being in the hands of German troops.

135

MR. COUNSELLOR SMIRNOV: I understand that this had no relation to your official activity as the commander of a signal regiment. But in spite of this you may perhaps have witnessed that various German troops combed the woods in the vicinity of the Smolensk-Vitebsk highway to capture Polish prisoners of war who had escaped from the camps?

OBERHÄUSER: I never heard anything about troops going there in order to, shall we say, recapture escaped Polish prisoners of war. I am hearing this here for the first time.

MR. COUNSELLOR SMIRNOV: Please answer me. Have you perhaps seen German military units escorting Polish prisoners of war who were captured in the woods?

OBERHÄUSER: I have not seen that.

MR. COUNSELLOR SMIRNOV: Please answer the following question: You were on good terms with Colonel Ahrens, were you not?

OBERHÄUSER: I have had good relations with all commanders of the regiment.

MR. COUNSELLOR SMIRNOV: And in addition to that, you were his immediate superior?

OBERHÄUSER: Right.

MR. COUNSELLOR SMIRNOV: Colonel Ahrens found out about the mass graves at the end of 1941 or at the beginning of 1942. Did he tell you anything about his discovery?

OBERHÄUSER: I cannot believe that Colonel Ahrens could have discovered the graves in 1941. I cannot imagine that—I especially cannot imagine that he would tell me nothing about it.

MR. COUNSELLOR SMIRNOV: In any case do you contend that neither in 1942 nor in 1943 did Colonel Ahrens report to you in regard to this affair?

OBERHÄUSER: Colonel Ahrens never told me anything about it, and he would have told me if he had known.

MR. COUNSELLOR SMIRNOV: I am interested in the following answer which you gave to a question by defense counsel. You remarked that the signal regiment had not enough weapons to carry out shootings. What do you mean by that? How many, and what kind of weapons did the regiment possess?

OBERHÄUSER: The signal regiment were mostly equipped with pistols and with carbines. They had no automatic arms.

MR. COUNSELLOR SMIRNOV: Pistols? Of what caliber?

OBERHÄUSER: They were Parabellum pistols. The caliber, I think, was 7.65, but I cannot remember for certain.

MR. COUNSELLOR SMIRNOV: Parabellum pistols, 7.65, or were there Mauser pistols or any other kind of weapons?

OBERHÄUSER: That varied. Noncommissioned officers, as far as I know, had the smaller Mauser pistols. Actually, only noncommissioned officers were equipped with pistols. The majority of the men had carbines.

MR. COUNSELLOR SMIRNOV: I would like you to tell us some more about the pistols. You say that they were 7.65 caliber pistols, is that so?

OBERHÄUSER: I cannot now, at the moment, give you exact information about the caliber. I only know that the Parabellum pistol was 7.65 or some such caliber. I think the Mauser pistol had a somewhat smaller caliber.

MR. COUNSELLOR SMIRNOV: And Walter pistols?

OBERHÄUSER: There were also Walters. I think they had the same caliber as the Mauser. It is a smaller, black pistol; and it is better than the somewhat cumbersome Parabellum pistol which is heavier.

MR. COUNSELLOR SMIRNOV: Yes, that is quite correct. Please tell me whether in this regiment the noncommissioned officers possessed those small pistols.

OBERHÄUSER: As a rule, noncommissioned officers had pistols but not carbines.

MR. COUNSELLOR SMIRNOV: I see. Perhaps you can tell us about how many pistols this signal regiment possessed?

OBERHÄUSER: Of course I cannot tell you that now. Let us assume that every noncommissioned officer had a pistol . . .

MR. COUNSELLOR SMIRNOV: And how many noncommissioned officers were there? How many pistols in all were there in your regiment if you consider that every noncommissioned officer had a pistol?

OBERHÄUSER: Assuming that every noncommissioned officer in the regiment had a pistol that would amount to 15 per company, a total of 150. However, to give a definite statement about that figure retrospectively now is impossible. I can only give you clues.

MR. COUNSELLOR SMIRNOV: Why do you consider that 150 pistols would be insufficient to carry out these mass killings which went on over a period of time? What makes you so positive about that?

OBERHÄUSER: Because a signal regiment of an army group deployed over a large area as in the case of Army Group Center is never together as a unit. The regiment was spread out from Kolodov as far as Vitebsk, and there were small detachments everywhere, and in the headquarters of the regiment there were comparatively few people; in other words, there were never 150 pistols in one and the same place.

MR. COUNSELLOR SMIRNOV: The main part of the signal regiment was located in the Katyn woods, was it not?

OBERHÄUSER: I did not understand your question.

MR. COUNSELLOR SMIRNOV: The main portions of your regiment were located in the Katyn woods, were they not?

OBERHÄUSER: The first company was mainly located between the regimental staff quarters and the actual command post of the army group. That was the company which was handling the communications, the telephone and teleprinted communications for the army group. It was the company, therefore, which was nearest.

MR. COUNSELLOR SMIRNOV: One more question. The officers of your regiment were obviously armed with pistols and not with carbines?

OBERHÄUSER: Officers had pistols only, and as a rule they only had small ones. Possibly one or the other may have had a Parabellum pistol.

MR. COUNSELLOR SMIRNOV: That is to say either a Walter or a Mauser?

OBERHÄUSER: Yes.

MR. COUNSELLOR SMIRNOV: Did you frequently visit the villa where the headquarters of Regiment 537 was located?

OBERHÄUSER: Yes, I was there at least once, sometimes twice, a week.

MR. COUNSELLOR SMIRNOV: Were you ever interested as to why soldiers from other military units visited the villa in Kozy Gory and why special beds were prepared for them as well as drinks and food?

OBERHÄUSER: I cannot imagine that there were any large-scale visits of other soldiers or members of other units. I do not know anything about that.

MR. COUNSELLOR SMIRNOV: I am not speaking about a great number. I am speaking of 20 or sometimes 25 men.

OBERHÄUSER: If the regimental commander summoned his company and detachment commanders for an officers' meeting, then, of course, there would be a few dozen of such officers who normally would not be seen there.

MR. COUNSELLOR SMIRNOV: No, I am not talking about officers who belonged to the unit. I would like to ask you another somewhat different question. Would the number 537 appear on the shoulder straps of the soldiers belonging to that regiment?

OBERHÄUSER: As far as I recollect the number was on the shoulder straps, but at the beginning of the war it could be concealed by a camouflage flap. I cannot remember whether during that particular period these covers were used or not. At any rate at the street entrance to the regimental headquarters there was a black-yellow-black flag, which bore the number 537.

MR. COUNSELLOR SMIRNOV: I am speaking of soldiers who came to the villa in Kozy Gory, and who did not have the number 537 on their shoulder straps. Were you ever interested in finding out what those soldiers did there in September and October of 1941? Did the commander of the unit report to you about this?

OBERHÄUSER: May I ask what year this was supposed to be, 1941?

MR. COUNSELLOR SMIRNOV: Yes, 1941, that is the year which is concerned.

OBERHÄUSER: I do not think that at that time there was much coming and going of outsiders at staff headquarters because during that period everything was in course of construction and I cannot imagine that other units, even small groups of 20 or 25 people should have been there. I personally, as I have told you, was there only once or twice weekly, and not before September or October.

MR. COUNSELLOR SMIRNOV: Beginning with what date of September did you start visiting there? You said it was in September but not from what date.

OBERHÄUSER: I cannot tell you. The commander of the army group moved at the end of September from Borossilov, shortly before the battle of Vyazma, which was on 2 October, into that district.

MR. COUNSELLOR SMIRNOV: Consequently, you could start visiting this villa for instance only at the end of September or the beginning of October 1941?

OBERHÄUSER: It was only then that the little castle was finally occupied, for the regiment did not arrive much earlier than we from the command of the army group.

THE PRESIDENT: Colonel Smirnov, is it necessary to go into this detail? Have you any particular purpose in going into so much detail?

MR. COUNSELLOR SMIRNOV: Mr. President, I ask this question for the following reasons: Later we shall interrogate witnesses for the Soviet Prosecution on the same point and particularly the chief of the medico-legal investigation. That is why I would like to ask the permission of the Court to clarify this point concerning the time when the witness visited the villa. That will be my last question to this point.

THE PRESIDENT: Yes, very well. Do not go into greater detail than you find absolutely necessary.

MR. COUNSELLOR SMIRNOV: Consequently, at the beginning of September and the first part of October 1941 you were not in the villa of Katyn woods and you could not be there at the time, is that true?

OBERHÄUSER: I cannot remember that exactly. The regimental commander had spotted the little castle and set it up for his staff headquarters. When exactly he moved in I cannot know, because I had other jobs to do.

MR. COUNSELLOR SMIRNOV: No, I asked whether you personally could not have been in the villa during the first part of September. Could you not possibly have been there before 20 September?

OBERHÄUSER: I do not think so.

MR. COUNSELLOR SMIRNOV: I have no further questions, Mr. President.

THE PRESIDENT: Do you wish to re-examine, Dr. Stahmer?

DR. STAHMER: Unfortunately, Mr. President, I shall have to come back to the question of time because it was not brought out too clearly during these last questions.

When did Regiment 537 move into the castle?

OBERHÄUSER: I assume it was during September.

DR. STAHMER: Beginning or end of September?

OBERHÄUSER: Probably rather more toward the end of September.

DR. STAHMER: Until then only the advance party was there, or...

OBERHÄUSER: The advance party of the regiment was there and my officers whom I had sent ahead.

DR. STAHMER: How many noncommissioned officers were with the advance party?

OBERHÄUSER: I cannot tell you exactly how many the regiment sent. I personally had sent one officer. Generally the regiment could not have sent very many. As a rule, as is always the case, the regiment was still operating at the old command post in

140

Borossilov and simultaneously it had to set up the new post. Consequently, during this period of regrouping, on the point of moving a command of an army group, there is always a considerable shortage of men. The old headquarters still has to be looked after, the new post requires men for its construction, so that as always during this period there were certainly too few people.

DR. STAHMER: Can you not even give us an estimate of the figure of that advance party?

OBERHÄUSER: There were 30, 40, or 50 men.

DR. STAHMER: How many noncommissioned officers?

OBERHÄUSER: Probably one or two officers, a few noncommissioned officers, and some men.

DR. STAHMER: The regiment was very widely spread out, was it not?

OBERHÄUSER: Yes.

DR. STAHMER: How far, approximately?

OBERHÄUSER: In the entire area of Army Group Center, shall we say between Orel and Vitebsk—in that entire area they were widely dispersed.

DR. STAHMER: How many kilometers was that, approximately?

OBERHÄUSER: More than 500 kilometers.

DR. STAHMER: Do you know Judge Advocate General Dr. Konrad of Army Group Center?

OBERHÄUSER: Yes.

DR. STAHMER: Do you know whether, in 1943, he interrogated the local inhabitants under oath about the date when the Polish officers were supposed to have been shot in the woods of Katyn?

OBERHÄUSER: No, I do not know.

DR. STAHMER: I have no further questions, Mr. President.

THE PRESIDENT: Were there any Einsatzkommandos in the Katyn area during the time that you were there?

OBERHÄUSER: Nothing has ever come to my knowledge about that.

THE PRESIDENT: Did you ever hear of an order to shoot Soviet commissars?

OBERHÄUSER: I only knew of that by hearsay.

THE PRESIDENT: When?

OBERHÄUSER: Probably at the beginning of the Russian campaign, I think.

141

THE PRESIDENT: Before the campaign started or after?

OBERHÄUSER: I cannot remember having heard anything like that before the beginning of the campaign.

THE PRESIDENT: Who was to carry out that order?

OBERHÄUSER: Strictly speaking, signal troops are not really fighting troops. Therefore, they really had nothing to do with that at all, and therefore we were in no way affected by the order.

THE PRESIDENT: I did not ask you that. I asked you who had to carry out the order.

OBERHÄUSER: Those who came into contact with these people, presumably.

THE PRESIDENT: Anybody who came in contact with Russian commissars had to kill them; is that it?

OBERHÄUSER: No, I assume that it was the troops, the fighting troops, the actual fighting troops at the front who first met the enemy. That could only have applied to the army group. The signal regiment never came into a position to meet commissars. That is probably why they were not mentioned in the order or affected by it in any way.

THE PRESIDENT: The witness can retire.

MR. COUNSELLOR SMIRNOV: Mr. President, I ask permission to call as witness the former deputy mayor of the city of Smolensk during the German occupation, Professor of Astronomy, Boris Bazilevsky.

THE PRESIDENT: Yes, let him come in then.

[The witness Bazilevsky took the stand.]

Will you state your full name, please?

BORIS BAZILEVSKY (Witness): Boris Bazilevsky.

THE PRESIDENT: Will you make this form of oath: I, a citizen of the USSR—called as a witness in this case—solemnly promise and swear before the High Tribunal—to say all that I know about this case—and to add or to withhold nothing.

[The witness repeated the oath.]

THE PRESIDENT: You may sit down.

MR. COUNSELLOR SMIRNOV: With the permission of the Tribunal, I should like to start with my interrogation, Mr. President.

THE PRESIDENT: Certainly.

MR. COUNSELLOR SMIRNOV: Please tell us, Witness, what your activity was before the German occupation of the city and district of Smolensk and where you were living in Smolensk.

BAZILEVSKY: Before the occupation of Smolensk and the surrounding region...

MR. COUNSELLOR SMIRNOV: Please speak slowly.

BAZILEVSKY: ... I lived in the city of Smolensk and was professor first at the Smolensk University and then of the Smolensk Pedagogical Institute, and at the same time I was director of the Smolensk Astronomical Observatory. For 10 years I was the dean of the physics and mathematics faculty, and in the last years I was deputy to the director of the scientific department of the Institute.

MR. COUNSELLOR SMIRNOV: How many years did you live in Smolensk previous to the German occupation?

BAZILEVSKY: From 1919.

MR. COUNSELLOR SMIRNOV: Do you know what the so-called Katyn wood was?

BAZILEVSKY: Yes.

MR. COUNSELLOR SMIRNOV: Please speak slowly.

BAZILEVSKY: Actually, it was a grove. It was the favorite resort of the inhabitants of Smolensk who spent their holidays and vacations there.

MR. COUNSELLOR SMIRNOV: Was this wood before the war a special reservation which was fenced or guarded by armed patrols, by watch dogs?

BAZILEVSKY: During the many years that I lived in Smolensk, this place was never fenced; and no restrictions were ever placed on access to it. I personally used to go there very frequently. The last time I was there was in 1940 and in the spring of 1941. In this wood there was also a camp for engineers. Thus, there was free access to this place for everybody.

MR. COUNSELLOR SMIRNOV: Please tell me in what year there was an engineer camp?

BAZILEVSKY: As far as I know, it was there for many years.

MR. COUNSELLOR SMIRNOV: Please speak slowly.

THE PRESIDENT: Wait a minute. Professor, will you wait a minute, please? When you see that yellow light go on, it means that you are going too fast; and when you are asked a question, will you pause before you answer it? Do you understand?

BAZILEVSKY: Yes.

MR. COUNSELLOR SMIRNOV: Will you please repeat your answer, and very slowly, if you please.

BAZILEVSKY: The last time I know that the engineer camp was in the area of the Katyn wood was in 1941.

MR. COUNSELLOR SMIRNOV: Consequently, if I understand you correctly, in 1940 and 1941 before the beginning of the war at any rate—and you speak of the spring of 1941—the Katyn wood was not a special reservation and was accessible to everybody?

BAZILEVSKY: Yes. I say that that was the situation.

MR. COUNSELLOR SMIRNOV: Do you say this as an eyewitness or from hearsay?

BAZILEVSKY: No, I say it as an eyewitness who used to go there frequently.

MR. COUNSELLOR SMIRNOV: Please tell the Tribunal under what circumstances you became the first deputy mayor of Smolensk during the period of the German occupation. Please speak slowly.

BAZILEVSKY: I was an administration official; and I did not have an opportunity of leaving the place in time, because I was busy in saving the particularly precious library of the Institute and the very valuable equipment. In the circumstances I could not try to escape before the evening of the 15th, but then I did not succeed in catching the train. I therefore decided to leave the city on 16 July in the morning, but during the night of 15 to 16 the city was unexpectedly occupied by German troops. All the bridges across the Dnieper were blown up, and I found myself in captivity.

After some time, on 20 July, a group of German soldiers came to the observatory of which I was the director. They took down that I was the director and that I was living there and that there was also a professor of physics, Efimov, living in the same building.

In the evening of 20 July two German officers came to me and brought me to the headquarters of the unit which had occupied Smolensk. After checking my *personalia* and after a short conversation, they suggested that I become mayor of the city. I refused, basing my refusal on the fact that I was a professor of astronomy and that, as I had no experience in such matters, I could not undertake this post. They then declared categorically and with threats, "We are going to force the Russian intelligentsia to work."

MR. COUNSELLOR SMIRNOV: Thus, if I understand you correctly, the Germans forced you by threats to become the deputy mayor of Smolensk?

BAZILEVSKY: That is not all. They told me also that in a few days I would be summoned to the Kommandantur.

On 25 July a man in civilian clothes appeared at my apartment, accompanied by a German policeman, and represented himself as a lawyer, Menschagin. He declared that he came by order of the military headquarters and that I should accompany him immediately to headquarters.

THE PRESIDENT: You are spending a lot of time on how he came to be mayor of Smolensk.

MR. COUNSELLOR SMIRNOV: Will you please allow me to pass to other questions, Mr. President? Thank you for your observations.

[Turning to the witness.] Who was your immediate superior? Who was the mayor of Smolensk?

BAZILEVSKY: Menschagin.

MR. COUNSELLOR SMIRNOV: What were the relations between this man and the German administration and particularly with the German Kommandantur?

BAZILEVSKY: These relations were very good and became closer and closer every day.

MR. COUNSELLOR SMIRNOV: Is it correct to say that Menschagin was the trustee of the German administration and that they even gave him secret information?

BAZILEVSKY: Yes.

MR. COUNSELLOR SMIRNOV: Do you know that in the vicinity of Smolensk there were Polish prisoners of war?

BAZILEVSKY: Yes, I do very well.

MR. COUNSELLOR SMIRNOV: Do you know what they were doing?

THE PRESIDENT: I do not know what this is going to prove. You presumably do, but can you not come nearer to the point?

MR. COUNSELLOR SMIRNOV: He said that he knew there were Polish prisoners of war in Smolensk; and, with the permission of the Tribunal, I would like to ask the witness what these prisoners of war were doing.

THE PRESIDENT: Very well; go on.

MR. COUNSELLOR SMIRNOV: Please answer. What were the Polish prisoners of war doing in the vicinity of Smolensk, and at what time?

BAZILEVSKY: In the spring of 1941 and at the beginning of the summer they were working on the restoration of the roads, Moscow-Minsk and Smolensk-Vitebsk.

MR. COUNSELLOR SMIRNOV: What do you know about the further fate of the Polish prisoners of war?

BAZILEVSKY: Thanks to the position that I occupied, I learned very early about the fate of the Polish prisoners of war.

MR. COUNSELLOR SMIRNOV: Please tell the Tribunal what you know about it.

BAZILEVSKY: In the camp for Russian prisoners of war known as "Dulag 126" there prevailed such a severe regime that prisoners of war were dying by the hundreds every day; for this reason I tried to free all those from this camp for whose release a reason could be given. I learned that in this camp there was also a very well-known pedagogue named Zhiglinski. I asked Menschagin to make representations to the German Kommandantur of Smolensk, and in particular to Von Schwetz, and to plead for the release of Zhiglinski from this camp.

MR. COUNSELLOR SMIRNOV: Please do not go into detail and do not waste time, but tell the Tribunal about your conversation with Menschagin. What did he tell you?

BAZILEVSKY: Menschagin answered my request with, "What is the use? We can save one, but hundreds will die." However, I insisted; and Menschagin, after some hesitation, agreed to put this request to the German Kommandantur.

MR. COUNSELLOR SMIRNOV: Please be short and tell us what Menschagin told you when he came back from the German Kommandantur.

BAZILEVSKY: Two days later he told me that he was in a very difficult situation on account of my demand. Von Schwetz had refused the request by referring to an instruction from Berlin saying that a very severe regime should prevail with respect to prisoners of war.

MR. COUNSELLOR SMIRNOV: What did he tell you about Polish prisoners of war?

BAZILEVSKY: As to Polish prisoners of war, he told me that Russians would at least be allowed to die in the camps while there were proposals to exterminate the Poles.

MR. COUNSELLOR SMIRNOV: What else was said?

BAZILEVSKY: I replied, "What do you mean? What do you want to say? How do you understand this?" And Menschagin answered, "You should understand this in the very literal sense of these words." He asked me not to tell anybody about it, since it was a great secret.

MR. COUNSELLOR SMIRNOV: When did this conversation of yours take place with Menschagin? In what month, and on what day?

BAZILEVSKY: This conversation took place at the beginning of September. I cannot remember the exact date.

MR. COUNSELLOR SMIRNOV: But you remember it was the beginning of September?

BAZILEVSKY: Yes.

MR. COUNSELLOR SMIRNOV: Did you ever come back again to the fate of Polish prisoners of war in your further conversations with Menschagin?

BAZILEVSKY: Yes.

MR. COUNSELLOR SMIRNOV: Can you tell us when?

BAZILEVSKY: Two weeks later—that is to say, at the end of September—I could not help asking him, "What was the fate of the Polish prisoners of war?" At first Menschagin hesitated, and then he told me haltingly, "They have already died. It is all over for them."

MR. COUNSELLOR SMIRNOV: Did he tell you where they were killed?

BAZILEVSKY: He told me that they had been shot in the vicinity of Smolensk, as Von Schwetz told him.

MR. COUNSELLOR SMIRNOV: Did he mention the exact place?

BAZILEVSKY: No, he did not mention the exact place.

MR. COUNSELLOR SMIRNOV: Tell me this. Did you, in turn, tell anybody about the extermination, by Hitlerites, of the Polish prisoners of war near Smolensk?

BAZILEVSKY: I talked about this to Professor Efimov, who was living in the same house with me. Besides him, a few days later I had a conversation about it with Dr. Nikolski, who was the medical officer of the city. However, I found out that Nikolski knew about this crime already from some other source.

MR. COUNSELLOR SMIRNOV: Did Menschagin tell you why these shootings took place?

BAZILEVSKY: Yes. When he told me that the prisoners of war had been killed, he emphasized once more the necessity of keeping it strictly secret in order to avoid disagreeable consequences. He started to explain to me the reasons for the German behavior with respect to the Polish prisoners of war. He pointed out that this was only one measure of the general system of treating Polish prisoners of war.

MR. COUNSELLOR SMIRNOV: Did you hear anything about the extermination of the Poles from the employees of the German Kommandantur?

BAZILEVSKY: Yes, 2 or 3 days later.

THE PRESIDENT: You are both going too fast, and you are not pausing enough. You are putting your questions whilst the answers are coming through. You must have longer pauses, and go slower.

MR. COUNSELLOR SMIRNOV: Thank you, Mr. President. *[Turning to the witness.]* Please continue, but slowly.

BAZILEVSKY: I do not know where I was.

MR. COUNSELLOR SMIRNOV: I asked you whether any of the employees of the German Kommandantur told you anything about the extermination of the Poles.

BAZILEVSKY: Two or three days later, when I visited the office of Menschagin, I met there an interpreter, the Sonderführer of the 7th Division of the German Kommandantur who was in charge of the Russian administration and who had a conversation with Menschagin concerning the Poles. He came from the Baltic region.

MR. COUNSELLOR SMIRNOV: Perhaps you can tell us briefly what he said.

BAZILEVSKY: When I entered the room he was saying, "The Poles are a useless people, and exterminated they may serve as fertilizer and for the enlargement of living space for the German nation."

THE PRESIDENT: You are doing exactly what I said just now. You are asking the questions before the translation comes through.

MR. COUNSELLOR SMIRNOV: Excuse me, Mr. President, I will try to speak more slowly.

[Turning to the witness.] Did you learn from Menschagin anything definite about the shooting of Polish prisoners of war?

BAZILEVSKY: When I entered the room I heard the conversation with Hirschfeld. I missed the beginning, but from the context of the conversation it was clear that they spoke about this event.

MR. COUNSELLOR SMIRNOV: Did Menschagin, when telling you about the shooting of Polish prisoners of war, refer to Von Schwetz?

BAZILEVSKY: Yes; I had the impression that he referred to Von Schwetz. But evidently—and this is my firm belief—he also spoke about it with private persons in the Kommandantur.

MR. COUNSELLOR SMIRNOV: When did Menschagin tell you that Polish prisoners of war were killed near Smolensk?

BAZILEVSKY: It was at the end of September.

MR. COUNSELLOR SMIRNOV: I have no further questions to put to this witness, Mr. President.

THE PRESIDENT: The Tribunal will adjourn.

[A recess was taken.]

MARSHAL: If it please the Tribunal, the Defendant Hess is absent.

THE PRESIDENT: Dr. Stahmer.

DR. STAHMER: Witness, in your testimony, just before recess, you read out your testimony, if I observed correctly. Will you tell me whether that was so or not?

BAZILEVSKY: I was not reading anything. I have only a plan of the courtroom in my hand.

DR. STAHMER: It looked to me as though you were reading out your answers. How can you explain the fact that the interpreter already had your answer in his hands?

BAZILEVSKY: I do not know how the interpreters could have had my answers beforehand. The testimony which I am giving was, however, known to the Commission beforehand—that is, my testimony during the preliminary examination.

DR. STAHMER: Do you know the little castle on the Dnieper, the little villa? Did you not understand me or hear me? Do you know the little castle on the Dnieper, the little villa on the Dnieper?

BAZILEVSKY: I do not know which villa you mean. There were quite a number of villas on the Dnieper.

DR. STAHMER: The house which was near the Katyn wood on the steep bank of the Dnieper River.

BAZILEVSKY: I still do not quite understand which house you mean. The banks of the Dnieper are long, and therefore your question is quite incomprehensible to me.

DR. STAHMER: Do you know where the graves of Katyn were found, in which 11,000 Polish officers were buried?

BAZILEVSKY: I was not there. I did not see the Katyn burial grounds.

DR. STAHMER: Had you never been in the Katyn wood?

BAZILEVSKY: As I already said, I was there not once but many times.

DR. STAHMER: Do you know where this mass burial site was located?

BAZILEVSKY: How can I know where the burial grounds were situated when I could not go there since the occupation?

DR. STAHMER: How do you know that the little wood was not fenced in?

BAZILEVSKY: Before the occupation of the Smolensk district by the German troops, the entire area, as I already stated, was not surrounded by any barrier; but according to hearsay I knew that after the occupation access to this wood was prohibited by the German local command.

DR. STAHMER: Therefore you have no knowledge of the fact that here in the Katyn wood a sanitarium or a convalescent home of the GPU was located?

BAZILEVSKY: I know very well; that was known to all the citizens of Smolensk.

DR. STAHMER: Then, of course, you also know exactly which house I referred to in my question?

BAZILEVSKY: I, myself, had never been in that house. In general, access to that house was only allowed to the families of the employees of the Ministry of the Interior. As to other persons, there was no need and no facility for them to go there.

DR. STAHMER: The house, therefore, was closed off?

BAZILEVSKY: No, the house was not forbidden to strangers; but why should people go there if they had no business there or were not in the sanitarium? The garden, of course, was open to the public.

DR. STAHMER: Were there not guards stationed there?

BAZILEVSKY: I have never seen any.

DR. STAHMER: Is this Russian witness who reported to you about the matter concerning the Polish officers, is this witness still alive?

BAZILEVSKY: Mr. Counsel, you probably mean Mayor Menschagin, if I understand you rightly?

DR. STAHMER: When you read your testimony off, it was not easy for me to follow. What was the mayor's name? Menschagin? Is he still alive?

BAZILEVSKY: Menschagin went away together with the German troops during their retreat, and I remained, and Menschagin's fate is unknown to me.

THE PRESIDENT: Dr. Stahmer, you are not entitled to say to the witness, "when you read your testimony off," just now, because he denied that he read his testimony off and there is no evidence that he has read it off.

DR. STAHMER: Did this Russian witness tell you that the Polish officers had come from the camp at Kosielsk?

BAZILEVSKY: Do you mean the camp at Kosielsk? Yes?

DR. STAHMER: Yes.

BAZILEVSKY: The witness did not say that.

DR. STAHMER: Do you know that place and locality?

BAZILEVSKY: Do you mean Kosielsk? I do, yes. In 1940, in the month of August—at the end of August—I spent my leave there with my wife.

DR. STAHMER: Do you know whether there were Polish officers at that place in a Russian prisoner-of-war camp?

BAZILEVSKY: Yes, I know that.

DR. STAHMER: Until what time did these prisoners of war remain there?

BAZILEVSKY: I do not know that for sure but at the end of August 1940 they were there. I am quite sure about that.

DR. STAHMER: Do you know whether this camp, together with its inmates, fell into German hands?

BAZILEVSKY: Personally, that is, from my own observation, I do not know it; but according to rumors, it appears to have been the case. That is, of course, not my own testimony; I myself did not see it, but I heard about it only.

DR. STAHMER: Did you hear what happened to these prisoners?

BAZILEVSKY: Yes, I heard, of course, that they remained there and could not be evacuated.

DR. STAHMER: Did you hear what became of them?

BAZILEVSKY: I have already testified in my answers to the prosecutor that they were shot on the order of the German Command.

DR. STAHMER: And where did these shootings take place?

BAZILEVSKY: Mr. Defense Counsel, you have apparently not heard my answers. I already testified that Mayor Menschagin said that they were shot in the neighborhood of Smolensk, but where he did not tell me.

DR. STAHMER: How many prisoners were involved?

BAZILEVSKY: Do you mean to say, how many were mentioned in the conversation with Menschagin? I do not understand your question. Do you mean to say according to the reports of Menschagin?

DR. STAHMER: What was the figure given to you by Menschagin?

BAZILEVSKY: Menschagin did not tell me any number. I repeat that this conversation took place on the last days of September 1941.

DR. STAHMER: Can you give us the name of an eyewitness who was present at this shooting or anyone who saw this shooting?

BAZILEVSKY: I believe that these executions were carried out under such circumstances that I think it scarcely possible that any Russian witnesses could be present.

THE PRESIDENT: Witness, you should answer the question directly. You were asked, "Can you give the names of anybody who was there?" You can answer that "yes" or "no" and then you can add any explanations necessary.

BAZILEVSKY: I will follow your instructions, Mr. President.

THE PRESIDENT: Can you give the name of anybody who saw the executions?

BAZILEVSKY: No, I cannot name any eyewitness.

DR. STAHMER: What German unit is supposed to have carried out the shootings?

BAZILEVSKY: I cannot answer that exactly. It is logical to assume that it was the construction battalion which was stationed there; but of course I could not know the exact organization of the German troops.

DR. STAHMER: Did the Poles involved here come from the camp at Kosielsk?

BAZILEVSKY: In general, this was not mentioned in the conversations of that time, but I certainly do not know that; besides these might have been any other Polish prisoners of war who had not been at Kosielsk previously.

DR. STAHMER: Did you yourself see Polish officers?

BAZILEVSKY: I did not see them myself, but my students saw them, and they told me that they had seen them in 1941.

DR. STAHMER: And where did they see them?

BAZILEVSKY: On the road where they were doing repair work at the beginning of summer, 1941.

DR. STAHMER: In what general area or location?

BAZILEVSKY: In the district of the Moscow-Minsk highway, somewhat to the west of Smolensk.

DR. STAHMER: Can you testify whether the Russian Army Command had a report to the effect that Polish prisoners at the camp at Kosielsk had fallen into the hands of the Germans?

BAZILEVSKY: No, I have no knowledge of that.

DR. STAHMER: What is the name of the German official or employee with whom you talked at the Kommandantur?

BAZILEVSKY: Not in the Kommandantur, but in Menschagin's office. His name was Hirschfeld.

DR. STAHMER: What was his position?

BAZILEVSKY: He was Sonderführer of the 7th Detachment of the German Kommandantur in the town of Smolensk.

DR. STAHMER: I have no further questions, Mr. President—just another question or two, Mr. President.

[Turning to the witness.] Were you punished by the Russian Government on account of your collaboration with the German authorities?

BAZILEVSKY: No, I was not.

DR. STAHMER: Are you at liberty?

BAZILEVSKY: Not only am I at liberty; but, as I have already stated, I am still professor at two universities.

DR. STAHMER: Therefore, you are back in office.

BAZILEVSKY: Yes.

THE PRESIDENT: Colonel Smirnov, do you wish to re-examine?

MR. COUNSELLOR SMIRNOV: No, Mr. President, I have no further questions to put to the witness.

THE PRESIDENT: Witness, do you know whether the man, whose name I understand to be Menschagin, was told about these matters or whether he himself had any direct knowledge of them?

BAZILEVSKY: From Menschagin's own words, I understood quite definitely that he had heard those things himself at the Kommandantur, particularly from Von Schwetz, who was the commander from the beginning of the occupation.

THE PRESIDENT: The witness can retire.

MR. COUNSELLOR SMIRNOV: Mr. President, I beg the Tribunal to allow me to call as witness Marko Antonov Markov, a Bulgarian citizen, professor at the University of Sofia.

[The interpreter Valev and the witness Markov took the stand.]

THE PRESIDENT: Are you the interpreter?

LUDOMIR VALEV (Interpreter): Yes, Sir.

THE PRESIDENT: Will you give us your full name?

VALEV: Ludomir Valev.

THE PRESIDENT: Will you repeat this oath after me: I swear before God and the Law—that I will interpret truthfully and to the best of my skill—the evidence to be given by the witness.

[The interpreter repeated the oath.]

THE PRESIDENT: *[To the witness.]* Will you give us your full name, please?

DR. MARKO ANTONOV MARKOV (Witness): Dr. Marko Antonov Markov.

THE PRESIDENT: Will you repeat this oath after me: I swear— as a witness in this case—that I will speak only the truth—being aware of my responsibility before God and the Law—and that I will withhold and add nothing.

[The witness repeated the oath.]

THE PRESIDENT: You may sit down.

MR. DODD: Mr. President, before this witness is examined, I would like to call to the attention of the Tribunal the fact that Dr. Stahmer asked the preceding witness a question which I understood went: How did it happen that the interpreters had the questions and the answers to your questions if you didn't have them before you? Now that question implied that Dr. Stahmer had some information that the interpreters did have the answers to the questions, and I sent a note up to the interpreters, and I have the answer from the lieutenant in charge that no one there had any answers or questions, and I think it should be made clear on the record.

THE PRESIDENT: Yes, I think so, too.

DR. STAHMER: I was advised of this fact outside the courtroom. If it is not a fact, I wish to withdraw my statement. I was informed outside the courtroom from a trustworthy source. I do not recall the name of the person who told me, I shall have to ascertain it.

THE PRESIDENT: Such statements ought not be made by counsel until they have verified them.

MR. COUNSELLOR SMIRNOV: May I begin the examination of this witness, Mr. President?

THE PRESIDENT: The examination, yes.

MR. COUNSELLOR SMIRNOV: Witness, I beg you to tell us briefly, without taking up the time of the Tribunal with too many details, under what conditions you were included in the so-called International Medical Commission set up by the Germans in the month of April 1943 for the examination of the graves of Polish officers in the Katyn woods.

I beg you, when answering me, to pause between the question I put to you and your own answer.

MARKOV: This occurred at the end of April 1943. While working in the Medico-Legal Institute, where I am still working, I was called to the telephone by Dr. Guerow.

THE PRESIDENT: The witness must stop before the interpreter begins. Otherwise, the voices come over the microphone together. So the interpreter must wait until the witness has finished his answer before he repeats it.

Now, the witness has said—at least this is what I heard—that in April 1943 he was called on the telephone.

MARKOV: I was called to the telephone by Dr. Guerow, the secretary of Dr. Filoff who was then Prime Minister of Bulgaria. I was told that I was to take part, as representative of the Bulgarian Government, in the work of an international medical commission which had to examine the corpses of Polish officers discovered in the Katyn wood.

Not wishing to go, I answered that I had to replace the director of my Institute who was away in the country. Dr. Guerow told me that according to an instruction of the Minister of Foreign Affairs, who had sent the telegram, it was precisely in order to replace him that I would have to go there. Guerow told me to come to the Ministry. There I asked him if I could refuse to comply with this order. He answered that we were in a state of war and that the Government could send anybody wherever and whenever they deemed it necessary.

Guerow took me to the first secretary of the Minister of Foreign Affairs, Schuchmanov. Schuchmanov repeated this order and told me that we were to examine the corpses of thousands of Polish officers. I answered that to examine thousands of corpses would take several months, but Schuchmanov said that the Germans had already exhumed a great number of these corpses and that I would have to go, together with other members of the commission, in order to see what had already been done and in order to sign, as Bulgarian representative, the report of the proceedings which had already been drafted. After that, I was taken to the German Legation, to Counsellor Mormann, who arranged all the technical details of the trip. This was on Saturday; and on Monday morning, 26 April, I flew to Berlin. There I was met by an official of the Bulgarian Legation and I was lodged at the Hotel Adlon.

MR. COUNSELLOR SMIRNOV: Please answer the next question: Who took part in this so-called International Commission, and when did they leave for Katyn?

MARKOV: On the next day, 27 April, we stayed in Berlin and the other members of the commission arrived there too.

MR. COUNSELLOR SMIRNOV: Who were they?

MARKOV: They were the following, besides myself: Dr. Birkle, chief doctor of the Ministry of Justice and first assistant of the Institute of Forensic Medicine and Criminology at Bucharest; Dr. Miloslavich, professor of forensic medicine and criminology at Zagreb University, who was representative for Croatia; Professor Palmieri, who was professor for forensic medicine and criminology at Naples; Dr. Orsos, professor of forensic medicine and criminology at Budapest; Dr. Subik, professor of pathological anatomy at the University of Bratislava and chief of the State Department for Health for

Slovakia; Dr. Hajek, professor for forensic medicine and criminology at Prague, who represented the so-called Protectorate of Bohemia and Moravia; Professor Naville, professor of forensic medicine at the University of Geneva, representative for Switzerland; Dr. Speleers, professor for ophthalmology at Ghent University, who represented Belgium; Dr. De Burlett, professor of anatomy at the University of Groningen, representing Holland; Dr. Tramsen, vice chancellor of the Institute for forensic medicine at Copenhagen University, representing Denmark; Dr. Saxen, who was professor for pathological anatomy at Helsinki University, Finland.

During the investigations of the commission, a Dr. Costeduat was missing; he declared that he could attend only as a personal representative of President Laval. Professor Piga from Madrid also arrived, an elderly gentleman who did not take any part in the work of the commission. It was stated later that he was ill as a result of the long journey.

MR. COUNSELLOR SMIRNOV: Were all these persons flown to Katyn?

MARKOV: All these persons arrived at Katyn with the exception of Professor Piga.

MR. COUNSELLOR SMIRNOV: Who besides the members of the commission left for Katyn with you?

MARKOV: On the 28th we took off from Tempelhof Airdrome, Berlin, for Katyn. We took off in two airplanes which carried about 15 to 20 persons each.

MR. COUNSELLOR SMIRNOV: Maybe you can tell us briefly who was there?

MARKOV: Together with us was Director Dietz, who met us and accompanied us. He represented the Ministry of Public Health. There were also press representatives, and two representatives of the Ministry for Foreign Affairs.

MR. COUNSELLOR SMIRNOV: I beg you to stop with these details and to tell me when the commission arrived in Katyn?

MARKOV: The commission arrived in Smolensk on 28 April, in the evening.

MR. COUNSELLOR SMIRNOV: How many work days did the commission stay in Smolensk? I stress work days.

MARKOV: We stayed in Smolensk 2 days only, 29 and 30 April 1943, and on 1 May, in the morning, we left Smolensk.

MR. COUNSELLOR SMIRNOV: How many times did the members of the commission personally visit the mass graves in the Katyn wood?

MARKOV: We were twice in the Katyn wood, that is, in the forenoon of 29 and 30 April.

MR. COUNSELLOR SMIRNOV: I mean, how many hours did you spend each time at the mass graves?

MARKOV: I consider not more than 3 or 4 hours each time.

MR. COUNSELLOR SMIRNOV: Were the members of the commission present at least once during the opening of one of the graves?

MARKOV: No new graves were opened in our presence. We were shown only several graves which had already been opened before we arrived.

MR. COUNSELLOR SMIRNOV: Therefore, you were shown already opened graves, near which the corpses were already laid out, is that right?

MARKOV: Quite right. Near these opened graves were exhumed corpses already laid out there.

MR. COUNSELLOR SMIRNOV: Were the necessary conditions for an objective and comprehensive scientific examination of the corpses given to the members of the commission?

MARKOV: The only part of our activity which could be characterized as a scientific, medico-legal examination were the autopsies carried out by certain members of the commission who were themselves medico-legal experts; but there were only seven or eight of us who could lay claim to that qualification, and as far as I recall only eight corpses were opened. Each of us operated on one corpse, except Professor Hajek, who dissected two corpses. Our further activity during these 2 days consisted of a hasty inspection under the guidance of Germans. It was like a tourists' walk during which we saw the open graves; and we were shown a peasant's house, a few kilometers distant from the Katyn wood, where in showcases papers and objects of various sorts were kept. We were told that these papers and objects had been found in the clothes of the corpses which had been exhumed.

MR. COUNSELLOR SMIRNOV: Were you actually present when these papers were taken from the corpses or were they shown to you when they were already under glass in display cabinets?

MARKOV: The documents which we saw in the glass cases had already been removed from the bodies before we arrived.

MR. COUNSELLOR SMIRNOV: Were you allowed to investigate these documents, to examine these documents, for instance, to see whether the papers were impregnated with any acids which had developed by the decay of the corpses, or to carry out any other kind of scientific examination?

MARKOV: We did not carry out any scientific examination of these papers. As I have already told you, these papers were exhibited in glass cases and we did not even touch them.

MR. COUNSELLOR SMIRNOV: But I would like you nevertheless to answer me briefly with "yes" or "no," a question which I have already put to you. Were the members of the commission given facilities for an objective examination?

MARKOV: In my opinion these working conditions can in no way be qualified as adequate for a complete and objective scientific examination. The only thing which bore the character of the scientific nature was the autopsy which I carried out.

MR. COUNSELLOR SMIRNOV: But did I rightly understand you, that from the 11,000 corpses which were discovered only 8 were dissected by members of the commission.

MARKOV: Quite right.

MR. COUNSELLOR SMIRNOV: Please answer the next question. In what condition were these corpses? I would like you to describe the state in which they were and also the state of the inner organs, the tissues, *et cetera*.

MARKOV: As to the condition of the corpses in the Katyn graves, I can only judge according to the state of the corpse which I myself dissected. The condition of this corpse was, as far as I could ascertain, the same as that of all the other corpses. The skin was still well preserved, was in part leathery, of a brown-red color and on some parts there were blue markings from the clothes. The nails and hair, mostly, had already fallen out. In the head of the corpse I dissected there was a small hole, a bullet wound in the back of the head. Only pulpy substance remained of the brain. The muscles were still so well preserved that one could even see the fibers of the sinews of heart muscles and valves. The inner organs were also mainly in a good state of preservation. But of course they were dried up, displaced, and of a dark color. The stomach showed traces of some sort of contents. A part of the fat had turned into wax. We were impressed by the fact that even when pulled with brute force, no limbs had detached themselves.

I dictated a report, on the spot, on the result of my investigation. A similar report was dictated by the other members of the commission who examined corpses. This report was published by the Germans, under Number 827, in the book which they published.

MR. COUNSELLOR SMIRNOV: I would like you to answer the following question. Did the medico-legal investigations testify to the fact that the corpses had been in the graves already for 3 years?

MARKOV: As to that question I could judge only from the corpse on which I myself had held a post mortem. The condition of this corpse, as I have already stated, was typical of the average condition of the Katyn corpses. These corpses were far removed from the stage of disintegration of the soft parts, since the fat was only beginning to turn into wax. In my opinion these corpses were buried for a shorter period of time than 3 years. I considered that the corpse which I dissected had been buried for not more than 1 year or 18 months.

MR. COUNSELLOR SMIRNOV: Therefore, applying the criteria of the facts which you ascertained to your experiences in Bulgaria—that is, in a country of a more southern climate than Smolensk and where decay, therefore, is more rapid—one must come to the conclusion that the corpses that were exhumed in the Katyn forest had been lying under the earth for not more than a year and a half? Did I understand you correctly?

MARKOV: Yes, quite right. I had the impression that they had been buried for not more than a year and a half.

THE PRESIDENT: The Tribunal will adjourn now.

[The Tribunal adjourned until 2 July 1946 at 1000 hours.]

Tuesday, 2 July 1946

Morning Session

[The witness Markov resumed the stand.]

MR. COUNSELLOR SMIRNOV: Witness, when did you, together with the other members of the commission, perform the autopsies of these eight corpses? What date was it exactly?

MARKOV: That was on 30 April, early in the day.

MR. COUNSELLOR SMIRNOV: And, on the basis of your personal observations, you decided that the corpses were in the ground 1 year or 18 months at the most?

MARKOV: That is correct.

MR. COUNSELLOR SMIRNOV: Before putting the next question to you, I should like you to give me a brief answer to the following question: Is it correct that in the practice of Bulgarian medical jurisprudence the protocol about the autopsy contains two parts, a description and the deductions?

MARKOV: Yes. In our practice, as well as in the practice of other countries, so far as I know, it is done in the following way: First of all, we give a description and then the deduction.

MR. COUNSELLOR SMIRNOV: Was a deduction contained in the record you made regarding the autopsy?

MARKOV: My record of the autopsy contained only a description without any conclusion.

MR. COUNSELLOR SMIRNOV: Why?

MARKOV: Because from the papers which were given to us there I understood that they wanted us to say that the corpses had been in the ground for 3 years. This could be deduced from the papers which were shown to us in the little peasant hut about which I have already spoken.

MR. COUNSELLOR SMIRNOV: By the way, were these papers shown to you before the autopsy or afterward?

MARKOV: Yes, the papers were given us 1 day before the autopsy.

MR. COUNSELLOR SMIRNOV: So you were...

THE PRESIDENT: Colonel Smirnov, you are interrupting the interpreter all the time. Before the interpreter has finished the answer, you have put another question. It is very difficult for us to hear the interpreter.

MR. COUNSELLOR SMIRNOV: Thank you for your indication, Mr. President.

MARKOV: Inasmuch as the objective deduction regarding the autopsy I performed was in contradiction with this version, I did not make any deductions.

MR. COUNSELLOR SMIRNOV: Consequently you did not make any deduction because the objective data of the autopsy testified to the fact that the corpses had been in the ground, not 3 years, but only 18 months?

THE PRESIDENT: Colonel Smirnov, you must remember that it is a double translation, and unless you pause more than you are pausing, your voice comes in upon the interpreter's and we cannot hear the interpreter.

MR. COUNSELLOR SMIRNOV: Very well, Mr. President.

MARKOV: Yes, that is quite correct.

MR. COUNSELLOR SMIRNOV: Was there unanimity among the members of the commission regarding the time the corpses had been in the graves?

MARKOV: Most of the members of the delegation who performed the autopsies in the Katyn wood made their deductions without answering the essential question regarding the time the corpses had been buried. Some of them, as for instance, Professor Hajek, spoke about immaterial things; as for instance, that one of the killed had had pleurisy. Some of the others, as for instance, Professor Birkle from Bucharest, cut off some hair from a corpse in order to determine the age of the corpse. In my opinion that was quite immaterial. Professor Palmieri, on the basis of the autopsy that he performed, said that the corpse had been in the ground over a year but he did not determine exactly how long.

The only one who gave a definite statement in regard to the time the corpses had been buried was Professor Miloslavich from Zagreb, and he said it was 3 years. However, when the German book regarding Katyn was published, I read the result of his impartial statement regarding the corpse on which he had performed the autopsy. I had the impression that the corpse on which he had performed the autopsy did not differ in its stage of decomposition from the other corpses. This led me to think that his statement that the corpses had been in the ground for 3 years did not coincide with the facts of his description.

MR. COUNSELLOR SMIRNOV: I would like to ask you to reply to the following question. Were there many skulls found by the members of the commission with signs of so-called *pseudocallus*? By the way, inasmuch as this term is not known in the usual books on medical jurisprudence and in general criminalistic terminology, I should like you to give us an exact explanation of what Professor Orsos, of Budapest, means by the term *pseudocallus*.

THE PRESIDENT: Would you repeat that question?

MR. COUNSELLOR SMIRNOV: Were there many skulls with signs of so-called *pseudocallus* which were submitted to the members of the commission? Inasmuch as this term is not known in the usual books on medical jurisprudence, I should like you to give us a detailed explanation of what Professor Orsos means by the term *pseudocallus*.

THE PRESIDENT: What are you saying the skulls had? You asked if there were many skulls with something or other.

MR. COUNSELLOR SMIRNOV: I see this term for the first time, myself, Mr. President. It is *pseudocallus*. It seems to be a Latin term of some sort of corn which is formed on the outer surface of the cerebral substance.

THE PRESIDENT: Can you spell the word in Latin?

MR. COUNSELLOR SMIRNOV: Yes, Mr. President.

[The prosecutor submitted a paper to the President.]

THE PRESIDENT: What you have written here is p-s-e-r-d-o. Do you mean p-s-e-u-d-o, which means false?

MR. COUNSELLOR SMIRNOV: Yes, that is right, pseudo.

THE PRESIDENT: Now then, put your question again, and try to put it shortly.

MR. COUNSELLOR SMIRNOV: Yes.

[Turning to the witness.] Were there many skulls with signs of so-called *pseudocallus* shown to the members of the commission? Will you please give an exact explanation of this term of Professor Orsos'.

MARKOV: Professor Orsos spoke to us regarding *pseudocallus* at a general conference of the delegates. That took place on 30 April, in the afternoon, in the building where the field laboratory of Dr. Butz in Smolensk was located.

Professor Orsos described the term *pseudocallus* as meaning some sediment of indissoluble salt, of calcium, and other salts on the inside of the cranium. Professor Orsos stated that, according to his observations in Hungary, this happened if the corpses have been in the ground for at least 3 years. When Professor Orsos stated this at the scientific conference, none of the delegates said anything either for or against it. I deduced from that that this term *pseudocallus* was as unknown to the other delegates as it was to me.

At the same conference Professor Orsos showed us such a *pseudocallus* on one of the skulls.

MR. COUNSELLOR SMIRNOV: I should like you to answer the following question: What number did the corpse have from which this skull with signs of *pseudocallus* was taken?

MARKOV: The corpse from which the skull was taken and which was noted in the book bore the Number 526. From this I deduced that this corpse was exhumed before our arrival at Katyn, inasmuch as all the other corpses on which we performed autopsies on 30 April had numbers which ran above 800. It was explained to us that as soon as a corpse was exhumed it immediately received a consecutive number.

MR. COUNSELLOR SMIRNOV: Tell me this, please. Did you notice any *pseudocallus* on the skulls of the corpses on which you and your colleagues performed autopsies?

MARKOV: On the skull of the corpse on which I performed an autopsy, there was some sort of pulpy substance in place of the brain, but I never noticed any sign of *pseudocallus*. The other delegates—after the explanation of Professor Orsos—likewise did not state that they had found any *pseudocallus* in the other skulls. Even Butz and his co-workers, who had examined the corpses before our arrival, did not mention any sign of *pseudocallus*.

Later on, in a book which was published by the Germans and which contained the report of Butz, I noticed that Butz referred to *pseudocallus* in order to give more weight to his statement that the corpses had been in the ground for 3 years.

MR. COUNSELLOR SMIRNOV: That is to say, that of the 11,000 corpses only one skull was submitted to you which had *pseudocallus*?

MARKOV: That is quite correct.

MR. COUNSELLOR SMIRNOV: I should like you to describe to the Tribunal in detail the state of the clothing which you found on the corpses.

MARKOV: In general the clothing was well preserved, but of course it was damp due to the decomposition of the corpses. When we pulled off the clothing to undress the corpses, or when we tried to take off the shoes, the clothing did not tear nor did the shoes fall apart at the seams. I even had the impression that this clothing could have been used again, after having been cleaned.

There were some papers found in the pockets of the clothing of the corpse on which I performed the autopsy, and these papers were also impregnated with the dampness of the corpse. Some of the Germans who were present when I was performing the autopsy asked me to describe those papers and their contents; but I refused to do it, thinking that this was not the duty of a doctor. In fact I had already noticed the previous day that with the help of the dates contained in those papers, they were trying to make us think that the corpses had remained in the ground for 3 years.

Therefore, I wanted to base my deductions only on the actual condition of the corpses. Some of the other delegates who performed autopsies also found some papers in the clothing of the corpses. The papers which had been found in the clothing of the corpse on which I performed the autopsy were put into a cover which bore the same number as the corpse, Number 827. Later on, in the book which was published by the Germans, I perceived that some of the delegates described the contents of the papers which were found on the corpses.

MR. COUNSELLOR SMIRNOV: I should like to ask you to reply to the following question. On what impartial medico-judicial data did the commission base the deduction that the corpses had remained in the earth not less than 3 years?

THE PRESIDENT: Will you put the question again? I did not understand the question.

MR. COUNSELLOR SMIRNOV: I asked on what impartial medico-judicial data were the deductions of the protocol of the International Medical Commission based, which stated that the corpses had remained in the ground not less than 3 years?

THE PRESIDENT: Has he said that that was the deduction he made—not less than 3 years?

THE TRIBUNAL (Mr. Biddle): He has not said that.

THE PRESIDENT: He has not said that at all. He never said that he made the deduction that the corpses remained in the ground not less than 3 years.

MR. COUNSELLOR SMIRNOV: He did not make this deduction; but Professor Markov, together with the other members of the commission, signed a report of the International Commission.

THE PRESIDENT: I know; but that is why I ask you to repeat your question. The question that was translated to us was: On what grounds did you make your deduction that the corpses had remained in the ground not less than 3 years—which is the opposite of what he said.

Now will you put the question again?

MR. COUNSELLOR SMIRNOV: Very well.

[Turning to the witness.] I am not asking you about your personal minutes, Witness, but about the general record of the entire commission. I am asking you on what impartial medico-judicial data were the deductions of the entire commission based, that the corpses had remained in the earth not less than 3 years. On the record of the deductions your signature figures among those of the other members of the commission.

THE PRESIDENT: Wait a minute. Now, then, Colonel Smirnov, will you put the question again.

MR. COUNSELLOR SMIRNOV: Yes, Mr. President.

[Turning to the witness.] I was asking you on what impartial medico-judicial data were the deductions of the commission based— not the individual report of Dr. Markov, in which there are no deductions—but the deductions of the entire commission, that the corpses had remained not less than 3 years in the ground?

MARKOV: The collective protocol of the commission which was signed by all the delegates was very scant regarding the real medico-judicial data. Concerning the condition of the corpses, only one sentence in the report was stated, namely that the corpses were in various stages of decomposition, but there was no description of the real extent of decomposition.

Thus, in my opinion, this deduction was based on the papers found on the corpses and on testimony of the witnesses, but not on the actual medico-judicial data. As far as medical jurisprudence is concerned, they tried to support this deduction by the statement of Professor Orsos regarding the finding of *pseudocallus* in the skull of corpse Number 526.

But, according to my conviction, since this skull was the only one with signs of *pseudocallus,* it was wrong to arrive at a definite conclusion regarding the stage of decomposition of thousands of corpses which were contained in the Katyn graves. Besides, the observation of Professor Orsos regarding *pseudocallus* was made in Hungary; that is to say, under quite different soil and climatic conditions, and withal in individual graves and not in mass graves, as was the case in Katyn.

MR. COUNSELLOR SMIRNOV: You spoke about the testimony of witnesses. Did the members of the commission have the opportunity personally to interrogate those witnesses, especially the Russian witnesses?

MARKOV: We did not have the opportunity of having any contact with the indigenous population. On the contrary, immediately upon our arrival at the hotel in Smolensk, Butz told us that we were in a military zone, and that we did not have the right to walk around in the city without being accompanied by a member of the German Army, or to speak with the inhabitants of the place, or to make photographs. In reality, during the time we were there, we did not have any contact with the local inhabitants.

On the first day of our arrival in the Katyn wood, that is to say, on 29 April, in the morning, several Russian civilians were brought under German escort to the graves. Immediately upon our arrival at Smolensk some of the depositions of the local witnesses were submitted to us. The depositions were typed. When these witnesses were brought to the Katyn wood, we were told that these witnesses were the ones who gave the testimonies which had been submitted to us. There was no regular interrogation of the witnesses which could have been recorded, or were recorded. Professor Orsos started the conversation with the witnesses and told us that he could speak Russian because he had been a prisoner of war in Russia during the first World War. He began to speak with a man, an elderly man whose name, so far as I can remember, was Kiselov. Then he spoke to a second witness, whose last name so far as I can remember was Andrejev. All the conversation lasted a few minutes only. As our Bulgarian language is rather similar to the Russian, I tried also to speak to some of the witnesses ...

THE PRESIDENT: Don't you think that should be left to cross-examination? Can't these details be left to cross-examination?

MR. COUNSELLOR SMIRNOV: Yes, Mr. President.

I would ask you, Witness, to interrupt the reply to this question and to answer the following one: At the time you signed this general report of the commission, was it quite clear to you that the murders were perpetrated in Katyn not earlier than the last quarter of 1941, and that 1940, in any case, was excluded?

MARKOV: Yes, this was absolutely clear to me and that is why I did not make any deductions in the minutes which I made on my findings in the Katyn wood.

MR. COUNSELLOR SMIRNOV: Why did you sign then this general report, which was incorrect in your opinion?

MARKOV: In order to make it quite clear under what conditions I signed this report, I should like to say a few words on how it was made up and how it was signed.

MR. COUNSELLOR SMIRNOV: Excuse me, I would like to put a question to you which defines more accurately this matter. Was this report actually signed on 30 April 1941 in the town of Smolensk or was it signed on another date and at another place?

MARKOV: It was not signed in Smolensk on 30 April but was signed on 1 May at noon, at the airport which was called Bela.

MR. COUNSELLOR SMIRNOV: Will you please tell the Tribunal under what conditions it was signed.

MARKOV: The compilation of this record was to be done at the same conference which I already mentioned and which took place in the laboratory of Butz in the afternoon of 30 April. Present at this conference were all the delegates and all the Germans who had arrived with us from Berlin: Butz and his assistants, General Staff Physician Holm, the chief physician of the Smolensk sector, and also other German Army officials who were unknown to me. Butz stated that the Germans were only present as hosts, but actually the conference was presided over by General Staff Physician Holm and the work was performed under the direction of Butz. The secretary of the conference was the personal lady secretary of Butz who took down the report. However, I never saw these minutes. Butz and Orsos came with a prepared draft to this conference, a sort of protocol; but I never learned who ordered them to draw up such a protocol. This protocol was read by Butz and then a question was raised regarding the state and the age of the young pines which were in the clearings of the Katyn wood. Butz was of the opinion that in these clearings there were graves too.

MR. COUNSELLOR SMIRNOV: Excuse me for interrupting you. Did you have any evidence that any graves were actually found in these clearings?

MARKOV: No. During the time we were there, no new graves were opened. As some of the delegates said they were not competent to express their opinion regarding the age of these trees, General Holm gave an order to bring a German who was an expert on forestry. He showed us the cut of the trunk of a small tree and from the number of circles in this trunk, he deduced the trees were 5 years old.

MR. COUNSELLOR SMIRNOV: Excuse me; I interrupt you again. You, yourself—can you state here that this tree was actually cut down from the grave and not from any other place in the clearing?

MARKOV: I can say only that in the Katyn wood there were some clearings with small trees and that, while driving back to Smolensk, we took a little tree with us in the bus, but I do not know whether there were any graves where these trees were standing. As I have already stated, no graves were laid open in our presence.

MR. COUNSELLOR SMIRNOV: I would request you to continue your reply, but very briefly and not to detain the attention of the Tribunal with unnecessary details.

MARKOV: Some editorial notes were made in connection with this protocol, but I do not remember what they were. Then Orsos and Butz were entrusted with the final drafting of the record. The signing of the record was intended to take place on the same night at a banquet which was organized in a German Army hospital. At this banquet Butz arrived with the minutes and he started reading them, but the actual signing did not take place for reasons which are still not clear to me. It was stated that this record would have to be rewritten, so the banquet lasted until 3 or 4 o'clock in the morning. Then Professor Palmieri told me that the Germans were not pleased with the contents of the protocol and that they were carrying on telephone conversations with Berlin and that perhaps there would not even be a protocol at all.

Indeed, having spent the night in Smolensk without having signed the record, we took off from Smolensk on the morning of 1 May. I personally had the impression that no protocol at all would be issued and I was very pleased about that. On the way to Smolensk, as well as on our way back, some of the delegates asked to stop in Warsaw in order to see the city, but we were told that it was impossible because of military reasons.

MR. COUNSELLOR SMIRNOV: This has nothing to do with the subject. Please keep to the facts.

MARKOV: Around noon we arrived at the airport which was called Bela. The airport was apparently a military airfield because of the temporary military barracks I saw there. We had dinner there and immediately after dinner, notwithstanding the fact that we were not told that the signing of the minutes would take place on the way to Berlin, we were submitted copies of the protocol for signature. During the signing a number of military persons were present, as there were no other people except military personnel on this airfield. I was rather struck by the fact that on the one hand the records were already completed in Smolensk but were not submitted to us for signing there, and on the other hand that they did not wait till we arrived in Berlin a few hours later. They were submitted to us for signing at this isolated military airfield. This was the reason why I signed the report, in spite of the conviction I had acquired during the autopsy which I had performed at Smolensk.

MR. COUNSELLOR SMIRNOV: That is to say, the date and the locality which are shown in the protocol are incorrect?

MARKOV: Yes, that is so.

MR. COUNSELLOR SMIRNOV: And you signed it because you felt yourself compelled to?

THE PRESIDENT: Colonel Smirnov, I don't think it is proper for you to put leading questions to him. He has stated the fact. It is useless to go on stating conclusions about it.

MR. COUNSELLOR SMIRNOV: Very well, Mr. President. I have no further questions to put to the witness.

THE PRESIDENT: Does anyone want to cross-examine him?

DR. STAHMER: Mr. President, I should like to ask a question concerning the legal proceedings first. Each side was to call three witnesses before the Court. This witness, as I understand it, has not only testified to facts but has also made statements which can be called an expert judgment. He has not only expressed himself as an expert witness, as we say in German law, but also as an expert. If the Court is to listen to these statements made by the witness as an expert, I should like to have the opportunity for the Defense also to call in an expert.

THE PRESIDENT: No, Dr. Stahmer, the Tribunal will not hear more than three witnesses on either side. You could have called any expert you wanted or any member of the experts who made the German examination. It was your privilege to call any of them.

DR. STAHMER: Witness, how long have you been active in the field of medical jurisprudence?

MARKOV: I have been working in the field of medical jurisprudence since the beginning of 1927 in the faculty for medical jurisprudence of the University in Sofia, first as an assistant and now I am professor of medical jurisprudence. I am not a staff professor at the university. My position can be designated by the German word "Ausserordentlicher Professor" (university lecturer).

DR. STAHMER: Before your visit to Katyn did your government tell you that you were to participate in a political action without consideration of your scientific qualification?

MARKOV: I was not told so literally, but in the press the Katyn question was discussed as a political subject.

DR. STAHMER: Did you feel free in regard to your scientific "conscience" at that time?

MARKOV: At what time?

DR. STAHMER: At the time when you went to Katyn?

MARKOV: The question is not quite clear to me; I should like you to explain it.

DR. STAHMER: Did you consider the task you had to carry out there a political one or a scientific one?

MARKOV: I understood this task from the very first moment as a political one and therefore I tried to evade it.

DR. STAHMER: Did you realize the outstanding political importance of this task?

MARKOV: Yes; from everything I read in the press.

DR. STAHMER: In your examination yesterday you said that when you arrived at Katyn the graves had already been opened and certain corpses had been carefully laid out. Do you mean to say that these corpses were not taken from the graves at all?

MARKOV: No, I should not say that, inasmuch as it was obvious that corpses were taken out of these graves and besides I saw that some corpses were still in the graves.

DR. STAHMER: Then, in order to state this positively, you had no reason to think that the corpses inspected by the commission were not taken from these mass graves?

THE PRESIDENT: He did not know where they came from, did he?

MARKOV: Evidently from the graves which were open.

DR. STAHMER: You have already made statements to the effect that, as a result of the medico-judicial examination by this International Commission, a protocol, a record was taken down. You have furthermore stated that you signed this protocol.

Mr. President, this protocol is contained in its full text in the official data published by the German Government on this incident. I ask that this evidence, this so-called *White Book*, be admitted as evidence. I will submit it to the Court later.

THE PRESIDENT: We will adjourn now.

[A recess was taken.]

THE PRESIDENT: Dr. Stahmer, the Tribunal rules that you may cross-examine this witness upon the report, and the protocol will be admitted in evidence, if you offer it in evidence, under Article 19 of the Charter. That, of course, involves that we do not take judicial notice of the report under Article 21 of the Charter but that it is offered under Article 19 of the Charter and therefore it will either come through the earphones in cross-examination or such parts of the protocol as you wish to have translated.

DR. STAHMER: Witness, was the protocol or the record signed by you and the other experts compiled in the same way in which it is included in the German *White Book*?

MARKOV: Yes, the record of the protocol which is included in the German *White Book* is the same protocol which I compiled. A long time after my return to Sofia I was sent two copies of the protocol by Director Dietz. These two copies were typewritten, and I was requested to make necessary corrections and additions if I deemed it necessary, but I left it without corrections and it was printed without any comments on my part.

MR. COUNSELLOR SMIRNOV: Just a moment Dr. Stahmer...

Mr. President, I believe that there is a slight confusion here. The witness is answering in regard to the individual protocol, whereas Dr. Stahmer is questioning him on the general record. Thus the witness does not answer the proper question.

DR. STAHMER: Mr. President, I would have cleared this matter up on my own account.

[Turning to the witness.] Do you mean your autopsy protocol?

MARKOV: I mean the protocol I compiled myself and not the general record.

DR. STAHMER: Now, what about this general protocol or record? When did you receive a copy of it?

MARKOV: I received a copy of the general record in Berlin where as many copies were signed as there were delegates present.

DR. STAHMER: Just a little while ago you stated that Russian witnesses had been taken before the commission in the wood of Katyn, but that, however, there had been no opportunity afforded the experts to talk with these witnesses concerning the question at hand.

Now, in this protocol, in this record, the following remark is found, and I quote:

"The commission interrogated several indigenous Russian witnesses personally. Among other things, these witnesses confirmed that in the months of March and April 1940 large shipments of Polish officers arrived almost daily at the railroad station Gnjesdova near Katyn. These trains were emptied, the inmates were taken in lorries to the wood of Katyn and never seen again. Furthermore, official notice was taken of the proofs and statements, and the documents containing the evidence were inspected."

MARKOV: As I already stated during the questioning, two witnesses were interrogated on the spot by Orsos. They actually said that they saw how Polish officers were brought to the station of Gnjesdova and that later they did not see them again.

THE PRESIDENT: Dr. Stahmer, the Tribunal thinks the witness ought to be given an opportunity of seeing the report when you put passages in it to him.

DR. STAHMER: Yes.

THE PRESIDENT: Haven't you got another copy of it?

DR. STAHMER: I am sorry, Mr. President, I have no second copy; no.

THE PRESIDENT: Can the witness read German?

MARKOV: No, but anyhow I can understand the contents of the record.

THE PRESIDENT: You mean you can read it?

MARKOV: Yes, I can also read it.

THE PRESIDENT: Can the witness read German, do you mean?

MARKOV: Yes, I can read German.

DR. STAHMER: Mr. President, may I make a suggestion?

THE PRESIDENT: Dr. Stahmer, if you have only got one copy, I think you had better have it back. You can't have the book passing to and fro like that.

DR. STAHMER: I should like to make the suggestion that the cross-examination be interrupted and the other witness be called, and I will have this material typed in the meantime. That would be a solution. But there are only a few sentences...

THE PRESIDENT: You can read it. Take the book back.

DR. STAHMER: Mr. President, I propose to read only a few short sentences.

[Turning to the witness.] Yesterday you testified, Witness, that the experts restricted or limited themselves to making an autopsy on one corpse only. In this report the following is set down—I quote:

"The members of the commission personally performed an autopsy on nine corpses and numerous selected cases were submitted for post-mortem examination."

Is that right?

MARKOV: That is right. Those of the members of the commission who were medical experts, with the exception of Professor Naville, performed each an autopsy on a corpse. Hajek made two autopsies.

DR. STAHMER: In this instance we are not interested in the autopsy, but in the post-mortem examination.

MARKOV: The corpses were examined but only superficially during an inspection which we carried out very hastily on the first day. No individual autopsy was carried out, but the corpses were merely looked at as they lay side by side.

DR. STAHMER: I should like to ask you now what is meant in medical science by the concept "post-mortem examination."

MARKOV: We differentiate between an exterior inspection, when the corpse has to be undressed and minutely examined externally, and an internal inspection, when the inner organs of the corpse are examined. This was not done with the hundreds of bodies at Katyn, as it was not physically possible. We were there only one forenoon. Therefore, I consider that there was no actual medico-judicial expert examination of these corpses in the real sense of the word.

DR. STAHMER: A little while ago you talked about the trees that were growing there on these graves, and you said that an expert explained the age of the trees by the rings counted on a trunk. In the protocol and the report the following is set down. I quote:

"According to the opinion of the members of the commission and the testimony of forest ranger Von Herff, who was called in as an expert on forestry, they were small pine trees of at least 5 years of age, badly developed because they had been standing in the shade of large trees and had been transplanted to this spot about 3 years ago."

Now, I would like to ask you, is it correct that you undertook a local inspection and that you convinced yourself on the spot whether the statements made by the forestry expert were actually correct?

MARKOV: Our personal impression and my personal conviction in this question only refer to the fact that in the wood of Katyn there were clearings where small trees were growing and that the afore-mentioned expert showed us a cross section of a tree with its circles. But I do not consider myself competent and cannot give an opinion as to whether the deductions which are set forth in the record are correct or not. Precisely for that reason it was judged necessary to call in a forestry expert, for we doctors were not competent to decide this question. Therefore, these conclusions are merely the conclusions of a competent German expert.

DR. STAHMER: But after having had a first-hand view, did you doubt the truth of these statements?

MARKOV: After the German expert had expressed his opinion at the conference of the delegates, neither I nor the other delegates expressed any opinion as to whether his conclusions were correct or not. These conclusions are set down in the record in the form in which the expert expressed himself.

DR. STAHMER: According to your autopsy report the corpse of the Polish officer which you dissected was clothed and you described the clothing in detail. Was this winter or summer clothing that you found?

MARKOV: It was winter clothing including an overcoat and a woolen shawl around the neck.

DR. STAHMER: In the protocol it says further and I quote:

"Furthermore, Polish cigarettes and matchboxes were found with the dead; in some cases tobacco containers and cigarette holders, and 'Kosielsk' was inscribed thereon."

The question is, did you see these objects?

MARKOV: We actually saw these tobacco boxes with the name "Kosielsk" engraved thereon. They were exhibited to us in the glass case which was shown to us in the peasant hut not far from the Katyn wood. I remember them because Butz drew our attention to them.

DR. STAHMER: In your autopsy report, Witness, there is the following remark, and I quote:

"In the clothing documents were found and they were put in the folder Number 827."

Now, I should like to ask you: How did you discover these documents? Did you personally take them out of the pockets?

MARKOV: These papers were in the pockets of the overcoat and of the jacket. As far as I can remember they were taken out by a German who was undressing the corpse in my presence.

DR. STAHMER: At that time were the documents already in the envelope?

MARKOV: They were not yet in the envelope, but after they had been taken out of the pockets they were put into an envelope which bore the number of the corpse. We were told that this was the usual method of procedure.

DR. STAHMER: What was the nature of the documents?

MARKOV: I did not examine them at all, as I have already said, and I refused to do so, but according to the size, I believe that they were certificates of identity. I could distinguish individual letters, but I do not know whether one could read the inscription, for I did not attempt to do so.

DR. STAHMER: In the protocol the following statement is made, and I quote:

"The documents found with the corpses (diaries, letters, and newspapers) were dated from the fall of 1939 until March and April 1940. The latest date which could be ascertained was the date of a Russian newspaper of 22 April 1940."

Now, I should like to ask you if this statement is correct and whether it is in accordance with the findings that you made?

MARKOV: Such letters and newspapers were indeed in the glass cases and were shown to us. Some such papers were found by members of the commission who were dissecting the bodies, and if I remember rightly, they described the contents of these documents, but I did not do so.

DR. STAHMER: In your examination just a little while ago you stated that only a few scientific details were contained in this protocol and that this was probably done intentionally. I should like to quote from this record as follows:

"Various degrees and types of decomposition were caused by the position of the bodies to one another in the grave. Aside from some mummification on the surface and around the edges of the mass of corpses, some damp maceration was found among the center corpses. The sticking together of the adjacent corpses and the soldering together of corpses through cadaverous acids and fluids which had thickened. and particularly the deformations that obtained from the pressure among the corpses, show that the corpses were buried there right from the beginning.

"Among the corpses, insects or remains of insects which might date back to the time of burial are entirely lacking, and from this it may be gathered that the shooting and the burial took place at a season which was cold and free from insects."

Now, I should like to ask you if these statements are correct and if they are in line with your findings.

MARKOV: I stated that little was said on the condition of the corpses, and indeed as can be judged by the quotation which I had in mind, only a general phraseology is used concerning the various degrees of decomposition of the corpses, but no concrete or detailed description of the condition of the corpses is made.

As to the insects and their larvae, the assertion of the general report that none were discovered is in flagrant contradiction to the conclusions of Professor Palmieri, which are recorded in his personal minutes concerning the corpse which he himself dissected. In this protocol, which is published in the same German *White Book*, it is said that there were traces of remains of insects and their larvae in the mouths of the corpses.

DR. STAHMER: Just a little while ago you spoke of the scientific examination of skulls undertaken by Professor Orsos. The record also refers to this matter, and I quote:

"A large number of skulls were examined with respect to the changes they had undergone, which, according to the background and experience of Professor Orsos, would be of great value in fixing the date of death. In this connection, we are concerned with stratified encrustations on the surface of the mush found in the skull as a residue of the brain. These symptoms are not to be found among corpses which have

175

been in their graves for less than 3 years. Such a condition, among other things, was found in a very decided form in the skull of corpse Number 526, which was found near the surface of a large mass grave."

I should like to ask you now if it is correct that, according to the report of Professor Orsos, such a condition was discovered not only as is said here on the skull of one corpse, but among other corpses also.

MARKOV: I can answer this question quite categorically. We were shown only one skull, the one precisely mentioned in the record under the Number 526. I do not know that other skulls were examined, as the record seems to imply. I am of the opinion that Professor Orsos had no possibility of examining many corpses in the Katyn wood, for he came with us and left with us. That means he stayed in the Katyn wood just as long as I and all the other members of the commission did.

DR. STAHMER: Finally, I should like to quote the conclusion of the summarizing expert opinion, in which it is stated:

"From statements made by witnesses, from the letters and correspondence, diaries, newspapers, and so forth, found on the corpses, it may be seen that the shootings took place in the months of March and April 1940. The following are in complete agreement with the findings made with regard to the mass graves and the individual corpses of the Polish officers, as described in the report."

Is this statement actually correct?

THE PRESIDENT: I did not quite understand the statement. As I heard you read it, it was something like this: From the statements of witnesses, letters, and so forth...

DR. STAHMER: "... in complete agreement with the findings made with regard to the mass graves and the individual corpses of the Polish officers and described in the report." That is the end of the quotation.

THE PRESIDENT: It doesn't say that the following persons are in complete agreement, but that the following facts are in complete agreement. Is that right?

· DR. STAHMER: No. My question is: "Is this statement approved by you? Do you agree with it?"

THE PRESIDENT: Yes, I know, but you read out certain words, which were these: "The following are in complete agreement." What I want to know is whether that means that the following persons are in complete agreement, or whether the following facts are in complete agreement.

DR. STAHMER: Special facts had been set down, and this is a summarizing expert opinion signed by all the members of the commission. Therefore, we have here a scientific explanation of the real facts.

THE PRESIDENT: Would you just listen to what I read out from what I took down? "From the statements of witnesses, letters, and other documents, it may be seen that the shooting took place in the months of March and April 1940. The following are in complete agreement." What I am asking you is this—

[Dr. Stahmer attempted to interrupt.]

Just a moment, Dr. Stahmer, listen to what I say. What I am asking you is: Does the statement mean that the following persons are in complete agreement, or that the following facts are in complete agreement?

DR. STAHMER: No, no. The following people testify that this fact, the fact that the shootings took place in the months of March and April 1940, agrees with the results of their investigations of the mass graves and of individual corpses. That is what is meant and that is the conclusion. What has been found here is in agreement with that which has been set down and determined scientifically. That is the meaning.

THE PRESIDENT: Go on.

DR. STAHMER: Is this final deduction in accord with your scientific conviction?

MARKOV: I have already indicated that this statement regarding the condition of the corpses is based on the date resulting from testimony by the witnesses and from the available documents, but it is in contradiction to the observations I made on the corpse which I dissected. That means I did not consider that the results of the autopsies corroborated the presumable date of death to be taken from the testimony or the documents. If I had been convinced that the condition of the corpses did indeed correspond to the date of decease mentioned by the Germans, I would have given such a statement in my individual protocol.

When I saw the signed protocol I became suspicious as to the last sentence of the record—the sentence which precedes the signatures. I always had doubts whether this sentence was contained in that draft of the protocol which we saw at the conference in Smolensk.

As far as I could understand, the draft of the protocol which had been elaborated in Smolensk only stated that we actually were shown papers and that we heard witnesses; and this was supposed to prove that the killings were carried out in March or April of 1940.

I was of the opinion that the fact that the conclusion was not based on medical opinion and not supported absolutely by medical reports and examination, was the reason why the signing of the protocol was postponed and why the record was not signed in Smolensk.

DR. STAHMER: Witness, at the beginning of my examination you stated that you were fully aware of the political significance of your task. Why, then, did you desist from protesting against this report which was not in accord with your scientific conviction?

MARKOV: I have already said that I signed the protocol as I was convinced that the circumstances at this isolated military airfield offered no other possibility, and therefore I could not make any objections.

DR. STAHMER: Why did you not take steps later on?

MARKOV: My conduct after the signing of the protocol corresponds fully to what I am stating here, I repeat. I was not convinced of the truth of the German version. I was invited many times to Berlin by Director Dietz. I was also invited to Sofia by the German Embassy. And in Bulgaria, the Bulgarian Foreign Office also invited me to make a public statement over the radio and to the press; and I was requested to say what conclusions we had come to during our investigation. However, I did not do so, and I always refused to do so. Because of the political situation in which we found ourselves at that moment, I could not make a public statement declaring the German version was wrong.

Concerning that matter there were quite sharp words exchanged between me and the German Embassy in Sofia. And when, a few months later, another Bulgarian representative was asked to be sent as a member of a similar commission for the investigation of the corpses in Vinnitza in the Ukraine, the German Ambassador Beckerly stated quite openly to the Bulgarian Foreign Office that the Germans did not wish me to be sent to Vinnitza.

That indicated that the Germans very well understood my behavior and my opinion on that matter. Concerning this question, Minister Plenipotentiary Saratov, of our Foreign Office, still has shorthand records about conversations which, if the Honored Tribunal considers it necessary, can be sent here from Bulgaria.

Therefore, all my refusals, after I had signed the protocol, to carry on any activity for the purpose of propaganda, fully correspond to what I said here, namely that the conclusions laid down in the collective protocol do not answer my personal conviction. And I will repeat that if I had been convinced that the corpses were buried for 3 years, I would have testified this after having dissected a corpse. But I have left my personal protocol incomplete and this is a quite unusual thing in the case of medico-judicial examination.

DR. STAHMER: The protocol was not signed by you alone, but on the contrary it carries the signatures of 11 representatives of science, whose names you gave yesterday, some of them of world renown. Among these men we find a scientist of a neutral country, Professor Naville.

Did you take the opportunity to get in touch with one of these experts in the meantime with a view of reaching a rectification of the report?

MARKOV: I cannot say on what considerations the other delegates signed the protocol. But they also signed it under the same circumstances as I did. However, when I read the individual protocols, I notice that they also refrained from stating the precise date of the killing of the man whose corpse they had dissected. There was one exception only, as I have already said. That was Professor Niloslavich, who was the only one who asserted that the corpse which he had dissected was that of a man buried for at least 3 years. After the signing of the protocol, I did not have any contact with any of the persons who had signed the collective protocol.

DR. STAHMER: Witness, you gave two versions, one in the protocol which we have just discussed, and another here before the Court. Which version is the correct one?

MARKOV: I do not understand which two versions you are speaking about. Will you please explain it?

DR. STAHMER: In the first version, in the protocol, it is set forth that according to the conclusion which had been made, the shooting must have taken place 3 years ago. Today you testified that the findings were not correct, and between the shooting and the time of your investigations there could only be a space of perhaps 18 months.

MARKOV: I stated that the conclusions of the collective protocol do not correspond with my personal conviction.

DR. STAHMER: "Did not correspond" or "do not correspond with your conviction"?

MARKOV: It did not and it does not correspond with my opinion then and now.

DR. STAHMER: I have no further questions.

MR. COUNSELLOR SMIRNOV: Mr. President, I have no further questions to put to this witness.

THE PRESIDENT: Witness, were any of the bodies which were examined by the members of this delegation exhumed from the ground in your presence?

MARKOV: The corpses which we dissected were selected among the top layers of the graves which had been already exhumed. They were taken out of the graves and given to us for dissection.

THE PRESIDENT: Was there anything to indicate, in your opinion, that the corpses had not been buried in those graves?

MARKOV: As far as traces are concerned, and as far as the layers of corpses were preserved, they were stuck to each other; so that if they had been transferred, I do not believe that this could have been done recently. This could not have been done immediately before our arrival.

THE PRESIDENT: You mean that you think the corpses had been buried in those graves?

MARKOV: I cannot say whether they were put into those graves immediately after death had come, as I have no data to confirm this, but they did not look as if they had just been put there.

THE PRESIDENT: Is it possible, in your opinion as an expert, to fix the date of March or April or such a short period as that, 3 years before the examination which you have made?

MARKOV: I believe that if one relies exclusively on medical data, that is to say, on the state and condition of the corpses, it is impossible, when it is a question of years, to determine the date with such precision and say accurately whether they were killed in March or in April. Therefore, apparently the months of March and April were not based on the medical data, for that would be impossible, but on the testimony of the witnesses and on the documents which were shown us.

THE PRESIDENT: When you got back to Sofia, you said that the protocol was sent to you for your observations and for your corrections and that you made none. Why was that?

MARKOV: We are concerned with the individual protocol which I compiled. I did not supplement it by making any conclusion, I did not add any conclusion because it was sent to me by the Germans and because in general at that time the political situation in our country was such that I could not declare publicly that the German version was not a true one.

THE PRESIDENT: Do you mean that your personal protocol alone was sent to you at Sofia?

MARKOV: Yes, only my personal protocol was sent to Sofia. As to the collective protocol, I brought that back myself to Sofia and handed it over to our Foreign Minister.

THE PRESIDENT: Is your personal protocol, in the words that you drew it up, incorporated in the whole protocol and signed by all the delegates?

MARKOV: In my personal protocol there is only a description of the corpse and of the clothing of the corpse which I dissected.

THE PRESIDENT: That is not the question I asked.

MARKOV: In the general protocol a rough description only is made, concerning the clothing and the degree of decomposition.

THE PRESIDENT: Well, do you mean that your personal protocol...

MARKOV: I consider that the personal protocols are more accurate regarding the condition of the corpses, because they were compiled during the dissection and were dictated on the spot to the stenographers.

THE PRESIDENT: Just listen to the question, please. Is your personal protocol, in the words in which you drew it up, incorporated in the collective protocol in the same words?

MARKOV: My own protocol is not included in the general record, but it is included in the *White Book* which the Germans published together with the general record.

THE PRESIDENT: It is there, then, in the report, is it? It is in the *White Book*?

MARKOV: Yes, quite right. It is included in this book.

THE PRESIDENT: The witness can retire. Yes, Colonel Smirnov, do you have another witness?

MR. COUNSELLOR SMIRNOV: Yes, Mr. President. I beg you to allow me to call as a witness, Professor of Medical Jurisprudence Prosorovski.

[The witness Prosorovski took the stand.]

THE PRESIDENT: Will you state your full name, please.

VICTOR IL'ICH PROSOROVSKI (Witness): Prosorovski, Victor Il'ich.

THE PRESIDENT: Will you repeat this oath after me:

I, citizen of the U.S.S.R.—called as a witness in this case— solemnly promise and swear before the High Tribunal—to say all that I know about this case—and to add and withhold nothing.

[The witness repeated the oath.]

THE PRESIDENT: You may sit down.

MR. COUNSELLOR SMIRNOV: Witness, just before questioning you, I beg you to adhere to the following order. After my question, please pause in order to allow the interpreters to make the translation, and speak as slowly as possible.

Will you give the Tribunal very briefly some information about your scientific activity, and your past work as a medico-judicial doctor.

PROSOROVSKI: I am a doctor by profession; professor of medical jurisprudence and a doctor of medical science. I am the Chief Medical Expert of the Ministry of Public Health of the Soviet Union. I am the Director of the Scientific Research Institute for Medical Jurisprudence at the Ministry of Public Health of the U.S.S.R.; my business is mainly of a scientific nature; I am President of the Medico-Judicial Commission of the Scientific Medical Council of the Ministry of Public Health of the U.S.S.R.

MR. COUNSELLOR SMIRNOV: How long did you practice as a medico-judicial expert?

PROSOROVSKI: I practiced for 17 years in that sphere.

MR. COUNSELLOR SMIRNOV: What kind of participation was yours in the investigation of the mass crimes of the Hitlerites against the Polish officers in Katyn?

PROSOROVSKI: The President of the Special Commission for investigation and ascertaining of the circumstances of the shootings by the German Fascist aggressors of Polish officers, Academician Nicolai Ilych Burdenko, offered me in the beginning of January 1944 the chairmanship of the Medico-Judicial Commission of experts. Apart from this organizational activity, I participated personally in the exhumations and examination of these corpses.

THE PRESIDENT: Colonel Smirnov, perhaps that would be a good time to break off.

[The Tribunal recessed until 1400 hours.]

Afternoon Session

THE MARSHAL: May it please the Tribunal, the Defendants Hess, Fritzsche, and Von Ribbentrop are absent.

MR. COUNSELLOR SMIRNOV: May I continue the examination of this witness, Mr. President?

THE PRESIDENT: Yes.

MR. COUNSELLOR SMIRNOV: Please tell me, how far from the town of Smolensk were the burial grounds where the corpses were discovered?

PROSOROVSKI: A commission of medico-legal experts, together with members of the special commission, Academician Burdenko, Academician Potemkin, Academician Tolstoy, and other members of this commission, betook themselves on 14 January 1944 to the burial grounds of the Polish officers in the so-called Katyn wood. This spot is located about 15 kilometers from the town of Smolensk. These burial grounds were situated on a slope at a distance of about 200 meters from the Vitebsk high road. One of these graves was about 60 meters long and 60 meters wide; the other one, situated a small distance from this first grave, was about 7 meters long and 6 meters wide.

MR. COUNSELLOR SMIRNOV: How many corpses were exhumed by the commission you headed?

PROSOROVSKI: In the Katyn wood the commission of medical experts exhumed and examined, from various graves and from various depths, altogether 925 corpses.

MR. COUNSELLOR SMIRNOV: How was the work of exhumation done and how many assistants were employed by you on this work?

PROSOROVSKI: Specialists and medico-legal experts participated in the work of this commission. In September and October 1943 they had exhumed and examined the corpses of the victims shot by the Germans...

MR. COUNSELLOR SMIRNOV: Where was the examination of the corpses performed?

PROSOROVSKI: They examined them in the town and the neighborhood of Smolensk. Among the members of this commission were Professor Prosorovski; Professor Smolianinov; the eldest and most learned collaborator of the Medico-Legal Research Institute, Dr. Semenovski; Professor of Pathological Anatomy Voropaev; Professor of Legal Chemistry Schwaikova, who was invited for consultations on chemico-legal subjects. To assist this commission, they called also medico-legal experts from the forces. Among them were the medical student Nikolski, Dr. Soubbotin...

MR. COUNSELLOR SMIRNOV: I doubt whether the Tribunal is interested in all these names. I ask you to answer the following question: What method of examination was chosen by you? What I mean is, did you strip the corpses of their clothes and were you satisfied with the customary post mortem examination or was every single one of these 925 corpses thoroughly examined?

PROSOROVSKI: After exhumation of the corpses, they were thoroughly searched, particularly their clothing. Then an exterior examination was carried out and then they were subjected to a complete medico-legal dissection of all three parts of the body; that is to say, the skull, the chest, and the abdomen, as well as all the inner organs of these corpses.

MR. COUNSELLOR SMIRNOV: Please tell me whether the corpses exhumed from these burial grounds bore traces of a previous medical examination?

PROSOROVSKI: Out of the 925 corpses which we examined, only three had already been dissected; and that was a partial examination of the skulls only. On all the others no traces of previous medical examination could be ascertained. They were clothed; and the jackets, trousers, and shirts were buttoned, the belts were strapped, and the knots of ties had not been undone. Neither on the head nor on the body were there any traces of cuts or other traces of medico-legal examination. Therefore this excludes the possibility of their having been subjected to any previous medico-legal examination.

MR. COUNSELLOR SMIRNOV: During the medico-legal examination which was carried out by your commission, did you open the skulls?

PROSOROVSKI: Of course. At the examination of quite a number of corpses the skull was opened and the contents of the skull were examined.

MR. COUNSELLOR SMIRNOV: Are you acquainted with the expression "pseudocallus?"

PROSOROVSKI: I heard of it when I received a book in 1945 in the Institute of Medico-Legal Science. Before that not a single medical legal expert observed any similar phenomena in the Soviet Union.

MR. COUNSELLOR SMIRNOV: Among the 925 skulls which you examined, were there many cases of pseudocallus?

PROSOROVSKI: Not one of the medico-legal experts who were examining these 925 corpses observed lime deposits on the inner side of the cranium or on any other part of the skull.

MR. COUNSELLOR SMIRNOV: Therefore, there was no sign of pseudocallus on any of the skulls.

PROSOROVSKI: No.

MR. COUNSELLOR SMIRNOV: Was the clothing also examined?

PROSOROVSKI: As already stated, the clothing was thoroughly examined. Upon the request of the Special Commission, and in the presence of its members and of the Metropolitan Nikolai, Academician Burdenko, and others, the medico-legal experts examined the clothing, the pockets of the trousers, of the coats, and of the overcoats. As a rule, the pockets were either turned, torn open, or cut open, and this testified to the fact that they had already been searched. The clothing itself, the overcoats, the jackets, and the trousers as well as the shirts, were moist with corpse liquids. This clothing could not be torn asunder, in spite of violent effort.

MR. COUNSELLOR SMIRNOV: Therefore, the tissue of the clothing was solid?

PROSOROVSKI: Yes, the tissue was very solid, and of course, it was besmeared with earth.

MR. COUNSELLOR SMIRNOV: During the examination, did you look into the pockets of the clothing and did you find any documents in them?

PROSOROVSKI: As I said, most of the pockets were turned out or cut; but some of them remained intact. In these pockets, and also under the lining of the overcoats and of the trousers we discovered, for instance, notes, pamphlets, papers, closed and open letters and postcards, cigarette paper, cigarette holders, pipes, and so forth, and even valuables were found, such as ingots of gold and gold coins.

MR. COUNSELLOR SMIRNOV: These details are not very relevant, and therefore I beg you to refrain from giving them. I would like you to answer the following question: Did you discover in the clothing documents dated the end of 1940 and also dated 1941?

PROSOROVSKI: Yes. I discovered such documents, and my colleagues also found some. Professor Smolianinov, for instance, discovered on one of the corpses a letter written in Russian, and it was sent by Sophie Zigon, addressed to the Red Cross in Moscow, with the request to communicate to her the address of her husband, Thomas Zigon. The date of this letter was 12 September 1940. Besides the envelope bore the stamp of a post office in Warsaw of September 1940, and also the stamp of the Moscow post office, dated 28 September 1940.

Another document of the same sort was discovered. It was a postcard sent from Tarnopol, with the post office cancellation: "Tarnopol, 12 September 1940."

Then we discovered receipts with dates, one in particular with the name—if I am not mistaken—of Orashkevitch, certifying to the receipt of money with the date of 6 April 1941, and another receipt in his name, also referring to a money deposit, was dated 5 May 1941.

Then, I myself discovered a letter with the date 20 June 1941, with the name of Irene Tutchinski, as well as other documents of the same sort.

MR. COUNSELLOR SMIRNOV: During the medico-legal examination of the corpses, were any bullets or cartridge cases discovered? Please tell us what was the mark on these cartridge cases? Were they of Soviet make or of foreign make; and if they were foreign make, which one, and what was the caliber?

PROSOROVSKI: The cause of death of the Polish officers was bullet wounds in the nape of the neck. In the tissue of the brain or in the bone of the skull we discovered bullets which were more or less deformed. As to cartridge cases, we did indeed discover, during the exhumation, cartridge cases of German origin, for on their bases we found the mark G-e-c-o, Geco.

MR. COUNSELLOR SMIRNOV: One minute, Witness.

I will now read an original German document and I beg the permission of the Tribunal to submit a series of documents which have been offered us by our American colleagues, Document Number 402-PS, Exhibit USSR-507. It concerns German correspondence and telegrams on Katyn, and these telegrams are sent by an official of the Government General, Heinrich, to the Government of the Government General.

I submit the original document to the Court. I am only going to read one document, a very short one, in connection with the cartridge cases discovered in the mass graves. The telegram is addressed to the Government of the Government General, care of First Administrative Counsellor Weirauch in Kraków. It is marked:

"Urgent, to be delivered at once, secret.

"Part of the Polish Red Cross returned yesterday from Katyn. The employees of the Polish Red Cross have brought with them the cartridge cases which were used in shooting the victims of Katyn. It appears that these are German munitions. The caliber is 7.65. They are from the firm Geco. Letter follows." signed—"Heinrich."

[Turning to the witness.] Were the cartridge cases and cartridges which were discovered by you of the same caliber and did they bear the mark of the same firm?

PROSOROVSKI: As I have already stated, the bullets discovered in the bullet wounds were 7.65 caliber. The cases discovered during the exhumation did indeed bear the trademark of the firm Geco.

MR. COUNSELLOR SMIRNOV: I now ask you to describe in detail the condition of the body tissues and of the inner organs of the corpses exhumed from the graves of Katyn.

PROSOROVSKI: The skin and the inner organs of the corpses were well preserved. The muscles of the body and of the limbs had kept their structure. The muscles of the heart had also kept their characteristic structure. The substance of the brain was, in some cases, putrified; but in most cases, it had kept its structural characteristics quite definitely, showing a clear distinction between the gray and white matters. Changes in the inner organs were mainly a sagging and shrinking. The hair from the head could be easily pulled out.

MR. COUNSELLOR SMIRNOV: From the examination of the corpses, to what conclusion did you come as to the date of death and date of burial?

PROSOROVSKI: On the basis of the experience I have gained and on the experiences of Smolianinov, Semenovski, and other members of the commission...

MR. COUNSELLOR SMIRNOV: One moment, Witness. I would like you to tell the Tribunal briefly what these experiences were and how many corpses were exhumed. Did you personally exhume them or were they exhumed in your presence?

PROSOROVSKI: In the course of the great War, I was often medico-legal expert during the exhumation and the examination of corpses of victims who were shot by the Germans. These executions occurred in the town of Krasnodar and its neighborhood, in the town of Kharkóv and its neighborhood, in the town of Smolensk and its neighborhood, in the so-called extermination camp of Maidanek, near Lublin, so that all told more than 5,000 corpses were exhumed and examined with my personal co-operation.

MR. COUNSELLOR SMIRNOV: Considering your experience and your objective observations, to what conclusions did you arrive as to the date of the death and the burial of the victims of Katyn?

PROSOROVSKI: What I have just said applies to me as well as to many of my colleagues who participated in this work. The commission came to the unanimous conclusion that the burial of the Polish officers in the Katyn graves was carried out about 2 years before, if you count from January, the month of January 1944—that is to say that the date was autumn 1941.

MR. COUNSELLOR SMIRNOV: Did the condition of the corpses allow the conclusion that they were buried in 1940, objectively speaking?

PROSOROVSKI: The medico-legal examination of the corpses buried in the Katyn wood, when compared with the modifications and changes which were noticed by us during former exhumations on many occasions and also material evidence, allowed us to come to the conclusion that the time of the burial could not have been previous to the autumn of 1941.

MR. COUNSELLOR SMIRNOV: Therefore, the year 1940 is out of question?

PROSOROVSKI: Yes, it is completely excluded.

MR. COUNSELLOR SMIRNOV: If I understood you rightly you were also medico-legal expert in the case of other shootings in the district of Smolensk?

PROSOROVSKI: In the district of Smolensk and its environs I have exhumed and examined together with my assistants another 1,173 corpses, besides those of Katyn. They were exhumed from 87 graves.

MR. COUNSELLOR SMIRNOV: How did the Germans camouflage the common graves of the victims which they had shot?

PROSOROVSKI: In the district of Smolensk, in Gadeonovka, the following method was used:

The top layer of earth on these graves was covered with turf, and in some cases, as in Gadeonovka, young trees were planted as well as bushes; all this with a view to camouflaging. Besides, in the so-called Engineers' Garden of the town of Smolensk, the graves were covered with bricks and paths were laid out.

MR. COUNSELLOR SMIRNOV: So you exhumed more than 5,000 corpses in various parts of the Soviet Union.

PROSOROVSKI: Yes.

MR. COUNSELLOR SMIRNOV: What were the causes of death of the victims in most cases?

PROSOROVSKI: In most cases the cause of death was a bullet wound in the head, or in the nape of the neck.

MR. COUNSELLOR SMIRNOV: Were the causes of death at Katyn similar to those met with in other parts of the Soviet Union? I am speaking of mass-shootings.

PROSOROVSKI: All shootings were carried out by one and the same method, namely, a shot in the nape of the neck, at point-blank range. The exit hole was usually on the forehead or in the face.

MR. COUNSELLOR SMIRNOV: I will read the last paragraph of your account on Katyn, mentioned in the report of the Extraordinary Soviet State Commission:

"The commission of the experts emphasizes the absolute uniformity of the method of shooting the Polish prisoners of war with that used for the shootings of Soviet prisoners of war and Soviet civilians. Such shootings were carried out on a vast scale by the German Fascist authorities during the temporary occupation of territories of the U.S.S.R., for instance, in the towns of Smolensk, Orel, Kharkóv, Krasnodar and Voroneszh."

Do you corroborate this conclusion?

PROSOROVSKI: Yes, this is the typical method used by the Germans to exterminate peace-loving citizens.

MR. COUNSELLOR SMIRNOV: I have no further questions to put to this witness, Mr. President.

DR. STAHMER: Where is your permanent residence, Witness?

PROSOROVSKI: I was born in Moscow and have my domicile there.

DR. STAHMER: How long have you been in the Commissariat for Health?

PROSOROVSKI: I have been working in institutions for public health since 1931 and am at present in the Ministry of Public Health. Before that I was a candidate for the chair of forensic medicine at Moscow University.

DR. STAHMER: In this commission were there also foreign scientists?

PROSOROVSKI: In this commission there were no foreign medico-legal experts, but the exhumation and examination of these corpses could be attended by anybody who was interested. Foreign journalists, I believe 12 in number, came to the burial grounds and I showed them the corpses, the graves, the clothing, and so on—in short everything they were interested in.

DR. STAHMER: Were there any foreign scientists present?

PROSOROVSKI: I repeat again that no one was present apart from Soviet experts of the medico-legal commission.

DR. STAHMER: Can you give the names of the members of the press?

THE PRESIDENT: Dr. Stahmer, he was giving a long list of names before and he was stopped by his counsel.

Why do you shake your head?

DR. STAHMER: I did not understand, Mr. President, the one list of names. He gave a list of names of the members of the commission. My question is that: The witness has just said that members of the foreign press were present and that the results of the investigation were presented to them. I am now asking for the names of these members of the foreign press.

THE PRESIDENT: Well, go on.

DR. STAHMER: Will you please give me the names of the members of the press, or at least the names of those who were present and to whom you presented the results of the examination?

PROSOROVSKI: Unhappily I cannot give you those names now here; but I believe that if it is necessary, I would be able to find them. I shall ascertain the names of all those foreign correspondents who were present at the exhumation of the corpses.

DR. STAHMER: The statement about the number of corpses exhumed and examined by you seems to have changed somewhat according to my notes, but I may have misunderstood. Once you mentioned 5,000 and another time 925. Which figure is the correct one?

PROSOROVSKI: You did not hear properly. I said that 925 corpses had been exhumed in the Katyn wood, but in general I personally exhumed or was present at the exhumation of over 5,000 in many towns of the Soviet Union after the liberation of the territories from the Germans.

DR. STAHMER: Were you actually present at the exhumation?

PROSOROVSKI: Yes..

DR. STAHMER: How long did you work at these exhumations?

PROSOROVSKI: As I told you, on 14 January a group of medico-legal experts left for the site of the burial grounds together with the members of a special commission.

THE PRESIDENT: Can you not just say how long it took—the whole exhumation? In other words, to shorten it, can you not say how long it took?

PROSOROVSKI: Very well. The exhumation and part of the examination of the corpses lasted from 16 to 23 January 1944.

DR. STAHMER: Did you find only Polish officers?

PROSOROVSKI: All the corpses, with the exception of two which were found in civilian clothing, were in Polish uniforms and were therefore members of the Polish Army.

DR. STAHMER: Did you try to determine from what camp these Polish officers came originally?

PROSOROVSKI: That was not one of my duties. I was concerned only with the medico-legal examination of the corpses.

DR. STAHMER: You did not learn in any other way from what camp they came?

PROSOROVSKI: In the receipts which were found, dated 1941, it was stated that the money was received in camp 10-N. It can therefore be assumed that the camp number was obviously of particular importance.

DR. STAHMER: Did you know of the Kosielsk Camp?

PROSOROVSKI: Only from hearsay. I have not been there.

DR. STAHMER: Do you know that Polish officers were kept prisoners there?

PROSOROVSKI: I can say only what I heard. I heard that Polish officers were there, but I have not seen them myself nor have I been anywhere near there.

DR. STAHMER: Did you learn anything about the fate of these officers?

PROSOROVSKI: Since I did not make the investigations, I cannot say anything about the fate of these officers. About the fate of the officers, whose corpses were discovered in the graves of Katyn, I have already spoken.

DR. STAHMER: How many officers did you find altogether in the burial grounds at Katyn?

PROSOROVSKI: We did not separate the corpses according to their rank; but, in all, there were 925 corpses exhumed and examined.

DR. STAHMER: Was that the majority?

PROSOROVSKI: The coats and tunics of many corpses bore shoulder straps with insignia indicating officers' rank. But even to-day I could not distinguish the insignia of rank of the Polish officers.

DR. STAHMER: What happened to the documents which were found on the Polish prisoners?

PROSOROVSKI: By order of the special commission the searching of the clothing was done by the medico-legal experts. When these experts discovered documents they looked them through, examined them, and handed them over to the members of the special commission, either to Academician Burdenko or Academician Tolstoy, Potemkin, or any other members of the commission. Obviously these documents are in the archives of the Extraordinary State Commission.

DR. STAHMER: Are you of the opinion that from the medical findings regarding the corpses the time when they were killed can be determined with certainty?

PROSOROVSKI: In determining the date on which these corpses had presumably been buried, we were guided by the experience which we had gathered in numerous previous exhumations and also found support by material evidence discovered by the medico-legal experts. Thus we were able to establish beyond doubt that the Polish officers were buried in the fall of 1941.

DR. STAHMER: I asked whether from the medical findings you could determine this definitely and whether you did so.

PROSOROVSKI: I can again confirm what I have already said. Since we had great experience in mass exhumations, we came to that conclusion, in corroboration of which we also had much material evidence, which enabled us to determine the autumn of 1941 as the time of the burial of the Polish officers.

DR. STAHMER: I have no more questions to put to this witness. Mr. President, an explanation regarding the document which was just submitted; I have here only a copy signed by Heinrich; I have not seen the original.

THE PRESIDENT: I·imagine the original is there.

DR. STAHMER: Thank you, Mr. President.

THE PRESIDENT: Yes, Colonel Smirnov, do you want to re-examine?

MR. COUNSELLOR SMIRNOV: Mr. President, I have no further questions to put to this witness; but with the permission of the Tribunal, I would like to make a brief statement.

We were allowed to choose from among the 120 witnesses whom we interrogated in the case of Katyn, only three. If the Tribunal is interested in hearing any other witnesses named in the reports of the Extraordinary State Commission, we have, in the majority of cases, adequate affidavits which we can submit at the Tribunal's request. Moreover, any one of these persons can be called to this Court if the Tribunal so desires.

That is all I have to say upon this matter.

THE PRESIDENT: Dr. Stahmer?

DR. STAHMER: I have no objection to the further presentation of evidence as long as it is on an equal·basis; that is, if I, too, have the opportunity to offer further evidence. I am also in a position to call further witnesses and experts for the Court.

THE PRESIDENT: The Tribunal has already made its order; it does not propose to hear further evidence.

DR. STAHMER: Thank you.

So clearly do the facts stand out that it is not proposed to offer any summary, but special mention must be made of the Swiss Professor Naville, the one neutral member of the International Medical Commission. He is one of the central figures to the drama and thus his part and what happened to him later must be emphasised.

In September 1946, when the Nuremberg Trial was nearing its end, a Communist member of the Swiss Grand Council, Mr Vincent (Swiss Communists ostensibly belong to the "Labour Party"), launched an attack against Professor François Naville on account of his participation in an International Medical Commission which in 1943 had conducted an investigation at Katyn and later published its well-known report. Mr Vincent chose the form of an interpellation addressed to the Geneva Executive Body (State Council).

This interpellation had its repercussion at a sitting of the Geneva Legislative Body (Grand Council) in 1947, when Mr Albert Picot, Head of the Cantonal Government, answered Mr Vincent's case. A substantial part of this answer consisted in reading extracts from Professor Naville's report, presented by the latter to the Government at their request, following the interpellation. The following is the substance of Mr Albert Picot's statement.

At the meeting of the Grand Council of 11 September 1946, Mr Vincent asked the Council of State how they "proposed to judge the case of Dr Naville, Professor of Forensic Medicine, who had agreed to act as legal expert at the request of the German Government in April 1943, where the origin of the 10,000 corpses of Polish officers discovered in Katyn Forest near Smolensk was concerned." Mr Picot explained that Katyn was in Russia, in a region which the Russians had occupied since the beginning of the Polish-German war in 1939, and where the Germans had not arrived until the summer or autumn of 1941, after the first successes of their offensive in the direction of Smolensk.

If the killings took place in 1940 or the winter of 1940-41, then these men were executed by the Russians. If the corpses dated from the autumn of 1941 or from 1942, then the murderers were Germans.

Considering the climatic conditions, the question could be decided by the advanced state of decomposition of the bodies.

In its report the State Council would deal only with the following three points.

1. The relations between Dr Naville and the Swiss authorities (federal, cantonal and military) before his departure.

2. Did Dr Naville receive any reward from Germany?

3. Did Dr Naville agree to work under conditions of constraint, thus soiling the honour of a Swiss professor?

On all these three questions Mr Picot said the State Council was in possession of a clear report from Dr Naville, and he was happy to read them extracts from it:

"I wish to state that in the present circumstances I have been obliged for the first time to abandon the restraint which I deliberately undertook to exercise for the last three years. I am not mixed up with politics. I consider that I did my duty by participating in the technical enquiry with a view to throwing some light on the matter concerned, and I have always refused to follow up the numerous requests addressed to me, either by Swiss or by foreigners, to make public my findings or my opinion. Rightly or wrongly, I considered that only the Poles, who had asked for an enquiry into the circumstances in which some ten thousand of their officers, prisoners-of-war, had been killed, could assume the responsibility of initiating a public discussion on the subject, of which the consequences could not be foretold.

But the intervention of Mr Vincent forces me to give certain information on the matter.

I recall that after the Germans had uncovered the ditches containing several thousand Polish officers, killed, according to them, by Russian secret police, the Polish Government in London as well as the Polish and German Red Cross asked the International Committee of the Red Cross to conduct an investigation on the spot. As Russia

194

seemed determined to veto such an enquiry, the German sanitary authorites in order to accede to the wishes of the Poles, decided to entrust the investigation to a committee of experts composed of one specialist in forensic medicine from almost every neutral country, that is, each country not directly interested in the matter.

The Russians, considering that the demand for an impartial investigation submitted by the Poles was a hostile act on their part, severed diplomatic relations with the Polish Government on Monday, April 26 1943. This I was told by the Swiss envoy in Berlin, Mr Fröhlicher, on whom I called immediately after my arrival in Berlin ...

It was on the night of 22 April 1943 that Dr Steiner, of Geneva, medical adviser to the German Consulate General there, asked me whether I could and would leave on April 26 to join the committee of experts concerned. May I add in this connection that I have never concealed from anybody my outspoken, and I may even say violent, hostility towards Germany after 1914, caused by their foreign policy which I always considered dangerous for Switzerland, and since 1933 by the attitude adopted by the Nazi bosses. I could give many proofs of this. It was well known to my students at the University, as even the late German Professor Askanasy occasionally protested to me about it. Your department can ascertain from Professor Liebeskind what I said after incidents provoked by one of his lectures to German students, and from the Dean of the Faculty of Law the way in which I intervened in connection with the affair of the German student-spies.

Therefore I refused at first, and suggested some other Swiss experts in forensic medicine. In the meantime, however, I contacted other persons. They told me that this was not a matter of rendering a service to the Germans, but of responding to the legitimate wish of the Poles, who demanded that an impartial investigation be made, and that it should be established whether anything had been done to produce a nominal roll of the dead officers, to proceed with the identifications as far as possible, and to inform the next-of-kin. Here I must remind you that, contrary to the practice followed by all the other belligerents, the Russians always refused to supply lists of prisoners-of-war taken by them to the International Committee of the Red Cross, and that for a long time no news had been received of the 10,000 officers they had taken prisoners.

When Dr Steiner again invited me, therefore, I decided to accept; if I am not mistaken it was on Friday night. It seemed to me that it would be cowardly to refuse to co-operate in an enquiry whose object was to establish the truth, under the pretext that I would necessarily be dissatisfied with one or the other of the belligerents accused of a crime so particularly odious and contrary to the modern usages of war. At that time, moreover, I did not know what the composition of the committee of experts would be, or even what would be submitted to me for examination and enquiry."

Professor Naville's report goes on to state that he was authorised to take part in the Medical Commission of Investigation both by the Swiss military authorities and by the Federal authorities (Political Department). In accordance with the regulations he advised the Dean of his Faculty, who neither at that time nor at any later period, raised any objection. Next, the report deals with the question of the fees which the Germans were supposed to have paid to the members of the Commission:

"Mr Vincent seems to be under the impression that I received a considerable amount of German gold. He can be relieved of his anxiety. I was certainly entitled to ask for a fee for such complicated work of such importance, on which I spent one month of my time carrying out various researches, after a journey taking eight days. But from the very beginning I decided to refuse it, on moral grounds. I did not want to obtain money either from the Poles or from the Germans. I do not know who paid the expenses of the journey of our committee of experts, but I personally never asked for nor received from anyone any gold, money, gifts, rewards, assets, or promises of any kind. If, at a time when

196

it is being mauled simultaneously by the armies of two mighty neighbours, a country learns of the massacre of nearly 10,000 of its officers, prisoners-of-war, who committed no crime other than to fight in its defence, and when that country tries to find out how this came about, a decent man cannot demand fees for going to the place and trying to lift the hem of the veil which concealed, and still conceals, the circumstances in which this act of odious cowardice, so contrary to the usages of war, was committed.

Mr Vincent asserts that I was acting under constant pressure from the Gestapo, which prevented us from having a free hand. This is absolutely untrue. I do not know whether the police were represented amongst those who received and accompanied us (doctors and guides), but I can definitely state that we were able to proceed undisturbed with our work as experts. I did not notice any signs of pressure being exerted on myself or on any of my colleagues. We were always able to discuss all matters freely amongst ourselves without the Germans being present. On many occasions I told my co-experts and the Germans who received us certain 'truths' which they considered rather outspoken. They seemed dumbfounded, but no one ever molested me. I did not conceal what I thought of the moral responsibility of the Germans in this matter, as it was they who went to war and invaded Poland, even if our conclusions should establish their innocence in the matter of the death of the officers.

We spent two days and three nights at Smolensk, about 50 km from the Russian lines. I moved about quite freely at Smolensk, as in Berlin, without being in any way accompanied or shadowed. As two of us could speak Russian, we were on several occasions able to talk to the peasants and Russian prisoners-of-war. We also contacted the medical personnel of the Polish Red Cross, who co-operated at the exhumation, and were specially detailed to identify the bodies, make nominal rolls and inform the next-of-kin. We assured ourselves that everything possible was being done in that respect.

197

We freely carried out about ten post-mortem examinations of bodies which we had had taken, in our presence, from the lower layers of the unexplored common graves. Undisturbed, we dictated reports on the post-mortem examinations, without any intervention from the German medical personnel. We examined, superficially but quite freely, about one hundred corpses which had been disinterred in our presence. I, myself, found in the clothes of one of them a wooden cigarette-holder engraved with the name 'Kozielsk' (one of the three camps from which the doomed officers had come), and in the uniform of another I found a box of matches from a Russian factory in the Province of Orel, the region where the three camps concerned were situated. [Only Kozielsk was in fact situated in the region of Orel. – LF.]

At the examinations, being concerned with the forensic medicine aspect, we paid particular attention to the transformation of the fatty substances of the skin and internal organs, to changes in the bones, to the destruction of joint tendons, to changes and atrophies of various parts of the body, and also to all other signs which would testify to the time of death.

Examination of the skull of a lieutenant, undertaken specifically by Professor Orsós from Budapest, at which I was present, brought to light a condition that virtually excluded the possibility of death having occurred less than three years previously, according to scientific works already published on that kind of mutilation ...

We experts were also at liberty to discuss amongst ourselves all our findings as well as the wording of our report. After having examined the graves and the corpses on Thursday and Friday, 29 and 30 April, all the experts met on Friday afternoon to discuss and decide on the composition of the report. Only medical personnel took part in that discussion, but without any interference. Some of us made a draft of the final report, and it was submitted to me for signature on Saturday May 1 at 3 am. I offered several comments and asked for some changes and additions, which were immediately made. I do not know whether the same consideration was given to the observations and criticisms made by Dr Markov of Bulgaria; I do not remember whether he intervened during our discussion at the meeting, but I was present when he signed the report on May 1 about noon, and I can state that he did not then make any objections or protests. I do not know whether he was subject to any constraint by the authorities of his own country, either before the journey to Katyn or at the time he revoked his signature, on being charged with collaboration and when he declared that he had acted under pressure; but he was certainly not under any pressure or constraint while the committee of which he was a member was at work. In any case he made in our presence a post-mortem of one corpse and quite freely dictated the report on it, of which I have a copy ...

By joining the twelve other experts in signing our report of 1943, I by no means wished to serve the Germans, but only the Poles and the truth. The report, by the way, occupies only five pages in the thick illustrated volume of 331 pages which the Germans published about Katyn, which I possess, and which I was told is also in the possession of the public library in Geneva.

Mr Vincent is a solicitor in Geneva. He knows that even in our country, in matters where a public confession or substantial evidence have not entirely clarified matters, the parties concerned try to take advantage of all the obscure points. He also knows that not everywhere in Europe are the rights of man and the truth unsullied by the ideological and political trends of the day respected as they are, happily, in Switzerland.

As for us, the forensic medicine experts, it is our right and our duty in our modest sphere to seek above all to serve the truth in conflicts where the parties sometimes serve other masters; it is the tradition and the pride of our profession, an honour sometimes dangerous. We must do this without yielding to pressure, from whatever quarter it may come, without regard for the criticism and hostility of those who may be put into an awkward position by our unbiased impartiality. May our motto always remain that

199

which honours certain tombs; *Vitam impendere vero*.

Here, Mr President, is the report you asked me to submit in justification of my actions. I leave it to you to decide whether it would be appropriate to contact the Federal Political Department, with whose consent I took part in the experts' examination in question, before you submit the text or its gist to the Grand Council, which might have political consequences I cannot foresee.

(signed) F. Naville"

Those, continued Mr Picot, were the parts of the report submitted by Dr Naville that concerned them most. On behalf of the State Council he concluded:

"The State Council considers that there is nothing with which to reproach Dr François Naville, distinguished man of science, excellent forensic medicine expert, who acted on his own responsibility and who did nothing to infringe any rule of professional conduct or of the code of honour. Dr Naville's report contains a statement justifying the conclusions of his original report of 1943. He may publish it when he wishes. The Grand Council is not entitled to make any pronouncement on this matter.

On the other hand, the Grand Council agrees with us that it is in accordance with the ideal of science and the moral principles of our country that a scientist should seek the truth by means of thorough investigation."

Another figure who must receive a special mention is the apostate, Markov. It is not known what eventually became of him, but it is not hard to hazard a guess.

Dr Markov provided the Russians with the only endorsement they achieved for their otherwise untenable, if elaborate, proposition that the Germans were responsible for the crime.

The day after the Russian forces invaded Bulgaria on 8 September 1944, they swept away the interim democratic non-Communist government of Muraviev and set up a Communist "Fatherland Front" headed by Kimon

Gheorghiyev. On 2 October 1944 the Bulgarian Radio announced a proclamation that the Bulgarian Government was committing for trial all those who had evidenced an attitude openly hostile to the USSR. As a signatory of the Commission's report implicating the USSR, Dr Markov was immediately arrested and imprisoned for over three months before he appeared before a "People's Tribunal". On the 26 January 1945, the Bulgarian Radio announced that the Third Section of the Supreme People's Tribunal would start a trial of those accused of having participated in "the monstrous German imposture of Katyn".

On 19 February 1945, the Bulgarian Radio announced: "The first of the accused, Dr Markov, has declared: 'I am guilty before the Bulgarian People, before their liberator, Russia, and before civilised humanity. My crime is that during the tyrannical government of Ficov [President of the Council of Ministers in Bulgaria, 1943. – LF] I succumbed to strong pressures to take part in the so-called inquiry at Katyn, and to not having found sufficient strength to resist and to support those more courageous Bulgars – enemies of that political government – who found themselves in prisons and concentration camps." The communiqué went on to state that Dr Markov had declared that he had no intention of helping German propaganda; that in his opinion the bodies had not been buried three years previously "as affirmed by the Germans" but later, and that it was materially impossible for the Russians to have committed the crime. "In these circumstances," ended the Bulgarian Radio statement "the Prosecutor has dropped his charges against Dr Markov."

On 23 February 1945, the Bulgarian Radio announced that Dr Markov, having been judged not guilty, was acquitted.

These "People's Courts" had sweeping powers, including the imposition of the death penalty and the condemning of guilty parties to terms of forced labour for ten years and more. Despite the fact that there is no evidence to show that Dr Markov signed the Protocol of the International Medical Commission under any kind of

201

duress and that Professor Naville, an unquestionably impartial witness, stated in Geneva that he carried out a post-mortem in Markov's presence, Dr Markov recanted. He revoked his earlier statements, and there can be no other reason for that other than fear of Soviet reprisals against his own person or family.

It will be recalled that in his report of 1946, Professor Naville stated that "Dr Markov ... was certainly not under any pressure or constraint while the committee of which he was a member was at work. In any case, he made in our presence, a post-mortem of one corpse and quite freely dictated the report on it, of which I have a copy." Markov himself spoke no German, and so when dictating his report, referred to by Professor Naville, he had to use the services of an interpreter. That interpreter, obviously a vital witness, was never asked by the Russian prosecutor to be produced at Nuremberg.

It may also be pointed out here that the Germans allowed a team from the Polish Red Cross to carry out investigations at Katyn through the medium of a "Technical Commission" (known as TC-PRC – Technical Commission of the Polish Red Cross). A member of that Polish Commission was Dr Marian Wodzinski, an expert in forensic medicine, who started work at Katyn on the 29 April 1943 and continued until mid-May of that year. In his report, which contains perhaps the most impressive and entirely credible evidence of the absence of German "pressure", Dr Wodzinski states that although constantly under the supervision of the Germans, no restrictions or limitations were set upon the personal freedom of members of his commission. Members of the commission wore Red Cross brassards, and had complete freedom to come and go to their quarters outside the forest at any time they chose. Dr Wodzinski states that the work of the Commission was never impeded or hampered by the Germans, who merely watched what was being done. He even added that Dr Buhtz, the German member of the International Medical Commission, came into occasional conflict with German propaganda experts when the latter tried (but failed) to interrupt his work which he approached from a purely scientific angle. The assistant to the head of German propaganda at Katyn was a Lt Sloventzyk, a journalist from Vienna; but neither Lt Sloventzyk or Lt Voss of the *Geheime Feldpolizei* ever interfered with Dr Wodzinski or his work. The absence in Dr Wodzinski's report of any mention of coercion by the Germans is directly contrary to the allegations made by Dr Markov in his recantations of 1945 and 1946.

Dr Wodzinski recognised among the disinterred corpses two former medical colleagues, Dr Kalicinski and Professor Pienkowski, of Kracow University. Another member of the TC-PRC, W. Kasur, also identified another body as that of Colonel Dr Stefanowski.

None of this in any way corroborates the statements made by Dr Markov, although in his recantation, Markov limited himself to answering points put forward by the Soviets, and did not comment on their allegations that the Germans had interfered with the corpses for the purpose of removing from them any document or evidence dated later than May of 1940. It is however quite evident from what Dr Wodzinski said, that such "interference" with the corpses for the purpose alleged by the Soviets would have been physically impossible.

Dr Markov, as Professor Naville testified, freely carried out examinations while a member of the International Medical Commission in 1943. At that time of German victory, Markov had no reason to believe that the bodies would again be disinterred by the returning Soviets, neither did he have any reason to think that he would, in Sofia, find himself in the hands of the Communists or be arraigned before a "People's Court". I have referred to the extreme penalties which such a court could impose. At Nuremberg in 1946, Markov, who still lived in the Soviet sphere of influence, had no course open to him but to repeat his earlier revocation.

This, then, was the manner in which the Tribunal dealt with the Katyn massacre – a confused story of truth and lies, of attempts to waylay witnesses, and of courage on the

part of the German defence counsel. There is the chimera of
"Camps Nos 1 O.N., 2 O.N. and 3 O.N."; there is a hint of
torture for the local inhabitants in that part of Russia
(Kisselev); there is the vanished figure of Menshagin.
German bullets; insects or the lack of them; pierced skulls;
tragic personal letters spilled on the ground; faceless,
medically incompetent Soviet "investigators"; advancing
armies; wolves scratching at graves, and behind it all a
horribly repeated digging in the ground for long-dead
innocent Poles. A truly terrible tale, spelt out word for word
beneath the scales of Justice for all the world to see. And at
the end of it all, no answer, no judgment and a withdrawal
of Katyn from the indictment.

But what of the number of victims, constantly stated as
being 11,000? This figure was first used by the Germans for
propaganda purposes, and then fastened upon by the
Soviets to cover up another mystery, not mentioned.

For it is known that of the 14,500 or so murdered in what
is collectively called the Katyn massacre, only somewhat
less than 5,000 from the camp at Kozielsk were found in the
ghastly pits in the Forest of Katyn. There arises the spectral
question of the whereabouts of the other 10,000! The
Russians have erected a squat and hideous monument in
Katyn Forest which, in Russian and illiterate Polish,
recites:
"Here are buried Polish officer prisoners murdered amidst
great suffering by German-Fascist occupiers in the autumn
of 1941."

The inscription on the memorial erected by the Russians at Katyn states:
"Here are buried Polish Officers murdered amidst great suffering by German
fascist occupiers in the autumn of 1941."

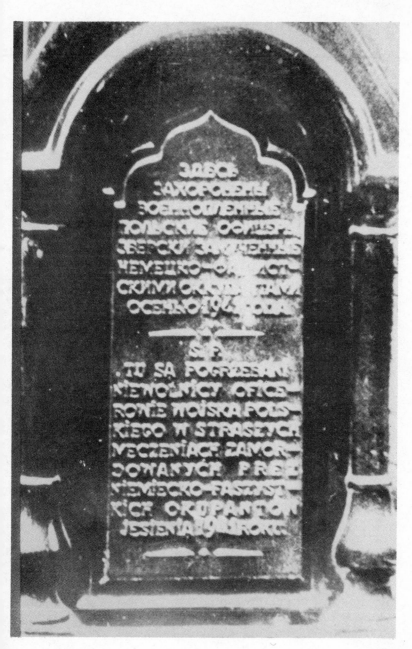

4 The US Select Committee 1952

The Nuremberg trials were over; the sentences were pronounced and death awaited the condemned, either at their own hands or at the hands of the executioner. But not all were sentenced to death. Even today Hess lingers on in Spandau prison, a tragic link with what was, a pawn in a disgusting political game with Berlin among the stakes. Grossadmiral Doenitz was awarded only ten years' imprisonment; perhaps this example of relative clemency relieves, somewhat, the more squalid aspects of the macabre process by which the victors sought to give moral indemnity to the victims of war.

No such indemnification, however, was offered to the surviving relatives of those so brutally murdered at Katyn – and they did not forget. Neither did General Anders, that gallant soldier who progressed from the Lubianka to Monte Casino and ended his days in London in exile. He remembered Katyn as did all other Poles, for whom one blow followed another. The disgraceful Treaty of Yalta tore from them the very country they had fought so bitterly to regain, and handed it like a prize to Stalin.

Herded together in London, the Poles must have wondered why justice never seemed to bless them, for after Yalta there was the victory march in England's capital – *and the Poles were not allowed to take part* for fear of offending the Polish puppet government or indeed the Russians. These Polish veterans of so many campaigns were urged to go back to Poland, but many of them had known what it

General Wladyslaw Anders.

was like to freeze in Siberia. They had looked into the brutish faces of their NKVD captors and had felt the point of the four-bladed bayonet in their backs as they stumbled in the snow beyond the Arctic Circle. Above all they thought of Katyn, mass grave of so many of their loved ones proscribed for ever beneath the still pines of Russia. There had been no justice, and their ex-allies were grotesquely anxious to obliterate even the memory of it for ever.

But not only are the Poles conspicuously brave, they are also tenacious, and in 1950 General Anders renewed the Polish plea, ending with these words:

"May I be allowed to appeal through you to the public opinion of the countries you represent as well as to that of other free and democratic countries and ask for their support of our endeavours tending to elucidate the Katyn Case and our plea for the appointment of a new International Tribunal which would be called upon to investigate this crime and to punish the culprits.

Because in my opinion, only if all the war criminals of this last war will meet with adequate punishment will this be understood as a warning for the future and will give a guarantee that human principles will be maintained in case we find ourselves involved in a new armed conflict."

Here indeed was a cry for help, a cry of anguish. It took perhaps two years to find an answer. On 18 September 1951 the US House of Representatives adopted a Resolution to establish a select committee to conduct a full and complete investigation concerning the Katyn massacre. It must have been a moment of sombre triumph for the exiled Poles to know that the full weight of American investigatory machinery was to be lent in yet another attempt to unravel this unjudged case.

In 1952 the United States Government Printing Office published the testimony received in evidence by the Select Committee in seven parts, totalling almost 2,400 pages. Having already in the previous chapter portrayed the evidence given at Nuremberg in considerable detail, it is obviously not possible here again to reproduce all the evidence collected by the US Select Committee. However, some of that evidence, collected in Germany and published in part 5 of the total is pertinent to what has already been said and must be included to present a clearer and more complete picture. The evidence which follows was collected in Frankfurt between 21 April and 26 April 1952, and the final report of the Select Committee is contained in Appendix I.

The Select Committee was composed of Congressmen Ray. J. Madden (Indiana) Chairman, Daniel J. Flood (Pennsylvania), Foster Furcolo (Massachusetts), Thaddeus M. Machrowicz (Michigan), George A. Dondero (Michigan), Alvin E. O'Konski (Wisconsin), Timothy P. Sheehan (Illinois), as well as John J. Mitchell, Chief Counsel.

What follows is an exact extract from the hearings before the Select Committee, with the exception of those parts which cover evidence from Colonel Ahrens, Reinhard von Eichborn, General Eugen Oberhäuser and Mr Sweet. It should be recalled that this evidence was taken some seven years after the Nuremberg Trial and that the Select Committee had the advantage of calling far more witnesses than were allowed in 1946. Much detail, therefore, which could and should have been available at Nuremberg is now given, and it throws into pin-point perspective many aspects of the Katyn case hitherto not taken into account. This is a lengthy chapter, crammed with detail – detail which is largely unknown to the public and which, in any event, has been waiting for such an opportunity for ventilation.

To start off with here, the evidence throws light upon Count Czapski's search in Russia for the "missing officers"; the proceedings continue with Werner Stephan, a journalist in Goebbels' Ministry of Propaganda.

Jozef Czapski

Mr. MITCHELL. Where did you have your education?

Mr. CZAPSKI. I studied at Peterburg and in Krakow.

Mr. MITCHELL. What did you do upon the completion of your studies?

Mr. CZAPSKI. After the completion of my studies, I moved to Paris, where I did considerable painting; and up until 1939, I had occupied myself as an artist, as a painter, and I did considerable writing in Warsaw after. After 1931 it was in Warsaw.

Mr. MITCHELL. Then your official position or profession was what?

Mr. CZAPSKI. I am an artist, a painter.

Mr. MITCHELL. Where were you on September 1, 1939?

Mr. CZAPSKI. I was in Warsaw, and as a Reserve officer, I was immediately called to active duty.

Mr. DONDERO. In what Army?

Mr. CZAPSKI. Naturally, to the Polish Army.

Chairman MADDEN. Pardon me.

I might say, on account of the large crowd in the courtroom, it is going to be necessary for the people to be as quiet as possible, the people that are assembled here, and also for the witness and interpreters to speak as loudly as possible, and slowly.

Mr. MITCHELL. What was the exact date that you joined the Polish Army?

Mr. CZAPSKI. I was called to active duty on September 3 in Krakow, where my regiment, the Eighth Regiment, was stationed.

Mr. MITCHELL. Mr. Chairman, I would like to ask the witness if he wants to tell what happened to him from that date forward in his own story.

Chairman MADDEN. Let me say to the witness that any procedure that makes it easier for him to reveal his knowledge with regard to the Katyn murders and facts leading up to his knowledge can be followed by him.

You can proceed in whatever way you desire.

Mr. CZAPSKI. I would prefer if you asked me the preliminary questions and get me to Starobielsk as quickly as possible, where I can then begin my testimony as to my direct association and knowledge of this matter.

I can now tell you how I was taken prisoner by the Russians.

Mr. MITCHELL. Please do.

Mr. CZAPSKI. As an officer of the Second Squadron of my regiment, I was with my regiment during our retreat on the heels of the German advance. On September 27, our units were surrounded by the armies of Russia and we were taken prisoner.

Mr. MITCHELL. What year was that?

Mr. CZAPSKI. September of 1939.

I was among those officers who were sent to one of the three camps where officers who had been armed had been taken. These officers were interned at Starobielsk, Kozielsk, and Otashkov.

Chairman MADDEN. I will have to admonish the photographers that these lights are interfering with the proceedings, so they will have to be turned out.

Mr. MITCHELL. Proceed.

Mr. CZAPSKI. I can describe for you our conditions in Starobielsk.

Mr. MITCHELL. Very briefly, please.

Mr. CZAPSKI. We remained at this camp until April 5, when the evacuation of the camp began, and the evacuation lasted from April 5 to May 12 of 1940. There were approximately 4,000 of us in this camp. There were 3,920 during the period of the evacuation.

There were amongst us people of all ranks and all units, starting with the rank of general, and there were several generals there. There were several hundred doctors, there were a few professors of the universities, there were many priests.

Among others evacuated before us was Father Alexandrowicz, the superintendent of the Protestant Church in Poland, the Reverend Potocki, and also the rabbi of the Polish Army, Rabbi Steinberg; several outstanding intellectuals, and a very large number of youths. Their only crime was that they were defending Poland against the aggression of Hitler. When the evacuation began, we were removed from the camp in groups numbering from 60 to 250 at each move.

Mr. MITCHELL. How many were in the group that left with you?

Mr. CZAPSKI. In my group there were only 16, but I will cover that later.

Mr. MITCHELL. On what date did you leave?

Mr. CZAPSKI. The 12th of May.

Mr. MITCHELL. What year?

Mr. CZAPSKI. 1940.

During this evacuation, a select group of 63 people was evacuated on the 25th of April. During this evacuation, the commanding officer of the camp, Berezkov, and another man, Kirszyn, assured us that we were being sent back to our homeland, to our own country, irrespective of by whom that country was being occupied, the Russians or the Germans.

At the same time, they were spreading rumors, however, that they were sending us to France, where we would form a special unit which would fight against Hitler.

After the 25th of April, when this select group had been evacuated, only a few more groups were evacuated. Included in those few remaining groups was my group of 16, which left on the 12th of May. We were first sent to Pavlishchev Bor, in the province of Smolensk. There we met the select and special group which had been evacuated from our camp on the 25th of April. Likewise, we also met there officers from the camps of Ostashkov and Kozielsk, numbering in all, approximately 400.

Mr. MITCHELL. Where was that?

Mr. CZAPSKI. That was in Pavlishchev Bor, in Smolensk.

After a couple of weeks, we were all sent to the camp of Griazovec, near Wologda. We at that time reasoned that all of our officers had been scattered among various camps in a similar manner. The uncertainty about the rest of our officers began that summer when we began receiving letters from relatives inquiring about them, from Poland.

211

Mr. MITCHELL. How long were you at the camp of Griazovec?

Mr. CZAPSKI. I remained at Griazovec until the end of August 1941.

Mr. MITCHELL. You are arrived at Griazovec what date?

Mr. CZAPSKI. Either at the very end of June or the early part of July 1940.

Mr. MITCHELL. Proceed with the rest of your story.

Mr. CZAPSKI. The alarm over our other fellow-officers grew from month to month.

Mr. FLOOD. Just a minute.

Before you begin to tell us about the search for the officers and the concern about the missing officers, I would like to know why you managed to survive, why you think the Russians kept you alive; and did your brother officers at Griazovec talk about that same question?

Mr. CZAPSKI. I must answer your second question first.

None of us, there wasn't a single one amongst us who at that time suspected these men had been murdered. We merely presumed that these men had been scattered in small groups such as ours in other camps and assigned probably to hard labor.

Do you now want to ask your first question?

Mr. FLOOD. I want your opinion today, as far as you are concerned.

Mr. CZAPSKI. In Griazovec there were interned people of all political beliefs, of all classes and not only but also members of minorities. It is my opinion that the decision to murder my fellow-officers was made in the Kremlin. This was during a period when there was great joy because of the close cooperation between Hitler and Stalin. It was their plan to first exterminate and execute these Polish officers, because for them it constituted a certain revenge, for these Poles constituted the elite of my country. But they did want to preserve a small group so that if a subsequent demand should ever be made, they could point to this group and say, "Here they are; you do have these people."

After the arrangement reached between Stalin and Sikorski, following Germany's invasion of Russia, a decision was reached that a Polish Army would be formed on the Russian territory, which would fight against the armies of Hitler.

Mr. MITCHELL. This committee has already heard testimony about a place called the "Haven of Bliss." Do you know anything about that? Answer yes, or no.

Mr. CZAPSKI. Yes.

Mr. MITCHELL. Tell the committee very briefly what you know about it.

Mr. CZAPSKI. I know only that about 20 officers had been taken there prior to the agreement reached between General Sikorski and Stalin.

Mr. MITCHELL. From which camp did those officers come; Pavlishchev Bor, or Griazovec?

Mr. CZAPSKI. From Griazovec and I think also from Moscow.

Mr. MITCHELL. Proceed and tell us what you know.

Mr. CZAPSKI. I know that the purpose of taking these people there and organizing this camp was to attempt to convert them to form a Red Polish Army in Russia.

Mr. FLOOD. Where was this villa?

Mr. CZAPSKI. Near Moscow.

From this group of approximately 20 officers, only a handful had agreed to this conversion. Among those who were converted was Berling, who subsequently became the commanding officer or commander in chief of the Red Polish Army in Russia at the time that General Anders' Polish forces were transferred from Russia.

And here lies one very important detail, which I would like to relate.

The chief of the NKVD, Beria, and his assistant, Merkulow, proposed to this particular group of officers, during the late fall of 1940, to prepare a plan for the formulation of a Polish Army in Russia which would fight against the armies of Hitler in case of a war against Hitler Germany.

Mr. MITCHELL. When did you say that was?

Mr. CZAPSKI. That was the late fall of 1940. At that time, Berling, who was the proposed commanding officer, said, "Very well; but under the condition that all of the Polish officers will be recruited into this proposed Army." To that, Beria replied, "Naturally, all of them; the leftists and the rightists, all of them."

To this, Berling replied: "Very well, we have the officers at Kozielsk, Starobielsk, and Ostashkov, and we have officers there of all units, so that we can form a complete army."

At this time, Merkulov told Berling: "Oh, no, no, not those at Kozielsk and Starobielsk. With those we have made a grave mistake."

Mr. MITCHELL. How do you know that?

Mr. CZAPSKI. I learned of this conversation in Turkestan in 1942. I heard this from three different people who, at various moments and at different places, had repeated this conversation to me.

Mr. MACHROWICZ. Mr. Chairman, I think at this point of the record it should be pointed out that this very same conversation, in those very same words, has been testified to before the committee, under oath, by other witnesses to whom they were repeated on the very same day they were uttered by Merkulow.

Chairman MADDEN. Very well.

Mr. MITCHELL. That is about all you know about the Haven of Bliss?

Mr. CZAPSKI. Yes, that is about all.

Mr. MITCHELL. You started to tell this committee, before I interrupted you, about the formation of the Sikorski-Stalin pact. Will you continue, please?

Mr. CZAPSKI. I began tell you this so that you would understand that when we were released from this camp as a cadre which was to form the Polish Army, already at that time, we were very seriously concerned about the safety of our fellow officers and, at that time, we already had prepared a list of several thousand of those whose names we could remember. But, I want to stress here and emphasize that we had considered the possibility that these men may have frozen to death, may have been starved to death, but at no time did we conceive of the possibility that these men may have been massacred.

The second phase that I can testify to is when we began forming our army in the regions near the Volga.

Mr. FLOOD. Before you start that second phase, I think you should know that the records of this hearing, or the hearings of this committee already show that the protocol, a copy of the protocol signed by the Soviet and the London Polish Government has been entered as a document in these hearings, and that, among other things, that protocol provided that on the part of Soviet Russia all prisoners—military, civil, or otherwise—held by the Russians in Russia, Poles, would be automatically freed, with the only exception listed being certain criminals.

Do you understand that in English?

Mr. CZAPSKI. Yes.

Mr. FLOOD. And having that in mind, the Poles now began to form their army, taking for granted the Poles would be released by the Russians for that purpose.

Mr. CZAPSKI. That is correct.

Mr. MITCHELL. Will you now proceed with the story of your assignment?

Mr. CZAPSKI. Yes; only mine.

Mr. MITCHELL. Then, the committee would like to know how you were appointed, why you were appointed, to whatever assignment you were appointed, and what time the appointment was made.

Mr. CZAPSKI. The reason was very clear. At the very beginning, I was assigned as chief of an office of assistance and information for the first Polish division that was being mobilized near Totsk. All the soldiers and all the officers that had reported from the various camps to this division had to first go through my hands.

Mr. MITCHELL. Who appointed you to that job?

Mr. CZAPSKI. General Tokaszewski, who was in charge of forming and mobilizing this particular division.

Mr. FLOOD. Just a minute.

For the purpose of today's hearing and to show some continuity, the record should show that at the time the rapproachment developed between the Soviet and the London Poles, Polish General Anders was a prisoner of the Russians in the Lubianka Prison in Moscow, and the Chief of the London Polish Government, General Sikorski, being unable to locate the Chief of Staff, General Haller, designated General Anders as the new commander in chief of the Polish Army to be organized in Russia. The Russians then released General Anders who proceeded to form the Polish Army, as indicated so far, and the testimony of General Anders taken in London indicates that he designated the witness, Czapski, to head up this unit and that his appointment from the other general mentioned was merely through the chain of command.

Mr. CZAPSKI. What I began testifying to before Mr. Flood's remarks was that at the time that I was describing I was just a very small, insignificant information officer of only one division, and it is very important that I be permitted to make my point here.

It was on the basis of the information that I obtained at that particular time that I went to General Anders with my information, and it was then that he appointed me in charge of the entire search for these men. When I was ordered by General Anders to organize a bureau to search for these men, I left Totsk and I proceeded to Buzuluk and joined the General Staff of the Polish Army.

Chairman MADDEN. Tell the witness if he would like to have a 5-minute recess, we can have a recess now.

Mr. CZAPSKI. It is immaterial.

Chairman MADDEN. Proceed.

Mr. CZAPSKI. I transferred to Buzuluk either in October or November—end of October or possibly the beginning of November, and with a large staff, I prepared a lengthy list of names which, subsequently, on the 4th of December, General Sikorski presented to Stalin.

But, there is a second reason why I had been named to this particular assignment by General Anders.

Mr. FLOOD. Just a minute.

Could that date of the meeting with Stalin have been December 3?

Mr. CZAPSKI. It is possible. It could have been the 3d or the 4th.

Mr. DONDERO. What year?

Mr. CZAPSKI. 1941.

The second reason was that I spoke Russian fluently. I had studied in Russia, and as early as 1919, I had made a search for Polish officers following the Bolshevik revolution.

As a result, I left behind my staff, which continued compiling and improving the list of the missing officers, and I personally then went into the terrain of Russia. I began at Czkalow, because the chief of the Soviet camps, the chief of the Gulag, was stationed at Czkalow. I went there with a letter from General Anders in which it was stated that on orders of Stalin all of the Polish prisoners should be released.

I was greeted, or received, by General Nasetkin. The General was sitting in front of a huge map of Russia on which were superimposed hundreds of stars and other marks indicating prison camps throughout Russia. Nasetkin received me somewhat cordially, because he was alarmed when I showed him the letter.

Chairman MADDEN. How did you know that these hundreds of stars on this map represented prison camps throughout Russia?

Mr. CZAPSKI. I knew because while I was the information officer at Totsk, and from where I came, I had received thousands of people who came from these very places—from Kolyma, from Kola, and from Komi which is in Soviet Russia near the Urals.

Mr. MITCHELL. Will you proceed, please?

Mr. CZAPSKI. General Nasetkin had promised to give me the answers to my questions on the following day.

Mr. MACHROWICZ. Did he say he needed that day's time to make telephone inquiries about these camps?

Mr. CZAPSKI. Yes; that is correct.

The following day, he received me very badly. It was obvious and apparent that he had received instructions from Moscow and from Kuybishev that he had no permission to talk to me.

Mr. FLOOD. Instead of asking a question, just for the record, the significance of Kuybishev was the fact that, because of the German advance, the Russian Government and the diplomatic corps had been moved to Kuybishev.

Mr. CZAPSKI. That is correct.

At the same time that I was getting this bad reception from Nasetkin, a general of the NKVD had contacted General Anders in Buzuluk and told him: "Czapski has no right to roam around the country. His dealings shall be confined to the central headquarters of the NKVD."

Following my return to Buzuluk, General Anders immediately dispatched me to the general headquarters of the NKVD. I went to Kuybishev, but I did not remain there very long because all traces led to Moscow. In Moscow, I attempted to talk either to Beria or to Merkulow.

Mr. MITCHELL. Whom did you talk to?

Mr. CZAPSKI. I was received neither by Beria nor Merkulow, but I did succeed in talking to one of Merkulow's most trusted and top assistants, General Rajchmann.

Mr. MITCHELL. When did you see him, approximately?

Mr. CZAPSKI. It was either at the beginning of February or the end of January 1942.

I beg your pardon. It was the 2d of April 1942.

Mr. MACHROWITZ. Wasn't it on February 3, 1942, witness?

Mr. CZAPSKI. No, it was the 2d of February, 1942.

Mr. MITCHELL. What transpired during your conversation with Rajchmann?

Mr. CZAPSKI. Rajchmann greeted me or received me, as the Russians always do, with another silent witness there. I handed him a memorandum which I now hold in my hand. It is the same memorandum.

Mr. MITCHELL. Do you have any objections to permitting the committee to see that, having it photostated, and returned to you?

Chairman MADDEN. Just a minute.

We'll take a recess for a few minutes now if the cameramen that came late desire to take pictures.

(Whereupon, a recess was taken.)

(After recess.)

Chairman MADDEN. The committee will come to order. Proceed.

• Mr. FLOOD. Now, Mr. Czapski, you have handed us what purports to be a memorandum handed by you to General Rajchmann; is that correct?

Mr. CZAPSKI. Yes; that is correct, Mr. Flood.

Mr. FLOOD. Will you have the stenographer mark this as exhibit No. 1?

(The document referred to was marked as "Exhibit No. 1, Frankfurt" and was returned to the witness at his request.)

Mr. FLOOD. I now show you exhibit No. 1 and ask you whether or not this is the memorandum to which you have just referred.

Mr. CZAPSKI. Yes, Mr. Flood, this is the original memorandum that I had handed him.

Mr. FLOOD. Do I understand that you will have a photostatic copy of this prepared for later submission to the committee?

Mr. CZAPSKI. That is correct.

Mr. FLOOD. We will have the photostatic copy then marked for the permanent record as exhibit 1–A, at which time the original document, exhibit 1, can be returned to the witness.

(Exhibit No. 1–A, photostatic copy of exhibit 1, is identical with exhibit 50–A already appearing in pt. 4, London hearings, p. 944, and will not be reprinted at this point.)

Mr. FLOOD (continuing). Now, in what language is that document, exhibit 1, now written?

Mr. CZAPSKI. In Russian.

Mr. FLOOD. Will you also have provided a translation from Russian into English to accompany the photostat of exhibit No. 1?

Mr. CZAPSKI. If you will help me, of course I will.

Mr. Flood. And that translation will be marked as "Exhibit 1–B."
(Exhibit 1–B, English translation of Exhibit 1, is shown below.

[Translation from Russian of Exhibit 1]

[On the top a pencil mark:] Memorandum submitted in Moscow to the Gen.
Raichmann in Lublianka [seat of N. K. V. D.] on April 2, 1942, by Capt. Czapski.

Memorandum Concerning the Polish Prisoners of War From Starobel'sk, Kozel'sk and Ostashkov, Who Did Not Return

The prisoners of war, who from 1939 until April 1940, were in Starobel'sk, Kozel'sk and Ostashkov (numbering more than 15,000, of whom 8,700 were commissioned officers) did not return from exile, and the place of their confinement is unknown to us; an exception are 400–500 men, that is approximately three percent of the total number of prisoners of war, who were released in 1941, after one year's imprisonment in Griasovets near Vologda or in other prisons.

Camp in Starobel'sk No. 1

Shipments of prisoners of war used to arrive in Starobel'sk camp from 30 September to 1 November 1939 and when the clearing of the inmates of the camp began, the number of the Polish Prisoners was 3,920 men including generals and colonels who were kept separately. There were also several scores of civilians, about 30 cadet-officers (podkhorunzhii) and ensigns (khorunzhii). All others were commissioned officers, of whom at least 50 percent were of the regular army, 8 generals, more than 100 colonels and lieutenant-colonels, about 250 majors, approximately 2500 first and second lieutenants of all branches of the service and auxiliary services. Among them there were 380 doctors, several professors of institutions of higher learning, etc.

Kozel'sk No. 1 and Ostashkov were camps for prisoners of war, both formed and cleared approximately at the same time.

The camp in Kozel'sk

On the day when the clearing of the camp began—on April 3rd, 1940—the camp had approximately 5,000 prisoners, among them 4,500 commissioned officers of all ranks and of all branches of the service.

Camp in Ostashkov

On the day when the clearing began—on April 6, 1940—this camp contained 6,750 men, among them 380 commissioned officers.

The clearing of the Camp in Starobel'sk

On April 5, 1940, the first group, consisting of 195 men, was sent from Starobel'sk Colonel Berezhkov the Soviet commandant, and commissar Kirshin official assured the prisoners of war, that they are being sent to the distribution center, from where they will be sent to the places of their residence, to Poland, both to the German or the Soviet part.[1] Up to April 26, inclusive, groups consisting of from 65 to 240 men were shipped.

On April 25, after the customary announcement concerning the sending of more than 100 men, a special list of 63 men was read, to whom the order was given to stand separately during the departure to the station.

After April 26 there was an interruption in the clearing of the camps until May 2, when 200 men were sent. After that the rest of the prisoners were sent with small groups on the 8th, 11th, and 18th of May. The group, which included me, among others, was sent to Pavlishchev Bor (Smolensky region), where we met the whole "special group" of 63 men, who were sent on April 25. Thus we numbered 79, almost all being commissioned officers from Starobel'sk, who were, after one year, released from Griazovecky camp. Adding to this number 7 more commissioned officers, who were shipped individually during the winter of 1939–40 from Starobel'sk, the total number of those commissioned officers who were released will make 86 out of 3920 men, i. e., slightly more than 2 percent of the total number of prisoners in Starobel'sk.

---

[1] According to the numerous letters received in Poland in the winter of 1940–41, we know for sure that nobody was then sent from Starobel'sk, Kozel'sk, and Ostashkov back to Poland.

The clearing of the camps of Kozel'sk and Ostashkov

It proceeded in like manner. In Pavlishchev Bor we found about 200 commissioned officers from Kozel'sk and about 120 men from Ostashkov. The proportion between the number of people brought to Pavlishchev Bor from these camps and the number of people confined there differed slightly from the proportion relating to Starobel'sk.

The camp in Griazovets

After a month's stay in Pavlishchev Bor the whole of the camp, approximately 400 people, was shipped to Griazovets near Vologda, where we remained until the day of [our] release. About 1,250 commissioned officers and enlisted men also arrived there, they were previously interned in Lithuania, Latvia, and Estonia and stayed as internees (not as prisoners of war) in Kozel'sk No. 2 from the fall of 1940 till the summer of 1941.

The camp in Griazovets was known to us as the only PW camp consisting mostly of commissioned officers of the Polish Army, which existed in the U.S.S.R. from June 1940 to September 1941, and the population of which, after their release, almost in full number, joined the Polish Army in the U.S.S.R.

Almost 6 months had passed since the "amnesty" to all Polish PW's and internees was proclaimed on August 12, 1941. Polish commissioned officers and enlisted men, released from confinement to which they were subjected when trying to cross the border after September 1939 or those arrested at places of their residence, were arriving, in groups or individually, to join the Polish Army. But despite the amnesty, in spite of the explicit promise given by the President of the Sovnarkom (Soviet of People's Commissars) Stalin himself, in November 1941, to our envoy Kot that PW's be returned to us, despite of a strict order to locate and liberate the PW's from Starobel'sk, Kozel'sk, and Ostashkov given by Stalin on December 4, 1941, in the presence of the Commanding General of the Polish Army Sikorski and General Anders, in spite of all this not a single prisoner of war appeared from Starobel'sk, Kozel'sk and Ostashkov (except the group from Griazovets mentioned before and a few scores of persons who were separately interned and liberated as early as in September).

No appeal for help from the PW's interned in the camps mentioned above has ever reached us.

In spite of the interrogation of thousands of persons returning from all the camps and prisons of the U. S. S. R. we shall have not obtained any reliable information on their [the prisoners, in Starobel'sk] whereabouts, except for the following rumors coming from second-hand sources: that from 6 to 12 thousands commissioned and noncommissioned officers were sent to Kolyma via Bukhta Nachodka in 1940;

That more than 5,000 commissioned officers were collected in the mines of the *Frants Iosif Islands;* that there were deportations to *Novaia Zemlia, Kamchatka,* and *Chukotka*; that in the summer of 1941, 630 commissioned officers, PW's from Kozel'sk, were working 180 kilometers from *Pestraia Dresva*; that 150 commissioned officers, clad in their uniforms, were seen north from the river *Sos'va* near *Gar'*; that some Polish commissioned officers, prisoners of war, were transported on huge towed barges (1,700–2,000 men to a barge) to *Severnye Ostrova* and that three such barges sank in *Barents sea*.

None of this information was confirmed sufficiently, although the information on *Severnye Ostrova* and *Kolyma* seems to be the most probable.

We know that every prisoner of war was registered, and that the "case records" of all us, with the numerous records on interrogations together with the documents, identified and checked photographs, were kept in special files. We know how carefully, and exactly this work of the NKVD was conducted, so that none of us, [former] prisoners of war, can believe for a second that the whereabouts of 15,000 PW's of which more than 8,000 are commissioned officers, could be unknown to the higher authorities of the NKVD. The solemn promise of the *Predsovnarkom* Stalin himself and his strict order to ascertain the fate of the former Polish prisoners of war permit us to hope that at least we could know where our brothers in arms are and, if they have perished, how and when it happened.

Number of commissioned officers of the Polish Army, former prisoners of war, who did not return

On April 5, 1940, the day of the beginning of the clearance of the camp of inmates in *Starobel'sk*, the total number of commissioned officers, prisoners of war, with the exception of some civilians and approximately 30 ensigns and cadet-officers was 3,920.

The number of prisoners of war in *Kozel'sk* on April 6, 1940, the day when clearing of the camp of inmates began, amounted to 5,000, among them commissioned officers constituted 4,500.

The number of prisoners of war in *Ostashkov* on April 6, 1940, the day when the clearing of the camp of inmates started, was 6,570; the commissioned officers constituted among them 380. Total 8,800 commissioned officers.

By deducting several scores of civilians from Starobel'sk the number of commissioned officers constitutes 8,700.

Some 300 commissioned officers from *Griasovets*, former prisoners of war from Starobel'sk, Kozel'sk, and Ostashkov, have returned to the Polish Army and furthermore several scores were released from prisons, into which they were sent from the above-mentioned camps, and returned, which makes the total number of returned commissioned officers not more than 400.

Consequently the following figure shows the number of commissioned officers who did not return from Starobel'sk, Kozel'sk, and Ostashkov camps—8,300 men.

All officers of the Polish Army, the number of which as of January 1, 1940, amounted to approximately 2,300 persons, were formerly confined or interned in Lithuania, Latvia, and Estonia, but they were not prisoners of war (with the exception of the above-mentioned 400 persons).

Being unable to define with similar precision the grand total number of all those who did not return, we give solely the figures of the prisoners of war from Kozel'sk, Starobel'sk, Ostashkov, the majority of which are officers, because we were able to determine their number with relative precision.

Because we were now expanding, by virtue of the decision of the Chairman of the Council of People's Commissars Stalin and of General Sikorski, our army in the south of the U. S. S. R., a continuously growing need is felt for these officers who disappeared; we are losing in them the best military experts, the best commanding personnel.

No special explanation is required to realize the extent to which the disappearance of many a thousand of brothers-in-arms obstructs the work of the creation in our army of confidence in the Soviet Union, which confidence is so much needed for a sound development of mutual relations between the two allied armies in their struggle against the common sworn enemy.

Commissioner for the Affairs of
Former Prisoners of War in the USSR
Captain of the Cavalry JOZEF CZAPSKI

Moscow, February 2, 1942.

Mr. CZAPSKI. I would like at this time to say, in a few words, what is in this memorandum.

Mr. FLOOD. You can proceed to testify from the best of your recollection as to what the memorandum contains, and refer to it, if necessary, to refresh your memory.

Mr. CZAPSKI. I began this memorandum with an accurate and detailed account of how these officers were transferred to these various camps, including the numbers. Then I cite all of the promises made by Stalin in the presence of Molotov that all of these people are ordered to be released. Then I proceed to explain that Poles are arriving to us from all over Russia and that among them there isn't a single member nor a single name of any of these three camps. I then proceed to name all of the islands and far-away camps where there are rumors that these officers may be interned. I want to emphasize here that at that particular time I still believed that these men would be found.

Mr. O'KONSKI. And that they were alive.

Mr. CZAPSKI. Yes; and I believed that they were alive, or I hoped that they were alive.

And then I further state in my memorandum that I cannot believe that the Russians do not know the whereabouts or the fate of these soldiers.

I further stated that I know very well how carefully the NKVD records the movements of every prisoner.

I then stated in the memorandum that the solemn promises of Stalin that these men would be released authorizes me to inquire of them to tell me at least whether or not these men are still alive.

General Rajchmann read my memorandum very calmly. He said that he knows nothing about this matter, although I have heard from other sources that he was for a certain time in charge of the entire Polish section.

Mr. FLOOD. Just a minute. What was the date of that memorandum?

Mr. CZAPSKI. The 2d of April 1942.

Mr. MACHROWICZ. Just a minute; the 2d of April, or the 2d of February?

Mr. CZAPSKI. I have noted here on my copy of the original that it is the 2d of April. It is possible that it was the 2d of February.

Mr. MITCHELL. What, exactly, have you got at the top of that memorandum?

Mr. CZAPSKI. I must make a correction. In the typewritten statement, typewritten in Moscow, the date is given as the 2d of February. My own notation at the top is incorrectly stated, in my own handwriting.

Mr. PUCINSKI. The witness, Mr. Chairman, is indicating in his copy here on the last page, under the signature, as the typewritten date, "February 2d," and a little notation on the face of the memorandum, written by hand, is the date "April 2d."

Mr. MACHROWICZ. Just one question, and I would like to have your answer on the record. Do you now wish to correct your statement so that it will read that this conversation you had with General Rajchmann and the date of handing him the memorandum is February 2d, 1942—is that correct?

Mr. CZAPSKI. Yes, I want that very much.

Mr. FLOOD. Now that we have established the date, I want to ask you this. In all of your conversations with any Russians of any category any place during your search thus far, had anybody told you that the Polish missing officers must be German prisoners, or prisoners of the Germans?

Mr. CZAPSKI. Never. Not once had I been told anything of that sort. And here I would like to add that it was common knowledge that the Russians had evacuated the prisoners when the Germans were advancing along all points sooner than they even evacuated the Russian families. For how these evacuations were conducted I suggest that you read a chapter in my book, Inhuman Land, which has the original stenographic record of this entire procedure of evacuation.

Mr. MACHROWICZ. Mr. Czapski, in that memorandum that you handed to General Rajchmann, did you specifically mention the fact that there were about 15,000 prisoners in Kozielsk, Starobielsk, and Ostashkov, and that none of them had been heard from?

Mr. CZAPSKI. I must reply to this very expressly. There were 15,000 in all. There were officers; there was police; and there were also soldiers. Of the officers in these three camps, there were 8,700.

Mr. MACHROWICZ. Did General Rajchmann tell you whether he would furnish you with an answer to the memorandum?

Mr. CZAPSKI. Yes. General Rajchmann assured me that he would give me a reply.

Mr. MACHROWICZ. Did you receive the reply?

Mr. CZAPSKI. I waited several days in Moscow, and suddenly one evening—that is, at midnight—I was awakened by the telephone. That was General Rajchmann calling me personally, who, in a very sympathetic manner, informed me that he would not see me again and that he had no knowledge in this matter, and he advised me to return to Kuybishev to see Vishinsky, since all the records on this matter were with Vishinsky at Kuybishev.

Mr. MACHROWICZ. Just a minute. Was Vishinsky then Commissar of Foreign Affairs?

Mr. CZAPSKI. He was the Vice Minister.

I told Rajchmann in reply that Ambassador Kot had talked to Vishinsky on eight different occasions in this matter and that Vishinsky's answer always was that he had no knowledge in this matter.

Mr. FLOOD. Just a minute. The record should show that Ambassador Kot is the Ambassador from the London-Polish Government to the Soviet, and at this time was with the Diplomatic Corps at Guybishev.

Mr. MACHROWICZ. Did that conversation end your seeking for information from the Russian authorities on the fate of these Polish officers?

Mr. CZAPSKI. Actually, yes. There were subsequent conversations. There was one with Ehrenburg, but the results of this conversation had contributed nothing new.

Mr. MACHROWICZ. By "Ehrenburg", you mean Ilya Ehrenburg, is that correct?

Mr. CZAPSKI. Yes.

Mr. MACHROWICZ. Who was Ilya Ehrenburg?

Mr. CZAPSKI. He was one of two of the most noted Russian writers at the time, and he had received a special Stalin prize (100,000 rubles) from Stalin for his book entitled "The Collapse of Paris."

Mr. MITCHELL. One question. When did you cease to be the head of this chief investigative unit for the locating of the missing Polish officers in Russia?

Mr. CZAPSKI. After my return to the Polish forces, which was either in April—it was in April of 1942.

Mr. MITCHELL. Why?

Mr. CZAPSKI. First of all, because I ceased believing that these men were alive. I base this conclusion of mine on my discussion and conversation with Hajchmann. Secondly, I had learned in Turkistan at this time of the discussions of Merkulow in the Villa of Bliss.

Mr. MACHROWICZ. Now, you are referring to the conversation in which Merkulow said or admitted that the Russians made a great mistake with these Polish officers?

Mr. CZAPSKI. Yes, that is correct.

Mr. FLOOD. Now, Mr. Czapski, I take for granted that this about terminated your general search—not that you ended it; I know that you still continued in a general way from then on.

Mr. PUCINSKI. The witness indicated, Mr. Flood, that he wants to reply to that.

221

Mr. Czapski. Officially my work was finished, and, naturally, I continued my interest in this search, and I first wrote the report which was sent to America and translated into English, called "The Death at Katyn."

Mr. Flood. Now, Mr. Czapski, where were you when the German announcement of Katyn was made in 1943?

Mr. Czapski. I was at that time with the Polish Army in Iraq, as the Chief of the Propaganda Agency of the Polish Army.

Mr. Flood. What was your reaction, and what was the reaction of your fellow Poles, when you heard the German announcement about Katyn?

Mr. Czapski. Naturally, our reaction was that this was done by the Russians. I do not remember that there was any one amongst us who doubted that anyone but the Russians could have done this.

Mr. Pucinski. The witness is questioning the German translation of his original answer and states here:

Mr. Czapski. We were fully aware that this could have been an act of the Germans because we knew of the German atrocities, but we knew that in this case this was done by the Russians because we were in Russia and we saw how the Russians had been evacuating these prisoners, and we knew that the Russians did not leave any prisoners to fall into the hands of the Germans.

Mr. Machrowicz. Now, Mr. Czapski, in the course of your many months of investigation in this matter, did you find any instances where the families of the officers at these three camps which you mentioned received letters from these people after April or May 1940?

Mr. Czapski. Never; never. We had heard, from time to time, rumors that such letters existed, and we had intensely searched for these letters, and we had found that those letters had never actually existed.

Mr. Machrowicz. Now, in April or May 1940, this territory in which these camps were located was in whose hands, German or Russian?

Mr. Czapski. The entire territory was in the hands of the Russians and was separated by hundreds of miles from the German territory, and it wasn't until the summer, or a year later, in the summer of 1941, that the Germans first arrived there.

Mr. Dondero. Now, Mr. Czapski, have you ever seen or heard of any of these officers and soldiers since April or May 1940?

Mr. Czapski. I have neither seen nor heard of these officers since April of 1940, and I would like to point out here that since my release from Griazovec the search for these men has been an obsession with me.

Mr. O'Konski. Will you state whether you see any similarity in the run-around which you and other Polish officials got from the Russians concerning Polish prisoners of war—do you see any similarity in the run-around which they got to the run-around which the United Nations are getting in Korea in dealing on the same subject?

Mr. CZAPSKI. I have not studied very carefully the situation in Korea, but it seems to me that if a massacre like this could have been perpetrated in Katyn it could also be repeated elsewhere.

Chairman MADDEN. Mr. Czapski, let me say this on behalf of the committee. You have testified here today under rather difficult circumstances by reason of using two interpreters in recording your testimony. You have reviewed the history of your experiences from back in 1939 on. Would you, from all these experiences, be in a position to say who, what government, is responsible for the massacre at Katyn, in your opinion?

Now briefly, briefly.

Mr. CZAPSKI. First of all, there is no doubt in my mind that these men were murdered by the Soviets.

Chairman MADDEN. I want to thank you for your testimony.

Mr. CZAPSKI. I must state my second point.

Chairman MADDEN. Very well.

Mr. CZAPSKI. Secondly, we keep forgetting that Russia is the most centralized country in the world whenever it comes to issuing orders or directives or policy. Therefore, the full responsibility for this crime does not rest with some NKVD sadist; the full responsibility rests with Beria and Stalin.

Werner Stephan

Mr. FLOOD. Were you in any way identified with the former German Government in any official capacity?

Mr. STEPHAN. Yes, I was Ministerialrat; that is, Ministerial Councilor in the Ministry of Propaganda.

Mr. FLOOD. Who was the chief in the Ministry of Propaganda under whom you served?

Mr. STEPHAN. That was Dr. Goebbels.

Mr. DONDERO. What was that answer?

Mr. STEPHAN. Dr. Goebbels.

Mr. FLOOD. Mr. Stephan, I direct your attention to the year of 1943 and ask you whether or not you were identified with the former German Government in that year in the capacity you have just indicated.

Mr. STEPHAN. Yes. At that time I had been working for 14 years for the President of the Reich Government.

Mr. FLOOD. What was your former business occupation?

Mr. STEPHAN. I was a journalist.

Mr. FLOOD. Now I direct your attention to the matter of the Katyn massacre and ask you how that matter first was brought to your attention in your official capacity.

Mr. STEPHAN. During the first days of April 1943, a journalist whom I had known for a very long time came to see me. At that time he was stationed near Smolensk as a soldier, and he came to see me in order to tell me something of great importance.

Mr. MITCHELL. What was his name?

Mr. STEPHAN. His name was Hans Meyer.

Mr. FLOOD. What was his rank and what unit was he connected with in the Germany Army at that time, and where was it located?

Mr. STEPHAN. Meyer had been working for several years as a department chief with the information center and had then been drafted to a press unit near Smolensk.

Mr. FLOOD. What was his business before he entered the armed forces, if you know?

Mr. STEPHAN. He was a journalist, and he belonged to the Deutsche Nachtrichten Bureau, which was the official German news agency.

Mr. FLOOD. All right. Tell us what happened, how you became acquainted with the Katyn matter, and what was Meyer's connection with it, so far as you were concerned.

Mr. STEPHAN. Meyer told me that he had to come to Berlin because in the area where he was stationed strange and, as it seemed to him, important things were happening. There had been rumors in this area spread by the Russian population that mass graves of Polish officers were there. Finally higher military commands had gotten knowledge of these rumors, and exhumations had been started. Now, it seemed to him that the whole affair was not started correctly and that the military commands were not aware of the importance of the whole matter. He was afraid that this was a political matter and that the military commands were not fully aware of the importance of this matter, and if there were exhumations carried out at all they had to be taken very seriously and records had to be taken and transcripts made and, if possible or necessary, international agencies or bodies would have to be formed.

Approximately the following: You know yourself, military commands grab everything and want to do everything, and they treat everything as a very secret matter and don't want to have anyone interfere; but really and actually, they don't understand anything about it. That is why Meyer had come to Berlin, because he thought that the political agencies had to be interested because the military commands did not begin it correctly.

Mr. FLOOD. What you mean is that Mr. Meyer was afraid of the Army, that he was afraid of the propaganda value of the discovery; was he not?

Mr. STEPHAN. Yes. Not exactly the propaganda value, but the political value.

224

Mr. FLOOD. You make a distinction between the two things, do you?

Mr. STEPHAN. Yes. Propaganda may be the utilization which need not necessarily be correct, whereas political evaluation, I think, is a different thing.

Mr. FLOOD. What agency were you working for?

Mr. STEPHAN. With the press department.

Mr. FLOOD. Why did Meyer come to you?

Mr. STEPHAN. Because I was an old acquaintance of his.

Mr. FLOOD. An old friend?

Mr. STEPHAN. Maybe "friend" is saying too much; but we knew each other for quite some time.

Mr. FLOOD. What did he ask you to do?

Mr. STEPHAN. He asked me to get him in contact with the high political agency, and I think that he was thinking in particular of Dr. Goebbels.

Mr. FLOOD. Did he ask especially about Dr. Goebbels?

Mr. STEPHAN. He did also ask for Dr. Dietrich, who was at that time press chief of the Reich Government.

Mr. FLOOD. What did you do?

Mr. STEPHAN. Dietrich was at that time in the Füehrer headquarters and therefore could not be reached. So I went to Goebbels' office and told them roughly what had happened. I told them in particular that Meyer asked to be received by Goebbels.

Mr. FLOOD. What arrangements did you make?

Mr. STEPHAN. I was first asked whether this man was really serious, because what I had told them briefly seemed rather sensational and, on first sight, not very credible. I told them that Meyer was a serious and reliable man and a good and well-proved journalist and that there were no objections to his being received. Thereupon, there was a reception with Dr. Goebbels.

Mr. FLOOD. Were you present?

Mr. STEPHAN. No; I was not.

Mr. FLOOD. Did Meyer ever report to you after he talked to Dr. Goebbels?

Mr. STEPHAN. Yes; he did. He came to me immediately after the reception and told me how the conversation had developed.

Mr. FLOOD. Could you tell us the day and the month and the year of Meyer's meeting with Goebbels?

Mr. STEPHAN. I should assume that it was the 1st or 2d of April 1943.

Mr. FLOOD. Will you give us the gist of Meyer's report to you after his meeting with Goebbels on this subject?

Mr. STEPHAN. Of course, I can do that only in very general terms, because 9 years have passed since then, and at that time I did not think or assume that I would ever have to testify as to that before an American commission.

Mr. FLOOD. Do you want to try?

Mr. STEPHAN. Yes.

Mr. FLOOD. Go ahead.

Mr. STEPHAN. Of course, it can only be a general impression. Meyer said approximately that Dr. Goebbels was extremely surprised. If I am permitted to say it less seriously, I should like to say he could hardly believe the fortune that had occurred to him. He was so very much surprised that such an important news should just come to him.

Several days passed and, as far as I know, Dr. Goebbels went to Hitler during these days, as he frequently did, and he reported to Hitler concerning this matter. And upon his return, he had the satisfaction, which was always felt during the Third Reich, that if, in a struggle of certain contests you were victorious over a rival, and in this case your rival was the army, the armed forces, and Dr. Goebbels had received authority to take over the case and the armed forces had to transfer the matter to him.

Mr. FLOOD. Where is Meyer today, if you know?

Mr. STEPHAN. As far as I know, he fell in action in Berlin in 1945.

Mr. FLOOD. And that, Mr. Stephan, is your connection with the official communication?

Mr. STEPHAN. Yes, that is all.

Mr. MACHROWICZ. Mr. Stephan, could you tell us whether Meyer told you when the German Army first learned of the presence of these graves?

Mr. STEPHAN. I think I have to make a distinction between the rumors and the time when these rumors were taken seriously. The rumors must have been there for quite some time, but the relationship between the Russian population and the German soldiers in this area was not particularly cordial, and the Russians obviously were shy and did not dare tell the official German agencies of these occurrences. But when the matter finally became official, I do not think that very much time elapsed until the time when he came to Berlin.

If I may estimate it roughly, I would say it would be about 2 weeks— 14 days.

But I am sure that the German officers who will testify here also and who were stationed in this area will be in a much better position to testify as to that.

Mr. MACHROWICZ. Just one other question.

To the best of your knowledge, was Mr. Meyer's information to the Minister of Propaganda the first information that had been received on the existence of these graves?

Mr. STEPHAN. Yes. I am convinced of that.

Mr. DONDERO. Mr. Stephan, did you see the graves at Katyn?

Mr. STEPHAN. No. I have never been in that region.

Col. Albert Bedenk

He was predecessor to Colonel Ahrens.

Mr. FLOOD. Were you at any time ever identified with the German armed forces?

Colonel BEDENK. I was a German soldier from 1914 to March 28, 1946.

Mr. FLOOD. Directing your attention to the outbreak of hostilities between Germany and Soviet Russia, in what rank and capacity were you serving at that time?

Colonel BEDENK. In October 1940 I took over the Signal Regiment 537, with the rank of lieutenant colonel and was commanding officer of the regiment to November 21, 1941.

Mr. FLOOD. Directing your attention to the hostilities on the eastern front, were you ever, in your official capacity, in the armed services, serving in that area?

Colonel BEDENK. Yes; I was. I went to that area as regimental commander of the Signal Regiment No. 537, and it was my duty to arrange all the communications between the various armies belonging to the central Army group.

Mr. FLOOD. Did you ever serve in the area of Smolensk in that capacity?

Colonel BEDENK. Yes, I did.

Mr. FLOOD. Will you tell us when you first entered the Smolensk area, from where you came, and when you got there?

Colonel BEDENK. The staff headquarters of the center army group was located in Borissow from July to approximately September 20, 1941.

Mr. FLOOD. When did you move into Smolensk?

Colonel BEDENK. During all the fighting around Smolensk, the army group had been thinking of where they could possibly get billets, and then they had decided on the area of Smolensk, to set up their headquarters there. Through this I had the opportunity of getting to Smolensk first because I had to see that all communications would be

227

established by the time the army group would move into the area, so that they would find all the communications ready and at their disposal, in proper working order.

Mr. FLOOD. How close was your movement behind the lines of the actual combat forces in that area on the day you got there?

Colonel BEDENK. Smolensk had already been taken some time ago, and the first-run troops had already gone as far as Vyazma, hundreds of kilometers east of Smolensk, in the direction of Moscow. The first time I got to that area was on July 28–29, 1941. On that day I had a conversation. It was with the signal chief of the army, not of the army group—at that time, still Col. General von Kluge. I had to supervise the work of my construction companies, who were establishing all the communications, and went right into the Smolensk area and surveyed the whole area.

Mr. FLOOD. What was the name of the chief military unit in the Smolensk area, and who was the commanding general?

Colonel BEDENK. It was the center army group, under the command of Field Marshal von Bock.

Mr. FLOOD. What was the capacity of General von Kluge at that time?

Colonel BEDENK. At that time, General von Kluge was commander in chief of the fourth army, belonging to the center army group.

Mr. FLOOD. How many armies were in that army group under Bock?

Colonel BEDENK. At the time of the advance, we had four armies within the center army group.

Mr. FLOOD. Where was von Kluge's headquarters set up with relation to the city of Smolensk?

Colonel BEDENK. It was located west of Smolensk to the south of the River Dneiper.

Mr. FLOOD. Who was the communications chief?

Colonel BEDENK. Major General Gercke.

Mr. FLOOD. Who was your immediate superior?

Colonel BEDENK. Major General Oberhaeuser.

Mr. FLOOD. Who was chief of intelligence in the Smolensk area at that time, if you know?

Colonel BEDENK. They did not have a direct chief of intelligence, but they had a 1–C, as he was called in the German Army.

Mr. FLOOD. Who was that?

Colonel BEDENK. At that time, still Lieutenant Colonel von Gersdorff; later on, major general.

Mr. FLOOD. Where did you set up your regimental command headquarters?

Colonel BEDENK. I put my regimental staff into a building approximately 4 kilometers west of the headquarters of the staff of the Center Army Group, in a house which was right on the banks of the River Dneiper.

Mr. FLOOD. Did the building in which your staff was housed have any particular name in the area?

Colonel BEDENK. There was some talk in the region that the building had been sort of a recreation home for the commissars in Smolensk.

Mr. FLOOD. What did the people in the area call the place? Did it have any particular name of any kind?

Colonel BEDENK. There was some talk of the G. P. U. house.

Mr. FLOOD. Did you ever hear of a place called either the "Little Dnieper Castle" or the "Dnieper Castle," or the "Red Castle"?

Colonel BEDENK. No.

Mr. FLOOD. Did you ever hear of the forest or the town of Katyn?

Colonel BEDENK. Yes; because we were actually billetted in the forest of Katyn.

Mr. FLOOD. Do you mean this regimental staff headquarters that you just described was actually in the forest of Katyn?

Colonel BEDENK. Yes, I do.

Mr. FLOOD. What was the name and number of your regiment at that time?

Colonel BEDENK. The official designation was Signal Regiment 537 of the Center Army Group.

Mr. FLOOD. And you were the first colonel to take that outfit into the Katyn Forest, were you not?

Colonel BEDENK. Yes, I was.

Mr. FLOOD. When did you get there?

Colonel BEDENK. We transferred from Borrisow with the regimental staff approximately in the middle of August. It may have been the beginning; approximately the middle.

Mr. FLOOD. When did you turn over the command of that regiment to your successor?

Colonel BEDENK. Colonel Ahrens came out to the eastern front on October 20, 1941, and during the period from between October 20 and November 20, I told my successor, who at that time was still Lieutenant Colonel Ahrens, all he ought to know about things there, and actually prepared him for his new job.

Mr. FLOOD. On what date did you turn it over to Colonel Ahrens?

Colonel BEDENK. I did not actually hand over on a specific day; this handling over business stretched over a whole month.

Mr. FLOOD. When did you relinquish the command of the regiment?

Colonel BEDENK. On the 20th of November 1941.

Mr. FLOOD. How many men did you have on your staff when you were in this headquarters in the Katyn Forest—with particular attention to the number of officers and noncommissioned officers?

Colonel BEDENK. The total strength was approximately 17, of which 5 or 6 were officers and 4 were noncommissioned, and the rest enlisted men.

Mr. FLOOD. About how many enlisted men did you have serving at the staff headquarters?

Colonel BEDENK. For security reasons, to do guard duty, I had requested and received two postal constructural units, which actually belonged to the regiment, and they had been detailed to my staff headquarters.

Mr. FLOOD. I do not mean that kind of personnel; I mean enlisted personnel actually on the staff at headquarters.

Colonel BEDENK. I don't remember the actual numbers; some drivers and cook and "flunkey."

Mr. FLOOD. How many? Can you give us an educated guess.

Colonel BEDENK. About 9 or 10 men, including NCO's.

Mr. FLOOD. Did you have any natives of the area, Russian peasants, male or female, working in any capacity at the staff headquarters?

Colonel BEDENK. I had brought with me from Borrisow three Russian POW's, one a carpenter, the other two, agricultural laborers who had been working for me, and I took them along to Katyn, to my staff headquarters.

Mr. FLOOD. Did you employ any natives of the immediate area of Katyn, of Smolensk?

Colonel BEDENK. Yes, I did. First, for kitchen duty, I had taken on some women from Smolensk, and later on, some women from the near vicinity, because Smolensk was too far away.

Mr. FLOOD. Will you describe, in as complete detail as you recall, the physical lay-out of this building, which was your regimental staff headquarters?

Colonel BEDENK. The building was located approximately 1,000 to 1,200 meters away from the highway, right on the banks of the Dnieper River.

Mr. FLOOD. Between what two big towns nearest did the highway run?

Colonel BEDENK. The two towns were Orscha and Smolensk.

Mr. FLOOD. Did it appear to be a new highway, or an old highway, a new road or an old one?

Colonel BEDENK. It was an old road.

Mr. FLOOD. Tell us more about the layout of this building inside and outside, around the area.

Colonel BEDENK. It was a double-story house. It was surrounded by·continuous balconies right around the building, on both floors. There was a main building and some outbuildings. On the lower floor there were 2 very large rooms measuring approximately 20 by 40 feet each, and 4 or 5 smaller rooms. The upper floor had only one of those large rooms, the same mentioned as downstairs, and also 4 or 5 smaller rooms, which could have been used as guest rooms.

The main outbuilding contained the kitchen and a number of smaller rooms, 6 to 8 of them, not of equal size, some smaller, others a bit larger, which could also accommodate several people, up to 4 people, for instance, overnight.

Mr. FLOOD. How far was the house from the highway?

Colonel BEDENK. As I said before, between 1,000 and 1,200 meters.

Mr. FLOOD. Do you know of the station or the town of Gniezdowo?

Colonel BEDENK. I don't remember it.

Mr. FLOOD. How far was the house from the city or the town of Smolensk?

Colonel BEDENK. Approximately 8 to 9 kilometers—that is five to six miles.

Mr. FLOOD. How far was the house from the town or the village of Katyn?

Colonel BEDENK. Between 4 and 5 kilometers, about—about 13 or 14 kilometers.

Mr. FLOOD. Will you describe just briefly the area in the forest within 500 meters of the house?

Colonel BEDENK. The house, as seen from the highway, was located in a dense pine forest. Partly it was mixed forest. There were no clearings, that I noticed. It was a typical Russian forest, not well kept, just the ordinary Russian forest.

Mr. FLOOD. The witness shows the committee a small photograph, which indicates in the front of the photograph a river, with a wooded shore on an elevation of about 15 degrees, and, on the top, what appears to be a fairly large-sized wooden building, with a castle-like tower on the left.

I am not concerned so much with the appearance of the forest between the house and the river; I am concerned now with the appearance of the forest within 1,000 meters on the other three sides.

Colonel BEDENK. The house was also surrounded on the other three sides by a dense mixed forest, pines and also evergreen trees.

Mr. FLOOD. Did you ever take any walks in the forest for recreation or other purposes during the period you were there?

Colonel BEDENK. Yes, I did.

Mr. FLOOD. Alone, or with others?

Colonel BEDENK. I frequently took walks with General Oberhaeuser whenever we had something to discuss with reference to our duties.

Mr. FLOOD. During the course of those walks in any part of the Katyn woods in any area of this house, did you ever see any mounds of any kind or earth piles of any sort that attracted your attention?

Colonel BEDENK. On the occasion of such walks, both I and General Oberhaeuser did notice some small mounds, which were about 1 to 2 meters long—that is, 3 to 6 feet long—and about 3 centimeters—that is one foot— high. But altogether, the country was slightly undulating.

Mr. FLOOD. How far, if you recall, from the headquarters house were any of these mounds of earth?

Colonel BEDENK. Between 80 and 150 meters.

Mr. FLOOD. Did they resemble in any way freshly dug graves or earth piled up over freshly dug graves?

Colonel BEDENK. No. We never had that impression.

Mr. FLOOD. Did you or General Oberhaeuser ever comment to each other or to anybody else, that you recall, in connection with those mounds or graves?

Colonel BEDENK. No, we did not, either.

Mr. FLOOD. Were there any odors of any kind emanating from the area, that were particularly noxious, if you recall, that you noticed?

Colonel BEDENK. No. If I had noticed anything like that I would never have set up my staff headquarters there.

Mr. FLOOD. If there had been any you would have noticed it, would you not?

Colonel BEDENK. Yes; definitely.

Mr. FLOOD. During the time when you first moved into the Katyn area, did you see or have any reports of Polish prisoners at that time?

Colonel BEDENK. I never heard anything of that kind.

Mr. FLOOD. Did you see any Polish prisoners in the area yourself?

Colonel BEDENK. No, I did not.

Mr. FLOOD. Did you occupy any Russian prison camps?

Colonel BEDENK. No, I did not. I never saw a prison camp.

Mr. FLOOD. You told me that you had some Russians from the area who were working in your staff headquarters somehow or other, domestic workers.

Colonel BEDENK. Yes, that is correct.

Mr. FLOOD. And you said that you had several Polish POW's working around there.

Colonel BEDENK. Not Polish ones; Russian POW's.

Mr. FLOOD. Did you have any conversations, or did you not hear from any of the people that worked for you, or any of your soldiers or anybody, at any time, any stories about Polish prisoners or Poles being killed, or anything of that kind?

Colonel BEDENK. My Russian prisoners told me that they had been told by Russian civilians of that area that shooting had taken place in the Katyn Forest, a lot of shooting, but they never referred to any Polish prisoners having been shot.

Mr. FLOOD. Did you ever receive, from any German superior officer, or did you ever hear of orders issuing through the German command, to kill Polish officers or commissars or Russian officers or commissars?

Colonel BEDENK. No, never.

Mr. FLOOD. You never heard discussed, at any time from higher echelons, any discussion or question among your brother officers about orders from superior German command for that purpose?

Colonel BEDENK. No, never.

Mr. FLOOD. Did you ever order any Polish prisoners killed yourself?

Colonel BEDENK. No, I never saw any.

Mr. FLOOD. Who was Von Eichborn?

Colonel BEDENK. Von Eichborn was communications expert with the Chief of Communications of the Central Army Group.

Mr. FLOOD. Was he ever stationed with you at your regimental staff headquarters, in residence?

Colonel BEDENK. Von Eichborn did not live at my staff headquarters. He lived about four kilometers away, but very frequently came to my staff headquarters because I also had an officer working on the same thing, also an expert on communications, and these two had to do quite a bit of work together.

Mr. FLOOD. Who was Lieutenant Hodt?

Colonel BEDENK. First Lieutenant Hodt was sometimes detailed to my staff from one of the companies as orderly officer attached to me.

Mr. FLOOD. As an experienced colonel in the army at that time, if you knew or had heard that there were graves or a grave containing several thousand bodies in a certain place in a forest, would you have placed your regimental staff command residence within 50 to 100 kilometers of that spot, had you known?

Colonel BEDENK. No, I would not.

Mr. FLOOD. Did you ever put up or give quarters to any groups of German soldiers of any other outfits, up to the number of 25 or 30, during the entire period you were at the staff headquarters?

Colonel BEDENK. No, never. I never had any other troops there.

Mr. FLOOD. Were there any Einstazgruppe Kommandos in your area in Smolensk when you moved in?

Colonel BEDENK. I am unable to say. I don't know. I didn't see any.

Mr. FLOOD. What were the general security orders, if any, that you gave in the area of your regimental staff headquarters?

Colonel BEDENK. In the daytime, I had a double guard posted on the highway at the spot where the road to my house branched off.

Mr. FLOOD. Why?

Colonel BEDENK. First of all, for the purpose of catching units of my regiment, or dispatch riders, or officers looking for me, to put them on the right road to my house, because the house was so hidden among the trees that it could not be seen from the highway.

Mr. FLOOD. How many guards in any one day, in any period of time you were there, would you have posted?

Colonel BEDENK. In daytime, I had only those two guards posted at the highway, and, at night, I had a patrol of two men going around the house all the time.

Mr. FLOOD. Did you ever throw up a cordon of armed guards in the entire forest area with relation to the highway, the river, 1,000 meters from the house, your house, at any time you were there?

Colonel BEDENK. No, never.

Mr. FLOOD. Was the area verboten to everybody, including civilians?

Colonel BEDENK. The area was not a verboten area. It was all open, particularly in view of the fact that near the house there was a crossing point for the river where the peasants used to cross over in boats, and there was always some civilian traffic passing by.

Mr. FLOOD. Was there much traffic, military or civilian, or both, on the highway passing in both directions within 1,000 meters of your house during the time you were there?

Colonel BEDENK. During the first time, in August and September, traffic was very heavy.

Mr. FLOOD. Day and night?

Colonel BEDENK. Day and night.

Mr. FLOOD. Did you have any electric lights or any kind of high-powered lights erected on trees in the area of your headquarters or within 1,000 meters of your headquarters in the forest in any direction?

Colonel BEDENK. No, we had no electric lights at all.

Mr. FLOOD. Did you ever have any staff conferences as high as division or group level at your headquarters while you were there?

Colonel BEDENK. Yes, there was one conference in September when all of the communications chiefs of the army group were convoked to my staff headquarters for a conference.

Mr. FLOOD. Was your outfit armed?

Colonel BEDENK. Yes, it was.

Mr. FLOOD. What did they carry?

Colonel BEDENK. Carbines, and the postal construction companys only carried pistols.

Mr. FLOOD. What did the NCO's carry?

Colonel BEDENK. They only had pistols.

Mr. FLOOD. How many NCO's did you have at your staff headquarters carrying pistols?

Colonel BEDENK. Six or eight.

Mr. FLOOD. Who were these postal workers you are talking about?

Colonel BEDENK. They were half civilians and half soldiers.

Mr. FLOOD. What kind of bread is that?

Colonel BEDENK. They were construction groups, civilians employed by the German Reich Post and working on the telephone and telegraph lines, and were detailed from the postal authorities to the army and had been put in uniform and were doing the same work out there that they were doing at home in ordinary times.

Mr. FLOOD. You mean the post office just turned them over to the army en masse and the army put uniforms on them, and there they were?

Colonel BEDENK. Not quite as roughly as that. As long as the German Army was still within the territory of the former Reich, the postal authorities were still running all these lines and looking after them, and so they were just attached to whichever regiment or division was there.

Mr. FLOOD. You wouldn't call them very skilled marksmen, would you?

Colonel BEDENK. Probably there must have been a number of old soldiers among them.

Mr. FLOOD. Among the postal workers?

Colonel BEDENK. Yes.

Mr. FLOOD. Now, Colonel, the Soviet report on a commission convened by the Soviet to investigate the Katyn massacres, and the indictment at Nuremberg of one Goering, which contained the Katyn matter, and the Soviet prosecution of that indictment at the Nuremberg trials, charged that these murders were committed by Construction Regiment 537 under the command of a Colonel Ahrens.

Colonel BEDENK. This accusation is wrong in every detail.

Mr. FLOOD. When did Colonel Ahrens take over from you, to repeat for the record?

Colonel BEDENK. Colonel Ahrens took over the regiment from me on November 20, 1941.

Mr. FLOOD. So, Colonel Ahrens was not in command in that area for several months prior to November, was he?

Colonel BEDENK. That's correct. He took over the regiment on November 20 although he had already arrived one month prior to that date, October 20, in order to get ready and to know about things and what duties he would have, and he had no executive power.

Mr. FLOOD. According to the Soviet report and the Soviet prosecution at Nurenberg, these murders were committed during a time and by a regiment of the same number as yours during the period of time when you were in command in that area.

Colonel BEDENK. I know that the Soviets came out with this accusation.

Mr. FLOOD. I ask you two final questions:

Did you receive or give any orders for the execution of any prisoners of war, particularly Polish officers, in the Katyn Forest during the time you were in command there?

Colonel BEDENK. No.

Mr. FLOOD. If any such executions or murders had taken place, being done by anybody else, especially Germans, day or night, in that area during the period of time you were in command, could it possibly have been done without your knowing or hearing about it?

Colonel BEDENK. If any firing had taken place at all, I would have known about it immediately because it would have been reported to me straight away.

Mr. FLOOD. Did you see any executions? Did you ever hear of any such executions, or were reports of any ever made to you?

Colonel BEDENK. No. The first I heard about the shooting of these Polish officers was after the graves had been opened.

Mr. FLOOD. What was the answer to my question—yes or no?

Colonel BEDENK. No.

Mr. FLOOD. That's all.

Mr. MACHROWICZ. Are you now serving in any capacity for the German Government?

Colonel BEDENK. No. I am war disabled and live on a pension.

Mr. MACHROWICZ. Have you, before you were called to this committee, consulted with anyone regarding your testimony?

Colonel BEDENK. No, I did not.

Mr. MACHROWICZ. Have you been instructed by anyone other than this committee in any way regarding your testimony today?

Colonel BEDENK. No, by nobody.

Mr. MACHROWICZ. Have you read the official Russian report on the Katyn Forest?

Colonel BEDENK. I merely read the articles which were published in the periodical Spiegel and in the Schwäbischer Nachtrichter, and found quite a few details were incorrect in them.

Mr. MACHROWICZ. Did you notice in that official Russian report the statement that the building you described as your headquarters was used as a place of orgy for German officers?

Colonel BEDENK. No.

Mr. MACHROWICZ. Did you read that report?

Colonel BEDENK. No, I never read it.

Mr. MACHROWICZ. Do you know Oberleutnant Rekst?

Colonel BEDENK. Rekst was my regimental adjutant and he was also regimental adjutant at the time of Colonel Ahrens.

Mr. MACHROWICZ. Do you know that a Russian official by the name of Anna Aleksiejewa stated in her affidavit in the Russian report that Oberleutnant Rekst was the adjutant of Colonel Ahrens? Is that true?

Colonel BEDENK. Yes.

Mr. MACHROWICZ. Do you know Lieutenant Hodt?

Colonel BEDENK. Yes, I do.

Mr. MACHROWICZ. Was he under your command?

Colonel BEDENK. Yes, he was in my regiment.

Mr. MACHROWICZ. And also a man by the name of Lumert?

Colonel BEDENK. That was the staff corporal sitting in the regimental office doing the secretarial work. Later on, he was made an officer, but not at that time.

Mr. MACHROWICZ. I'll mention a few other names she noted in her affidavit and ask you if you remember them.

Rose, who had charge of the electric plant.

Colonel BEDENK. That's possible. We had a pumping station. It might be this one here on this picture.

Mr. FLOOD. The witness shows the committee a picture of what is obviously a pumping house or power house, with two soldiers standing there, obviously employed in some capacity with that machinery.

Mr. MACHROWICZ. Was Oberleutnant Ahrens in the Katyn area at the same time you were?

Colonel BEDENK. Yes, he was there for one month together with me, from October 20 to November 20. I left the area after handing over the regiment to him on November 21.

Mr. MACHROWICZ. Did you have a man there whom you used as an interpreter whose first name was Johann?

Colonel BEDENK. That might have been my flunky, but his first name was Josef.

Mr. MACHROWICZ. For your information, Aleksiejewa claims that Johann, at the request of Ahrens, instructed the peasants in the area not to say anything about the shooting they had been hearing while you were in charge. Is there any truth in that statement?

Colonel BEDENK. I do not know, but it is possible, in my opinion, that this Johann or Josef was later on taken into the staff of the regiment, but that was after I had gone, so I do not know about that.

Mr. MACHROWICZ. You have testified previously that you were told by some of the local people that shootings had taken place in this forest, is that correct?

Colonel BEDENK. Yes, that's correct.

Mr. MACHROWICZ. Did they tell you when those shootings had been taking place?

Colonel BEDENK. No, they did not give any details.

Mr. MACHROWICZ. Didn't you consider it important to inquire?

Colonel BEDENK. No, for the simple reason that I assumed that all this shooting was in connection with the fighting that had taken place around about there—that they meant that.

Mr. MACHROWICZ. Didn't these mounds that you saw in the area stir any suspicion in your mind?

Colonel BEDENK. No, none.

Mr. MACHROWICZ. Did you ever investigate what those mounds were there for?

Colonel BEDENK. No, I didn't, because I wasn't interested in that.

Mr. MACHROWICZ. Did you find in the area of Katyn within, say, ten or twelve kilometers, any encampments?

Colonel BEDENK. I didn't find any encampment in my region, but it is possible that where the army group was billeted, that being old army territory, there might have been some encampment, and something was being said about a childrens' recreational institution located in that area before the war.

Mr. MACHROWICZ. The Russians claimed that there were three camps within a close proximity of this Katyn Forest and that the Polish officers were located in these three camps and were left behind them when the Germans advanced forward. Now, do you know anything about the existence of any camps which might answer that description?

Colonel BEDENK. I never saw any such installations which might have been camps.

Mr. MACHROWICZ. You had charge of communications for how many miles in that area?

Colonel BEDENK. My communications stretched over hundreds of kilometers, as far a Vyazma and Orel and north to the Ninth Army and even to a tank army that was operating hundreds of kilometers away.

Mr. MACHROWICZ. If there were any camps of that type near the railroad line wouldn't you have known about them?

Colonel BEDENK. Along the railroad lines, no, because we never used the railroad. We had nothing to do with them.

Mr. MACHROWICZ. If they were along the lines of communication, would you have known?

Colonel BEDENK. But we had only something to do with communications.

Mr. MACHROWICZ. Do you know what the first railroad station is, west of Smolensk?

Coloned BEDENK. I do not recollect exactly. Something like Krosny Bor, I believe.

Mr. MACHROWICZ. Do you remember what the second station was?

Colonel BEDENK. I do not recollect. I was never on the railroad, so I do not know.

Mr. MACHROWICZ. Does the name Gniezdowo bring any recollection to you?

Colonel BEDENK. The village of Gniezdowo was near this highway and near Katyn.

Mr. MACHROWICZ. Did you ever return to the place where the graves were, after you had left there in November?

Colonel BEDENK. Yes, I returned to this area in August 1943, to check out with General Oberhaeuser because I had been transferred at that time.

Mr. MACHROWICZ. Was that after the graves were found?

Colonel BEDENK. Yes, after the graves had been found and after the exhumations had taken place and the whole business was finished.

Mr. MACHROWICZ. Did you see any of the bodies?

Colonel BEDENK. No, everything was closed up by the time I got there.

Mr. MACHROWICZ. What kind of soil was there in this forest?

Colonel BEDENK. As far as I know and remember, sandy soil.

Mr. MACHROWICZ. Was it a light soil or a dark soil?

Colonel BEDENK. A light colored soil, and light soil.

Mr. MACHROWICZ. I believe you testified also, previously, that it was a dense forest, is that correct?

Colonel BEDENK. Yes. In parts the forest was very dense, and it was mostly young trees in those parts.

Mr. MACHROWICZ. In the parts which you later learned the graves were found, was it thick or thin?

Colonel BEDENK. I don't know where the graves are, because I never went there.

Mr. MACHROWICZ. You were there in August 1943, just a few months after they were exhumed?

Colonel BEDENK. Only in the area to report to General Oberhaeuser, who was living 4 kilometers away from that spot. I didn't go to the graves.

Mr. MACHROWICZ. Well, because of the fact that you had previously been in that area in 1941, didn't it interest you to find out where those graves were found?

Colonel BEDENK. No. We were in a very great hurry because we were being transferred with the whole staff headquarters of the Army to the Balkans, and we had to hurry to Smolensk to catch a plane to be flown down to the Balkans, so we were in a very great hurry.

Mr. MACHROWICZ. Did you ever employ 500 Russian prisoners of war in the work in the Katyn forests?

Colonel BEDENK. No.

Mr. Machrowicz. Are you familiar with the fact that in the Russian charge it is claimed that the officer in command hired 500, or rather, employed, 500 Russian prisoners of war to help dig the graves?

Colonel Bedenk. No, I don't know.

Mr. Machrowicz. At any rate, during the time that you were there you claim you never employed 500 Russian prisoners of war or any figure near that?

Colonel Bedenk. The most I ever employed were 3 prisoners I always had there, that I brought along from Borisow.

Mr. Machrowicz. I think you mentioned before that Rose was one of the officers in your detachment.

Colonel Bedenk. I don't know Rose.

Mr. Machrowicz. You never heard the name Rose?

Colonel Bedenk. No.

Mr. Machrowicz. Was there a mechanic employed by you by the name of Greniewski?

Colonel Bedenk. I don't know, but not at my time; definitely not.

Mr. Machrowicz. The reason I ask you that question, witness, is because in the Russian charge one Michailowa claims that when she and some others came near the place where the graves were subsequently found, a noncommissioned officer Rose and a mechanic Greniewski chased them away and threatened them if they came near that scene.

Colonel Bedenk. I know nothing about that. The name of Rose is unknown to me, and the name of Greniewski too. That must have happened after I had gone away from there, if it happened.

Mr. Machrowicz. The name "Greniewski" is spelled G-r-e-n-i-e-w-s-k-i.

Who was your billeting officer?

Colonel Bedenk. At that time it was a Captain of the reserves, Emil Schaeffer.

Mr. Machrowicz. Who was Irvin Algier?

Colonel Bedenk. I don't know him.

Mr. Machrowicz. That is all.

Chairman Madden. Any further questions?

Let me ask you this. I don't think you have testified to it.

Oh, pardon me; go ahead.

Mr. O'Konski. As the Germans started their offensive against the Russians, was it the policy of the Russians to leave behind any amount of able-bodied men, whether they were Poles, Lithuanians, Latvians, Estonians, or Russians?

Colonel Bedenk. I don't know anything about that, as I was never with the first fighting troops, or with the first-line troops.

Mr. O'Konski. Do you know any order of any disposition that might have been made in case they did, for instance, capture 15,000 Polish officers?

Colonel Bedenk. No.

Mr. O'Konski. Just one more question.

If disposition had been made of some 15,000 Polish officers, with the German economy as it was at that time is there any likelihood that the Germans would have done them the honor of burying them with brand new overcoats and a brand new pair of boots? Or do you think that those might have been removed?

Colonel BEDENK. I cannot answer that question. I don't know how to answer that question.

Mr. MACHROWICZ. In the Russian charge there are also affidavits of about 4 or 5 local people who testify under oath that in the fall of 1941 they frequently heard much shooting in those forests. Was there any shooting going on in that forest at that time?

Colonel BEDENK. No, there was no firing going on whatever in the fall of 1941.

Mr. MACHROWICZ. You were there during all of the fall of '41, were you not?

Colonel BEDENK. I spent the whole fall of '41 there.

Mr. MACHROWICZ. And were you in charge?

Colonel BEDENK. Yes, I was in charge.

Mr. MACHROWICZ. Up to November of that year?

Colonel BEDENK. Yes.

Mr. MACHROWICZ. The charge also states that some of those shootings took place in the beginning of September of 1941. Do you know anything about that?

Colonel BEDENK. I cannot understand that; I know nothing about it.

Mr. MACHROWICZ. The witness Aleksiejewa also charged in her affidavit that she herself saw, in the fall of 1941, while she was on her way to work, how the German officers sent a great number of Polish prisoners to the forests and later several shots were heard. Do you know anything about that incident?

Colonel BEDENK. That is a clear invention. That is impossible.

Mr. MACHROWICZ. Did you ever read these affidavits?

Colonel BEDENK. No, never.

Mr. MACHROWICZ. That is all.

Chairman MADDEN. I don't think you mentioned the size of this Katyn Forest. How large was this forest area? How large?

Colonel BEDENK. It was about 1200 meters from the high road to the house. There was dense forest on both sides, but it was generally called the Katyn Forest. But how large that forest was, and how far——

Chairman MADDEN (interposing). How many meters thick, through it?

Colonel BEDENK. I don't know, because I never went to the other end of the forest.

Rudolph von Gersdorff

Mr. FLOOD. Were you ever identified with the German armed forces?

General VON GERSDORFF. Yes, I was an officer on active service, a professional officer.

Mr. FLOOD. What was the highest rank you reached in the armed services?

General VON GERSDORFF. Major General.

Mr. FLOOD. What was your rank and what was the nature of your duty in 1941 on the so-called eastern or Russian front?

General von GERSDORFF. From April 1941, to September 1943, I was third general staff officer of the army group center which corresponds to the position of G-2 in the United States Army.

Mr. FLOOD. By G-2, you mean intelligence?

General VON GERSDORFF. Yes, my main duties were to collect information about the enemy. Besides, I was in charge of counterintelligence, propaganda, and care of the troops.

Mr. FLOOD. You were, in other words, chief of intelligence of the army group center?

General VON GERSDORFF. Yes.

Mr. FLOOD. What was your rank?

General VON GERSDORFF. At first, I was a major and was then promoted to the rank of colonel subsequently.

Mr. FLOOD. Then you were the Colonel von Gersdorff who has been referred to in the Smolensk area as chief of intelligence between July and December of 1941?

General VON GERSDORFF. It couldn't possibly be anyone else but me, but, at that time, I was merely a major on the general staff.

Mr. FLOOD. And you were the Colonel von Gersdorff referred to in 1943 as being chief of intelligence in the Smolensk area?

General VON GERSDORFF. Yes, that is correct.

Mr. FLOOD. When did you move into the Smolensk army group center command?

General VON GERSDORFF. I moved into the Smolensk area with the staff of the central army group in the first days of September 1941, but, on a previous occasion, I had already visited this area once.

Mr. FLOOD. When, and why?

General VON GERSDORFF. I do not exactly recollect the date, but it must have been late in July or early in August of the same year, and it was my practice to enter an area which had just been conquered as quickly as possible, being chief of intelligence, so as to have an opportunity of interrogating important Russian prisoners that had been brought in.

Mr. FLOOD. How many days were you in the Smolensk area on that visit after the combat troops moved forward?

General VON GERSDORFF. I do not recollect the exact number of days, but it was only a few days after the combat troops had gone forward.

Mr. Flood. As chief of intelligence and one of your duties being, as you described, the interrogation of combat troops taken in that area, on that visit to the Smolensk area did you interrogate any Polish prisoners of any category?

General von Gersdorff. During the whole Russian campaign, I never saw or interrogated a Polish prisoner.

Mr. Flood. Did you ever see any dead ones?

General von Gersdorff. After the dead bodies of the Polish officers in Katyn Forest had been exhumed, I saw Polish dead for the first time.

Mr. Flood. That's the only time you saw any live Polish officers, soldiers, or enlisted personnel, between July 1942, and the time the bodies were exhumed at Katyn in April 1943?

General von Gersdorff. Yes; they were the first and only Poles, dead ones in this case, that I ever saw during the period mentioned.

Mr. Flood. During that period, did you ever hear from any of your widespread sources of intelligence in the Smolensk area that there were Polish prisoners, officers or enlisted personnel, hiding in the woods or hiding in the Russian villages?

General von Gersdorff. No, never.

Mr. Flood. During the same period of time did you ever, as chief of intelligence, direct any of your personnel to conduct regular round-ups and searches for Polish prisoners in the area?

General von Gersdorff. No.

Mr. Flood. Would anybody else have been able to issue such orders and conduct such intelligence operations without your knowledge or approval?

General von Gersdorff. The only possibility would have been that the so-called Einsatzgruppen of the SD who were not under the juris-diction of the Central Army Group could have performed such duties, but, in view of the fact that the then chief of the police units was an officer by the name of Nebe who, already since 1938, secretly belonged to the resistance movement, I am certain that he would never have engaged in any such action without previously having contacted me about that.

Mr. Flood. What resistance movement?

General von Gersdorff. The German resistance movement against Adolf Hitler and against National Socialism.

Mr. Flood. Were you a member of the movement?

General von Gersdorff. Yes; I was.

Mr. Flod. You mentioned something about the Einsatzgruppen. Were there Einsatzgruppen or Einsatzkommandos in the area of Smolensk when you moved in?

General von Gersdorff. In every area of an army group there were certain units of the so-called Einsatzgruppen which were under the direct order of higher SS and police chiefs. This high-ranking SS or police officer was under the direct command of Heinrich Himmler. His only instructions consisted in making contact with the staff of the army group. The army group, however, had the possibility of demanding that such Einsatzgruppen should be withdrawn in the case of these Einsatzgruppen hampering the strategical and tactical movements of the combat trops. We made very wide use of this opportunity of getting rid of these Einsatzgruppen and, particularly within the area of the Four Army under Field Marshal von Kluge, these Einsatzgruppen were practically always far in the rear. Nebe always supported this action of ours. On the other hand, of course, he had to see that his Einsatzgruppen were also commissioned with some tasks so as not to make too bad an impression upon his higher command.

Mr. FLOOD. Did your outfit get rid of the Einsatzgruppen in your area at the time we are speaking about?

General VON GERSDORFF. I do not quite clearly recollect whether at that time the Einsatzgruppen which was attached to the Fourth Army was in action or not. I believe that at the time when the Fourth Army took Smolensk, this Einsatzgruppen was not actually fighting in the front line but I have no clear recollection of that.

Mr. FLOOD. Even if they were, in view of the nature of the commanding officer and his liaison with the Wehrmacht, would it have been possible for Himmler to have ordered the commander of that Einsatzgruppe to have committed a murder at Katyn of 4,000 troops without your knowing about it?

General VON GERSDORFF. This is utterly impossible, particularly in the spot where the murders actually took place and where the graves were subsequently found in view of the fact that this spot is located so near the highway leading from Vitebsk to Smolensk that it would have been absolutely impossible to kill 4,000 people without lots of people passing along the highway noticing it.

Mr. FLOOD. It would have been impossible for an order coming from the supreme command to the army group having to do with the killing of Polish prisoners, particularly officers, without you, as chief of intelligence, having heard about it, isn't that so?

General VON GERSDORFF. No; because such an order would have been transmitted to my command immediately and I would have known about it immediately, too.

Mr. FLOOD. Was any such order transmitted to your command or from a supreme command to an army group during the period of service you had in the Katyn-Smolensk area?

General VON GERSDORFF. No, never.

Mr. FLOOD. You heard General Oberhaeuser testify this morning, did you not?

General VON GERSDORFF. Yes, I did.

Mr. FLOOD. And you heard Colonel Ahrens testify this afternoon, did you not?

General VON GERSDORFF. Yes; I did.

Mr. FLOOD. Now, directing your attention to that part of the testimony of those two officers having to do with the description of the Dnieper Castle and the area surrounding the castle, do you wish to add anything, any details, to what they said in that description?

General VON GERSDORFF. I fully agree with the statements of Gen-

Lt Voss of the Feldgeheimepolizei shows a nominal list of exhumed corpses to Lt Sloventczyk (left) and Prof Buhtz (right).

eral Oberhaeuser and Colonel Ahrens about the Dnieper Castle, but I would like to add the following: In the vicinity of Gniezdowo, there were prehistoric Russian cairns, old prehistoric tombs in caves. They were overgrown with shrubs and heavily so. They were actually in that area, so that was the reason why, when the graves of the Polish officers were discovered, we did not call it the murders of Gniezdowo, but to distinguish it from these old prehistoric tombs of Gniezdowo, we called it the murders of Katyn, so as not to get these two things mixed up.

243

Mr. FLOOD. Then these graves were actually closer to Gniezdowo than they were to the village of Katyn?

General VON GERSDORFF. Yes; that is correct.

Mr. FLOOD. Who finally conferred the title of the Katyn Massacre on this thing? Did you do that?

General VON GERSDORFF. This was done by my unit with the chief of our staff agreeing to it.

Mr. FLOOD. How did you first hear the story of Katyn?

General VON GERSDORFF. My units contained a small command of military field police of about 8 to 10 men. In charge of this small police unit was the Field Police Secretary Voss. The duty of this field police unit consisted of security measures so as to guard security of the field marshal and of the staff headquarters. Therefore, I had instructed Voss to watch carefully over the surroundings of these staff headquarters so as to make sure that no strangers, that is, people who did not belong there, should enter the area.

Mr. FLOOD. Who was Voss?

General VON GERSDORFF. Voss was in charge of the small unit of military field police. He was a so-called military field police secretary, and his duties corresponded to the rank of lieutenant. Owing to his duties, Voss was in close contact with the population of the surroundings of our staff headquarters. One day Voss came to me and made the following report.

Mr. FLOOD. Just a moment.

When, if you remember?

General VON GERSDORFF. I do not recollect the exact date, but it must have been in February 1943.

Mr. FLOOD. All right, go ahead.

General VON GERSDORFF. Voss reported to me that Polish auxiliary volunteers who belonged to several infantry divisions which were marching up to the front line and who had taken up temporary quarters in Gniezdowo and the surroundings, had made inquiries on behalf of Poles in Poland for possible Polish prisoners in that area.

Mr. FLOOD. I now show you exhibit 5 and ask you whether or not you can identify the German officers on that picture?

General VON GERSDORFF. Yes.

The one in the center is Military Field Police Secretary Voss. The one on the left is a lieutenant whom I recognize, but I do not recollect his name. The one on the right resembles Professor Buhtz.

Mr. FLOOD. Did you ever hear of a Lieutenant Slovenczik?

General VON GERSDORFF. I recognize the name now and I presume that he is the third man on this photograph which was just shown me. He belonged to a propaganda unit which was under the command of General Schenkendorff, commanding officer of the rear area.

Mr. FLOOD. Who was the immediate superior commander of Slovenczik at Smolensk?

General VON GERSDORFF. Major Kotts, the commanding officer of this propaganda unit.

Aerial view of Gniesdovo station near Katyn.

244

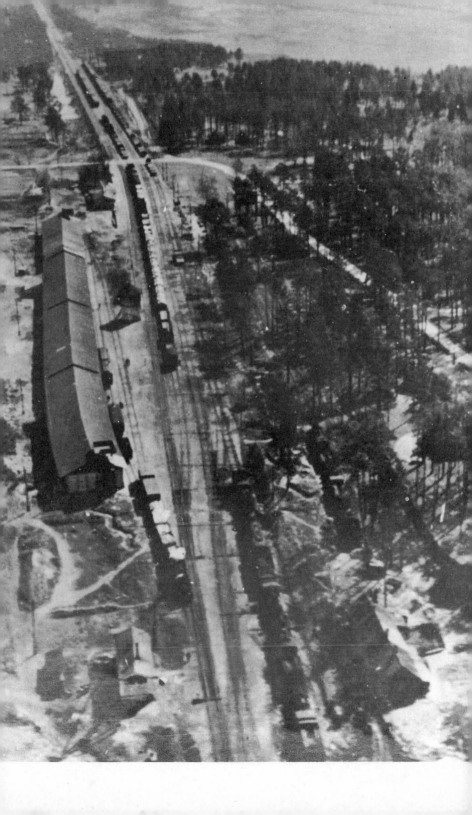

Mr. FLOOD. Will you examine exhibit 5 again, in view of this conversation, and direct your attention to the officer you have not yet identified, and tell us whether or not that could be Slovenczik?

General VON GERSDORFF. I believe that Slovenczik is the officer on the left side of the photograph.

Mr. FLOOD. Very well. What did Voss have to say to you?

General VON GERSDORFF. Voss reported to me that Russian inhabitants of Gniezdowo had told the previously mentioned Polish auxiliary volunteers that in spring, 1940, large transports of Polish prisoners had arrived by full train-loads at Gniezdowo station. They clearly recognized them as Poles from their uniforms and also heard them speaking Polish to each other. Then, these Poles were taken away in large black prison vans from the station and they were taken to this forest which was located approximately 1 kilometer from the station and disappeared. The forest and the so-called Dnieper Castle were at that time cordoned off by guards and nobody could approach there.

Mr. FLOOD. I show you exhibit 3 and ask you if you can identify it.

General VON GERSDORFF. The picture shows the so-called Dnieper Castle where I was a visitor of Colonel Ahrens on two occasions. It was located only a few hundred meters away from the graves.

Mr. FLOOD. I show you exhibit 4 and ask you if you can identify that.

General VON GERSDORFF. Yes; I clearly recognize this picture. It shows the crossing point of the railroad line at Gniezdowo station with the highway leading from Vitebsk to Smolensk. The road at that spot has an S-shaped bend.

Mr. FLOOD. We'll offer exhibit 4.

After you cordoned off Dnieper Castle, after you had this information from Voss, whom did you report to, if anybody?

General VON GERSDORFF. I passed on this report to the 1–A; that is, the first general staff officer, and also to the chief of staff, and was instructed to investigate this matter further.

Mr. FLOOD. What is the opposite number of the German 1–A on the table of organization?

General VON GERSDORFF. I believe, G–3.

Mr. FLOOD. Go ahead.

General VON GERSDORFF. I thereupon instructed Voss to interrogate these Russian inhabitants of Gniezdowo under oath. The interrogations confirmed everything we had heard about these Polish prisoners.

Mr. FLOOD. Did you talk to any Russian peasants yourself?

General VON GERSDORFF. No; I did not talk to any because I do not know Russian, but, later on, I did speak to some of the Russian workers, with the help of an interpreter who were engaged upon the exhumation work.

Mr. FLOOD. What did you talk to them about?

General VON GERSDORFF. I merely repeated the questions that they had already been asked during the first interrogations and, in addition, asked them whether they could give me more interesting details in the matter.

Mr. FLOOD. What instructions did you get from your superiors, if any, with reference to the exhumations of these bodies?

General von Gersdorff. As it became clear from the interrogation of these Russian civilians that something had happened there, orders came from above, from higher quarters, to investigate this matter thoroughly and to dig in the forest. At that time, we had no idea yet that it was matter of such a dreadfully large number of dead bodies. Professor Buhtz of Breslau University was put in charge of the exhumations. He belonged to the chief quartermaster's division and had to investigate any infringements of the Hague Convention.

Mr. Flood. Was he attached to the headquarters at Smolensk?

General von Gersdorff. The division of the chief quartermaster was located or billeted in the city of Smolensk proper.

Mr. Flood. Then I gather you were in charge in the Katyn Forest area of the exhumations in a general way?

General von Gersdorff. Yes; that is correct.

Mr. Flood. Whom did you designate in charge of security or in charge of the guard you told us about around the graves—that area?

General von Gersdorff. In the beginning, the previously mentioned military field police unit took up the security duty. Afterwards, a company of Polish volunteers took up guard duty and mounted guard near the graves.

Mr. Flood. Do you remember the name of the German officer you designated in charge?

General von Gersdorff. No; I do not recollect the name.

Mr. Flood. When did the exhumations, the diggings, start, if you remember?

General von Gersdorff. As far as I recollect, in March 1943.

Mr. Flood. Do you recall the Polish Red Cross being connected in any way with the exhumations?

General von Gersdorff. The Polish Red Cross was advised at once and requested to send delegates to Katyn who would supervise and arrange the exhumations. In addition, the International Red Cross in Geneva was also advised, but I presume this was done via the Foreign Office in Berlin.

Mr. Flood. When did the exhumations stop?

General von Gersdorff. The exhumations stopped in June or July at the height of the summer, and this was done on the advice of military physicians which we had there, who feared that the terrible stench of the dead bodies would have some noxious effects on the health of the men engaged in the task.

Mr. Flood. Did you visit the graves during the course of the exhumations between—when did you say they started?

General von Gersdorff. In March.

Mr. Flood. In March. And in the summer, when they were finished, did you visit the area?

General von Gersdorff. I visited the graves three or four times, possibly more often.

Mr. Flood. Were visiting delegations received in the area during the course of the exhumations?

General von Gersdorff. The Ministry of Propaganda in Berlin had very many, or a large number of commissions come to the graves to see them. I welcomed a delegation of journalists to the graves, and also a delegation of experts of judicial medicine. This latter commission consisted of members from all the countries which could be reached from Germany at that time. Furthermore, commissions of American, British, French, and Polish prisoners of war also came to see the graves. I also saw the Archdeacon of Krakow, Dr. Yazinski.

Mr. FLOOD. Any other delegations of any kind?

General VON GERSDORFF. There was also a great number of German delegations, many of them from troop units, but also delegations that came directly from Germany.

Mr. FLOOD. Were any prisoner of war visitors received at the Katyn grave during the exhumation?

General VON GERSDORFF. Yes, in the first place, Polish officers, but they were also British and French officers, and, as far as I recollect, also several American officers.

Mr. FLOOD. Would you say that during the 4 months during which the exhumations were going on there were hundreds or thousands of visitors of all kinds received in the area?

General VON GERSDORFF. I would say, rather, thousands.

Mr. FLOOD. Did you see the bodies yourself during the exhumation?

General VON GERSDORFF. Yes; I did.

Mr. FLOOD. Will you describe for us, briefly, what you saw as the bodies were exhumed?

General VON GERSDORFF. In the first place, the mass grave was opened, which was approximately 10 meters long and 20 meters wide, and very deep. In this grave the dead bodies of the Polish officers were stacked in 12 layers on top of each other. Then later on a second grave was opened, which was not quite as large as the first one, but in that grave all the dead bodies were fettered. They had their hands tied up. It may be assumed that in that case these Polish prisoners had perhaps tried to resist at the very last moment.

Mr. FLOOD. Did you see bodies with their hands tied behind their back yourself?

General VON GERSDORFF. Yes, I did.

Mr. FLOOD. What were they tied with?

General VON GERSDORFF. As far as I recollect, it was either wire or cord, but they were tied up, fettered, in a typically Russian manner.

Mr. FLOOD. Could it have been wire in some cases and cord in others?

General VON GERSDORFF. That I do not recollect any more.

Mr. FLOOD. Will you demonstrate on the interpreter the manner in which those hands and arms were tied behind their backs, the backs of the corpses?

General VON GERSDORFF. Not exactly, but approximately.

Mr. FLOOD. Well, stand up and do the best you can, as you best recollect.

[The witness indicated.]

Mr. FLOOD. The witness demonstrates on the interpreter the crossing of the left arm and the right arm at the wrists at about the small of the black.

And they were tied in that manner; is that it?

General VON GERSDORFF. Yes.

Mr. FLOOD. In what way were they tied, as you best recollect? Will you point out?

General VON GERSDORFF. I do not remember the details. Many of the dead bodies had sacks or tunics pulled over their heads, and these sacks or tunics were tied fast around the waist.

Mr. Flood. You saw that yourself?

General von Gersdorff. Yes; I did.

Mr. Flood. Did you observe any of the corpses with sawdust in the mouths?

General von Gersdorff. Yes. I remember now that Professor Buhtz established this fact in one or a few cases.

Mr. Flood. Did you see the International Commission conducting post mortems or autopsies there at the grave?

General von Gersdorff. Yes. I welcomed them personally and also spoke to them.

Mr. Flood. Did you see post mortems or autopsies being performed upon the bodies of several hundred of these dead officers by German commissions by Dr. Buhtz and two other Germans?

General von Gersdorff. On that occasion I was not present personally, but I saw myself foreign physicians carrying out autopsies.

Mr. Flood. Now, the committee has a great deal of detailed evidence, scientific and from observation of scientists and laymen who visited the graves at Katyn, having to do with the depth of the graves, the surroundings, when the graves were opened, and the detailed conditions of the decomposed state of the corpses and the conditions of the uniforms, but we would like you to add, because of your important position in the area, your comments briefly on the condition of the corpses and uniforms or documents found there, if any.

General von Gersdorff. The dead bodies were still being held together by the uniforms, but the state of decay was already very far advanced, although the soil in which the bodies were buried was very sandy. All the corpses had at least one or two bullet holes where the bullets had left the skull, which were either in the forehead or near the eyes.

Mr. Flood. Will you demonstrate again on the interpreter the point of entry and the point of exit of the bullet?

(The witness indicated.)

Mr. Flood. The witness indicates with his finger on the interpreter the point of entry as being at about the base of the skull and the neck line, and the point of exit as being in the forehead between the hairline and the eyebrow.

General von Gersdorff. Almost every dead body had an amulet, or these little crosses—what do you call them?

Mr. Mitchell. Crosses?

Mr. Flood. Scapular or crucifix.

General von Gersdorff. Scapular; yes. It was under their underwear, on their chests. Otherwise no real valuables were found on them.

Mr. Flood. I suppose you are aware that many Poles are Roman Catholic?

General von Gersdorff. I would assume that practically all of them were Roman Catholic.

Mr. Flood. And one of the practices of Roman Catholics is the wearing of a scapular or crucifix around the neck?

General von Gersdorff. Yes. These crucifixes and other items had not been removed from the dead bodies, probably, because they had been wearing them under their shirts.

Mr. FLOOD. And would only be of little value to whoever removed them?

General VON GERSDORFF. I beg your pardon?

Mr. FLOOD. And probably would be of little value to whoever was removing things from the bodies at the time?

General VON GERSDORFF. Only in the case of the dead bodies of two generals, evidently one gold cigarette case and a golden ring were found. On the other hand, a large number of documents were found on all the other bodies. These documents consisted of diaries, notebooks, and letters from their next of kin or friends. In addition to that, there were also many photographs. They also had large amounts of paper bank notes, Polish zloty, which at that time had been taken out of circulation.

Mr. FLOOD. I am sure the general is aware that the date of the burial of these bodies is so material as to be, perhaps, controlling in determining the guilt of the parties responsible for the murder.

General VON GERSDORFF. Yes; that is quite clear to me.

Mr. FLOOD. In view of that situation, or that possibility, General, do you have any observations to make with reference to the latest date found on any documents on these bodies that you are now describing?

General VON GERSDORFF. I saw very many of these documents myself—that is, the originals. The most interesting items were diaries which had been written in great detail. I remember a diary of one Polish officer who related the events as follows: He relates, at first, how they were being kept in a Russian POW camp located at Kozielsk. He further relates how, in March 1940, they were taken away in railroad cars.

When they left they had not the slightest idea as to where they were going. However, hopes were rising high when they ascertained that they were traveling in a westward direction. They could also establish that they were passing through the town of Roslavl, and that they continued in the direction of Smolensk. They wrote down in their diaries that they were now hoping to be returning to their Polish homeland. Then there were further entries that their transport trains had certainly stopped at a small station outside Smolensk. Evidently this was the station of Gniezdowo.

Mr. FLOOD. General, do you remember the name of the first station after you leave Smolensk in that direction? What is the name of the first station after you leave Smolensk?

General VON GERSDORFF. I never used the railroad in those days. I believe that the first station was Gniezdowo, but I am not certain about it.

Mr. FLOOD. Now I return to my question and I ask you again, General, with particular reference to the dates on the documents, papers, and so on, what was the latest date that you observed on any of these papers or documents?

General VON GERSDORFF. All the entries in the diaries ceased at the end of March or, at the latest, the beginning of April 1940. Likewise, the very numerous letters and postcards which were found on the dead bodies, and which came from their relatives and friends in Poland, were all dated from November–December 1939 and January 1940.

Mr. Flood. What was done with the documents by the Germans after they took them from the bodies?

General von Gersdorff. The documents had first to be treated chemically, because they were partly soaked in——

Mr. Flood (interposing). Body fluid?

General von Gersdorff. Body fluid, yes. They were then exhibited in glass cases on the porch of the building where this military field police unit was billeted.

Mr. Flood. Were records kept of the documents with reference to each body, if you know?

General von Gersdorff. Yes. Every dead body was identified, and it was entered what had been found on the body.

Mr. Flood. Did each body have a number?

General von Gersdorff. As far as I can remember; yes.

Mr. Flood. Did the envelope containing the documents taken from that body have a number corresponding to the number of the body from which they were taken?

General von Gersdorff. I presume that that was so, but I have no knowledge of these details. I would think, however, that Mr. Pfeiffer would be able to say more about these details.

Mr. Flood. Who is Pfeiffer?

General von Gersdorff. He was a member of the military police unit of Voss.

Mr. Flood. What did the Germans do with all the documents they had collected in the late summer of 1943 after they had closed up the grave?

General von Gersdorff. As far as I remember, all these items, documents, and other things were packed into chests and put on the way to Germany, but I do not know much about that.

Mr. Flood. Do you know a Dr. Naville, a distinguished Swiss pathologist and an authority on forensic medicine?

General von Gersdorff. Yes; I met Dr. Naville right at the graves in Katyn, and also sat next to him at a dinner party which was given for these international groups by the Center Army group.

Mr. Flood. Did you have a conversation with Dr. Naville?

General von Gersdorff. Yes; I had long discussions with him.

Mr. Flood. What language did you talk in?

General von Gersdorff. We spoke German and French.

Mr. Flood. What was the gist of the subject of the conversation?

General von Gersdorff. At that time I had the impression that Dr. Naville was absolutely convinced that only the Russians could have committed this crime.

Mr. Flood. Do you know or remember the date of the dinner given by the Germans to the visiting Commission?

General von Gersdorff. I do not recollect the date of the dinner, but I remember that it was on an extremely hot day.

Mr. Flood. Do you know a Professor Markhov, the Bulgarian member of the Commission?

General von Gersdorff. I remember Dr. Markhov, and I also remember that he was the Bulgarian member of this Commission.

Mr. Flood. Was he at Dnieper?

General von Gersdorff. Yes; he was.

Mr. Flood. Did you have a conversation with him?

General von GERSDORFF. Yes; I also had a conversation with him.

Mr. FLOOD. In what language?

General von GERSDORFF. There were very many representatives of Slav nations and I do not quite recollect, but I believe that Dr. Markhov knew some German or French.

Mr. FLOOD. What did Markhov have to say, if anything?

General von GERSDORFF. I do not recollect the details of our conversation, but I recollect this much, that Dr. Markhov, too, was firmly convinced that the Russians were responsible for this crime.

Mr. FLOOD. You will be interested to know that on the 5th of March, in Sofia, Professor Markhov outlined his experiences as a member of the German International Medical Commission. He says that he had been forcibly included in the Commission, that he had been completely isolated from the local population while at Katyn; he recants any statement he made, and says the Germans did the killing. What do you have to say about that?

General von GERSDORFF. How far single members of the Commission had come of their own free will or otherwise I am not in a position to say, but I could hardly imagine that the Swiss representative would have come against his will. In Smolensk itself, from the moment of the arrival of the Commission, I can confirm that the gentlemen of this Commission had any liberty they could wish for to move and do what they liked. They were permitted to talk to anyone, Russian or no Russian, that they wanted to talk to. They could go wherever they wanted to go, and they could engage in any activity that they felt like engaging in.

Mr. FLOOD. Did you receive or give any orders which would in any way have curtailed the activity of the International Commission of Scientists at Katyn, or any of its individual members?

General von GERSDORFF. No. On the contrary, I issued special orders that the free movement and liberty of these gentlemen should be safeguarded at all costs and that they should be given the opportunity of going where they wanted to go and doing what they wanted to do without any hindrance, and that they should even be assisted.

As an example, I recollect that some of these international delegates left the graves and drove back to Smolensk earlier than others. They were probably tired or something, and went back earlier, while others still remained longer at the graves and carried on their investigations.

Mr. FLOOD. Professor Markhov, separate and distinct from any writing that he made or any protocol that he may have signed about the investigation in addition, at the dinner party, told you, in a social conversation, that he felt that the crime at Katyn had been committed by the Russians, is that it?

General von GERSDORFF. As far as I recollect, Dr. Markhov was sitting at my left side during the dinner, and we did actually discuss this matter, and Dr. Markhov confirmed to me that in his opinion the Russians had committed the crime.

Mr. FLOOD. I now hand to the stenographer, to be marked as "Exhibits 7, 8, 9, and 10," four photographs.

(Due to incorrect numbering, there is no exhibit 6.)

(The photographs referred to above were marked "Frankfurt Exhibits 7, 8, 9, and 10," and are shown on pp. 1315–1317.)

Mr. FLOOD. I now show the witness exhibit No. 7 and ask him whether or not he can identify any of the three persons shown thereon examining one of the corpses, two in military uniform, and the third person in civilian clothes.

First, who is the civilian, if you know?

General VON GERSDORFF. I clearly recollect the civilian. That was a Hungarian, Professor Orsos, who was a member of the International Delegation.

Mr. FLOOD. How do you spell Orsos?

General VON GERSDORFF. O-r-s-o-s. As far as I remember, the man-in uniform is the Finnish delegate. The third man in uniform appears to be a medical corps soldier who is just busy typing out the report which Professor Orsos, who knew German very well, was dictating.

Mr. FLOOD. I now show you exhibit No. 8, which depicts a group of two or three dozen civilians talking to a German officer in uniform. Who was the officer, if you know, and can you identify the nature of the group of civilians?

General VON GERSDORFF. The officer is the lieutenant of this propaganda unit, with a Polish name, and the civilians of the picture, as far as I remember, are members of a delegation of journalists from neutral and other countries.

I now show the witness exhibit No. 9 and ask him if he can identify the military uniforms present, what countries they represent, and the civilian, if he can.

General VON GERSDORFF. The officers are American and British prisoners of war. The officer in the center is a British major, who had declared himself to be the leader of his delegation, or the chief of the delegation. When he arrived he told us that he alone would comment on the whole matter, and that the other officers present did not wish to make any comments. The civilian is a Russian worker, an inhabitant of Gniezdowo, who was working on the exhumations, and, as far as I recollect, also made statements about the murder having happened, and upon his statements investigations were started and the graves were discovered.

Mr. FLOOD. Do you know or recall, General, whether or not the visiting American and British officer POW's were permitted to talk to those Russians without German interference?

General VON GORSDORFF. This would have been quite possible, they could have talked to the Russian civilians because these officers were absolutely free, there were not even guards with them. But, in any case, such a conversation with the Russian civilians would have depended upon the presence of an interpreter, in view of the fact that the officers did not know Russian.

Mr. FLOOD. General, you may be interested to know that the two American officers, now colonels, have already testified before this committee and have said they were permitted to talk to the Russians present without interference from the Germans.

I now show the witness exhibit No. 10 and ask him whether or not he can identify the persons on that picture.

General von Gersdorff. I recognize, on this picture, the Polish Archdeacon Yazinski in his ecclesiastical garb; and the tall civilian I do not remember. In the foreground there is one of the Russian workers, and at the far right of the picture the head of Voss is visible.

Mr. Flood. General, do you recall a visit by the executive secretary or director of the Polish Red Cross from Warsaw named Skarzynski?

General von Gersdorff. No; I do not recollect this visit, because I was away very often on inspection and had to go around a lot.

Chairman Madden. Do you have any questions, Mr. Dondero?

Mr. Dondero. I have one question.

General, you testified that you noticed that the bodies in one of the graves had their hands tied behind them, either with wire or with cord. Was that cord round or flat?

General von Gersdorff. I do not quite recollect that, but I believe that they were flat.

Mr. Dondero. You might be interested to know that the record already shows that a part of that cord has been presented to this committee and received in evidence. It was flat.

Chairman Madden. Are there any further questions?

General, you read the Russian report, did you not, regarding the Russian investigation?

General von Gersdorff. I did not read this report very carefully; I just went through it quickly. But I know more or less what it contained.

Chairman Madden. Were you present in the room this afternoon when several members of the committee asked the preceding witnesses regarding certain phases of the Russian report?

General von Gersdorff. Yes; I was present.

Chairman Madden. What comment would you have to make regarding some of the conclusions reached in the Russian report?

General von Gersdorff. It appears to me quite impossible that, as from the date of the German occupation of that territory or of that area, a crime of such magnitude could have been committed in the immediate vicinity of the main supply road of the army group, and likewise, in the immediate vicinity of the army group proper. This highway carried an extremely heavy supply traffic day and night. And even in the case of SS troops or some other unit carrying out such an action, it would at all events have come to our knowledge.

Apart from the previously stated facts, the documents recovered from the bodies, the expert advice given by physicians is so convincing that there should not be any doubt as to who committed the crime.

German soldiers pose at Katyn site outside their quarters.

Albert Pfeiffer

He was a member of Lieutenant Voss's unit.

Mr. FLOOD. Were you ever a member of the German armed forces?

Mr. PFEIFFER. Yes; I was.

Mr. FLOOD. Were you ever serving in that capacity on the eastern or Russian front?

Mr. PFEIFFER. Yes.

Mr. FLOOD. When did you arrive in the Smolensk area?

Mr. PFEIFFER. At the end of October or at the beginning of November 1942.

Mr. FLOOD. Did you ever hear of Lieutenant Voss?

Mr. PFEIFFER. Yes; I did.

Mr. FLOOD. Were you with his unit?

Mr. PFEIFFER. Yes; for 2 years.

Mr. FLOOD. What were the duties of the unit and what were your duties in it?

Mr. PFEIFFER. The unit had security duties in the vicinity or the surroundings of the staff headquarters of the center army group and to watch over the civilians in that area, and they also had the care of the civilians who were working in the different German units and agencies.

Mr. FLOOD. What do you mean by "watch over" the civilians in the area?

Mr. PFEIFFER. Our activities were confined to patroling the near vicinity of the staff headquarters and see that no strangers would come into this area; that those pepole who lived there and who had been registered were actually there.

Mr. FLOOD. How many men were in Lieutenant Voss' unit?

Mr. PFEIFFER. Our unit had been split up into two halves. The one to which I belonged was in Gluschtschenki. We numbered five and the others that went to Gniezdowo numbered from five to seven.

Mr. FLOOD. Do you speak Russian?

Mr. PFEIFFER. Yes. I was employed as an interpreter.

Mr. FLOOD. Did you have any conversations with any of the Russians in the area of Katyn?

Mr. PFEIFFER. Yes; with the civilians of Gluschtschenki and the near vicinity of the staff headquarters, but not with those of Katyn because I only went to Katyn once.

Mr. FLOOD. When did you first hear about Katyn?

Mr. PFEIFFER. The first time I heard anything about Katyn was in February 1943 when I was confined to the infirmary.

Mr. FLOOD. Where?

Mr. PFEIFFER. The infirmary was with the staff headquarters. My buddy, Roeske, who was also an interpreter, came to me and told me that investigations would have to be made after some Poles who had disappeared.

Mr. FLOOD. Were you identified with the exhumations in any way?

Mr. PFEIFFER. Yes; from the very first day.

Mr. FLOOD. What was your assignment, and who assigned you to it?

Mr. PFEIFFER. I had been detailed for this duty by Lieutenant Voss in the capacity of interpreter, and it was my duty to explain to the Russian civilian workers, who had been brought to that spot, to explain to them what kind of work they had to do there and that now they had to go about the exhumation.

Mr. FLOOD. Were you there the first day that the digging started? Were you present when the first work was begun?

Mr. PFEIFFER. Yes; when the first spade entered the ground I was present.

Mr. FLOOD. Had you ever been in that immediate vicinity at any other time before that first day?

Mr. PFEIFFER. Not in the area.

Mr. FLOOD. Will you describe the appearance of the grave and its immediate surroundings within a very few feet before the first spade was put into the ground?

Mr. PFEIFFER. It was a clearing in the forest, and the mound of earth was up to a height of 3 feet, overgrown with small fir trees and heather and bushes and scrub.

Mr. FLOOD. Indicate with your hands, from the floor, the height of the trees you saw on this mound or grave the first day you appeared there, when the excavations began.

(The witness indicated a height from the floor.)

Mr. FLOOD. The witness indicates about—what; 3½ feet?

Mr. PFEIFFER. The largest were about that size [indicating].

Mr. FLOOD. The witness indicates from the floor a height of 3½ feet. Were these small trees all over the mound of earth?

Mr. PFEIFFER. They were scattered. You could clearly see that they had not been planted according to any plan and they were not numerous.

Mr. FLOOD. Were they removed before the digging began?

Mr. PFEIFFER. That was the first job.

Mr. FLOOD. I now show the witness exhibit No. 5 and ask him if he can identify the officers on that exhibit?

Mr. PFEIFFER. I know two of them. On the left side is First Lieutenant Slovenczik and in the middle is Field Police Secretary Voss, my superior, my commander.

Mr. FLOOD. Have the stenographer mark this next photograph as exhibit 11.

Mr. FLOOD. I now show the witness marked for identification Exhibit No. 11 and ask him whether or not he can identify the people on that photograph; I just want him to tell me how many of that group were on Lieutenant Voss' squad.

Mr. PFEIFFER. Among this group were some that belonged to the unit of Lieutenant Voss.

Mr. FLOOD. What are their names?

Mr. PFEIFFER. The one, I do not want to name because I know that he would object. The second one is Pfc. or Corp. Karl Nikolatz, our driver, and in front, sitting on the ground, myself.

Mr. FLOOD. Who is the female in the picture?

Mr. PFEIFFER. Mrs. Irina Erhardt.

Mr. FLOOD. What was her duty?

Mr. PFEIFFER. She had to translate the documents and diaries found on the dead bodies because she knew Polish well.

Mr. FLOOD. I will ask the stenographer to mark for identification exhibit No. 12, which is another photograph.

Mr. FLOOD. I now show the witness marked for identification Exhibit No. 12, a photograph, and ask him whether or not that properly depicts the grave site and the grave after the trees had been removed and just as the first digging commenced?

Mr. PFEIFFER. The picture could, of course, have been taken anywhere. I do recognize people wearing clothes as they usually wear them in Russia.

In view of the fact that the picture only shows a very small area, I am not in a position to say that it is actually one of the Katyn graves; but the character of the place looks very much like the site of the graves at Katyn.

Mr. FLOOD. How far down, after the digging commenced, did they go before they struck the first bodies; how many meters?

Mr. PFEIFFER. Two-and-a-half meters.

Mr. FLOOD. How many graves were opened during the period of time that you were there?

Mr. PFEIFFER. I do not recollect the exact number of graves, but I do recollect exactly three graves.

Mr. FLOOD. What were your duties after the graves had been opened and the bodies had been removed?

Mr. PFEIFFER. I had to go through the pockets of the clothes of the dead bodies and to remove the items found in them and had to identify the dead bodies from the documents found on them.

Mr. FLOOD. How long did you work at that job?

Mr. PFEIFFER. Right to the end of the exhumations.

Mr. FLOOD. When was that?

Mr. PFEIFFER. It was approximately in the beginning of June. It may have been even at the end of May, but, at any rate, it was not later than the 11th of June.

Mr. FLOOD. Can you give us the exact date, the day and month and year, when the exhumations began?

Mr. PFEIFFER. Not the day.

Mr. FLOOD. How close can you come?

Mr. PFEIFFER. The second half of March 1943.

Mr. FLOOD. Were any visitors or visiting delegations of personages received at the Katyn grave area during any period of time that you were working there?

Mr. PFEIFFER. Yes. There were commissions; among others, one of them, officers who were prisoners of war, British, French, and Polish; then the Commission of International Physicians, either from neutral countries or countries fighting on the side of the Germans, and then a very large number of Russian civilians and German soldiers.

Mr. FLOOD. After the first days, where did you do your work on the documents?

Mr. PFEIFFER. In the hut which was built onto a Russian house, in the village or in the hamlet of Gluschtschenki, where I was billeted. It was about 20 meters away from the place where I was actually billeted.

Mr. FLOOD. Wait a minute. You had better spell that for the record.

Mr. PFEIFFER. G-l-u-s-c-h-t-s-c-h-e-n-k-i.

Mr. FLOOD. What was the nature of your work with the documents at this hut?

Mr. PFEIFFER. I took the documents out of their envelopes and dictated to a mate every item I discovered, and attempted to establish the name of the individual, usually on the strength of the pay books which I had discovered.

Mr. FLOOD. What procedure did you use for preserving the documents?

Mr. PFEIFFER. No procedure.

Mr. FLOOD. Did you separate them? Did you put them all in one pile? Did you keep them in relationship to one name? What did you do?

Mr. PFEIFFER. The documents were put back into their own envelopes and numbers put on them, and the identical number that was on the dead body was put on the envelope, and then, all the envelopes with the numbers on them were put into a large chest and stored away, and certain documents and items were picked out and I exhibited them outside of this hut.

Mr. FLOOD. Do you know what disposition was made by the Germans at the end of the exhumations in the summer? Where did the chests of documents go, if you know?

Mr. PFEIFFER. It was said that they would be taken to Krakow so as to distribute them among the next of kin and the relatives of the murdered men.

Mr. FLOOD. How many chests of documents were there?

Mr. PFEIFFER. I estimate four. I do not know exactly, but I estimate four.

258

Mr. FLOOD. Did you make a close examination of the documents of various kinds that came to your hut?

Mr. PFEIFFER. Yes; certainly; I did examine them very carefully.

Mr. FLOOD. Was there anything significant with reference to any of the documents that came to your attention, especially?

Mr. PFEIFFER. The one significant fact that struck me was that these documents were comparatively in a very good state of preservation and the most interesting part of the documents found were the diaries.

Mr. FLOOD. Do you have any comment to make with reference to the dates on any of the documents?

Mr. PFEIFFER. Yes. The letters and post cards and also some newspapers found on the dead bodies all carried dates and the dates never went beyond April 1940.

Mr. FLOOD. I now have the reporter mark for identification exhibit 13, a photograph; exhibit 14, a photograph; exhibit 15, a photograph; and exhibit 16, also a photograph.

(The documents referred to were marked: "Frankfurt Exhibit No. 13," "Frankfurt Exhibit No. 14," "Frankfurt Exhibit No. 15," "Frankfurt Exhibit No. 16.)

Mr. FLOOD. I show you exhibit 13 and ask you if you can identify the photograph.

Mr. PFEIFFER. Those were our billets.

Mr. FLOOD. Where?

Mr. PFEIFFER. Gluschtschenki, opposite the headquarters of the field marshal.

Mr. FLOOD. Is that near Katyn?

Mr. PFEIFFER. Half-way between Smolensk and Katyn.

Mr. FLOOD. I now show you exhibit 14 and ask you if you can identify that.

Mr. PFEIFFER. That's the large grave, the mass grave after the end of the exhumations and after we had reburied the dead bodies and rearranged the burial place.

Mr. FLOOD. I would like to ask you this: The Soviet statement indicates that when the Soviet began the exhumations of their commission there was only one grave. Will you tell us how many graves were there, in number, at the time the Germans finished the exhumations and the Polish Red Cross reburied the bodies in the summer of 1943—approximately?

Mr. PFEIFFER. I only recollect three graves, but I know that we were talking about more graves.

Mr. FLOOD. The photograph, exhibit 14, that I now show you shows how many graves and how many crosses?

Mr. PFEIFFER. I want to apologize. I believe that you are meaning something different than what I mean; that we are mixing up the old graves and the new graves.

Mr. FLOOD. Then, let's go back.

What I mean is this: The Polish Red Cross, it was just testified to by the general, participated in the exhumations and the burials, do you recall that?

Mr. PFEIFFER. Yes. Two Poles worked with me on the identification of the bodies all the time, too.

Mr. FLOOD. The Polish Red Cross and the Germans worked together on the exhumations and the reburials?

Mr. PFEIFFER. Yes.

Mr. FLOOD. And after all the exhumations had been completed and after all the reburying had been done, how many graves were there then shown?

Mr. PFEIFFER. After that period, there were the old open graves left and the new ones, but I do not recollect the number of the new ones.

Mr. FLOOD. I mean just the new ones. Do you remember the number of the new ones?

Mr. PFEIFFER. No; I cannot.

Mr. FLOOD. Well, at least three or four are showing on exhibit 14 that I just showed you.

Mr. PFEIFFER. I was there once more in September, 1943, but, in spite of that, I am unable to give the exact number of graves.

Mr. FLOOD. You will be interested in knowing that the vice president of the Polish Red Cross, who was there and did this work, was before this committee and testified that when the Polish Red Cross finished the work there were seven graves.

Mr. PFEIFFER. That is quite possible. I recollect that Voss had been deliberating whether to bury all the dead bodies discovered there in one huge mass grave or whether to make several smaller graves, and then it was decided for reasons of piety, to make several graves.

Mr. FLOOD. It is of interest to the committee in view of the fact that the Soviet report states that when they came to Katyn to open the mass grave there was only one grave there.

I now show you Exhibit 15 and ask if you can identify that.

Mr. PFEIFFER. Yes. This is a photostat of the first page of a Polish pay book as we found them by the thousands, and I do not recall the name but there were chaplains, one or several chaplains, among the dead. It is the typical first page of a Polish pay book and there were thousands of them.

Mr. FLOOD. I now offer the reporter to be marked "Exhibit 17."

(The above-described document was marked: "Frankfurt exhibit No. 17.")

Mr. FLOOD. Are you aware that the bodies of two Polish general officers were discovered at Katyn? Did you ever hear of that?

Mr. PFEIFFER. Yes; right in the beginning.

Mr. FLOOD. Did you ever hear that the Polish Red Cross, when the reburials were being made, buried the two generals each in a separate grave marked by a separate smaller cross?

Mr. PFEIFFER. Now that you mention it, I recall that very clearly. Before, I did not.

Mr. FLOOD. I now show you exhibit 17 and ask you whether or not this picture shows six white crosses on six newly made graves with one large grave in the front with a cross and two small crosses on two separate smaller graves?

Mr. PFEIFFER. I recognize the burying place with the graves and the two small crosses indicate the new graves of the two Polish generals.

Mr. FLOOD. We are describing the reburial of the bodies discovered at Katyn—these are the newly reburied graves, is that it?

Mr. PFEIFFER. Exactly.

Mr. FLOOD. I now show you exhibit 16 and ask you if you can identify the people shown on that picture.

Mr. PFEIFFER. On this picture I only recognize Voss and the exhibits which I put out in front of this so-called hut.

Mr. DONDERO. One question: When you reburied these bodies, did you rebury them right where you found them or did you move them away?

Mr. PFEIFFER. We reburied the dead bodies in a different spot which was about 100 meters away from the original place where we found them, in the direction of the highway that was coming from Katyn.

Mr. DONDERO. That's all.

Mr. O'KONSKI. Will you tell the committee how many Russian workers were used in this exhumation proceedings that you carried on?

Mr. PFEIFFER. I am only in a position to give the exact number of the first day when we started. That was 30 Russian peasants from the surroundings.

Mr. O'KONSKI. Will you tell the committee if ever as many as 500 Russians were used for that purpose?

Mr. PFEIFFER. That is absolutely out of the question. Never simultaneously.

Mr. O'KONSKI. The reason why I state that is that in the Russian report they state that 500 Russians were used for that purpose and they were all shot by the Germans after they completed their work. What comment do you have on that?

Mr. PFEIFFER. It is possible that over the whole period of exhuming the bodies 500 workers were used successively, but never at one time, and that these 500 workers were shot, I do not believe and it is nonsense.

Mr. O'KONSKI. Will you tell the committee if any bodies of Polish women soldiers were found in the graves of the bodies you exhumed.

Mr. PFEIFFER. No. Exclusively officers, ranking from lieutenant up to general.

Mr. O'KONSKI. What was the total number of bodies that was exhumed from the graves at Katyn?

Mr. PFEIFFER. I ought to be able to give you the exact figure because I actually numbered all the exhumed bodies and put the same number on the documents, but I do not, at this time, recollect the exact number, but I am certain it was between 4,500 and 5,000.

Mr. O'KONSKI. That is all I have, Mr. Chairman.

Chairman MADDEN. One question: Did you notice in these papers that you removed from the bodies medical certificates like vaccination or innoculations for typhus?

Mr. PFEIFFER. Yes; I did find such medical certificates.

Paul Vogelpoth

Mr. FLOOD. What is your present occupation?

Mr. VOGELPOTH. Editor.

Mr. FLOOD. Of what paper and where?

Mr. VOGELPOTH. Mittag, Duesseldorf.

Mr. FLOOD. Were you ever a member of the German armed forces?

Mr. VOGELPOTH. Yes.

Mr. FLOOD. Did you ever serve with the German armed forces in the Smolensk area on the Russian front?

Mr. VOGELPOTH. Yes, I did.

Mr. FLOOD. Were you there in March and April to the summer of 1943?

Mr. VOGELPOTH. Yes, I was.

Mr. FLOOD. With what unit were you identified?

Mr. VOGELPOTH. Propaganda unit W.

Mr. FLOOD. Stationed where?

Mr. VOGELPOTH. Smolensk.

Mr. FLOOD. When did you first come to the Smolensk area?

Mr. VOGELPOTH. In the middle of February 1942.

Mr. FLOOD. When did the massacres of the Katyn Forest first come to your attention?

Mr. VOGELPOTH. As far as I recollect, in the middle of March 1943.

Mr. FLOOD. In what manner were these first brought to your attention?

Mr. VOGELPOTH. I learned of it through my fellow officer, First Lieutenant Slovenczik, Gregor Slovenczik.

Mr. FLOOD. Were you assigned to any special duties in the area of the graves at Katyn?

Mr. VOGELPOTH. Yes. At the end of March 1943, when the big rush or influx of people started, many people started coming to the graves. I was detailed to Katyn Forest to put some order into the whole thing. It was about the 25th of March 1943.

Mr. FLOOD. Would you say that you had charge of the security arrangements in the area of the graves?

Mr. VOGELPOTH. Yes, I could say that.

Mr. FLOOD. Will you just detail for us the nature of your duties? What did you do, whom did you have charge of, and how long did you do it?

Mr. VOGELPOTH. My duty extended from 9 in the morning to 6 at night in the forest of Katyn every day. I had the task of selecting groups of 150 to 200 people from the very large numbers of soldiers and civilians—everyone was coming to the forest to see the graves—and of taking these groups to the graves.

Mr. FLOOD. During the time that you were there, would you say that hundreds or rather thousands had visited the graves?

Mr. Vogelpoth. I estimate about 200,000 all together, from the end of March right through April, May, and June, to the end of June.

Mr. Flood. Were there any special groups of any significance that visited the area during the time that you were there?

Mr. Vogelpoth. Yes, all the delegations. The delegations, however, were managed by Slovenczik and Voss. I had nothing to do with them.

Mr. Flood. What kind of delegations?

Mr. Vogelpoth. There were delegations consisting of officers, prisoners of war, French, American, British, and Poles, and also the Spaniards of the so-called Blue Division.

Mr. Flood. Any other delegations of any particular kind of work or effort or business?

Mr. Vogelpoth. Yes, there were other delegations, such as the delegation of prominent international medical men, and then a commission of experts of judicial medicine, commissions of authors, of artists, and there were also commissions sent there by the ministry of propaganda.

Mr. Flood. As a former journalist, do you remember seeing any delegations of journalists?

Mr. Vogelpoth. Yes, we had a delegation of journalists there.

Mr. Flood. What were your particular duties, witness, with reference to these visitors, delegations, or groups?

Mr. Vogelpoth. Generally speaking, I had nothing to do with all these delegations, with the exception of the delegation of journalists and of authors. Those two delegations I took over the graves and over the areas.

Mr. Flood. Did you volunteer, or was it part of your job to explain if anybody asked any questions as to what this was all about?

Mr. Vogelpoth. Yes, it was part of my duty to give explanations to them and to answer any question they put to me.

Mr. Flood. Then you acted as a sort of guide and informer in the area during the visits?

Mr. Vogelpoth. Yes, that is correct.

Mr. Flood. What was Slovenczik?

Mr. Vogelpoth. He was a first lieutenant in the propaganda detail W, and he was assigned to this post right at the beginning, just a few days after Voss had been detailed to the Katyn Forest.

Mr. Flood. Why, if you know, witness?

Mr. Vogelpoth. He was an exceptionally good talker, orator, and— well, he knew his way about very well.

Mr. Flood. He was a narrator and a good talker. Did he act as a guide for these groups as well?

Mr. Vogelpoth. Yes, he did, with the delegations, not with the many visitors coming there on their own, like soldiers and civilians, but expressly for the delegations and commissions.

Mr. Flood. I now show the witness exhibit No. 5 and ask him if he can identify any of the officers on that exhibit.

Mr. Vogelpoth. On the left is Slovenczik; in the center is Voss; and on the right-hand side—I don't know him, I do not believe that it is Dr. Buhtz.

Mr. Flood. I now show the witness exhibit No. 8 and ask him if he can identify the German officer in uniform and the group of civilians.

Mr. VOGELPOTH. Slovenczik is on the left. In the light overcoat is the rather well known German author, Luetzkendorf. And one of the other gentlemen in this picture is sitting among the audience here, but I don't know who he is, and he does not want to be mentioned.

Mr. FLOOD. I now show the witness exhibit No. 12 (see p. 1325) and ask him if he can identify that picture.

Mr. VOGELPOTH. That is the beginning of the exhumation in the middle of March. That is the largest grave that was found and opened.

Lt Vogelpoth examines young saplings transplanted to cover up the mass graves at Katyn.

Mr. FLOOD. I now show the witness exhibit No. 20 and ask him if he can identify anybody on that picture.

Mr. VOGELPOTH. On the left, Slovenczik. The man in the black overcoat was a former Polish minister-president, who was killed in an air raid in Berlin in 1944, but the name is unknown to me.

Mr. FLOOD. I now show the witness exhibit No. 19 and ask him if he can identify the person on that picture.

Mr. VOGELPOTH. That is myself.

Mr. FLOOD. What were you doing at the time that picture was taken?

Mr. VOGELPOTH. We were investigating the growth of the grass and of the trees, not as experts.

Mr. FLOOD. That is all.

Chairman MADDEN. Any further questions.

Mr. O'KONSKI. I would like to ask a question.

Chairman MADDEN. Congressman O'Konski.

Mr. O'KONSKI. If they exhumed something like 250 bodies, in round figures, why did the propaganda ministry, or whoever had charge of propaganda, continue to say that there were 11,000 or 12,000 or 15,000 bodies found in Katyn?

Mr. VOGELPOTH. We knew from the Poles, who had told us that between 12,000 and 13,000 Polish officers were missing, and we assumed that all of them were lying buried in the forest of Katyn. The figure of 11,000 was mentioned at the time when the reburying was still carried out. It had not been complete. It is definitely established that the forest of Katyn contained more dead bodies of Polish officers than the 4,250 which were actually found, because, right at the beginning of June, we discovered a new grave of Polish officers, but we just only opened it a bit and had to close it again, because it was getting so hot at that time of the year that we were afraid of epidemics and we would not take the risk, and this grave has never been opened. And this new grave, which we just opened in one spot and closed up again without investigating it, was located about 200 meters between the so-called Korzy Gòry—that is, it was located between these hills and the Dnieper Castle. Not near the low part, inside the forest, in the direction leading toward Dnieper Castle.

Mr. O'KONSKI. In other words, they used the figure in their propaganda of 11,000 because they felt that if they had an opportunity to dig up all of the graves they might find 11,000 bodies there, because they heard a report that there were that many Polish officers missing, is that correct?

Mr. VOGELPOTH. The figure of 11,000 originated from my unit. They were asked by Berlin to name a figure or an estimate, and they actually named 11,000, that is, my unit, but later on they found out that they had erred, it could not be correct. As it is, the Katyn Forest only holds the bodies of the Polish officers who came from the camp of Kozielsk, but not those of the other two camps. Later on we learned that apart from the camp of Kozielsk there were another two very large camps of Polish officers.

Mr. FLOOD. May I say that that last statement has some significance in view of the fact that at the other two camps referred to by the witness, the one, Starobielsk, and the third, Ostohkov, contained as prisoners, both military and civilian, unaccounted for to date, in the neighborhood of 6 to 8 thousand Poles. The 6 to 8 thousand from the other two camps of Starobielsk and Ostoshkov have not been heard from to this day and their bodies have never been discovered.

Chairman MADDEN. Is there anything further you would like to say?

Mr. VOGELPOTH. The previous witness was questioned as to the exact number of graves. I am in a position to give you the exact number of graves.

Chairman MADDEN. We will be glad to have it.

Mr. VOGELPOTH. There were four old graves and a fifth one, which we discovered later in the forest, and new graves. They laid out four large ones and two smaller, single, ones, six all together.

Hans Bless

In his testimony he stated that the last date in a diary found at Katyn upon one of the exhumed corpses was 20 April 1940.

Mr. FLOOD. Were you ever identified with the Wehrmacht?

Mr. BLESS. Yes.

Mr. FLOOD. Were you a member of the German armed forces in 1943?

Mr. BLESS. Yes, I was.

Mr. FLOOD. Were you on the Russian, or eastern front?

Mr. BLESS. I was also on the eastern front.

Mr. FLOOD. With what unit?

Mr. BLESS. Reconnaissance unit.

Mr. FLOOD. When did you move into the Smolensk area?

Mr. BLESS. I will have to elaborate a little bit on that.

On the 1st of March of 1943, the Rzew bridgehead was abandoned. At that time, during all that retreat, I was the leader of the covering rear unit. It was in the vicinity of Dorogubush when the front line again became consolidated. Inasmuch as during all of that retreat I was covering the rear, subsequently I was sent to a resting place.

This happened sometime during the middle of March of 1943.

During that retreat, rumors were rife that somewhere at the Smolensk area, mass graves of Polish prisoners had been discovered. I no longer accurately recall whether or not I was officially ordered to proceed to Katyn; however, I still do know that I eventually traveled to Katyn in an automobile. However, I do definitely remember that the division at that time prepared special groups, which subsequently had been dispatched to Katyn.

Mr. FLOOD. Did you see the location of the graves?

Mr. BLESS. Yes, I did.

Mr. FLOOD. When were you there?

Mr. BLESS. I estimate I was there around the end of March; it might perhaps have been around the 20th or 25th of March.

Mr. FLOOD. The exhumations were already going on when you got there, were they?

Mr. BLESS. Yes, they were.

Mr. FLOOD. Did you talk to any Russian civilians in the area at any time?

Mr. BLESS. Yes.

Mr. FLOOD. What was the nature of those conversations?

Mr. BLESS. It was during a survey of the graves. There was a small group of us standing together.

And when I say "us" I am referring to a group of German soldiers and a serviceman.

I don't know who said, "Well, there is a Russian civilian standing out there in front." It was an old Russian of about—well, in my estimation, 70 years of age.

This Russian is also in a position to tell something. It would, however, be practical to offer him a cigarette right at the outset.

The Russian civilian testified approximately as follows: "Several years ago—it was in the spring—a transport of prisoners of war arrived on a train at the nearest railroad station," that subsequently, the entire area where the graves were located had been cordoned off, as well as—as he expressed himself—a cottage where Kommissars were purportedly residing; that Polish prisoners of war had subsequently been taken to that area on trucks. The shooting reportedly took place every day in the early hours of the morning.

And I believe that is all.

Mr. FLOOD. Was that the only Russian civilian to whom you spoke?

Mr. BLESS. Yes, that was the only one I spoke to. However, I happened to see some more Russian civilians around. They were busy, they were working.

Mr. FLOOD. At what stage was the exhumation when you were there; what degree of exhumation?

Mr. BLESS. I was there when the exhumation of the second grave was just begun.

Mr. FLOOD. Did you see the bodies closely enough to observe how they may have been killed?

Mr. BLESS. Yes.

Mr. FLOOD. Did you pay any attention as to whether or not the hands were tied?

Mr. BLESS. Yes; I did.

Mr. FLOOD. Did you observe anything with reference to documents or what may be described as the personal effects of any of the dead bodies?

Mr. BLESS. Yes. There was a series of—as I should put it—personal property of no practical value at all, such as handkerchiefs, papers, letters. But on the chest of either a colonel or a lieutenant colonel, there was a diary lying on his chest. It might perhaps be of interest to note that the pockets of all of the uniform coats had been cut by scissors in order to gain easier access to the pockets of the uniforms.

With respect to the tying of the hands, I wish to indicate that partially the hands were tied by wire. In one instance, I recall he must have been tied by his own belt. In various other instances, the hands were tied by pieces of string or rope.

Mr. FLOOD. Were you close enough to actually observe that yourself?

Mr. BLESS. Well, in one instance, for example, of a body that had been lying on its back, I actually investigated how his hands were bound.

Mr. Flood. You mentioned a diary. Did you have a chance to look at or see the diary?

Mr. Bless. Yes, I did. I said, "Well, it is too bad nobody around here speaks Polish." Subsequently, however, we found a German noncommissioned officer who spoke Polish; whose name, however, I don't know.

Then we picked up the diary, which had been lying on the chest of this colonel or lieutenant colonel, as I indicated before, and the noncommissioned officer subsequently translated practically all of the diary to us.

Mr. Flood. Can you give us the gist of what it said. the meat of what it said?

Mr. Bless. Yes.

He set forth in writing, first, the circumstances of his capture; that subsequently all of them were herded into a large camp; later, part of the inmates of the camp were taken away somewhere, so that eventually nothing but officers remained in the camp.

Mr. Flood. Do you happen to remember, or did you notice; and if you did notice, do you remember the last date of entry on the diary?

Mr. Bless. Yes. As a matter of fact, I recall it precisely.

Mr. Flood. What was it?

Mr. Bless. Adolph Hitler's birthday was on the 20th of April.

Mr. Flood. What was the date recorded?

Mr. Bless. The last entry in the diary was the 20th of April, because I recall I made a remark. In a jocular mood, I said, "Well, as a reward from the Russians to Adolph Hitler for having given them a portion of Poland, the Russians killed those officers."

Mr. Flood. What was the date of the diary?

Mr. Bless. The last date was the 20th of April.

Mr. Flood. What year?

Mr. Bless. 1940.

Mr. Flood. In your conversations with any Russians, or the Russian to whom you talked, did that Russian indicate any opinion as to who did the shootings?

Mr. Bless. If I remember correctly, this one Russian I spoke to held it was the Red army who did the shootings.

Mr. Flood. Did you happen to hear of any Russians or any rumors in the area that any Russians blamed the Germans for the shooting?

Mr. Bless. No, I did not; not at that time, at least. I think the first time I heard about that was sometime in 1946.

Mr. Flood. Where, in 1946, did you ever hear that kind of talk?

Mr. Bless. It was here in Germany. I read it in the papers. It was in connection with the Nuremberg Tribunal proceedings.

Mr. Flood. But you never talked to any Russians who said that or heard of any Russians who said that in 1943; is that it?

Mr. Bless. No; at least, I don't remember.

The corpses are arranged in the open to await examination, as first observed by Dr Tramsen.

Dr Helge Tramsen

His evidence, together with that of Dr Palmieri (see Chapter 6), is extremely important to this narrative.

Dr. TRAMSEN. I am a practitioner in Copenhagen and, at the same time, a lecturer at the university, teaching at the high school of physical training, and a surgeon commander in the Royal Danish Navy.

Mr. FLOOD. You practice medicine, I suppose?

Dr. TRAMSEN. Yes, I do.

Mr. FLOOD. How long have you been engaged in the practice of medicine?

Dr. TRAMSEN. I did my final examination in 1936 at the Copenhagen University, and later I had training in hospitals and scientific institutes in Copenhagen.

Mr. FLOOD. You indicated that you are a reserve surgeon in the Danish armed forces, did you?

Dr. TRAMSEN. Yes.

Mr. FLOOD. Where did you get your surgery?

Dr. TRAMSEN. I got my surgery at the university clinic in Copenhagen, Rigs Hospital, and several other hospitals; and from 1940, November, I studied and did scientific work at the Institute of Medico-Legal Medicine. In 1943 I was prosector—you call it—at this institute.

Mr. FLOOD. In 1943, what had been your experience in the general or special field of pathology?

Dr. TRAMSEN. Three years of training in pathology and medico-legal medicine at the University Institute in Copenhagen.

Mr. FLOOD. Had you experience in the performance of post mortems or autopsies on human bodies?

Dr. TRAMSEN. Yes, I had.

Mr. Flood. All areas of the human body?

Dr. Tramsen. Yes.

Mr. Flood. What is your experience in the field of forensic or legal medicine?

Dr. Tramsen. In those 3 years I worked—it was altogether 4 years—I worked at the University Institute of Medico-Legal Medicine. I did every day post mortems of murder cases and sudden death of unnatural cause.

Mr. Flood. I direct your attention to the year of 1943 and ask you whether or not, in that year, the matter of the Katyn Forest massacres was brought to your attention?

Dr. Tramsen. Yes. I have read about it in the Danish press.

Mr. Flood. Did the then German Government subsequently, in any way, communicate with you with reference to your serving professionally in connection with that incident?

Dr. Tramsen. Yes. On April 22, 1943, I had the offer from the Danish Foreign Office to be a member of a committee, consisting of scientists and medico-legal specialists, that should go to Katyn to investigate the tombs and do post mortems on the dead bodies there. And the secretary of foreign affairs in Copenhagen told me that this invitation had come straight from the Reichsgesundheitsfuehrer, Dr. Conti, in Berlin.

Mr. Flood. Then I understand that the invitation from the then German Government did not come directly to you but was transmitted to you by the then Danish Foreign Office. Is that correct?

Dr. Tramsen. Yes.

Mr. Flood. And what did you reply?

Dr. Tramsen. The first invitation had come to my chief, Professor Sand, and he was a very old man and didn't feel like going on this long journey. So he pointed me out because at that time I was a military doctor as well, and he thought it would be possibly the best thing to have a military surgeon as well going on this job.

Mr. Flood. Your chief where?

Dr. Tramsen. At the University Institute for Medico-Legal Medicine.

Mr. Flood. You were so designated, then, as I understand it?

Dr. Tramsen. Yes.

And may I add there that I had an official order from the Danish Minister of Foreign Affairs, as well as the admiralty, to join the committee.

Mr. Flood. So your appearance upon this international medical commission was not the result of any direct or personal negotiations between you and the then German Government?

Dr. Tramsen. No.

Mr. Flood. I presume you then took your place with the commission. Will you, in your own words, just tell us what developed up until the point you reached Katyn?

Dr. Tramsen. Yes. On April 27, 1943, I was taken by a special plane from Copenhagen to Berlin.

Mr. Flood. May I interrupt? I, of course, take for granted that you were aware that on April 15, 1943, the Germans had made the announcement of their discovery at the Katyn Forest; followed 2 days later, on April 17, by the Russian announcement or the Russian reply to the German charges?

Dr. TRAMSEN. Yes.

Mr. FLOOD. Will you proceed?

Dr. TRAMSEN. In Berlin I was presented in the Hotel Adlon to the other members of this medical scientific committee by Dr. Zietz, from the Reichsgesundheitsamt. I knew several of these gentlemen beforehand by name through international scientific circles.

Mr. FLOOD. Do you at this time think you can give us the names of the men who were on the commission with you?

Dr. TRAMSEN. From Belgium, Professor Speleers.

Mr. FLOOD. When you read that, will you also state the name of the university, or his identity?

Dr. TRAMSEN. Yes.

This Professor Speelers was professor in ophthalmology in the University of Ghent.

Dr. Markov, lecturer at the Institute of Forensic Medicine and Criminology, University of Sofia, Bulgaria.

No. 3 was me.

No. 4, Professor Saxen, Professor of Pathologic Anatomy in Helsinki, Finland.

Professor Palmieri, professor in medico-legal medicine and criminology in the University of Naples.

Professor Miloslawich, professor of medico-legal medicine and criminology, University of Agram, Croatia.

Mr. FLOOD. Doctor, you might like to know that Dr. Miloslawich has already testified before this committee, at its hearings in America, in the city of Chicago.

Dr. TRAMSEN. Yes. Professor Burlet, professor of anatomy in Groningen, Holland. Professor Hajek, professor of medico-legal medicine and criminology in Prague. Dr. Birkle, forensic specialist for the Rumanian Minister of Justice and prosecutor at the Institute of Medico-legal Medicine and Criminology, Bucharest, Rumania. Professor Naville, professor of medico-legal medicine, University of Geneva. Professor Subik, professor of pathologic anatomy, University of Pressburg, Czechoslovakia.

No. 12, Professor Orsos, professor of forensic medicine and criminology, University of Budapest. This is the total list.

And Professor Orsos was chosen chairman of the committee because he was, I should say, the most well known specialist and he had the advantage that he could speak Rusian fluently, having been a Russian prisoner of war in Russia for 4 years during the First World War.

Mr. FLOOD. Who selected Dr. Orsos as the chairman of the delegation?

Dr. TRAMSEN. We did that between us.

Mr. FLOOD. Then Dr. Orsos was elected or selected as chairman by his fellow scientists who were members of the delegation, as you have just described?

Dr. TRAMSEN. Yes.

Mr. FLOOD. Were there any consultants or German delegations or scientists who cooperated or were with you at the time?

Dr. TRAMSEN. Yes; several doctors and specialists, of which I don't recall all the names, from the University Institute of Forensic Medicine in Berlin. Professor Miller Hess was the chief, and his second assistant was there, I remember, Dr. Huber.

Mr. FLOOD. Do you recall a Dr. Buhtz?

Dr. TRAMSEN. Yes. But he was not in Berlin; he was in Smolensk and we met him out there. He was ordinary professor of forensic medicine in the University of Breslau.

Mr. FLOOD. Did you see him present at any time at Katyn when you were there?

Dr. TRAMSEN. Yes. He was actually the leader of the whole expedition and examinations during the days we stayed in Smolensk.

Mr. FLOOD. Representing the German Government?

Dr. TRAMSEN. Yes; representing the German Government.

Mr. FLOOD. Do you recall any French delegate or any French representative?

Dr. TRAMSEN. Yes. There was a rather elderly professor, Dr. Costedoat, who did not take much part in the negotiations as he said he was sent only from the French Government to investigate what we were doing. He was a specialist in psychology.

Mr. FLOOD. Did you go to Berlin?

Dr. TRAMSEN. Yes. And early next morning we were taken in German military airplanes from Tempelhof, landing midway in Warsaw and finishing up in Smolensk at 6 or 7 o'clock in the evening, a 1,600-mile flight.

Mr. FLOOD. When did you get to the graves at the Katyn Forest?

Dr. TRAMSEN. Next morning, about 10 o'clock.

We were collected at the house of the Wehrmacht, where we stayed for the night, and taken in Germany military buses out to the Katyn woods about 16 kilometers west of Smolensk.

Mr. FLOOD. Will you describe, in your own words, your first impression and your obervations of what you saw immediately upon arriving at the scene of the graves?

Dr. TRAMSEN. The first thing we saw was a rather sparse wood of fir trees, and there was a terrible smell of decay. And then we saw, in a sort of lane, a long line of dead bodies that had already been extracted from the tombs.

This is the first few I saw (producing photograph).

We were taken immediately to the tombs.

Mr. FLOOD. May I interrupt?

Will the stenographer mark for identification this photograph as exhibit No. 43?

(The photograph referred to marked for identification "Exhibit 43.")

Mr. FLOOD. I now show you a photograph marked for identification as exhibit No. 43 and ask you, Doctor, to describe what that is.

Dr. TRAMSEN. In this picture you see about 20 rows of dead bodies and anything up to 15 dead bodies in each row; all fully dressed in typical uniform dresses and with their boots in rather good condition. That was about the first thing I observed.

Mr. MACHROWICZ. Who took that picture?

Dr. TRAMSEN. The Germans took that.

Mr. MACHROWICZ. In your presence?

Dr. TRAMSEN. Yes.

Mr. FLOOD. Has this been in your possession ever since?

Dr. TRAMSEN. Yes.

Mr. FLOOD. Until you presented it here this morning?

Dr. TRAMSEN. Yes.

Mr. FLOOD. Very well.

Dr. TRAMSEN. Secondly, we were taken to the tombs, of which we soon counted seven. They were lying in various heights on a sloping hill. We went down into some of the tombs, as you see me on this picture standing along by the dead bodies.

Mr. FLOOD. Just a moment.

We now ask the stenographer to mark for identification a photograph as exhibit No. 44.

Mr. FLOOD. I now show the witness exhibit No. 44, a photograph, and ask him to identify the photograph and the persons who are on the photograph.

Dr. TRAMSEN. In this picture, you see the bottom of one of the tombs, filled up with dead bodies, and by the side of these dead bodies are two of the members of the committee: Professor Subik and me.

Mr. FLOOD. I take for granted, Doctor, that these two exhibits thus far introduced and the others—if you have any that will be introduced—are photographs, as you say, taken by the Germans, given to you, and have been in your custody up until you presented them to the committee this morning?

Dr. TRAMSEN. Yes.

Mr. FLOOD. Proceed.

Dr. TRAMSEN. We tried to make an impression of how many dead bodies some of these tombs could hold, and in one of these tombs it seemed to be quite an easy job because the dead bodies were all lying in very even sheets, and we could count the dead bodies in the line and in the sheets because at the site of the tombs the tomb would deck down to the lowest sheet.

Mr. DONDERO. Do you mean tiers, Doctor?

Dr. TRAMSEN. Yes.

Mr. FLOOD. Just a moment.

Will the stenographer mark another photograph as exhibit 45?

Mr. FLOOD. I now show you a photograph marked as exhibit 45 and ask you if he can identify that photograph and describe it.

Dr. TRAMSEN. This photograph only shows various layers of the dead bodies with all the heads lying in the same line.

Mr. FLOOD. Will you let me have the other photographs so that we will be able to make them as exhibits as we did with the doctor's earlier. We do this only for the purpose of saving time. We did the same thing with the documents just presented by the other witnesses.

Will the stenographer mark these photographs for identification as exhibit 46 and in sequence. They are photographs for the purpose of exhibits.

Mr. FLOOD. Proceed, please.

Dr. TRAMSEN. Approximately, we could reckon that not less than 2,500 dead bodies could be held in the biggest of these tombs, and a varying number, small numbers, in each of the other tombs. But how many altogether we did not make any statement at that time, unfortunately.

The next thing was that, under the leadership of Professor Buhtz, one of the dead bodies was extracted from a place in one of the tombs that the committee pointed out itself. This body was put on a wooden table and the committee collected around it were able, with Professor Buhtz, to identify the body as you see on the picture, exhibit 46. It could be done because we found in the pockets of the uniform jacket several personal papers and between them some letters, but I do not recall the name of that special first dead body we examined. This was what actually happened that morning, and we returned about midday to Smolensk.

The further investigations of the tombs took place the next day with the post-mortem autopsies. As you already have been told about the titles of the members of the committee, some of these committee members were not specialists in forensic medicine, so we had decided upon that only those with forensic medical specialist training should do the postmortems, and that was nine of us.

Mr. FLOOD. The decision to have you nine of the entire commission conduct the postmortems was a decision made by agreement of the scientists on the commission?

Dr. TRAMSEN. On the whole commission; yes.

Mr. FLOOD. And not by any German decision?

Dr. TRAMSEN. No.

So, we, next morning, went to the wood at quarter past nine to proceed with the examinations. As you see, on exhibit 47, six tables for autopsies were put up in an open space in the wood. The Germans had supplied us with typists, interpreters, secretaries, and all instruments, rubber gloves, rubber aprons, and everything necessary for postmortem autopsies. I went down about 10 o'clock in one of the tombs, as you see on exhibit 48.

Mr. FLOOD. You are using the term "tomb" interchangeably with "grave"; is that so?

Dr. TRAMSEN. Yes, that is the same.

In one of the graves, and with me was a German secretary and an assistant doctor and one of the civilian Russian workers that was working for the Germans in the place. I chose myself the very place where I wanted to extract a body and this is what you see on exhibit 48. This dead body was put on a table and I examined it from the outside. I could see the body was dressed in a Polish uniform.

Mr. FLOOD. How did you know it was a Polish uniform?

Dr. TRAMSEN. I could see the buttons with the Polish eagle and I could see the badge of the uniform cap which was lying next to the body.

Mr. FLOOD. You are holding in your hand at this moment what appears to be a uniform badge.

Dr. TRAMSEN. Yes.

Mr. FLOOD. Is that one of the badges taken from one of the bodies?

Dr. TRAMSEN. That is a badge taken from the cap of that dead body I extracted.

Mr. FLOOD. May we see that, please?

Dr. TRAMSEN. Yes.

Corpses on trestles awaiting examination. Prof Naville fifth from left.

Mr. FLOOD. And this has been in your possession ever since you yourself took it from the uniform of one of the dead bodies at Katyn under the circumstances you have described; is that correct?

Dr. TRAMSEN. Yes; that's right.

Mr. FLOOD. And you described this as the Polish eagle insignia taken from the cap of a Polish officer's body at Katyn?

Dr. TRAMSEN. Yes.

Mr. FLOOD. Doctor, I now show you exhibit 61 marked for identification and ask you whether or not that is the insignia taken from the cap of a Polish officer's body at the grave at Katyn?

Dr. TRAMSEN. Yes.

Mr. FLOOD. That is in evidence.

Dr. TRAMSEN. My next job was to try and identify this dead body and it didn't take me a long time because in the right side of the uniform jacket, the inside pocket, I found the military pass of this officer, with a red mark of mobilization, and his name very clearly to be read, as Ludwig Szyminski, and his address as Krakow-Miasto, stamped on the front page. On the other side, there was a place for a photograph but, unfortunately, this had been so spoiled that nothing could be seen on the photograph. But, underneath, with a special significance for identification, it has "eyebrows," "beard," "height," and so forth.

Mr. FLOOD. I show you exhibit 62 for identification and ask you if that is the identification slip and the mobilization order to which you just referred?

Dr. TRAMSEN. Yes.

Besides, I found a lot of papers, newspapers, and, as well, a pocketbook. This showed very clearly that the owner must have been a chemist. It was a Polish pocketbook from Bayer Meister Lucius, a German medical firm, giving all the details about the doses of this medical firm. Another little extraordinary detail was that the officer probably must have been a stamp collector, because he had an envelope with some Russian and Polish stamps in his pocketbook.

Mr. FLOOD. Doctor, I now show you an envelope, marked for identification as "Exhibit 63," containing these stamps you have just described. Take a look at those stamps. Are those the stamps you have just mentioned?

Dr. TRAMSEN. Yes, they are.

Mr. FLOOD. Go ahead.

Dr. TRAMSEN. In the pocketbook I found several Polish bank notes.

Mr. FLOOD. What is the name of that type of currency?

Dr. TRAMSEN. These are zloty.

That was not extraordinary, because they were found in masses on pretty well all the bodies extracted from the grave.

Mr. FLOOD. Mark for identification as "Exhibit 64" this envelope containing the zloty just described by the doctor.

Mr. FLOOD. I now show you, doctor, this envelope, marked for identification as exhibit 64, containing the zloty you just described. Look at that envelope. Is this the zloty you have described?

Dr. TRAMSEN. They are.

It was remarkable that we didn't find anything of great value, like fountain pens or watches. I didn't find any on this body either, but I found two small coins in the waistcoat pocket—5 and 10 grozy.

Mr. FLOOD. Doctor, I show you an envelope marked for identification as exhibit 65 containing the coins to which you have just referred. Will you examine the envelope and does it contain those coins?

Dr. TRAMSEN. Yes; it does.

Chairman MADDEN. We'll have a 3-minute recess.

(Whereupon, a recess was taken.)

Mr. FLOOD. Doctor, when we recessed, you were in the process of continuing your story. Will you go on from there?

Dr. TRAMSEN. Yes; I was telling about doing the identification of this dead body that was removed from one of the graves.

Having cut open the uniforms and clothes, I could remark that they must have been on the dead body for quite a while, a long time, because the underclothes were more or less compact with the skin. But they were all in the proper size and all buttoned up. I could remark that he was definitely warmly dressed, having two kinds of underwear and a thick, wooly scarf. The boots were in good condition. I remarked that the hands were tied in the back with a sort of thick white rope; I should think about a quarter of an inch in diameter, possibly, and the string was cut right through the skin, nearly to the bone. That has surely happened after death.

Mr. Flood. At that point, you were describing that the hands of the body you were examining were tied with a rope, the nature of which you described. During your stay at Katyn, did you have occasion to observe that any other bodies found there were similarly tied?

Dr. Tramsen. Yes. I should think that the committee altogether, and I as well, saw some 800 dead bodies, out of which only a few were not tied with their hands on their back.

Mr. Flood. Did you happen to observe whether or not any of the bodies with the hands tied were tied with any wire?

Dr. Tramsen. Yes, I saw that in at least two cases, and, in some other cases, they were tied with leather straps—possibly, the soldier's belt.

Mr. Flood. You mentioned that the particular body that you were working on at the time was warmly dressed—woolen scarf, winter underwear, etc. During the course of your stay at Katyn and your observation of the other bodies, did you observe whether or not any of them wore overcoats?

Dr. Tramsen. Yes, most of them carried overcoats, some of a bit civilian kind—thick-skinned coats, and even a few fur coats in between.

Mr. Flood. Did you observe any of the bodies wearing leather jackets or knitted pull-over sweaters or that kind of thing?

Dr. Tramsen. I cannot remember having seen any leather jackets, but I have seen lots of woolly pull-overs and woolly knitted jumpers and things like that under the uniform jackets.

Mr. Flood. There is no doubt, at least in your mind, from your observations, that the bodies wore winter clothing?

Dr. Tramsen. No. They wore winter clothes.

Mr. Flood. Proceed.

Dr. Tramsen. The state of the body itself was in an extraordinary kind of decay. I would call it more or less mummified, and I may say that this has been caused by the immense pressure of the weight of hundreds of dead bodies and the tons of heavy sand over them.

Mr. Flood. Then you had occasion to observe the nature, the texture, and the color of the soil?

Dr. Tramsen. Yes.

Mr. Flood. Would you describe that?

Dr. Tramsen. It was yellowish, more or less dry, very sandy soil, with a rather deep ground-water stand. We observed water only in that grave which was lying lowest on the sloping hill. The yellow sand had some stripes of brownish color which might hold that lime was in the minerals in the ground, but I don't know much about that.

Mr. Flood. Doctor, you described in some detail the manner in which the uniforms were upon the bodies as you observed them. Would you say from such observation, and from observations you have made in your medical experience of dead bodies containing clothing over a period of time, that these bodies had been buried in the uniforms as you saw the uniforms at the grave?

Dr. TRAMSEN. Yes, it is beyond doubt that they were buried in the uniforms in which they were found.

Mr. DONDERO. I think you mean at the time they were buried and not the time you found them.

Dr. TRAMSEN. I mean both.

Mr. FLOOD. So do I.

Doctor, you described in some detail the bodies as you saw them lying in the grave. Could you say from your observation of the bodies and the manner in which they were lying in the graves, that it indicated clearly a systematic arrangement of the bodies in the grave?

Dr. TRAMSEN. Yes. I can specially say that in some parts of the graves we found systematic order very clearly, especially along the sides and ends of the graves, more. Less, I should say, in the center.

Mr. FLOOD. Did you find or did you see any bodies in the graves or laid out when you were there that were not the bodies of Polish officers?

Dr. TRAMSEN. No, not in those seven tombs that were shown us by the Germans, but the Germans showed us some bodies that were extracted from other tombs in the same wood, lying a bit apart from those same tombs.

Mr. FLOOD. Did you find any bodies that from their insigna or dress or documentation or anything else would indicate that they were the bodies of clergymen?

Dr. TRAMSEN. Yes, I did. Yes, I saw at least three at the time I was there that were clergymen, carrying their black collar and the rosebuds and the cross as Catholic clergymen do.

Mr. FLOOD. Would it be obvious to military people, or people who had associated with military people, that the markings of the black collar—the rosebuds and the cross—would indicate that the wearer would be a clergyman or a chaplain of some degree?

Dr. TRAMSEN. Yes, I well imagine that they were military clergymen because they wore particularly uniforms and then these insignia I told you about.

Mr. FLOOD. In the particular graves in question did you see or did you hear that a female body in military Polish uniform was unearthed?

Dr. TRAMSEN. No, I have not.

Mr. FLOOD. Was it brought to your attention that there were gold teeth or gold dentures in any of the bodies?

Dr. TRAMSEN. There were very few gold teeth found in those bodies we saw.

Mr. FLOOD. There were some?

Dr. TRAMSEN. I have seen some, yes.

Mr. FLOOD. In looking at any of the documents or diaries or papers of any nature that you observed on your body or saw as having been taken from any others, did you have occasion to observe the dates with any particularity?

Dr. TRAMSEN. Yes. I have got two papers extracted from dead bodies, not the one I just did a post-mortem on, but from two others, with dates on them.

Mr. FLOOD. May I see those, please?

Dr. TRAMSEN. The one is evidently a Polish poem and apparently is signed Kozielsk, the 26th of April 1940.

Mr. FLOOD. The stenographer will mark these for identification as exhibits 66 and 67.

(The documents referred to were marked "Frankfurt Exhibits 66 and 67."

(NOTE.—Subsequent examination of the two documents showed they were insufficiently legible for complete translation. Thus they are not included in this published report. The documents are in the committee's permanent file.)

Dr. TRAMSEN. You asked me if I had some more documents with dates on.

Mr. FLOOD. That is correct.

Dr. TRAMSEN. Another officer, a Capt. Ludwig Gajenski, was found in one of these tombs, and one of the German scientists, Dr. Huber, who did a post-mortem on this man, found this list in his pocket. It is a roll call list of officers of a fifth company of some artillery regiment and signed "Kozielsk, 12 April 1940." It contains a list of some thirty officers with their birthdays and their military rank, and what is interesting is that some ten or eleven of the names have been crossed out. Whether this means anything or not, I am not able to say, but possibly a Polish officer will be able to decipher the numbers written underneath in various groups.

Mr. FLOOD. Doctor, I take for granted that these documents we are now discussing were taken by you from bodies at the graves or else were given to you by others who took them from the bodies at the graves, and have been in your custody until they have been presented here this morning.

Dr. TRAMSEN. Yes, that is so, and if not extracted by me, the others I did not extract, I saw being extracted.

Mr. FLOOD. You saw them extracted yourself?

Dr. TRAMSEN. Yes, so I can definitely state that they have been extracted from the bodies.

Mr. FLOOD. Doctor, I show you an envelope marked for identification as exhibit 68 and ask you to examine it and tell us whether or not it contains the list of officers taken from the body as you just described it?

Dr. TRAMSEN. It does.

Chairman MADDEN. I think we should recess now.

Mr. FLOOD. Now, I show the witness these exhibits marked 70, 71, and 72, photographs, and I ask you, witness, if you will identify them, please.

Just take 70 and tell us what it is, and then 71, and so on. Take all three and tell us what they are.

Dr. TRAMSEN. Number 70 is corresponding to the beginning of the medical examination of the dead body, and it shows the skull of a Polish officer. The soft tissues from the neck have been removed, and it is clearly to be seen in the picture that a pistol-shot wound in the occipital bone has entered the skull this way. You can see that, because the bones of the skull consist of an outer and an inner layer, between which you see, in the bone, small parts, and what is called cells. And a shot that enters the bone like that will make an absolutely round hole on the outside and a greater hole on the inside of the bone, and we have seen that in practically all of the skulls that were examined by cutting the bone through. That is all I want to say about this picture.

Mr. FLOOD. While we are discussing that picture—I was going to take the details of the post-mortems later, all at one time, but since you have a picture, this last exhibit, which indicates the point of entry and the condition of the skull at the time you found it insofar as the bullet wound is concerned, I am going to ask you now to demonstrate on the interpreter the point of entry and the point of exit of the bullet on that skull and any others that you examined.

Dr. TRAMSEN. In the soft tissues in this area back of the neck [indicating].

Mr. FLOOD. The witness is pointing to the back of the neck at the base of the skull of the neckline.

Now, Doctor, for the purpose of the record, and since this is a highly technical and a very scientific piece of testimony, I wish that you would forget that we are laymen, unless you have to translate later, and, as though you were addressing a collection of pathologists, will you describe, in technical, pathological terms, the analysis of the point of entry and the point of exit?

Dr. TRAMSEN. Yes. In the soft tissues, in this area we always found a lot of marking of black gunpowder, which has more or less been pushed into the skin because the shot has been fired with the muzzle straight touching the skin and pointed forward, upwards, with the exit of the gunshot near the right or left temple at the fore of the head [indicating].

Would you like any further demonstration of this?

Mr. FLOOD. I would like you to indicate which is the occipital bone.

Dr. TRAMSEN. The occipital bone is the bone going in this direction [indicating] carrying forward on to the base of the skull surrounding the hole for the central nervous system.

Mr. FLOOD. Now, you were indicating the point of entry in the nape of the neck into the bone structure of the occipital bone. Is there any other technical description you could give to that area which might be described as the foramen magnum?

Dr. TRAMSEN. No.

The exit of the bullet—would you like to hear anything about the exit of the bullet?

Mr. FLOOD. Yes. Tell us technically the scientific description of the point of exit and the description of the area in scientific terms, the physiological examination.

Dr. TRAMSEN. In practically all of the dead bodies we found the exit of the bone along the line of the hair border in the left or right temple, and only in one or two we saw the exit line lower, below the eye.

Mr. FLOOD. Were there any skulls upon which there was more than one point of entry or exit?

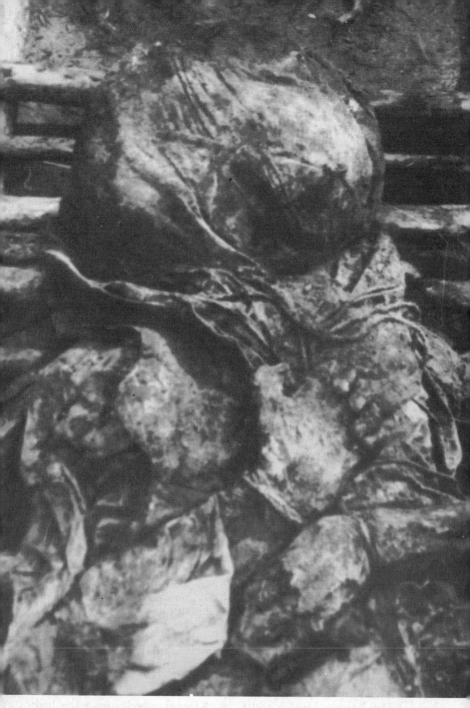

Body of a dead woman, head covered in sacking and hands tied behind back with the cord carrying up behind the neck: an NKVD victim before the mass murder of Polish officers.

Dr. TRAMSEN. We saw one skull with two points of entry and exit.

Mr. FLOOD. But in most cases, as I understand it, there was only one point of entry and one point of exit.

Dr. TRAMSEN. Yes.

Mr. FLOOD. Did you open any of the skulls in your post-morterms for the purpose of examining the interior to determine the course of the bullet or the condition of the interior of the skull with reference to the course of the bullet?

Dr. TRAMSEN. Yes; I have done that myself in one case, this Captain Szyminski that I told you about.

Mr. FLOOD. Will you give us the results of your examination of the interior of the skull in the body you examined?

Dr. TRAMSEN. The direction of the bullet in that skull was such as it couldn't possibly have avoided a lesion, a serious lesion, of the bottom of the brain and the so-called medulla oblongata, the nerve center of respiration, with an absolutely deadly effect.

Mr. FLOOD. Doctor, you indicated to us earlier that you had been shown the remains of bodies in the area from older graves, which you described as older Russian graves.

Dr. TRAMSEN. Yes.

Mr. FLOOD. Did you examine the skulls or see the skulls of any of those bodies found in the much older Russian graves in the immediate area of the Katyn grave?

Dr. TRAMSEN. Yes; I did.

Mr. FLOOD. What did you find?

Dr. TRAMSEN. Yes; I have got a picture; exhibit 72.

Mr. FLOOD. The witness now refers to exhibit No. 72.

Dr. TRAMSEN. That is a picture of a dead body that I saw. The Germans dug it out of a tomb further into the wood.

Mr. MACHROWICZ. Did they dig it out in your presence?

Dr. TRAMSEN. Yes. It is a body of a dead woman, and the head is covered with a sort of sacking, and the hands are tied on the back with a string carrying up around the neck. And the cause of death was the same, the shot through the neck and out through the temple. From the state of the dead body it could be concluded that it must have been lying in the ground pretty much longer than the dead bodies we saw in the Polish officers' tomb.

Mr. FLOOD. There are two questions that I want to ask you in connection with this exhibit.

First, does the point of entry and the point of exit and the course of the bullet indicated thereby found on the skull of this female body that you have just described in the exhibit—were they similar to the points of entry and exit and the course of the bullets found in the skulls in the Katyn graves?

Dr. TRAMSEN. Yes, they were exactly similar.

Mr. FLOOD. By "the Katyn graves" I mean the Katyn graves of the Polish officers.

Dr. TRAMSEN. Yes, quite right.

Mr. FLOOD. And secondly, in the graves containing the bodies of the Polish officers, did you find any bodies where the heads were covered with sacking or coating and tied with a rope around the neck, similar to the body you have just described in exhibit No. 72 as having come from an old Russian grave nearby?

282

Dr. Tramsen. No; I have not seen that.

Mr. Flood. You have told us that many of the bodies of the Polish officers were found with their hands tied behind their backs, and you described them in a certain way. Were the hands of this female body that you describe in exhibit No. 72 tied in the same manner that the bodies of the Polish officers were tied in the graves at Katyn?

Dr. Tramsen. No, I have not seen them tied in that way, but, if I may refer to the picture exhibit 53, I will give you a description of how the hands, generally, were tied on the Polish officers.

Mr. Flood. Will you demonstrate again upon the interpreter the manner in which you saw the hands tied on the bodies of the Polish officers?

Dr. Tramsen. Yes. As you see on this picture, the hands were tied on the back with a tight loop of string on one wrist, carrying the strings over on the other wrist, around that one [indicating], and a loop around both hands, tied in a long tie with long loose ends, evidently giving a lot of rope for each.

Mr. Flood. You mentioned that some of the hands were tied with wire. I suppose the hands were found in about the same position on the back of the body when tied with a wire?

Dr. Tramsen. Yes, pretty well the same way.

Mr. Flood. Doctor, in your official and professional capacity as an expert and an experienced pathologist, did you ever have occasion to examine bodies where the cause of death had been bullet wounds or gunshot wounds?

Dr. Tramsen. Yes, plenty. We had a lot of murder cases during the occupation in Denmark, and I did the post-mortems on pretty well all those murdered by gunshots or shots.

Mr. Flood. From the nature and the condition of the gunshot wound, the kind of wound and its appearance upon the body, is it possible for an expert pathologist to determine whether or not that shot was proximate to the body?

Dr. Tramsen. Yes, that is absolutely possible because you would not find a complete tattooing of the skin with the gunpowder unless the muzzle had been put absolutely close to or on the skin itself.

Mr. Flood. Doctor, in the body you examined, and in any examination of other bodies that were at Katyn, but with particular reference to the one upon which you performed the post-mortem, would you be able to say, from the blasting of the skull, from the finding of the powder marks as you have described them, and from the course of the bullet, that this had been fired proximate to the skull?

Dr. Tramsen. Yes, I can; because in many of the cases we observed a very big blast effect on the skull, in some cases, with long lines of fractures, and in a few cases with a complete loosening of the top of the skull, which could not have been done unless gunshot had been fired straight at the skull itself.

Mr. Flood. For the reasons you have just given, in the language of a layman would you say that the shot fired into the skull of the body you examined, and of the others that you saw in the graves at Katyn, had been fired at a very close or a point-blank range?

Dr. Tramsen. There is no doubt that they have all been fired at point-blank range; all those I have seen, anyway.

Mr. Flood. Now, is it possible for a pathologist of your experience and training, examining thousands of bodies containing gunshot wounds, as you have, keeping in mind the nature and the type of the wound and the similarity in all cases of the point of entry and the point of exit and the course of the projectile—is it possible for a pathologist, under those circumstances, to say whether or not those shots had been fired by a practiced hand or hands?

Dr. TRAMSEN. No, I wouldn't say that, because you need not have much practice for doing that sort of thing.

Mr. FLOOD. Did you make any examination with calipers or any other instrument as to the diameter of the wound so that you might be able to tell the caliber of the projectile?

Dr. TRAMSEN. Yes; we have, and I have, too. We could say that the entry wound in the skull is a pretty good picture of the caliber of the bullet. And, furthermore, we found, in one of the dead bodies, a bullet in the front part of the skull. This is what I can show you on the picture, Exhibit 52. I saw this picture being taken in Katyn, and it shows a bullet clearly lying in the exit wound of the skull, and all of our examinations prove that they must have been shots fired with bullets of a caliber 8 millimeter.

Mr. FLOOD. Do you know enough about the science of ballistics, or are you acquainted with pistol ammunition sufficiently well to be able to say if that would resemble what ammunition people call a 7.65?

Dr. TRAMSEN. Just a moment, please, and I will tell you.

Yes; I think it is quite true that it might have been a caliber 7.65. Anyway, as we put it in the protocol, below 8 millimeter.

Mr. FLOOD. Did you see the bullet you just described, that was embedded in that skull, after it was extracted?

Dr. TRAMSEN. Yes; I saw it, but I did not measure that myself, and it looked exactly like an ordinary pistol bullet.

Mr. FLOOD. Did you see, when you were at Katyn, or was there shown to you in the graves, or described as having been taken from the graves, the shell cases of any of the ammunition supposed to have been used there?

Dr. TRAMSEN. Yes; I have seen them, but I cannot recall very much about them. There were many of them among the dead bodies in the tomb.

Mr. FLOOD. Did you ever hear them described, when you were there, as cartridge cases of German-make ammunition?

Dr. TRAMSEN. Yes; I have. Germans themselves told me they were of German origin, but, at the same time, they stated that a lot of ammunition for pistols and other hand weapons had been delivered to Russia before Russia entered the war.

Mr. FLOOD. But the fact remains that you were shown, at the Katyn graves, cartridge shells said to have been taken from the graves; you were shown these shells by Germans who told you two things, first, that the cartridge shells found by the graves were ammunition, pistol ammunition, of German manufacture, but that, frequently, that caliber of ammunition had been sold to Russians and others?

Dr. TRAMSEN. Yes; that is right.

Mr. FLOOD. Now, Doctor, did you notice personally, or were you advised by any of your other brother scientists, whether or not there were any other wounds on any of these bodies other than pistol wounds?

Dr. TRAMSEN. Yes. We saw several bodies with typical wounds of bayonets in their backs, of a special square kind.

Mr. FLOOD. Did you examine the point of entry of the bayonet wound?

Dr. TRAMSEN. Yes; I did.

Mr. FLOOD. Would you say it could have been triangular or square?

Dr. TRAMSEN. I saw several that could be doubtful, but I saw, anyway, at least one that definitely was of a square kind.

Mr. FLOOD. Are you in a position to express any opinion as to the type of bayonet used by the Russian armed services about that time?

Dr. TRAMSEN. No; I did not know at that time, but I had later been told that the Russians used those of a square type.

Mr. FLOOD. Would that same statement be true, as far as you knew or have heard since, with reference to the type of bayonet used by the Russian armed services in 1940?

Dr. TRAMSEN. It is possible; I do not know.

Mr. FLOOD. How many bodies were post mortems performed upon by your group of scientists, about?

Dr. TRAMSEN. We did nine total post mortems, examining the whole body and organs and all signs of lesions and diseases.

Mr. FLOOD. Now, after all of these bodies, the nine of them, upon which the dissections were made by you and your colleagues, you told us that you were permitted to select any body you wished. Was the same true of your colleagues; if you know?

Dr. TRAMSEN. Yes; they were completely free to choose.

Mr. FLOOD. Now, I want to return to the examination of skulls for a minute and ask you whether or not any matter was brought to your attention by any of your colleagues, having particular reference to the internal examination of the skulls.

Dr. TRAMSEN. Yes. We examined several of the insides of the skulls which were brought to Smolensk from the tombs after the post mortems, and Professor Orsos of Budapest, who is a specialist in doing post mortems in regard to deciding the time of death, had instructed us as to a new manner of examining the inside of a skull which has been interred for a long time. I had read about this method but had never practiced it before.

Mr. FLOOD. Was this method important for the purpose of establishing the time of death of the corpse?

Dr. TRAMSEN. Yes; to a certain extent.

Mr. FLOOD. Will you just indicate to us what the method was, with particular reference to the brain pulp or calcium formations?

Dr. TRAMSEN. Yes. If a skull is left in the ground for a certain time, at least for 2 years, the pulp of the brain will sort of lay down in a compact mass at the lowest part of the skull, and if you cut the skull through, with the lowest part still lying low, then you will cut through this pulp of the brain lying at the bottom of the skull and notice certain layers of grayish and yellowish stripes formed by the various chemical parts of the brain, the liquids and the phosphor acids and salts of various kinds, laying down in a special layer that you can notice. But, as Professor Orsos has stated, this will not take place unless the skull has been lying in the same position for at least 2 years, and we had noticed that symptom in several of the skulls that were cut through.

Mr. Flood. So that, could any of the substance that you have described as being present in the brain under those circumstances be described as a calcium type of formation of some nature?

Dr. Tramsen. Yes, I think so.

Do you mean a calcification in the brain pulp could have developed in a couple of years?

Mr. Flood. That is correct.

Dr. Tramsen. Yes, it can; and we saw that, too.

Mr. Flood. Could you say that the brain pulp remaining in that part of the skull after such a lengthy burial could be described as being of a claylike nature or a claylike state?

Dr. Tramsen. Yes. It was like rather heavily compressed clay.

Mr. Flood. Did you observe, or were any observations made by your brother scientists, or others, in your presence, with reference to the presence of or the lack of insects in the graves?

Dr. Tramsen. Yes. We had particularly been looking out for insects, eggs, mites, and ants, but we found nothing of that kind.

Mr. Flood. Could it be reasonably concluded, based upon that finding, that the bodies were buried at a time of the year which would be insect-free or perhaps cold?

Dr. Tramsen. Yes, indeed. And it corresponds very well to the observation that the lack of original decay was obvious, particularly when you take into notice the climate of that part of Russia, which is very hot in summertime and very cold in wintertime.

Mr. Flood. Did you examine, did you see, or was it brought to your attention at the time you were at Katyn, that any of the skulls or bodies had indications of a ricochet shot thereon?

Dr. Tramsen. No; I do not recall that.

Mr. Flood. The type of wound that perhaps might indicate that shot had been fired at such a body, ricocheted therefrom or therethrough, and struck another body, which may have been lying nearby?

Dr. Tramsen. Yes; that I remember.

In one case we found a bullet sitting, so far as I remember, in the shoulder muscles of one of the bodies in the tomb, and this bullet had penetrated so slowly and so little in the body that it could not have been fired pointblank, or must have penetrated something else before, in any case.

Mr. Flood. Doctor, it has been indicated to the committee by a number of witnesses of various kinds that trees of a certain height had been planted in the area, had been seen in the area, and had been removed from the grave just immediately prior to the grave being opened, of these Polish officers at Katyn.

Dr. Tramsen. Yes; I remember seeing quite a lot of lines of young fir trees about the height of one-and-a-half foot, and I saw them stretching out from the graves because they had been removed when those graves had been opened possibly.

Mr. Flood. Were any observations made or comments made by your colleagues or others there at the time with reference to those trees, anything of any special significance, that you recall?

Dr. Tramsen. Yes. But I do not understand much of forestry, and I have no special knowledge about. But the Germans produced a German specialist, a forester, who showed us these trees in cuts.

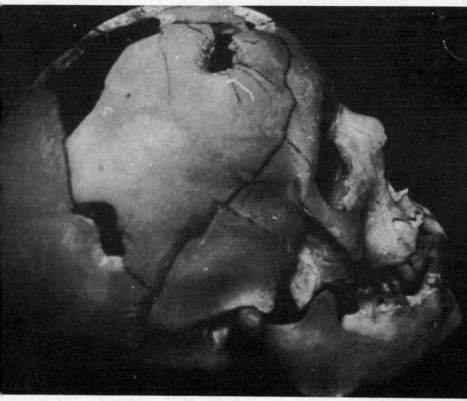

Skull showing exit hole of bullet in forehead, side view.

Mr. Flood. Do you remember the name of the German forester?

Dr. Tramsen. Hafferer, or something like that. I don't quite remember the name, I am sorry.

Mr. Flood. If you heard the name, do you think you would recognize it?

Dr. Tramsen. Yes; I think so.

Mr. Flood. Could it have been Von Herff?

Dr. Tramsen. Yes; that is it.

Mr. Flood. What did von Herff say or do when you were there?

Dr. Tramsen. I cannot exactly remember that von Herff demonstrated the trees himself, but I can remember that Professor Buhtz gave a conclusion that the German forester had put up and stated on the examination of these trees.

Mr. Flood. Do you recall the nature of Dr. Buhtz's observations about the trees?

Dr. Tramsen. Yes. And it was clearly demonstrated under microscope that the growth rings of these trees had some sort of arrest, had a special place, which could be assembled from one cut to the other.

Mr. Flood. How many graves, if you know, were opened at the time you were at Katyn, about?

Dr. Tramsen. Seven graves, with Polish officers.

Mr. Flood. You do not include the other so-called older Russian graves?

Dr. Tramsen. No.

Mr. Flood. You gave us some details with reference to certain types and kinds of documents, doctor. Did you observe, for any reason, any particular date which could be called the latest date, that you know?

Dr. Tramsen. Yes. We saw Russian papers dated as late as the 20th of April 1940.

Mr. Flood. By Russian "papers" I presume you mean Russian newspapers.

Dr. Tramsen. That is right.

And I remember having been shown a diary from one of the Polish officers showing a date as late as the 21st of April, and that was the very last date we could find on any of the papers or books or diaries found in these graves.

Chairman Madden. Mr. Machrowicz.

Mr. Machrowicz. Mr. Chairman, in connection with the statement which I made to the committee just before adjournment, I have since that time been informed that the particular witness in question, namely, Hans Bless, has prepared a written statement which he wishes to present to the committee. I understand he may not be available later. I would like to ask the indulgence of the present witness if we could interrupt for a few minutes to take advantage of his presence.

I would like to ask the chairman that, in all fairness to him and in order to complete our record, he be permitted to present to the committee the statement which he has prepared.

Mr. Flood. Dr. Tramsen, will you return to the stand, please?

Doctor, did you ever talk to any Russian peasants who lived in the area of the Katyn graves at any time you were there?

Dr. Tramsen. No, I have not done that personally as I don't speak Russian.

Mr. Flood. Did you see any of your colleagues, or were you with them at the time any of them, in your presence, spoke to any Russians in the area?

Dr. Tramsen. Yes. In the afternoon on the very first day, Professor Orsos spoke to three Russian civilians, and the talk was translated by interpreters into German.

Mr. Flood. What was the nature or the gist of the conversation, if you recall?

Dr. Tramsen. Professor Orsos asked these Russians whether they had seen, in 1940, Polish prisoners of war being carried from Gniezdowo railway station to the Katyn wood, and at the same time, they told that they had heard a lot of shooting in the early morning hours in the Katyn wood area, but that the wood had been guarded by Russians for a long time and no civilians had been allowed into that special area.

And that is what I remember of these talks with the Russians.

Mr. FLOOD. Doctor, we would just like one more scientific and professional opinion with reference to the degree of decomposition of any of the bodies you observed individually or a mass condition of decomposition with reference of one body to another in such a mass, as to coagulation and congealing.

Dr. TRAMSEN. I am sorry to say I have not got much experience according to mass graves, but from what I have been told and what I have read about before, the bodies interred in such graves must have been left there for a considerable time to be compressed and congealed in such a manner as they were here.

Mr. FLOOD. Would these circumstances and degrees of decomposition that you have just mentioned permit the conclusion of a contemporaneous burial, all at one time?

Dr. TRAMSEN. Yes. They were all decayed and compressed to such a degree and in the same manner that one could conclude that they must have been buried pretty well at the same time.

Mr. FLOOD. Do you remember a member of the International Medical Commission, a colleague of yours, from Bulgaria, one Dr. Markov?

Dr. TRAMSEN. Yes.

Mr. FLOOD. Do you remember whether or not Dr. Markov expressed any opinions with reference to who might have been responsible for these murders; what country, what people?

Dr. TRAMSEN. Yes. I spoke quite a lot to Dr. Markov in Smolensk and later in Berlin, and I am of the absolutely complete idea that he meant the Russians had done these murders. And so far as I remember, he said it directly at several occasions.

Mr. FLOOD. You have no doubt about that, Doctor?

Dr. TRAMSEN. That is quite correct.

Mr. FLOOD. Did Dr. Markov, to you or to anyone in your presence, then indicate that he was under any kind of duress or compulsion or threat from the Germans because of his position on this commission with you?

Dr. TRAMSEN. No; not at all.

Mr. FLOOD. You are aware, are you, that Dr. Markov has subsequently recanted his signature of this international medical protocol and states that he was forced by the Germans to participate and to sign?

Dr. TRAMSEN. Yes; I have been told that. But at the final meeting in Smolensk, nevertheless, Dr. Markov signed, as you see his personal signature here, the protocol that we concluded in stating that the shooting of the Polish officers must have taken place in the months of March and April of 1940.

Mr. FLOOD. Doctor, were you placed under any duress, direct or indirect, at that time by the Germans or by your own Danish Government and forced, against your will or with promise of advantage or gratuity, to participate in this investigation?

Dr. TRAMSEN. No; I did not. I took part in the commission on my own free will and have never been under any stress during those days by the Germans, the Danish Government, or any other authority.

Mr. FLOOD. Did you have the full cooperation of the German authorities during your scientific examinations of these bodies at Katyn?

Dr. TRAMSEN. Yes. I had the absolutely free allowance to move about, take pictures with my own camera, and was assisted by the

Germans in any way during my scientific examinations and autopsies of the bodies.

Mr. FLOOD. Were you prevented by the Germans at any time from doing any particular thing you wanted to do?

Dr. TRAMSEN. No; not at all.

Mr. FLOOD. As far as you know, was the same cooperation extended to your brother scientists on this commission?

Dr. TRAMSEN. Yes. They were all given the same facilities.

Mr. FLOOD. Have you been placed under any duress, or have you been the recipient of any promise by your Danish Government today, or by the West German Government, or by the Government of the United States, or anybody else, to appear here today?

Dr. TRAMSEN. No. I did that on my own free will.

Mr. FLOOD. From your examination, made as you have described in this length and detail, of the bodies in the graves at Katyn, is it possible for you to reach a conclusion as to the cause of death?

Dr. TRAMSEN. Yes. In all the cases I saw, which amounted up to nearly 800, it was undoubtedly, in every case, a rank murder and could not have been suicide or any other way of cause of death.

Mr. FLOOD. What was the nature of the instrument used in the murder, and what was the direct cause of death?

Dr. TRAMSEN. The way of murder was done by shots with pistols, at pointblank, and the cause of death was mortal lesions of the brain and the main nerve, consisting of the nerve centers for the respiration and circulation.

Mr. FLOOD. Is it possible, from the testimony you have given and from your experiences at Katyn, to approximate the date of death and the date of burial of the bodies you saw there?

Dr. TRAMSEN. From a medical point of view, that will be very difficult, but from the examinations of the decaying of the dead bodies, it can be concluded.

Mr. FLOOD. What is your conclusion?

Dr. TRAMSEN. First, that the murders and the burial must have taken place in a cold time of the year, in the winter or early spring, and, second, that the dead bodies must have been buried in these graves for at least 2 years, possibly anything up to 5 or 10 years.

Mr. FLOOD. Would it have been possible, for those reasons, under your conclusions, for those bodies to have been buried in March or April of 1940?

Dr. TRAMSEN. Yes; that is possible.

Mr. FLOOD. We offer in evidence all exhibits now up to and including No. 73.

Chairman MADDEN. Mr. Dondero.

Mr. DONDERO. Doctor, I have just one question.

You have told this committee that you examined the cord or rope with which the hands of these men were bound. Was that cord or rope flat or round?

Dr. TRAMSEN. I think it was a round woven cord, made of rather whitish sort of cotton thread.

Mr. DONDERO. Did you make a personal examination of it, or just a casual examination of the cord?

Dr. TRAMSEN. I have examined one of them very closely and brought one with me back to Denmark, and I have previously, about a year ago, put it at the disposal of the committee by Mr. Arthur Bliss Lane, who took it back with him to the United States.

Mr. DONDERO. Would it be possible that it was flat, like a shoestring?

Dr. TRAMSEN. I can't remember.

Mr. MITCHELL. I would like to have the record show that Mr. Arthur Bliss Lane has offered that rope to this committee.

Mr. DONDERO. Arthur Bliss Lane was either at that time or later the Ambassador from the United States to Poland; is that correct?

Dr. TRAMSEN. Yes, that is correct; not a year ago but further back, about 3 years ago I think he was.

Mr. DONDERO. That is all.

Chairman MADDEN. Mr. O'Konski.

Mr. O'KONSKI. Doctor, have you been aware of or have you read the report of the Russian medical commission that made a report in January of 1944?

Dr. TRAMSEN. Yes, I have.

Mr. O'KONSKI. I would like to pick out some of the statements in that report and would like to have your comment on them, if possible.

One of the statements in their report is as follows: that only 20 out of 925 bodies had their hands tied behind their backs—speaking of the bodies that they dug up from the graves.

Does that square with the facts that you saw? That is only one out of every 50 bodies that had their hands tied behind their backs.

Dr. TRAMSEN. No; that is definitely incorrect.

Mr. O'KONSKI. They make much of the fact, in their report, that only 20, or about one out of every 50 bodies, had their hands tied behind their backs. That is incorrect, is it, according to your observation?

Dr. TRAMSEN. Yes. I saw only a few that were not tied.

Mr. O'KONSKI. Another statement that they make much of in their report is as follows:

In 1943, the Germans made an extremely small number of post-mortem examinations.

Does that square with the facts?

Dr. TRAMSEN. No.

You see, at that time the German commission had already done a lot of post mortems, and about 800 identifications, and we checked these identifications and raised the post mortems with another nine, with a total autopsy of the bodies.

Mr. O'KONSKI. Another part of their report states that although, in the post mortems, the coats and the shoes were cut for the removal of documents, after they dug up the bodies they still found many documents on the bodies.

Is that very likely to have happened?

Dr. TRAMSEN. Which dead bodies are those the Russians are speaking about; those the Germans had already examined?

Mr. O'KONSKI. The same bodies.

Dr. TRAMSEN. So far as I could see, the examination of the dead bodies was very thorough, and all papers and identification marks were removed from the dead bodies and checked in the German reports.

Mr. O'KONSKI. Another part of their report states that in spite of the search by the Germans for documents, they still left, on some of the bodies, the same bodies, some documents, including diaries.

Is there any likelihood that your commission or the Germans would have buried back any diaries with those bodies?

Dr. TRAMSEN. No. I think that is very unlikely because the German examination was very thorough and they were particularly interested in diaries that could give personal reports from the prisoners of where they had been captured and in which camp they had stayed and what had happened to them altogether.

Mr. O'KONSKI. When it comes to the cause of death, the shooting, the Russian report and your report are almost identical; the only other part where they disagree with your report is the extent of decay. And this Russian medical commission claims that the deaths were sometime in the early fall of 1941. Is that possible?

Dr. TRAMSEN. From a medical point of view, I wouldn't say it would be impossible. As I tell you, we could reckon that the dead bodies must have been in there 2 years, for at least 2 years. That makes exactly 2 years, at the spring of 1941.

Mr. O'KONSKI. They claim it was the fall of 1941.

Dr. TRAMSEN. I should hardly think so, because it is not anywhere close to what could have been possible.

Mr. O'KONSKI. Doctor, before the war, in your study of pathology, you had an opportunity to become acquainted or have heard or read of almost every expert on pathology in Europe, have you not?

Dr. TRAMSEN. Yes; if I may say so.

Mr. O'KONSKI. These medical men that you attended this exhumation with at Katyn, you had heard most of those names as being experts before you got over there, did you not?

Dr. TRAMSEN. Yes. I knew a few of them personally before.

Mr. O'KONSKI. Did you ever hear or become acquainted with in reading, writing, mail, or personal contact or conversations, or did you have occasion to meet any Russian experts on pathology?

Dr. TRAMSEN. No.

Mr. O'KONSKI. You never had?

Dr. TRAMSEN. No; I never had.

Mr. O'KONSKI. You never heard of the name of V. I. Prozorlobsky as being an expert on pathology?

Dr. TRAMSEN. No.

Mr. O'KONSKI. Did you ever hear of the name of V. M. Smolyanobov as being an expert on pathology?

Dr. TRAMSEN. No.

Mr. O'KONSKI. Did you ever hear of the name of D. N. Vyropaybe as being an expert on pathology?

Dr. TRAMSEN. No.

Mr. O'KONSKI. Did you ever hear of the name of P. S. Smemevosky as being an expert on pathology?

Dr. TRAMSEN. No; I did not.

Mr. O'KONSKI. Or did you ever hear of the name of M. D. Shviakova as being an expert on pathology?

Dr. TRAMSEN. No; I did not.

Mr. O'KONSKI. In other words, Doctor, those names are all strange to you, are they not?

Dr. TRAMSEN. They are all strange to me.

Mr. O'KONSKI. Together with Dr. Markov, do you remember a Dr. Hajek of Czechoslovakia who was with you on the commission?

Dr. Tramsen. Yes.

Mr. O'Konski. In your conferences and meetings with Dr. Hajek of Czechoslovakia, what was his reaction to the cause of the crime at Katyn and when it was committed?

Dr. Tramsen. Professor Hajek was a professor of legal medicine in Prague and he did a post mortem himself and took part in the committee's meetings, and he was of absolutely the same idea as the other members and signed the protocol personally with the same impression that the murder has been done by the Russians as stated in the protocol.

Mr. O'Konski. Have you heard rumors that he has also recanted the signing of that?

Dr. Tramsen. That I know. I was told that last night and I have heard and read in the papers previously that he has taken back his statement and given a completely other idea about the whole Katyn affair.

Mr. O'Konski. Did that news surprise you, after talking to him as you did at this investigation at Katyn?

Dr. Tramsen. Yes; it certainly has astonished me.

Mr. O'Konski. It is interesting to note from the signing of that protocol, just from the standpoint of chronology, that both Dr. Markov and Dr. Hajek signed the protocol before you did. Therefore, if they did it under duress, it seems strange because they signed it before you did. You were among the last to sign the protocol.

Dr. Tramsen. I was not quite aware of that because I think we signed it all pretty well at the same time. So far as I remember, we were produced a copy of the protocol that evening we finished our meeting in Smolensk and we signed it then and, on our way back to Berlin and the landing at Bialistok, were produced a copy each to sign for each other.

Mr. O'Konski. In other words, Doctor, the opinion among the 12 of you medical experts was such that it made no difference who signed it first? You were all unanimously agreed, willingly, without duress?

Dr. Tramsen. Yes.

Mr. O'Konski. That's all.

Mr. Dondero. Dr. Tramsen, who prepared the protocol?

Dr. Tramsen. We had a meeting in Smolensk, which was led by Professor Buhtz, the German, and the written way of the conclusions was suggested by Professor Orsos, and corrected or edited by all of us giving our statement each. So we had written down, all of us, in our own writing, the copy of the conclusions and it was later copied by the Germans so we could see that it was correctly written before the signature was made.

Mr. Machrowicz. Doctor, prior to your designation to this committee, were you an active member of any political party or an active supporter of any political ideology in Denmark or outside Denmark?

Dr. Tramsen. Well, I must confess that I had my own political ideas, but it was in neither one direction nor the other. It was only anti-German because we had a German occupation, and at the time when I took part in this committee, I had been a member of the Danish resistance movement for about 1 year.

Mr. Machrowicz. So then, there was nothing in your past activities or any political statements which would indicate at the time of your appointment any particular sympathies toward the German cause, is that correct?

Dr. TRAMSEN. No. I should rather say the opposite.

Mr. MACHROWICZ. Before you accepted your appointment on this committee, did you converse with anyone else in Denmark other than those people whom you have already testified to?

Dr. TRAMSEN. Yes; I did. I made contact with two of the best men in the Danish resistance movement and put the case in front of them and they suggested that I should go because it would be of general interest to know what had taken place in Katyn.

Mr. MACHROWICZ. Anyone besides those?

Dr. TRAMSEN. No, but I may add that to prove that I did not have any special German sympathies, I continued my work in the Danish resistance movement after I came back and was taken prisoner by the German Gestapo and held for 1 year in a concentration camp—the last year of the war.

Mr. MACHROWICZ. All right now, you arrived in Berlin, as you testified. Whom did you see in Berlin in connection with your mission?

Dr. TRAMSEN. As I may show you on this photograph, the commission took part in a meeting with the German Reichsgesundheitsamt Fuehrer Dr. Conte in his office, and here the protocol was handed over to Dr. Conte by the joint committee and Professor Orsos in person.

Mr. MACHROWICZ. Did all the members of the committee participate in that meeting?

Dr. TRAMSEN. Yes; all the members took part in that meeting.

Mr. MACHROWICZ. Was there anything said or done at that meeting which you could interpret as an attempt to influence, advise you, or compel you to do anything against your own wish?

Dr. TRAMSEN. No; not at all. The meeting took place under very friendly forms and the committee just handed over the protocol to Dr. Conte who thanked us for the work and nothing else.

Mr. MACHROWICZ. Did you see anyone else in Berlin in connection with your mission?

Dr. TRAMSEN. Only scientific people. We visited the University of Berlin Forensic Medical Institute and met a lot of German doctors and specialists, but we did not have any official meeting anywhere else in Berlin.

Mr. MACHROWICZ. After you arrived in Smolensk, were you then met by anyone and given any instructions or warnings of any kind which might be considered by you as any undue pressure upon you?

Dr. TRAMSEN. No; we were met at the airport with quite a lot of high German officers, General Holm and Professor Buhtz, and a lot of German military doctors, and at the first meeting they stated we could move about freely and do all examinations we wanted to do in the Katyn area freely. They just did advise us not to walk around very much alone in the town of Smolensk, which we didn't feel very much like doing either.

Mr. MACHROWICZ. Were those orders ever changed?

Dr. TRAMSEN. No.

Mr. MACHROWICZ. Did you receive any compensation or reward of any kind, monetary or otherwise, for your services in connection with this matter.

Dr. TRAMSEN. No; I did not.

Mr. Machrowicz. Have you read Dr. Hajek's complete statement of March 10, 1952, as reported by the Tass Soviet Agency?

Dr. Tramsen. No; I have not.

Mr. Machrowicz. In that statement, he claims that most of the members of your committee were not well conversant with the German language and, therefore, could not understand what they signed. Can you comment on that statement?

Dr. Tramsen. I know only one of the so-called members that did not speak German very well. That was a Frechman and he didn't take part in the committee's meetings nor the signature of the protocol.

Mr. Machrowicz. He was not a member of the committee, was he?

Dr. Tramsen. He was not an actual member. He was only, as the Germans said, a Voelkischer Beobachter.

Chairman Madden. What was he in English?

Dr. Tramsen. He was a psychologist.

Chairman Madden. No, this remark that they made.

Dr. Tramsen. That is a German joke because Voelkischer Beobachter is the name of an official Nazi paper and means public observer.

Mr. Machrowicz. He states also that he was forced under duress to accept this assignment and was told that he might be placed in jail unless he accepted it. Was there anything that he said to you or to anyone else that indicated that was true?

Dr. Tramsen. No; not at all.

Mr. Machrowicz. Did you have occasion to have conversations with Dr. Hajek?

Dr. Tramsen. Yes, I had.

Mr. Machrowicz. And were those conversations just the two of you or were there others present?

Dr. Tramsen. On several occasions I spoke to him personally, one to the other, because I was interested to know the conditions in Prague in the university at that time.

Mr. Machrowicz. Did he ever give you that impression as now made in his statement?

Dr. Tramsen. No; certainly not.

Mr. Machrowicz. He states further that the first thing that struck him after he arrived at the scene was the fact that it all appeared as a prearranged affair.

Dr. Tramsen. It must have been a mighty big arrangement anyway. I never saw anything like that.

Mr. Machrowicz. He states further that on the basis of his observations "and the work done by me upon several bodies, I immediately, with all positiveness, confirmed the fact that these bodies could not have been there 3 years, as the Hitlerites claimed, but only a short time—not more than 1 year." Now, did he ever make that statement to you?

Dr. Tramsen. No. I do not know anything at all about that and he stated quite another thing when he signed the protocol himself and he took part in the discussion in the committee that last evening in Smolensk, and he totally agreed with us that the bodies must have been in these graves for at least 2 years—possibly longer.

Mr. Machrowicz. Now, he stated further that he found in many instances the fingers, the nose, the lips, and even the skin, in a good state of preservation which would indicate that the bodies could not have been there 3 years. What did he say about that?

Dr. TRAMSEN. I must say that there was a certain decay of the dead bodies, including skin, noses, and lips, and this decay was particularly developed in those bodies lying at the outside of the graves, while those bodies lying in the midst of the heap were very well preserved. As you could think when there would be no bacteriological decay because of the weight of the dead bodies, the pressure, and the weight of the tons of sand again, which has worked the whole thing out like pressed meat, with no air and no opportunity for the bacteria to work and accomplish the decay on noses, lips, and fingers.

Mr. MACHROWICZ. Did he ever indicate to you or to anyone else in your presence that those factors I have just mentioned were indicative of the fact that the bodies were not there as long as claimed in your report?

Dr. TRAMSEN. No. We were all of the same opinion that the dead bodies must have remained in the graves for at least 2 years.

Mr. MACHROWICZ. He points also in his statement to the fact that the buttons and other brass items on uniforms did not show sufficient rust to indicate that the bodies had been in those graves the period of time your report claims they were. Do you remember that factor?

Dr. TRAMSEN. The buttons and the insignia on the uniform caps and various other metal parts were, for the greater extent, in a good condition. They were made of pewter or aluminum, which, as far as I know, do not get rusty.

Mr. MACHROWICZ. He states further that in some cases he found tobacco which was still of its natural color and had not lost its odor, which indicated it could not have been there long. Was your attention called to any such instance?

Dr. TRAMSEN. Well, I have seen several tobacco purses and pipes, and even purses with cigarette paper and cigarette tobacco, but this tobacco was mainly in a bad state—brownish and of a very bad smell. I wouldn't like to smoke it, anyway.

Mr. MACHROWICZ. Now, he says further that one of the matters that struck him immediately was the fact that the bayonet wounds were not as deep as they would have been if Russian bayonets had been used because Russian bayonets were sharper and longer. Now, has that been brought to your attention, or did you notice anything about that?

Dr. TRAMSEN. I can only remember one case during the autopsies where a bayonet wound was really made clear, and that was a rather longish wound, as I told before, square in the outline and going under the right shoulder, right deep through the lung. If that is possible for a Russian or any other bayonet, I shall not be able to tell the difference there, but it was, anyway, a rather deep bayonet wound.

Mr. MACHROWICZ. I might say that in his statement he does concede that the former Russian bayonets were four-cornered and would produce a square opening. Is that the kind of opening you saw?

Dr. TRAMSEN. Yes.

Mr. MACHROWICZ. Now, in all your time with Dr. Hajek, do you remember him at any one single instance calling to your attention or to the attention of the other members of the committee in your presence these facts which I have now outlined and which he includes in his statement?

Dr. TRAMSEN. No; I have not heard Professor Hajek at Smolensk give any evidence in that line he has just done lately.

296

Mr. MACHROWICZ. That's all.

Mr. O'KONSKI. Dr. Tramsen, when you got back from this trip you were delegated to go on to Katyn, were you approached by the then German Government to enlist with them in some lecture tour or propaganda tour? Would you care to make any comment on that, if that happened?

Dr. TRAMSEN. Yes. I was called to meet the German High Commissioner in Denmark, Dr. Best, who very strongly put it to me that it was necessary that I spread the details about these observations among the Danish population.

Mr. O'KONSKI. Did these officials of the then German Government offer you any remuneration if you would participate in any such political activity?

Dr. TRAMSEN. Yes; they did. Not the official German Government, but at that time in Copenhagen the Main Institution for German Culture. They offered me rather a big reward for going about making lessons and demonstrations about the observations in Katyn.

Mr. O'KONSKI. Would you care to mention to this committee the extent of the remuneration that was offered and the other enticement that was given—roughly?

Dr. TRAMSEN. Yes. Quite a good offer in money, extending to— well, I may say, about $50 for each lesson.

Mr. O'KONSKI. Well, in every instance, you refused to participate in that type of propaganda activity or political activity after you returned from Katyn?

Dr. TRAMSEN. Yes. I did not make any public or any other statement about my observations although I was very well attacked by a lot of reporters. This is the first time I give a public statement on my observations on my Katyn travel for this committee now today.

Mr. O'KONSKI. Doctor, one more question:

Do you think you might have been spared 1 year in a German concentration camp if you had participated in accepting the offer which they made to you?

Dr. TRAMSEN. No; but I am sure I had a very easy escape with that 1 year after what happened to my fellow patriots.

Mr. O'KONSKI. In other words, Doctor, it is safe to say, is it not, that your interest in Katyn was purely one of honor in regard to your profession, which was medicine, and not political in any manner, shape, or form?

Dr. TRAMSEN. That is so.

Mr. O'KONSKI. In that respect, I want to say that you are a credit to the medical profession.

Chairman MADDEN. Any more questions?

Now, Doctor, if there is any more that you wish to add to what you have already said, the committee would be glad to hear you.

Dr. TRAMSEN. I don't think I have anything more to add.

Chairman MADDEN. On behalf of the committee, I want to say that we appreciate your great sacrifice in coming here today. We fully realize that your business has been neglected, by reason of taking time to come down to Frankfurt. Your testimony has been very valuable in fixing the time of the burial of these bodies at Katyn, and this committee owes you a debt of gratitude in contributing facts concerning this international crime.

Thank you very much.

The corpses as they were revealed.

Dr Wilhelm Zietz

Dr. ZIETZ. From 1939 through 1945 I was with the Reich Health Service and the Reich Chamber of Doctors.

Mr. FLOOD. In 1943, what was your official title with the then German Government?

Dr. ZIETZ. I was Deputy Chief of the Riech Public Health Service and Reich Physicians' Chamber with the Foreign Office.

Mr. FLOOD. Who was your chief?

Dr. ZIETZ. Dr. Conte.

Mr. FLOOD. What was his title?

Dr. ZIETZ. Reich Leader of Public Health Service and Secretary of State.

Mr. FLOOD. I direct your attention to the year 1943 and ask you when and under what circumstances was the Katyn matter brought to your attention in your official capacity?

Dr. ZIETZ. We of the department first heard a radio address of former Reich Minister Dr. Goebbels who broadcast to the public for the first time that a massacre beyond imagination had been discovered at Katyn. To the best of my recollection, it must have happened within the first 14 days of the month of April. Subsequently, I learned that it was Professor Buhtz who was in charge of the exhumations at Katyn. Professor Buhtz just happened to be a good old friend of mine since the days of our common studies. I knew him to be a very reliable scientist of extremely good character.

Subsequently, I called him at Smolensk and asked him what I should believe of this report. He told me over the phone that discoveries of extreme importance had been made in connection with gruesome executions of former Polish officers, and that it was his opinion that the Russians had been those who committed the executions. He told me, however, that the figures indicated by Dr. Goebbels did not square with the truth. In fact, those figures were less, and this fact, he told me might perhaps be explained by the fact that about 11,000 or 12,000 Polish officers were still missing.

I asked him whether or not it would be desirable to dispatch a committee of international scientists to the scene which he answered in the affirmative.

I subsequently proceeded to Dr. Conte who gave me an absolutely free hand to act, provided that both of us would agree upon the dispatch of an international committee being desirable.

I subsequently proceeded to the Foreign Office and the cultural political department which, in fact, was competent for such affairs and I discussed with the cultural political department the expediency of such an international committee. The cultural political department of the Foreign Office right away agreed to it.

Subsequently, someone spoke over the phone with Foreign Minister Ribbentrop at Fuschel—I don't know any more who it was—and received on the next day already his complete agreement.

It was agreed upon that the host would be the Reich health leader so as not to give a political tang to this whole affair, and the Foreign Office had nothing to do but merely convey the invitations of the Reich health leader to all people—friendly nations, neutral nations, as well as our allies. In case they were occupied territories, appropriate German occupation authorities were contacted who, in turn, conveyed the messages to the proper local agencies. In essence, the Foreign Office was responsible for the conveyance of most of these invitations to foreign countries. It all went very fast, and, if I am not mistaken, during the latter days of April 1943, we had collected all the participants in Berlin. Eventually, it is a well known fact, we had 13 countries participating, 12 representatives who felt they had full authority to act, and a thirteenth, as Dr. Tramsen already testified, the representative of the French Vichy Government, who felt he was merely competent as an observer.

I no longer possess any written documents which I might refer to, such as Dr. Tramsen possessed in huge quantities, so I have to rely upon my power of recollection and particularly so as I haven't seen the white book ever since 1945.

All our guests were quartered at the Adlon Hotel in Berlin and, up to the time of their leaving for Smolensk, they were taken care of by myself there.

The flight to Smolensk must have taken place on the 27th or 28th of April. Dr. Tramsen would be in a better position to know that. I wouldn't know any more. I was taking care of the guests by asking every individual guest as to his wishes and desires, and sometimes also attending to dinner parties or supper parties and also inviting a series of German physicians to attend, as, for instance, Dr. Mueller-Hesse.

Mueller-Hesse was Berlin's most prominent doctor of forensic medicine and still is today. He, subsequently, too was at Katyn.

Neither the Foreign Office nor Dr. Conte had given us any instructions as to Katyn. I was officially instructed to accompany the committee and to take care of all their desires. There was no discussion whatever of a protocol or any kind of agreement or stipulation because none of us knew what we had to anticipate at Katyn. We flew to Smolensk in a Condor plane. There was a stop-over sometime in Brest-Litovsk where we had breakfast. There was nobody present but an observer of the Foreign Office, whose name, however, I don't know and who actually did nothing at all but just observe, so that most likely, the members of the committee did not get to know him at all. There was also a female doctor from Berlin/Lichtenfelde traveling along, whose name I indicated to the committee at Godesburg some time ago. That was the desire of some ministry. Neither I nor she knew why she came along. Actually, she was not anxious to go there to see what there was to see. Then there was a photo reporter in order to take snapshots. To the best of my knowledge, his name was Pabl, but I believe he was killed in action. He is no longer alive.

In Smolensk we were greeted by a general surgeon, Dr. Holm. Recently at Godesburg I said that to the best of my recollection his name was Reinhardt, because I could not properly recollect. I want to correct that statement: his name was Holm, and he is purportedly still alive.

In addition, there was a number of members of the German Army, principally doctors.

We were escorted to a so-called hotel at Smolensk. It was a hotel of which the Russians boasted, which consisted of nothing but a facsimile, and which was so dreary that you actually couldn't expect to find anything else in a destroyed town.

In the evening, as every day, we had supper at the casiono of the general surgeon. Dr. Holm took very much care of foreign guests, and during the meeting in the evening he promised every freedom of movement during inspection or survey, and placed every support and every cooperation of the army group central at their disposal. We did not see Field Marshal General von Kluge. On our way to Smolensk we constantly had to pass by his residence. It was called, I believe, the red castle, or something to that effect.

To the best of my knowledge on the first evening, at the occasion of a greeting by Holm, there was practically no discussion of Katyn. It was more or less meant that the individual members got acquainted with each other. Holm and Buhtz were very much concerned about these gentlemen getting an absoluetely independent impression. Subsequently there were inspections, surveys, post mortems, and the familiarizing of them with the environment of Katyn, always under the leadership of Buhtz and Holm. I myself always had been present, even though I was not a medical doctor.

I recall we also visited the so-called museum of the field police, where all items had been placed on display in glass showcases, which so far had been discovered by way of diaries, also pocketbooks, tobacco pouches, and so forth. That is where I believe we got to know Mr. Voss, who, I take it, was in command of the field police.

The members of the committee were free to take anything out of the showcases they were interested in or which they desired to read.

There was no document that would not have been accessible to them.

The graves were exhaustively inspected and the entire area of the woods was surveyed. By the side of the largest of the main graves—and I take it that it was grave No. 5, but I am not positive, I may be mistaken about that—wooden tables were place for the post mortems or the autopsies, as well as small tables for the typewriters on which autopsy reports could be typed up.

Dr. Holm and Dr. Buhtz had thoroughly prepared everything so that each of these foreign gentlemen who desired to do so could perform autopsies.

Some of the gentlemen worked all by themselves; others worked in teams of two. They were assisted by gentlemen from the Institute of Forensic Medicine, which had moved from Breslau to Smolensk, medics, noncoms, and Polish and Russian laborers as well, who were carrying corpses.

The smell of the corpses was impossible to bear, so, for the first time in my life, I became a chain smoker. Shortly beyond the residence of von Kluge the smell of the corpses became discernible. It was a very hot summer.

I myself am no expert in autopsies. However, I looked at everything closely and I was even able to stand it through to the end. It was my principal duty to see to it that all wishes of our foreign guests were met.

Incidentally, I recall there was a broadcasting truck present, where discs might be made and broadcast right away. I myself had such a conversation with Professor Saxen, from Helsinki, a professor of the University of Helsinki, a professor of pathology. I also made a disc with a female doctor from Berlin, who, however, told me these corpses were so gruesome, and she asked me to only mention the corpses in the introduction, so that our conversation over the radio consisted more or less only of a discussion of a wide Russian country, the city walls of Smolensk, the relics of Napoleon, and the Cathedral.

I take it I need not discuss the details of Katyn because Dr. Tramsen did so exhaustively.

On the last day at noon, still at Katyn, certain members of the delegation asked me what we now anticipated or expected from them as a result of it. They themselves suggested to me that it was most likely they would be of a unanimous opinion in regard to a protocol. This intimation did not start on the German side. As a matter of fact, it was made by the foreign, by the alien parties.

We met Professor Buhtz at the Institute of Forensic Medicine in the afternoon. With one exception, there were no Germans present but Professor Buhtz and myself. Professor Buhtz was requested to take charge of the negotiations, that is, more or less only of the technical side of the discussion, not of the contents. As to the contents, it was more or less performed by the spokesman of the committee, the senior member, Professor Orsos. It was, at any rate, a discussion between the foreign participants as to what should be contained in the protocol. There were no material discrepancies of opinion, it was more as to the form or as to the extent of the statements to be made.

For instance, I myself did not know this at Katyn, I mean, the question of the planting of trees. During that session, however, Professor Orsos requested a microscope. He produced out of a bag one of these saplings that Dr. Tramsen had mentioned before, and demonstrated, by the specimen, that these saplings had been replanted on one previous occasion and that, according to his findings, these saplings had been standing in one place for 3 years, and prior to that, for another 2 years, in a different place.

It was very interesting to notice, during that discussion as well as during all of the previous discussions, that all of the participants of the committee were unanimous as to a recognition of the international reputation of Dr. Orsos. But even in the course of this issue here there was a clear political difference between the Hungarian and the Rumanian. The Rumanian guest was a lecturer of the Institute of Forensic Medicine at Bucharest, which enjoyed a very good reputation. His name was Dr. Birkle. He emphasized, however, that he was no German but a full-blooded Rumanian. Dr. Birkle frequently objected to the findings of Dr. Orsos, and frequently found them to be too far reaching or of a too dictatorial nature.

All of us frequently smiled at these bickerings, because it was our opinion that this was clearly manifested in former differences about Sienburgen and other parts of the country. This was expressed particularly when the question of these fir trees arose. Birkle said, in essence, as follows:

"Professor Orsos, you may be a really competent doctor of forensic medicine, and you might also be a very good artist, but that you, however, wish to be a very competent botanist, that is going too far."

Now, Professor Orsos demanded that his theory be adopted. I mean, the theory about the 3 and 2 years, respectively. Then one of the participants asked whether or not there was a forestry expert of the army group present. Professor Buhtz replied in the affirmative, and called up from the very same room that a forestry expert should report at once. He actually appeared within a few minutes, and he had no inkling as to what he was supposed to say. That was Mr. von Herff.

Now, Mr. von Herff took one look at the microscope, and, I wish to emphasize, right on the spur of the moment, without having been told before what the subject of the discussion was, said, "This tree here has been standing in one place for 3 years, here is a notch, and it has been standing in another place 2 years prior to that." That, at least, is what I remember.

After this clear-cut, expert statement of Mr. von Herff, Dr. Birkle admitted that he had been licked, and he furthermore admitted that Dr. Orsos was also a competent botanist.

Essentially, I can fully concur in what Dr. Tramsen testified to before in the course of those proceedings. Not a single one of the foreign participants was forced to make a statement for the protocol or to sign anything. What could we, the two German participants, have done if anyone had said, "No, I won't sign it"? He would merely have had to say, "I haven't received such authority from my Government; I was merely instructed to go and take a look at the things at Katyn." That was the attitude taken by the French representative, who has been previously sufficiently characterized by Dr. Tramsen. He was a good-natured old gentleman who, however, had no essential private opinion. He stated, however, that he, for his person, was in full agreement with what he saw and with what the committee determined. I am referring to the end of the protocol where, if I remember correctly, he and Professor Buhtz are mentioned as the two gentlemen who fully concurred in what had been said. I, for my part, could not indicate my agreement, due to the fact that I am not a medical man.

This instrument, when we were back in Berlin, was transmitted by the foreign participants of the committee to my chief, Dr. Conte, on the occasion of a formal visit, and it also included a formal speech. Subsequently, and by his order, I transmitted one copy of it to the Foreign Office. Then we had photostatic copies made so that the signatures would also be pictorially visible, and gave one copy to every member.

Part of the members of this delegation remained in Berlin for another week, and we further took care of their wishes. For instance, I made an appointment for a visit to the Institute of Forensic Medicine in Berlin; they purchased medical textbooks; they went to look at this or that. Then they individually left Berlin.

Some time later, it might have been about 10 or 14 days later, a German medical committee had been flown up there. It was I who also intimated that such a commission should go. However, I did not take part in it. The most prominent member of it, I believe, was the formerly-mentioned Mueller-Hesse. That delegation, too, went on record with a statement.

The Foreign Office was preparing a so-called White Book of the Katyn incident, and these visits, as well as the determinations set forth in the protocol, were also mentioned in the White Book. I then cooperated in the preparation of the White Book, and principally saw to it that a great medical report of Professor Buhtz was contained in it, in which he set forth all of his experiences. I had a series of pictures made, which I deemed expedient, and I was also proofreading, along with others.

When my book had been completed, I submitted one copy to each of the foreign participants and received friendly letters of gratitude from all of the members as I remained in a pleasant exchange of letters and thoughts with many of them.

Mr. FLOOD. May I say this, doctor: I am interested in that very extensive and detailed report. When you invited the foreign and neutral governments to participate in the commission, did any of them refuse?

Dr. ZIETZ. We don't know who had been invited by the Foreign Office. In Switzerland, for instance, as also in other countries, invitations were conveyed through the Ambassador. For instance, we would have liked to have Spain and Portugal also represented; however, the efforts of Dr. Conti in this respect were of no avail. Perhaps there were too many objections engendered by neutrality.

Mr. FLOOD. Did you ever hear that Portugal refused?

Dr. ZIETZ. No.

Mr. FLOOD. Did you ever hear that the Spanish delegate never participated?

Dr. ZIETZ. No, he did not participate. Spain was not present.

Mr. FLOOD. Did you know that the Swedish delegate was seriously injured in a motor accident just before he left Stockholm for the Berlin meeting?

Dr. ZIETZ. Yes; we deeply regretted it. I believe he sustained an injury of his spinal column, vertebrae, or something to that effect, and for a whole year he lay in a plaster cast. We already had been notified of his participation, and we would have liked very much to have had him, and I have been with him in amicable correspondence for a long time.

Mr. FLOOD. Were you here this morning when Dr. Sweet, of the allied institute for the possession of war-captured documents, was testifying?

Dr. ZIETZ. No. Due to a failure of a locomotive, I arrived 2 hours late.

Mr. FLOOD. Did you know that the Foreign Office, in transmitting the invitation that you are talking about, has asked certain of its diplomats to look for anti-Jewish or pro-Nazi scientists?

Dr. ZIETZ. That is unknown to me. These suggestions definitely were not made by my chief.

Mr. FLOOD. Do you remember the Bulgarian member, Markov, and the Czech member, Hajek?

Dr. ZIETZ. Very well.

Mr. FLOOD. Did either Markov or Hajek, at any time during your association with the commission, object to any treatment they were receiving from the Germans, or in any way protest or disagree with the findings of their colleagues on the commission?

Dr. ZIETZ. No; no. In the first place, I wish to deal with Professor Markov. I, for myself, hold Professor Markov in high esteem as a man of impeccable character. After Katyn, he repeatedly wrote friendly letters to me and never expressed any skepticism on his part.

I can fully understand he made a different statement at Nuremberg because he had occasion to see at Katyn how such things are done.

Professor Hajek also wrote me once or twice afterward. He certainly had no easy position in the protectorate. However, he never gave any indication that he would not fully go along and agree with what was signed.

Mr. FLOOD. You are aware, of course, that Markov and Hajek have both changed their original story and have recanted from their signatures and opinions of the international protocol?

Dr. ZIETZ. That, in my opinion, is merely a lack of scientific conviction due to a threat to life and limb.

Fritz von Herff

This forestry specialist's evidence is pertinent to the young trees planted over the graves in 1940.

Mr. FLOOD. What is your present occupation or business?

Mr. VON HERFF. Forester.

Mr. FLOOD. Were you ever identified with the German Armed Forces?

Mr. VON HERFF. Yes, I was.

Mr. FLOOD. I direct your attention to the year of 1943 and ask you whether or not you were serving with the German armed forces on the Russian front in the Smolensk area?

Inspection of an opened mass grave.

Mr. von Herff. Yes, I did.

Mr. Flood. Were you serving in your capacity as a forester for the Armed Services in that area?

Mr. von Herff. Yes, I was.

Mr. Flood. Are you aware of the Katyn Forest and the massacre of the Polish officers in that area?

Mr. von Herff. I am pretty well familiar with the woods surrounding Katyn because I was extensively occupied in furnishing wood to German troops billeted around the area.

Mr. Flood. When did you first arrive in the Smolensk area?

Mr. von Herff. In the end of December 1941, I came to Smolensk.

Mr. Flood. When did you leave?

Mr. von Herff. On the 1st of August 1943.

Mr. Flood. In all the time you were in the area, did you have occasion to visit the area of the Katyn Forest in the vicinity of the Dnieper Castle?

Mr. von Herff. Yes.

Mr. Flood. Did you have occasion, in your professional capacity as a forester, to observe carefully the nature of the terrain and the nature of the trees and growth within a thousand meters or more of the Dnieper Castle?

Mr. von Herff. According to my notes, I and my superior, a captain, inspected the Katyn graves on the 14th of April.

Mr. Flood. When was the first day that the graves were opened by the Germans in April of 1943, if you know?

Mr. von Herff. I don't know the exact date. It must have been eight or 14 days before.

305

Mr. FLOOD. During the time that you were in the Katyn Forest area, in December of 1941, until April 15, 1943, did you ever observe any extensive growths of small pine, evergreen, or birch trees?

Mr. VON HERFF. The entire region of Krasny Bor is a wooded area, the woods principally consisting of fir trees of various ages.

Mr. FLOOD. Is it possible for a forester of your experience, by observation, to be able to tell whether or not evergreen trees or birch trees have been transplanted within 3 years, if there had been any extensive transplanting in one area?

Mr. VON HERFF. That is not easy to say.

Mr. FLOOD. Is it easy to say one way or the other?

Mr. VON HERFF. No. It is impossible to say so definitely.

Mr. FLOOD. Certainly, in the length of time you were in the Katyn area, you examined the forests or the woods within a thousand meters of the Dnieper Castle; did you not?

Mr. VON HERFF. I was not around the castle much because that was the residence of the commander in chief and it was not so easy to gain access to the area.

Mr. FLOOD. Did you gain access and make any inspections or surveys for timber or lumber or fuel, or did you examine the woods and forest in the area?

Mr. VON HERFF. I did not survey any timber or lumber or wood of any kind in the area surrounding the graves. My area of operation was far away from Katyn, up to 60 kilometers from Katyn.

Mr. FLOOD. When was the matter of the Katyn graves first brought to your attention in your official capacity as a forester?

Mr. VON HERFF. On the 30th of April.

Mr. FLOOD. In what manner?

Mr. VON HERFF. I received a telephone call from the chief quartermaster telling me that I was supposed to proceed forthwith to a hospital in the eastern portion of Smolensk. There I was supposed to render an expert statement. The evening was approaching. I proceeded there, and there I found an international committee, about a dozen gentlemen. Presiding was General Surgeon Holm. General Holm presented to me several fir saplings—as has been mentioned by a previous witness—about 30 or 40 centimeters, one foot and a half in height. There might have been 2 or 3 pieces.

In the first place, I determined the age. To the best of my recollection, it was from about 5 to 7 years. Then I was asked whether the growing process had been a normal one. To this end, a crosscut of the sapling was made and I took a look at the crosscut under a microscope. There you could clearly see the year rings.

Every wooden plants adds every year one ring of wood, which is clearly discernible. Now, it could be easily traced back that one of these yearly rings, 3 years ago, was of a very small size. This year, consequently, the growth of the plant must have been stunted.

Being foresters, we know that every plant, after being transplanted, does not grow normally the first year after the transplanting has been effected because the roots of the plant have to get accustomed to the new soil in which the plant grows. Therefore, I expressed my opinion that 3 years ago—that is, 3 years prior to 1943—something must have happened to the plant.

Hence, when asked by the chairman whether a transplantation of a plant might have been done about 3 years ago, I replied in the affirmative.

The gentlemen of the committee were in full agreement but for a single party, who asked whether this stunted growth of the plant perhaps could be ascribed to inclement weather conditions. I right away admitted such a possibility.

That concluded my expert statement and I was asked no further questions.

Mr. Flood. Did you know where the tree came from that was shown to you by the scientist that night?

Mr. von Herff. No. I had not been told.

Mr. Flood. Did you know a Dr. Buhtz?

Mr. von Herff. I knew nothing of the gentleman.

Mr. Flood. You did not talk to Dr. Buhtz on the phone or in person at any time prior to your visit to the scientist that night?

Mr. von Herff. I did not speak with any one of these gentlemen, either before or after this issue.

Mr. Flood. What was the rank of the officer that talked to you and gave you your orders to go to Smolensk?

Mr. von Herff. Well, I could not say; it was most likely an orderly officer who merely transmitted an order presumably given by the chief quartermaster.

Mr. Flood. How many rings were on the crosscut of the tree that you examined that night in Smolensk?

Mr. von Herff. As I said before, I don't remember quite accurately, but I indicated before, to the best of my recollection, the saplings were from 5 to 7 years of age.

Mr. Flood. If a sapling had seven rings on it, how old would it be?

Mr. von Herff. Seven years of age.

Mr. Flood. Does it show a full ring for its first year of growth?

Mr. von Herff. That is merely intimated by a point—a dot.

Mr. Flood. Do you count the dot as one full year?

Mr. von Herff. One full year.

Mr. Flood. And you don't recall the exact number of rings in addition to the dot on the sapling you saw that night?

Mr. von Herff. No; I do not.

Mr. Flood. But you are positive it was not less than five?

Mr. von Herff. I am quite positive of that.

Mr. Flood. Was there any indication on the cross-cut sapling you saw of a darkening of the ring at the third ring?

Mr. von Herff. I do not remember any longer.

Mr. Flood. Did you ever see the graves at Katyn with trees the size that you are indicating you examined in Smolensk planted on the graves?

Mr. von Herff. Inasmuch as I visited the graves prior to having made this examination of the sapling, I didn't pay so much attention to the trees planted there. However, I recall that they were of approximately the same size as that sapling.

Mr. Flood. Did you visit the graves before they were opened?

Mr. von Herff. After they had been opened.

Mr. Flood. After they had been opened?

Mr. von Herff. Yes.

Mr. FLOOD. Did you see any trees lying around the area that you had been told had been removed from the top of the graves?

Mr. VON HERFF. No; I do not recall.

Mr. FLOOD. Had anybody discussed with you the existence of trees of the type and kind you examined at Smolensk as having been planted on the graves of the Polish officers?

Mr. VON HERFF. No; I know nothing about that.

Mr. FLOOD. Of course, at the time you went to the meeting of international scientists in Smolensk you had heard about the Katyn graves and they had been opened?

Mr. VON HERFF. Yes.

Mr. FLOOD. Weren't you curious or didn't you think in your mind what these scientists were doing there that you, as a forester, were called in to talk to them?

Mr. VON HERFF. Well, from the whole proceedings I was given to understand that I was supposed to help find out from the sapling I examined when these corpses had been buried.

Mr. FLOOD. The German side in this case takes the position, among others, in support of their conclusion that the Russians had perpetrated this massacre and, in order to conceal the graves in which the bodies were buried, took saplings 2 years of age, transplanted them on the graves, with the result that when the Germans, in April 1943, uncovered the graves, the saplings would then be 5 years of age. In your professional opinion as a forester, could the sapling or the two or three of them showed to you that night in Smolensk, especially the one you examined the cross-cut of, have been such a sapling as could be 5 years of age and could have been transplanted 3 years previously to 1943?

Mr. VON HERFF. Definitely so. It might have been such a one, definitely.

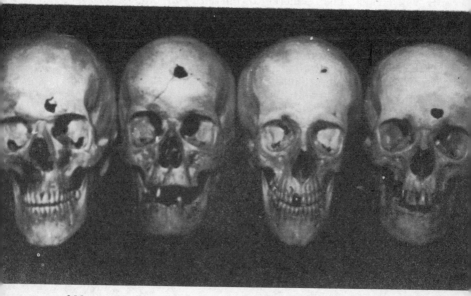

Wladyslaw Kawecki

A Polish lieutenant.

Mr. MACHROWICZ. During the year 1939, were you in the Polish army?

Mr. KAWECKI. Yes.

Mr. MACHROWICZ. In what rank?

Mr. KAWECKI. Second lieutenant.

Mr. MACHROWICZ. Prior to the war, what was your occupation?

Mr. KAWECKI. I was a journalist.

Mr. MACHROWICZ. In April 1943, were you in Poland?

Mr. KAWECKI. Yes; that is correct.

Mr. MACHROWICZ. In what part of Poland?

Mr. KAWECKI. In Krakow.

Mr. MACHROWICZ. Sometime in April, were you called by anyone to go to Katyn?

Mr. KAWECKI. That is correct.

Mr. MACHROWICZ. Who asked you to go to Katyn?

Mr. KAWECKI. I was summoned to the office of the Press Chief of the Government General in Krakow on the 9th of April, at noon.

Mr. MACHROWICZ. Was that before, or after it was announced that the graves of Katyn were found?

Mr. KAWECKI. It was from him that I learned of the fact that the graves were discovered at Katyn.

Mr. MACHROWICZ. Witness, for your information, the Germans announced the finding of the graves on the 15th of April 1943. Do you remember that date?

Mr. KAWECKI. That may be true, because the first announcement of the discovery of the graves was made only after the return of the second Polish group to Katyn.

Mr. MACHROWICZ. Then you would say that you left about the 9th of April, is that right?

Mr. KAWECKI. I left on the 10th of April, in the morning.

Mr. MACHROWICZ. Who was with you?

Mr. KAWECKI. The day that I was notified of my departure I did not know who was going to be with me.

Mr. MACHROWICZ. Who accompanied you on the trip?

Mr. KAWECKI. We had to assemble at 7 in the morning in front of the propaganda headquarters in Krakow. From there we left for the airport near Krakow.

Mr. MACHROWICZ. Who was with you on this trip?

Mr. KAWECKI. I left with the chief of an organization that provided for the evacuees from the Poznan area, the Poles who were evacuated from Poznan, the RGO, whose name was Edmond Sayfred, a Pole; and a worker in the Zielinski factory, whose name was Jan Prochownik.

Skulls with exit holes in forehead.

I want to make clear that this was a Polish organization that Say-fred headed.

Mr. MACHROWICZ. Were you told what the purpose of your trip was?

Mr. KAWECKI. I was told on the 9th of April when I was summoned to the press chief's office.

Mr. MACHROWICZ. What were you told?

Mr. WAWECKI. I was told that in the region of Smolensk had been found graves of Polish Army officers.

Mr. MACHROWICZ. Were you told what the purpose of your trip was?

Mr. KAWECKI. For the purpose of convincing ourselves whether or not these were Polish officers.

Mr. MACHROWICZ. After the plane left Krakow, did it make any stop before it arrived at Katyn?

Mr. KAWECKI. Yes; it did.

Mr. MACHROWICZ. Where?

Mr. KAWECKI. The airplane landed in Warsaw.

Mr. MACHROWICZ. Did you take on any additional passengers in Warsaw?

Mr. KAWECKI. Yes.

Mr. MACHROWICZ. Can you tell us the names of any of those who got on at Warsaw?

Mr. KAWECKI. Yes; I can. All told, eight people boarded the plane in Warsaw. Among them were Ferdinand Goetel, who was president or the Polish literary club, and Jan Emil Skiwski. The rest of the group consisted of officials from the local Warsaw Polish Government.

Mr. MACHROWICZ. For your information, witness, Mr. Goetel, whom you mentioned, has already testified before this committee during its proceedings in London regarding this trip.

Mr. KAWECKI. Thank you.

Mr. MACHROWICZ. Did you then go to Smolensk?

Mr. KAWECKI. In about 20 minutes. After about a 20-minute delay, the plane left for Smolensk.

Mr. MACHROWICZ. What happened after you arrived at Smolensk?

Mr. KAWECKI. We arrived at Smolensk approximately at 2 in the afternoon. There we waited for the arrival of automobiles at the airport. We waited for a half hour. About two or three cars arrived in a half hour and they took us to the hotel.

Mr. MACHROWICZ. What happened after that?

Mr. KAWECKI. We arrived at the hotel and were received there by the officials. Then we were taken to dinner in the Casino. Later on, a German lieutenant, whose name we later learned was Sloven-czyk, came to us.

Mr. MACHROWICZ. Did he later take you to the scene of the graves?

Mr. KAWECKI. Not that evening, but the following day at 9:30 in the morning we left for Katyn.

Mr. MACHROWICZ. Will you tell us what you saw and noticed and did when you arrived at the scene of the Katyn graves?

Mr. KAWECKI. After our arrival at the graveyard of Katyn, we were greeted by a delegation of high-ranking German officers, and included in that group was the gentleman who was here the other day, General von Gersdorff. After a brief reception by this group of higher officers, we were immediately taken to the largest grave, where we were confronted with a horrible sight.

It did not take us long to establish clearly in our minds that these

310

were the Polish officers. We established this by the uniforms that they wore, the buttons, the insignia, and the characteristic Polish boots.

Mr. MACHROWICZ. Will you just tell us what part you took personally in the examination of these bodies?

Mr. KAWECKI. After viewing this large grave, we were taken to another spot, where several exhumed bodies were lying. Among these we noticed the bodies of General Smorawinski and General Bohaterowicz. Both of these men were readily recognizable because of their uniform and because of the high distinguished medals which they still had on them.

General Bohaterowicz had on a fur coat, from which we concluded that he must have been executed or the period of his death must have been during the winter months or in the early spring.

Immediately, we were given complete freedom and permission, with the help of the Russian workers, to select at will the bodies from the graves and proceed to search these bodies for records or any other means that we wanted to use to try to determine the method of their death. After examining some 40 bodies, we concluded that these men met their death through a bullet shot through the back of the head, with the bullet leaving through the forehead.

Next, we had an opportunity to mingle with the Russian workers in the area, and in reply to our questions as to when these murders were committed, they told us that the period was from March to May of 1940.

I recall particularly the name of one of these Russians that I talked to. His name was Kisielev. I spoke to him in Russian and I had an opportunity to see, from my personal conversation with him, in his own language, whether he was telling me these things willingly. I felt that if a German translator were present he might be coerced or embarrassed and might not tell me everything.

Mr. MACHROWICZ. Just a moment. Did Kisielev and whomever else you talked to tell you how they knew that these killings took place between March and May 1940?

Mr. KAWECKI. Kisielev said that he had been told by his friends in Gniezdowo how they had seen some unknown soldiers—soldiers that were not Russian or Soviet—being transferred to trucks at Gniezdowo and then being taken to the forest of Katyn, from which they were never seen to return.

Mr. MACHROWICZ. Did they give you any other information upon which they based their belief that the killings took place within that period?

Mr. KAWECKI. Independent of the conversations that I had with Kisielev, I talked to another Russian. I cannot recall his name, but I think it was Kriwozercew. He also worked on the farm nearby the forest and said that he had seen the NKVD vans, known as the "black ravens," bringing soldiers into the Katyn woods.

Mr. MACHROWICZ. Do you want to tell us any further observations that you made while you were at Katyn during that time?

Mr. KAWECKI. At the time, I was so unnerved by my whole experience that I did not have the strength to carry on any sort of detailed investigation. However, the observations that I did make confirmed the horrible drama which we had witnessed at Katyn.

Mr. MACHROWICZ. How many days did you remain in Katyn on that trip?

Mr. KAWECKI. The following day we returned by plane to Poland.

Mr. MACHROWICZ. Did you make another trip to Katyn?

Mr. KAWECKI. Yes, I did.

Mr. MACHROWICZ. When?

Mr. KAWECKI. The middle of May 1943.

Mr. MACHROWICZ. Can you tell us how that second trip to Katyn was brought about?

Mr. KAWECKI. After my return from my first trip to Katyn, I brought with me the list of the Polish officers who up to that time had been identified.

Mr. MACHROWICZ. How many were there?

Mr. KAWECKI. The first list that I and those with me compiled included approximately 50 names.

Mr. MACHROWICZ. Before we leave the first trip, can you tell us how many bodies were exhumed at the time you were there the first time?

Mr. KAWECKI. During my first visit to Katyn, three graves were uncovered and there were approximately 70 people exhumed. Among these were the bodies of General Smorawinski and General Bohaterowicz.

Mr. MACHROWICZ. Now will you proceed to tell us why you were called the second time to Katyn?

Mr. KAWECKI. After my return, the list which I brought with me was published in the Polish newspapers, and the families of those men who were interned in Russia began making voluminous inquiries as to more names, because the Germans at that time, the German propaganda, had indicated that there were between ten and eleven thousand bodies at Katyn.

Mr. KAWECKI. Further, Dr. Adam Szebesta, who was head of the Polish Red Cross at the time, was making inquiries of me for more names. Dr. Szebesta not only inquired of me for additional names, but also sought permission from the Germans to make avaliable to him the obtaining of additional names because there was a list of names, or several lists, that were sent through by a Polish Red Cross commission which had been working at Katyn since the latter part of April and the list was in such form that it could not be properly evaluated. The lists being sent to us by the commission in Katyn were being telephoned in and had to go through Minsk, Wilnow, Koenigsberg, Danzig, and finally Krakow.

Mr. MACHROWICZ. And, in the process, did the names frequently end up in a different form than they should be?

Mr. KAWECKI. Yes, the names were misspelled and incorrect by the time we received them.

Mr. MACHROWICZ. And, as a result, did Dr. Szebesta ask the Germany authorities for permission to send some one to Katyn who would get the spelling of the names?

Mr. KAWECKI. That is correct.

Mr. MACHROWICZ. Were you delegated to do that?

Mr. KAWECKI. Originally, Dr. Moliszewski was assigned to this mission, but because he had broken a leg prior to his departure, I was substituted for him.

Mr. MACHROWICZ. With whom did you go to Katyn?

Mr. Kawecki. I was instructed to leave by train from Krakow to Waclaw, Breslau, and then I proceeded from there by plane.

Mr. Machrowicz. When did you arrive at Smolensk and Katyn the second time?

Mr. Kawecki. On the plane trip from Breslau to Smolensk I was accompanied by a group of Allied prisoners of war who were being taken from Berlin to Smolensk.

Mr. Machrowicz. The question that I asked you is what date did you arrive at Smolensk?

Mr. Kawecki. I do not recall the exact date, but I do know that it was in the middle of May.

Mr. Machrowicz. Of 1943?

Mr. Kawecki. Yes; that is correct.

Mr. Machrowicz. Do you remember the names of any of these Allied prisoners of war who accompanied you by plane from Breslau to Smolensk?

Mr. Kawecki. At Breslau, I was not permitted to mingle or communicate with the Allied prisoners of war. However, by the time we concluded the trip to Bialek-Polawski the rules were not as rigidly adhered to and, at lunch, I was sitting between a British medical captain and an Australian pilot who had the rank of lieutenant.

Mr. Machrowicz. Were there any American officers in this group?

Mr. Kawecki. Yes, there were among these American prisoners and I recall that one of them was in the rank of major.

Mr. Machrowicz. Do you remember his name?

Mr. Kawecki. I recall it was Major Van Vliet.

Mr. Machrowicz. Was there another American officer in that group?

Mr. Kawecki. As far as I recall, yes; there was another American in this group.

Mr. Machrowicz. Do you remember his name or rank?

Mr. Kawecki. No, I do not.

Mr. Machrowicz. Would it have been Lieutenant Stewart?

Mr. Kawecki. It is possible, but I cannot recall the exact name.

Mr. Machrowicz. This airport you mentioned as the place where you landed, was that the airport used for the Smolensk area?

Mr. Kawecki. Yes, that is correct. That was one of the two air fields used by the German authorities.

Mr. Machrowicz. How long did you stay in the Katyn area on this trip?

Mr. Kawecki. The period of my stay at Katyn was indeterminate. I was supposed to have remained there until I had completed the entire list. However, toward the end of May, the communications were very bad with Krakow and the weather became very bad, so, toward the end of May, I had returned to Krakow via Warsaw.

Mr. Machrowicz. And then, those 2 or 3 weeks you spent at Katyn at that time, were confined to trying to get a correct list of the names of the officers; am I right?

Mr. Kawecki. That is correct.

Mr. Machrowicz. Now, you mentioned the name of Dr. Adam Szebesta, the head of the Polish Red Cross. Was he with you on either the first or the second trip to Katyn? I am not interested in knowing the names of the people who were with Dr. Szebesta. All I want to know is whether Dr. Szebesta was with you on any of these trips to Katyn?

Mr. KAWECKI. No.

Mr. MACHROWICZ. Was he in Katyn a few days after your first trip, if you know?

Mr. KAWECKI. Yes; that is correct.

Mr. MACHROWICZ. And after you returned from the second trip to Katyn, did you work in close contact with Dr. Adam Szebesta in publishing the names of these Polish officers found in Katyn?

Mr. KAWECKI. Dr. Szebesta was very much interested, as president of the Polish Red Cross, in this list of names. As a result, I had frequent opportunities to be in his office in Krakow.

Mr. MACHROWICZ. As a result of your two trips to Katyn, did you establish in your own mind a belief as to who was the guilty party for the murders at Katyn?

Mr. KAWECKI. Yes; I did.

Mr. MACHROWICZ. What was your opinion?

Mr. KAWECKI. During my 2 weeks' stay at Katyn I had an opportunity, without any difficulty, to work in the entire terrain of the graves. I also had an opportunity to examine the letters and documents. I also found on the bodies newspaper clippings, letters which had been dated but not mailed, and various other documents.

Mr. MACHROWICZ. As a result of your observations, what was your opinion at that time as to who was guilty of the Katyn massacre?

Mr. KAWECKI. On the basis of my 2 weeks' stay at Katyn I came to the conclusion, and a conclusion that cannot be doubted, that the murderers of these soldiers in Katyn were the Bolsheviks.

Mr. MACHROWICZ. By Bolsheviks you mean the Russians?

Mr. KAWECKI. That is correct.

Mr. MACHROWICZ. Now, in the course of your conversations with Dr. Adam Szebesta, did you communicate to him what your beliefs were in this respect?

Mr. KAWECKI. Yes; we frequently discussed the subject. I told him my observations and Dr. Szebesta personally was of the opinion likewise that the massacre at Katyn was perpetrated by the Soviets.

Mr. MACHROWICZ. Were these conversations between you and Dr. Szebesta done under such conditions and such an atmosphere that it indicated a free express on his part?

Mr. KAWECKI. In 1942, both Dr. Szebesta and I had been arrested by the Gestapo and jailed in Krakow for several months. However, at the time of these particular discussions relative to Katyn, the situation was such that we did not feel that we were under any particular surveillance or that we could not express our free opinions.

Mr. MACHROWICZ. So that you are convinced, are you, that in your number of conversations with Dr. Szebesta he told you what his honest opinion was; is that right?

Mr. KAWECKI. Dr. Szebesta was no stranger to me. I knew him during my army service and before the war, and there was no need on the basis of our personal acquaintance or friendship for either one of us to lie to each other.

Mr. MACHROWICZ. I have had handed to me by one of the German correspondents who is present at this hearing a press release issued by the Polish Military Mission in Eastern Germany, dated March 28, 1952, in which Dr. Szebesta is quoted as now having changed his opinion on the question of guilt for the Katyn massacre.   Are you familiar with that statement?

Mr. KAWECKI. A few days ago I had occasion to see a newspaper published by the Polish Red Cross, a daily in Frankfurt, in which there appears the entire text of Dr. Szebesta's renunciation of his original views.

Mr. MACHROWICZ. Are the views and expressions which are contained in that statement by Dr. Szebesta in absolute and direct contrast to the expressions which he freely expressed to you when you were in Poland?

Mr. KAWECKI. Unfortunately, that is correct.

Mr. MACHROWICZ. Now, after 1943, did you leave Poland?

Mr. KAWECKI. Yes; I did.

Mr. MACHROWICZ. Were you later in Rome, Italy?

Mr. KAWECKI. Yes.

Mr. MACHROWICZ. In what year?

Mr. KAWECKI. 1947 and 1948.

Mr. MACHROWICZ. While you were in Rome during the years 1947 and 1948, did anyone approach you with the direct purpose of trying to get you to change the statements made by you previously in Poland as to the guilt for the murder of the Polish officers in Katyn?

Mr. KAWECKI. Yes.   In May 1947, I was approached in the village of Recceone.   I was approached by an officer in the uniform of the Second Polish Corps, but, after he began asking me certain questions, it became apparent to me that I was talking to a soldier of the Warsaw Government in Poland.   His name was Alex Dobrowolski, who at that time, said he was the adjutant to the Polish Military Attaché in Rome whose name was Rosen Zawadzki.

Mr. MACHROWICZ. What did he tell you?

Mr. KAWECKI. Dobrowolski wanted to arouse my Polish sympathies.   He tried to convince me that my conclusions and the statement made in 1943 were under duress by the Germans.   He proposed to me at that time that I sign a separate declaration renunciating those views, and he showed me two copies of a statement already prepared which he had in his possession.

Mr. MACHROWICZ. What happened then?

Mr. KAWECKI. After reading this declaration which contained therein a complete renunciation of all the views I expressed originally on this Katyn matter, he asked and requested me to sign it.   I read it and then refused to sign it.

Mr. MACHROWICZ. Did he make any offers or propositions to induce you to sign the instrument?

Mr. KAWECKI. Yes.   While I was reading the declaration, Dobrowolski took out of his pocket a packet of American dollars and laid them on the table.

Mr. MACHROWICZ. Did he tell you how much they were or did you know how much they were?

Mr. KAWECKI. No, he did not tell me and I didn't ask, but from my observation, I felt that there were about one hundred twenty dollar bank notes.

Mr. MACHROWICZ. Did you accept it?

Mr. KAWECKI. No.

Mr. MACHROWICZ. Have you been offered or promised any consideration of any kind, monetary or otherwise, in order to testify before this committee today?

Mr. KAWECKI. No.

Mr. MACHROWICZ. Is the statement made by you here today, free and voluntary?

Mr. KAWECKI. That is correct.

Erwin Allgayer
A member of the then Fifth Company of the 8th Railroad Engineer Regiment.

Mr. FLOOD. Were you ever identified with the German armed forces at any time?

Mr. ALLGAYER. Yes, I was.

Mr. FLOOD. Did you ever serve with the German forces on the Russian front in the Smolensk area?

Mr. ALLGAYER. Yes, I did.

Mr. FLOOD. What was the name and description of your unit and when did you go to Smolensk?

Mr. ALLGAYER. It was the Fifth Company of the Eighth Railroad Engineer Regiment.

Mr. FLOOD. After you advanced from Bialistok in the direction of Smolensk, what were your duties that took you into Smolensk?

Mr. ALLGAYER. I, being a private, first class, belonged to a company troop of the company.

Mr. FLOOD. Were you a billeting officer?

Mr. ALLGAYER. No, I was not. I was a private, first class. I was not an officer.

Mr. FLOOD. I know, but were you engaged in searching for billets in the Smolensk area for your outfit?

Mr. ALLGAYER. Yes, I did that.

Mr. FLOOD. When did you get into Smolensk first?

Mr. ALLGAYER. It was definitely in the beginning of August 1941. I am convinced it was either the 1st or 2d of August.

Mr. FLOOD. How soon after the combat or first line troops moved out did you get into Smolensk? How many days, about?

Mr. ALLGAYER. Judging from what I have been able to learn, at that time, it must have happened several days later.

Mr. FLOOD. Was the front moving very fast forward about that time?

Mr. ALLGAYER. Yes, the front line was moving forward at a fast pace.

Mr. FLOOD. Tell us in your own words about your arrival in Smolensk, your search around the Smolensk area for billets, and when you first got to the forest known as Katyn?

Mr. ALLGAYER. At that time, I and several buddies of mine traveled down to Smolensk, traveling along a highway leading through the Katyn woods. We traveled along that highway down to Smolensk. I still clearly remember that there were constantly serious traffic jams by reason of the fast movement forward of the front line and the ensuing movement of troops. I found Smolensk was pretty heavily destroyed. Only a very few buildings were still intact. They were, however, not fit for billeting purposes. Subsequently, we traveled back from Smolensk, back to the woods. I still have the impression that it was at a distance of about 10 to 15 kilometers from Smolensk. That's only an approximation. That is a figure which I still remember. Then I discovered, on the left-hand side of the road, a fence which was either painted white or light blue, as it is customary in Russia. Well, there was an entrance in the fence and we, being servicemen, surmised that where there is a fence there will also be some building nearby behind it. Subsequently, we went through this gate and we traveled along a path. I remember it was a path or dirt road. It was not a highway—no proper road. This path was winding through the woods for quite some distance until, eventually, it ended by a building.

This building was entirely empty and it struck us as peculiar. It was of a type that was not common in Russia. It was partly constructed of timber and partly of bricks. One portion of the building had two stories. If I was facing the building, the left-hand portion had two stories. The right-hand portion contained garages, and, if I correctly remember it, the foundations of the garage were walled in. What particularly attracted my attention was a piano in the house because that's an object very infrequently found in Russia.

Subsequently, we put up our billets there. However, it occurred to us that the space would not be sufficient to billet an entire company, so, subsequently, we used the garages to have sufficient billeting purposes. At the time of our arrival, it was in summer and it was very hot. Therefore, we soldiers found it very fortunate that we had been billeted on the banks of the River Dnieper. We could very properly use these facilities for bathing purposes.

Mr. FLOOD. How long did your outfit stay there?

Mr. ALLGAYER. To the best of my recollection, about 3 weeks.

Mr. Flood. Do you remember about the date you moved out of there?

Mr. Allgayer. No, I could not accurately indicate that.

Mr. Flood. Do you know what part of the month?

Mr. Allgayer. I take it it was some time toward the end of the month.

Mr. Flood. Of what month?

Mr. Allgayer. August.

Mr. Flood. Was there any evidence of any German troops having been in residence in this castle or this building for any length of time when you got there—Germans?

Mr. Allgayer. Normally, if you move into billets which had previously been occupied by troops, you are apt to discover remains left behind, such as empty cigarette packages or signs or posters containing instructions. We didn't find any such indications in that building. However, I am not in a position to say there had been no German troops there a few days prior to our arrival in this building.

Mr. Flood. This outfit moved into this building right on the heels of the advancing German troops?

Mr. Allgayer. Yes.

Mr. Flood. All the time your outfit was there, did you see any Polish prisoners of any kind in the area?

Mr. Allgayer. No, I did not.

Mr. Flood. Did you see any Polish officers or Polish prisoners of any kind working on the highway?

Mr. Allgayer. Are you referring to the vicinity of Katyn?

Mr. Flood. In the vicinity of your heaquarters around the wood?

Mr. Allgayer. No, I did not.

Mr. Flood. Did you have any conversations with any Russians who lived in the area—men or women?

Mr. Allgayer. Yes, I did. I have a vague and faint recollection only of a woman calling upon us on one occasion asking whether she could get authority to exhume her husband.

Mr. Flood. Did you ever hear any conversations that took place between any of your comrades or the Russians or did you have any conversations with Russians in which they talked about Poles being shot in the area?

Mr. Allgayer. I do not recall anyone having mentioned that those men had been Polish. However, I do recall a Russian, whose quarters, sort of a log cabin, was situated close near the highway, having told us servicemen upon one occasion that some people had been shot there.

Mr. Flood. Did he say when or about when?

Mr. Allgayer. It is possible he said so. However, I do not remember it.

Mr. Flood. Did you know anything about the graves at Katyn Forest or did you see any graves at Katyn Forest during the time you were there?

Mr. Allgayer. No; I neither saw the graves nor did I know anything about the graves at that time.

Mr. Flood. If there had been any shooting by Germans in the area during the time you were there, wouldn't you have known about it since you were right nearby?

Mr. Allgayer. Yes, we would have had to know it.

Mr. FLOOD. What were the sanitary conditions around your headquarters, so far as general health and sanitary conditions were concerned? Any trouble?

Mr. ALLGAYER. Yes. We had a lot of trouble, such trouble as we had nowhere and at no time in Russia.

Mr. FLOOD. What kind of trouble?

Mr. ALLGAYER. The majority of the company was taken ill with dysentery.

Mr. FLOOD. Anything else?

Mr. ALLGAYER. No.

Mr. FLOOD. Did you have any trouble with insects?

Mr. ALLGAYER. Oh, yes. We had an incredible number of insects which I believe was predicated upon the hot season of the year.

Mr. FLOOD. What did the people around there, that is, your comrades, think caused this dysentery to such a large extent in your unit?

Mr. ALLGAYER. Well, it was an enigma to us. We were questioning what might be the reason. First, we believed it might be the water. Subsequently, we believed our meat rations or the bread might have been spoiled. However, all our guesswork got us nowhere and even by the medical investigation of our doctor we got no results.

Mr. FLOOD. Did you have any trouble with flies?

Mr. ALLGAYER. Yes, we had an awful lot of trouble from flies, and I believe that was the reason why the company was moved out of this region so fast.

Mr. FLOOD. But nobody said anything to you about graves or thousands of men being murdered in the Katyn Forest right near your headquarters?

Mr. ALLGAYER. No.

Mr. FLOOD. Did you hear of any orders given to your headquarters to shoot any prisoners in the area?

Mr. ALLGAYER. This would have been something incredible at that time.

Mr. FLOOD. Did your unit take part in the execution of several thousand Polish officers in the Katyn woods?

Mr. ALLGAYER. Our only task was to maintain and repair the railroad line running through Smolensk and we had no other tasks whatever.

Mr. FLOOD. Did you take part in any executions or did your unit?

Mr. ALLGAYER. No.

Mr. FLOOD. Could any such executions have taken place within a thousand meters of your headquarters without your knowing about it, or hearing about it?

Mr. ALLGAYER. That is utterly impossible.

Mr. FLOOD. Did you make any observations with reference to any open spaces in the forests or the woods around your headquarters? Did you notice any?

Mr. ALLGAYER. Yes; I had a vague recollection of one such clearing. It happened because I and one of my buddies were walking through the woods and we came to such a clearing, and, actually, we couldn't see any reason why there should be a clearing right in the middle of a forest.

Mr. FLOOD. Was that a subject of conversation among the troops in your outfit?

Mr. Allgayer. Well, we soldiers just briefly discussed the mere fact. However, we did not put any importance on this fact.

Mr. Flood. What were the general regulations, as far as you knew or saw, as far as the Wehrmacht was concerned, in its treatment of Russian prisoners in the area of Smolensk-Katyn when you were there?

Mr. Allgayer. 'At that time no Russian POW's had yet been assigned as laborers to our maintenance unit, and therefore I know nothing about the treatment of Russian POW's.

Some of the personal possessions recovered from the corpses. Note the faint Polish eagle on the left and the Polish banknotes.

Karl Herrmann

Mr. FLOOD. Were you ever identified with the German armed forces?

Mr. HERRMANN. Yes; I was a member of the security police.

Mr. FLOOD. Where were you stationed in 1943 and 1945?

Mr. HERRMANN. In 1943 I was at Lemberg and Krakow.

Mr. FLOOD. As a member of the security forces, what were your duties?

Mr. HERRMANN. Toward the end I was serving with the administration of the security forces in Krakow in my capacity as administrator of the material depot.

Mr. FLOOD. What year was that?

Mr. HERRMANN. In 1944 and 1945, until the end and the escape.

Mr. FLOOD. Had you ever heard of the Katyn massacres in any way by that time?

Mr. HERRMANN. Yes; I had heard about it for the simple reason that we, in our institute, had documents in our safekeeping.

Mr. FLOOD. What institute?

Mr. HERRMANN. The Institute for Forensic Medicine in Krakow.

Mr. FLOOD. Who was the chief of that institute?

Mr. HERRMANN. Dr. Beck.

Mr. FLOOD. What connection, if any, did you yourself have, in your capacity as a member of the security forces, with the Polish documents?

Mr. HERRMANN. I had no proximate connection; all this ensued only later on, in 1945.

Mr. FLOOD. Tell us what happened in 1945, as far as you recall, with reference to the transportation of these documents taken from your institute, that you described, in any way, from Krakow?

Mr. HERRMANN. Well, I will have to elaborate on that a little, to some extent. As I indicated before these documents had been in safekeeping with the institute.

Mr. FLOOD. Go ahead.

Mr. HERRMANN. After, however, we found out the guerrillas attacked the storage place—and I cannot say whether these guerrillas were Bolshevik guerrillas or belonged to the Polish underground—it was determined to take these documents to Breslau. On the 18th of January 1945, we were forced to flee from Krakow, and we were traveling via Breslau. In Breslau we were taken to emergency billets, where we were waiting for orders indicating to us where we were supposed to move subsequently. There I received an order to go and pick up the documents at the institute of anatomy and to haul the documents on a postal truck to the loading platform at a railroad depot. There was a train standing at the depot ready to take the members of the government somewhere else. It was the last train scheduled to leave the town, and we were assigned one coach of this train.

We traveled on that train to Dresden, and that is where the guard assignment of the boxes began.

Incidentally, I wish to emphasize that I do not know whether there were all of the documents. There were 16 boxes of documents.

Mr. FLOOD. How big was each box?

Mr. HERRMANN. They were 1 meter in length and from about 30 to 35 centimeters in height.

Mr. FLOOD. What were they made of?

Mr. HERRMANN. Wood.

Mr. FLOOD. How were they labeled, if you remember?

Mr. HERRMANN. They weren't—there weren't any labels, practically; there was only a sign on it, "Reichssicherheitshauptamt."

Mr. FLOOD. What does that mean? Translate it.

Mr. HERRMANN. Head Office of the Reich Security Office.

Mr. FLOOD. These boxes were all placed in that coach on that train, were they?

Mr. HERRMANN. Yes.

Mr. FLOOD. You saw that yourself?

Mr. HERRMANN. Yes. Well, we lent a hand in doing so.

Mr. FLOOD. Did you ride on the train with the boxes?

Mr. HERRMANN. Yes, in the very same coach.

Mr. FLOOD. To where?

Mr. HERRMANN. To Dresden.

Mr. FLOOD. What happened when you got to Dresden?

Mr. HERRMANN. The boxes were unloaded at a loading platform at Dresden-Neustadt.

Mr. FLOOD. What happened then, when you took them off at Dresden?

Mr. HERRMANN. Gestapo headquarters were notified to send us a truck. Originally, as far as I heard, the boxes were supposed to proceed straight to Berlin. In the meantime, however, the Russians had made a forced advance, so it was no longer feasible to take the boxes, as originally intended, to Berlin. The boxes were laden on a truck and taken to Radebeul.

Mr. FLOOD. When and where was the last time you saw these boxes?

Mr. HERRMANN. Well, I cannot indicate an accurate date. It might have been, however, toward the end of February.

Mr. FLOOD. What year?

Mr. HERRMANN. 1945.

Mr. FLOOD. Where was the last place you saw them?

Mr. HERRMANN. In Radebeul.

Mr. FLOOD. What town?

Mr. HERRMANN. That is near Dresden.

Mr. FLOOD. That is all.

Mr. HERRMANN. It is between Dresden and Meissen.

Dr Werner Beck

He was in 1943 Director of the Institute for Forensic Medicine and Scientific Criminology in the General Government of Poland set up by the Third Reich.

Mr. FLOOD. Were you ever, at any time, identified with the former German Government?

Dr. BECK. Yes; I was serving with the Ministry of the Interior.

Mr. FLOOD. Did you ever, in your official capacity, have occasion to serve in Poland in any way?

Dr. BECK. Yes; I did.

Mr. FLOOD. Will you give us the title of your position in Poland and a short description of your duties there?

Dr. BECK. I was director of the Institute of Forensic Medicine and of Scientific Criminology.

Mr. FLOOD. Will you give us the German name of that institute, and your title?

Dr. BECK. Director of the State Institute for Forensic Medicine in the General Gouvernment.

Mr. FLOOD. And where was that located?

Dr. BECK. At Krakow.

Mr. FLOOD. In 1943, of course, you heard of the Katyn massacre?

Dr. BECK. Yes; I did.

Mr. FLOOD. When in 1943 had you heard of the Katyn massacre?

Dr. BECK. In April of 1943.

Mr. FLOOD. Where were you at that time?

Dr. BECK. In Krakow.

Mr. FLOOD. Doing what?

Dr. BECK. In my capacity as director of the Institute of Forensic Medicine.

Mr. FLOOD. By that time you had heard of the report of the International Commission of Scientists and their protocol of April 30, 1943, with reference to their findings at Katyn?

Dr. BECK. Yes; I had, for the simple reason that the leader of the German Commission, Professor Buhtz, had been my chief at Breslau University.

Mr. FLOOD. That is the Dr. Buhtz who was cooperating with the International Commission of Scientists at that time; is that correct?

Dr. BECK. Yes.

Mr. FLOOD. Do you know whether or not the Polish Red Cross was in any way connected with the exhumations at Katyn?

Dr. BECK. Yes; I do.

Mr. FLOOD. Did any officials of the Polish Red Cross get in touch with you after the protocol of the international scientists had been signed?

Dr. BECK. Yes.

Mr. FLOOD. Who, when, where, and why?

Dr. BECK. To the best of my recollection it was the president of the Polish Red Cross, Dr. Czinski.

Mr. FLOOD. When was this?

Dr. BECK. Sometime in the first days of May of 1943.

Mr. FLOOD. Where did it take place, and why did they get in touch with you?

Dr. BECK. The office of the president of the Polish Red Cross was located at Warsaw. The president came to Krakow and requested me to place all these auxiliary personnel at his disposal in order to perfect the exhumation.

I wish to indicate that after the German Commission and the International Commission had terminated their activities, the entire exhumations were turned over to the Polish Red Cross.

Mr. FLOOD. Did you cooperate with and grant the request of the president of the Polish Red Cross?

Dr. BECK. Yes, I did, in every way.

Mr. FLOOD. Did you name any of your associates from your institute to assist?

Dr. BECK. Yes, I did.

Mr. FLOOD. Will you name them?

Dr. BECK. Those were the Polish doctors: Dr. Praglowski; then Dr. Wodzinski, both from Krakow; Lecturer Dr. Felz, as well as Dr. Manczarski, both from the subsidiary of my institute at Warsaw. In addition, there were a certain number of assistants for the dissections.

Mr. FLOOD. Did you instruct all of these people to work under the supervision of the Polish Red Cross?

Dr. BECK. Yes, I did.

Mr. FLOOD. Did you ever have any complaints from the Polish Red Cross that these people refused to cooperate, or would not work with them?

Dr. BECK. No, I did not.

Mr. FLOOD. After the exhumations were completed, in the summer of 1943, what happened?

Dr. BECK. All of the material discovered on the dead bodies, such as notebooks, passports, personal papers, personal property such as rings, bracelets, watches, wallets containing banknotes of various currencies and denominations, such as Polish, Russian, and American currencies—all of that collected material was taken to my institute at Krakow.

Mr. FLOOD. What was your procedure with reference to these documents and these personal belongings of the dead Polish officers? How did you take care of them?

Dr. BECK. First I wish to state that all of these objects were sent to Krakow by the Polish Red Cross in 14 boxes. The boxes were locked and I was handed the keys. Subsequently, and upon the request of the president of the Polish Red Cross at Warsaw, Dr. Czinski, I turned all of the objects over to the chemical department of my institute. In charge of the chemical department was Lecturer Dr. Robel.

Mr. FLOOD. Why were they turned over to the chemical section?

Dr. BECK. We had been requested to take those documents, which had been spoiled by a formation of decomposition wax, to a chemical laboratory and to make them again discernible and readable.

Mr. FLOOD. By "decomposition wax" you mean the result of the decomposition of the bodies found in the graves?

Dr. BECK. Yes; that is correct.

Mr. FLOOD. Do you have the names of the persons at your chemical division of the institute under Dr. Robel who were concerned with this matter?

Dr. BECK. Yes, I do.

Mr. FLOOD. Will you place those in the record, please?

Dr. BECK. Yes.

Mr. Flood. Spelling them, please, for the reporter.

Dr. Beck. Dr. Senkowska, a woman; Magistra Cholewinski; Dr. Szwed; lecturer Dr. Ackermannowna; and Dr. Paszkowska.

Mr. Flood. You turned over all of the documents that you had, the boxes and the keys that were in your possession, to the chemical institute, is that right?

Dr. Beck. Yes, and I handed the keys to the man in charge of my chemical section, a Polish doctor, Dr. Robel.

Mr. Flood. All right. What transpired?

Dr. Beck. During the course of this extensive work, extending over a series of months, there was a search for identification marks by which those documents might have been identified. For instance, at first we had to clean all of the objects, and subsequently we photographed them. Subsequently we applied chemical treatment to all of the documents, such as notebooks, passports, all written matter, and particularly as to letters, so as to make the faded writing, either pencil or ink writing, again legible. These jobs were frequently very tedious and extensive, and were not successful in all events.

In those instances, however, when we succeeded in making the writing legible again, we made photostatic copies of the documents, and subsequently we notified the members of the families of the killed Polish officers, as far as I had been able to ascertain them from the letters and the senders indicated on the letters.

Mr. Flood. What method did you use for keeping the items, documents, and personal belongings, of each separate body separate from the others?

Dr. Beck. The appropriate measures had already been taken at the place of the exhumations. The bodies were taken out of the graves one at a time, in sequence. Each body was individually searched for personal property and belongings, and after discovery the belongings in each instance were placed in a separate pouch, and subsequently, when the examinations were made, each pouch was produced individually and the contents of each pouch were treated and examined individually.

Mr. Dondero. By "pouch" do you mean that they were placed in a large envelope?

Dr. Beck. Yes; I mean an envelope.

Mr. Flood. Did you keep in touch with these proceedings all the time that these matters were going through processing in your institute?

Dr. Beck. In the interests of the Polish Red Cross I daily supervised that work.

Mr. Flood. The term "doctor" is very common around here. What kind of a doctor are you?

Dr. Beck. A doctor of medicine.

Mr. Flood. Did you ever have occasion in your official capacity, in view of the fact that you were a doctor of medicine, to issue any death certificates in connection with this matter?

Dr. Beck. Yes; I did.

Mr. Flood. Now, Doctor, I direct your attention to the change of the Eastern Front, insofar as the military campaigns were concerned, in June and July of 1944, and ask you in what way the change in the military situation had anything to do with these documents and your work?

Dr. Beck. In the year 1944 I received an order by the commander of the security police to destroy the documents.

Mr. Flood. The commander of the security police, where?

Dr. Beck. At Krakow. The commander of security police for the entire general government.

Mr. Flood. That is the German occupation government?

Dr. Beck. Yes.

Mr. Flood. All right. What were the instructions?

Dr. Beck. It was a written instruction saying that all of the kept documents, including documents and personal property, originating from Katyn should be destroyed altogether in one lump, lest they fall into the hands of the Russians.

Mr. Flood. What was your reaction and that of your associates, and what did you do about it?

Dr. Beck. I refused to comply with those orders, on the following grounds:

It was my position that these documents, and particularly as to the written instruments, should be kept for the benefit of the Polish Nation, and particularly so for reasons in connection with any possible civil actions or legal actions.

At that time I was approached by Count Ronicker, chief of the Polish welfare organization, which was a sort of liaison organization between the Polish Nation and the German occupation government, as well as by the director of the Academy of Fine Arts, Dr. Pronaskou, with a request to do all I could and see to it that these documents would not be destroyed.

To begin with, we negotiated with the man in charge of the chemical department, Dr. Robel, and we made up our minds to distribute those documents amongst the reliable Poles and subsequently report to the security police that the destruction of the documents had been concluded. This plan, however, could not be effected because such a stench emanated from these documents that they could not be kept in private homes.

Eventually, after plenty of negotiations with the security police, and German Government agencies in the general government, I succeeded in receiving a permit to transfer these documents further west, to wit, to Breslau. In Breslau those boxes were placed in the Anatomical Institute, in view of the stench emanating also from these boxes.

Mr. Flood. How many boxes, and how were they marked?

Dr. Beck. There were 14 boxes, and there were larger inscriptions in black letters on them, "Institute Krakow Library."

Mr. Flood. Of what were the boxes made?

Dr. Beck. Out of stout lumber, with lids. There were no padlocks, but just normal locks were fitted in the boxes.

Mr. Flood. What was the size of the boxes?

Dr. Beck. I would estimate the size of the boxes as 1 meter and 50 in length, 70 centimeters in height, and about 60 centimeters in width.

Mr. Flood. What was done with the boxes at the Anatomical Institute at the University at Breslau?

Dr. Beck. The boxes were kept in a large, separate room placed at our disposal by the then director of the Breslau University.

Mr. Flood. And was any work done on them there?

Dr. BECK. Yes; the identification was continued. It was done by myself and Dr. Robel, the man in charge of my chemical department, going to Breslau time and again. We always received the finished, complete work, and we took out of the boxes new envelopes on which subsequent work was supposed to be done.

Mr. FLOOD. Now, in January of 1945, when the Germans evacuated Krakow, what did you do?

Dr. BECK. I was one of the last to leave Krakow, together with the officers of my administration. To begin with, we traveled to Breslau, and, once there, the first thing I took care of were the documents, these original documents, from Katyn. By reason of the further movement of the front line I had to make up my mind to transfer the boxes from Breslau.

We brought the boxes to Dresden. While we were standing guard over them in Dresden I contacted the police agencies in order to obtain proper and fitting storage room. However, I did not get any cooperation from the police agency, with one exception, that I was given one truck in order to haul the documents away. I then brought these original Katyn documents to a suburb of Dresden, Radebeul.

Mr. FLOOD. Where did you place them there?

Dr. BECK. At first they were placed in a private household, and subsequently, because the stench was too penetrant, they were placed in a storage room of the railroad forwarding depot, or the railroad forwarding department.

Mr. FLOOD. All right. Suppose you tell us what disposition you tried to make of these documents, where you wanted to take them, and why you couldn't get them there.

Dr. BECK. I intended to turn this collection of documents over to some agency of the International Red Cross.

Mr. FLOOD. Where?

Dr. BECK. According to my information, there was a single agency of the International Red Cross in the vicinity, and that was in Prague. Prague, at that time, was a hospital city, and that is why there was an agency of the International Red Cross. No German agency placed a vehicle at my disposal in order to take the documents to Prague. Therefore, I at first attempted to travel to Prague myself in order to have these documents subsequently picked up by the International Red Cross. This happened in the first days of May 1945. By reason of the vicissitudes of war I was not in a position to contact the agencies of the International Red Cross.

I then proceeded from Prague to Pilsen, after one specific road had been opened to traffic. I traveled there with the German Army. Pilsen had already been occupied by the United States Armed Forces. I then reported to some commanding officer, whose name I no longer know, and subsequently, after having told him my story, he gave me a pass to travel to Dresden.

While on my way to Dresden I learned that Dresden, in the meantime, had been occupied by the Russians, so I personally had no chance whatever to get into Dresden.

I then proceeded to the United States zone of occupation in Bavaria.

Mr. FLOOD. When did you enter the American zone?

Dr. BECK. In June of 1945.

Mr. FLOOD. What disposition, if any, did you hear subsequently was made of the boxes that were at the railway station in Dresden?

Dr. BECK. The boxes had been burned immediately prior to the Russians moving in.

Mr. FLOOD. By whom?

Dr. BECK. By the railroad forwarding agent.

Mr. FLOOD. Who told you that?

Dr. BECK. I myself had given this order. At that time we had quite a clear picture of the development of the war. We still anticipated and hoped that the Americans would occupy Dresden. However, in order to cover all possibilities, I had given an order that should the Russians come and occupy Dresden, the boxes should be burned.

Mr. FLOOD. Did you ever receive any information from anybody in Dresden after the Russian occupation that your orders had been carried out?

Dr. BECK. Yes, I did.

Mr. FLOOD. Now, the committee has been advised of the name of the person who gave you that order, and of the repute and standing of that informant. We can understand why you may not want to tell us, but, if you wish to, we would be glad to have the name of the person for the record, although the committee is aware of it anyhow. That is up to you.

Dr. BECK. For security reasons, and in the best interests of persons residing in the Russian zone who are connected with this business, I take it that it would be advisable not to mention or to divulge the name here in an open session.

Mr. FLOOD. This same informant was in touch with you or gave you information in connection with efforts made by the Russian secret service in connection with these documents at Katyn, and later, when they thought they were in Dresden?

Dr. BECK. Yes. The Russian secret police, by ways and means unknown to me, had learned of the storage place of these documents, or of these boxes, and had made several searches of the house of my parents, who were residing near Dresden. The Russians also traced the exact route of my flight up to the border of the Russian zone. The Russians searched the homes of all persons who sheltered me at that time, particularly so the houses of friends of mine. They lost track of me only at the zonal border.

Mr. FLOOD. Was anything done to your family?

Dr. BECK. My mother had been incarcerated at Dresden for more than half a year because the Russians wanted to learn my address.

Mr. FLOOD. How old was she then?

Dr. BECK. Sixty-two years of age.

Mr. FLOOD. How long was she in jail, if you know?

Dr. BECK. A bit more than 6 months.

Mr. FLOOD. Whatever happened to the railroad agent that burned these things at the station, if you have heard?

Dr. BECK. Yes; he has been deported, and the members of his family, even today, still don't know where he is.

Mr. FLOOD. Deported where and by whom?

Dr. BECK. By Russian police in those gray uniforms, with green bands around the caps; Russian secret police.

Mr. FLOOD. Why didn't you report these matters to the Nuremberg trials?

Dr. BECK. I did not report it because I had to figure I would be automatically arrested by virtue of my official position, the major position I had held with the occupation government in Poland, and I had to figure on being extradited to the Russians right away. At that time surrender or extradition took place, without proper court proceedings, by the simple request of one of these commissions, which went about scouring the camps.

Mr. FLOOD. Doctor, it has been testified before this commission by various witnesses upon various occasions that certain of these bodies of the Polish officers found in the graves at Katyn had their hands tied behind their backs with either rope or wire. Have you ever heard of that?

Dr. BECK. Yes. I obtained current reports from my Polish collaborators, who had been working on these exhumations, and it had been reported that numerous of those Polish officers found at Katyn had their hands tied behind their backs with string. I was familiar with the protocol of this International Commission of Scientists, which had arrived at the same finding.

Subsequently, I requested my assistants to take the material used for the tying-up, and bring it to me.

I formerly engaged in criminological scientific investigation of material used for strangulation purposes or for tying purposes, and that is why I have been surprised that this international commission of scientists had arrived at the finding that the string used for the tying of the hands of the Polish officers was made of Russian hemp. Subsequently I made a thorough examination of that strangulation material, which I myself developed and published in 1947. My method has been repeatedly used; for instance, by the supreme court of Massachusetts, file No. 13 N. E., 206–382. I made a thorough examination of that material brought me, based upon my method, and I was in a position to determine and corroborate that that material was made of Russian hemp, and I was particularly in a position to positively determine that this material was not of German industrial manufacture.

Mr. MACHROWICZ. In this institute that you were operating in Krakow, the various sections of that institute, with the exception of the serologic department and the department of identification of arms, were actually headed by Poles; am I right in that?

Dr. BECK. Yes.

Mr. MACHROWICZ. And were these Polish doctors given a free hand to handle those departments?

Dr. BECK. Yes.

Mr. MACHROWICZ. You mentioned in your statement Dr. Marion Wodzinski. Do you remember him?

Dr. BECK. Yes; I do.

Mr. MACHROWICZ. Did he ever ask you to be relieved of his duties in that department that he headed?

Dr. BECK. No. However, I wish to add that, to the best of my recollection, Dr. Wodzinski left sometime before Christmas of 1944 and did not return.

Mr. MACHROWICZ. Did he leave voluntarily?

Dr. BECK. Voluntarily.

Dr Robert Kempner

A lawyer and political scientist, he was a member of the American prosecution staff at Nuremberg. His evidence throws light on the legal methods at that trial and pinpoints how Katyn came to be missing from the final judgement.

Dr. KEMPNER. In comparative law and international law and also in political science, I lectured at the University of Pennsylvania; also in Michigan, in Ann Arbor.

Mr. DONDERO. Was that the University of Michigan?

Dr. KEMPNER. Yes, your Honor.

Mr. DONDERO. At Ann Arbor?

Dr. KEMPNER. At Ann Arbor.

Mr. DONDERO. How long?

Dr. KEMPNER. At West Point and various other schools.

Mr. DONDERO. On what subjects did you lecture at West Point?

Dr. KEMPNER. Various times on German-Russian relations.

Mr. DONDERO. Do you understand that West Point is the Military Academy of the United States?

Dr. KEMPNER. Yes, Your Honor, that is the Military Academy of the United States.

Mr. DONDERO. How long did you lecture in the United States at the three places you named?

Dr. KEMPNER. I lectured at various schools and places between 1939 and 1951.

Mr. DONDERO. All in the United States, or here in Europe as well?

Dr. KEMPNER. In the United States; also in Switzerland and also in Germany.

Mr. DONDERO. Where were you in 1939?

Dr. KEMPNER. In France and in the United States.

Mr. DONDERO. Where were you during the recent war, or World War No. II?

Dr. KEMPNER. In the United States.

Mr. DONDERO. When did you come back to Europe?

Dr. KEMPNER. The first time I came back after World War II was in July or the beginning of August 1945.

Mr. DONDERO. What was the purpose of your return to Europe?

Dr. KEMPNER. I was at that time connected with the War Department and was on loan to Justice Robert H. Jackson's prosecuting staff.

Mr. DONDERO. Do you mean to say that you were connected with the War Department of the United States?

Dr. KEMPNER. Yes, your Honor.

Mr. DONDERO. Were you connected at one time with the German Government?

Dr. KEMPNER. Yes, your Honor.

Mr. DONDERO. How long?

Dr. KEMPNER. Until 1933.

Mr. DONDERO. And in what capacity?

Dr. KEMPNER. I was senior Government counselor and of kind of general counsel of the German police system.

Mr. DONDERO. Was that in the further practice of the law?

Dr. Kempner. The general counsel's job was a legal job with the pre-Hitler German Government.

Mr. Dondero. And that would be before 1933, would it?

Dr. Kempner. Yes, your Honor.

Mr. Dondero. Just what date did you become connected with the War Department of the United States, as far as you can remember?

Dr. Kempner. I think I switched from the Department of Justice in Washington to the Department of War in the beginning of 1945.

Mr. Dondero. Was that when you came back to Europe?

Dr. Kempner. That was before.

Mr. Dondero. What is your recollection as to when you came back to Europe as a representative of the War Department in Washington?

Dr. Kempner. It was in July or beginning of August 1945.

Mr. Dondero. Who employed you at that time?

Dr. Kempner. I was on the payroll of the Judge Advocate General.

Mr. Dondero. Of the United States?

Dr. Kempner. Of the United States.

Mr. Dondero. Did you take any part in the Nuremberg trials?

Dr. Kempner. Yes, Your Honor.

Mr. Dondero. With whom were you associated there?

Dr. Kempner. I was a member of the American prosecution staff.

Mr. Dondero. Who was the head of that staff?

Dr. Kempner. Justice Robert H. Jackson.

Mr. Dondero. Then you were one of the assistant prosecutors; is that correct?

Dr. Kempner. I was at that time one of the assistant prosecutors.

Mr. Dondero. And from either July or August 1945 you were then at the Nuremberg trials after that date, were you?

Dr. Kempner. That is correct, Your Honor.

Mr. Dondero. How long?

Dr. Kempner. I came for 30 days and remained until September–October 1949.

Mr. Dondero. How many years and months would that be?

Dr. Kempner. About 4 years and 3 or 4 months.

Mr. Dondero. And while you were at Nuremberg did the subject of the Katyn massacre come before the court?

Mr. Flood. Before you proceed with the matters of the Nuremberg trial itself, suppose you outline, just for the record, so we'll know what we're talking about later, briefly, but reasonably detailed, the agreements at the London meeting between the powers how the jurisdiction of the counts decided upon were distributed among the nations; how the Katyn matter became identified as a count or an indictment; the differences in procedure at the Nuremberg trials as distinguished from the English common law as practiced in the United States of America, with particular reference to motions to quash indictments or motions for nol. pros.; and in what manner were counts, as we say in the English common law, or charges, presented under the Nuremberg practice.

Dr. Kempner. I must mention in the beginning that I was not present in London when the agreement was made, and I am sure my superior at that time, Justice Robert H. Jackson, can tell this much better than I; but since I practiced this matter for 4½ years, I think I can answer the question of the committee.

After the London Agreement of 1945, which was backed by 20 or more Allied states, not only by the Big Four powers, but also by the Danish, by the Dutch, and all the other nations who were at war in Germany, a dividing line had to be made how to handle that big trial. The first Nuremberg trial, the so-called big international trial, had four counts, and these counts were more or less drawn up according to Anglo-Saxon law. There were certain continental points in it, but I don't want to go into that now.

The first count was a common plan and conspiracy to commit crimes against peace, war crimes, and crimes against humanity. The second count was crimes against peace. The third count was called war crimes, and if I saw war crimes, I mean war crimes in the old conservative sense—violation of the Hague Convention, the Geneva Convention, and similar. The fourth count was crimes against humanity. That was something new in the form. We old reactionary criminal lawyers just called it murder and similar things.

Mr. MACHROWICZ. May I just interrupt there for the record so there will be no misunderstanding? Will you explain what you mean by reactionary criminal lawyers?

Dr. KEMPNER. The people who call murder just murder, but I will refrain from any antistatements.

Now, the big battle started how should these four counts be divided up among four nations that participated—the United States, the British, the French, and the Russians, and the division which came out was as follows, and I saw the very great outline. There were a lot of details which I think are of no interest to the particular problem here. Common plan and conspiracy (count I) and crimes against peace (count II) were handled by the United States and the British.

Chairman MADDEN. I didn't get that last.

Dr. KEMPNER. Count I, conspiracy, and count II, crimes against peace, were handled by the United States and by the British. Count III, war crimes, and count IV, crimes against humanity, were divided up according to geographical regions or districts. The French handled the war crimes and crimes against humanity as far as Western Europe was concerned. They were, so to speak, spokesmen, the prosecuting spokesmen, for the French, for the Dutch, for the Belgians, and other German occupied western territories. The Russians were in charge of war crimes and crimes against humanity which were allegedly committed in the eastern areas, and if I say eastern areas I mean the Soviet Union, Poland, and at the time they handled also Yugoslavia, and Bulgaria, Czechoslovakia.

Mr. FLOOD. Let me ask you as you best remember, and it is only your best recollection, was there any actual geographic demarcation line drawn or was it just a general distinction?

Dr. KEMPNER. If I remember, it was a clear-cut agreement between the four nations at that time.

Mr. FLOOD. I understand the agreement was clear-cut, but what I am trying to find out is was there any actual demarcation line actually drawn from point A to point B geographically to make the difference between the East and the West, as far as jurisdiction was concerned?

Dr. KEMPNER. I don't think so, Your Honor. I think it was kind of a general practice. Everybody handled it this way.

Mr. O'KONSKI. In what was Germany proper before the war—who had the responsibility there, the Russians or the French?

Dr. KEMPNER. There the question of nationality played a role. If the victims were, for instance, Russian prisoners of war, the Russians handled it, and if they were slave labor camps with French inmates, the French handled it.

Mr. O'KONSKI. Suppose the victims were Poles? Who handled them, the Russians or the French?

Dr. KEMPNER. Mostly the Russians, but since sometimes camps had French and Polish inmates and even Hungarian inmates; then it was just up to the prosecutors who said maybe, "No, that's Russian stuff. Don't bother me with that." You know how that is in a trial.

Mr. MACHROWICZ. Specifically then, under the circumstances which you know of as existing then, would the Katyn Forest incident come under the Russians or the French jurisdiction?

Dr. KEMPNER. The Katyn affair was a clear-cut Russian affair and was handled right from the beginning by the Russians.

May I ask Your Honor very humbly to give me leading words what the first topic is?

Mr. FLOOD. The first topic is have you, in your opinion, described for the committee how the different jurisdictions were set up? Are you satisfied with that?

Dr. KEMPNER. I think I am, if you are.

Mr. FLOOD. You have told us in what jurisdiction the Katyn matter fell and why. Now, we are down finally to the difference in procedure in Nurnberg and the English common-law system.

Dr. KEMPNER. The first topic, the indictment. The Nurnberg indictment which was drawn up by all the four nations was pretty similarly done to an Anglo-Saxon indictment. However, I would say there were more particulars in the indictment than we would do it normally in the United States. Not to the satisfaction of the defendants who wanted even more according to continental law. The indictment had four counts, as I already have said. In the rules and procedures of the court there was no provision, as we would say, to quash the indictment. We had no such provisions. However, there were instances where German counsel asked for something which might come pretty near to such a procedure. For instance, the lawyer of Goering, Mr. Stahmer, made a motion or, as he called it, an application, after the evidence in the Katyn case was heard, to move that this part should be stricken.

Mr. FLOOD. You mean stricken from the record?

Dr. KEMPNER. As I remember, a kind of removing from the indictment.

Mr. MACHROWICZ. May I ask at that point, was that before or after the testimony on that particular point of the indictment was offered?

Dr. KEMPNER. This was after the witnesses on Katyn were heard.

Mr. FLOOD. Now, what about a nol pros?

Dr. KEMPNER. That didn't exist. It practically never came up; something like that.

Mr. FLOOD. So that a motion for a nol pros under the English common law system made either by one of the parties or the prosecution did not exist under the Nurnberg procedure?

Dr. KEMPNER. During the first trial it never came to my attention. Later we did it.

Mr. FLOOD. There's only one more part of that procedural question: In what manner were the counts presented or the charges brought before the Court or the Tribunal by each of the member nations?

Dr. KEMPNER. First, certain general questions were handled and presented to the court, based on trial briefs. Each trial brief was supplemented by a document book, mostly captured original German documents, and it was presented like in an American or English court—first, the opening statement of the chief prosecutor for the Americans, Justice Jackson. The British was Sir David Maxwell-Fyfe, who is now Minister of the Interior, and I think for the Russians it was General Rudinko. For the French, among others, Edgar Faure, the French Prime Minister, who was French Prime Minister during the last 2 months or so. Then another way of presentation started. We wrote trial briefs against each individual defendant, together with document books, a kind of catalog lining up each defendant with the various things. In fact, I was in charge of the division which had to write these trial briefs on the individual defendants.

Mr. DONDERO. Now, Mr. Kempner, coming right down to the Katyn question, how specific was the count drawn in that case?

Dr. KEMPNER. The Katyn case was mentioned in the indictment under count III, subsection C, that means mistreatment, and so forth, of prisoners of war. Count III, subsection C, and if I remember, it was drawn up just in three or four lines, printed line, in the indictment.

Mr. DONDERO. Who drew it up?

Dr. KEMPNER. To my best knowledge, the Russians.

Mr. DONDERO. What was the specific charge in that count?

Dr. KEMPNER. The specific charge was and, if I may, I want to refresh my memory—the specific charge was as printed in the indictment in volume I, page 54, of the record of the International Military Tribunal, page 54, which reads, and I have to correct myself because these are only two lines and not three or four lines as I said.

Now, I am refreshing my memory and see that the indictment says:

In September 1941, 11,000 Polish officers * * *

Mr. FLOOD (interposing). As a matter of fact, you are reading directly from the record, are you not?

Dr. KEMPNER. I am reading now from the record, volume I, page 54:

In September 1941, 11,000 Polish officers were killed in the Katyn Forest near Smolensk.

Mr. MACHROWICZ. Have you read the complete charge in the indictment, so far as Katyn is concerned?

Dr. KEMPNER. Yes, your Honor, I did so.

Mr. DONDERO. Now, when did this case come before the court, during the beginning of the Nurnberg trials or toward the end?

Dr. KEMPNER. The first time evidence was submitted or alleged evidence was submitted by the Russian prosecution was in the middle of the trial. In fact, on February 14, 1946.

Mr. DONDERO. In what form did they submit the evidence?

Dr. KEMPNER. The evidence submitted at that time by the Russian prosecutor, Colonel Pokrovsky, was a Russian document which had the document number U. S. S. R. 54, and this document was a report written by a Russian state commission, as they called it, and in this report there were details about the alleged massacre which I have mentioned as part of the indictment, and this is in the record of the International Military Tribunal, volume VII, pages 425 to 427.

Mr. MITCHELL. Isn't that volume XVII?

Dr. KEMPNER. Volume VII.

Mr. DONDERO. Now, that report, Mr. Kempner, is the report of the Russian Commission appointed by the Russian Government to examine the question of Katyn?

Dr. KEMPNER. Yes, your Honor.

Dr. DONDERO. What is the date of that report?

Dr. KEMPNER. I don't know the date. I have forgotten the exact date.

Mr. DONDERO. After the Russians presented their charge in the form of this report, was there anything done on the part of the Governments of the United States, the British, or the French?

Dr. KEMPNER. Nothing at all.

Mr. DONDERO. When did it come up again, the question of the Katyn massacre?

Dr. KEMPNER. This question just came up just about 1 month later, namely, on March 8, 1946.

Mr. MACHROWICZ. One question there; so there will be no misinterpretation: Nothing was done by the Americans, British, or French because, under the method you have described here previously, there was nothing that should have been done or could have been done by the Americans, British, or French, is that correct?

Dr. KEMPNER. That is correct. We had no right to interfere in any way.

Mr. DONDERO. When it came up a month later, then what happened?

Dr. KEMPNER. On March 8, 1946, the defense took it up.

Mr. FLOOD. May I interrupt at this time to point out, in fairness to the witness, that the chief counsel of the German defense was whom?

You may not be able to decide who that was.

Who was the counsel for Goering?

Dr. KEMPNER. I don't want to answer the first question because of certain professional——

Mr. FLOOD (interposing). All right.

Who was the counsel for Goering?

Dr. KEMPNER. The very distinguished lawyer from Schleswig-Holstein, Mr. Otto Stahmer.

Mr. FLOOD. I think you would like to know that Dr. Stahmer is now in the courtroom at this moment.

Dr. KEMPNER. I am glad to see again the fighter from the other side.

Mr. FLOOD. Will you stand up, Dr. Stahmer?

Mr. DONDERO. Tell the committee then what happened when the defense brought it up.

Dr. KEMPNER. On that very day, Mr. Stahmer stood up and made something, which was translated into English, an application, I would rather call it a motion, and his motion was—I say it shortly: "I do not believe that my client and the persons mentioned in the Russian document are guilty or connected with this Katyn case, and I want to have witnesses," he said, and he asked at that time for a Colonel Ahrens, a Lieutenant Rex, and a General Oberhaeuser, and a Lieutenant Graf Berg, and he also mentioned that he wanted to have as a witness for the defense or an expert witness, a Professor Naville, from

Geneva, and Chief Justice Lawrence, as always, said: "Put it in writing," and all this happened on March 8, 1946, and I am referring to volume IX pages 3 and 4, of the blue volumes of the record of the International Military Tribunal.

Mr. DONDERO. Who was Justice Lawrence?

Dr. KEMPNER. That was the chief justice, who was a Britisher.

Mr. DONDERO. Tell the committee just what happened?

Dr. KEMPNER. There was another very short discussion because Mr. Stahmer complained that he had not received copies of the famous Russian State Commission report.

Mr. MITCHELL. Were you present in court at the time of this discussion?

Dr. KEMPNER. I remember I was at that time in court.

The answer was that 30 copies were already at the translators' room. I think that is written down in volume IX, page 28.

Mr. MITCHELL. One question: Did Dr. Stahmer put it in writing when the judge told him to, to your knowledge?

Dr. KEMPNER. I cannot say. I can only draw the conclusion that he did so.

Mr. MITCHELL. You don't know yourself, though?

Dr. KEMPNER. I don't know myself, and I can draw the conclusion from the thing which follows right now.

Mr. DONDERO. In other words, Dr. Stahmer, the attorney, demanded that witnesses be called?

Dr. KEMPNER. Yes; and he did so very energetically.

Mr. DONDERO. Tell the committee just what happened in regard to the arrangements for witnesses.

Dr. KEMPNER. This motion about witnesses was translated into four languages, which always took some time, and on May 11, 1946, the Russian, Colonel Pokrovsky, announced the motion in open court, and he said literally: "The prosecution protests very energetically * * *" In fact, he didn't say "the prosecution," he said: "The Soviet Union, the prosecution of the Soviet Union, categorically protests against witnesses," and then Chief Justice Lawrence made one remark, and after that very remark, Colonel Pokrovsky gave in in some way.

Chairman MADDEN. What remark did Justice Lawrence make there?

Dr. KEMPNER. I don't know. I am not able to quote it really, but it was some remark which is in the record in volume XIII, page 430.

Chairman MADDEN. Have you that volume here?

Mr. DONDERO. The witness refreshes his memory from the record.

Dr. KEMPNER. I refresh my memory, and with your permission, I am reading this remark from page 430: "PRESIDENT OF THE COURT: Colonel Pokrovsky, we have this matter fully in our mind and we have already had to consider it. Therefore, it is not necessary for you to deal with it in detail, for I understand that these are new witnesses who have not before been applied for."

Chairman MADDEN. Now, what did President Lawrence mean by that remark?

Dr. KEMPNER. It's rather difficult for a prosecutor or lawyer to interpret a judge, but, if I understand it well, then he meant: "You better be careful and I think we will do something about it."

Mr. DONDERO. Were witnesses agreed upon and the number?

Dr. KEMPNER. At that time there was a further discussion, and the Russian, Colonel Pokrovsky, said, more or less to the court: "If the defense wants 2 witnesses, we, the Russians, want 10 witnesses."

Mr. MITCHELL. Was it the customary procedure of the court to grant such requests?

Dr. KEMPNER. Not such wild ones, I would say.

Mr. DONDERO. Did they finally agree upon the number of witnesses upon each side?

Dr. KEMPNER. The judge, in what at that time I thought was a very wise way, said: "Each of you three." That was the ruling which was later pronounced—each side three. That's all.

Mr. MITCHELL. Three witnesses?

Dr. KEMPNER. Three witnesses.

Mr. DONDERO. Did each side present three witnesses?

Dr. KEMPNER. Anyhow, he made this ruling: "Three witnesses," and then something happened, Your Honor, which I do not know, because the American prosecution had nothing to do with it, but I know that some coming together between the Russian prosecution and the German defense happened.

Mr. MITCHELL. I would like to ask here a procedural question.

When the defense or the prosecuting lawyers on either side wanted to have a conference, official conference, to whom did they go to arrange such a meeting?

Dr. KEMPNER. When we Americans had something, I just went to the German lawyers and said, "What are you doing, and what should I do?" However, when a question with the Russians was involved, the German lawyers went, as we would say in the United States, to the clerk of the court, he should arrange a meeting, or, as it was said or as the official name was in Nuremberg, the secretary general.

Chairman MADDEN. Before Mr. Mitchell asked his question, you stated something happened then between the Russian prosecution and the German defense. What did you mean by that?

Dr. KEMPNER. A talking about the ruling of the court, that each side has a right to have three witnesses, whether they really would have three or maybe two are enough, or whether they might do it in affidavit form or something like that. But I was not present.

Chairman MADDEN. What happened? Was there a decision made?

Dr. KEMPNER. Anyhow, on June 29, 1946, which was 1 month later, Justice Lawrence asked the Russian colonel, who was a prosecutor, a kind of judge advocate, "Did you come to an agreement?" He asked him in open court, "Did you, Russian Prosecutor, make an agreement with German counsel about the three witnesses?"

Mr. MITCHELL. May I pause a minute there?

You referred to the so-called clerk of court, as called in the American system, or as he was called at Nuernberg—what was it?

Dr. KEMPNER. Secretary General.

Mr. MITCHELL. Who was that?

Dr. KEMPNER. I think at the time there were certain changes. There was some clerk of the Supreme Court from Washington first, but I think at that time, his successor was—I am not a hundred percent sure, but I think it was a General Mitchell.

Mr. MITCHELL. An American?

Dr. KEMPNER. An American general.

Mr. Dondero. Now, Mr. Kempner, you are in court, the court has called up the case, he asked you, for the prosecution and the defense, if you had come to an agreement; and your answer was that you had?

Dr. Kempner. Not my answer but the answer of the Russian attorney, and I think also of Mr. Stahmer. And the answer was there was some agreement between prosecution and defense, "And we just can go ahead."

Mr. Flood. I think the record should be very clear at this point that whatever discussion you are talking about, or whatever discussion there was with the court about agreements as to the number of witnesses was a matter between the court, the Russians, and the Germans, and nobody else; is not that it?

Dr. Kempner. That is right. And I testify only on matters which I saw in court, or heard.

Chairman Madden. You were acting in the capacity of an observer or a spectator, were you?

Dr. Kempner. The American prosecution was always represented. We had our own table and we were present.

Chairman Madden. You were participating then?

Dr. Kempner. Yes.

Mr. Mitchell. No.

Mr. Flood. One moment.

I want the record to show—I repeat it again for the purpose of emphasis—that whatever agreements were made in the open court, that you are talking about and that you saw or heard, were made between the court, the Russian prosceution, and the German defense; is not that right?

Dr. Kempner. That is absolutely correct, and the records shows so.

Mr. Flood. And you were present in the court merely as an attaché of the American side.

Dr. Kempner. I was one of the representatives of the American side.

Mr. Flood. Apparently, I have to spell this out three times. You did not, for the Americans, participate in any of these agreements that we were talking about, with the Russians and Germans.

Dr. Kempner. I did not; and, to my best knowledge, none of my American or British colleagues did so.

Mr. Dondero. After this matter came up the second time, that you have just described, did it come up again before the court?

Dr. Kempner. Yes, your Honor. Just 2 days later this defense presented the three witnesses.

Mr. Dondero. Did the Russians present any witnesses?

Dr. Kempner. Yes; your Honor.

Dr. Dondero. Who were the German witnesses?

Dr. Kempner. The German witnesses—and the record of the Tribunal, volume 17, page 274, shows so, that the first German witness Mr. Stahmer presented was Mr. Friedrich Ahrens.

Mr. Dondero. I think you have already testified to that. My attention has just been called to it.

Now, that was 2 days after the agreement or discussion about the witnesses.

Dr. Kempner. Yes, your Honor; on July 1.

Mr. Dondero. What year?

Dr. Kempner. 1946.

338

Mr. DONDERO. What happened in regard to the Katyn case in court after that, if you know?

Dr. KEMPNER. After Mr. Stahmer was through with his three witnesses and the Russians were through with their three witnesses——

Mr. DONDERO. In other words, what did the court do?

Dr. KEMPNER. Mr. Stahmer made, 3 days later, on July 5, his final plea for Goering.

Mr. DONDERO. The question is: What did the court do?

Dr. KEMPNER. I made a little mistake. There is something that happened before.

The Soviets were not very enthusiastic about the thing and said, "We brought only these two or three witnesses; this is pretty bad. We want to have many more witnesses, up to 120 or something like that." And Mr. Stahmer stated for the defense, "Okay, if we get equal numbers." And Justice Lawrence, if I am right, said, more or less, "We are through; each side had three witnesses."

And 3 days later, Mr. Stahmer made already his final statement, because these were really the last witnesses of the whole trial.

Mr. DONDERO. Do you mean the Nuremberg trial?

Dr. KEMPNER. The Nuremberg trial.

Mr. DONDERO. After that happened, what did the court do, if anything?

Dr. KEMPNER. I want to say shortly, Mr. Stahmer said, "No proof," in his final statement on July 5. And a couple of days later, on July 29, 1946, the Russian prosecutor made his statement, his final statement.

Mr. DONDERO. What did he say?

Dr. KEMPNER. Volume 19, page 583—and he didn't mention Katyn at all——

Mr. DONDERO. The question has been left unanswered. What did the court do after that, if anything?

Dr. KEMPNER. The court didn't mention the Katyn case any more, and so far as I know the judgment, the word "Katyn" had not been mentioned in the judgment October 2, 1946.

Mr. DONDERO. So that the case of the Katyn massacre was left undecided?

Dr. KEMPNER. The court made no finding.

Chairman MADDEN. Mr. O'Konski.

Mr. O'KONSKI. From your observation, when the Katyn matter came up did the judges sitting at the trial show a sincere interest in establishing guilt one way or the other for those murders or were they more interested in letting it drop just as fast as possible?

Mr. MACHROWICZ. Mr. Chairman, may I say that I think it was agreed with counsel that he should express whatever facts he knows of and whatever observations he made, and I think it would be unfair for the committee to ask the counsel to express an opinion, unless he wishes to do so—an opinion particularly of this kind.

Mr. O'KONSKI. I will drop the question, but I have some more questions. I withdraw the question.

Mr. MACHROWICZ. Do you care to answer?

Dr. KEMPNER. No. It is a little difficult to talk about my own judges. It might be contempt of court and it might be admiration, and I don't want to say anything.

Mr. O'Konski. I will withdraw the question, then.

Dr. Kempner. Thank you.

Mr. O'Konski. I have some more questions, and these are not questions of opinion; these are questions of fact from your observation.

The United States and Great Britain were given the responsibility of preferring charges at the trial for a plan of conspiracy and crimes against peace; is that not correct?

Dr. Kempner. Yes; and a conspiracy to commit such crimes and war crimes and crimes against humanity.

Mr. O'Konski. Did the United States and British delegations at Nuremberg trials prefer the charges of an act of aggression and a breaking of nonaggression treaties by Russia against Finland in 1938 and 1939?

Dr. Kempner. Not to my knowledge.

Mr. O'Konski. Did the British and American delegations bring the charges, since it was within their category, since they were charged with plans of conspiracy and crimes against peace, prefer the charge of Russia's aggression against Latvia and the breaking of the non-aggression pact with Latvia by the Russians?

Dr. Kempner. Not to my knowledge.

Mr. O'Konski. Did they prefer any charges before the Nuremberg trials on Russia's aggression and breaking of a nonaggression treaty with Estonia?

Dr. Kempner. Not to my knowledge.

Mr. O'Konski. Did they bring any charges of Russia's aggression and violation of a nonaggression pact with the country of Lithuania?

Dr. Kempner. No.

Mr. O'Konski. Here is an important one: Did the British and the American delegations bring the charge before the Nuremberg trials of Russia's attack on Poland in league with Hitler when he first started the war and the breaking of the nonaggression pact with Poland?

Dr. Kempner. No.

Mr. O'Konski. In other words, at the Nuremberg trials, the only charges of aggression and treaty violation that the United States and Great Britain brought before the Nuremberg trials were those which were committed by the Germans?

Dr. Kempner. At that time; yes.

Mr. O'Konski. That is all.

Mr. Machrowicz. Just one question.

I would like to return to the Katyn case, but I am going to ask just one question to clear some of the matters.

In view of the fact that this was a four-power tribunal, could the United States or Great Britain prefer any charges against another member of that tribunal, Russia?

Dr. Kempner. Of course not. It was a time of a warm peace and not of the cold war.

Mr. O'Konski. In that connection, I wish to state that there were four judges—were there not—one Russian, one Frenchman, one Englishman, and one American, and they could have decided, if it had not been brought up, that it could be brought up?

Dr. Kempner. That is a very difficult type of technical, $64, question and I really have not the answer, Your Honor, I am sorry.

Mr. Machrowicz. Returning to the Katyn case, I am going to ask just a few questions.

Am I correct in assuming, from the testimony which you have given thus far, that you have given this committee the understanding that the entire responsibility for the presentation of the case, insofar as Katyn is concerned, was placed upon the Russian representative?

Dr. KEMPNER. Yes, Your Honor. The Russians had the sole responsibility.

Mr. MACHROWICZ. And am I correct also in assuming that the Russian representative upon whom this responsibility was placed failed completely in his final argument to the courts to even mention the Katyn case.

Dr. KEMPNER. Yes, Your Honor. After that debacle with the witnesses they didn't press it any longer.

Mr. MACHROWICZ. And am I correct in understanding that the four-power court failed completely in its judgment to mention the Katyn case?

Dr. KEMPNER. To the best of my knowledge and after having read the judgment—volume 1, again—Katyn is not mentioned.

Mr. MACHROWICZ. The Russians had a representative in that four-power court, did they not?

Dr. KEMPNER. Yes, they had, Your Honor.

Mr. MACHROWICZ. Do you remember who he was?

Dr. KEMPNER. I think it was General Nikitchenko.

Mr. MACHROWICZ. Did the Russian member of that tribunal make any objection or protest against the four-power tribunal having failed to determine guilt in the Katyn case?

Dr. KEMPNER. Not so far as the official record is concerned.

Mr. MACHROWICZ. And do you know anything to the contrary?

Dr. KEMPNER. I never have heard anything about it.

Mr. MACHROWICZ. Now, did I understand also that the Russian prosecutor, who had the sole responsibility of the presentation of the case, had the right, after the judgment was entered, to make a request that the judgment be amended to include a finding in the Katyn case?

Dr. KEMPNER. I think every power, every prosecutor, had the right to ask for some motion of error or some motion to amend the judgment.

Mr. MACHROWICZ. Do you not know, as a matter of fact, that there were instances during the Nuremberg trial when the prosecutor did make such a request whenever he felt that the court failed to make a ruling on a material matter?

Dr. KEMPNER. I do not know exactly whether we did, but I know exactly that in two Nuremberg trials later the defense did it, with success, in two cases.

Mr. MACHROWICZ. So that the Russian representative, then, did have that power, in your opinion?

Dr. KEMPNER. Despite the fact that these judgments were, so to speak, final, you always could make motions to the same court.

Mr. MACHROWICZ. And isn't it true also that there were instances in the Nuremberg trial when one representative of the tribunal, who felt not in accord with the majority opinion, did express his own minority opinion? Is that correct?

Dr. KEMPNER. That happened, and, in fact, in the first Nuremberg trial the Russians filed a dissenting opinion because they were not satisfied with the acquittal of Schacht and von Papen and, I think, Fritsche. And they were also not satisfied, I think, with the life sentence for Hess. I think they wanted something else.

Mr. Machrowicz. And in this case the failure of the Russian member of the tribunal to file a dissenting or minority opinion must be construed as constituting his agreement to the failure of the tribunal to determine guilt in the Katyn case? Am I correct?

Dr. Kempner. I don't care to interpret the Russian sphinx and Mr. Nikitchenko, what he thought at that time, why he did or why he did not, but he just did not, and they filed a dissenting opinion of 11 or 12, or of more than 12, printed pages on other issues.

Mr. Machrowicz. But you do state that, despite the fact that the Russian member of the tribunal could have filed a minority opinion in this instance, he filed no dissenting opinion?

Dr. Kempner. Yes, Your Honor, I do.

Mr. Flood. Now, counselor, I want to ask you a question. It will call for a combinaiton, perhaps, of fact and of opinion for you to answer. You don't have to answer anything if you don't want to.

When I arrived in Bremerhaven I went to Bremen and I met with the German press. Later on I met with the German press at Bonn, and the international press at Bonn, and I told the press as that time that one of the things that the American Congress was interested in, and one of the things that this Commission was going to try and inquire into, was whether or not there was any collusion between any members of the American staff and the Russians for the purpose of ignoring or dropping or failing to prosecute the Katyn indictment.

Now, as far as your official connection or capacity permitted, from your observations and experience, are you aware of any such conspiracy or attempt to collude between anybody on the American side and anybody on the Russian side, or anybody else, to ignore, to brush off, or to quash or to dispose of the Katyn indictment?

Dr. Kempner. Not the slightest, and, in fact, we admired Mr. Stahmer at that time because this was one of the few scores he really made for Goering, that the Russians more or less dropped the Katyn matter.

Mr. Flood. Was the atmosphere or the attitude among the attachés of the court such that it could be construed as a victory for Stahmer insofar as that court was concerned?

Dr. Kempner. So far as I am concerned, absolutely, and I think there were several people of the American prosecution who expressed this to Mr. Stahmer, and to other people. And, if I remember very well, I myself said to old Goering—something which I cannot translate very well into English.

Mr. Machrowicz. May I state for the record that because of an appointment that the Chairman and I have, to leave for Berlin, we will have to leave the hearing at this time, and I hope the witness does not construe our departure as taking away from his testimony at all, which I considered very informative and very important to hear.

Mr. Flood. Now, as one trial lawyer to another, I want you to express an opinion. You don't have to if you don't want to.

Wouldn't you say that the failure of the Russian prosecution to argue the Katyn matter in the closing argument, and the failure of the Russians to pursue the Katyn matter further, in view of their peculiar position as a member of the tribunal, is about as clear a confession of guilt of the Katyn matter as it would be possible to imagine?

Dr. KEMPNER. At that time, in 1945, Katyn was no issue for my point. I was not acquainted with all these things too well. However, after I have studied it again—and I am writing some history on the Nurnberg trials—I would say at least it looked mighty funny.

Mr. DONDERO. I want to say that it is to be regretted that the court did not dispose of this case at the time they had it before them.

Mr. FLOOD. Your name appeared in the German press here in connection with these hearings. What is the nature of your appearance here, voluntary or otherwise?

Dr. KEMPNER. It is absolutely voluntary.

Chairman MADDEN. Congressman O'Konski.

Mr. O'KONSKI. I have a question.

At no time during the Nurnberg trials when the Katyn matter came up were the Polish people or the Polish Government-in-exile consulted, were they?

Dr. KEMPNER. I don't know; I never met them.

Mr. O'KONSKI. There was a Polish white book that was published, and it was presented to the American delegation at the Nurnberg trials, the French, and the English. Now, under the rules of procedure, there was no way in which the Americans could have presented that document because it was a Russian case, was it not?

Mr. KEMPNER. Yes; that is correct.

Mr. O'KONSKI. You didn't, at any time, see the Polish white book that was gotten out, establishing what they thought as to who was guilty for the masacre at Katyn?

Dr. KEMPNER. No; I have never seen any white book.

Mr. DONDERO. One question more.

Did you have before you, as assistant prosecutor, a book consisting of some 400 pages entitled, "Facts and Documents Concerning Polish Prisoners of War Captured by the USSR in the 1939 Campaign"?

Dr. KEMPNER. I have never seen it.

Dr Otto Stahmer

Defence counsel for Reichsmarshal Goering in 1945.

Mr. FLOOD. You are a member of the German bar?

Dr. STAHMER. Yes, I am.

Mr. FLOOD. For how long have you been engaged in the practice of law in Germany?

Dr. STAHMER. Since March 1907, with the Oberlandesgericht, Kiel.

Mr. FLOOD. Have you ever been identified with a German bar association or confederation of lawyers?

Dr. STAHMER. No, immediately after having finished my training I became an attorney at law.

Mr. FLOOD. Were you ever an official of the German Bar Association or an association of German lawyers?

Dr. STAHMER. After 1945 I was appointed by the British Occupation Power to the Bar Association in Schleswig-Holstein. In October 1945, I was elected to the chairmanship, and later on became the president of the Bar Association, and left it again in 1947, owing to pressure of work.

Mr. FLOOD. Now, I direct your attention, doctor, to the Nuremberg trials and ask you whether or not you were ever identified with those proceedings?

Dr. STAHMER. I was defense counsel for the former Reichsmarshal Goering at the war crimes trials at Nuremberg.

Mr. FLOOD. Will you tell us in what way you came to be identified with the defense of Goering?

Dr. STAHMER. Yes, I can.

The various bar associations called for attorneys who would be prepared to act as defense counsel in Nuremberg, prior to the opening of the trial. The Oberlandesgericht president of Kiel, in Schleswig-Holstein, made a list of the men willing to act as defense counsel. Five names were suggested, and I was one of them. This list was forwarded to Nuremberg and, from all the lists collected from the various districts, an ultimate list, or an accumulated list, was established. This list was submitted to the accused, and they were authorized to select defense counsel from this list. Goering selected me from the list, and he told me later that I had been recommended to him by the Reichsgerichtent-fuehrer; that was the leader of the Reich legal men, Frank.

Before that I had no contacts with Goering.

Mr. FLOOD. Now, doctor, we are concerned with that part of the Goering indictment or the Nuremberg proceedings that have to do only with the Katyn massacre. I am sure you are entirely capable of presenting that story to us without my interrupting with questions. I will try not to, unless there is some particular thing that we happen to think of.

Therefore, will you take us from the beginning to the end of that part of the Nuremberg proceedings that had to do with Katyn?

Dr. STAHMER. As Dr. Kempner pointed out, quite correctly, the charge in Nuremberg contained a short sentence, running as follows: "In the Katyn forest 11,000 Polish officers were murdered in September 1941."

Mr. FLOOD. May I interrupt, for the record, and read you the exact language, so you may begin? I quote from the statement of Dr. Stahmer on page 274 of the International Military Tribunal Trial of the Major War Criminals, volume 17: "In September 1941, 11,000 Polish officers, prisoners of war, were killed in the Katyn woods near Smolensk."

Dr. STAHMER. Yes, that is correct. As it was, here, a question of prisoners of war, it could safely be assumed that the crime could only have been perpetrated by German troops. I discussed this matter with Goering and asked him whether the German Army could possibly have had anything to do with this matter. Goering declared to me, being his defense counsel, that he could state with a clean conscience that the German Army was not responsible for this crime. I thereupon told him that in that case it was our duty to deal with this matter in detail for the sake of the honor of the German Wehrmacht.

I suggested that I would take up this matter in connection with his, Goering's, own case, being defense counsel for Goering, and in view of the fact that Goering was the highest ranking officer in the German Army there. Goering agreed, and thus I engaged in this matter.

Mr. FLOOD. Now, may I interrupt for the procedural problem again?

As I understand it, the Katyn charge brought by the Russians was not brought against any specific defendant.

Dr. STAHMER. No. That is correct. The accusation did not contain any more than the sentence which was read out a few minutes ago, and I could only get a little further in this matter when, as Dr. Kempner correctly pointed out previously, the Russians submitted the document U. S. S. R. 54 on April 14, 1946.

I established the following facts from this document:

A construction battalion of engineers with the number 537 was mentioned in this accusation. The document also mentioned that this battalion was under the command of a certain Colonel Arnes. The document also mentioned the names of three officers: First Lieutenant Rex, First Lieutenant Holdt, and Lt. Graf Berg.

I got hold of these three names and established and proved that they could not possibly have perpetrated the crime. The news of this evidence was published over the radio. It was also heard by Lieutenant Arnes, who actually was Colonel Ahrens.

A few days after that Colonel Ahrens came to see me and offered to testify as a witness, and with his assistance I succeeded in bringing some more light into the matter. In the meantime, a 1st lieutenant von Eichborn had also reported to me, and these two gentlemen also brought me into contact with General Oberhaeuser.

The situation now developed as follows:

Colonel Ahrens stated that he had arrived in the area of Katyn in November 1941 and had taken command of Signal Regiment 537. The former designation of Engineer's Construction Battalion was incorrect; it was actually Signal Regiment No. 537. I learned from him, too, that immediately upon the occupation of Smolensk, in July of 1941, a small advance unit had been in that area near Katyn, and at the beginning of August of the same year the regimental staff headquarters had been established in the Dnieper Castle. The commander of the regiment and in that regimental staff at that time was Colonel Bedenk, who, as I said before, was succeeded by Colonel Ahrens in November 1941.

That, in brief, was the material which I had at my disposal for proving my case. My aim was to prove to the Nuremberg Tribunal that the German Wehrmacht was not responsible for this crime. The Russians were not accused, and therefore I had neither the task nor the duty to clear up the matter.

At first the court allowed me to call the five witnesses which I had named before. It was then suggested that in view of the fact that the case was a comparatively simple one, the number of witnesses should be reduced to three. The selection of the witnesses was left to the defense counsel or to the prosecution.

In this connection I should like to mention the following incident. One day the secretary general of the court telephoned me and asked whether I was prepared to discuss the Katyn matter with the Russian prosecution. I said that I was prepared to do so, but requested in view of the fact that although it did not concern all the defense counsel it still did concern a large number of them, I requested Professor Exner, who was a defense counsel for General Jodl, to accompany me. The two of us met Colonel Prochownik. Colonel Prochownik pointed out that a few days before the chairman, Lord Lawrence, had requested that the proceedings be made shorter if possible. He was of the opinion that we could shorten the proceedings by not hearing the witness, or by submitting affidavits instead of having the witnesses testify, with the request that the court should take official knowledge of these affidavits.

I refused this suggestion, and Professor Exner did likewise, for the result of such an action would have been that the documents would have been submitted without the public getting to know anything about their contents.

I gave my response for refusing by pointing out that the Russian prosecution had accused the German Wehrmacht publicly of having murdered eleven thousand prisoners of war, and for the sake of the honor of the German Wehrmacht I thought it imperative that the public should be informed in the same way, that this accusation was without foundation.

This suggestion of mine was rejected. Colonel Prochownik said that such a procedure would again take a much longer time. I had declared that, provided the other German defense counsel would agree, I would agree to have affidavits submitted, but only on condition that they should be read out during the proceedings. I forgot to mention that previously. That was for the reason that it would take more time again, and that the Lord Justice's wishes would not be fulfilled that way, of shortening the proceedings.

A further suggestion of mine, to limit the proceedings to a certain time, was also rejected. This was the contents of our discussion, which was also mentioned by Dr. Kempner, although I do not believe that Dr. Kempner had knowledge of what was said during those discussions.

The chairman then declared that, in view of the fact that no agreement had been reached, the suggestion that both sides should only call three witnesses each should be adhered to.

My witnesses were Colonel Ahrens, General Oberhaeuser, and First Lieutenant von Eichborn.

The Russians proposed the former Buergermeister of Smolensk, who was Buergermeister while Smolensk was occupied by the Germans. I forget the name at present, but it is in the documents, in the protocol. Then, a Bulgarian professor, Dr. Markov. Professor Markov had been a member of the commission which had gone to Smolensk and Katyn, on the instigation of the Germans, and had given expert evidence on the probable time, gathered from the state of the decayed bodies, or the condition of the dead bodies, when the crime had been promulgated.

The evidence and the results of this investigation were laid down in the German official white book. Professor Markov had, by then, been captured by the Russians, and that was how he got to Nuremberg as a witness. I cannot say exactly whether he was still a prisoner at that time.

The third witness produced by the Russians was a professor of anatomy who had been working there in Smolensk after the Germans had evacuated. The Russians, after Smolensk and Katyn had been evacuated by the Germans, had hauled a commission of physicians, which had to work on the same lines as the previous commissions under the Germans had been working. This Russian commission arrived at a different result, to the effect that the murder had been committed in September 1941, that is, at the time when the area was already under German occupation.

As I established by cross-examining during the proceedings, this Russian commission consisted exclusively of Russian physicians, no neutrals or members of the Allied nations taking part in it. The result was as laid down by me in my arguments. From the testimony of the witnesses Ahrens, Oberhaeuser, and von Eichborn, I had my opinion proved clearly that the crime could not possibly have been perpetrated by the German Wehrmacht.

It was already stated that the Russians, in their final argument, which took place after the arguments of the Germans had been given, did not refer to the Katyn case with a single word.

That was generally how this case was handled in Nuremberg.

Mr. FLOOD. Did the tribunal, in its findings, refer to the Katyn matter?

Dr. STAHMER. No.

Mr. FLOOD. Do you know of any reason, as a matter of fact, that they did not?

Dr. STAHMER. No; of course, I do not know them.

We must, however, not forget that a large number of crimes were put to the debit of the Germans which were also not dealt with in the finals, even if they were not dealt with in such detail.

Mr. FLOOD. Were you satisfied, as far as you were concerned, that the tribunal did not mention the Katyn matter one way or the other?

Dr. STAHMER. Yes; it is so.

Mr. FLOOD. As counsel for the defense and defending an indictment, you were satisfied that the whole matter was dropped, as far as that detail was concerned; is that right?

Dr. STAHMER. It had been dropped because the Russians had simply not referred to it any more. But it was not so, either, as it should have been in accordance with German law, that the accusation had also been dropped.

Mr. FLOOD. This conference that you spoke about, at which the submission of affidavits was discussed with the Russians, that conference, as I understand it, was called at the request of the Russians.

Dr. STAHMER. Yes. General Mitchell had actually asked me whether I would be prepared to confer with the Russians so as to shorten the proceedings. I was of the opinion that the Russian prosecution had approached General Mitchell with a request to arrange such a conference.

Mr. FLOOD. The Americans did not take part in that conference, did they?

Dr. STAHMER. No. The only ones were the Russian, myself, and Professor Exner.

Mr. FLOOD. And during your entire handling of the Katyn matter with the Russians, the matter was handled only between you and the Russians and the court; is that correct?

Dr. STAHMER. Yes, that is so.

Mr. FLOOD. Your three witnesses for the German side were presented in open court and the testimony was fully developed?

Dr. STAHMER. Yes; that is correct.

Mr. FLOOD. Were you satisfied with the presentation of your case and did you consider that you had an ample opportunity to present the German side?

Dr. STAHMER. Yes. It was like that, that there was one gap for me. That was a gap of time between July and November 1941, before Colonel Ahrens took over the command of the regiment. But the reason for that was that I did not know the address of First Lieutenant Hodt and, as far as I recollect, was also unable to contact Colonel Bedenk.

Mr. FLOOD. And the Russians had an opportunity to present the same number of witnesses, that is, three, that the German side did?

Dr. Stahmer. Yes. The court had distributed the witnesses on an equal basis.

Mr. Flood. And the Russians did present their three witnesses?

Dr. Stamhiner. Yes, they did so.

Mr. Flood. And the Russians had an opportunity to cross-examine the German witnesses?

Dr. Stahmer. They did have the opportunity, and they availed themselves of the opportunity.

Mr. Flood. And the Germans had the opportunity and availed themselves of the opportunity of cross-examining the Russian witnesses?

Dr. Stahmer. Yes. I did cross-examine the Russian witnesses. There was a certain restriction imposed on that, because some German defending counsels wanted to cross-examine the witnesses and were only allowed to do so in case their witnesses had actually been connected with a specific case.

Mr. Flood. And the eminent counsel for Goering made an eloquent and persuasive argument to the tribunal?

Dr. Stahmer. Yes, I did so.

Mr. Flood. With reference to the Katyn matter.

Dr. Stahmer. Yes.

Mr. Flood. And the Russians, in closing to the tribunal, never mentioned the Katyn matter?

Dr. Stahmer. That is correct; because they gave their final argument after me.

Mr. Flood. And the result was that you had, insofar as the Katyn indictment was concerned, a victory as against the Russian charge?

Dr. Stahmer. In my opinion, I had fulfilled my task of proving that the Germans were not the perpetrators of the crime.

Mr. Flood. You were not concerned with trying to find out who was?

Dr. Stahmer. I believe that the court would have objected to that, in view of the fact that the Russians were not the accused. We had this experience on several occasions, when we ventured to point out that the other side had also occasionally sinned, that it was immediately pointed out to us that the other side was not sitting on the bench of the accused.

Mr. Flood. And, of course, the doctor knows, as a distinguished trial lawyer, that when you are trying an indictment, in which A is indicted, you cannot convict B who was not indicted?

Dr. Stahmer. The Russians had not charged anyone else.

Mr. Flood. Doctor, when I arrived in Germany for this committee, I spoke to the German press at Bremen. I subsequently spoke to the German and international press at Bonn. Among other things, I stated that this committee felt that it had been charged by the American House of Representatives to find out whether or not any of the Americans participating in the Nurenberg trials, or anybody else, for that matter, were engaged in any consipracy with the Russians or anybody else to drop or not to prosecute this Katyn indictment.

Dr. Stahmer. I think that impossible.

Mr. Flood. Will you state, then, whether or not, in your opinion, any of the Americans, as far as you know, were so engaged?

Dr. Stahmer. No. I could not even imagine how that could have been done, in view of the fact that I was not at all restricted or hampered in my defense. The only thing I was actually interested in was to prove that the German Army and the German officers who had been accused were not guilty.

That I was successful in that respect is proved to me by the fact that the Russians never again leveled this accusation and left the officers which they had mentioned in their allegation out of it altogether later on. Otherwise, the Russians were very prolific in accusing everybody and anybody. In my opinion, the Russians would never have dropped the case and would have pursued it with all energy if there had only been a shadow of tagging the thing onto the Germans.

Mr. FLOOD. As a matter of fact, in the early part of your statement, you told us that the Katyn case had been brought as a charge by the Russians.

Dr. STAHMER. That is not quite correct. At first, in this document, the accusation was a general one. A more detailed description and explanation was added to it later on.

Mr. FLOOD. That's exactly what I want to say and the additional documentation and additional detail consisted entirely of a document which was the official report of the Extraordinary State Commission which was officially authorized by the Russians to investigate the Katyn case; isn't that it?

Dr. STAHMER. Yes; that is correct. The Russians said, as already pointed out by Dr. Kempner, that they had another 120 witnesses, but they did not produce an eyewitness.

Mr. FLOOD. As a matter of fact, as a practical trial lawyer, what really happened was that the Russians were pretty good trial lawyers themselves in that case, they had pretty good lawyers there, didn't they?

Dr. STAHMER. I should rather say that they were slightly unlucky in their choice of witnesses.

Mr. FLOOD. As a matter of fact, as good lawyers, the Russian prosecution knew they had no case on the Katyn indictment, and that's why they dropped the whole matter; isn't it?

Dr. STAHMER. I do not know that.

Mr. FLOOD. Any other questions?

Mr. DONDERO. Congressman Flood has stated on the record what he understands to be the purpose of this committee. The resolution passed by the House of Representatives of the United States Congress is the best evidence of our authority here in Europe, and that resolution authorizes this committee to collect the evidence, make an investigation of the Katyn massacre, and report back to the Congress of the United States. Justice delayed is justice denied, and had the court at Nuremberg disposed of this case, we would not be here today.

Mr. FLOOD. Mr. O'Konski.

Mr. O'KONSKI. Doctor, do I understand that the indictment on Katyn was part of a general indictment?

Dr. STAHMER. Yes; that is correct.

Mr. O'KONSKI. Could the Russian prosecution, under the procedure under which you were operating, have asked that that part of the indictment regarding Katyn be dismissed?

Dr. STAHMER. No; I do not think so.

Mr. O'Konski. Could the defense have asked that that part of the indictment pertaining to Katyn be dropped from the general charge?

Dr. Stahmer. No; not that either.

Mr. O'Konski. After these three witnesses were called on each side and you gave your closing argument, did the Russians ask that the charge be dismissed?

Dr. Stahmer. No; they did not.

Mr. O'Konski. Now, when the decision was handed down by the Tribunal, that is, the court at Nuremberg, was the decision based on the entire indictment or did they leave some parts of the indictment out in their findings?

Dr. Stahmer. The entire indictment.

Mr. O'Konski. Is it reasonably safe to assume then that the Russians assumed that the world would assume that, since it was a part of the indictment, and since it was not stricken from the indictment, and the decision was handed down on the whole indictment, was it possible for the Russians to assume that the world would think that that was one of the crimes of which the Germans were guilty?

Dr. Stahmer. I do not know what to reply to that question.

Mr. O'Konski. It would seem to me, as an observer, not being schooled in law, that if the general indictment contained a clause indicating the crimes at Katyn, and if that part of the indictment was never dropped, and a decision was handed down on the entire indictment, that I, as a layman, would draw the conclusion that the Germans were guilty and that was one of the crimes for which they were convicted.

Mr. Dondero. Well, Dr. Stahmer, no decision was ever reached by the court.

Dr. Stahmer. No, it was never reached.

Mr. O'Konski. That's all.

Mr. Flood. Is there anything further you would care to say, Doctor?

Dr. Stahmer. No.

Mr. Flood. I can say that the committee appreciates very much the time and the patience you have taken in coming to us and helping us with your testimony. Thank you very much.

You might like to know that for tomorrow morning the witnesses, I am advised, will be a Herr Genshow, president of the Genshow Ammunition Co., which was the company that manufactured the ammunition found in the graves at Katyn.

The second witness is a Mr. Christer Jaederlunt, a distinguished Swedish newspaperman who was a member of the international commission of journalists that visited Katyn.

The third witness is a Mr. Rudi Kramer, who is listed as a staff director of Frankfurt, Germany, and who was identified with one of the propaganda units at Smolensk.

One of the opened mass graves with examination trestles in the background.

Christer Jaederlunt
He wrote an account of the Katyn case for his newspaper
Stockholm Tidingen published on Sunday 18 April 1943.

Mr. FLOOD. What is your occupation at the present time?

Mr. JAEDERLUNT. Journalist and representative of the Swedish newspaper, the Stockholm Tidningen.

Mr. FLOOD. Where were you born?

Mr. JAEDERLUNT. Viby, Sweden.

Mr. FLOOD. Are you still a native of Sweden, a Swedish citizen?

Mr. JAEDERLUNT. Yes; I am.

Mr. FLOOD. When did you first come to Germany, representing your paper?

Mr. JAEDERLUNT. 1928.

Mr. FLOOD. What is the name of the paper?

Mr. JAEDERLUNT. The Stockholm Tidningen.

Mr. FLOOD. Did you represent that paper in April 1943?

Mr. JAEDERLUNT. Yes; I did.

Mr. FLOOD. I now show you documents marked for identification as exhibits 82 and 83 which are photostat reproductions of articles from the paper you say you represented in 1943. Are they? Is that correct?

Mr. JAEDERLUNT. That is correct.

Mr. FLOOD. You wrote the stories that are reproduced in those papers?

Mr. JAEDERLUNT. Yes; I did.

Mr. FLOOD. What is the date of the paper and the title of the story dealing with Katyn?

Mr. JAEDERLUNT. The date of the newspaper is Sunday, April 18, 1943, and the article was written on the previous day. "Berlin welcomes the corps of the Polish Red Cross about the Katyn case."

Mr. FLOOD. Were you in Berlin on that day?

Mr. JAEDERLUNT. Yes; I was.

Mr. FLOOD. That information came to you as a result of your investigations as a Swedish newspaperman in Berlin on that day?

Mr. JAEDERLUNT. Does the question apply to the heading of the article or to the contents?

Mr. FLOOD. The whole story.

Mr. JAEDERLUNT. The heading is from official information on which I received. The contents of the article are based on my personal experiences and investigations in Katyn.

Mr. FLOOD. What was the attitude of the then German Government toward the request of the London Polish Government to the International Red Cross to intervene in the Katyn matter?

Mr. JAEDERLUNT. The then German Government welcomed this request.

Mr. FLOOD. Do you know whether or not the then German Government made a request of a similar nature to the International Red Cross?

Mr. JAEDERLUNT. Yes; the then German Government also submitted a request to the International Red Cross.

Mr. FLOOD. Do you know whether or not the International Red Cross replied to the requests of the London Polish Government and the then German Government?

Mr. JAEDERLUNT. From articles in the German press and from German authorities I heard that the International Red Cross was unable to take part in the investigations because the Russians were not able to take part in them.

Mr. FLOOD. Did you go to Smolensk?

Mr. JAEDERLUNT. Yes; I did.

Mr. FLOOD. Now, suppose, in your own words, you just take us on your journey from the moment you left Berlin to Smolensk, describe to us what you saw at the graves at Katyn, and, in general, give us the details of the story that appeared under the byline in the Swedish paper from Berlin on April 17, 1943.

Mr. JAEDERLUNT. May I use some notes to refresh my memory?

Mr. FLOOD. Are those your own notes?

Mr. JAEDERLUNT. Yes; they are written by myself on my own typewriter.

Mr. FLOOD. There is no objection to the witness referring to notes made by himself for the purpose of refreshing his memory.

Mr. JAEDERLUNT. I belonged to the first group of journalists which went to Katyn after the discovery of the mass graves. This happened approximately in the second week of April 1943. I do not recollect the exact date, but it could be ascertained, if necessary. In the preceding weeks I had been to the so-called Atlantic defense wall on the French coast. On the day when I returned to Berlin from France, I received a telephone call and was asked whether I was prepared to go to Russia the next morning.

Mr. FLOOD. Telephone call from whom?

Mr. JAEDERLUNT. From the Ministry of Propaganda in Berlin.

Mr. FLOOD. The German Ministry?

Mr. JAEDERLUNT. Yes, the German Ministry of Propaganda.

The reason for the journey to Russia was not disclosed, and the head of this expedition was, as far as I recollect, a German officer from the German supreme command. Not before we arrived in Smolensk the next night did the officer who accompanied us give us the reason for this journey, to be the effect that mass graves had been found. Whereupon, we journalists looked at each other with long faces and all agreed that if we had known that beforehand we would never have gone there.

Mr. FLOOD. When you speak of journalists, who do you mean? Do you recall some of them, their papers, their nationalities?

Mr. JAEDERLUNT. I have been trying to recollect the names of the others and who they were, but I can only remember one of them, a journalist from Yugoslavia by the name of Milan Micasinovitch, and I remember him better than the others because he was able to speak Russian and, thus, he was rather helpful to all of us.

Mr. FLOOD. Were there other journalists from various countries?

Mr. JAEDERLUNT. Yes, they had been selected from neutral countries.

Mr. FLOOD. About how many?

Mr. JAEDERLUNT. Approximately 5 or 6. I do not recollect the exact number.

Mr. FLOOD. Very well.

Mr. JAEDERLUNT. The next day we were taken by car to Krasny-Bor and to the forest and were shown the mass graves. In a large pit, we saw dead bodies, clad in uniforms, lying in several layers. They were sticking together like leaves. Certain dead bodies were taken out of the pit in our presence and examined. They were in a good state of preservation, probably owing to the nature of the soil—so to speak, half-mummified.

Professor Buhtz, director of the Criminological Institute and Institute for Judicial Medicine in Breslau was in charge of the exhumations. He requested us to select the dead bodies we wished to see personally and those that we wanted to see ourselves. We did so, and I was able to establish that the dead bodies had not been touched before or perhaps brought there from some place else.

The young Russians working in the pit had trouble in getting the dead bodies out because they stuck together so tightly. It happened at times that they only managed to extract a head alone.

The documents and papers found in the pockets of the clothes of the dead bodies were also well preserved. Only part of them showed traces of decay.

354

Mr. FLOOD. Do I understand that when these Russian workers were removing the bodies that in some cases the bodies came apart when they were trying to pull them out?

Mr. JAEDERLUNT. No. I said that now and again a head came off of the bodies, because they were sticking so closely. Many bodies just formed big lumps.

I read through a great number of letters, documents, pay books, diaries, and so forth, and I could also make out that many of these papers carried stamps of a Russian prisoner-of-war camp, and that no entry in diaries or pocketbooks bore a later date than April 20, 1940. I also established that the dead bodies I saw all came from the prisoner-of-war camp Kozielsk.

The dead bodies were lying in the grave in tightly packed layers. Many of them had their hands tied behind their backs and their mouths were filled with sawdust and they all showed the typical shots in the neck, and it was quite easy to gather an idea of how these mass executions had taken place.

Mr. FLOOD. We are interested in this business of sawdust in the mouths. Did you see any of the skulls or the open mouths of bodies with sawdust in them yourself? Did you actually see that?

Mr. JAEDERLUNT. Yes; there was a great number of dead bodies which had been taken out where I saw this sawdust. Some of the dead bodies had already been taken out the previous day, but we also selected a large number of dead bodies in the pits and had them taken out.

Mr. FLOOD. Now, on those bodies that you yourself selected and had removed from the pit in your presence, did you see unmistakable evidence of sawdust in the mouths of any of those bodies?

Mr. JAEDERLUNT. At least in once instance.

Mr. FLOOD. Did that body have the hands tied behind the back?

Mr. JAEDERLUNT. I do not recollect whether this particular body had its hands tied behind its back, but, in several cases, I recollect bodies which had sawdust in their mouths and the hands tied behind their backs, as we presumed, for the reason that they had been resisting prior to being shot.

Mr. FLOOD. The purpose for our interest is that this committee heard testimony taken in Washington by an eyewitness to this shooting who claims that he saw officers with their hands tied behind their backs, and NKVD soldiers or officers forcing open their mouths and forcing sawdust into the mouths and pushing them into the graves.

Did you notice any bodies with the hands tied behind their backs that may have been tied with wire?

Mr. JAEDERLUNT. What kind of wire?

Mr. FLOOD. Any kind of wire.

Mr. JAEDERLUNT. Yes; several dead bodies were pointed out to us whose hands were tied with wire.

Mr. FLOOD. On the other bodies with their hands tied behind their backs, what was used to tie the hands in some of the other cases?

Mr. JAEDERLUNT. Ordinary hemp rope.

Mr. FLOOD. Will you demonstrate on the interpreter two things: First, how the hands were tied behind the back, and, secondly, the point of entry and the point of exit, as you remember, of any bullet wounds you saw in the skulls?

Mr. Jaederlunt. It is rather difficult for me because I am a layman and not a physician.

Mr. Flood. All I want you to do is point how, if you remember, where in the back of the head the bullet went in and, if he remembers, where it came out.

Just show on the back of the head of the interpreter where you remember the bullet entered.

Mr. Jaederlunt. Here [indicating].

Mr. Flood. And where it came out—in the front some place?

Mr. Jaederlunt. I do not recollect.

Mr. Flood. Will you indicate how the hands were tied behind the back?

Mr. Jaederlunt. I do not quite recollect where they were lower down or higher up [indicating].

Mr. Flood. Where did you see these documents that you described?

Mr. Jaederlunt. Part of them was located in a wooden barracks that had been erected near the graves, where the documents of the previous day had been collected, and part of the documents came from the pockets of the clothes of the dead bodies which we had taken out of the pits.

Mr. Flood. You had seen these documents of various kinds removed from the bodies you selected, and the documents were removed in your presence?

Mr. Jaederlunt. Yes, I did.

Mr. Flood. And it was from those documents that you concluded the latest date was April 1940?

Mr. Jaederlunt. Yes; that is corerct.

Mr. Flood. That wasn't from a lot of documents the Germans handed to you from some place else?

Mr. Jaederlunt. No. We were the first, actually, to see these documents, immediately after they had been taken out of the pockets of the bodies.

Mr. Flood. What story did you hear, and from whom did you get it, as to how the Germans first discovered the graves?

Mr. Jaederlunt. I was told the story as follows: Two Poles had been walking past this forest of Katyn——

Mr. Flood (interposing). Who told you the story?

Mr. Jaederlunt. I do not recollect, but I recollect that we questioned a few Russians later on and they confirmed it to us. We had the opportunity of staying in Smolensk and Katyn for several days because, at that time, no plane was available to take us back at once.

Mr. Flood. Were these Russians you talked to Russians from the area of Katyn and Smolensk?

Mr. Jaederlunt. Yes; that is so, and one of them related to us as I shall say now: Two Poles were walking along there in that area and, as the Poles usually did, asked the local people about other Poles.

Mr. Flood. What were Poles doing wandering around that area then?

Mr. Jaederlunt. Probably some workers enlisted by the Germans.

So, one of these Poles asked one of the Russian inhabitants of that region whether he knew anything about Poles having been in this region, and the Russian said: "Yes, in Krasny-Bor, some Poles are buried." And one of the Poles took a spade and went to the spot that had been indicated to him by this Russian. He began digging

356

and discovered some dead bodies wearing Polish uniforms. He then closed up the hole again, secured two pieces of timber and made a rough cross over that and, as the Russian said, literally, he cursed and wept, and then he walked away. After this incident, I was told that it took quite some time before these rumors started spreading and getting to the ears of the Germans. Whereupon, the Germans decided to start digging in the area and to investigate this matter.

Mr. FLOOD. What were the uniforms on the bodies that you saw at Katyn, if you know?

Mr. JAEDERLUNT. Do you mean any distinct nationality?

Mr. FLOOD. Yes.

Mr. JAEDERLUNT. Polish.

Mr. FLOOD. How do you know?

Mr. JAEDERLUNT. I had been in Poland previously and knew Polish uniforms.

Mr. FLOOD. Did you see or hear of any female bodies being found in the graves at Katyn?

Mr. JAEDERLUNT. Personally, I did not see any, but I was told there that one or two had been dug up.

Mr. FLOOD. Did you hear whether or not one of the female bodies found at Katyn was in the uniform of a Polish aviatrix, female?

Mr. JAEDERLUNT. No, never.

Mr. FLOOD. Did you see or hear that the bodies of any chaplains or clergymen of various denominations were found in the graves at Katyn?

Mr. JAEDERLUNT. I do not recollect that, but I wish to point out that I was in Katyn at a very early date when not many bodies had yet been brought up from the pits.

Mr. FLOOD. About how many had been brought up?

Mr. JAEDERLUNT. I do not recollect the number. A fair number.

Mr. FLOOD. What was the day, if you recall, that you got to Katyn?

Mr. JAEDERLUNT. As far as I recollect, but I am not sure that I am right, it might have been around about the 10th of April. It is easy to get the exact date from the authorities, because it was the first commission of journalists that went there.

Mr. FLOOD. Now, the newspaper story that you printed in the Swedish paper was dated, I believe, the 17th of April.

Mr. JAEDERLUNT. The report bears the date of the 17th of April, but prior to that we had spent several days in Berlin and several days in Smolensk.

Mr. FLOOD. As a matter of fact, the newspaper article dated on the 17th of April 1943 describes your experiences at Smolensk and Katyn.

Mr. JAEDERLUNT. Yes, that is so.

Mr. FLOOD. And, in view of the fact that the official German announcement of the discovery of the graves at Katyn did not occur until the 15th of April, then you actually were there even before the official announcement was made?

Mr. JAEDERLUNT. Yes, that is so. That is quite correct, and I have the impression that the then German Government wanted one of us neutrals to see and confirm the matter before making it known to the public at large, but, as I was told by my newspaper a few days ago, the editors of my paper kept back my articles for some time in order to wait until the Germans would publish something about the matter themselves.

Mr. FLOOD. Did the Germans in any way interfere with your examinations or observations at Smolensk or Katyn?

Mr. JAEDERLUNT. No, on the contrary, and I am in a position to give you some more details about that.

Mr. FLOOD. Please.

Mr. JAEDERLUNT. I walked about the whole Katyn Forest by myself and without any escort, and owing to the fact that we were unable to get a plane from Berlin to go back for several days, we spent several days at Smolensk and went out for walks over the area, either alone or two or three of us, without any German escort, and the captain of the propaganda company in that area actually lent me a horse and I rode about in the whole area without ever being hampered or hindered by anyone. I came across a good many soldiers standing at guard duty at crossroads and other points, but whenever I addressed them and asked them to direct me, they merely answered in Russian: "I do not understand." They were Russians doing service in the German Army. The local population was distinctly friendly and we went into their houses on various occasions and they were always very friendly and invited us to share their meals and to share the little they had at that time, and among ourselves we talked and said: "Well, in view of the fact that we have this opportunity of moving around for ourselves, let's do it and find out as much as possible for ourselves." That was before we saw the graves and we were skeptical because we thought it was merely a propaganda story and we wanted to find out as much as possible for ourselves. The population was fairly open hearted in talking to us and one day I asked a Russian worker what he thought their future would be, and the worker said: "Well, what we think, I and my fellow countrymen here, is that there is practically no difference between the Bolsheviks and the Nazis and we don't like either of them." He also said that it was their hope that the Bolsheviks and the Nazis would finish each other in this war, and he concluded by saying that in the end, after the Bolsheviks and Nazis had been finished, they hoped that the British would come with lots of money and that the social democratic party would then be supreme in Russia.

I related this in order to show that the Russian population was not in any way against foreigners and talking to them, and they were not exactly afraid of talking to us. That was not my impression, if you approached them in the right manner.

Mr. FLOOD. In your conversations with any of the Russian natives of the area did you inquire of them or did they volunteer any information about any shootings in the Katyn area, cries and disturbances and, if they did, when did those things take place?

Mr. JAEDERLUNT. Such statements came about the first time when the Germans called for witnesses on the day we went to the graves. These witnesses were called in from their houses and one of them, who lived very close to the forest, stated that he had seen transports of prisoners of war being brought in about April 1940, and possibly, as far as I recollect, he might also have mentioned May 1940. He also stated that the local population at that time had been strictly forbidden to approach the forest, but he lived so near the forest that he couldn't help passing very near the forest occasionally, and he had actually heard shootings and screams and shouts and he never noticed any prisoners of war coming out of the forest again, and several of these local peasants told the same story and they were very eager in telling it and did not give any impression of having been coerced or worked on in any way.

Mr. FLOOD. Did they mention anything about any GPU or any NKVD Russians in the area at the time these things took place?

Mr. JAEDERLUNT. Yes, they said the NKVD actually forbade the local population to go near the forest. They also stated that there was a house in this forest which was a recreational home of NKVD. They further stated that if they went to look for dead bodies in that forest, they would not only find these bodies of that specific time in 1940, but they would also find a number of bodies executed before the war and in former times.

I might add another incident: The Germans told me when I was there that only a few days after the exhumations had begun, a Russian plane appeared over the forest and kept on circling over it for a long time, evidently eager to see what the Germans were doing in that forest—an observation plane.

Mr. FLOOD. As a distinguished Swedish neutral newspaperman at that time, in view of the magnitude of this observation, this matter at the Katyn Forest, and in view of your personal observations there, would it have been possible for the Germans to have staged this whole thing as a propaganda show?

Mr. JAEDERLUNT. We actually went there with this suspicion. We didn't all trust Goebbels and thought it would be possible he would be capable of doing such a thing. So our idea when we went from Smolensk to Katyn the first time was: "Let's try and get as much news as possible about conditions here in Russia and should we find or see any dead bodies, we shall report that matter just on a back page, not as an important item, because our Swedish press at home is sure to say: 'Leave atrocity stories to Goebbels'." But when I stood in front of the mass graves and when I realized what an atrocious crime had been perpetrated there, all my suspicions vanished and my own newspaper, at first, was not prepared to publish this report, but I insisted upon the report's being published because I said: "The world at large must know about this matter."

Mr. FLOOD. Did you then and now have an opinion as to who committed the murders at Katyn? We would like to have you express it, if you wish to. You don't have to, but if you wish to and have an opinion, will you tell us?

Mr. JAEDERLUNT. Then and now I was and I am absolutely convinced that the Russians committed it. I do not wish to say the Russians. I would rather amend it to the NKVD.

Mr. DONDERO. Did all of the bodies that you saw at Katyn have their hands tied behind them?

Mr. JAEDERLUNT. No; only single ones.

Mr. DONDERO. Did you see any more than one?

Mr. JAEDERLUNT. Yes; I saw several.

Mr. DONDERO. Were they tied with rope or wire?

Mr. JAEDERLUNT. Those, as far as I could see, were tied with rope.

Mr. DONDERO. What was the color of it?

Mr. JAEDERLUNT. I don't recollect.

Mr. DONDERO. Was it flat or round?

Mr. JAEDERLUNT. I must state that I went there as a journalist and not as a scientist.

Rudi Kramer

Sonderfuehrer "Z" who had heard from the local Russian people near Katyn of the existence of "crosses" in the forest.

Mr. KRAMER. I am a director of the municipality, retired on pension.

Mr. FLOOD. What municipality?

Mr. KRAMER. I was in charge of the sports department in the town of Breslau.

Mr. FLOOD. Where are you now residing?

Mr. KRAMER. Here in Frankfurt.

Mr. FLOOD. Were you ever identified with the German armed forces?

Mr. KRAMER. Yes; I was.

A mass grave.

Mr. FLOOD. Did you ever have occasion to serve on the Russian or Smolensk front?

Mr. KRAMER. Yes; I did.

Mr. FLOOD. Were the matters of the Katyn massacre ever brought to your attention while you were in that area?

Mr. KRAMER. I was present from the beginning to the end.

Mr. FLOOD. What was your rank, and what was the nature of your unit serving in the Smolensk area at the time of the discovery of the graves by the Germans?

Mr. KRAMER. I was Sonderfuehrer "Z"—that is the rank of lieutenant—with the propaganda detail W in Smólensk.

Mr. FLOOD. Who was the commanding officer of the propaganda unit at Smolensk when you served there?

Mr. KRAMER. My direct superior was Lieutenant Anschuetz, and the C. O. was Gans.

Mr. FLOOD. During your service in the Smolensk area did you ever have occasion to visit the Katyn Woods or the Dnieper Castle in that area generally before the graves were discovered?

Mr. KRAMER. Yes; I did.

Mr. FLOOD. Do you know where the Dnieper Castle was located?

Mr. KRAMER. Yes; I do.

Mr. FLOOD. Did you walk, at any time, in the woods within, say, a thousand meters all around the castle?

Mr. KRAMER. I did not get to the forest of Katyn before I had not heard from the local population of the existence of such graves.

Mr. FLOOD. Will you detail for us, as best you remember, the conversation you had with any Russian person of the area with reference to these graves in Katyn?

Mr. KRAMER. Yes, I can.

Mr. FLOOD. In your own words. Please proceed.

Mr. KRAMER. I was detailed to the propaganda detail W at the beginning of March 1943. Originally I had been detailed to this unit as a sports officer, with the task of interesting myself in sports activities of the military units, and also in connection with sports of the local population.

I was instructed by the propaganda unit to work among the Russian population, which was not anti-German at that time, to try and gain some influence on the Russian population and to foster pro-German feelings among them. We published a newspaper in the Russian language and also had theatrical groups come out to the area to present shows for the Russian population, and thus we established close contacts with the Russian population.

Behind the locality called Krasny Bor there was another place called Gniezdowo. I had to go to that place frequently on duty and had many conversations with the local people. On one of those occasions an old peasant, who was living right on the railroad line near the forest, told me that there were mass graves in the forest. He also said that there were several small crosses erected in the forest, and that the local population had the habit of going there on holidays and putting some flowers down near them.

Mr. FLOOD. Did he indicate when these graves had been made?

Mr. KRAMER. Yes, later. Later on I asked him, once, whether he could recollect when these graves had come into existence, and he said, "3 years ago."

Mr. FLOOD. What was the date of the conversation when he said that?

Mr. KRAMER. This conversation must have taken place about the middle or towards the end of March 1943, after we had transmitted the report of this peasant to the army group and had been instructed to investigate the matter.

Mr. FLOOD. Do you talk or understand Russian?

Mr. KRAMER. No, I always went out with an interpreter.

The peasant related that, 3 years before, large transports had arrived at Gniezdowo station and that the men had been taken out of the boxcars at the station. In his opinion these men in the trains were not Russians, but Polish soldiers. Some of them were put into trucks and taken to the forest; other had to march from the station to the forest.

Later on, some time later, I asked several of those peasants whether they recollected the approximate number of men who had been taken to the forest. They did not give any figure, but they said, "Very many, very many, and they kept on arriving for days and days," and not one of those that they had seen taken to the forest had ever returned from it.

After having reported the matter to higher quarters, and after we had been instructed to investigate, we went into the forest and found sort of a clearing in it, planted with small trees, and we actually discovered two primitive crosses and also some dried flowers lying about.

Mr. FLOOD. What do you mean by "primitive crosses"?

Mr. KRAMER. They were not carved in any way. Probably the people who had erected them had just cut off some wood and put it together.

Mr. FLOOD. Do you use the word "primitive" to mean "ancient", or do you use it to mean "rude and clumsy"?

Mr. KRAMER. I meant the second version, that they were made in a crude manner and that they also had been standing there for some time or other.

Mr. FLOOD. What were the crosses made out of?

Mr. KRAMER. I believe it was birchwood, but I am not quite certain about that.

Mr. FLOOD. Proceed, please.

Mr. KRAMER. Some small distance from the graves, approximately 200 or 300 meters, there was a house, a building, which was subsequently used by the Germans, which was called the Dnieper Castle.

I reported all that I had discovered to my unit, which, in its turn, transmitted the report to the army group. The army group then issued orders to start digging.

Mr. FLOOD. These trees that you referred to as small trees, were they on or around the grave where the crosses were?

Mr. KRAMER. There were no actual graves. The whole soil of the clearing was flat and uniform, no mounds of earth or anything and on this even clearing small trees were growing all over.

Mr. FLOOD. Will you indicate with your hand, witness, from the floor, as you best recollect today, about the height of those trees, the small trees?

Mr. KRAMER. About so high [indicating].

Mr. FLOOD. The witness indicates in the area of 2½ to 3 feet.

Mr. KRAMER. On the very first day when digging started I was not out there, but I came there on the second or third day, and they were busy digging in an area of approximately the size of this room. They were digging down in many spots, and whenever they dug down they came upon dead bodies. The area might have been considerably larger than this room. It is not quite easy to estimate the size.

The digging was done, then, in a systematic way. First of all, they dug down very deep so as to ascertain how far down the dead bodies reached into the ground, and then they opened up towards the sides.

The dead bodies were lying in the grave, sticking together in one solid mass. They were sort of mummified and dried out, probably for the lack of air which had not been able to get to the bodies, and that had caused a sort of mummification of the dead bodies. They were fully clad in uniforms, even with leather belts and everything that belonged to a uniform, and they all wore boots. Some of them had their hands tied behind their backs, but that was not uniform. We found some without their hands tied, and then there was one, again, with his hands tied, so it was diverse.

I wish to state that these statements I made during the last few minutes came from my observations and investigations over some longish time. I have just been giving a survey of my observations covering some longish period.

Mr. FLOOD. Yes.

Mr. KRAMER. In the meantime, Professor Buhtz, from Breslau, whom I had already known in Breslau because I had business with him there, had been put in charge of the exhumations, and because of the fact that I had known him before, I had quite a few good opportunities of seeing things and learning things which, in the ordinary course of my duties, I would perhaps never have learned.

All ranks were found in the graves among the dead bodies, ranging from generals down to assistant medical officers and cadets. Physicians were also found.

The dead bodies were all lying in layers, very close together, and it was established by and by that 12 layers of dead bodies were stacked on each other. We also established that all the men had been killed by shots in the neck, and we assumed that the execution took place in such a way that one row of men had to lie down at the bottom of the pit with their faces down and had then been shot. Then the next row of men had to lie down on top of the men who had just been shot, and were killed subsequently, and so on, one layer after the other. This assumption is based on the fact that we found several bodies with more than one bullet hole.

Several actions were coordinated there. First of all, we of the propaganda unit had been given the task to try and get international commissions to the graves so that they should investigate the thing. There were commissions—one international commission of medical experts; another commission consisted of foreign journalists; then there was also a commission of writers, authors, and artists, and also a commission of Western Allied Officer who were prisoners of war in Germany. I also recollect a large group of Polish clergymen who had been brought there, and then, subsequently, the relatives and next of kin of the murdered men started arriving from Poland. They kept on coming all the time, as soon as the identification of the dead bodies had begun.

Simultaneously, we carried on our investigations among the local population, so as to find out when these transports of prisoners had arrived in the area, and it was established from many statements that this happened in April 1940. This was further confirmed by the fact that all entries in diaries, pocket-books, etc., which we later found on the dead bodies, ended between April 16th and April 19th, 1940. The third proof was established by getting forestry experts to come to this forest and examine the small trees, and they all established that the trees had been in that spot for about 3 years.

The commissions that came to the graves were taken there by German officers. Once on the spot, they had full liberty to investigate on their own, to go about, to talk to the auxiliary volunteers who did the digging up, and also to talk to the local population. They were not hindered in any way; they could just do as they liked. Professor Buhtz also helped them in every way, and insofar as when these commissions were especially interested in special dead bodies, and pointed them out, they were immediately taken out of the pits and the members of the commission were allowed to designate special bodies which they wanted to have taken out, and that was always done at their request.

As the weather became warmer, gradually conditions became very unpleasant. There was a terrible smell, and millions of flies started collecting, so that it was imperative to rebury the bodies that had been taken out of the pits as quickly as possible.

Up to the day when the exhumations ceased because it was becoming too hot, I estimate that about 3,000 bodies had been taken out of the pits, of which 800 had, by then, been identified. From the situation and the measurements of the graves, we made an estimate that there would probably be between 8,000 and 10,000 bodies in the ground.

The population, in the course of all these investigations, became more talkative, and also pointed out to us that there were more graves in the vicinity. Upon investigating those graves it was found that they merely contained civilians who had probably come to death during the fighting. At any rate, no more soldiers or any uniformed persons were found in the surroundings.

On account of the great heat in the summer, the exhumations ceased approximately in July—it might have been a little earlier—and were to be restarted some time in September. However, my unit was transferred to Italy from Smolensk early in September, so I am unable to state whether the exhumations ever began again or not.

Mr. FLOOD. You say you don't know whether the exhumations began again or not in September?

Mr. KRAMER. No; I do not know that.

Mr. FLOOD. Well, the military situation on the eastern front changed about that time, so that it was necessary for the Germans to withdraw. Do you remember hearing about that?

Mr. KRAMER. Yes; that is correct. We heard in Italy, from some of our fellow soldiers who had remained in the Smolensk area, that when the Russians came back into that area they were very eager to get to the Katyn Forest as quickly as possible.

Mr. FLOOD. That being the case, and since the graves were closed in the summer before the exhumations were completed, it is entirely possible that if the graves were opened in September, or subsequently reopened, that additional missing Polish bodies might have been found?

Mr. KRAMER. Yes, that is correct. In my estimation we only succeeded in clearing about one-third of the area. Two-thirds was never touched by us because we didn't have time.

Mr. FLOOD. You have heard of the other two prison camps, besides Kozielsk, of Starobielsk and Ostoskov?

Mr. KRAMER. No, I have not.

Mr. FLOOD. Now, according to your theory as to how the executions took place, with the prisoners forced to lie down flat on their faces over the previously executed prisoners, you say that that indicated that bullet wounds, several bullet wounds, were found in other bodies. Well, how would that theory produce that conclusion?

Mr. KRAMER. It was merely on the top layers that we made the discovery that some of the dead bodies had more than one wound, because further down it was impossible, you could not expect any human being to actually climb down into the pits, because the stench was so terrible, the whole thing, that nobody could actually go down there, they could only be pulled out with hooks, or something like that. Therefore, we only noticed these several wounds in some bodies on the top layers.

We noticed in several cases—not in each one, but in quite a few cases—on the top layers of the dead bodies, that the bullet which had penetrated the skull of the top body had gone on in the same direction and hit the bodies underneath, not in the same place where the bullet had hit the first body, but the way of the bullet, or the course of the bullet, was lying in exactly the same direction, so that it was unmistakable that the bottom body had been hit by the same bullet. That was why we established this theory.

Mr. FLOOD. That is interesting, because there is medical testimony that certain bodies, some bodies, were found with more than one bullet wound, and that is an interesting observation to explain that.

Mr. Dondero?

Mr. DONDERO. Were you at the Katyn graves, Mr. Kramer, during April of that year?

Mr. KRAMER. Yes, I was.

Mr. DONDERO. What kind of weather do they have in that area?

Mr. KRAMER. Partly there was still snow and ice in the area.

Mr. DONDERO. Were all of the bodies buried with their faces down?

Mr. KRAMER. I did not see any body that was not buried with its face down.

Mr. DONDERO. Did you see any bodies with overcoats on?

Mr. KRAMER. Yes, I recollect one general; altogether two generals were found, and one general was still wearing a fur coat.

Matvey Skarginsky

Once a member of the White Russian Army, who later served in the Wehrmacht as a Russian interpreter. He testified as to the arrival of the Poles near Katyn and, as a friend of Menschagin, spoke of his disappearance.

Mr. FLOOD. Where were you born?

Mr. SKARGINSKY. In Elizavetgrad.

Mr. FLOOD. You are a Russian?

Mr. SKARGINSKY. Yes, I am.

Mr. FLOOD. Were you ever a member of the Russian armed forces?

Mr. SKARGINSKY. At the end of the Czarist Army, and later on a member of the White Russian Army.

Mr. FLOOD. Were you ever taken prisoner by the Germans?

Mr. SKARGINSKY. No, I was not.

Mr. FLOOD. In what way did you become identified with the German armed forces?

Mr. SKARGINSKY. I rec ived a mobilization order in Berlin in October 1941, a mobilization order extending to non-German citizens.

Mr. FLOOD. Did you ever serve in the Smolensk area?

Mr. SKARGINSKY. Yes; on several occasions during the last war.

Mr. FLOOD. In what capacity did you serve with the Germans on the Smolensk front?

Mr. SKARGINSKY. At first, when Smolensk was occupied in 1941, with the motorized heavy artillery detachment No. 808.

Mr. FLOOD. Well, when did you first get to the city of Smolensk?

Mr. SKARGINSKY. I do not quite recollect, but it was at the end of July—it was at the end of July or at the beginning of August 1941.

Mr. FLOOD. Witness, will you raise your voice a little bit, please?

Mr. SKARGINSKY. Yes.

Mr. FLOOD. Just talk louder.

Mr. SKARGINSKY. Yes.

Mr. FLOOD. You said you were born in Russia and you were mobilized by the Germans in Berlin. How and under what circumstances did you get to Berlin?

Mr. SKARGINSKY. I lived in Yugoslavia up to May 1941, and after the occupation of Yugoslavia by the Germans the Labor Office sent me to Germany for work, and that is how I got to Berlin.

Mr. O'KONSKI. In other words, you served in the German armed forces not by choice but you were conscripted for that service, were you not?

Mr. SKARGINSKY. That is correct.

Mr. O'KONSKI. And you were serving against your will?

Mr. SKARGINSKY. I was conscripted. I did not volunteer. I was conscripted and mobilized.

Mr. O'KONSKI. Now, will you tell us briefly what you know about the Katyn massacre?

Mr. SKARGINSKY. Yes.

I was a member of this artillery unit which I mentioned up to October 1942. In October 1942 I was transferred to the staff headquarters of the Ninth Army. The staff headquarters of this army were located in Sitschewka, in the Smolensk area.

Mr. O'KONSKI. Then, as I understand it, you were employed by the German staff as an interpreter because of your knowledge of the Russian language; is that correct?

Mr. SKARGINSKY. That is correct.

Mr. O'KONSKI. Then in your job as interpreter, what assignment were you given by the German Staff regarding the Katyn massacre?

Mr. SKARGINSKY. When the staff headquarters were transferred to Smolensk in February 1943, then rumors started spreading that somewhere in the Smolensk area there were mass graves and that these mass graves were located near the former NKVD recreation home in the vicinity of Katyn. I thereupon was given orders to interrogate the local population living in the vicinity of Katyn.

I thereupon interrogated some 30 local peasants from three villages lying in that specific area. The name of the one village is Gniezdowo; the other two I do not recollect.

And I also interrogated three railroad officials who were already railroad officials under the Russians and remained railroad officials in German services after the occupation had taken place. There were several railroad officials who were employed right at the Gniezdowo Station.

The most interesting statement was given by one of those railroad employees, one of the officials. All the statements tallied in that respect, that early in the summer of 1940, freight trains started arriving at the railroad station, containing Polish prisoners. The trains used to arrive shortly before midnight on every occasion. The boxcars were locked from the outside. In the small cabins where the brakemen sit, as is usual in Europe, there were NKVD guards guarding the train. The trains arrived at the station without any official papers, so that it could not be ascertained from where they were coming.

Mr. O'KONSKI. Did the railroad station attendants tell you it was early spring of 1940 that these cars arrived?

Mr. SKARGINSKY. As far as I recollect, they told me that it was at the end of the spring or at the beginning of summer 1940.

Mr. O'KONSKI. Did they mention any specific months?

Mr. SKARGINSKY. I only recollect the year of 1940 and, as I said before, the end of the spring or beginning of summer.

The prisoners who were in the boxcars were taken out of those railroad cars and marched off to the forest of Katyn in marching order; it was four and four. Strict orders had been issued at that time that nobody was to approach the railroad line and the road leading from the station to the forest. All the railroad officials were also forbidden, those who were not right on duty at the station. Nobody was to approach the line or the road.

Mr. O'KONSKI. There is one thing I would like to check with you. You testified a little earlier that you were conscripted in Berlin in October of 1941; then later you said you reached the Smolensk area in August 1941. Will you clear up those two dates? Evidently, you must have been confused.

Mr. SKARGINSKY. Yes, I made a mistake. I meant to say I had been mobilized in October 1941 and the first time I got to Smolensk was in November 1941, not in August; not in August but in November 1941.

Mr. O'KONSKI. You said that you interviewed about 30 natives and 3 depot agents. Did they all agree as to the time of the arrival of the Polish soldiers, and did they also agree that they were disposed of by the Russians at that time?

Mr. SKARGINSKY. The statements by all those various people differed only to a very slight extent. It was only a matter of a month or two. Some of the people stated that the prisoners had arrived in

The corpse of General Bohaterewicz being examined at Katyn.

May; others said they had arrived in June. But all the statements taken together very much tallied with each other.

Mr. O'KONSKI. There was no native that you interviewed, or official that you interviewed, that said anything otherwise, to the contrary?

Mr. SKARGINSKY. It was like this: Very detailed statements came from those railroad officials, because they were actually on the spot and saw the Polish prisoners being taken out of the boxcars or being marched away, because they were on duty at the trains, at the station.

The peasants, however, were not allowed to come near the station

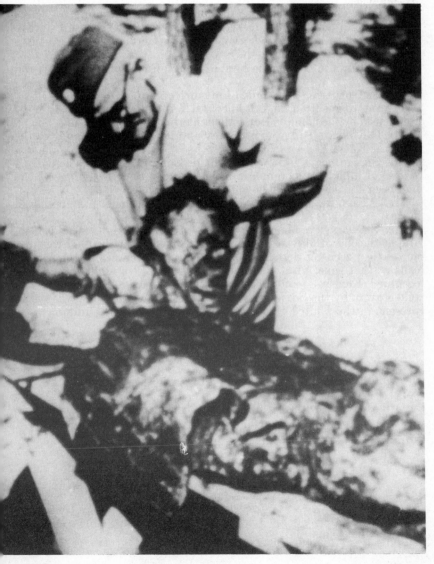

or the forest and could only see things going on from afar. So they only said, "We saw some trains arriving and some people being taken out of the trains and some people being marched away." But they could not say whether they had been Polish prisoners or whatever they were because they were too far away and the area was cordoned off, so they could not get near the spot.

But nobody ever made a statement different to this one.

Mr. O'KONSKI. Did you, in your process of interviewing, ever get acquainted with a deputy mayor in Smolensk, by the name of Boris Basilevsky?

Mr. SKARGINSKY. Yes; I did. He was second acting buergermeister of Smolensk.

Mr. O'KONSKI. Did you have any conversations with him?

Mr. SKARGINSKY. I only talked to him very little because I hardly knew him, but I know that shortly before the Germans had to evacuate Smolensk, he crossed over to the Soviets.

Mr. O'KONSKI. You came here of your own accord to testify, did you not?

Mr. SKARGINSKY. Yes; quite of my own accord.

I want to mention that I knew well the first buergermeister of Smolensk, by the name of Boris Menschagin.

Mr. O'KONSKI. Did he express any opinion as to who committed the crime at Katyn?

Mr. SKARGINSKY. I knew Menschagin very well; he was actually a friend of mine. His opinion all the time was that the Polish officers had been murdered by the Soviets.

Mr. O'KONSHI. Do you know what has become of Menschagin since?

Mr. SKARGINSKY. Menschagin I saw in Berlin in 1944 and 1945, and at the end of May 1945, Menschagin was in Karlsbad—it was just across the Czech-Slovakian border—which was occupied by the Americans at that time. But then, all of a sudden, one night the Soviets occupied Karlsbad, and a few hours afterwards, Menschagin was taken away by the Soviets and was never seen again. His wife is at present in the United States, in New York, with the children.

Karl Genschow

He gives interesting evidence regarding the bullets used for the mass-murder at Katyn. The question of the German bullets (Gecko – 7.65) has always caused confusion.

Mr. FLOOD. What is your business?

Mr. GENSCHOW. I was formerly president of the Gustav Genschow Co., and at present I am trustee of the same firm, which is under French supervision.

Mr. FLOOD. Will you spell the name of the company?

370

Mr. Genschow. G-u-s-t-a-v Genschow & Co.

Mr. Flood. What is the business of that company?

Mr. Genschow. Formerly the firm manufactured ammunition and weapons and exported these goods.

Mr. Flood. Where was the main office of this company?

Mr. Genschow. In Berlin.

Mr. Flood. Where is the chief manufacturing plant?

Mr. Genschow. The ammunition works were in Durlach, near Karlsruhe.

Mr. Flood. How long has the company been in business?

Mr. Genschow. The factory has been in existence since 1887 and the ammunition works since 1906.

Mr. Flood. During that period of time, did the company ever manufacture pistol ammunition?

Mr. Genschow. Yes.

Mr. Flood. Did it ever manufacture pistol ammunition of the caliber of 7.65?

Mr. Genschow. Yes.

Mr. Flood. Is that a very common type of caliber for pistol ammunition?

Mr. Genschow. It is a very common type.

Mr. Flood. What was the trade-mark of the pistol ammunition on that caliber?

Mr. Genschow. The trade-mark was changed several times in the course of the years.

Mr. Flood. Will you give us some of the trade-mark names?

Mr. Genschow. Yes. The cartridges of the shells of this pistol ammunition carried, since the year 1933–34, the word "Geco" on the bottom of the shell, and underneath the "Geco" was "7.65".

Mr. Flood. Can 7.65 ammunition of the type manufactured by this firm be used in various kinds and makes of pistols?

Mr. Genschow. Yes, it could; because it was a standard type of cartridge which could be used in very many different makes of pistols.

Mr. Flood. Was it used internationally by various nations, police, or armed forces, in pistols?

Mr. Genschow. Yes; certainly.

Mr. Flood. Did this firm ever export pistol ammunition of the caliber 7.65 to Eastern Europe?

Mr. Genschow. Yes; that is the case.

Mr. Flood. Do you know what caliber of ammunition was used and what kind of pistol was used by the NKVD or the GPU from the year 1933 until the end of the war?

Mr. Genschow. No; I do not know that also, because since 1928 we did not export large quantities of pistol ammunition to Soviet Russia.

Mr. Flood. Did you export any quantities of 7.65 pistol ammunition to Soviet Russia?

Mr. Genschow. Yes; before 1928, somewhat larger amounts. But I wish to point out that at that time the stamp on the bottom of the cartridge was different from the one I stated before, and after 1928 the quantities which were exported were small.

Mr. Flood. But there were some quantities shipped to Soviet Russia after 1928, of 7.65 ammunition bearing the "Geco" trade-mark?

Mr. Genschow. Yes.

I wish to point out that the trade-mark which was used before 1933–34, when the latest trade-mark was introduced, also had the word "Geco" in it and "7.65." There was only the addition of two D's slightly underneath the right and left end of the word "Geco."

Mr. Flood. So that the trade-mark "Geco," regardless of the other details you are giving us, was on 7.65 ammunition shipped to Soviet Russia for some time?

Mr. Genschow. Yes. Most probably, it may be that some deliveries took place in former years, before we put the word "Geco" on the bottom of the cartridges. There may have been some older deliveries many, many years ago, where it only stated "7.65" with a "D" underneath.

Mr. Flood. Can you keep 7.65 pistol ammunition for any length of time if it is properly cared for?

Mr. Genschow. If you store it properly and if the cartridges remain in their original packings, you can safely store it for 10 to 20 years.

Mr. Flood. Did you ship any ammunition to other eastern European countries, other than Soviet Russia?

Mr. Genschow. Yes; in particular, to the three Baltic States.

Mr. Flood. What do you mean by the three Baltic States?

Mr. Genschow. Esthonia, Latvia and Lithuania.

Mr. Flood. Did you ever ship any 7.65 pistol ammunition to the three Baltic States?

Mr. Genschow. Yes; I did export quantities which were considerably larger than those going to Soviet Russia, although not unduly large.

Mr. Flood. What do you consider a small shipment in the number of units?

Mr. Genschow. We did not export more than two or three thousand rounds to Soviet Russia after 1928; but to the Baltic States, to my recollection, we exported approximately 50,000 rounds to each of the three.

Mr. Flood. Did you ever export any pistol ammunition to Poland?

Mr. Genschow. We did not export any pistol ammunition to Poland during the time under review because conditions for such exports were not advantageous. We did, however, export shells and bullets separately to that country; which however, were marked differently so as to distinguish them from our original make which we used to export.

Mr. Flood. Did you ever export any 7.65 pistol ammunition to Poland from 1933 up to 1940?

Mr. Genschow. I do not recollect. I do not think that we did it.

Mr. Flood. What about from 1923 to 1940?

Mr. Genschow. It may be, but I do not recollect that because we had to stop our exports of ammunition to Poland all of a sudden owing to new customs regulations having come into force in Poland. But I do not recollect the year when that happened.

Mr. Flood. Of course, you know that "Geco" shells, cartridge shells, were found in the graves at Katyn, do you not?

Mr. Genschow. Yes. I learned that after the German Wehrmacht had made its investigations in Katyn.

Mr. FLOOD. Was this matter ever brought to your attention by the then German authorities?

Mr. GENSCHOW. Not immediately. I only discussed this matter with the army high command and the weapons division. They requested me to submit extracts from our statistics on exports to foreign countries, which we had carried out. And only in the course of these negotiations with the high command did I learn that this type of bullet and shells had been found in the Katyn graves.

Mr. FLOOD. Did they inquire as to whether or not your firm exported 7.65 ammunition to any of the countries in the Baltic or Eastern Europe?

Mr. GENSCHOW. Yes; and we had to give accurate details of the quantities which had been exported to each single country and in what year.

The actual rope used to bind a victim's hands. All the rope used was ready-cut in identical lengths.

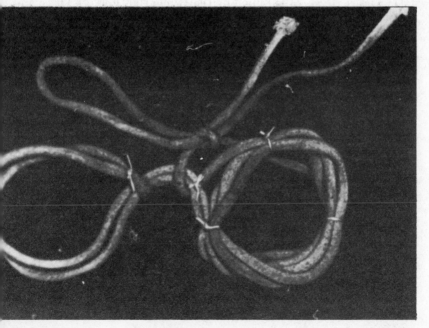

Dr Ferenc Orsos

His theory of post-mortal decalcification, callus and pseudocallus on bones is so vital to the proof in this case.

Mr. Flood. Doctor, will you please tell us from what schools or universities you graduated, and what were your degrees and courses?

Dr. Orsos. Only the degrees obtained from universities, or everything?

Mr. Flood. In the field of pathology and forensic medicine.

Dr. Orsos. Yes. In Budapest University. Then I became an assistant doctor, physician, in Budapest, and from 1906 I was chief prosektor and expert for judicial medicine in Pecs.

Mr. Flood. In your long experience as a pathologist did you ever have occasion, Doctor, to perform autopsies and post mortems upon dead bodies and disinterred corpses?

Dr. Orsos. In many hundreds of cases.

Mr. Flood. Doctor, will you now please direct your attention to the year 1943 and the matter of the Katyn massacres?

Dr. Orsos. Yes; I will.

Mr. Flood. And, Doctor, where were you living and in what practice were you engaged in April of 1943?

Dr. Orsos. I was a professor of judicial medicine and director of the department for judicial medicine at Budapest University and at the Institute for Judicial Medicine in Budapest. At the same time I was expert for judicial medicine for all high courts in the surroundings of Budapest.

Mr. Flood. How were you invited, and under what circumstances, to participate in the scientific investigations at Katyn?

Dr. Orsos. I was called upon by the Hungarian Foreign Office and the Ministry of Culture to take part in this international commission, in view of the fact that I was the only professor of forensic medicine and expert in this field, and there was no other expert like me in all the five universities in Hungary. I was exclusively engaged in forensic medicine in Hungary and did not do any other work, whereas my colleagues from the other universities were only doing this kind of work occasionally, acting for others, and that was the reason why I was asked to be a member of this commission.

Mr. Flood. Then you were invited by the Foreign Office of your own Government and not directly and personally by the then German Government?

Dr. Orsos. That is correct. I presume that the then German Government had previously negotiated with the Hungarian Government about this matter.

Mr. Flood. Do you know a Dr. Conte, a German, a Dr. Buhtz, a German, and a Dr. Zietz, a German? Do you recall them?

Dr. Orsos. Yes; I do.

Mr. Flood. Will you tell us who they were and in what way they were identified with this commission?

Dr. Orsos. Dr. Conte was the so-called Reich health leader, and, at the same time, president of the Reich medical chamber.

Buhtz, Professor Buhtz, was an expert for forensic medicine at Breslau, in Silesia.

Dr. Zietz is a German, and he accompanied us to that area and made all arrangements for our accommodations, etc., and just cared for us.

Mr. FLOOD. Doctor, in your own words, then—and I am sure you are capable of doing so very well—would you take us, now, to Katyn and describe your observations and autopsies performed there?

Dr. ORSOS. Yes. After our return to Berlin from Katyn, and after we had handed the protocol to Dr. Conte, all of us, that is, all the commission, undertook not to disclose anything about our Katyn investigations, neither by the spoken word nor in writing, unless some new scientific points would come up and we would find it necessary to make additions to our original protocol. That is because we were only asked to act as experts for forensic medicine. We only had to answer two questions. Everything that we saw at Katyn we entered in our protocol after a very careful and thorough discussion among ourselves. We were aware of the fact that if we were to talk about the things that we had seen we would destroy the scientific value of our protocol and would probably be a party to propaganda.

That is all.

Mr. FLOOD. Doctor, did you observe the bodies in the graves?

Dr. ORSOS. Yes, I did; certainly I did.

Mr. FLOOD. And did you yourself perform any autopsies or post mortems on any of the bodies?

Dr. ORSOS. Yes; I did.

Mr. FLOOD. Did you reach any conclusion as to the cause of death?

Dr. ORSOS. Yes, I did, and you will find that in the protocol.

Mr. FLOOD. Was the cause of death in any of the bodies, or any body out of the group that you examined, a gunshot wound in the head?

Dr. ORSOS. That is also stated in detail in the protocol.

Mr. FLOOD. And did you have occasion to observe whether or not the gunshot wounds—if they were the cause of death, as described in the protocol—were fired proximate to the skull?

Dr. ORSOS. The protocol even states the distance in inches or measurements in centimeters.

Mr. FLOOD. And did you observe, Doctor, that the bodies that were discovered in the graves and that you saw there were dressed in the uniforms of Polish officers?

Dr. ORSOS. That is also stated in detail in the protocol.

Mr. FLOOD. And did you, Doctor, as indicated by pictures now in evidence, and as indicated in the protocol, talk to certain Russian inhabitants of the area?

Dr. ORSOS. Yes; I did.

Mr. FLOOD. And did you observe, Doctor, on certain of the bodies, that the hands were tied behind the back in a certain way?

Dr. ORSOS. This was also laid down in the protocol.

Mr. FLOOD. And as is evidenced by certain photographs taken on the spot and now in evidence?

Dr. ORSOS. Yes.

Mr. FLOOD. And did you observe, Doctor, that certain of the bodies were wearing overcoats or greatcoats, or what could be described as winter clothing?

Dr. Orsos. We investigated all these matters in full detail and put all these details into the protocol.

Mr. Flood. And did you observe, Doctor, on the bodies of some of the corpses taken from the grave and in the area and in certain exhibits, documents, and personal belongings of the dead officers?

Dr. Orsos. Yes.

Mr. Flood. And did you, Doctor, in the presence of your fellow scientists, expound to them, using as an exhibit a skull opened by you, a certain theory of calcification of brain pulp?

Dr. Orsos. Those were no theories; those were experiences of a period of more than 30 years.

Mr. Flood. And you expounded them as a scientific fact?

Dr. Orsos. Yes; that is so.

Mr. Flood. Do you care to outline for the benefit of the committee generally, Doctor, the Orsos theory on the calcification of brain pulp in the skull and organic changes brought about by interment, which would indicate the time in which the body had been buried?

Dr. Orsos. No; I am not prepared to do it. But I am handing you the heading of an article which I published in a scientific paper, copies of which you will find in any scientific library, and all details of this teaching of mine can be found in this article.

Mr. Flood. Will you place in the record and translate into English the name and the address of this article, dealing with this theory of organic change of the skulls?

Mr. von Hahn. It is in Hungarian.

Mr. Flood. Then place it in the record as it is given you by the witness.

(The following was contained on the document produced by the witness and was translated into German by the witness:)

Orvosi Hetilap   (Athenaeum Budapest)
1941, No. 11

A halál utáni csontmésztelenedés, szuvasodás és pseudocallus.

Mr. von Hahn. The English version is approximately:

The post mortal decalcification, callus, and pseudocallus on bones.

That is the title of the article.

Mr. Flood. Doctor, did you point out to the scientists at Katyn, as indicated in the protocol and in the photograph, evidences of that scientific conclusion?

Dr. Orsos. Yes; I did.

Mr. Flood. And did you, Doctor, at the conclusion of your autopsies and analysis, sign such a protocol, as you have referred to it?

Dr. Orsos. Yes; I did.

I would like to add something. We discussed all the matters the whole afternoon in every detail after we had finished with the post mortems. I wrote down every remark made by all the members of the commission. Then I dictated the medical part of the protocol.

We finished up at 3 o'clock in the morning. Then we went to the mess hall. Some of my colleagues had already gone to bed. And very early in the morning we left on our return flight in three planes.

The protocol had been read out to us in this mess hall, in this canteen, the manuscript, the draft, and when we reached the town of Bialystok on our return flight, a military plane caught up with us with mimeographed copies of the protocol. There, at that place, we had about one and a half hours to read through the protocols and to sign them, and then we continued our return flight to Berlin.

Mr. FLOOD. Doctor, did you read the protocol and did you sign it?

Dr. ORSOS. Yes, I did.

Mr. FLOOD. Do you subscribe today to your signature and to the protocol?

Dr. ORSOS. Yes, I do.

Mr. FLOOD. Your distinguished, the Danish scientist Tramsen, has placed in the hands of the committee a copy of the protocol signed by the members of the commission, including you, Dr. Orsos. I show you, Dr. Orsos, Dr. Tramsen's copy and ask you if that is your signature on page 7?

Dr. ORSOS. Yes. I confirm this to be my signature. Each one of us was handed such a copy of the protocol.

Mr. FLOOD. Is it not true that the distinguished doctor himself was chairman of the commission and was elected as such by his fellow members?

Dr. ORSES. Apparently, if my colleagues agreed with that, it was probably because I was the oldest in age and the most experienced scientist in this field, in view of the fact that I had carried out more than 80,000 autopsies. So if my colleagues agreed to that, then I was the chairman of this committee.

Mr. FLOOD. I might state, Doctor, that your distinguished colleagues Miloslavich, the Croat, and the Dane, Tramsen, have so advised us and agreed.

Dr. ORSOS. I cannot confirm that I was officially appointed chairman of the commission, but it was a gentlemen's agreement.

Mr. FLOOD. There is no doubt in the mind of the committee that because of the doctor's distinction and vast experience, if he had not been he should have been so appointed.

Dr. ORSOS. Actually, we were all the same in the commission and, actually, I was only requested to take the chair during our discussions and at our meetings. It was on that afternoon which I mentioned before.

Mr. FLOOD. I show you, Doctor, certain photographs placed in evidence by Dr. Tramsen, the Danish scientist and a member of the commission, upon which the distinguished witness now on the stand appears at various times, and ask you whether or not you can identify yourself on those photographs?

Dr. ORSOS. Yes. I am to be seen on each one of them.

Mr. FLOOD. Doctor, do you have any further statements to make?

Dr. ORSOS. Yes. And, in fact, the one thing which I have much at heart is that my name should not be published in the papers. I do not want to be pointed out in the papers because it would prejudice my present position.

Mr. FLOOD. I might point out, Doctor, that the committee indicates that the press is present. We have no control over the action of the public press, but we merely direct the attention of the press to the request of the witness.

Dr. ORSOS. I would like to add, in connection with Katyn, that we, the members of the commission, were allowed to select single dead bodies in the pits, so that those were brought up which we had specially designated.

One of the corpses being examined in Katyn Forest. Prof Orsos second from left, Prof Buhtz third from left, Dr Markov third from right and Dr Saxen on right. Note the cut-away front quarter of the skull.

Dr François Naville
He reaffirmed that the latest date on any document found on the corpses was 22 April 1940.

Mr. FLOOD. Where were you born?
Dr. NAVILLE. In Switzerland; Neuchatel.
Mr. FLOOD. Are you a Swiss citizen?
Dr. NAVILLE. Yes.
Mr. FLOOD. What is your profession?
Dr. NAVILLE. A professor of forensic medicine in Geneva.
Mr. FLOOD. In what universities did you take your degrees in pathology and forensic medicine?
Dr. NAVILLE. In Geneva.
Mr. FLOOD. How long have you been engaged in your profession?
Dr. NAVILLE. 40 years.

Mr. FLOOD. In the practice of your profession, Doctor, have you ever had occasion to perform post mortems or autopsies upon dead bodies or upon corpses disinterred?

Dr. NAVILLE. I want to say that at the Forensic Institute in Geneva, we have approximately 150 corpses to examine during the period of a year.

Mr. FLOOD. I direct your attention to the year of 1943 and ask you whether or not, at any time in that year, your attention was directed to the massacres at Katyn?

Dr. NAVILLE. Yes.

Mr. FLOOD. How were you invited, and by whom, to become a member of the international medical commission at Katyn?

Dr. NAVILLE. Through the Polish Red Cross and the German Red Cross, the government had been asked to form an international commission, and the Russian Government at that time disagreed. And at that time a private commission was formed, and I was asked to become a member of this commission.

Mr. FLOOD. Who asked you to become a member?

Dr. NAVILLE. Through the German consulate in Geneva.

Mr. FLOOD. Doctor, do you know a Dr. Conti, a Dr. Buhtz and a Dr. Zietz?

Dr. NAVILLE. I made their acquaintance only on the occasion of Katyn.

Mr. FLOOD. Will you tell us who each one is, as you remember?

Dr. NAVILLE. Dr. Conti was the chief of the Reich Health Ministry. Dr. Buhtz at that time was in charge in Smolensk, of all forensic affairs in general, or only with Katyn; I am not sure about that.

Dr. Zietz is not a physician, he is a phililogist, and he was in charge only of the administrative part of these affairs, and he was a member of the Medical Chamber of Germany. He should be asked what he did exactly at the time because I don't know.

Mr. FLOOD. Doctor, Dr. Zietz has already testified.

Doctor, will you tell us now what transpired when you arrived at Katyn with your fellow-scientists on the commission?

Dr. NAVILLE. We spent 2 days or a part of 2 days in the wood of Katyn, and we saw about 800 or a thousand corpses; and we made about 10 autopsies, not all myself but among my colleagues.

I want to emphasize the fact that we did not make autopsies on corpses that were pointed out to us, but we selected the corpse on which we desired to make an autopsy.

Mr. MACHROWICZ. I have one question there, Doctor.

Did you select them from the corpses that were already exhumed, or those that were obviously untouched before you came there?

Dr. NAVILLE. The corpses that were still in the grave.

Mr. FLOOD. Doctor, can you tell us whether or not the Germans cooperated in any way, or did they interfere with your scientific experiments in any way at all?

Dr. NAVILLE. No. We were completely free to do what we wanted to. We could stay on the left hand side or the right. Then I myself walked out on the forest, the wood. I was together with a French doctor by the name of Costedoat, who spoke Russian. I went along with him. And I also interrogated some Russian natives who were working there.

Mr. FLOOD. Did you have an opportunity, Doctor, to talk to any Russian inhabitants of the area?

Dr. NAVILLE. Not directly. Those people had been heard by all our people together but not by me personally.

Mr. FLOOD. Do you recall the substance of any of the conversation that was had before the whole group with any of these Russian peasants in the neighborhood?

Dr. NAVILLE. Not very clearly. Professor Orsos, who spoke Russian, interrogated these people and I was told that they had said that; but, naturally, of course, I could not speak any Russian and I don't know what they were talking about.

Mr. FLOOD. Doctor, did you examine any of the corpses, with particular attention to the cause of death?

Dr. NAVILLE. Yes.

Mr. FLOOD. What, in your opinion, Doctor, was the cause of death?

Dr. NAVILLE. Shots that were fired in the skull from a very near distance.

Mr. FLOOD. What were the facts that led you to conclude that the shots were fired from a very near distance?

Dr. NAVILLE. First of all, because it had been aimed very carefully, and then because there were some powder burns.

I want to remark here that in the newspapers it was published that these people had been killed by machine guns; but this is not correct.

Mr. FLOOD. What is your opinion, Doctor, as to how they were killed?

Dr. NAVILLE. I think that they must have been standing. I don't believe that they had been lying. I believe they had been standing when they were shot.

Mr. FLOOD. Doctor, had you ever had any experience, before you went to Katyn, in the examination of bodies where the cause of death had been gunshot wounds, particularly fired by pistol?

Dr. NAVILLE. Yes.

Mr. FLOOD. Do you have any opinion, Doctor, as to what kind of weapon was used in the killing?

Dr. NAVILLE. If this has been referred to in the protocol, I don't remember the caliber any more.

Mr. FLOOD. Could it have been a pistol?

Dr. NAVILLE. Yes.

Mr. FLOOD. Is it possible for you to say, Doctor, from the similarity of the wounds, the shots having been fired close to the skull in all cases, and from the course of the bullets and the other circumstances; is it possible for you to say, Doctor, from your long experience in such matters, that these killings had all been done by pistol and with a very practiced hand?

Dr. NAVILLE. Naturally, a person with some experience. And from these powder marks, you could determine that these shots had been fired from at least 10 centimeters (about 6 inches).

Mr. FLOOD. Doctor, will you demonstrate upon the interpreter, if you will be so kind, the point of entry and the point of exit of the shot?

(Dr. Naville indicated on Interpreter von Hahn.)

The doctor indicates the point of entry as the base of the skull, at the hair line of the neck, the general area.

Dr. NAVILLE (indicating on Mr. von Hahn). And the exit of the bullet depended on the occasion. Sometimes it was here, here, or there.

380

It depended on from where the shot was fired, from what direction. And there were corpses who had received many shots.

Mr. FLOOD. The point of exit was indicated by the doctor on the subject as being between the hair line and the eyebrows, in the general area of the forehead.

Dr. NAVILLE. Yes.

Mr. FLOOD. Did you observe, on any of the bodies, wounds made by any other instrument than a pistol or a gunshot wound?

Dr. NAVILLE. No. I had been shown a piece of clothing showing a square hole made by a four-edged bayonet, but I am not sure whether this piece of cloth was from one of the corpses lying in the grave there, or from any other thing.

Mr. FLOOD. Did you observe, Doctor, that any of the corpses had their hands tied behind their backs?

Dr. NAVILLE. Yes. We saw a small number. I remember, I am not quite sure, I know, I had been told that there had been a number of those corpses who had the hands tied behind their backs. I think I saw a small number myself, but I am not quite positive.

Mr. FLOOD. Were you shown any bodies that were described to you as having been found in the general area of the graves but were said to be the bodies of Russian civilians buried some time before the Katyn bodies?

Dr. NAVILLE. One or two.

Mr. FLOOD. Do you recall, Doctor, whether or not any of those bodies were female?

Dr. NAVILLE. No.

Mr. FLOOD. Do you remember whether or not those bodies had their hands tied behind their backs?

Dr. NAVILLE. Yes, they had.

Mr. FLOOD. Do you recall, doctor, whether or not any of those bodies had a cloth thrown over the head, with a rope tied around the cloth at the neck?

Dr. NAVILLE. Yes. I saw it.

Mr. FLOOD. Do you have any observation to make with reference to the growth of the trees that were identified with the Katyn graves?

Dr. NAVILLE. In this forest there were big trees and also small trees about that high [indicating]. And I remember someone had stated that they had been somewhere else before. Whether they had been taken away from there I cannot recall.

Mr. FLOOD. Do you recall, doctor, whether or not, at a meeting in Smolensk, after the commission had visited the graves, whether or not a professional German forester demonstrated anything with reference to small trees said to have been taken from the grave?

Dr. NAVILLE. Yes. I recall it very well. And I have here a photograph showing these exactly, the special examination of these made by this man.

Dr. NAVILLE. I am not an expert on botany, I am not a forester; so I don't know anything about it.

Mr. FLOOD. Do you recall, doctor, anything that was said by the forestry expert at that meeting in Smolensk, with reference to the small trees said to have been taken from the top of the grave and discussed at the time the picture was taken?

Dr. NAVILLE. Yes. He said that these trees are about 5 years old and that they had been transplanted about 3 years prior to that time. But the one that I saw had, in my opinion, more than 5 years. And, actually, I have seen the cut of these trees, and I have seen some lines were closer to each other, and they might have been more than 3 years.

Mr. FLOOD. What kind of uniform, if you know, was on the bodies at Katyn?

Dr. NAVILLE. I believe they were all Polish uniforms.

I have here some buttons I have brought along.

Mr. FLOOD. Will you let me have one of them?

Dr. NAVILLE. The eagle is better on this one [producing button.]

Mr. FLOOD. Do you mean the Polish eagle?

Dr. NAVILLE. I believe so.

Mr. FLOOD. Do you know, Doctor, from what material those buttons are made?

Dr. NAVILLE. No, I do not know. They are probably aluminum; I am not sure.

Mr. FLOOD. Aluminum does not generally rust, does it?

Dr. NAVILLE. No.

Mr. FLOOD. Will you have this envelope marked as "Exhibit 100" containing a uniform button taken from a Polish officer's uniform, as mentioned by the doctor?

Mr. FLOOD. I now show the witness this envelope marked for identification as "Exhibit 100," and ask him whether or not it contains the button he just showed the committee.

Dr. NAVILLE. I am not quite sure. I see the eagle better than before.

Mr. FLOOD. Then, doctor, for the record, will you select from the envelope that you brought with you, a button from one of the uniforms and place it in the envelope marked "Exhibit 100"?

Did you observe whether or not any of the bodies had any overcoats, or great coats, or winter uniforms?

Mr. MACHROWICZ. I think the record should show that in answer to Congressman Flood's question, the doctor has selected a button and placed it in the envelope marked "Exhibit 100".

Dr. NAVILLE. Yes, they wore winter clothing.

Mr. FLOOD. Did you observe whether or not there were any documents or personal belongings or objects on any of the bodies, and did you see any such things?

Dr. NAVILLE. I have here a picture on which I am seen just taking out of the pocket of one of the bodies a box of matches, and I have a photograph of this box of matches in my possession. I also found a cigarette holder which has an inscription Kozielsk on it, and, when I found this cigarette holder, I remember that there was an inscription on it of 1939–1940, but you can't see it any more. There is a pencil copy of the Russian text and also of the French translation on the photograph.

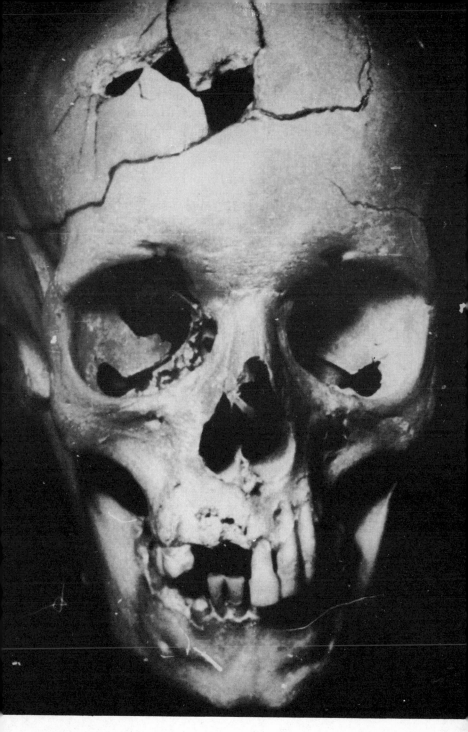

Front view of skull showing exit hole of bullet.

Mr. FLOOD. I now show the doctor that exhibit and ask him whether or not that envelope contains the papers and the photograph of the match box top he just handed to us?

Dr. NAVILLE. That is correct.

Mr. FLOOD. I now ask the stenographer to mark for identification this envelope as exhibit 103 containing an obviously handmade wooden cigarette holder, and still visible thereon the marking of Kozielsk that the doctor described, as having been taken from one of the bodies at the graves at Katyn.

Mr. FLOOD. I show you exhibit 104 and ask you to describe who is the person on that photograph and what he is doing.

Dr. NAVILLE. That is myself, searching the body of this corpse which had not been searched before, and finding a box of matches.

Mr. FLOOD. From the examination or observation of any or all of the documents that you saw on the body or in the exhibits at the Katyn area, did you notice what was the latest date appearing on any of the written documents?

Dr. NAVILLE. I have seen many documents and newspapers, and the last date that was on any of them was the 22d of April 1940.

Mr. FLOOD. Do you have any photographs showing in detail the degree of decomposition of any of the bodies?

Dr. NAVILLE. Yes, I have two of them.

Mr. FLOOD. May I see those, please?

Dr. NAVILLE. The first photograph shows a corpse at the moment an autopsy is made on the corpse, made by Dr. Hajek, I think.

The second picture I do not remember and I don't know whether it was one of the corpses that we saw there, but, on the reverse side of this photograph, there is a remark in German that the picture was taken by the Germans and this represents a corpse from Katyn.

Mr. FLOOD. Will the stenographer mark the first one as exhibit 105 and the second one, as described by the doctor, containing the German inscription, as 106?

Dr. NAVILLE. At some spots the tissue was already removed. In some spots there was already a process of calcification, but in some spots you could see a crust on it.

Mr. FLOOD. Do you recall any statements made by the Scientist Orsos with reference to a scientific process having to do with the calcification of the brain pulp in the skull?

Dr. NAVILLE. Yes, that referred to corpse No. 526.

Mr. FLOOD. Will you tell us in brief what the premise of that theory was?

Dr. NAVILLE. That was a process of calcification in the inside of the back part of the skull. I have here a publication by Professor Orsos concerning this subject that he had observed this process of calcification on a corpse lying in the ground more than 3 years.

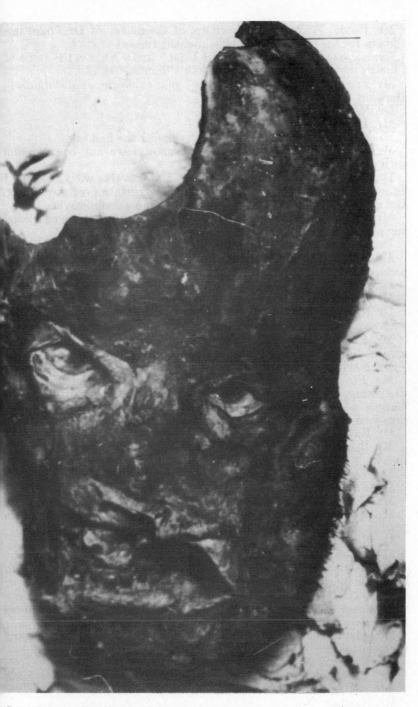

Partly mummified head with smashed jaw, presumably by a rifle butt just before death. Part of the skull cut away for examination.

Mr. FLOOD. Wasn't the importance of the theory of Dr. Orsos important for the purpose of establishing the time of death?

Dr. NAVILLE. Yes, naturally; but I don't know what is the value of a theory which only can be seen once in a thousand cases.

Mr. FLOOD. Do you remember one of your colleagues, the Bulgarian, Markhov?

Dr. NAVILLE. Yes.

Mr. FLOOD. And the Czech, Hajek?

Dr. NAVILLE. Yes, not as well as I remember the first one.

Mr. FLOOD. Did the Bulgarian, Markhov, have any conversation with you during your stay at Katyn?

Dr. NAVILLE. Yes. I remember that I took walks with him, but I do not remember that we discussed the interpretation of these cases. But anyway, he didn't make any objections or special remarks.

Mr. FLOOD. Did the Czech, Dr. Hajek, make any protests or special complaints or remarks?

Dr. NAVILLE. I do not have the slightest recollection of that.

Mr. FLOOD. Did Markhov or Hajek both object to signing the protocol, or did they sign it?

Dr. NAVILLE. Yes; they signed it in my presence.

Mr. FLOOD. Do you have a photograph of such a signing?

Dr. NAVILLE. It happens by accident that I have a photograph here where you can see me signing, and, on my right-hand side, is Markhov.

Mr. FLOOD. I show you a photograph marked for identification as exhibit 107 and ask you if that is the photograph you just described?

Dr. NAVILLE. That's right.

Mr. FLOOD. I now show the doctor a copy of the protocol we are discussing, that was handed to the committee by the distinguished Danish scientist Tramsen, and ask you whether or not you can recognize your signature on page 7 of that document?

Dr. NAVILLE. Yes.

Mr. FLOOD. Do you subscribe to your signature and to that protocol today?

Dr. NAVILLE. Yes.

Mr. FLOOD. That's all.

Mr. Dondero.

Mr. DONDERO. Doctor, did you see any rings, watches, or fountain pens on any of the bodies you saw at Katyn?

Dr. NAVILLE. No.

Mr. FLOOD. Mr. Machrowicz.

Mr. MACHROWICZ. Doctor, was any pressure exerted upon you to have you accept the assignment on this international commission?

Dr. NAVILLE. No. I was very much surprised, because it is a very well-known fact among the public that since World War I, I have hated the Germans so much.

Mr. MACHROWICZ. Did you receive any compensation or reward for your services on that committee?

Dr. NAVILLE. None whatsoever.

Mr. MACHROWICZ. Has any undue pressure been exercised upon you to testify before this committee?

Dr. NAVILLE. No.

Mr. MACHROWICZ. Have you been offered any reward or remuneration for your services in testifying before this committee?

Dr. NAVILLE. No.

Mr. MACHROWICZ. Is your testimony before this committee free and voluntary?

Dr. NAVILLE. That's right.

Mr. MACHROWICZ. Have you ever been approached by anyone with regard to changing your testimony which you gave at the time you signed the protocol in April 1943?

Dr. NAVILLE. No.

Mr. MACHROWICZ. That's all.

Dr. NAVILLE. I remember that the German consulate asked me whether I wished to make a broadcast of my observations in Katyn, and I refused. I am a scientist, a doctor, a physician. I am not making any propaganda.

The trestles are set out in the forest. Note the helmeted field police, far right background.

Dr Vincenzo Mario Palmieri

He agreed with Dr Orsos that the massacre had taken place not later than April or May 1940. Both he and Dr Tramsen confirmed their evidence as recently as 1974.

Chairman MADDEN. Doctor, very briefly for the record, please state how long you have been practicing medicine.

Dr. PALMIERI. Since 1922.

Chairman MADDEN. What universities did you attend?

Dr. PALMIERI. The University of Naples.

Chairman MADDEN. Do you specialize or carry on a general practice of medicine?

Dr. PALMIERI. I specialize in forensic medicine and criminology.

Chairman MADDEN. In the year 1943 were you invited to join a medical commission to make a medical investigation and examination of the bodies that were found in a large grave in the Katyn Forest near Smolensk in Soviet Russia?

Dr. PALMIERI. Yes.

Chairman MADDEN. From whom did you receive the invitation?

Dr. PALMIERI. From the Italian Ministry of Foreign Affairs.

Chairman MADDEN. What was the name of the man issuing this invitation?

Examination of an exhumed corpse. Prof Orsos shows cut-off top of cranium to Dr Saxen to demonstrate calcification of brain matter. Prof Buhtz is looking over Prof Orsos' right shoulder; Dr Markov is facing camera, far left background.

Dr. Palmieri. The invitation came from the Ministry on April 23, telling me to leave on the following day for Rome and go to the Ministry of Foreign Affairs, and when I arrived at the Ministry I was informed further what it was all about.

Chairman Madden. But what was the name?

Dr. Palmieri. A functionary told me that this man was D'Astis, who was Director General within the Ministry.

Chairman Madden. Where did you go from there?

Dr. Palmieri. From the Ministry of Foreign Affairs we went to the German Embassy to get the visas and other documents. When we left the German Embassy, we were told to leave the day after for Berlin by air.

Chairman Madden. Whom did you meet?

Dr. Palmieri. The entire commission was at the Hotel Adlon.

Chairman Madden. Whom did you meet?

Dr. Palmieri. Dr. Naville, Dr. Orsos, Dr. Tramsen, Dr. Costendat, Dr. Markhov, Dr. Speelers, Dr. Hajek, Dr. Saxen, Dr. De Bulet. [Dr. Palmieri had forgotten some of these names but easily recalled them with the help of the subcommittee.] I knew some of these persons and met the others there.

Chairman Madden. Then what did you do?

Dr. Palmieri. There was a second meeting at the hotel in the evening when we met Professor Buhtz a medical specialist, who was killed by the Germans in the last revolt, but at that time was present. He was a liaison officer.

Chairman Madden. From there did you go to Katyn?

Dr. Palmieri. Yes, by air, accompanied by all of the members of the commission and Buhtz.

Mr. Machrowicz. Do you know why you were selected?

Dr. Palmieri. No.

Mr. Machrowicz. You are unquestionably a specialist in this field of medicine?

Dr. Palmieri. There is proof of this matter at the University of Naples.

Mr. Machrowicz. Did anyone use any duress or coercion to have you on this commission?

Dr. Palmieri. No.

Mr. Machrowicz. Was this a voluntary act?

Dr. Palmieri. Yes, I might have said no.

Mr. Machrowicz. When you arrived in Berlin did anyone use any pressure on you?

Dr. Palmieri. No.

Mr. Machrowicz. After you arrived in Smolensk in Katyn did anyone use any duress on you?

Dr. Palmieri. Practically, we did not have any contact with the Germans, only technically.

Mr. Machrowicz. Were you given the authority to go forward in the inspection of the graves?

Dr. Palmieri. They showed us the bodies in the graves. Each one of the committee had as assistants two men and a stenographer.

Mr. Machrowicz. Would you tell us exactly what you saw and what you did at Katyn?

Dr. Palmieri. That is a long story.

Mr. MACHROWICZ. Only the important details to determine the time of the alleged killings.

Dr. PALMIERI. When a certain time has passed from the time of death, the possibility of determining the time of death becomes always more difficult. Therefore one must study the corpse. Generally, two conclusions may be reached by the magistrate on the time of death and can be determined in two ways: Firstly, when did the person die; secondly, between the two dates which we are giving you which is the most probable. The first question is far more difficult to answer if it is a question of establishing dates which are very near to each other when much time has passed. It is much easier to reach a conclusion on the second question, and this is what was done. Two dates are possible—April 1940 or October 1941. Between the two dates there are 18 months, this allows precise orientation. The answer to the question (1940–41) was influenced by two circumstances: (1) The state of the corpses, and (2) the plant life which had been planted over the bodies. In the bodies, or at least in many of the bodies, Professor Orsos observed the presence of growths (corns)—in the inside of the cranium pseudo-growths in the internal part of the skull which are due to manifestations of reduction of the mineralization of the brain—of the cerebral tissues and of the other substances contained in the skull. In a special publication of Professor Orsos in 1934 he had called attention to the fact that these cerebral growths are noticeable on bodies which have been dead for at least 2 years. Orsos had been a prisoner of the Russians during the First World War and had been in Siberia and there had made these special studies which he published in 1934. Secondly, the question of the plants concerns the age of these plants. It is a fact that one notes when a tree is cut that each year a circle is noted for its age. There was this coincidence and led to the conclusion from a technical point of view, and there were others which are not technical arguments, for instance, material found in the pockets—letters, newspapers, diaries—none of these had a date later than April 1940. This was not a medical question.

Mr. MACHROWICZ. From your own experiences and experiments at Katyn did you come to any conclusion as to the time of death of the persons found in these graves?

Dr. PALMIERI. I can say no more than when a person is buried between 18 and 30 months to establish the exact time of burial is difficult.

Mr. MACHROWICZ. What conclusion did you arrive at?

Dr. PALMIERI. I came to a conclusion especially similar to Orsos' theory on the formation of cerebral growth.

Mr. MACHROWICZ. Was Dr. Orsos' conclusion that the deaths occurred not later than April or May 1940?

Dr. PALMIERI. Yes.

Mr. MACHROWICZ. Did you agree?

Dr. PALMIERI. Yes, based on the researches that Dr. Orsos had made.

Mr. MACHROWICZ. Did you sign a report on the results of the investigation?

Dr. PALMIERI. Yes.

Mr. MACHROWICZ. Before you signed, did you read and note the contents?

Dr. PALMIERI. Yes; we worked until 3 in the morning to find a formula in which everyone could sign.

Mr. MACHROWICZ. Then you agreed to that formula?

Dr. PALMIERI. Yes.

Mr. MACHROWICZ. Then your agreement was voluntary, not forced?

Dr. PALMIERI. No; voluntary.

Mr. MACHROWICZ. You met Dr. Markhov there; did you not?

Dr. PALMIERI. I met him there. I did not know him before.

Mr. MACHROWICZ. Did you have any conversation with him?

Dr. PALMIERI. Yes.

Mr. MACHROWICZ. In the course of the conversation you had with Dr. Markhov did he ever tell you that he was compelled or forced to take part on the committee?

Dr. PALMIERI. We spoke of other matters.

Mr. MACHROWICZ. Did he tell you whether or not he agreed with the conclusions of the report?

Dr. PALMIERI. No; we did not speak of that.

Mr. MACHROWICZ. Did you meet Dr. Frantisek Hajek there also?

Dr. PALMIERI. I knew him [Hajek] before. He was an assistant at the Medical-legal Institute in Prague.

Mr. MACHROWICZ. How long before had you known Hajek?

Dr. PALMIERI. Several years.

Mr. MACHROWICZ. Did Dr. Hajek ever tell you that he was forced to become a member of the committee or to sign the report?

Dr. PALMIERI. No.

Mr. MACHROWICZ. Did he indicate to you that his action at the Katyn Forest was free and voluntary?

Dr. PALMIERI. No. Only one person did not sign the results voluntarily—Professor Costedort—because he was not authorized by the French Government. He was free not to sign but to be solely an observer.

Chairman MADDEN. All other members signed willingly?

Dr. PALMIERI. As far as I know and believe the only one was Costedort—not because he did not agree but because he was not authorized.

Mr. MACHROWICZ. Since signing the report have you changed your opinion as to the results.

Dr. PALMIERI. No. Also I have been obliged to make examinations of other corpses, and I have noted the same things found at Katyn; that is the growths.

Mr. MACHROWICZ. Are these pseudo-growths calcium deposits?

Dr. PALMIERI. Yes.

Mr. MACHROWICZ. Has anyone used force or duress to make you appear before this committee today?

Dr. PALMIERI. No; I would also like to add that I am sorry that I could not come to Frankfurt as I was so busy.

Mr. MACHROWICZ. Has this been a free and voluntary statement?

Dr. PALMIERI. Yes.

Mr. MACHROWICZ. Did your conclusion as to the time of death of those found in the Katyn graves rest also on the age of the trees upon the graves and upon the dates of the documents. In other words, was your decision based on all three factors?

Dr. PALMIERI. Yes.

Mr. MACHROWICZ. Did you have the opportunity to select any documents from the grave?

Dr. PALMIERI. Yes.

Mr. MACHROWICZ. Where did you find the documents?

Dr. PALMIERI. The bodies were pulled out from the ground and the documents were in the pockets. We went down in the graves and pointed out which one we wanted to pull out since the heads were out—the grave was only 3 meters deep. Looked like a wine cellar with the necks of the bottles showing.

Mr. MACHROWICZ. Was it possible for someone to have put documents into the pockets after burial?

Dr. PALMIERI. No; because the bodies were so near to each other that it would have been impossible to get between. They were packed in like anchovies in a barrel.

Mr. MACHROWICZ. Did you personally take documents from the bodies?

Dr. PALMIERI. Yes. It was the first thing we examined after looking at the exterior of the bodies.

Mr. MACHROWICZ. Did you find any documents dated after April 1940?

Dr. PALMIERI. No. First we examined the documents, then the clothing, and then followed with the autopsy.

Mr. MACHROWICZ. Is it your conclusion today that the persons were killed in April 1940?

Dr. PALMIERI. It is the same as then; I have not changed.

Mr. MACHROWICZ. That is April 1940?

Dr. PALMIERI. Yes; based on the three points.

The CHAIRMAN. Doctor, we are very grateful and wish to thank you for coming here today to testify.

Dr. PALMIERI. I would also like to add that I was never a Fascist and that in a certain way I was persecuted for not being a Fascist because in 1933 they withdrew my card as a Fascist. I just had it for 1 year because as a theoretical man I could not agree with the Fascist doctrine.

As will be seen from page 12 of the Final Report dated 22 December 1952 (See Appendix I), the Select Committee recommended that the President of the United States forward the evidence to the US delegate to the UN; that he issue instructions to US delegates to present the Katyn case to the General Assembly of the UN; that the General Assembly of the UN seek action in the International World Court of Justice against the Soviet Union and finally that he instruct US delegates to seek the establishment of an international commission which would investigate other mass murders and crimes against humanity. Not one of these recommendations was acted upon!

Exhumed hand and wrist showing rope.

5   Twenty years on: 1952-72

The efforts of the US Select Committee did not fall upon entirely stony ground, for Professor Sir David Savory, MP, raised it in the British House of Commons on 6 November 1952. His interest had been aroused at the time of the German revelations and he went to considerable trouble to piece together the facts as best he could; the more he read in *Soviet War News* the more sceptical he became of the Russian story. He visited the Polish Minister of Information and obtained more evidence. After several weeks he compiled a report which he handed to the then British Foreign Secretary, Ernest Bevin. He told the House how his report had eventually found its way to Nuremberg and he then went on to give a short history of the events which led up to the Katyn massacre followed by an account of the International Medical Commission of 1943 and its findings. He drew the attention of MPs to the work of the US Select Committee and the conclusions it reached, and he ended his speech by urging the Foreign Secretary (who was going to New York the following day) to support the recommendation that the United Nations form an international tribunal further to investigate the Katyn massacre. There is nothing to show that any action was taken, nor that the Foreign Secretary did anything at all about it.

There then appears to be a gap of a full ten years. During this period, although spasmodic references may have been made to Katyn in one country or another, no important definitive statement was made sufficient to attract much attention.

However, on 14 May 1962, Congressman Derwinsky made a significant speech in the House of Representatives in which he tried to establish a special House Committee on Captive Nations and used as his main argument the Katyn case and the findings of the Select Committee of 1952. He referred to a resolution passed in 1949 by the National Council of the Polish Republic on the motion of the Polish Government-in-Exile. This resolution expressed gratification that the initiative for an independent investigation of the Katyn massacre had been undertaken in the United States, and expressed confidence that: "people with sufficient moral strength would be found in the free world, able to bear the burden of struggle for the truth and to wage this struggle victoriously". He told Congress how the Soviets had refused to take part in the Select Committee of 1952 and quoted their memorandum dated 29 February 1952: "The question of the Katyn crime had been investigated in 1944 by an official commission, and it was established that the Katyn case was the work of the Hitlerite criminals, as was made public in the press on January 26, 1944. For 8 years the Government of the United States did not raise any objections to such conclusion of the Commission until recently."

Congressman Derwinsky went on to quote the words of Representative Madden who, in 1952, addressed a mass meeting of Poles in London and, *inter alia,* said: "Katyn is not only a Polish issue, but one that affects the conscience of the entire civilised world being at the same time a threat to this world." Continuing his speech, Derwinsky then made a statement of vast importance, although it appears not to have been singled out for the attention it deserved at the time. He referred to the publication in 1957 of a Secret Soviet document in a German weekly periodical. Giving the date of the document as 10 June 1940, it was said to contain details of how the three camps (Kozielsk, Starobielsk and Ostashkow) were wound up, and thus a solution to that mystery which has bothered so many, namely the

395

whereabouts of the "other 10,000" who were not found at Katyn.

Why no positive action was taken as a result of this particular statement it is *impossible to understand*.

Once again silence descended on the subject in the international field. But the Poles never forgot. In 1965, the twentieth anniversary of the crime, a collection was started to provide funds for some kind of memorial; £635 were spent upon a sculpture which still adorns a special chapel in the Polish church of St Andrew Bobola in London. Its message is plain enough, but only Poles pray there and although such a monument should be seen by the world, it is not. In 1966, the millennium of Polish Christianity, a commemorative plaque was placed in the Polish church in Leicester – again probably only seen by the Polish community.

But the time was approaching when Katyn would again thrust itself on world attention, for the BBC was planning in 1970 to make a documentary film on the subject. It was in the autumn of that year also when I started to write my book *Katyn – a crime without parallel*. The subject was opened up by a letter of mine in the *Daily Telegraph* on 31 October 1970. On 28 January 1971 Professor J. K. Zawodny republished a book about Katyn which attracted several reviews and which started a flood of correspondence in the national press.

This awakened interest was not pleasing to the Soviets. On 8 February 1971 *The Times* published a letter from the London correspondent of the Russian press agency, *Novosti*, in which Mr Felix Alexeyev attempted to portray the Katyn massacre as a crime perpetrated by the German army. This was a foolish move, as it rejuvenated the subject and brought forth a further stream of letters plainly stating that it was the Soviets who were responsible for that ghastly crime. Felix Alexeyev again tried to convince the readership of *The Times* of Russian innocence, to which a telling rejoinder came from Mr Peter Reddaway published on the same day. In his letter, Mr Reddaway mentions Georgiyevich Menshagin who was silenced by the Soviets

Commemorative tablet in the Polish Church in Leicester erected during the millenium of Polish Christianity, 1966.

by incarceration in the Lubianka (1945-51) and in the city jail in Vladimir (1951-May 1970) after which he was put into an old people's home in Knyazhaya Guba in Murmansk region – which is inside the arctic circle.

This spate of accusatory letters brought forth a curiosity: a letter from a Mr Henry Metelmann who wrote to *The Times* saying that he had been in the German army in Russia and knew that the massacre had been committed by his compatriots. Mr Metelmann lives in Godalming, but as yet I have not met him. I should like to as his story is so odd that a full explanation would be welcome. On 19 April 1971 my book was published, timed for the same day as the BBC

397

film previously mentioned, and on 22 April Airey Neave, MP, tabled a motion in the House of Commons which called for an inquiry into the Katyn massacre by the United Nations and "if the evidence is conclusive, condemn those responsible."

This motion, therefore, brought matters back to the recommendation of the 1952 US Select Committee. But in the same way, nothing was done. The British Government could find no time even for a debate on Mr Neave's motion.

These events were noted in Switzerland where, on 28 April, the *Zuricher Zeitung* reported on the BBC film as a result of which the Polish Government petulantly cancelled a proposed visit to Poland by the Director of the BBC.

On 17 June 1971 Lord Barnby initiated a debate in the House of Lords and for over two hours no less than twelve peers pressed for some action or at least statement from the British Government. It was a discussion of importance, for never before had Katyn been discussed in that House. But once again it led to nothing as the Government steadfastly refused to be drawn into the matter. That, however, is not to say that it brought no result at all. The Hansard report was immediately sent to America; on 1 July Congressman Roman Pucinski placed the whole report on Congressional record together with the text of Mr Airey Neave's motion and the names of the 165 MPs who, up to that date, had supported it (Congressional Record, 1.7.71 pages E7015 – E7023). Mr Pucinski had been a member of the 1952 Select Committee, to which he referred in his opening remarks when he said: "I hope we can renew this demand and I shall shortly circulate a petition among our colleagues to join our British counterparts in demanding a UN investigation". This was taken up by the powerful Polish American Congress, the president of which, Mr Aloysius Mazewski, wrote to the US representative to the UN, repeating the demand. The growing campaign in America was taken up by the Assembly of Captive European Nations (ACEN) as reported in *ACEN News* for September-October 1971 (Issue No 152). Protest meetings were held by members of the Polish American Congress in

398

Milwaukee, San Francisco, Los Angeles, Cleveland, Washington and other PAC centres. During this summer of 1971, Katyn was also extensively mentioned in the newspapers of South American countries, of South Africa and in Australia.

Meanwhile in Britain the Poles had been encouraged to write to the BBC asking for a second showing of the documentary film. It was repeated on BBC 1 on 13 October and is said to have reached an audience of perhaps six million people. Many strange concidences have attended this resurgence of interest in Katyn, some of them not completely explained by the word coincidence and which give cause for deep reflection. In the space of half a year this terrible crime of over thirty years before was again world news and the conspiracy of silence under which the perpetrators had hoped to bury it was shattered as completely as if it had happened in April 1940.

Despite all the outcry and all the demands for action, nothing positive was done by any government. The whole matter would probably have died out, as it had so often before, had not the Russians felt compelled to say something. On 16 October 1971 the *Soviet Weekly* published an article entitled "The Truth about Katyn". Once again the old story was trotted out including the accusation against the 537th Engineering Battalion of the German Army, the findings of the Soviet Commission of 1944, the revocation of Professor Markov at Nuremberg coupled with a further revocation by Professor Gaek (presumably they meant Professor Hajek) and winding up with the text of a statement issued in 1952 by the Polish (Communist) Government, from which a quoted extract said:

"The annihilation of thousands of Polish officers and men in Katyn was the deed of Hitlerite criminals who, together with the Crimes of Katyn, committed hundreds of similar crimes on Polish and Soviet territory." Almost incredibly the article rounded off with a reprint of the extraordinary letter from Mr Henry Metelmann, as if it constituted evidence of any value.

Nothing new was produced. It was just the same dull

tale, a compound of lies, out-of-context remarks and a revelation of Russian terror as exemplified by the revocation of Professor Markov and the "statement" forced out of the Polish Government in 1952, presumably meant to counteract the efforts of the US Select Committee of that year. It was a year of renewed hope for the Poles, so long deprived of even a word about Katyn in public discussion. They had seen this subject given as much publicity, if not more, than was accorded to it in 1943. Again and again during the year they must have hoped that some international body would attempt to procure a judgment. But it was not to be. By October it appeared that the usual silence was again about to descend and that the cry from far-off Katyn was once more to me muted and extinguished. What could be done to keep it strong and

Demonstration about Katyn
in Chicago, 1971.

loud? How to prevent all the effort of 1971 being wasted?

It was at this point that a surprising thing happened – a letter from an anonymous Polish exile in Johannesburg reached the author. It contained a donation of 60 Rand (about £30) for the relief of any widow of a Katyn massacre victim who might be in distress and it ended with a short paragraph suggesting that a memorial in honour of the victims be erected in some free country of the West until such time as one could be raised in a free Poland. It was an idea both poignant and provoking. It held the promise of positive action at last. Something *could* be done to perpetuate the memory of those thousands of innocent men, martyred because they would renounce neither their country nor their Faith. Their burial places in Russia were unhallowed and proscribed. Only a small chapel in the

Polish church in London marked their passing for anyone in the West to see, and who, apart from now sadly ageing Poles in exile, was there to see it? The more the idea was contemplated, the more important it seemed.

The author had only one course to pursue: to contact immediately all those who, during the year, had put so much effort into obtaining justice in the Katyn case and for many of whom it had become a mission. Mindful of past disappointments and snubs, the Poles reacted at first with sad scepticism, but later with growing enthusiasm. They felt that they must discuss it amongst themselves, and this they did, reaching the conclusion that the initiative must be seen to be British. The Poles in exile in Great Britain are ever mindful of the hospitality offered them, and with the passing of the years their innate chivalry and excellent manners have never been diminished. They did not therefore feel that on Englsih soil they could sponsor the idea alone. Their leaders met under the chairmanship of that redoubtable war-hero, General Kopanski, and they made up their minds. They would welcome such a monument – *if* it could be achieved!

In the meantime the author had sounded his parliamentary friends, and a meeting was called in the House of Commons. The Poles turned up in force. General Kopanski quietly gave it as the opinion of the Polish community that the idea of a memorial would be most welcome. It was the work of less than an hour to give birth to an Anglo-Polish Committee which christened itself the Katyn Memorial Fund. A suggestion that Lord Barnby be invited to be chairman was greeted with acclaim; Lord St Oswald and Airey Neave accepted the posts of Vice-Chairmen, and the author was proud to accept the post of Honorary Secretary. In retrospect it was an historic moment, for none present in that room could have known whither their steps were leading. Immediate problems of course came to mind, but what was not foreseen was the perfidy to come, nor the hypocrisy nor even the cowardice of those who should have been the first to want to help.

At once problems presented themselves: what kind of

monument? how to pay for it? where to put it? Simple questions of fact, totally unrelated to other powers which started to work against what was proposed. It is a fact that honest men are generally unarmed, at first, to defend themselves in the face of evil; such, indeed, had befallen the Katyn victims during their interrogation in Russia until death finally revealed the black face of Asmodeus.

The Committee launched an appeal for funds throughout that scattered world of Polish exiles wherever they may find themselves, and the response was electric. Mainly through the universal organisation of the Polish Combatants, news spread fast. In all continents locally made efforts produced support, both written and financial. The money started to come in.

The author began a personal search for a site in London to place this historic and vitally important monument. With members of the committee he looked at a place within the borough of Hammersmith. But, as sometimes happens in marriage, first choices are not correct, so in this case attention had not been fully paid to local party political ideas. Hammersmith did not want it, although the refusal was cloaked in the usual ambiguous terms. Obviously a higher authority must be approached and the Greater London Council, after some hesitation, offered two sites: one in Wormwood Scrubbs, seat of a famous prison, and the other in Battersea Park adjacent to a funfair. Whether these offers were made in good faith or in derision is now a matter for conjecture, but quite obviously neither could be contemplated. In the politest terms they were refused and forgotten.

Opposite that famous church of the Oratorians in Brompton Road, London, there is a neglected triangle of ground – like a fingernail tapering off the long finger where Cromwell Road and Thurloe Place come together like the White and the Blue Niles in the Sudan. An interesting spot devoid of its own identity. Perhaps here should be the receptacle of so fascinating an object as the Katyn Memorial?

If it appears that the memorial itself attempts to

403

resurrect things past, so does this tiny piece of land. After considerable correspondence about the ownership it was found to belong to none other than that august but obscure body, the Royal Commission for the Exhibition of 1851. There was an amusing moment when the author telephoned the Secretary and hoped that the Governors were not quite as old as Methuselah, only to find, in the dry reply, that "offices within the Commission were, *obviously, passed on*". In fact the Royal Commission does an excellent work in promoting study in Italy through funds obtained from now most valuable rents. But again an obstacle – the site was on a road subject to heavy traffic and thus unlikely to receive official blessing.

It was all getting rather frustrating until a day when the Leader of the Royal Borough of Kensington and Chelsea, Sir Malby Crofton, joined Lord Barnby, Airey Neave and the author at an informal lunch in the House of Commons. As soon as Sir Malby grasped just what his borough meant to the Poles, and why they wanted the memorial within its bounds, he immediately offered to help. The result was an offer of St Luke's Gardens, Chelsea, adjacent to St Luke's Church.

The third and perhaps most knotty problem was the question of the design of the monument. A sub-committee of the Katyn Memorial Fund was created, whose members were Count Zamoyski, Adam Treszka and the author. An international competition was launched, mainly amongst Poles (even in Poland) and after a time drawings and sketches began to arrive. Some of the projects were, in their way, sublime; others were grotesque; all were conceived rather after the Slavonic or Eastern European manner and it seemed to the author that one salient point had been overlooked. What would be acceptable to the British and, even more important, to the planning authority of a London borough? Again, it had to be realised that statues and other sculptures can be vastly expensive and, indeed, vulnerable to malicious damage (who could say that this precious monument might not be the subject of physical attack or planned destruction?). The answer was suddenly quite clear – an obelisk. London and indeed cities throughout the world abound in obelisks, some tall and thin, some short and broad, but all having the same essentials, even to the point at the apex which prevents fouling by birds. A design was submitted by the author and, most happily, was accepted by the borough planning officer in principle.

Thus the triple problem of money, site and design seemed solved. This was felt to be not too bad a result after only one year. The Committee was confident, little knowing of the vindictive attitude which was later to be adopted by the Church through the excitement of local residents to oppose this whole plan.

Towards the end of autumn the Poles in London reproduced both the once-secret despatches of Sir Owen O'Malley in booklet form, for sale.

The profits went to the Katyn Memorial Fund. A foreword was contributed by Lord Barnby, who said in part:

"In one way or another everyone in the free world has benefited by the sacrifices made by the Poles in the last war, and it cannot be right to abandon them now when they seek help in establishing the guilt of those who brutally murdered so many of their countrymen.

I hope this reproduction of Sir Owen O'Malley's reports will be widely read, and that it will remain a constant reminder of the need for justice until the day that justice is achieved. I commend this pamphlet to anyone with an interest in what is right and what is wrong, and if it causes a few to think again of their charitable and Christian duties to gallant ex-allies then something will have been gained."

Charity – Christian duty; who at the end of 1972 was in doubt that these virtues would be displayed, and who then could have forseen the cowardice, duplicity and malice which were later and so disgracefully to sour this noble plan? Certainly I felt that all must go well, so that when offered an opportunity of serving the UN in a refugee relief operation in the Sudan I felt free to accept, confident that my task as to the Katyn Memorial was largely done.

But even in Khartoum and Juba news reached me of increasing difficulties encountered by the committee, placed in its path by the Diocesan Advisory Committee upon which sits the Archdeacon of Middlesex. Middlesex is remote from the vast Sahara, and the gardens next to St Luke's church are tiny by comparison with the endless central plain of Africa. Only the tomb of the Mahdi in Omdurman somehow recalled the Katyn monument – a place of homage, a treasured spot for those with memories and with loyalty.

6   The Katyn Memorial 1973-5

I returned from Africa in the early summer of 1973 to find that more and more arguments were being mounted against the memorial project. The Diocesan Advisory Committee put up one feeble complaint after another; it took its time in considering rebuttals; it created innumerable delays. Slowly at first the confidence of the committee was undermined, and the Poles shook their heads and looked back to other instances when they had been snubbed. What lay behind all this procrastination? The land of St Luke's Gardens has belonged to the borough for nearly a hundred years, and it had voluntarily offered the site. Further it was the planning authority and it had given its blessing to the final drawings so excellently produced after immense effort by Ryszard Gabrielczyk, a consulting engineer of great merit who gave of his best without any fee.

Somehow an uneasy feeling crept in; something was going wrong; unseen forces were at work to try and prevent the memorial ever reaching completion. Was it possible these forces emanated from the church authorities? There could be no other explanation, and yet it should have been unthinkable.

Now St Luke's Gardens was a burial ground up until 1857, and despite the fact that the church sold the land to the borough it nevertheless retains certain if archaic rights over it. The Disused Burial Grounds Act of 1884 demands that a "faculty" be granted before anything can be placed in or taken out of such a disused burial ground, and it was upon this unsuspected rock that the memorial project found itself stuck.

Perhaps the church thought that by creating a delay of nearly two years the Katyn Memorial Fund would just "go away", but it misjudged the single-minded purpose which inspired the committee, just as another misjudgment was to follow in due course. The committee was not to be deflected from its purpose, and the day drew ever nearer when a trial of strength in the London Diocesan Consistory Court would bring the parties face to face. And so 1973 came to an end, with a conflict looming on the horizon, and with a hardening of attitudes on both sides. As has been said, the date of the Katyn massacre was to be plainly inscribed on the monument – 1940. Was it of this that the Church was so frightened? Was it the truth, the awful truth in this case, which caused the Archdeacon of Middlesex to tremble? It was beginning to look very much as if this was the key.

Thus 1974 dawned with both sides preparing for battle: on one side the Royal Borough of Kensington and Chelsea with its redoubtable leader Sir Malby Crofton joined by the Katyn Memorial Committee headed by Lord Barnby, with Lord St Oswald and Airey Neave MP as vice-chairmen; on the other stood the Archdeacon of Middlesex, the Rector of St Luke's backed by the whole machinery of the Church of England. It may seem strange that this should be so, but it was. Solicitors took instructions and counsel were briefed; the typewriters clicked, and a battlefield was chosen: St Paul's Church, Covent Garden, that singular "barn" built by Inigo Jones.

Spring turned to summer, and the first hearing took place in the church in June. From the very outset it was obvious that the Church was to use every possible means and subterfuge to defeat the monument if it could. On that first day also appeared the underlying difficulty. As had been suspected, it was the date "1940" which stuck, like a bone, in the throat of the Church. The Chancellor of the Diocese said that he would divide the case into two parts:

Isometric projection of the Katyn Memorial as originally designed in 1972.
(The small pines have now been abandoned.)

first whether or not the memorial itself was allowable, and only then would he consider a second aspect, that of the inscription (containing the lowering date of "1940"). Counsel for the Archdeacon said she would prefer some looser statement instead of "1940" such as "in the early years of the war". Such a statement of course would have included "1941" the date when the Soviets said the massacre was committed by the Germans, so it was in this way that the Church sought once again to cover up the dreadful reality of Katyn and to smudge the truth.

The Poles turned away in disgust when they sensed that this was to be another attempt to bury Katyn, to lose it and to existinguish again the pain and the sorrow which lies behind it in so many Polish hearts. But the raft upon which the Church was launched was unstable; it could not look good that the Church, presumably the fount of that same Christian charity to which Lord Barnby had referred, was seen to stamp on the feet of waiting mourners and turn them away. Already the newspapers were sniffing at the Chancellor's gown, and growling at his peremptory dismissal of the date question. Some other and more palatable method must be discovered to thwart the monument and distract attention from the Church's ignoble purpose. What better than the united voice of local residents, always vociferous in Chelsea?

This appeared an excellent way out, and the Chancellor seized upon it avidly. He adjourned the court and instructed the church-wardens to "find out what the local residents thought". Now these residents had already had every chance to consider the memorial, and as a public record, the detailed drawings were available to them in the Town Hall. They had done nothing, not even when a notice of the forthcoming hearings was nailed to the church door. But now they were to be mobilised and militated against the monument, and no effort was spared. The churchwardens hurried about their business, persuading people of the horrifying proportions of the memorial, of how unsuitable it was, of how it would ruin their peaceful and lovely garden where the "elderly" so liked to sit in the sun. They worked themselves and the residents into a foam of disapproval and they started a petition – that popular method of consolidating public thought. They were joined by the Chelsea Society; by other bodies and the clamour grew. The uncourageous, and there are not a few of them, began to wobble. There was much whispering, and many letters to the national press. *The Times* alone published no less than 18, nicely balancing 9 for the project and 9 against. The battle was attracting attention in ever increasing circles, like a stone dropped into a limpid pool. Accusations were hurled; invective was used and tempers flared. But one thing was certain; Katyn was talked of perhaps almost as much as on and after that fateful day in April 1943 when the mass-graves were opened and their ghastly contents shown to the world. Amidst the din the Poles said little; they had seen it all before; no one wanted Katyn. But did these local residents, I wondered, fully understand what they were at? On 19 October 1974 *The Times* published my article explaining what it was all about, an article which drew an unexpected echo from a highly placed leader of the UN, at that time attending the General Assembly in New York. It was a gratifying moment, and it also brought a new ally, the Provost of Brompton Oratory, whose church had been offered as an alternative site without his having been first approached. And there were converts to the cause, as well as new enemies. The Germans too were watching with growing interest. Would the date "1940" be allowed? Would someone, at last, proclaim that it was not they who had done this awful thing in Russia? It was a fascinating fascinating spectacle: the Royal Borough, and the Anglo-Polish memorial committee against the Church which seemed intent on preventing any announcement in stone of Soviet guilt. The imagination stumbles on the implications.

The case, too, stumbled on throughout the autumn and the costs increased. The costs had to come from money subscribed from all parts of the world by exiles many of whom could hardly afford their daily bread; costs put upon

411

them by the "charity" of the Church. Obviously the intention was to whittle away the Fund's slender finances to a point where surrender was the only reply. But such is the smallness of small men's minds that they did not realise that Faith is larger than Mammon, nor that in this matter was the concept of justice fully understood. Neither the Royal Borough nor the Memorial Fund bent one inch, and 1975 was awaited with considerable expectancy. There was indeed a meeting in Kensington Town Hall, convened within the popular spirit of "consultation". This spirit is the modern manner of putting off that which is inevitable; it is the soft option in the hope that some compromise can be found. But there was no offer of compromise for the 14,471 who lost their lives in Russia during the early part of 1940, and thus this effort in 1974 was an echo of nothing.

But in the meantime truth was at stake, and the assiduous efforts of legal minds were at work. Forensic specialists had voluntarily taken part in examining the corpses found in the forest. Were any of them still available to say again what they then stated? This historic task was entrusted to a girl who, by the whims of life, had recently found herself an assistant solicitor within the framework of the Royal Borough of Kensington and Chelsea. Meticulously she set about finding the truth as could be expressed in a court of law. In the event she traced Dr Tramsen in Denmark and obtained from him a sworn statement.

"I, Helge Andreas Boysen Tramsen in the Kingdom of Denmark Doctor of Medicine of the University of Copenhagen make oath and say as follows:

1. I am and I have at all material times been a Danish national. I am a practitioner in Copenhagen and at the same time a lecturer at the University. I did my final examination in 1936 at the Copenhagen University and had surgical training at the University clinic in Copenhagen, Rigs Hospital and several other hospitals. Prior to 1943 I had three years training in pathology and forensic medicine at the University Institute in Copenhagen. I am now 63

412

years of age. I am able to read and understand documents including scientific documents written in the English and German languages.

2. In April 1943, when Denmark was in German occupation I was Prosector at the University Institute of Forensic Medicine in Copenhagen. I was asked by the Danish Foreign Office on behalf of Dr Conti who was the Head of the Health Department of the German Reich, to take part in an investigation of mass graves which had been discovered by German troops who were then in occupation of a large area of Russia including the town of Smolensk. For the purpose of the investigation the German government assembled an International Medical Commission. It had twelve members. One was Professor Francois Naville, the Professor of Forensic Medicine and Criminology at the University of Geneva. Apart from this one representative of a neutral country, the members of the Commission were all drawn from countries then occupied by Germany or within the sphere of German influence, including Germany's ally Italy. There were, however, no German members of the Commission.

3. The members of the Commission were assembled at Berlin and from there we travelled to the Katyn Forest approximately 16 kilometres west of Smolensk. We remained there from the 28th to the 30th April 1943. At a place called Kosy Gory within the Forest seven graves filled with bodies had been opened. In common with the other members of the Commission I examined the graves and the bodies which they contained. The corpses had been buried fully dressed and in a great many cases it was possible to identify the uniforms as being those of Polish officers. Of a total of 982 bodies which were exhumed and examined some 70 per cent were identified. In the case of every body which I examined death had been caused by a shot in the nape of the neck. I have no doubt whatsoever that at the time when the members of the Commission examined the bodies in April 1943 they had lain in the ground for three years. This means that death must have occurred in the spring of 1940. The pathological evidence pointing to this

413

date was confirmed by documents found on the bodies which bore dates covering the period between the autumn of 1939 and April 1940. Furthermore, the members of the Commission personally questioned a number of Russians living in the vicinity who stated that in March and April 1940 large numbers of Polish officers had arrived almost daily at the railway station of Gniezdovo, which is near Katyn, and were sent from the station towards the forest in lorries and not heard of again. I understand that the Germans found over 4000 bodies at Kosy Gory. I see no reason to doubt this figure.

4. Throughout their investigation the members of the Commission were afforded complete freedom of movement by the German authorities, who provided such technical means as might be of assistance. Neither while we were at Katyn nor at any later date were we the members of the Commission placed under any kind of pressure by the Germans. Having completed our examination we returned to Berlin and handed over our Report to Dr Conti. The Commission was then disbanded. The Report of the Commission was written in the German language. A photographic copy of the Report is now produced and shown to me marked 'T.1'. I am able to confirm its accuracy and also the fact that it bears my signature. A copy of the Report translated into the English language is now produced and shown to me marked 'T.2'. I am able to confirm that this is an accurate translation.

Sworn at the British Embassy, Consular Section, Copenhagen 12 July 1974 before the British Vice Consul, a Commissioner for Oaths."

An identical testimonial was provided by Vincenzo Mario Palmieri, another of the eminent doctors who took part (with Markov) in the examination of the bodies which the German Army had caused to be dug up. But these two affidavits are dated 1974, and they affirm the same facts as the signatories stated in 1943, thirty-one years previously.

Based upon the known facts, and the indisputable evidence of these surviving members of the International

Commission, counsel for the petitioners (in the matter of the "Faculty") stated the case as follows:

"1. Your Petitioners refer to their Amended Petition herein and in particular to paragraph 3 thereof and the Schedule thereto from which it appears that your Petitioners desire that the Memorial which they seek to erect should bear the words "Katyn 1940" and a further commemorative inscription as follows:

'In remembrance of 14,500 Polish prisoners-of-war who disappeared from camps at Kozielsk, Starobielsk and Ostashkow in 1940, of whom 4,500 were later identified in mass graves at Katyn near Smolensk.'

Your Petitioners will show that the said inscription is an accurate historical record of the event which it is intended to commemorate.

2. On the 1st September 1939 armed forces of the Third German Reich crossed the border between Germany and Poland and advanced rapidly eastwards although strongly resisted by the armed forces of the Republic of Poland. A state of war thus existing between Poland and Germany, the Government of the United Kingdom of Great Britain and Northern Ireland declared war on Germany on the 3rd September 1939. On the 17th September 1939 armed forces of the Union of Soviet Socialist Republics crossed the border between Russia and Poland and advanced rapidly westwards. On the 28th September 1939 the Polish armed forces capitulated. Poland was thereupon divided by the Ribbentrop-Molotov line into zones of German and Russian occupation. Your Petitioners say that the facts and events related in this paragraph, together with the fact of the German attack on and invasion of Russia and the fact of the German broadcast to which reference is hereinafter made, are notorious facts relating to the existence of a state of war affecting the Government of the United Kingdom of Great Britain and Northern Ireland and accordingly facts of which the Courts take judicial notice. Your Petitioners intend to prove the other facts and events herein related.

3. The Russians deported from Poland into Russia

upwards of 200,000 prisoners-of-war. These prisoners included not only members of the Polish armed forces, but also personnel of the Polish police and a considerable number of professional men. Approximately 15,000 of the aforesaid prisoners were accommodated in camps (hereinafter referred to as 'the Special Camps') at Kozielsk (about 4,500 prisoners) Starobielsk (about 4,000 prisoners) and Ostashkow (about 6,500 prisoners). The approximate locations of the Special Camps are shown on the map annexed hereto.

4. Of the prisoners at Kozielsk the great majority were officers of the Polish armed forces (land, naval and air).

5. Of the prisoners at Starobielsk the great majority were also officers (including eight generals) and included Roman Catholic Priests, Protestant Ministers and Jewish Rabbis. Amongst the reserve officers were several hundred university professors and lecturers, about 400 surgeons and physicians, several hundred engineers with university degrees, several hundred lawyers (including judges, public prosecutors, solicitors and civil servants), a great number of high school and grammar school teachers, many poets, writers and journalists and a great number of social welfare workers and politicians.

6. Of the prisoners at Ostashkow about 400 were officers (300 being officers of the militarised Polish police). In addition there were non-commissioned officers private soldiers of the Intelligence Service, the Military Police, the Frontier Guards, the State Police and Prison Warden Corps, several scores of priests, ex-servicemen settlers, landowners and Court magistrates.

7. The aforementioned prisoners were held in the Special Camps from November 1939 until April 1940. During that period they were extensively interrogated by the Russians. In April or early May 1940 107 prisoners from Kozielsk were moved to Pavlishchev Bor (the location of which is shown on the said map). Later they were joined by 79 prisoners from Starobielsk, about 132 prisoners from Ostashkow and about 90 more prisoners from Kozielsk, making a total of about 408. Later these prisoners were

moved to a camp at Griazovetz (the location of which is also shown on the said map). On the 22nd June 1941 the armed forces of the Third German Reich attacked the Russians. In August and September 1941 the said prisoners at Griazovetz were released by the Russians. Until approximately the end of April 1940 the prisoners in the Special Camps maintained communication with their relations and friends. After that date all communication with the prisoners remaining in the Special Camps ceased. The dead bodies of upwards of 4,000 prisoners who had been confined at Kozielsk were found in the circumstances hereinafter related. Your Petitioners submit that those prisoners who remained at Starobielsk and Ostashkow and of whom no further news has ever been received by their relations and friends must be presumed to be dead.

8. Following the German attack on Russia the Government of the Union of Soviet Socialist Republics released not only the prisoners at Griazovetz but also numerous other Polish prisoners of war with a view to the formation of a new Polish Army under the command of the late General Anders. It rapidly became apparent to the Polish authorities in Russia who were raising the new army that many Polish officers who had been taken prisoner by the Russians were missing. Information obtained from the prisoners who had been released from the camp at Griazovetz showed that the missing officers had been confined in the Special Camps and enquiries disclosed that communication with them had (as hereinbefore stated) ceased at about the end of April 1940. No satisfactory information as to their whereabouts was (or ever has been) forthcoming from the Russian authorities.

9. Following the attack on the 22nd June 1941 the Germans advanced rapidly into and occupied Western Russia including the region of Smolensk and Forest of Katyn (both of which are shown on the said map). On the 13th April 1943 the Germans in a broadcast by Radio Berlin announced that a mass burial of Polish officers had been discovered at Katyn.

10. In all the Germans discovered seven mass graves at

Katyn. The German Government assembled an International Medical Commission to investigate these graves. The said Commission visited the Katyn Forest from the 28th to the 30th April 1943 and the members of the Commission examined the graves and the bodies which they contained. In a great many cases the bodies were clothed in the uniforms of Polish officers. Death had been caused by shooting in the nape of the neck. The pathological evidence showed that the corpses had lain in the ground for three years so that death had occurred in the spring of 1940. This pathological evidence was confirmed by documents on the bodies which bore dates covering the period between the autumn of 1939 and the spring of 1940.

11. In the premises your Petitioners submit that the inscription which they desire to be included as part of the proposed Memorial is not other than a correct historical record of an event proper to be commemorated by a memorial on consecrated land to soldiers and others who have died honourably in war and that the said inscription ought accordingly to be permitted by this Worshipful Court."

The Statement was then sent to counsel for the Archdeacon of Middlesex. It can therefore be said categorically that the Church was in possession of the truth before the end of 1974.

Not content with the unanswerable evidence given by Drs Tramsen and Palmieri, the Assistant Borough Solicitor assembled further facts from eminent Poles in exile who still live amongst us in Great Britain. Major Prince Eugene Lubomirski provided a definitive statement of great authority.

"1. I reside at 18 Hornton Street London W.8. I was born in Poland in 1895 of a Polish landowning family.

2. In September 1939 I was arrested by the Soviet political authorities when the Russian Army invaded Poland. I was deported to Russia and imprisoned. In the autumn of 1941 as a result of the Sikorski-Stalin Agreement

418

following Hitler's attack on Russia I was released from a hard labour camp in the Arctic Circle and in November 1941 I was appointed ADC to General Anders who was forming a Polish Army under his command.

3. In my capacity as ADC I was closely involved with the search for surviving officers to take command in the new army. It was very quickly apparent that there were still missing many officers who it was known had been taken prisoner by the Russians. The Russians stated that they had no knowledge of any prisoners remaining under their control. Eventually it became apparent from information given by officers coming from a camp at Griazovetz that many of the missing officers had been interned in prisoner of war camps at Kozielsk, Starobielsk and Ostashkow prior to the liquidation of those camps in April 1940. With the exception of the 400 or so men who had been sent from those camps to Griazovetz, nothing had been heard of the 14,000 other prisoners.

4. In November 1941 General Anders set up a Bureau to deal with the families of officers who had been in the three camps and to try to locate the whereabouts of the missing men. Part of my work was involved with the Bureau under Captain Kackowski. During the time I was working for the Bureau a large number of letters went through my hands during the period from May 1942 to June 1942. These letters were written by people in search of their relatives, officers and enlisted men. These people knew from earlier correspondence with their relatives that the latter were placed by the end of 1939 and in the winter and spring of 1940 in the camps at Kozielsk, Starobielsk and Ostashkow. All of the letters emphasised, I do not know for what reason, that before March and May 1940 which dates were continously repeated, they received information about the missing men fairly regularly and replies to letters sent to them but that from March and May 1940 all correspondence ceased.

5. Included with the letters from the relatives, were many postcards written by the men while they were at the three camps sent by the relatives as evidence that the men

had been there. Most of the postcards that I saw had the last dates in February, March or the last few days in April 1940. In every case when the relatives had written to the Bureau they informed us that they had made enquiries of the Russian Authorities who had replied that they had no knowledge of the whereabouts of the missing men.

6. Diplomatic talks went on with the Russians but no information was revealed as to the whereabouts of the men beyond a statement in 1941 that all prisoners of war had been released.

7. Simultaneously with the work of the Bureau and the diplomatic talks, General Anders was able to make direct enquiries of the NKVD which had prisoners of war under its control. By February 1942 a more or less complete list of the missing officers was available compiled from the information given by the officers coming from Griazovetz and this was handed to Stalin by General Anders in March 1942. Stalin said that he had given orders for the release of the men and he did not know where they were. General Anders told me this as soon as he left Stalin.

8. Despite all these enquiries, none of the officers missing from March and April 1940 who were desperately needed for the new army were ever heard of until 1943 when the mass graves in the Katyn Forest were discovered. As the bodies were identified it was clear that about 4,500 of the missing officers had been buried there.

9. After the War, I found myself in the United Kingdom in the Polish Resettlement Corps together with the majority of the Polish soldiers who refused to return to Poland which was now under a Communist regime. After demobilisation, I settled in Kensington where I work in Polish institutions.

10. In common with many Polish ex-combatants who remained in Britain after the war, I was personally acquainted with several victims of the Katyn Massacre among whom were three members of my son-in-law's family. Some of these Polish officers came from the Reserve and were doctors, lawyers, eminent academicians and politicians. Although the majority were of the Roman

Catholic faith, many other faiths were represented among the victims.

11. On the termination of the Resettlement Corps the Polish soldiers who remained in the West were given the opportunity to settle in the free world. The majority remained in Great Britain. I personally decided to settle in this country because of the close links which had in the past existed between our two countries, links which extended back over many centuries, and also because of my respect for the British principles of justice and freedom. I have always regarded the Royal Borough of Kensington and Chelsea as being especially linked with Polish ex-combatants who now live in this country as so many of our institutions, associations and communal centres are situated in the Borough. I am certain that if my fellow countrymen who died in 1940 had survived, many would have settled like myself in England. For these reasons I feel that St Luke's Gardens is a very appropriate site for the memorial to the victims of Katyn."

As did Wladyslaw Jerzy Cichy, of the Lutheran persuasion.

"1. I reside at 17 Kensington Court Gardens, London W8.

2. In September 1939 I was a cadet officer in the Polish Army and I was taken prisoner by the Russians on the 20th September 1939. By early October 1939 I had been sent to a prisoner of war camp at Tietkino in the Ukraine. At the beginning of November 1939 the whole camp was transferred to Kozielsk where we were joined by many other prisoners. The prisoners numbered about 4,500, mainly officers of the Polish forces but some civilians – professors, lawyers, doctors and other professional men. Sanitary conditions at Kozielsk were appalling due to the over-crowding and there were rumours re-inforced by Russian hints that we would be sent to other camps before the following summer for health reasons.

3. On the 3rd April 1940, the names of individual

prisoners were called out and they left the camp. We did not know why they had been taken nor where but there were rumours that they were going home to Poland. I never saw nor heard of them alive again. After that day, parties of prisoners would leave almost every day numbering between 80 and 300 in each party. The camp was obviously being liquidated but we could get no definite information from the Russians.

4. On the 26th April 1940 my name was called out and I left with a party of 107 consisting of all ranks. There was no pattern to the formation of any of the parties but it was common knowledge that the lists were given to the camp authorities from Moscow.

5. I left the camp and we were loaded into lorries and taken to railway sidings at Kozielsk station and put into prison wagons. We did not know where we were going but from chalked messages knew that we were in the same wagons as had been used to transport the earlier parties. The others had left scribbled messages on the sides of the wagons and one message which I read said in Polish "We are being detrained at Gniezdowo." I also saw the names of some of my former colleagues. After one or two days travelling we stopped at Babyno at about noon. We were detrained and transported to Pawlizczew Bor. There we found a pleasant camp at which there was much more room than at Kozielsk. At that time we believed that our colleagues who had left before us had been taken to similar smaller camps for sanitary reasons. This was at the end of April 1940.

6. We were soon joined by 79 prisoners of war from a camp at Starobielsk in the Ukraine and then by a party of about 132 from a camp at Ostashkow. A further group of about 90 from Kozielsk arrived last bringing the number in the new camp to about 400. We then exchanged views with the prisoners from the other camps and found that the same process of liquidation had been followed there.

7. In mid-May 1940 we were transferred to another camp at Griazowietz halfway between Moscow and Archangel where we remained until we were released in

August/September 1941. During that time we believed that our former colleagues were in similar camps and expected to hear something of them at least indirectly.

8. Until we left Kozielsk we were allowed to write to our families about once a month and we were allowed to do so again after we reached Griazowietz. As soon as we were allowed to receive letters again from Poland, we heard from friends of our former colleagues asking us for news of them and why they did not write. We began to get more and more such enquiries and became very worried as we began to realise that something must have happened to them. I first received such an enquiry in August 1940.

9. After I left Kozielsk in April 1940 I never saw or heard of most of my colleagues again until the list of bodies found at Katyn Forest was published and I saw that many of their names appeared on the list.

10. With regard to religion, it is true that the majority of the prisoners in the camp were Roman Catholics. Nevertheless, all other creeds were represented in the camp e.g. Orthodox Church, Jews, the Lutheran and Calvinistic Churches. I am myself of the Lutheran faith and I knew other Protestants among my fellow prisoners. There were quite a number of Jews also especially among the civilian prisoners mostly professional men e.g. doctors, lawyers, actors etc."

Ryszard Gabrielczyk, who has given so much of his valuable time and knowledge to the design of the Katyn Memorial, also testified *inter alia:*

"10. I was born in East Poland and in the winter of 1939/40 I was resettled with my family and many other people from East Poland into the depths of Russia. My family and I arrived in Charitonowo camp on the River Wychegda, about 60 kilometres north from Kotlas in the Solvichegorsky region of Archangel.

11. My godfather, Witold Sierpinski, a captain in the Polish Army, had been taken prisoner in the autumn of 1939 and was in a prisoner of war camp near Smolensk in

the Soviet Union. Whilst in Charitonowo, and indeed before, I was personally in correspondence with my godfather as were my father and the Captain's brother, Kazimicrz Sierpinski who was in the same camp as us. We were in adjacent barracks and used to exchange the news we had of the Captain almost weekly.

12. In the summer of 1940 one or two of my letters to the Captain were returned by the Russians with a note saying they could not be delivered at the address stated. My father and the Captain's brother had their letters returned also. Kazimierz Sierpinski and my father then wrote to the Russian authorities asking for the whereabouts of Captain Sierpinski and in about August or September 1940 an official Russian notification which I saw arrived saying that the Captain's present whereabouts were unknown and that he was no longer in the custody of the Russian authorities responsible for prisoners of war. The Russian authorities suggested that he might have escaped into Manchuria. I personally saw the letters sent and returned as I delivered them to and from the camp Commandant to the people involved. I was also present when my father and Kazimierz Sierpinski exchanged news.

13. I personally gave up hope for my godfather in the summer of 1940 and was most upset to see his name on the official list of the victims of the Katyn Massacre. His number on the list is 1356."

If nothing else remains in the reader's mind, crowded by now with horror and desolation, the thought of corpse No 1356 must bring a moment of absolute silence.

Thus 1974 ended, with the combatants still aface, and the matter of a judgment in the hands of the Chancellor of the London Diocese of the Church of England. Doubtless he pondered in depth while Christianity celebrated the birth of the Good Shepherd. Just how deeply he pondered can be seen from his judgement, delivered in St Luke's Church on 15 January 1975. Shamefully, he refused to grant the faculty. (He held that the obelisk was a building within the meaning of the Act; he considered that the

Montage to show relative size of Katyn Memorial to St Luke's Church, Chelsea.

Royal Borough was in breach of its trust as to an "open space" and these legal arguments he backed up with the whipped-up opposition of the local residents, itself the result of misrepresentation.)

There is one simple postscript to this chapter and it is contained in a letter received by the author (in his capacity as Honorary Secretary of the Katyn Memorial Fund) from His Excellency the President of Poland dated 16 January 1975:

"Thank you for your letter dated 15 January, in which you inform me about the disastrous results of the Court case in respect of the erection of Katyn Memorial on English soil.

I convey to you and the Committee my most sincere thanks for your courageous and manly initiative and endeavours in this matter.

I trust that both you and the Committee will spare no effort in furthering this great cause, which should serve as a warning not only to the inhabitants of Great Britain, but to all humanity as well.

I take this opportunity to express ... (etc)
Sgd: Stanislaw Ostrowski"

A final word can be added. On 5 February 1975 the Katyn Memorial Committee met again. It had before it telegrams from the Katyn Committee in Chicago and the Polish American Congress. Both urged that an appeal against the judgement be lodged. News was also available that the Royal Borough would support any appeal by the committee. The committee took its only proper decision. It would appeal. The author, as Honorary Secretary, issued a press release on the following day, which it is hoped truly reflects the wishes of the Polish President.

"Release date: 7 February 1975

Katyn Memorial

By a unanimous decision of those present on 5 February, the Katyn Memorial Fund decided to give notice of appeal against the judgement delivered by the Chancellor of the London Diocese in the consistory court which sat in St Luke's Church, Chelsea, on 15 January. In so doing the Fund reflects the cabled desires of the Katyn Memorial Fund Committee in Chicago and the Polish-American Congress.

The Fund heard that any appeal to the Court of Arches would be supported by the Royal Borough of Kensington and Chelsea and it is proud again to join with the local authority in so important a cause. It is particularly grateful to Sir Malby Crofton for his unswerving help.

In the absence of Lord Barnby abroad, the Fund's committee sat under the chairmanship of Airey Neave MP, and it also decided to launch a "fighting fund" with the aim of replenishing its financial resources which have been somewhat eroded by the prolonged legal proceedings caused by the objections of the Church. A sub-committee of the Fund's officers will direct this new appeal with the welcome addition of Sir Frederick Bennett MP.

The costs imposed upon the Fund through action taken and encouraged by the Church (which will include the cost of the appeal to the higher court) amount to some £6,000. The Fund is wholly confident that those who recall Poland's sacrifices during and after the war, and who sympathise with the sorrow of those bereaved by the massacre, will respond and thereby assist our gallant ex-allies who so fervently seek to honour the memory of the 14,471 men who were murdered at Katyn and two other places in 1940.

Louis FitzGibbon
Honorary Secretary,
London 6 February 1975   The Katyn Memorial Fund"

The London Diocesan Consistory Court sitting in St Paul's Church, Covent Garden, summer 1974.

7 "The other 10,000" and the secret NKVD report of 1940

So far this book has concerned itself with Katyn, which is to say the massacre of 4,500 Polish prisoners whose bodies were found by the Germans in Katyn forest in 1943. A comment on that is contained in Solzhenitsyn's now famous book *Gulag Archipelago* where, on page 77, he says:

"They took those who were too independent, too influential, along with those who were too well-to-do, too intelligent, too noteworthy; they took particularly many Poles from former Polish provinces. (It was then that ill-fated Katyn was filled up; and then too that in the northern camps they stockpiled fodder for the future army of Sikorski and Anders.)"

But "Katyn" is a collective word used to embrace not only those 4,500 found in the forest of that name, but a further 10,000 murdered at the same time. These were the men imprisoned at Starobielsk (about 4,000) and at Ostashkow (about 6,000). It is customary to refer to them shortly as "the other 10,000 – whose whereabouts has remained a mystery".

10,000 murdered prisoners cannot be dismissed in so short a sentence. This figure represents perhaps the population of a sizeable town, or if seen as an army advancing across the plain it would appear a mighty host indeed. One thing is certain: just as no word ever came from the 4,500 Poles in Kozielsk camp after May 1940, so also was nothing again heard after that date from the 4,000 in Starobielsk camp, nor from the 6,000 in Ostashkow camp. They could not just vanish, and their corpses must be somewhere. But where? In his excellent book, *The Katyn Wood Murders,* Joseph Mackiewicz has this to say.

"Lieut Mlynarski, mentioned already, acted as DAC to the so-called 'Senior Officer' of the Starobielsk camp. The post of Senior Officer was held in turn by Major Zalewski, Major Niewiarowski and Major Chrystowski. On 5 April 1940, it was Major Niewiarowski who held the post.

At about 9 am that day, the Soviet camp commander, Lt-Col Boreshkov, with Kirshov, the political commissar, called upon the Senior Officer and told him that the camp was going to be wound up, and that same day the first group of 195 officers was to leave the camp.

'Where to?' asked Major Niewiarowski.

'Where? ...' Boreshkov drawled his answer. 'Home! To your own homes. You will be sent first to transit camps, and then – to where you came from, to your wives – he, he, he!'

And from then on, transports were sent out daily. In the mornings, roll-calls were held in the spacious room of the commander of block No 20. The selected men were immediately searched there. The daily groups varied from 60 to 240 persons.

One day Lieut Mlynarski asked Boreshkov: 'Why do you send us away in groups of 240 at the most? Having brought us all here together in thousands, you could surely send us back the same way?'

'We can't,' he answered. 'The whole world is at war. We have to be ready too. We cannot spare the transport.'

The 26 of April came. Suddenly the transports were cancelled. This lasted till 2 May when a certain number were sent again. Then there was another delay until 8, 11 and 12 May on which days the last transports left Starobielsk. Those amongst the prisoners who later on reached Griazovietz were strictly ordered to keep apart from the others. When those still remaining in camp were

431

heartily saying goodbye to those departing, the camp commander used to say ironically: 'You will all soon meet again!'

What also was very striking, was that for each transport prisoners were chosen from various blocks. Special care was taken that no 'brothers', no people belonging to the same 'gang' or others who had formed small intimate circles of friends, were sent together. This was brought to the notice of the camp commander, always with the same result.

'No good! You will all meet again soon anyhow.'

Where? That was the next question asked.

On 25 April in block No 20 a 'special list' of names was read out aloud. It included 63 names. The prisoners were loaded into railway trucks and sent to Voroshilovgrad and from there to Kharkov, where the train was held up. One of the prisoners managed to poke his face through a chink in the door. A railway worker happened to pass by, walking with slow measured steps. He was tapping the wheels of the train with a hammer.

'Comrade!' whispered the prisoner. 'Is this Kharkov?'

'*Da* ... (Yes) Kharkov. Prepare for leaving the train. That's where all "yours" are being unloaded and sent further in cars.'

'Where to?'

The railway worker shrugged his shoulders. Then he spat between the wheels and got on with his job.

This is all that is known ...

The 'special group' was not unloaded in Kharkov. In the end it reached Griazovietz where ... they never found the other inmates of their camp.

What happened at the same time in Ostashkow was absolutely similar to the events described in Starobielsk and Kozielsk. The Ostashkow camp was in an ex-monastery, with the only difference that it was on an island in a lake. A bridge joined the island with the mainland. And in quite the same way, from 4 April 1940, onwards, groups were formed, searched, and also assured that they were being sent home ... There also some were chosen separately and finally sent to Griazovietz while the

rest were crowded into railway prison coaches and sent ...
Where?

Senior Constable of the Polish Police Forces, A.
Woronecki, related a conversation which he had at the time
with one of the camp guards. The latter, after having
accepted a pinch of the stinking black Soviet tobacco,
agreed in exchange, as he called it himself, 'to let the secret
out'.

'You'll never see your comrades again ...'

'Why? Where are they?'

'It isn't true that they were sent home. Neither were they
sent to other labour camps.'

'Well, then ... What is the truth?'

The guard smoothed out a scrap of newspaper which he
used as cigarette paper, licked it with a solemn precision,
rolled in the tobacco, stuck and pressed it. He then dug out
from the depths of his thick trousers a home-made lighter,
lit the cigarette, and only after he had led the first cloud of
smoke from his nostrils, did he drawl through his teeth:

'They have drowned them all ...'

Of course there is a possibility that the guard was only
joking ...

Military Police Sergeant J. B., who was also a prisoner in
Ostashkow and whose report is kept in the archives of the
Polish Army in the East, under catalogue No 11,173,
confirmed everything related by others:

The transports were sent in groups ranging from 60 to
300 each. He once wandered up to the bakery where he was
on friendly terms with Nikityn, the chief baker. Of course
their talk touched on the problem of the camp's
disbandment.

'Where are they sending us? Don't you know?' asked the
Sergeant.

'*Na sievier, bratku* (To the north, my friend). They are
sending you somewhere to the north,' answered Nikityn.

Later on the Sergeant found himself in a "special group"
which was sent together with a larger group of some 300
Polish policemen on 28 April 1940. They actually did go *na
sievier* – northwards, along the Leningrad railway line. At

433

Bologoye, the wagon with the "special group" was detached from the rest of the train and sent in the direction of Rhzev. As it left, the Sergeant could see all that remained of the train still standing on a side-track of the Bologoye station.

From the total of prisoners interned in those three camps, the Soviet authorities picked out the following number of prisoners, who were first sent to a camp in Pavlishchev Bor and later on to Griazovietz.

From Ostashkow	120 persons
From Starobielsk	86 persons
From Kozielsk	200 persons
In all	406 persons

These 406, together with another 50 or so singled out and sent individually to Moscow prisons for the purpose of interrogation long before the disbandment of the camps, were the only ones who survived until the 'amnesty' which was granted to all Poles on the strength of the Soviet-Polish Agreement signed on 30 July 1941. They were also the only ones to regain freedom.

The rest, that is about 14,700 men, amongst whom were some 8,400 officers, have disappeared since that spring of 1940 without a trace."

Here at least are the names of two places: *Kharkov* and *Bologoye*. Mackiewicz was a member of the Polish Red Cross team which visited the opened graves at Katyn, and he soon came to the conclusion while walking amongst those serried rows of exhumed corpses, that *there were not enough of them!* His enquiry of the German Professor Buhtz was answered only by a shrug for at that time the Germans were maintaining that there were 11,000 bodies at Katyn. It will be recalled also that at Nuremberg and before the Soviets had also used this figure which perhaps they thought would conveniently embrace the Katyn crime and simultaneously remove questions about the remainder.

Mackiewicz goes on later in his book to make further comment on the possible fate of the prisoners from Ostashkow and Starobielsk.

The fate of the prisoners from Ostashkov

"On 26 April 1943, a woman named Katarzyna Gaszciecka reported to the Record Office No 5 of the Polish Army which had succeeded in crossing the border of the USSR. This woman was the wife of one of the missing Polish officers and she was also one of the many Polish citizens deported from Poland by the Soviet authorities. She told the following story.

'In June 1941, among a crowd of four thousand men and women all deported from Poland, I was shipped over the White Sea. We were sailing from Archangielsk to the estuary of the Peczora River. They were sending us for further slave-labour and for further misery. I was sitting on the deck of the barge. While watching the receding shore, I suddenly felt a bitter yearning to be free again, to see my own country, to know what had happened to my husband, to – live again … I began to cry. It attracted the attention of a young Russian soldier, a member of the crew, who came up to me and asked: "Here, you! What are you wailing about?"

"My fate. Is that also forbidden in this free country of yours? I'm crying over my husband's fate."

"And who was he?"

"A Captain."

The Bolshevik burst into scornful laughter.

"Your tears won't help him any more. All your officers have been drowned here. In this very sea." And he meaningly thumped the deck with his heel. Then he cynically told me that he himself had taken part in the convoy which had transported about seven thousand people, mostly Polish officers and members of the Police Force. They were towed out in two barges. Once in the open sea, the barges were cut adrift and sunk. "All went straight to the bottom," he ended, and went away.

While he was speaking to me, another, older man, also a Russian, came up and stood near us. He also belonged to the crew of our barge but he wasn't a soldier. When the other man had gone away, the old man came up to me and, leaning over the railing, said a few comforting words in a low voice.

"It's true what you have just heard. I also saw it with my own eyes. The crew was taken off, into the towing ship. The barges had been pierced through. It was an awful sight." He actually wiped away a tear and sighed ... "No one could have saved himself." '

This story does roughly corroborate the details gathered about the fate of the prisoners from Ostashkow Camp. First of all it is curious that the Polish Police Force should be mentioned because all the policemen were kept in Ostashkow. Further, the number of 'about seven thousand' quoted by the Russians comes close to the number of the prisoners in that camp, of which there were over six thousand. We also know that Police Constable Woronecki – one of the lucky prisoners from Ostashkow who was sent to Griazovietz and thence out of Russia – had also heard it mentioned by the camp guards that the other prisoners had been drowned. The statement made by Police Sergeant J. B., although it does not mention drowning, points to the north as the direction in which the Ostashkow prisoners were taken when they disappeared.

There is proof that they had been sent to a station called Bologoye which lies north from Ostashkow, but what happened to them later on?

At the time when the Polish Army was being organised on Soviet territory, a time to be always remembered for its feverish searching, and the vain attempts at re-assembling the missing thousands, there were many stories of Polish prisoners being either seen or heard about somewhere in the North – tales about some undefined accident having taken place in the White Sea. Originally it was commonly assumed that all the Polish prisoners had been deported to the far North. The discovery of the Katyn graves cut short this flow of hazy surmises. It also became known by then that Polish prisoners had, in fact, been sent to the North in 1940, but these were not prisoners from any of the three camps in question, but those who had been previously interned in the Baltic States. And those who came from the

Polish ex-Soviet prisoners reporting to join the Polish army in Russia, 1941–2.

Baltic States, although deported to the North, had not been murdered.

Up till now, there has not been sufficient evidence gathered to come to any definite conclusion and it cannot be claimed with any certainty that the Polish prisoners from Ostashkow had really been drowned in the White Sea. The evidence supplied by Mrs Katarzyna Gaszciecka is undoubtedly important but far from being sufficient proof. Although if the prisoners from Ostashkow had really been sent to Archangielsk, their way would actually have led through Bologoye. But ...

Logically, the theory of their drowning seems improbable. As is known, the fate of all three camps, both during their existence and in the method of their disbandment, was identical. The similar way in which all the prisoners were treated makes it nearly certain that their fate was decided by the very same order issued from above, which probably did not only decree their deaths, but the method by which their executions were to take place.

From that point of view, it would seem absurd to murder

437

the prisoners from Kozielsk in a relatively small wood in the densely populated Smolensk district, and at the same time transport over six thousand prisoners from Ostashkow all the way to Archangielsk, in order to drown them in the White Sea. Why bother, when it would be so much easier to dispose of them in the same way as had been done at Katyn – just shoot them somewhere? There are immeasurable forests in which it would be much easier to lose all traces of them than in that little wood in the Smolensk area.

These reasons therefore seem to point to the conclusion that the prisoners from Ostashkow lie buried not far from some small railway station, just as the prisoners from Kozielsk lie not far from the Gniezdovo station.

The fate of the Starobielsk Camp

Where did the 3,500 Polish officers from Starobielsk disappear? The only answer can also be found by drawing a parallel.

We already know that the last traces left by the transports evacuating the prisoners from Starobielsk are to be found at Kharkov railway junction. Beyond that, all trace ceases. 'All your men are unloaded here,' said the Soviet railway worker. Perhaps he told the truth. Perhaps it was a lie ... It was not a very satisfactory clue. Perhaps a little nearer or a little further away, they also lie with their skulls pierced by the infallible bullet, and their bodies pressed together under the earth of a great common grave on which little pine trees have been planted ...''

Once again the two names: Kharkov and Bologoye, of which Kharkov somehow stands out clearly as not only possible but probable. The name Bologoye, however, is less sharply defined; it appears as perhaps a stopping place only on the way to the White Sea as hinted by Katarzyna Gaszciecka. Somehow this idea of the 6,000 from Ostashkow being taken to Archangel, loaded into barges, being sealed down and then sunk by gunfire has stuck. The author has questioned many of his Polish friends, and without exception they refer to this story of the White Sea.

Yet a glance at the map raises only doubt. It is essential to look at the complete liquidation of the camps as one centrally planned operation and, if possible, to enter the mind of the NKVD officer who sometime in the spring of 1940 set himself the task of making all the logistic arrangements. To take the 4,500 from Kozielsk to Katyn is logical (if such a satanic scheme has anything to do with logic); to take the 4,000 from Starobielsk to Kharkov is also logical; but to transport 6,000 men all the way from Ostashkow to the White Sea is not. It does not fit into the kind of pattern that a military mind would draw. But Bologoye – that is different. It would be "logical" to finish them off at Bologoye, or near Bologoye.

But here the trail ends – only in speculation, in guesses and sombre reflection. 10,000 men buried; piles and piles of compressed bodies every bit as horrific and tragic as at Katyn – *but over twice as many*. A glimpse into this mystery has already been made earlier in this book with a reference to Congressman Derwinsky's speech in 1962 and his mention of a report published in a German weekly newspaper as far back as 1957 (See Chapter 5). Dated, so it was said, 10 June 1940, this secret document was thought to provide the answer to the riddle of the 10,000. But where was this report? Where indeed was the German newspaper to be found in which it was reproduced? Obviously this is evidence of the first magnitude, and the question immediately arises as to why it has not been investigated further. Books, many books, relate to the 4,500 at Katyn, but somewhere there is one single sheet of paper which tells of the fate of "the other 10,000".

The author again asked his Polish friends. Indeed there was a vague reference to the secret report, but it was shrouded in mystery itself, overlaid with promises to an unknown man that the information would not be revealed in his lifetime. It did not seem that Polish sources could produce the answer, for they did not have it. What could be done to find the end of this trail which seemed to lead nowhere? The answer was simple, just as it so often is in history when mysteries appear insoluble. The weekly

439

newspaper was German, so the key must lie in Germany. But how to find it? With the help of the German Embassy in London the vital article was found. It is given here in translation.

"*Secret!*

Union of the Socialist
Soviet Republics

People's Commissariat for
Internal Affairs

Headquarters of the NKVD
region of Minsk

[Department?]

10 June 1940

The Headquarters of
the NKVD Moscow

Official Report

By order of the Headquarters of the NKVD of February 12th 1940 the liquidation of the three Polish prisoner-of-war camps was carried out in the regions of the towns of Kozielsk, Ostaschkovo and Starobyelsk. The operation of liquidating the three above-named camps was completed on 6th June of that year. Comrade Burjanoff, who had been seconded from the Central Office, was appointed to be in charge.

Under the above-mentioned order the camp at Kozielsk was liquidated first of all by the security forces of the Minsk headquarters of the NKVD in the area of the city of Smolensk during the period between March 1st and May 3rd of that year. As security forces territorial troops, in part from the 190th Rifle Regiment, were employed.

The second action under the above order was carried out in the area of the town of Bologoye by the security forces of the Smolensk headquarters of the NKVD, and was also covered by troops of the 129th Rifle Regiment (Velike Luki); it was completed by June 5th of that year.

The Charkow headquarters of the NKVD was entrusted with the carrying out of the third liquidation at the camp of Starobyelsk. It was carried out in the area of the Dergachi settlement with the assistance of security forces of the 68th Ukrainian Rifle Regiment of the territorial troops on June 2nd. In this case the responsibility and leadership in this action was entrusted to the NKVD Colonel B. Kutschkov.

A copy of this report is being sent simultaneously to the NKVD Generals Raichmann and Saburin for their attention.

The Organisational Head of the Office of
the NKVD, area of Minsk:

Tartakow

verified by   Secretary of
[illegible]   the Department"
                                       [illegible]

Just as at Katyn in 1943 the Germans had found the 4,500, so in 1974 they resolved the mystery of "the other 10,000".

What more is there to say?

8 Who writes the final chapter?

Although this is the last chapter of this book, it should not be. The final chapter must be an account of how international authority eventually found the courage and the purpose to take stock of this enormous mass-murder, seek a judgement, obtain it and condemn the perpetrators. In this book the last chapter must therefore pose the important question: who will do this and thus write the final chapter? However hard men may try, and shame upon them for so doing, it must be an impossibility that some 14,500 innocent prisoners-of-war could be murdered as recently as thirty-five years ago and nothing be done about it.

These men have a place in history; their relatives are due at least some moral indemnification. Both would be provided if this disgraceful *res non judicata* were legally resolved. Throughout this book it will have been seen how individuals and nations have consistently run away from the facts which so grimly stared them in the face. They have sought refuge in man-made confusion; they have hidden their faces or looked away; they have been guilty of a profound lack of fortitude. If this book spells out the name of the criminal, so also does it point a finger at all those who could have, but did not, act upon evidence presented again and again. Such an act is condonation. It is a vast sin of omission; a stain upon the conscience of the free world.

Some summary of the facts would be useful here. The first piece of evidence is the refusal of the Soviets to allow

Extract from *Time*, 15 July 1974, of President Nixon at Khatyn war memorial.

Tolling Bells. After the tough arms negotiations, Nixon flew to the Belorussian capital of Minsk to take part in ceremonies mourning the destruction of the region by the Nazis 30 years ago. In the village of Khatyn, standing before a huge black granite statue of a gaunt man holding his dead son in his arms, the President said quietly: "This is very, very moving."

Favoring his left leg, Nixon also walked around a section of the memorial area containing the outlines of 26 peasant houses that the Germans had burned to the ground. Inside each was an obelisk, shaped like a burnt smokestack, that contained a bell. Every 30 seconds, one of the bells tolled to honor the dead. Nixon wrote in the guest book: "May this moving memorial to the victims of war reinforce the determination of all those who come here to build a living monument to those who died—a world of peace for their children and their grandchildren."

NIXON AT KHATYN WAR MEMORIAL

443

the International Committee of the Red Cross to examine the exhumations at Katyn in 1943. The second was the findings of the International Medical Commission of the same year, and the third was the obvious untruth contained in the results of the Russian Commission of 1944. In the loaded atmosphere of Nuremberg in 1946, when the victors panted to nail the Germans to the ground, the Soviet prosecution itself failed to prove its case; it was just dropped without, it appears, much reaction from the other participants. In this respect at least, the pageant of justice was a total and culpable failure. Another attempt was made in 1952; again the Soviets refused to participate, and again nothing was done as a result. That US Select Committee reached a crystal-clear conclusion, and made recommendations which are still viable today. Another attempt was made in the British House of Commons as recently as 1971. The question which there received no answer was repeated in the House of Lords a few months later. And still the world shut its eyes and blocked its ears.

What has been the Soviet reaction? Apart from refusing to help the International Red Cross in 1943 and the US Select Committee in 1952, it has gone on solemnly and monotonously repeating the so-called "findings" of its own 1944 Commission. The lie was again offered in reply to mounting interest in 1971, and when it seemed that the Katyn Memorial Fund was not to be put off its course by the Church of England, another and even more fatuous diversion was constructed to assist those who clung precariously to the "confusion in this case". Somewhere in Byelorussia there is said to be a village called Chatyn, as it would be spelt in Cyrillic script. This village along with scores of others was said to have been overrun and destroyed by the advancing German armies in 1941. "Chatyn" is very similar to "Katyn", or so it must have appeared to the Russians; the more so if, when transcribed into Western writing, the "C" becomes a "K"; even more so when it is realised that the "h" would be silent. Thus Chatyn became "Katyn" when spoken by Europeans, and it was here that the Soviets erected a hideous and gigantic

444

Map of the western region of the USSR showing the three camps, the three places of the mass murders (with numbers killed) and both Katyn and Khatyn.

monument to commemorate some 126 peasants whom they said the Germans had slaughtered. In 1974 they took President Nixon on a conducted tour of this place, and made sure that news of it reached as large an audience as possible in the hope that people would say: "What is all this fuss about? Even the President of the United States has been taken to Katyn to see the monument placed there to German brutality – so what are these people in England talking about, with their monument proposed for St Luke's Gardens, Chelsea?"

To the Euro-Asian mind this must have seemed an admirable ruse, but it failed, serving to underline once again the lengths to which the Russians will go to cover up the massacres at Katyn, Dergachi and Bologoye. Some attention should be given to the numbers of the murdered; the use of the word "approximately" is too often repeated.

Of the 4,500 prisoners at Kozielsk, 245 were capriciously spared, leaving 4,255. The bodies found at Katyn numbered 4,254 at the final count. Of the 6,500 prisoners at Ostashkow, 124 reached General Anders' army, leaving 6376 buried somewhere near Bologoye. Of the 3,920 imprisoned at Starobielsk, only 79 lived after 1940, so about 3,841 must be in mass-graves at Dergachi. The total of the dead is therefore 14,471.

Once again a few seconds pause is required to comprehend this figure of 14,471. A journalist once asked the author why he was so excited about a "mere 15,000 when millions were killed in the war". But this was different. Here were close on that number, who *in time of peace* had been transported to three carefully selected places and there *coldly and individually shot in the back of the head*.

It is true that in the Spring of 1940, "they fell into the grave unpitied and unknown". Now they are known; I pray that they are pitied.

But what will be done? Who writes the last chapter?

Appendices

Appendix I
Final Report of the US Select
Committee 1952

FINAL REPORT

[Pursuant to H. Res. 390 and H. Res. 539, 82d Cong.]

INTRODUCTION

On September 18, 1951, the House of Representatives unanimously adopted House Resolution 390. This resolution provided for the establishment of a select committee to conduct a full and complete investigation concerning the Katyn massacre, an international crime committed against soldiers and citizens of Poland at the beginning of World War II.

The Katyn massacre involved some 4,243 of the 15,400 Polish Army officers and intellectual leaders who were captured by the Soviets when Russia invaded Poland in September 1939. These officers were interned in three Soviet prison camps in the territory of the U. S. S. R. They were permitted to correspond with their families in Poland until May 10, 1940. Then all trace of these men was lost after that date. Nothing further of their whereabouts was known until several mass graves containing remains of Polish bodies were discovered in the Katyn Forest near Smolensk, U. S. S. R., by the German troops in April of 1943.

The Katyn massacre was one of the most barbarous international crimes in world history. Since the discovery of the graves, and until this committee completed its investigation, the massacre remained an international mystery. The Soviets blamed the Germans for the crime. They charged the Poles fell into Nazi hands when Germany invaded Russia in the summer of 1941. The Germans organized a medical commission investigation consisting of leading doctors from 12 European nations including the neutral country of Switzerland. This medical commission met at Katyn on April 29 and 30,

1943, and unanimously determined that the Poles were massacred in the spring of 1940. At that time the Katyn area was under the complete domination of the Soviets.

Immediately following passage of House Resolution 390, the Speaker of the House of Representatives appointed the following members of this committee: Ray J. Madden, Democrat, Indiana, chairman; Daniel J. Flood, Democrat, Pennsylvania; Foster Furcolo, Democrat, Massachusetts; Thaddeus M. Machrowicz, Democrat, Michigan; George A. Dondero, Republican, Michigan; Alvin E. O'Konski, Republican, Wisconsin; and Timothy P. Sheehan, Republican, Illinois.

The committee selected John J. Mitchell as chief counsel and Roman C. Pucinski as chief investigator.

PROCEDURE

The committee's investigation was divided into two phases: First, to establish which nation actually was guilty of the massacre; and, second, to establish whether any American officials were responsible for suppressing the facts of the massacre with all of its ramifications from the American people.

INTERIM REPORT

On July 2, 1952, this committee filed with the House of Representatives an interim report (H. Rept. 2430) in which it fixed the guilt for the Katyn massacre on the Soviet NKVD) Peoples' Commissariat of Internal Affairs). On the basis of voluminous testimony, including that of recognized medical expert witnesses, and other data assembled by our staff, this committee concluded there does not exist a scintilla of proof, or even any remote circumstantial evidence, that this mass murder took place no later than the spring of 1940. The Poles were then prisoners of the Soviets and the Katyn Forest area was still under Soviet occupation.

In the interim report this committee recommended the Soviets be tried before the International World Court of Justice for committing a crime at Katyn which was in *violation of the general principles of law recognized by civilized nations.* The United Nations Charter presently carries provisions for the legal action recommended by this committee.

Furthermore, this committee called attention to the striking similarity between the Katyn massacre and events taking place in Korea today. For 2 years the Soviets disavowed any knowledge of the vanished Polish officers and deceived the Polish Government in its search for these men. Today the Communists are similarly prolonging the Korean peace talks because they cannot account for the 8,000 American soldiers reported by General Ridgway "killed as war crimes victims." There are many indications that Katyn was a blueprint for Korea.

INTERNATIONAL RED CROSS

The International Committee of the Red Cross, in April 1943, requested Soviet permission to conduct a neutral investigation at Katyn and their request was ignored by Moscow. In March 1951, the International Committee of the Red Cross sent two delegates to Peiping, China, to request permission to conduct a neutral investigation of alleged war atrocities in Korea. In July 1951 Communist Red China refused permission to conduct such an investigation.

Excerpts of our interim report appear in the appendix. This final report will deal primarily with the second phase of our investigation.

SECOND PHASE

The Congress requested that our committee determine why certain reports and files concerning the Katyn massacre disappeared or were suppressed by departments of our Government.

Records and documents assembled from the State Department and War Department files provided a clear-cut picture of the tremendously important part the Katyn massacre played in shaping the future of postwar Europe.

From these hitherto secret documents this committee learned that as early as the summer of 1942 American authorities considered a Polish Army extremely vital to the Allied war effort against Hitler and Mussolini. Documents introduced in our hearings describe conclusively the efforts made to create such an army on Russian soil as quickly as possible. We learned further that American authorities knew as early as 1942 of Poland's desperate efforts to locate her missing officers who could lead the Polish Army being formed on Russian soil.

These same documents show that when high-level Polish officials failed to obtain an adequate reply from the Soviets regarding the whereabouts of their missing officers, American emissaries intervened. In every instance, American officials were given the same reply: The Soviets had no knowledge of their whereabouts.

United States Ambassador to Moscow, Admiral William H. Standley, advised the State Department on September 10, 1942, that Soviet officials were opposed to United States intervention in Russo-Polish problems. This attitude was stated to Admiral Standley by Molotov when Standley inquired about the missing Polish officers.

Throughout 1942–43—or until the mass graves were discovered at Katyn—this committee's record recites a long series of efforts being made by the United States to aid the Poles. But it also shows the total lack of cooperation the United States received from the Soviets.

When Russia finally broke diplomatic relations with Poland (April 26, 1943) following the Polish request for an International Red Cross investigation of the Katyn massacre, Ambassador Standley warned the State Department that Russia had been seeking a pretext to break with Poland for some time. He emphasized that the Soviets were plotting to create a pro-Communist satellite Polish government which would take over Poland after the war. He warned that Russia was planning to create an entire belt of pro-Soviet governments in eastern Europe, which would jeopardize the peace of Europe.

It is apparent that American authorities knew of the growing tension between the Soviets and the Poles during 1942–43—and they likewise knew about the hopeless search for the Polish officers—but at the time, all of these factors were brushed aside, on the theory that pressing the search would irritate Soviet Russia and thus hinder the prosecution of the war to a successful conclusion.

451

The Katyn investigation revealed that many individuals throughout the State Department, Army Intelligence (G–2), Office of War Information and Federal Communications Commission, and other Government agencies, failed to properly evaluate the material being received from our sources overseas. In many instances, this information was deliberately withheld from public attention and knowledge. There was a definite lack of coordination on intelligence matters between Army Intelligence (G–2) and the State Department, at least as far as the missing Polish officers and the Katyn massacre was concerned.

The possibility exists that many second-echelon personnel, who were overly sympathetic to the Russian cause or pro-Communist-minded, attempted to cover up derogatory reports which were received concerning the Soviets.

Former American Ambassador Averell Harriman—now Mutual Security Director—and former Under Secretary of State, Sumner Welles, explained why the United States acquiesced so frequently to outrageous Soviet demands.

Both said the underlying consideration throughout the war was military necessity. They agreed that American foreign policy called for a free postwar Poland to assure stability in Europe. Both concurred in the fact that the United States wanted a Polish Army very urgently in the Near East campaign. They insisted, however, that these considerations had to give way to military necessity and to the maintenance of our alliance with Russia. These witnesses further maintained the Allies feared Russia might make a separate peace with the Germans.

American emissaries who reported the status of conditions concerning the Soviets were either bypassed or disregarded if their views were critical of the Soviets. When some of the emissaries expressed anti-Soviet observations, President Roosevelt sent his personal representative to confer directly with Marshal Stalin.

This was borne out by testimony of Ambassador Standley, who said that when he warned against Russia's postwar plans for forming a pro-Soviet bloc of nations around the U. S. S. R., President Roosevelt sent Wendell Willkie to confer with Stalin. Mr. Standley said he was not given the details of Mr. Willkie's mission.

In retrospect, we now realize the prophetic truth of Admiral Standley's warning about the Soviets which he made in 1943, when the Katyn massacre was announced to the world for the first time. (See vol. VII of the published hearings.)

Both Mr. Harriman and Mr. Welles, in testifying before our committee, conceded in effect that the United States officials had taken a gamble on Russia's pledge to work harmoniously with the western democracies after the war—and lost.

However, they presented arguments to justify their actions. Mr. Harriman insisted that agreements made at Tehran and Yalta would have assured a lasting peace if only the Soviets had kept their promises.

Mr. Harriman insisted that territorial concessions made to the Soviets at the Big Three conferences were predicated on the military reality that the Soviets were actually in physical control of these

452

lands. To have resisted their demands, or to have tried to drive the Soviets out by force, would have meant prolonging the war, Mr. Harriman maintained.

He further testified that concessions made to the Soviets at Yalta were made at a time when the American Joint Chiefs of Staff insisted on getting the Soviets into the Japanese war at all costs.

Mr. Harriman said he personally "was full of distrust of the Soviets at the time." He declared the Yalta agreements were breached by the Soviets. He stated that the present government in Poland is not representative of its people. He added, "It is a puppet government of the Soviet Union."

Mr. Harriman testified:

The fact that they [the Soviets] broke these agreements has been one of the reasons why the Free World has become more and more united. (See vol. VII of the published hearings.)

This committee believes the tragic concessions at Yalta might not have taken place if the Polish officer corps had not been annihilated by the Soviets at Katyn. With proper leadership, the Polish Army could have relieved a great deal of the early reverses suffered by the Allies. The Kremlin's hand would not have been as strong at the Yalta Conference, and many of the concessions made because of "military necessity", as maintained by Mr. Harriman, would have been obviated.

This contention is borne out by a portion of a telegram sent to the State Department on June 2, 1942, by A. J. Drexel Biddle, Jr., American Ambassador assigned to the Polish Government in Exile in London. (See exhibit 21, pt. VII of the published hearings.)

The absence of these officers is the principal reason for the shortage of officers in the Polish forces in Russia, wither officers from Scotland had to be sent lately. The possible death of these men, most of whom have superior education, would be a severe blow to the Polish national life.

PRESIDENT ROOSEVELT INTERCEDES

This committee heard testimony and studied documents which clearly show President Roosevelt himself appeared concerned about Polish-Soviet relations. When Marshal Stalin informed the President of his decision to break off diplomatic relations with the Poles following their demand for an International Red Cross investigation of Katyn, Mr. Roosevelt sent a personal message urging Stalin to reconsider his action.

The tone of Mr. Roosevelt's message clearly demonstrated his desire, above all, to retain cordial relations with the Soviets. (See exhibit 17, pt. VII of the published hearings.)

When again, in 1944, former Ambassador George Howard Earle, who served as a special emissary for President Roosevelt in the Balkans, tried to convince Mr. Roosevelt that the Soviets were guilty of the Katyn massacre, the President dismissed the suggestion.

Testifying before this committee that he based his statement to the President on secret documents and photographs of Katyn clearly establishing Soviet guilt, Mr. Earle quoted the President as replying:

George, this is entirely German propaganda and a German plot. I am absolutely convinced the Russians did not do this.

It becomes apparent to this committee that the President and the State Department ignored numerous documents from Ambassador Standley, Ambassador Biddle, and Ambassador Winant, American emissary to London, who reported information which strongly pointed to Soviet perfidy.

It becomes obvious Mr. Roosevelt's dealings with the Soviets throughout the war were based on a strong desire for mutual cooperation with Russia in the war effort. This desire was based on a belief in Soviet Russia's sincerity. It is equally obvious that this desire completely overshadowed the dictates of justice and equity to our loyal but weaker ally, Poland.

CONCLUSIONS ON THE DEPARTMENT OF STATE

When Sumner Welles was asked by a member of this committee if a more firm attitude toward the Soviets during the war would have helped avoid some of today's postwar problems, Mr. Welles replied:

It is a very difficult thing to answer in the light of hindsight. As I look at it today, I think you are entirely correct. As we looked at it then, of course, the success of the war effort was the major effort; and I must remind the committee that the one overshadowing fear on the part of our military authorities at that time was a separate peace on the part of the Soviet Government with Germany.

It appears from the record that the Katyn massacre undermined Polish-Soviet relations throughout the war and thereafter. *Katyn was a means to an end. The Soviets had plotted to take over Poland as early as 1939. Their massacre of these Polish officers was designed to eliminate the intellectual leadership which subsequently would have attempted to block Russia's ultimate designs for complete communization of Poland. This was but a step of the Soviets toward the complete communization of Europe and eventually the entire world, including the United States.*

The record of this committee shows that the United States had been forewarned of Soviet Russia's treacherous designs on Poland and the rest of Europe. Whatever the justification may be, this committee is convinced the United States in its relations with the Soviets found itself in the tragic position of winning the war but losing the peace.

THE VAN VLIET REPORT

On May 22, 1945, an American Infantry officer, Col. John H. Van Vliet, Jr., arrived in Washington from Europe and promptly reported to Maj. Gen. Clayton Bissell, Army Assistant Chief of Staff in charge of Army Intelligence (G-2), to record his observations at Katyn. Colonel Van Vliet and Captain Donald Stewart, while German prisoners of war, had been taken to the mass burial grounds by the Nazis in May 1943. It was apparent the Nazis had hoped to bolster credence in their charges by taking Colonel Van Vliet and Captain Stewart, as well as British officers, to the scene of the graves. Neither Colonel Van Vliet nor Capt. Donald Stewart would commit themselves to any conclusion while in Nazi detention. But as soon as Colonel Van Vliet was liberated he came to the Pentagon to make his report.

In his report, dictated on General Bissell's orders, Colonel Van Vliet described his observations and concluded, emphatically and unequivocally, that he was convinced the Polish officers were murdered by the Soviets.

General Bissell promptly labeled the report "Top secret." This report was made in a single original manuscript without copies. General Bissell ordered Colonel Van Vliet to maintain absolute secrecy concerning his report.

This "Top secret" document has disappeared from the Army Intelligence (G-2) files, and to this date has not been found. The search for the Van Vliet report has been one of the most important tasks of this committee. An independent investigation conducted by the Army's Inspector General in 1950 concluded the report had been "compromised" and that there is nothing to indicate it had ever left Army Intelligence (G-2). This finding was in response to General Bissell's allegation that he "believes" he had forwarded Van Vliet's report to the Department of State.

Appearing before this committee on two different occasions, General Bissell steadfastly maintained his belief that he had forwarded the document to the Department of State on May 25, 1945.

GENERAL BISSELL TESTIFIES

General Bissell introduced into evidence a letter he had written to Assistant Secretary of State Julius Holmes on that date, inquiring if the State Department had any record of another Van Vliet document, and interrogation by a Swiss Protecting Power official shortly after Colonel Van Vliet had visited Katyn. Bissell's letter of May 25 bears no notation that an enclosure was attached. Nor is there any record of a receipt for the "Top secret" report to prove the document actually was received by the Department of State. (See exhibit 5, pt. VII of the published hearings.)

General Bissell introduced into evidence another letter he had written on August 21, 1945, to Mr. Frederick B. Lyon, Mr. Holmes' assistant in the Department of State. In this letter General Bissell includes a report by a British officer who likewise was taken to Katyn by the Nazis. General Bissell concludes his letter of August 21 with the statement:

This report substantiates in effect the statement of Col. John H. Van Vliet, Jr., forwarded to General Holmes on the 25th day of May 1945.

In his testimony before this committee General Bissell contended that the particular phrase in his letter of August 21 substantiates his claim that he sent the Van Vliet report to the State Department.

Both Mr. Holmes, who is now Minister of the American Embassy in London, and Mr. Lyon testified before the committee. Under oath, they disavowed any knowledge of ever having received the Van Vliet report from General Bissell. They also stated that if they had discussed this report with General Bissell they would have remembered it because of the "political significance" involved at that time.

It is this committee's conclusion that General Bissell is mistaken in his claim that he might have forwarded the Van Vliet report to the State Department. The committee believes the Van Vliet report was either removed or purposely destroyed in Army Intelligence (G-2).

General Bissell himself admitted to the committee that had the Van Vliet report been publicized in 1945, when agreements for creating a United Nations organization reached at Yalta were being carried out in San Francisco, Soviet Russia might never have taken a seat in this international organization.

In justifying his actions for designating the Van Vliet report "Top secret," General Bissell said he was merely carrying out the spirit of the Yalta agreement.

He admitted the report was explosive and came at a time when the United States was still trying to get a commitment from the Soviets to enter the Japanese war. General Bissell contradicted his own theory when he told the committee that the Van Vliet report couldn't have been sent to the Secretary of the Army "because it had nothing to do with the prosecution of the war at that time." This committee was dismayed to learn that the United States Assistant Chief of Staff, Army Intelligence (G-2), was considering political significance of the Van Vliet document, which should have been treated objectively from a strictly Military Intelligence standpoint.

In the opinion of this committee, it was the duty and obligation of General Bissell to process this document with care so that it would have reached the Department of State.

General Bissell testified:

I saw in it [the Van Vliet report] great possibilities of embarrassment; so I classified it the way I have told you, and I think I had no alternative.

More amazing to this committee is testimony of three high-ranking American Army officers who were stationed in Army Intelligence (G-2) during General Bissell's command of this agency. Testifying in executive session, all three agreed there was a pool of "pro-Soviet civilian employees and some military in Army Intelligence (G-2), who found explanations for almost everything that the Soviet Union did."

These same witnesses told of tremendous efforts exerted by this group to suppress anti-Soviet reports. The committee likewise heard testimony that top-ranking Army officers who were too critical of the Soviets were bypassed in Army Intelligence (G-2).

There is no question that Army Intelligence (G-2) knew of the military potential of the Polish Army which was being formed in Russia in 1941. In March 1942, an American Army officer, Col. Henry I. Szymanski, was sent to join that army as a United States liaison officer. Colonel Szymanski told this committee he never did carry out his mission in Russia because the Soviets refused him a visa. Szymanski was recalled in November 1942 to give a full account of Soviet obstruction to the creation of the much-needed Polish Army. Evidence unearthed by this committee shows that Szymanski's highly critical reports of Soviet Russia were buried in the basement of Army Intelligence (G-2), and subsequently moved to the "dead file" of that agency.

OFFICE OF WAR INFORMATION, FEDERAL COMMUNICATIONS COMMISSION

When the Nazis, on April 13, 1943, announced to the world the finding of the mass graves of the Polish officers at Katyn and accused the Soviets, the Allies were stunned by this action and called it propaganda. Mr. Elmer Davis, news commentator, then head of the Office of War Information, an agency established by Executive order, told this committee he reported direct to the President. Under questioning he admitted frequent conferences with the State Department and other Government agencies. However, testifying before this committee, when faced with his own broadcast of May 3, 1943, in which he accused the Nazis of using the Katyn massacre as propaganda, he admitted under questioning that this broadcast was made on his own initiative.

This is another example of the failure to coordinate between Government agencies. A State Department memorandum dated April 22, 1943, which was read into the record (see vol. VII of the published hearings), stated:

and on the basis of the various conflicting contentions [concerning Katyn] of all parties concerned, it would appear to be advisable to refrain from taking any definite stand in regard to this question.

Mr. Davis, therefore, bears the responsibility for accepting the Soviet propaganda version of the Katyn massacre without full investigation. A very simple check with either Army Intelligence (G-2) or the State Department would have revealed that the Katyn massacre issue was extremely controversial.

Furthermore, members of the staff of both OWI and FCC did engage in activities beyond the scope of their responsibilities. This unusual activity of silencing radio commentators first came to light in August 1943 when the House committee investigating the National Communications Commission discovered the procedure.

The technique utilized by staff members of OWI and FCC to silence was as follows: Polish radio commentators in Detroit and Buffalo broadcasting in foreign languages after the announcement of the discovery of the mass graves of Polish officers at Katyn reported facts indicating that the Soviets might be guilty of this massacre.

In May 1943 a member of the FCC staff suggested to a member of the OWI staff that the only way to prevent these comments was to contact the Wartime Foreign Language Radio Control Committee. This committee was made up of station owners and managers who were endeavoring to cooperate with the OWI and FCC during the war years. Accordingly a meeting was arranged in New York with two of the members of this industry committee. They were specifically requested by the OWI staff member to arrange to have a Polish radio commentator in Detroit restrict his comments to straight news items concerning Katyn, and only those by the standard wire services. The fact that a member of the FCC staff attended this meeting is significant because the FCC in such a case had no jurisdiction. In fact, the FCC member was in New York to discuss the renewal of the radio license of one of these industry members. The owner of the radio station in Detroit was contacted and requested to restrict the comments of the Polish commentator on his station, and this was done.

By applying indirect pressure on the station owner, these staff members accomplished their purpose, namely, keeping the full facts of the Katyn massacre story from the American people. (See vol. VII of the published hearings.)

Office of Censorship officials testified and supported the conclusion of this committee that the OWI and FCC officials acted beyond the scope of their official Government responsibilities on this matter of Katyn.

Testimony before this committee likewise proves that the Voice of America—successor to the Office of War Information—had failed to fully utilize available information concerning the Katyn massacre until the creation of this committee in 1951. The committee was not impressed with statements that publication of facts concerning this crime, prior to 1951, would lead to an ill-fated uprising in Poland. Neither was it convinced by the statements of OWI officials that for the Polish-Americans to hear or read about the Katyn massacre in 1943 would have resulted in a lessening of their cooperation in the Allied war effort.

MR. JUSTICE JACKSON

Mr. Justice Jackson appeared before this committee and advised that he had received no instructions or information concerning the Katyn massacre. When asked to explain how the Katyn affair happened to come on the agenda of the Nuremberg trials under the indictment of Herman Goering, he stated that the Soviets were responsible for drawing indictments on war crimes committed in eastern Europe. Mr. Justice Jackson stated as follows:

To the United States was allocated the over-all conspiracy to incite and wage a war of aggression. The British were assigned the violation of specific treaties and crimes on the high seas. Violations of the laws of war and crimes against humanity were divided on a geographical basis. The French undertook crimes in western Europe, and the Soviet prosecution was assigned the duty of preparing and presenting evidence of crimes in eastern Europe—an area largely in Soviet occupation. and to much of which the others of us had no access. The geographical area thus assigned to the Soviet representatives included Katyn wood and Poland as well, but at that time it was not known that the Katyn massacre would be involved.

When asked by the committee if he had received the various reports then in the files of the State Department and Army Intelligence (G–2), Mr. Justice Jackson testified that he had not. When asked by the committee what he would have done if he had received these reports, he replied as follows:

Of course, any information would have been helpful. If we had had information of that kind, I cannot pass on whether this would have been adequate, but if we had had adequate information of Russian guilt, we would not have consented at all to have the charge against the Nazis. It would have strengthened our hand in keeping it out immensely and probably would have resulted in the Soviets not making the accusation.

Before this committee was formed, many allegations were made that Americans on Mr. Jackson's staff at Nuremberg assisted the Soviets in the preparation of this case on Katyn against the Nazis. The committee desired to clarify this point and specifically asked Mr. Jackson this question, and he denied that any member of his staff participated in the preparation of the Katyn indictment.

The committee viewed with interest Mr. Justice Jackson's statement in his testimony which is as follows:

This history will show that, if it is now deemed possible to establish responsibility for the Katyn murders, nothing that was decided by the Nuremberg Tribunal or contended for by the American prosecution will stand in your way.

CONCLUSIONS

1. In submitting this final report to the House of Representatives, this committee has come to the conclusion that in those fateful days

nearing the end of the Second World War there unfortunately existed in high governmental and military circles a strange psychosis that military necessity required the sacrifice of loyal allies and our own principles in order to keep Soviet Russia from making a separate peace with the Nazis.

For reasons less clear to this committee, this psychosis continued even after the conclusion of the war. Most of the witnesses testified that had they known then what they now know about Soviet Russia, they probably would not have pursued the course they did. It is undoubtedly true that hindsight is much easier to follow than foresight, but it is equally true that much of the material which this committee unearthed was or could have been available to those responsible for our foreign policy as early as 1942.

And, it is equally true that even before 1942 the Kremlin rulers gave much evidence of a menace of Soviet imperialism paving the way for world conquest. Through the disastrous failure to recognize the danger signs which then existed and in following a policy of satisfying the Kremlin leaders, our Government unwittingly strengthened their hand and contributed to a situation which has grown to be a menace to the United States and the entire free world.

2. Our committee is sending a copy of this report, and volume 7 of the published hearings, to the Department of Defense for such action as may be proper with regard to General Bissell. We do so because of the fact that this committee believes that had the Van Vliet report been made immediately available to the Department of State and to the American public, the course of our governmental policy toward Soviet Russia might have been more realistic with more fortunate postwar results.

3. This committee believes that the wartime policies of Army Intelligence (G-2) during 1944–45 should undergo a thorough investigation. Testimony heard by the committee substantiates this belief, and if such an investigation is conducted another object lesson might be learned.

4. Our committee concludes that the staff members of the Office of War Information and Federal Communications Commission who participated in the program of silencing Polish radio commentators went beyond the scope of their duties as official Government representatives. Actually, they usurped the functions of the Office of Censorship and by indirect pressure accomplished domestic censorship which was not within the jurisdiction of either of these agencies.

5. This committee believes that if the Voice of America is to justify its existence it must utilize material made available more forcefully and effectively.

6. This committee began its investigation last year, and as the committee's work progressed, information, documents, and evidence was submitted from all parts of the world. It was at this same time that reports reached the committee of similar atrocities and violations of international law being perpetrated in Korea. This committee noted the striking similarity between crimes committed against the Poles at Katyn and those being inflicted on American and other United Nation troops in Korea. Communist tactics being used in Korea are identical to those followed at Katyn. Thus this committee believes that Congress should undertake an immediate investigation of the Korean war atrocities in order that the evidence can be collected and

the truth revealed to the American people and the free peoples of the world. This committee will return to Congress approximately $21,000 in surplus funds, and it is suggested that this money be made available by Congress for such an investigation.

RECOMMENDATIONS

RECOMMENDATIONS

The final report of the Select Committee Investigating the Katyn Forest Massacre hereby incorporates the recommendations contained in the interim report, filed on July 2, 1952 (H. Rept. No. 2430).

This committee unanimously recommends that the House of Representatives approve the committee's findings and adopt a resolution:

1. Requesting the President of the United States to forward the testimony, evidence, and findings of this committee to the United States delegates at the United Nations;

2. Requesting further that the President of the United States issue instructions to the United States delegates to present the Katyn case to the General Assembly of the United Nations;

3. Requesting that appropriate steps be taken by the General Assembly to seek action before the International World Court of Justice against the Union of Soviet Socialist Republics for committing a crime at Katyn which was in violation of the general principles of law recognized by civilized nations;

4. Requesting the President of the United States to instruct the United States delegation to seek the establishment of an international commission which would investigate other mass murders and crimes against humanity.

RAY J. MADDEN, *Chairman.*
DANIEL J. FLOOD.
THADDEUS M. MACHROWICZ.
GEORGE A. DONDERO.
ALVIN E. O'KONSKI.
TIMOTHY P. SHEEHAN.

APPENDIX

I. INTRODUCTION

*　　　*　　　*　　　*　　　*　　　*　　　*

HEARINGS

The committee's first public hearing was held in Washington on October 11, 1951. It heard the testimony of Lt. Col. Donald B. Stewart, a United States Army officer, who as a German prisoner of war, was taken by the Germans to view the mass graves at Katyn in May 1943. (See pt. I of the committee's published hearings.)

The next set of hearings was held in Washington on February 4, 5, 6, and 7, 1952. Seven witnesses appeared and rendered an account of their knowledge relating to the Katyn massacre. (See pt. II of the published hearings.)

In Chicago on March 13, 14, 1952, eight other witnesses were heard by this committee. (See pt. III of the published hearings.)

In London on April 16, 17, 18, and 19, 1952, 29 witnesses were heard. (See pt. IV of the published hearings.)

In Frankfurt, Germany, on April 21, 22, 23, 24, 25, and 26, 1952, 27 witnesses were heard. (See pt. V of the published hearings.)

In Berlin, Germany, on April 25, a subcommittee heard testimony from members of the German Commission on Human Rights and received approximately 100 depositions which had been taken by that organization.

In Naples, Italy, on April 27, testimony of Dr. Palmieri was heard.

In Washington on June 3 and 4, 1952, testimony was heard from five witnesses.

In the course of the hearings held by this committee to date, testimony has been taken from a total of 81 witnesses; 183 exhibits have been studied and made part of the record, and more than 100 depositions were taken from witnesses who could not appear at the hearings. In addition, the committee staff has questioned more than 200 other individuals who offered to appear as witnesses but whose information was mostly of a corroborating nature.

LETTERS OF INVITATION

The committee unanimously agreed that in order to make this a full, fair, and impartial investigation, it would be willing to hear any individual, organization, or government having possession of factual evidence or information pertaining to the Katyn massacre.

Letters of invitation were forwarded to the Government of the U. S. S. R., the Polish Government in Warsaw, the Polish Government-in-Exile in London, and the German Federal Republic. The German Federal Republic and the Polish Government-in-Exile accepted the invitation.

The Soviet Government rejected the invitation of the committee with the statement that a Special Soviet Commission (composed of all Russian citizens) had thoroughly investigated the Katyn massacre in January 1944 and consequently there was no need for reopening the issue. However, the Soviet Government did attach to their reply the special commission's report and it later was made part of the permanent record of this committee. (See pp. 223 through 247, pt. III of the published hearings.)

The Polish Government in Warsaw transmitted to the American Embassy a note likewise rejecting the committee's invitation, part of which is quoted as follows:

"The attitude of the Polish Government re the activities of this committee was expressed in the declaration of the Polish Government published on March 1, 1952, and the Polish Government does not intend to return to this matter again."

The entire note may be found on page 504 of part IV of the public hearings of this committee.

The attitude of the Polish Government as quoted above was revealed by the vicious propaganda blast issued in the form of a press release and circulated to all newspaper correspondents by the Polish Embassy in Washington. The chairman of the committee published this press release in its entirety in the Congressional Record on March 11, 1952, and called upon the Secretary of State to take prompt action relative to the propaganda activities of the Polish Embassy here in Washington. The Secretary of State on March 20, 1952, delivered a stern reprimand to the Polish Embassy regarding such press releases and greatly restricted its activities in this field.

HOUSE RESOLUTION 539

The first two series of hearings definitely established in the minds of this committee that it would be impossible to conduct a thorough investigation without obtaining the testimony of available witnesses in Europe. Consequently, the committee went before the House of Representatives on March 11, 1952, with House Resolution 539 which amended the original, House Resolution 390, and requested permission to take testimony from individuals and governments abroad. The House approved House Resolution 539 on March 11, 1952.

FINDINGS

This committee unanimously agrees that evidence dealing with the first phase of its investigation proves conclusively and irrevocably the Soviet NKVD (Peoples' Commissariat of Internal Affairs) committed the massacre of Polish Army officers in the Katyn Forest near Smolensk, Russia, not later than the spring of 1940.

This committee further concludes that the Soviets had plotted this criminal extermination of Poland's intellectual leadership as early as the fall of 1939—shortly after Russia's treacherous invasion of the Polish nation's borders. There can be no doubt this massacre was a calculated plot to eliminate all Polish leaders who subsequently would have opposed the Soviets' plans for communizing Poland.

In the course of its investigation, this committee has observed a striking similarity between what happened to the Polish officers in Katyn and the events now taking place in Korea. We unanimously agree that this committee would be remiss in its duty to the American people and the free people of the world if it failed to point out that the identical evasions by the Soviets to the Polish Government while the Poles were searching for their 15,000 missing officers in 1941, appear again in the delaying tactics now being used by the Communists in Korea.

This committee feels that Katyn may well have been a blueprint for Korea. Just as the Soviets failed for almost 2 years to account for the missing Polish officers, so to this day the Communists in Korea have failed to account for many thousands of captured United Nations soldiers. Among these are 8,000 Americans whom General Ridgway described as atrocity victims in his report to the United Nations last July, and the estimated 60,000 South Koreans still unaccounted for.

The Communists' delaying tactics in the Korean peace talks today may be from the same cloth as the nebulous replies received from the Soviets by the Poles in 1941–42 while they searched for their missing officers.

II. Statement of Historical Facts

On September 1, 1939, Germany declared war on Poland and consequently World War II began.

On September 13, 1939 the Polish Ambassador in Moscow was handed a note by the Soviet Government which stated that the Soviet Government was no longer in a position to remain neutral and that the Soviet Government had given orders to the supreme commander of the Red army to close the frontier of the Polish Republic. This note was without provocation and terminated the Soviet-Polish Treaty of Nonaggression.

Then on September 17, 1939, the Soviets crossed the Polish border and, under the guise of coming to the Poles' assistance, occupied the eastern part of Poland.

On September 28, 1939, the German-Soviet Boundary and Friendship Treaty (commonly known as the Ribbentrop-Molotov Pact) was announced to the world. Under this treaty Poland was divided—with Germany taking 72,806 miles,

462

population 22 million; the U. S. S. R. taking 77,620 square miles, population 13 million.

From September 1939 through March 1940 a deliberate well-organized plan was executed by the NKVD to separate Polish Army officers and intellectual leaders from the mass of other Polish prisoners and the placing of those selected in three camps in Soviet Russia, namely, Kozielsk, Starobielsk, and Ostashkov.

On June 22, 1941, the Germans attacked the U. S. S. R. On July 30, 1941, the U. S. S. R. and Poland signed an agreement renewing diplomatic relations. Under this agreement, all Poles interned in Soviet prison camps within the territory of the U. S. S. R. were to be released by the Soviets. The same agreement provided for the formation of a Polish Army whose commander was to be appointed by the Polish Government-in-Exile in London.

On August 14, 1941, the Polish-U. S. S. R. military pact was signed.

On August 16, 1941, General Anders began his fruitless search for the missing Polish officers.

On April 13, 1943, the Germans announced the discovery of the mass graves at Katyn Forest in Russia containing bodies of Polish Army officers, intelligentsia, Government officials, and clergy.

On April 15, 1943, the Polish Government-in-Exile in London appealed to the International Committees of the Red Cross to send a delegation to investigate on the spot the true state of affairs at the Katyn Forest, near Smolensk, Russia.

On April 25, 1943, V. M. Molotov, the People's Commissar for Foreign Affairs of the U. S. S. R. sent a note to Mr. T. Romer, Polish Ambassador to the U. S. S. R. Ambassador Romer refused to accept the note.

On April 26, 1943, the U. S. S. R. severed diplomatic relations with Poland because Poland had approached the International Committee of the Red Cross to conduct a neutral investigation.

On April 30, 1943, a medical commission of leading representatives of medical jurisprudence and criminology from 12 European universities and neutral countries, selected by the Germans, signed a protocol establishing these Polish officers were massacred in the spring of 1940.

On January 24. 1944. the Soviet Special Commission To Investigate the Katyn Massacre release its own report stating that the Nazi Germans had committed the atrocity after the Poles fell captive to the Nazis in July–August 1941.

On July 1 and 2, 1946. the International Military Tribunal at Nuremberg heard testimony from both German and Russian witnesses concerning the Katyn massacre. No decision as to guilt was announced by the tribunal.

III. Testimony of Survivors of the Three Camps

Thousands of Poles were taken prisoners by the Soviet after its invasion of Poland in September 1939. These prisoners were grouped in some hundred-odd camps in Poland's eastern territories and the western provinces of the Soviet territory. However, three of these camps were especially designated for the confinement of Polish officers, lawyers, doctors, clergy, professionals, government officials, and intellectual leaders—most of whom were reserve officers in the Polish Army.

These camps and the number of Polish prisoners interned in each are as follows: Kobielsk, located east of Smolensk, imprisoned 5,000; Starobielsk, near Kharkov, held 4,000 Polish officers; and Ostashkov, near Kalinin, where 6,400 Poles were interned.

The committee heard testimony from 26 Polish officers who had originally been interned in one of these three camps. Their testimony revealed that—

(1) A deliberate effort has been made by the Soviets to segregate the officers into groups. The majority of higher ranking Polish military officers were interned along with hundreds of Polish doctors—all army reservists—in Kozielsk. Noncommissioned officers and Poland's peacetime political and educational leaders—also reservists—were interned in Starobielsk. And, finally, Poland's frontier guards, home police, and public officials of eastern Poland were interned in Ostashkov. Religious leaders were interned in all three camps.

(2) There is general agreement that these special prisoners in the three camps totaled about 15,400. They comprised the elite of the Polish military and civilian leaders.

(3) This NKVD action was a planned, well-conceived, and highly organized separation of the Polish intelligentsia to pick out potential leaders of Poland after the war.

463

(4) These were not ordinary prisoner-of-war camps, but installations heavily guarded by the select NKVD, as contrasted to ordinary Soviet prisoner-of-war camps which were guarded by ordinary Russian soldiers.

(5) These prisoners remained at the three camps from September–October 1939, until April–May 1940.

INTERROGATION OF PRISONERS

(6) This 6 months' interment was meant as a period of political investigation and observation. Each prisoner was examined exhaustively and in each instance several times—mostly during the night, with some interviews lasting several hours.

(a) The NKVD placed great emphasis on the social origin, political views, party adherences, professional qualifications and in particular—if the prisoner had participated in Poland's successful defeat of the Bolsheviks in 1920.

(b) During the long and exhausting interrogations, discussions were held on the subject of war, its reasons and probable outcome, the attitude of the prisoner toward Russia and particularly his knowledge of the Soviet Union.

(7) It is obvious to the committee from this line of questioning and from the conclusions of the witnesses that the Soviets were trying to determine if any of these prisoners eventually could be converted to communism. Evidence clearly established that from this entire group of Poles interned at the three camps, only six subsequently joined Soviet forces.

(8) About March 1940, the interrogations were completed and it was announced almost simultaneously in Kozielsk, Ostashkov, and Starobielsk the camps would shortly be liquidated. Rumors began to circulate in the camp that the prisoners would be sent home. According to testimony presented to this committee by witnesses both in America and Europe, the camp authorities, when speaking to the prisoners, encouraged these rumors.

During evacuation of the 3 camps, groups of 200 to 300 Poles left each day, sometimes every second day and sometimes every third day.

(9) The evacuation continued in the three camps until the middle of May 1940. From among this entire group of 15,400 Poles interned in the 3 camps only 400 survived. These were taken to another NKVD camp at Pavlishev-Bor where the Soviets continued questioning them in hopes of converting them to communism.

(a) Apart from this small group of 400 Poles who survived (listed in exhibit 2, part IV of the published hearings), the world has never heard from a single other Pole who was interned in these camps between the period September-October 1939, and April–May 1940.

(b) The Polish Government-in-exile and relatives who subsequently fled from Communist Poland have tirelessly searched for these missing men for 12 years. In not a single instance have any of these prisoners been heard from or seen since May 1940, except the 4,143 identified in the mass graves of Katyn.

(c) In October of 1940, when the Soviets began to fear an assault by the Nazis, certain members of this group of 400 survivors were asked to form a staff for a proposed Polish Army in Russia. It was apparent this group did not have enough qualified men for such a staff. One witness testified in London that he asked the Soviet Minister of State Security Mirkulow why the Russians didn't select this staff from among those Poles evacuated from Kozielsk, Starobielsk, and Ostashkov. Mirkulow replied: *"We have committed an error. These men are not available. We will give you others."* This statement was made by Mirkulow 6 months after the Russians evacuated the three camps. (See p. 553, vol. IV of the published hearings.)

RUSS ADMIT THEIR "BLUNDER"

(d) This same witness related similar statements made by Soviet Minister Beria of the NKVD to Lieutenant Colonel Berling, one of the six Poles who turned traitor and joined the Soviet forces in 1941. Berling likewise asked Beria in October of 1940, why the Soviets didn't enlist the officers from these camps in the proposed Polish Army. Beria replied: *"We have committed a great blunder. We have made a great mistake."* (See p. 554, vol. IV of the published hearings.)

(10) All correspondence from those interned in the three camps ended May 1940.

(a) While interned at Pavlishev-Bor, the 400 survivors continued to correspond with their families in Poland and those testifying before this committee

464

said they received countless inquiries regarding the fate of their compatriots who were previously interned in the three camps.

(b) A Special Family Bureau established by the Poles in Russia following the rapprochement of 1941 received thousands of inquiries regarding the missing officers. In not a single instant was it reported that any news of these officers was received in Poland subsequent to May 1940.

(11) Only those Poles interned at Kozielsk were massacred in the Katyn Forest.

(a) Numerous survivors of the Kozielsk camp testified they saw inscriptions written by those who departed earlier: "We are being unloaded in Gniezdovo." This rail station is 12 miles west of Smolensk and 2 miles from Katyn Forest.

(b) One of the survivors from Kozielsk who was actually taken to Gniezdovo and then spared in the last moment said he saw NKVD guards with fixed bayonets guarding the Poles while they were being removed from the train into lorries which had backed up to the train.

"The prisoners were asked to go into the autobus, and not stopping on the ground, but just to go from the railroad wagon immediately into the back door of the autobus. The autobus was of quite an ordinary type. The windows were painted, or rather smeared with some white color—I imagine it was just smeared with lime—and the autobus took about 30 people. Then it went away, and returned after more or less half an hour—I cannot tell exactly, because I had no watch with me, but about half an hour—take the next party and this proceeded for some hours. * * * (See p. 606, vol. IV of the published hearings.)"

It is significant to note that this witness mentions that the NKVD had guarded the Polish officers being removed from the train and that the NKVD were armed with fixed bayonets. Testimony presented to this committee by doctors who had performed autopsies on the bodies of the massacred Poles found in Katyn, was conclusive that besides the bullet hole shown in the head which was the cause of death of most of these men, there were some who showed signs of bayoneting. Dr. Miloslavich testified in Chicago that the bayonet wounds were of the four-bladed type which are used exclusively by the Soviets.

(c) The last entry in the diary found on the massacred body of Maj. Adam Solski in the Katyn Forest, dated April 8, 1940, stated:

"From 12 noon we are standing at Smolensk on a railway siding.

"April 9, 1940, a few minutes before 5 in the morning reveille in the prison cars and preparation for departure. * * * We are to go somewhere by car, and what then?

"April 9, 1940, 5 a. m.

"April 9, 1940. From the very dawn, the day started somewhat peculiarly. Departure by prison van in little cells (terrible) ; they brought us somewhere into the woods—some kind of summer resort. Here a detailed search. They took the watch, on which time was 6 :30 a. m. (8 :30), asked me for my wedding ring, which they took, roubles, my main belt and pocket knife."

The diary ends there. It is included in the transcript of the committee's hearings in London as exhibit 28 (pp. 726 to 731, pt. IV). This diary was brought to the committee's attention by General Bor-Komorowski, who testified in London, and by other witnesses previously heard in Washington and Chicago.

(12) Prisoners evacuated from Starobielsk testified they also saw inscriptions in train prison cars but in this case they stated: "We are being removed or unloaded in Kharkov." See p. 525, pt IV.)

(13) The trail of prisoners evacuated from Ostashkov ends at Wiasma.

(a) Zygmunt Luszczynski, of London, testified that after he was evacuated from Ostashkov on April 24, 1940, his train composed of seven cars, stopped at Wiasma. He stated:

"We were taken from Ostashkov to Wiasma, where we remained at the siding for 3 days; then six of the seven cars were disconnected and they went in some other direction, and the care in which I was present was taken to Babynino (en route to Pavlishev Bor). (See p. 614, part IV.)"

(b) Other testimony strongly supports the theory that the Ostashkov prisoners were drowned in the White Sea.

(c) Adam Moszynski, himself a former prisoner at Starobielsk, author of the most authentic list of names of prisoners interned in the three camps (See exhibit 5A in the appendix of part III) testified:

"I am sure there are three Katyns in the world. One Katyn is in the Katyn Forest, near Gniezdovo (Smolensk) ; the second Katyn, of Starobielsk, could be near Kharkov, and the prisoners of Ostashkov, near the White Sea. * * *

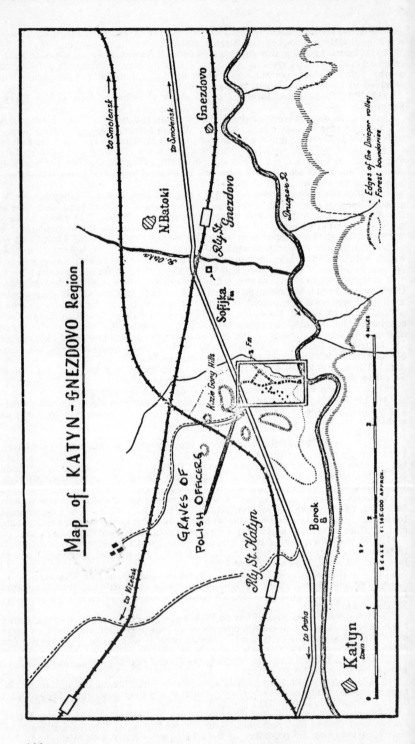

Map of KATYN - GNEZDOVO Region

to Smolensk →

to Smolensk →

Gnezdovo

N.Batoki

R.OLsa

Rly.St. Gnezdovo

Sofijka
Fm

Fm

Kozie Gory Hills

GRAVES OF POLISH OFFICERS

Borok

Rly.St.Katyn

to Vitebsk →

to Orsha →

Dnieper R.

— Edges of the Dnieper valley
— Forest boundaries

4 MILES

3

2

Katyn
town

SCALE 1:165.000 APPROX.

0

1

LEGEND

 — The route of the murdered Polish officers subsequently found buried in the mass graves at Katyn.

— Probable route of those missing but not found at Katyn.

— Route of the 400 Polish officers who survived.

— Route of these 400 survivors when they eventually were released by the Soviet and permitted to join the Polish Army in Russia in 1941.

"To the best of my knowledge, based on considerable research on the subject, the prisoners in Ostashkov were placed on two very old barges, and when the barges were towed out to sea they were destroyed by Russian artillery fire."

(14) Col. George Grobicki, who had been interned in Kozielsk, testified that: "Everybody was dressed when leaving the camp just as he was when taken prisoner. Most of the people were in overcoats when they left the camps."

This testimony corroborates to a great extent the testimony of numerous witnesses who had actually been taken to the scene of the graves and who had observed that most of the bodies of the massacred Polish officers were buried either wearing overcoats or winter underwear.

Grobicki's testimony becomes very pertinent when we, recall that in the Soviet countercharge accusing the Nazis for this crime, Russian witnesses claim these prisoners were executed by the Germans as early as August of 1941. This committee considers it doubtful the victims would be wearing winter garb in August.

(15) Even more startling was Grobicki's testimony that when he read the list of Poles being removed from the graves in Katyn published by the Germans shortly after the discovery of the graves in 1943, he noted that these bodies were being exhumed in the same group formations as they were when evacuated from Kozielsk. It is difficult to accept the theory that these men who allegedly left Kozielsk in April of 1940, to be assigned to special work units west of Smolensk by the Russians, should remain in the identical groupings until 1941 when they were allegedly murdered by the Germans.

(16) This committee has tried to establish how the 400 who survived from the three camps were selected. General Wolkowicki, testifying in London, said he believed he was spared because prior to Poland's rebirth, following World War I, he was a Russian Naval officer who won distinction in the Russo-Japanese War.

"I was the only officer who opposed the surrender of (this Russian) ship, and that is why their attitude toward me was one of considerable interest. (See p. 645, pt. IV.)"

(A) General Wolkowicki showed this committee an immunization card given to him by the Russians while he was interned at Kozielsk. He testified hundreds of similar cards subsequently were found on the bodies of Poles exhumed in Katyn. (See exhibit 17, pt. IV.)

This committee considers itself fortunate in getting the testimony of the above-mentioned witnesses who constitute only a small group of the 400 survivors taken to Griazovec by the Soviets in June 1940, and who remained there until they were released on July 20, 1941, to join the Polish Army. Their testimony has been instrumental toward helping this committee arrive at a conclusion.

IV. Search for the Missing Polish Officers

Having established that approximately 15,400 Polish officers and leaders had been imprisoned in these three major camps and that after June 1940 only 400 were known to be alive, the next major trend of the committee's evidence deals with the efforts of the Polish Government in Exile in London to find traces of the missing Polish officers from August 1941, through the entire year of 1942. This official Polish search resulted from one of the quirks of history:

Nazi Germany and Soviet Russia had been allies from August 1939, and particularly during the fourth dismemberment of Poland. In mid-June 1941, this unholy totalitarian alliance fell apart when Hitler's legions swept across the Russian boundaries to overwhelm the Russian armies. Within 2 months the Nazis had driven into the Ukraine past the area of Smolensk.

Following the Germans' attack and their overwhelming military victories, which were driving the Russians into dangerous retreats, the Soviet leaders were temporarily desirous of securing military aid from anywhere and anybody. As part of the Kremlin's negotiations with the British Government, the Soviets recognized the Polish Government in Exile in London.

The Soviets and the Polish Government entered into an agreement in July 1941, whereby all the Polish prisoners in Russia, except acknowledged criminals, were to be granted an amnesty by the Soviets and be transferred to specially designated camps where they would be organized into Polish army divisions under Polish officers. It was expected that this reborn Polish Army would join Russian armies in their fight against the Nazis. As part of this official arrangement, General Wladislaw Anders, who was at that time a prisoner in the Lubianka prison in Moscow, was accepted by the Russians as commanding general of the proposed Polish armed forces.

When he was released, General Anders immediately sought to collect as his staff officers those men whom he personally knew had been captured by the Soviets. Shortly after the arrangement between the Soviets and the Poles and the appointment of General Anders as Polish commander in chief, small groups of Polish soldiers from Griazovec and other prison camps joined the Anders command. Only 400 of the officers reporting had been numbered among the 15,400 men who had been at Kozielsk, Starobielsk, and Ostashkov prior to May 1940. Very few of these men were the staff officers whom Anders knew personally and whom he needed. Where were the other 15,000 Polish leaders? From then until the summer of 1942 when General Anders commenced to move his Polish troops out of Russia into the Middle East he continued his search for these officers. Repeated requests, personal and official, were made to the Russian general staff, to the Russian foreign office, and even to the NKVD, for information about these missing officers.

General Anders in addition to making official representations to the Russian Government authorized one of his officers, Maj. Josef Czapski, to make a search for these officers throughout Soviet prisons. General Anders also secured an interview with Premier Stalin in December 1941.

At this meeting, General Anders accompanied the head of the Polish Government in Exile, General Sikorski, and the Polish Ambassador in Moscow, Mr. Kot. Stalin personally was asked about these missing Polish officers. The Soviet Premier insisted he was not detaining them nor did he have them.

General Anders testified in London before this committee:
"We inquired, 'Well, where could they have gone?' To this Stalin replied, 'They escaped.' We asked, 'Where could they have escaped?' And Stalin replied, 'To Manchuria.' I said that this was impossible."

Anders had a second meeting with Stalin at the Kremlin in Moscow on the 18th of March 1942. At this meeting with Stalin, Anders presented him with a list of missing Polish officers and told Stalin that none of the officers had as yet reported to the Polish Army.

Stalin replied: *"Well, what good would they be to us? Why would we want to be keeping them or retaining them?"* At this same meeting Stalin hinted that maybe the Polish officers had fled and become separated when the Germans invaded Russia.

It is noteworthy, however, when a committee member explicitly asked whether any Russian official at any time said that the Polish officers might have become German prisoners, General Anders replied: "Never." Anders testified: "This to us was one of the most disturbing factors because we knew that the Bolsheviks had made very long and lengthy and complete lists of all their prisoners."

General Anders' testimony about his discussions with the highest Soviet officials regarding the missing Polish officers was independently verified by the testimony of Ambassador Stanislaus Kot, the first Polish Ambassador to Moscow under the new arrangement of July 1941.

VISHINSKY AND MOLOTOV QUESTIONED

Testifying in London, Kot said from the 20th of September 1941, until his departure from Moscow in the fall of 1942, he (Kot) made repeated inquiries to all levels of Soviet officialdom, to the NKVD, to Vishinsky, to Molotov, and even to Stalin himself, for information regarding these missing Polish officers. The incident of the conference between Kot and Deputy Foreign Minister Vishinsky on October 6, 1940, was characteristic of these meetings.

Kot complained to Vishinsky that only 2,000 Polish officers of an estimated 9,500 whose names were known to the Poles had reappeared among the Polish forces. Kot asked Vishinsky what had happened to the other officers saying:

"We have been making constant effort to find these people. We have searched for these men in the German prison camps in occupied Poland. Every place where they could conceivably have been found."

Kot said that he did not see how thousands of men could disappear. Vishinsky never answered the question but parried it with a confused: "Well, what do you think happened to these men?" Subsequently, Vishinsky stated: "They must be among the 300,000 Polish nationalists who have already been freed."

When Kot discussed the same question with Soviet Foreign Minister Molotov on October 22, 1941, Molotov put him off with the statement: "We will try to everything possible."

Similarly, during the meeting with Stalin on November 14, 1941, when Kot emphasized the anxiety of the Poles regarding the missing officers, Stalin at first asked: "Are there still some Poles not released?" And stated: "Amnesty knows no exceptions. We released all, even those people who were sent to * * * destroy bridges and kill Soviet people, even those people were released by us."

It is worth noting that Stalin's categorical assertion was made several months after the Germans had overrun the Smolensk area; and still the Soviet leaders gave no indication that they even thought the Polish officers might have been captured by the Germans.

The diplomatic memoranda of the conversations between General Anders and Ambassador Kot with Molotov, Vishinsky, and Stalin are part of the committee's record. They reveal any number of fictitious Soviet reasons why the Polish officers had not been located. Never once did these high Soviet officials, nor did any other Communist official of a high or low echelon, indicate to any of the Poles that those Polish prisoners of war might have been captured by the Germans.

It has been established by the record that the Polish Government in London employed its underground in Poland to check German prisoner-of-war camps to discover if any of these Russian-captured Poles might have been recaptured by the Germans. These efforts, like the negotiations in Russia, ended in negative results.

It was not until the Germans announced the discovery of the Katyn graves on April 13, 1943, that the Soviets first claimed these Polish prisoners had been moved into the Smolensk area in the spring of 1940. This evidence proves that the Soviet Government either was lying to the Poles during 1941 and 1942, when the Kremlin leaders said that they did not know where the prisoners of war might be, or else the Soviets were lying in their 1943 and 1944 reports, when they claimed the Poles had been moved to the Smolensk area in the spring of 1940 and subsequently captured by the Germans in 1941.

ALL LETTERS RETURNED

The committee has testimony from a Special Family Bureau which had been established by the Polish Government in Gangi Gul, Russia, to try to trace the missing Polish officers.

Major General Kaczkowski and Capt. Eugene Lubomirski, Directors of this Family Bureau, testified in London that they personally had examined hundreds, virtually thousands of letters from relatives in Poland, inquiring about these missing officers. In every instance, they testified, each of the letters and postal cards had stated that the last time the families heard from the Polish officers was in April and May of 1940.

These witnesses further testified that they had personally examined hundreds of letters addressed by the families to the prisoners interned in these three camps subsequent to May 1940, and all of those letters were returned by the Russian authorities with the inscription that the whereabouts of these Polish officers were unkown.

It is inconceivable that the highly developed bureaucracy of the Soviets would have permitted the NKVD to lose complete trace of so potent a force as these 15,000 Polish officers after they had left the three camps in the Spring of 1940. (See testimony starting on p. 628, pt. IV.)

All of the foregoing testimony which the committee has heard from Anders, Kot, and Czapski was reported to the American colonel, Henry I. Szymanski, when he was assistant United States military attaché at Cairo, Egypt. Szymanski testified that he was assigned in March of 1942 to be United States liaison officer with the Poles in Russia, but that he was never granted a visa to enter Russia.

Szymanski's specific assignment was to ascertain what had happened to the Polish officers in Russia, because the United States considered these Polish officers e̶   ̶ial to the Allied war effort. Consequently, Szymanski met with all the
    ̶king Polish officer survivors as they came out of Russia during the latter
    ̶1942 and 1943, and he reported all of the foregoing testimony to the
    ̶Chief of Staff for G-2.
    ̶e 22-month effort by the Poles to locate their missing officers, General
    ̶his staff had carefully commenced preparing a list of names of those
    ̶rned in the three camps. This list was prepared on the basis of
    ̶plied General Anders by the 400 survivors who were grouped

During his conference with Stalin in December, General Sikorski personally handed the Russian premier a list bearing more than 3,000 names and again Sikorski was assured that it was Stalin's understanding all of these men had been released.

Testimony heard by this committee proves conclusively that not once during all of these top-level conversations had the Russians either stated or hinted that these missing men might have fallen into German hands.

The committee believes if the Soviets were innocent, there was no reason why they should not have admitted to the Poles that their officers had fallen into German hands. But if they were guilty, they had a cogent reason for not telling such a story. So long as the Soviets insisted they didn't know the whereabouts of the Polish officers, nobody could prove they were dead.

V. Discovery of Graves at Katyn

The Polish Government's search for the missing officers came to an abrupt end on April 13, 1943, when the following Berlin broadcast by the Germans shocked the world:

"From Smolensk comes news that the native population has revealed to German authorities the spot where in secret mass executions the Bolsheviks murdered 10,000 Polish officers. German authorities made a horrible discovery. They found a pit 28 meters long and 16 meters wide in which, 12 deep, lay, the bodies of 3,000 Polish officers. In full uniform, in some cases shackled, all had wounds from pistol bullets in the back of the neck. Search and discovery of other pits continue."

This German announcement was followed by an intense campaign of Nazi propaganda aimed at the political exploitation of the discovery.

German Foreign Office documents which were captured by the Allies and turned over to the United States and Britain for joint custody were traced by the committee in England. These documents which are included in part V of the public hearings clearly show that Goebbels and other top Nazi officials had given instructions to exploit the propaganda value of this discovery to its fullest.

These documents also show the desperate efforts made by the Nazis to persuade the International Committee of the Red Cross to make an impartial investigation of the shocking discovery.

Hitler himself is quoted as having instructed his Foreign Office to use every means to get an investigation by the International Red Cross. One of the documents states:

"In following up the invitation issued by the German Red Cross to Geneva, that the International Red Cross should take part in the identification of the Russian atrocities against Polish officers, the Führer tonight ordered an actual invitation to be dispatched to Geneva by the German Red Cross. This extra invitation is to be signed by the Duke of Coburg so that the weight of his international name should be used."

The German claim was: The presence of these graves was called to the attention of the Nazis by Russian natives of the area; there was no question that these were Polish officers and that they were executed in the spring of 1940 by the Soviets. The Germans drew this immediate conclusion from an investigation of letters, diaries, and newspapers found on the bodies of the victims and from statements made by Russian natives in the area.

POLES SEEK RED CROSS INVESTIGATION

The Polish Government's immediate reaction was one of shock. In view of its long search for the missing officers, the Polish Government likewise issued an invitation to the International Committee of the Red Cross. After a meeting of the Council of Ministers the Polish Minister of National Defense issued a statement in which he said (see exhibit 30A, p. 748, pt. IV):

"We have become accustomed to the lies of German propaganda and we understand the purpose behind its latest revelations. In view, however, of abundant and detailed German information concerning the discovery of the bodies of many thousands of Polish officers near Smolensk and the categorical statement that they were murdered by the Soviet authorities in the spring of 1940, the necessity has arisen that the mass graves discovered should be investigated and the facts alleged verified by a competent international body such as the Internation Red Cross. The Polish Government has therefore approached this inst with a view of their sending a delegation to the place where the massacre of the Polish prisoners of war is said to have taken place."

The Soviet's immediate reaction was voiced by Molotov when he termed this a discovery of archeological remains. On April 19, 1943, the Soviet newspaper, Pravda, carried a front-page editorial which attacked the Polish Government's request for assistance of the International Red Cross in "investigating something that never happened." A day later, Izvestia carried a reprint of the editorial and said it fully reflects the position of leading Soviet circles. Thus, even at this late date the Soviets attempted to conceal their hideous crime.

Molotov's first reaction can be understood in the light of the testimony presented before this committee by General Rudolph von Gersdorff, German Intelligence Officer, who was among the first to arrive in the Smolensk area following the German invasion. Discussing the discovery of the graves Von Gersdorff said:

"In the vicinity of Gniezdowo, there were prehistoric Russian cairns, old prehistoric tombs in caves. They were overgrown with shrubs and heavily so. They were actually in that area, so that was the reason why, when the graves of the Polish officers were discovered, we did not call it the murders of Gniezdowo, but to distinguish it from these old prehistoric tombs of Gniezdowo, we called it the murders of Katyn, so as not to get these two things mixed up."

This committee has heard considerable evidence from other sources that the whole area of Katyn had been used by the Bolsheviks as early as 1929 for mass executions.

Only after the Germans had definitely established that the discovery was indeed valid did the Russians present a countercharge which they maintain to this day: the Poles interned in the three camps had been transferred by the Russians to other camps in the vicinity of Smolensk during March and April of 1940 and were taken prisoner by the Germans during the Russian retreat. The Russians flatly accused the Germans of executing "11,000" Polish officers in 1941.

The Polish Red Cross was informed by the International Committee of the Red Cross that a neutral investigation of the Katyn discovery could be made only if all three nations involved participated, namely, Poland, Germany, and Russia.

Russia's formal reaction to the Polish Government's request for a neutral investigation of Katyn by the International Red Cross was the abrupt break of diplomatic relations with the Poles. The Soviets bitterly denounced the Poles for "collaborating with the Nazis."

All subsequent efforts by the British Foreign Office and the American State Department to heal the Russo-Polish breach were met with invectives hurled by the Soviets.

This loud reaction of Soviet injured innocence is construed by this committee as being the resource of a cornered culprit begging the question. There is no question that Russia's retaliatory move severing diplomatic relations with the Poles was motivated primarily to divert attention from the Poles' request for an International Red Cross investigation.

VI. Testimony of Observers Present at Katyn When the Bodies Were Exhumed

Even before the Germans made their announcement, a leading Swedish correspondent, Christer Jaederlunt, correspondent of the Stockholm Tidningen, was invited by the German Ministry of Propaganda to visit Katyn. When he learned the purpose of the visit, the Swedish journalist admitted that he felt he was being used by German propagandists to spread their anti-Soviet themes. Yet this newspaperman, after viewing the Katyn graves and making such investigation as he himself wanted, refused to even consider that this could have been o[?] propaganda show staged by the Germans.

committee explicitly asked Jaederlunt, when he testified in Frankfurt, a neutral newspaperman, could have conceived this Katyn affair as a "propaganda show." Jaederlunt's answer was very significant, and it ed the attitude of all the committee's witnesses who had visited the s. Jaederlunt said:

went there with this suspicion [that Katyn was a German 'prop- We did not trust Goebbels and thought that it would be possible ble of doing such a thing. * * * But when I stood in front s and when I realized what an atrocious crime had been perpetrated there, all my suspicions vanished and my own newspaper, at first, was not prepared to publish this report, but I insisted upon the reports being published because I said: "The world at large must know about this matter.'" (See pt. V of the published hearings.)

The testimony of the Swedish journalist Jaederlunt clearly established that he would have preferred to have considered the Katyn massacre as a German atrocity. Mr. Jaederlunt concluded his testimony as follows:

"Then and now I was and I am absolutely convinced that the Russians committed it. I do not wish to say the Russians. I would rather amend it to the NKVD." (See pt. V of the published hearings.)

During the Chicago hearings, Casmir Skarzynski reported on his official visit to the Katyn graves. This witness was the deputy chairman of the Polish Red Cross in German-occupied Poland. The Polish Red Cross, when the Germans first informed them about the Katyn graves, refused to accept the German statement on the basis that *this is a pure propaganda move, and the Red Cross must keep away from any propaganda.*

Skarzynski was directed by Polish Red Cross officials to go to Katyn to supervise the exhumation and proper reburial of these Polish officers. *While at Katyn, the Polish Red Cross official was moved by the facts he personally witnessed to admit that the German Army in this instance was innocent.* (See pt. III of the published hearings.)

AMERICAN ARMY OFFICERS VISIT KATYN

The most significant testimony of the independent witnesses who visited Katyn shortly after the German announcement of the graves' discovery was provided by two American army officers, Lt. Col. Donald B. Stewart and Col. John H. Van Vliet, Jr.

These officers had been captured by the Germans in north Africa and were taken to Germany as prisoners of war. These two Americans with two British officers had been compelled by German authorities to visit Katyn in May 1943. Stewart's suspicions of the German purpose was indicated by his testimony to the effect "that I was there [Katyn] under orders; that I felt the matter was a propaganda effort, and, in any event, it was a political effort. * * * I had no desire to have anything to do with a propaganda effort or a political matter." (See pt. I of the published hearings.)

Similarly, Van Vliet in his written report stated:

"I hated the Germans. I didn't want to believe them. * * * When I became involved in the visit to Katyn I realized that the Germans would do their best to convince me that Russia was guilty. I made up my mind not to be convinced by what must be a propaganda effort * * *."

Likewise, in his oral testimony to the committee, Van Vliet stated:

"As a prisoner of war, I had a personal grudge against them [the Germans] and as an American army officer I had a professional grudge against them. * * * So the German story was one that I did not want to believe. * * *" (See pt. II of the published hearings.)

It is particularly noteworthy that both officers independently emphasized the same convincing factor, which they both stated had not been brought to their attention by the Germans but which was an independent deduction from their own observations. This was the evident fact that the clearly undisturbed corpses were clothed in winter attire which was in an excellent state of repair, showing practically no wear. The two officers also independently made these same observations about the condition of the boots of the Polish officers. In both instances the officers stated from their own personal experience as prisoners of war in a German camp that clothing could not have remained in that condition if it had been worn for a year in a prison camp.

Hence, Colonel Stewart stated:

"The decision I reached, I can never forget. My decision was that those [Polish] men were killed by the Russians while they were prisoners of the Russians * * *." (See pt. I of the published hearings.)

In similar fashion Colonel Van Vliet in his oral testimony stated:

"If those Polish officers had been alive and in prison camp until the Germans overran the Polish prison camps, and if the Germans had in fact killed these Polish officers, then by the very virtue of the fact that their clothes had been worn and their shoes had been walked in, they would show much more wear. * * *" Likewise in his written report, Van Vliet explicitly recorded his sincere conviction:

"The sum of circumstantial evidence, impressions formed at the time of looking at the graves, what I saw in peoples' faces—all force the conclusion that Russia did it." (See pt. II of the published hearings.)

SOME VICTIMS BURIED ALIVE

Zbigniew Rowinski, who testified in London, said he had been taken to Katyn by the Germans in April of 1943. Rowinski at the time was a German prisoner of war interned at Woldenberg. He said not all the victims were shot in the head:

"I suppose only those people who tried to defend themselves were bound, because I saw some bodies with the sawdust in their mouth and some of them had even their heads covered with their overcoats, then a string round the neck connected with string at the hands. So when they started to struggle to free the hands, they must have choked themselves." (See p. 692, pt. IV, of the published hearings.)

In London the committee heard the testimony of Ferdinand Goetel, an official of the Polish Red Cross who visited the graves at Katyn. The following is an exact quotation of the conversation the Polish Red Cross group had with Lieutenant Slovencik who was in charge of receiving of members of all delegations of all nationalities who went to Katyn at the time of the exhumations:

"Another even more interesting detail of our conversation with Slovencik was that although he was inclined to describe the whole case as a most dramatic incident from the Polish point of view—he had no idea where could have come from all these bodies of Polish officers. All he knew was what the local inhabitants had told him that they had been brought in transports arriving from the direction of Smolensk. As he already had in hand photographs and, I think, even originals of some of the letters and postcards found on the bodies he asked us whether we could explain why the address of Kozielsk repeated itself so often on many of the cards. I told him in short what I knew about the camps of Kozielsk, Ostaszkov, and Starobielsk and I closely watched his reaction to this piece of news. It was most lively and convinced me beyond all doubt that Slovencik had learned about Kozielsk only from us. It was the only detail of our conversation of which he made a note. A moment later, after we had finished our talk, I heard him repeating the news about Kozielsk to Olenbusch and to the other Germans. * * * (See p. 845, pt. IV of the published hearings.)"

Thus, from the above-quoted testimony, it is evident that the Germans were unaware of the camp in Russia where these Polish officers had been imprisoned during the period, September 1939 through May 1940.

VII. OTHER WITNESSES

This committee heard several witnesses whose testimony will be grouped under a special heading. Among these was a Pole who testified as an eyewitness to the massacre. His identity had to be concealed with a mask to prevent reprisals against his relatives still living in Poland. However, all the committee members are familiar with his identity.

Testifying as "John Doe" at the committee's second hearing in Washington, this witness maintained that he and two of his compatriots personally viewed the execution of 200 Poles by Russian soldiers in what he believed to be the Katyn Forest. These observations were made by the witness and his friends at the beginning of November after the trio escaped from a Russian prisoner-of-war camp at Pavlischchev Bor. (See p. 143 of pt. II.)

After relating how the trio observed the Poles being led into the forest, the witness continued:

"Two of them [Russian soldiers] seized their hands and held them in back and one of the Russian soldiers lifted his chin up [the victim's] took him by the head, opened his mouth and shoved a handful of sawdust into his mouth."

"John Doe" said most of the victims were executed with a shot through the backs of their heads. Some, however, according to his testimony, were thrown into the graves alive and left to suffocate.

"John Doe" further stated he saw the Poles' hands being bound in the back with wire prior to the execution.

This witness introduced several new factors hitherto unknown to the committee: he said the executions he witnessed were in the early part of November; he said the victims' hands were bound with wire; he said their mouths were stuffed with sawdust; and he said some of the victims were left to suffocate rather than shot in the head.

These observations, up to the time that John Doe testified, had never been published in any of the material prepared by the Polish Government during its lengthy research on the Katyn massacre. Subsequently, however, they were substantiated by witnesses appearing before this committee.

Colonel Grobicki, testifying in Washington, said groups of Polish officers were evacuated from Kozielsk as early as November. In London, Mr. Rowinski, an observer at the graves taken there as a German prisoner of war in 1943, testified he observed several victims with their mouths stuffed with sawdust. In Frankfurt, Dr. Tramsen, a member of the German International Medical Commission, testified several victims had their hands bound with wire. During the same hearing, Dr. Naville, of Switzerland, and also on the same Commission, said he believed some of the victims died of suffocation instead of gunshot wounds. Several German witnesses likewise observed the victims' mouths stuffed with sawdust and hands tied with wire.

This committee heard testimony of many witnesses whose revelations were of a circumstantial nature. But in order to get the atmosphere surrounding all the facts of the Katyn massacre, their testimony was accepted and placed in the record.

Among these was Jerzy Lewszecki who testified in London. He said he was a German prisoner of war interned at the prison camp near Lubeck. In 1943 he had occasion to discuss the Katyn massacre with Stalin's oldest son by a prior marriage who likewise was a German prisoner of war interned in the same camp.

Lewszecki said he discussed the disappearance of the Polish officers with Stalin's son who frankly admitted that the Poles were executed by the Soviets. *"Why those were the intelligentsia, the most dangerous elements to us, and they had to be eliminated,"* Lewszecki quoted Stalin's son as saying. (See p. 777, pt. IV.)

During our latest hearing here in Washington, this committee heard testimony from Boris Olshansky of New York, a former Soviet army officer who escaped to this country in 1946. Olshansky related conversations he had in Moscow with N. N. Burdenko, director of the Special Soviet Commission which made an investigation for the Russians in January 1944. Burdenko supervised the exhumation of 925 bodies for the Soviet investigation and in the official report stated all of the Poles were executed in the autumn of 1941.

Olshansky testified Burdenko told him the Soviet report was false. He quoted Burdenko as saying:

"I was appointed by Stalin personally to go to the Katyn place. All the corpses were 4 years old. For me, as a medical man, this problem was quite clear. Our NKVD friends made a mistake."

Olshansky further stated he was told by Burdenko that there are more Katyns in Russia.

"Katyns existed and are existing and will be existing," Olshansky quoted Burdenko as stating in Moscow in April of 1946. *"Anyone who will go and dig up things in our country, Russia, would find a lot of things that we had to straighten out the protocol given by the Germans on the Katyn massacre,"* the aging Burdenko further told Olshansky.

VIII. TESTIMONY OF INTERNATIONAL MEDICAL COMMISSION

The Germans formed an International Medical Commission, composed of the leading scientists, pathologists, and professors of criminology from 12 different countries of Europe. The committee heard testimony from 5 of these doctors who participated in the exhumation of the bodies. They were provided with the necessary instruments to perform their own individual autopsies. The five doctors are:

Dr. Edward Lucas Miloslavich (Croatia). (Part III of the published hearings.)

Dr. Helge Tramsen (Denmark). (Part V of the published hearings.)

Dr. Ferenc Orsos (Hungary). (Part V of the published hearings.)

Dr. Francois Naville (Switzerland). (Part V of the published hearings.)

Dr. Vincenzo Mario Palmieri (Italy). (Part V of the published hearings.)

All of the above-named doctors categorically and unequivocally stated to the committee that they had complete freedom of action in performing whatever scientific investigation they desired. Also, that they had complete freedom to interrogate any individual they considered appropriate.

Their unanimous conclusion was that the Poles were murdered at least 3 years ago—thus placing the time of death as the spring of 1940 when the Katyn area was under Soviet control.

Dr. Tramsen presented as an exhibit for the committee the original protocol signed by the 12 doctors in their own handwriting. He also presented a photograph of the 12 doctors signing the protocol to prove that there was no duress.

Dr. Orsos, Dr. Naville, and Dr. Tramsen definitely identified this protocol and stated that they had signed it and that they were of the same opinion today as they were when they signed this protocol on April 30, 1943.

Dr. Miloslavich gave the following testimony to the committee relative to the condition of the bodies as they were found in the mass graves:

"One body was placed on top of the other one, with their faces down. They were close together, nothing between them. All the bodies were dressed in Polish officers' uniforms, the clothing being winter clothing, underwear, and the uniforms; and coats on some. The heads were downward. One body like this, the next one like this, and the next one like this [indicating]. This was the width of the grave. Then 12 layers down, and then multiply by the length. I don't remember how many we found in the length. Anyway, at that time when I was examining and making my own estimations I didn't follow anybody, and no one tried to give me any advice because I knew what to do. I estimated approximately 2,870, something like that, a little less than 3,000 officers. They were packed completely together by decaying fluids of the human body, the decomposing fluids, which started to penetrate, to imbibe, to infiltrate every dead body in there. That was a solid mass in which you just saw skulls you could recognize and that they were human beings.

"Then I went into the graves and studied which ones of them would give me the best information, what the dead body could tell us. With the help of two Russian peasants I picked a body, and slowly and gradually—it took them close to an hour—they removed the body and brought it out. I examined it very carefully to find out two main points. First, what was the cause of death. Second, how long a time was this individual buried. Third, who he was?

"In examining the body I found a gunshot wound at the boundary between the back of the neck and the head. The Germans gave the expression 'nackenschuss.' That is the precise description of the shot which was fired. The majority of them had just one shot, because it entered in here [pointing with finger] and came out here at the root of the nose, which means the head was bent downward. It was administered with such precision that the medulla was completely destroyed. (See pt. III of the published hearings.)"

Both Tramsen and Naville presented to the committee numerous papers, military buttons, officers' insignia, and, in the case of Dr. Naville, a cigarette holder, which they had taken from the Polish bodies in Katyn at the time of their own individual autopsies. Both of these doctors had preserved this material since the day they left Katyn and voluntarily offered these items to the committee. (All of this material has been made part of the permanent record and may be found as exhibits in part V of the published hearings.)

Dr. Palmieri testified as follows:

"In the bodies, at least in many of the bodies, Professor Orsos observed the presence of growths (corns)—in the inside of the cranium, pseudo growths in the internal part of the skull, which are due to manifestations of reduction of the mineralization of the brain—of the cerebral tissues and of the other substances contained in the skull."

Dr. Palmieri stated when interrogated by the committee as follows:

"Question. What conclusion did you arrive at?

"Dr. PALMIERI. I came to the conclusion especially similar to Orsos' theory on the formation of cerebral growth."

"Question. Was Dr. Orsos' conclusion that the deaths occurred not later than April or May 1940?

"Dr. PALMIERI. Yes.

"Question. Do you agree?

"Dr. PALMIERI. Yes, based on the researches that Dr. Orsos had made (see part V of the published hearings)."

The five doctors heard by this committee stated emphatically that many of their observations were made independently and outside the presence or possible influence of German authorities who were supervising the exhumations.

Before the committee held its hearings in Europe, word was received that Drs. Markov and Hajek, who are today in countries behind the iron curtain, were giving radio talks implying that they were not in full agreement with the German International Medical Commission's protocol which they had signed on April 30, 1943.

In the published hearings of this committee—particularly parts III and V—there is contained the testimony of five international doctors. Categorical statements are made by all five doctors who testified before this committee that all members of the International Medical Commission signed the protocol of their own free will and without duress. The five doctors specifically stated that both Drs. Markov and Hajek had made no objections and were in full agreement with the protocol when they signed it.

IX. RUSSIAN REPORT

While the testimony heard by this committee is conclusive in itself to establish that the Polish officers were massacred by the Soviets, nothing appears as incriminating against the Russians as their own report published in 1944 following an investigation at Katyn by an all-Soviet commission.

The committee has made a careful analysis of the Soviet report (which is exhibit 4 in part III of the published hearings). This analysis was important because when the Soviets declined this committee's invitation to participate in the investigation, they maintained that their own report conclusively established the Germans were responsible for the Katyn massacre.

It is interesting to see how the Soviet's official findings stand up under the light of facts uncovered by this committee.

At the very outset, the Soviet claim is incongruous with the facts. The Soviets quote Russian natives who allegedly saw Polish officers working on road gangs and construction projects in the Smolensk area prior to the German invasion. These witnesses are quoted to substantiate the Soviet allegation that all the officers were transferred from Kozielsk, Starobielsk, and Ostashkov by the Russians in March and April 1940 to three camps in the Smolensk area designated only as ON1, ON2, and ON3. If the Polish officers worked on road gangs—as the Russians maintain—it is logical to ask if their boots and uniforms would have shown as little wear as Colonel Van Vliet observed when he examined their bodies in Katyn.

While conducting hearings in London, this committee was fortunate in obtaining the testimony of Mr. Joseph Mackiewicz who visited the Katyn Forest on instructions of the Polish underground in May 1943 and observed the German exhumations. Mr. Mackiewicz is an authority on the Katyn massacre having tirelessly studied all related facts for the past 9 years. Some of his observations (starting on p. 867 of part IV) follow:

"The Russian communiqué claims that there were found at Katyn 11,000 bodies, but actually there were found only slightly more than 4,000. The Bolsheviks, therefore, used the figure 11,000, because even if assuming that those 4,000 that were found in Katyn had been murdered by the Germans, the question arises: What happened to the rest? Furthermore, the question of the correspondence becomes associated here. The Russians claimed that they had found correspondence on these bodies which indicated that these men had corresponded with their families in Poland up to 1941. If there were 11,000 bodies in Katyn, each one of them then most probably had some family in Poland ranging anywhere from 1 to 6 people.

"The number of potential witnesses in Poland who could have been summoned to testify that they had corresponded with any members of their family in these camps up to and including 1941 would have reached the figure, roughly, of 20 000 to 30,000. The Germans, who had, of course, capitalized on a tremendous propaganda to their own advantage, would have taken into consideration the fact that, in a country where the people were generally adversely disposed toward the Germans, the news that the Germans had lied would have certainly spread very quickly through Poland, and the Germans would have never permitted themselves to be compromised to that extent."

Mackiewicz adds further:

"The Russian Commission claims that these Poles had been brought to the rail station at Gniezdowo in the year 1940, that they were not murdered but instead placed into three camps, No. 1 ON, No. 2 ON and No. 3 ON, at a distance of from 25 to 45 kilometers to the west of Smolensk, and that during the time of the

German offensive they fell captive into the hands of the Germans. This, of course, is a lie, because there were no such camps in that locality. The Russian communiqué does not specify exactly where were those three camps. Naturally, if those three camps had actually existed, they could have notified Ambassador Kot, General Sikorski, General Anders, and Mr. Czapski, who had conducted a long search for these men."

The allegation made in the Russian report that the commanding officer of the three camps was unable to get transportation to evacuate the Poles from the camps while the Germans were advancing, conflicts with known facts. This committee had testimony presented in London which clearly spelled out that Russian commanders were ordered to save prisoners-of-war at all costs.

Statements taken by the committee here in Washington, from a former high Soviet official assigned to the Russian foreign office during World War II, also established that Russian prisoners of war were not to fall into enemy hands under any circumstances.

Mackiewicz's comment on this point was:

"Furthermore, the Russian communiqué or report claims that the commanding officer of the Russian camp No. 1 ON was a major of the NKGB, Wietosznikow, and that when the Germans were approaching that area the commanding officer had communicated with the commanding officer of the transport forces in Smolensk, Iwannov, with a request for rail cars in order to evacuate these Polish prisoners. Since he was unsuccessful in obtaining these railroad cars, consequently these Polish prisoners fell into the hands of the Germans, but Wietosznikow himself remained with the Russian forces and did not fall into captivity of the Germans. Therefore, if Wietosznikow, who was the commanding officer of the security forces, knew about the whereabouts of these soldiers, why did not Stalin and Molotov and Vischinsky know about their presence virtually within the shadow of Moscow? And as a consequence, for 2 years they ostensibly searched to find an answer as to the whereabouts of these soldiers. Wietosznikow certainly must have reported to his superiors as to what happened to these prisoners, and when Czapski made his frequent inquiries to the NKVD, they would have immediately told him that these men fell captive to the Germans.

"Assuming that Wietosznikow could not get the rail cars from Iwannov as he had requested, he could have evacuated the soldiers from these prison camps by foot, especially when you consider that the claim is that Wietosznikow appealed to Iwannov for these cars on the 12th of July; but the official Soviet communiqué of the 23d of July 1941, claimed that the Russians were still in control and possession of Smolensk."

The Russians further claim their Polish camps were near the Gussino line and that trains could not be sent because that line already was under fire. If, in fact, these three camps were along the Gussino line, which is west of Smolensk and which leads right into Gussino, it is reasonable to ask why were these Polish prisoners removed at Gniezdovo, 45 miles away, after being evacuated from their original camps, and transported by truck the rest of the way when there are sufficient railway stops from Gniezdovo all the way to Gussino itself.

Mackiewicz testified:

"There actually were no camps in the location that the Russians claim that they had taken these men to, and I had substantiated that to my satisfaction on the basis of my conversations with inhabitants of the general area and my conversations with Kriwozercow. All of them told me that there had never been any such camps in that area. Furthermore, I would like to call your attention to one more little detail.

"The attitude in Poland and in Russia was so bitterly anti-German in 1943 that when they released the news of Katyn, that is, the Germans, in the spring of 1943, the announcement gave birth to a mess of various versions of what happened, which could have refuted the German version.

"At that time, because communications, especially radio communications, had been severely curtailed, many people had not heard the German version. As a consequence, the Russian agents, who were very actively operating in all these parts, started rumors of their own version, merely to destroy and discredit the German version.

"As an example, when I was in Katyn, there were with me two Portuguese correspondents. One of these men told me that he had been taken to look at a little village, to which the Germans had taken him, and then he asked me repeatedly whether I felt certain that this was the work of the Russians. I asked him, 'Why do you ask?' He said that he had talked to a young girl in this village, who told him that those murdered men 'are really Jews who have been dressed in Polish uniforms.'

"Even such fantastic stories were circulated when if, in effect, and in actuality, there were those three camps in this area, they would have said that the Poles were in these camps and the Germans came by and captured these Poles and that they murdered them. Nobody at all has ever heard of any such camps in that area."

In the Russian report, witness T. E. Fatkov testifies that round-ups of the Polish war prisoners took place up until September 1941. And, he goes on to say in the Russian version that, "*After September 1941, the round-ups were discontinued and no one saw Polish war prisoners any more.*"

Thus, Fatkov fixes the last possible date of the executions at September 1941. If this is true, and it must be true, since it is in the Russian's own report, why then were all of these Polish war prisoners found in winter garb in the Katyn Forest? Weather reports show that the temperatures during August and September of 1941 in the Smolensk area ranged between 65 and 75 degrees Fahrenheit. It is inconceivable that the Polish prisoners of war would have had scarfs tied around their necks and would be wearing overcoats if they actually were massacred in August and September of 1941.

Russian witnesses further testified that they knew that the men they saw were Polish war prisoners because they wore the same Polish uniforms and their characteristic four-cornered hats. This committee has photographs of Poles who reported to General Anders from other camps in 1941 when he was forming his Polish army. None of these men reported in their original Polish uniforms since they were worn out during their 2-year captivity.

The Russians claim that Witness Kisselev, who had testified before the German Commission, had been brutally beaten to say that he actually had seen and witnessed the executions. The Germans never claimed to have an "eyewitness." Any allegations which the Russians attribute to Kisselev, therefore, are false.

The Soviet report is inconsistent with the facts in its claim there were 11,000 Poles massacred at Katyn. The Polish Red Cross has definitely and conclusively established in the minds of this committee that there were no more than 4,143 bodies exhumed at Katyn, and another 110 found but not exhumed.

The Polish Red Cross had made a thorough search of the area in order to find more graves and no additional graves or bodies could be found.

Out of some 11,000 bodies which the Russians claim that they had found in Katyn, they were able to find only nine documents which showed a date later than May of 1940.

RUSSIAN REPORT CONTRADICTORY

Furthermore, the Russian report quotes a citizen, Moskovskaya, who claims she talked to a man named Yegorov in March of 1943. He reportedly said that in April of 1943 he had been sent into the Katyn Forest by the Germans to remove all documents which were dated subsequent to May of 1940 from the bodies of the dead soldiers. It is interesting to note that her conversation was in March of 1943 and Yegorov was describing activities in which he allegedly had participated a month later, in April of 1943.

Yegorov allegedly stated that there was some 500 Russian natives from the area in all who were ordered by the Germans to remove these records. After the task was completed, according to Yegorov, the 500 Russians were executed by the Germans. Nowhere in its report does the Soviet Commission claim that the graves of these 500 Russians ever were found.

Evidence before this committee already has substantially established that only 4,253 bodies were buried in Katyn. If the Russian claim that there were 11,000 Poles buried in that forest is to be accepted, why then didn't the Russians recover the additional 7,000 bodies?

It is also significant to note that while not a single Russian witness mentions a date later than September 1941 as the time of the alleged massacre by the Germans, in their final report the Soviets claim "September to December" as the period of the executions.

Henry Cassidy told this committee that the correspondents taken to Katyn by the Russians pointed out this inconsistency, and he said further:

"Thereupon, the text of the Soviet Atrocities Commission report, which was to be released simultaneously with our dispatches, was held up for a couple of days, I suppose to be rewritten, and our dispatches were released when that report was finally ready, and it was then that we got our copy into the telegraph office." (See p. 214, part II, of the published hearings.)

In all the allegations in the Soviet Commission's report, not once do they make mention of the type of ammunition used. The type of ammunition, was manufactured in Germany by Genschow & Co. But testimony heard before this committee clearly proved that the German-made ammunition had been sent to Russia and the Baltic states for many years before World War II. Mr. Genschow, president of the Gustav Genschow & Co., as a witness before the committee in Frankfurt, testified as follows:

"Mr. GENSCHOW. * * * 'The cartridges of the shells of this pistol ammunition carried, since the year 1933–34, the word "Geco" on the bottom of the shell, and underneath the "Geco" was '7.65.'

"QUESTION. Can 7.65 ammunition of the type manufactured by this firm be used in various kinds and makes of pistols?

"Mr. GENSCHOW. 'Yes, it could; because it was a standard type cartridge which could be used in very many different makes of pistols.'

"QUESTION. Was it used internationally by various nations, police, or armed forces, in pistols?

"Mr. GENSCHOW. 'Yes, certainly.'

"QUESTION. Did this firm ever export pistol ammunition of the caliber 7.65 to Eastern Europe?

"Mr. GENSCHOW. 'Yes; that is the case.' "

(See part V of the published hearings.) From the foregoing testimony it is evident that both Russia and Germany had access to this type of ammunition.

Finally, this committee cannot accept the Russian claim that these Polish officers fell into German hands during the Soviet retreat because there isn't an iota of proof in the Soviet report that any Russian soldiers or officers guarding these alleged camps had fallen captive to the Germans. It is inconceivable that these 15,000 Polish officers would have waited around these three camps to be taken prisoners by the Germans while their Russian guards themselves fled the impending German onslaught. There should be no doubt that the moment the Russian soldiers abandoned the camps the 15,000 Poles likewise would have fled for freedom.

X. NUREMBERG

This committee reports that during the International Military Trials held in Nuremberg after World War II, evidence was heard relative to the Katyn massacre.

The committee has heard testimony from two of the attorneys who participated in the Nuremberg trials. (See pt. V of the published hearings.) In accordance with the London agreement of 1945, the Soviets were in charge of war crimes which were allegedly committed in the eastern areas, such as: U. S. S. R., Poland, Yugoslavia, Bulgaria, and Czechoslovakia. Hence the Katyn massacre, since it occurred in Soviet territory, was the direct responsibility of the Government of the U. S. S. R. to prosecute the individuals responsible for this crime.

The Katyn massacre appears in the Nuremberg trials as a charge against Herman Goering since he was the highest ranking German officer. The Soviet prosecutor produced three witnesses to establish the Germany guilt for the Katyn massacre. The German defense counsel produced three witnesses for the defense. These are all the witnesses the tribunal would hear. Witnesses for both the Germans and the Soviets were duly examined and cross-examined.

This committee in the course of the hearings at Frankfurt heard testimony from the three German witnesses who appeared at Nuremberg, that is, Colonel Ahrens, General Oberhaeuser, and Lieutenant Von Eichborn. (See pt. V of the published hearings.)

These three witnesses testified that they were with German Signal Regiment 537, not the Five hundred and thirty-seventh Engineer Battalion as alleged in the Russian report. (See p. 247, pt. II of the published hearings.)

SOVIETS FAIL TO PROVE CASE AT NUREMBERG

All of them arrived in the Smolensk area after September 1, 1941. In the case of Colonel Ahrens, he testified that he did not arrive in the Katyn Forest until early November 1941. He was specifically named in the Russian report as the individual who directed the mass shootings of the Polish prisoners. (See p. 247, pt. III of the published hearings.) Colonel Ahrens was again accused before the

International Military Tribunal by the Soviet prosecutor and it is significant to note that he was never indicted by the tribunal nor was his indictment requested by the Soviet prosecutor. (See pt. V of the published hearings.)

This committee heard testimony from Col. Albert Bedenk who was the predecessor to Colonel Ahrens as commanding officer of Signal Regiment 537. He testified that he arrived in the Smolensk area on July 28, 1941, several days after the fighting front had moved many miles east of Smolensk on the way to Moscow. Colonel Bedenk set up the headquarters of Signal Regiment 537 in the Dnieper Castle about the middle of August 1941. He testified: "the total strength of the regiment at that time was 17, of which 5 or 6 were officers, 4 were noncommissioned, and the rest were enlisted men." (See pt. V of the published hearings.)

The Russian report states, "The Polish prisoners of war who were in the three camps west of Smolensk employed on road building up to outbreak of war, remained there after the German invaders reached Smolensk, until September 1941." (See p. 247, pt. III of the published hearings.) Colonel Bedenk categorically denied ever seeing a Pole in the area, as did General Oberhaeuser and Colonel Ahrens. Colonel Bedenk also testified that Colonel Ahrens relieved him as commanding officer of Signal Regiment 537 on November 20, 1941, as did General Oberhaeuser. (See pt. V of the published hearings.) Thus the testimony taken before this committee under oath speaks for itself.

The Soviet prosecutor in his summation of the charges against Goering never mentioned the Katyn massacre. Testimony before this committee reveals that the Soviet prosecutor failed to prove his case against the Germans, therefore the matter was dropped by the tribunal.

XI. Conclusions

This committee unanimously finds, beyond any question of reasonable doubt, that the Soviet NKVD (Peoples' Commissariat of Internal Affairs) committed the mass murders of the Polish officers and intellectual leaders in the Katyn Forest near Smolensk, Russia.

The evidence, testimony, records, and exhibits recorded by this committee through its investigations and hearings during the last 9 months, overwhelmingly will show the people of the world that Russia is directly responsible for the Katyn massacre. Throughout our entire proceedings, there has not been a scintilla of proof or even any remote circumstantial evidence presented that could indict any other nation in this international crime.

It is an established fact that approximately 15,000 Polish prisoners were interned in three Soviet camps: Kozielsk, Starobielsk, and Ostashkov in the winter of 1939–40. With the exception of 400 prisoners, these men have not been heard from, seen, or found since the spring of 1940. Following the discovery of the graves in 1943, when the Germans occupied this territory, they claimed there were 11,000 Poles buried in Katyn. The Russians recovered the territory from the Germans in September 1943 and likewise they stated that 11,000 Poles were buried in those mass graves.

Evidence heard by this committee repeatedly points to the certainty that only those prisoners interned at Kozielsk were massacred in the Katyn Forest. Testimony of the Polish Red Cross officials definitely established that 4,143 bodies were actually exhumed from the seven mass graves. On the basis of further evidence, we are equally certain that the rest of the 15,000 Polish officers—those interned at Starobielsk and Ostashkov—were executed in a similar brutal manner. Those from Starobielsk were disposed of near Kharkov, and those from Ostashkov met a similar fate. Testimony was presented by several witnesses that the Ostashkov prisoners were placed on barges and drowned in the White Sea. Thus the committee believes that there are at least two other "Katyns" in Russia.

No one could entertain any doubt of Russian guilt for the Katyn massacre when the following evidence is considered:

1. The Russians refused to allow the International Committee of the Red Cross to make a neutral investigation of the German charges in 1943.

2. The Russians failed to invite any neutral observers to participate in their own investigation in 1944, except a group of newspaper correspondents taken to Katyn who agreed "the whole show was staged" by the Soviets.

3. The Russians failed to produce sufficient evidence at Nuremberg—even though they were in charge of the prosecution—to obtain a ruling on the German guilt for Katyn by the International Military Tribunal.

4. This committee issued formal and public invitations to the Government of the U. S. S. R. to present any evidence pertaining to the Katyn massacre. The Soviets refused to participate in any phase of this committee's investigation.

5. The overwhelming testimony of prisoners formerly interned at the three camps, of medical experts who performed autopsies on the massacred bodies, and of observers taken to the scene of the crime conclusively confirms this committee's findings.

6. Polish Government leaders and military men who conferred with Stalin, Molotov, and NKVD chief Beria for a year and a half attempted without success to locate the Polish prisoners before the Germans discovered Katyn. This renders further proof that the Soviets purposely misled the Poles in denying any knowledge of the whereabouts of their officers when, in fact, the Poles already were buried in the mass graves at Katyn.

7. The Soviets have demonstrated through their highly organized propaganda machinery that they fear to have the people behind the iron curtain know the truth about Katyn. This is proven by their reaction to our committee's efforts and the amount of newspaper space and radio time devoted to denouncing the work of our committee. They also republished in all newspapers behind the iron curtain the allegedly "neutral" Russian report of 1944. The world-wide campaign of slander by the Soviets against our committee is also construed as another effort to block this investigation.

8. This committee believes that one of the reasons for the staging of the recent Soviet "germ warfare" propaganda campaign was to divert attention of the people behind the iron curtain from the hearings of the committee.

9. Our committee has been petitioned to investigate mass executions and crimes against humanity committed in other countries behind the iron curtain. The committee has heard testimony which indicates there are other "Katyns." We wish to impress with all the means at our command that the investigation of the Katyn massacre barely scratches the surface of numerous crimes against humanity perpetrated by totalitarian powers. This committee believes that an international tribunal should be established to investigate willful and mass executions wherever they have been committed. The United Nations will fail in their obligation until they expose to the world that "Katynism" is a definite and diabolical totalitarian plan for world conquest.

Appendix II
Katyn and Khatyn

I mentioned earlier the Soviet attempt to confuse the Katyn issue in 1974 by publicising Khatyn as a place where the Germans are said to have committed a massacre of local inhabitants. It is a matter which deserves some further explanation. Shortly after President Nixon's visit to Khatyn, the *Daily Telegraph* published an illuminating article by David Floyd, which is given here *in toto*.

Confusion on Khatyn and Katyn
By David Floyd, Communist Affairs Correspondent

"President Nixon's visit to the memorial in the Byelorussian village of Khatyn has caused a mistaken impression that Russia has erected a memorial to the victims of the wartime massacre of Polish officers in the Katyn forest.

In fact, Khatyn and Katyn are two entirely different places, Khatyn, in which the "kh" is pronounced like an English "h," is a small village some 30 miles to the north-east of Minsk, the capital of Byelorussia.

Katyn, which is pronounced as written, is a town about 15 miles west of Smolensk, a provincial city in Russia proper. Khatyn is about 160 miles west of Katyn.

When Stalin and Hitler divided up Poland at the outbreak of the Second World War in 1939, some 240,000 Polish officers and men fell into Russian hands. After Hitler's invasion of Russia in June, 1941, 15,000 were found to be missing and the Russians denied all knowledge of them.

Mass grave

Katyn fell into German hands in the late summer of 1941 and at the beginning of 1943 the German army discovered a mass grave of 4,443 Polish officers and men.

When the Polish Government-in-exile appealed for an international tribunal to determine how the Poles died Stalin broke off relations. After re-taking Katyn the Russians set up their own inquiry and said the Poles had been executed by the Germans.

Later researches by Polish and independent authorities in the West, as well as wartime Foreign Office documents, leave no doubt that the Poles were executed by the Soviet secret police, the NKVD.

The Russians have tried to erase Katyn from maps and history books. The reference to it in the 1953 edition of the Soviet Encyclopaedia was dropped in the 1973 edition. No visitors are allowed to the area and no memorial has been erected.

It was not until 1969 that the Russians announced the unveiling of a "memorial complex" on the site of the village of Khatyn. It was one of the 9,200 Byelorussian villages destroyed by the Germans, and one of 136 of which all the inhabitants were killed.

The Russians appear to have chosen Khatyn because of the similarity of its name to Katyn. They hoped in this way to obscure the fact they have erected no memorial to the victims of Katyn, which was no less a crime than the one committed at Khatyn."

Daily Telegraph, Wednesday, 3 July 1974

It is interesting to look back into Soviet maps to discover just what official attitude was adopted and how Khatyn rather suddenly made an appearance:

1954 A map of the Minsk Region in the *Large Soviet Encyclopedia* does not show Khatyn at all.

1956 A map of the Smolensk Region in the *Large Soviet Encyclopedia* shows Katyn.

1969 A large atlas of the USSR shows neither Khatyn nor Katyn.

1974 A map of the Minsk Region in the *Large Soviet Encyclopedia* shows Khatyn but not Katyn.

It may now be profitable to indulge in a few moments speculation. In 1954, that is to say after the findings of the US Select Committee (of 1952) had been made known, there is no sign of Khatyn, while even in 1956 Katyn is still shown. In 1969 neither place finds any reference in the atlas, whereas by 1974 Katyn has been erased while Khatyn makes an appearance. It can thus be supposed that whereas two decades ago the Soviets had overlooked Katyn, they have since "corrected" this by producing Khatyn and obliterating Katyn. It should be noted that in cyrillic script "K" is written as in ordinary script as "K" while "X" is the symbol for "Kh" as we in the West read it.

It can only be that this extraordinary sleight-of-hand is a device to remove the real KATYN and substitute KHATYN in an attempt, albeit clumsy, yet further to distract and confuse the world as to the whereabouts of a crime committed by the NKVD and substitute another alleged crime to Nazi Germany.

As David Floyd says, Khatyn is about 160 miles west of Katyn.

Bibliography

For those who wish to verify the statements contained in this book, the following documents and books are recommended:

Der Massenmord im Walde von Katyn – Ein Tatsachenbericht. A short pamphlet of 6 pages only, and with a further 26 pages of pictures. Undated and with no indication of publisher. Probably originating from NSDAP in 1943.

Amtliches Material zum Massenmord von Katyn.
The official German Government Report, published in Berlin in 1943. (Copy in the possession of the Polish Library, London.)

Soviet War News. No 541 dated 17 April 1943.

Indictment presented to the International Military Tribunal sitting at Berlin on the 18th October, 1945 pursuant to the agreement by the Governments of the United Kingdom of Great Britain and Northern Ireland, of the United States of America, of the Republic of France and of the USSR for the prosecution and punishment of Major War Criminals of the European Axis. London. HM Stationery Office. Treaty Series No 27 (page 22). 1946.

Document: *The Mass Murder of Polish Prisoners of War in Katyn.* Produced in London by the Polish Government in

Exile. March 1946 (then marked "Most Secret").

Judgement of the International Military Tribunal in the trial of the Major German War Criminals (with dissenting opinion of the Soviet members). Nuremberg 30/9 and 1/10/46. HM Stationery Office, London.

La Tribune de Genève. Issue of 20 January 1947.

The Inhuman Land. Count Josef Czapski. Chatto & Windus. 1951.

The Katyn Wood Murders. Josef Mackiewicz. The World Affairs Book Club, London. Undated.

Katyn – Ein ungesuhntes Kriegsverbrechen gegen die Wehrkraft eines Volkes. Pamphlet published by Wehrwissenschaftlicher Verlag Walther de Bouche, Munich. 1952.

The Katyn Forest Massacre. Final Report of the Select Committee to conduct an Investigation and study the facts, evidence and circumstances of the Katyn Forest Massacre (Pursuant to House Resolutions 390 and 539 of the 82nd Congress). Washington. 1952.

Speech of the late Professor Sir Douglas Savory MP in the British House of Commons. Hansard (Commons), 6 November 1952, Columns 333-41.

Crimes discreetly veiled. F. J. P. Veale. Cooper Book Company, 293 Grays Inn Road, London. WC1. 1958.

Death in the Forest. J. K. Zawodny. University of Notre Dame Press. 1962.

Congressional Record, Vol. 108, dated 14.5.1962, page 7643.

The Crime of Katyn – Facts and Documents. Published by the Polish Cultural Foundation, London. 1965.

The Nuremberg Trials. Heydecker and Leeb. Verlag Kiepenneuer & Witsch. Köln-Berlin. 1958.

Operation Barbarossa. Ronald Seth. Anthony Blond, 1964.

Stalin and the Poles. Dr Bronislaw Kusnierz. Hollis and Carter. 1949.

Katyn – A Crime without Parallel. Lous FitzGibbon. Tom Stacey. 1971.

The Katyn Cover-up. Louis FitzGibbon. Tom Stacey. 1972.

A further list containing some 25 documents and over 60 books can be obtained through the Polish Government-in-Exile in London, or from the Polish Library, 9 Princes Gardens, London SW7.

Index of names and places

If the spelling of individual words varies it is because such words appear differently depending upon from what language they were translated and sometimes by what national they are quoted. As the name "Katyn" appears constantly throughout the book it was not thought necessary to include it in this index. Page numbers in brackets refer to illustrations.

491

493

Oberhauser, Maj Gen, E, 86, 97, 101, 122, 130-42, 209, 228, 231, 237, 243, 335, 346-7, 480-1.

O'Konski, A E, 209, 219, 222, 238, 261, 265, 291-3, 297, 333, 339-40, 342, 350, 351, 366-70, 450.

Olshansky, Boris, 475.

O'Malley, Owen, 36-7, 53, 55-6, 58-9, 72, 78, 405.

Omdurman, 406.

Orashkevitch, 186.

Orel, 13, 45, 84, 141, 189, 198, 236.

Orsha, 65-6, 230.

Orsos, F, Dr, 28, 34, 155, 162-3, 165-7, 171, 175-6, 198, 253, 271, 285, 288, 293-4, 301-2, 374-7, (378), 379, 384, 386, (388), 389-90, 475-6.

Oslo, 14.

Ostashkow, 18-9, 21, 37-8, 40, 43-5, 62, 76-8, 210-1, 213, 217-20, 265-6, 365, 395, 415-7, 419, 422, 430-40, 446, 463-5, 467-9, 474, 477, 481.

Ostrowski, S, President, 426.

Pabl, 300.

Palmieri, V, Dr, 28, 36, 155, 161, 168, 175, 269, 271, 388-92, 414, 418, 461, 475-6.

Paszkowska, Dr, 325.

Paulischev Bor, 39, 62-3, 211-2, 217-8, 416, 422, 434, 464-5, 474.

Peczora, 435.

Persia, 42.

Pestraia Dresva, 218.

Pfeiffer, 251, 255-61.

Philby, Kim, 26.

Picot, A, 193-4, 200.

Pienkowski, Prof, 203.

Piga, Prof, 156.

Pilsen, 327.

Pokrovsky, Col, 82, 85, 92, 334, 336-7.

Poland, 48-9, 462-4, 468, 470, 477-8, 480, 483.

Polish Red Cross, 21, 40, 42, 73, 77, 186, 194, 197, 202, 247, 254, 259, 260, 312-5, 323-5, 353, 379, 434.

Pollard, Prof, 51.

Posen, 129.

Potemkin, W, 60, 83, 183, 191.

Potocki, Rev, 211.

Poznan, 73, 309.

Praglowski, Dr, 324.

Prague, 28, 210, 271, 295, 327, 391.

Pressburg, 271.

Prochownik, Col J, 309, 346.

Pronaskou, Dr, 326.

Prosorovsky, Prof, 96, 181-92.

Prozorlobsky, V I, 292.

Pucinski, R, 220, 222, 398, 450.

Raczynski, 40, 50.

Radebeul, 322, 327.

Radziwill, Prince S, 21.

Raeder, Admiral, (92), 107, 123.

Raichmann, Gen, 216-7, 220-1, 441.

Reddaway, P, 396.

Rex, O/Lt, 84, 86, 108, 120, 235, 335, 346.

Rhzev, 434.

Riga, 45.

Robel, Dr, 324-5, 327.

Roberts, Sir Frank, 57.

Roeske, 256.

Romania, 27-8, 271.

Romer, T, 40, 463.

Ronicker, Count, 326.

Rose, Corporal, 109, 238.

Roslaul, 250.

Rowinski, Zbigniew, 474-5.

Royal Commission for Exhibition of 1851, 404.

Rudenko, Gen, 88, 90, 96, 334.

Rueger, Mr, 21.

Rzew, 266.

Saburin, Gen, 441.

St Andrew Bobola, 396.

St Luke's Gardens, Chelsea, 404, 406–7, 421, 426, 446.

St Oswald, Lord, 402, 408.

Sailsbury, Marquess of, 59.

Sand, Prof, 270.

Saratov, Minister, 178.

496